The exploding field of AI and IA has arguably caught humanity unawares. This timely edited collection, drawing on expertise in the sciences, technology and the humanities once more meets the challenge of asking publicly important questions. Distinctions within AI, its threat to human society, its carbon footprint and the implicit bias that is inevitably built into its creation are among the many questions that are discussed. It is time for theologians and ethicists to contribute to the boundaries in the growth of AI for the sake of our human futures. This rich collection of essays is a much-needed resource for public debate, especially but not limited to religious communities.

Celia Deane-Drummond, Director, *Laudato Si'* Research Institute, Campion Hall, University of Oxford.

As AI and IA take the world by storm, this book is essential reading for all who take the power of technology seriously and who care about the common good. Faith leaders and tech lovers alike: read this book and be part of a conversation that will dominate this century.

Chris Mulherin is Executive Director of ISCAST–Christianity and Science in Conversation, Australia.

The Promise and Peril of
AI and IA

Edited by Ted Peters

The Promise and Peril of AI and IA

New Technology Meets Religion, Theology, and Ethics

Ted Peters, Editor

Adelaide
2025

Text copyright © 2025 remains with the authors and for the collection with ATF Press. All rights reserved. Except for any fair dealing permitted under the Copyright Act, no part of the publication may be reproduced by any means without prior permission. Inquiries should be made in the first instance with the publisher.

Agathon: A Journal of Ethics and Value in the Modern World
Volume 10, 2025

Agathon refers to the Greek word used by Plato in the Republic to refer to 'the good beyond being', most notably deployed in recent times by Iris Murdoch and Emmanuel Levinas, both of whom use this touchstone to situate ethics at the heart of all of philosophy

We live in an evolving and increasingly complex world but our ethical concepts have frequently struggled to keep pace with the change. As a result, much of what passes for public debate at present remains in the grip of either deterministic or consequentialist thinking, both built on outdated assumptions and both representing attempts to address major issues in the absence of ethical concepts. We suffer, as Iris Murdoch lamented, a 'loss of concepts, the loss of a moral and political vocabulary'.

The interdisciplinary journal, *Agathon*, seeks to bring together scholars from across the humanities, social sciences and sciences, including disciplines such as philosophy, theology, law and medicine, to engage with the ethical questions that now beset the modern world.

The journal is a home for considering questions such as how we deal with competing values in ethical discourse, how ethical theory finds expression in practice, what constitutes ethical character and how it is cultivated, and what excellence and wisdom look like for the ethical person or society in the twenty-first century.

Agathon is an international and interdisciplinary refereed journal published annually by ATF Press.

Chief Editor
Dr Paul Babie, University of Adelaide Law School Professor of the Theory and Law of Property

Editorial Board
- Professor Terence Lovat, Emeritus Professor, The University of Newcastle, Australia & Hon Fellow University of Oxford, UK.
- Professor Robert Crotty, former Director, Ethics Centre of South Australia, Emeritus Professor of Religion and Education, University of South Australia, Adelaide.
- Managing Editor and Publisher Mr Hilary Regan, Publisher, ATF Press Publishing Group, PO Box 234 Brompton, SA 5007, Australia. Email: hdregan@atf.org.au

Subscription Rates
Local: Individual Aus $55 Institutions Aus $65 Overseas: Individuals US $60 Institutions US $65

Agathon is published by ATF Press an imprint of the ATF Press Publishing Group which is owned by ATF (Australia) Ltd (ABN 90 116 359 963) and is published once a year. ISSN 2201-3563

ISBN
978-1-923206-86-1   Soft
978-1-923206-87-8   Hard
978-1-923206-88-5   Epub
978-1-923206-89-2   PDF

Published by:

An imprint of the ATF Press Publishing

Group owned by ATF (Australia) Ltd.
PO Box 234
Brompton, SA 5007
Australia
ABN 90 116 359 963
www.atfpress.com
Making a lasting impact

Table of Contents

David Brenner, Foreword, *AI and Faith* — ix

Ted Peters, *Editorial 2018: Human Utopia or Human Extinction?* — xiii

Ted Peters, *Editorial 2024: Does Posthuman Utopia Require Human Extinction?* — xxi

Part One: AI, IA, and Frankenfear

1. Noreen Herzfeld, *The Enchantment of AI* — 3
2. Ted Peters, *Artificial Intelligence, Transhumanism, and Frankenfear* — 17
3. Brian Patrick Green, *Should God have Given Humans Technology? The Stories We Tell Ourselves* — 45
4. Neville Grant Rochow, *Somnambulating Towards AI Dystopia? The Future of Rights and Freedoms* — 71
5. Matthew J. Gaudet, *Lethal Autonomous Weapons Systems, Just War, and a Culture of Encounter* — 97
6. Levi Checketts, *Idle Hands and the Omega Point: Labor Automation and Catholic Social Teaching* — 111
7. Noreen Herzfeld, *Call Me Bigfoot: The Environmental Footprint of AI and Related Technologies* — 131
8. Tracy Trothen and Calvin Mercer, *AI, IA, and Theological Anthropology* — 141
9. Alan Weissenbacher, *Artificial Intelligence and Intelligence Amplification: Salvation, Extinction, Faulty Assumptions, and Original Sin* — 163

Part Two: AI and IA in Culture, Religion, and Ethics

10. Martinez Hewlett, *AI in Recent Literature* — 183
11. Benjamin Chicka, *Video Games and Theology of Culture* — 201
12. Daniel J. Peterson, *On the Faith of Droids* — 219
13. Rajesh Sampath, *From Heidegger on Technology to an Inclusive Pluralistic Theology* — 229
14. Ali-Reza Bhojani, *Between Fear and Hope: AI Ethics in Islamic Thought* — 245
15. Lawrence A. Whitney, *Confucian Role Ethics and Artificial Intelligence* — 257
16. Sunday Akande and Oluwatobi Ife-Adediran, *AI in African Liberation* — 279
17. Mark Graves, *AI Reading Theology: Promises and Perils* — 293
18. Randall Reed and Claire Kennedy, *ChatGPT as Study Buddy* — 313
19. Daren Erisman, *AI for Pastors* — 327
20. Evan Underbrink, *The Chatbot: An Eschatological and Apocalyptic Overview* — 337

Part Three: Is there really an "I" in "AI" or "IA"?

21. Hermina Nedelescu, *Intelligence Amplification and the Inner Life of the Soul* — 353
22. Michael Spezio, *Theology Engaging AI: Constructs of Human Intelligence and Metaphors of Translation* — 365
23. Anselm Ramelow, *AI Algorithms and Human Free Will* — 385
24. Yousef Jamali and Mohammad Jamali, *Free Will Selfhood, and AI: The Avicenna-Bohm Theory* — 399
25. Daekyung Jung, *Artificial Religious Agents: A Study on Theoretical Feasibility and Normative Considerations* — 415
26. Alan Weissenbacher, *AI as Storyteller and Mentor: The Pedagogical Potential for AI in Moral Development* — 447
27. Braden Molhoek, *Reflections on the Virtuous AI Project* — 465

Contributors — 485

Foreword
AI and Faith

When a handful of technologists, theologians and related professionals launched *AI and Faith* in 2018, we chose the name as a deliberate provocation: those words and worlds seemed not at all to relate. On the heels of our launch came the first edition of this remarkable collection of essays, *AI and IA, Utopia or Extinction?*, many by pioneer thinkers such as Ted Peters and Noreen Herzfeld who had anticipated our provocative question by a decade or more and were already well down the road with answers.

Six years on, AI technology has advanced to a shocking degree, moving rapidly from theory to consequential applications in every part of life. The faith conversation around AI's rewards and risks—its promises and perils—is also burgeoning, as the opportunity and need for the world's oldest wisdom to deepen the AI ethics debate become ever more apparent. This new edition of essays comes in the fullness of both time and faith insights from a variety of faith traditions.

Especially the recent surprising advances of generative AI and now the promise of bots stepping up as even more powerful 'agents', raise humankind's oldest questions. These include 'what is distinctive about humans relative to other creatures (and now our own creations)?' 'What is the meaning and purpose of life and work?' 'Do we even have free will, let alone the ability to preserve it?' And 'what harm or hope awaits us individually and as a race?' The essays in this edition grapple with these questions and more, demonstrating along the way that religion, philosophy and ethics offer not just interesting insights but essential grounding for rules, regulations, and practices that can master humanity's drive for ever greater knowledge and control.

These essays—many by intellectuals and technologists I am pleased to call friends and colleagues in AI and Faith— crackle with the power of a high voltage line. I like to think there is an equally valuable function, like a 'step-down voltage transformer', for all us readers in distributing this thinking into our daily world. This is the role I played professionally as a litigator in corporate risk management and insurance, where my strong suit was stepping down the deep insights of experts into opinions understandable to a judge and jury. Attempting that skill now, I offer the following contention: much of what drives our fascination with AI is *fear* and *functionality*.

Fear is obvious and indeed right in the theme of this collection—many seemingly credible sources suggest our very future is at risk. But such fear is still in the mainstream only the *frisson* of a scary movie. Sheer terror may be coming, but we really don't yet believe it. And even if it comes, people of faith always have this escape clause—that a sovereign deity remains sufficiently in control that whatever threat AI presents will not be truly existential.

Certainly, I hold to that belief, and it is a great comfort. And yet, in the Jewish and Christian faith traditions, there is also that compelling mandate to 'love your neighbor'. So equally certainly we must do all in our power to promote AI's contribution to human flourishing and boundary it's destructive risk, even if that risk does not rise to the demise of humanity. A lot of bad things can happen short of that.

Functionality is the shortcut around such thorny questions as consciousness, self-awareness, sentience, and the meaning of intelligence itself. If an AI application can produce outcomes that present all the hallmarks of these human qualities, and if it can draw from us an emotional response sufficient to enliven it with what feels to us like a real relationship, isn't that enough to say it is an intelligent being? It is here that our reason must master our emotions, and our faith rescue us from category confusion and premature embrace.

Oddly, functionality has its own way of giving over to a misplaced faith. Especially as generative AI has metamorphized so rapidly and almost mystically, I have thought often of the forest log selected by a craftsman in Isaiah 44:16–18:

> Half of the wood he burns in the fire;
> over it he prepares his meal,
> he roasts his meat and eats his fill.
> He also warms himself and says,

"Ah! I am warm; I see the fire."
From the rest he makes a god, his idol;
he bows down to it and worships.
He prays to it and says,
'Save me! You are my God!'

Is AI our digital equivalent of that craftsman's log? For those relying solely on technology solutions, whether guised as promoters of the 'Singularity', or 'move fast and break things', or now 'AI accelerationists', I think the answer must be yes.

But the authors in these essays guide us past this newest version of such ancient foolishness, ever present in man's inclination to find the sacred and the profane in the same material thing. What we have in these essays are relevance, depth, courage, and hope to face the challenges of this most interesting of times. Read them and see more clearly.

David Brenner

Board Chair, *AI and Faith*
https://aiandfaith.org/

Agathon: A Journal of Ethics and Value in the Modern World, Vol 10/2025

Human Utopia or Human Extinction?
Editorial 2018

Ted Peters

> 'As AI becomes invisibly ubiquitous, new ethical challenges emerge. The protection of human self-determination is one of the most relevant concerns and must be addressed urgently.'
> — Mariarosaria Taddeo and Luciano Floridi[1]

The fast-moving frontier of Artificial Intelligence (AI) in league with Intelligence Amplification (IA) prompt anxiety in some quarters. Our initial hopes are quickly dowsed with fear of hazards.

When it comes to smart phones or autonomous gadgets for vacuuming our living room carpets, a brief moment of "wow" is quickly superseded by 'oh, hum'. Robotic intelligence, though initially fascinating, seems to prompt no worries about the short-range future. But, what about the long-range future? When we forecast the evolution of posthuman superintelligence that will either bring a technological utopia or render *Homo sapiens* extinct, anxiety causes us to ask existential questions.

Could the techie whizzes among us invent enough gadgets to relieve human beings from the drudgery of work? Can we look forward to a near future where robots and sex-bots and nanny-bots and chef-bots and mow-the-lawn-bots provide everything we previously had to strive for? Could we create our own utopia? Or, might there be a risk that the AI we create will, like the Sorcerer's Apprentice, get out of control? Might the superintelligent children of our technological procreation discard their parents as outdated junk?

---

1. Mariarosaria Taddeo and Luciano Floridi, 'How AI can be a force for good', in *Science* 361:6404 (24 August 2018): 751–752, at 751.

Will AI and IA bring us to a fork in the road where one route leads to utopia and the other to extinction?

We pause here to ask: what is intelligence anyway? Could *Homo sapiens* with moderate intelligence give birth to a posthuman species of more intelligent hybrids, cyborgs, or robots? If we humans are able to create cybernetic geniuses as our progeny, will we the creators attain the status of technological gods? Could *we* humans advance to the status of *Homo Deus*? Or, because that race of superintelligent and super-powerful creatures will survive us, should we designate *them* as 'gods'? Will we creatures have created a divine race to surpass us? Will the posthuman discard us mere humans as obsolete trash?

These questions raise the specter of transhumanism. 'The field of artificial intelligence is deeply rooted in transhumanist visions for the future', avers Natasha Vita-More, Executive Director of Humanity + Incorporated.[2]

Like riding a jet-propelled escalator, the transhumanists (abbreviated H+) among us are rocketing evolution toward an unprecedented new stage, namely, superintelligence. Whether through deep brain implants to amplify existing human intelligence (IA) or through creating robots with artificial intelligence (AI), a new posthuman species is scheduled to emerge. The event of posthuman emergence is dubbed, the *Singularity*. After crossing the Singularity threshold, superintelligence will take the reins of evolution and continue the advance to yet higher levels of intelligence until all of reality has been imbued with the cyber mind. Among other vicissitudes to be conquered is death, which will be surpassed by radical life extension or even cybernetic immortality. The transhumanists offer us a utopian vision of cosmic consciousness, even if we atavistic *Homo sapiens* may not be there to enjoy it.

These forecasts should give theologians pause, especially when it comes to anthropology and eschatology. Are the presuppositions about human nature adopted by transhumanists accurate? Is disembodied intelligence the same intelligence we in human bodies have come to know? Is the concept of whole brain emulation leading to cybernetic immortality realistic? Is the eschatological vision of the transhumanist compatible with, or contradictory to, the biblical promise of the Kingdom of God?

---

2. Natasha Vita-More, *Transhumanism: What Is It?* (published by author, 2018) 64.

Some theologians, such as D Gareth Jones, warn of competition between saviors. Who will save us? Science or Christ? 'The excesses of transhumanism with its picture of a new world order, in which medicine will be devoted to conquering mortality, overcoming ageing, vanquishing neurodegenerative diseases and enabling people to live to 600 or so years of age as healthy and fulfilled individuals, rightly repel Christians . . . These extreme vistas represent a rerun of the science-as-saviour mentality.'[3] Or, to put the issue in First Commandment terms, does the H+ veneration of technology tempt us to idolatry, tempt us to revere the progress of science as salvific?

AI and IA in Cybertheology

In the chapters to follow, we will ask whether the disjunction between utopia and extinction provides the most realistic set of alternatives. According to Alan Weissenbacher, managing editor of *Theology and Science*, there is no reason to think that development of AI or IA will represent anything dramatic at all, especially once one assesses critically several of the assumptions that lead some futurists to overenthusiastic optimism. In his contribution, 'Artificial Intelligence and Intelligence Amplification: Salvation, Extinction, Faulty Assumptions, and Original Sin', Weissenbacher analyses three questionable assumptions made by techno-optimists and transhumanists. First, the definition of intelligence we find in AI and IA technology is vague and confusing. Wet brain human intelligence and dry machine intelligence are so different, they cannot rightly be compared. They are two different things, even if they functionally overlap at times.

Second, according to Weissenbacher, there appears to be an implicit assumption especially among transhumanists that higher intelligence equates to greater morality. This assumption, every theologian knows, is clearly false. Some of the brightest minds in history have devised and disguised the most horrendous evils. There is no relationship between enhanced intelligence and enhanced morality.

Third, closely related to this is the assumption that greater intelligence will bring with it the will to address societal problems.

---

3. D Gareth Jones, 'A Christian Perspective on Human Enhancement', in *Science and Christian Belief*, 22:2 (2010): 14-16, at 14.

This is by no means the case. One could easily forecast that the generation of human beings who initiates the era of superintelligence could use this newfound power for greedy or tyrannical purposes. Technological advance does not entail moral advance.

Unless, of course, you are Mark Graves. Graves, currently pursuing research at the University of Notre Dame in the US, is author of 'AI Reading Theology: Promises and Perils'. Graves is both a computer scientist and a theologian who raises the question: should we ask AI to read and interpret theology, especially the theology of St Thomas Aquinas. Given the current computational ability to analyse and generate theological text, reasonably near future AI may plausibly read theology comparable to a first-year seminary student and have the capacity to learn more.

Should theologians contribute to AI learning theology? Yes. Benefits include technologically enhanced theological interpretations and, note, improved AI morality. AI reasoning necessarily entails moral reasoning, he says. Really? I find this doubtful, frankly, because AI does not include selfhood; and it takes selfhood for a sense of moral responsibility and culpability. Be that as it may, Graves invitation for AI to enter the very heart of theological and ethical deliberation is both unique and exciting.

Asking a computer to reason morally would be to ask too much, according to Noreen Herzfeld, a hybrid theologian and computer science professor. Herzfeld fears that too much hype is leading us to unrealistic expectations. Despite nearly three quarters of a century of research, to date no electronic device yet invented exhibits intelligence. Computers compute, to be sure; but they cannot pass the Turing Test. They are not intelligent. Even though it's too early to predict what will happen in the future, Herzfeld bets that authentic machine intelligence remains science fiction. In her article, 'The Enchantment of Artificial Intelligence', Herzfeld suggests that the H+ vision is extravagant, unrealistic. Even if Weissenbacher and Herzfeld are correct about long range forecasts, AI developments will have implications in the near future for human work and human dignity.

Despite our enchantment with AI, IA, and the H+ vision, all this might be considered dystopian rather than utopian. According to Australian barrister Neville Rochow, such dystopias are familiar to us. But, rather than focus on the technology associated with Amazon, Apple, Facebook, and Google plus the horizon of new AI advances,

Rochow worries about the business side of technology. In his contribution, 'Somnambulating Towards AI Dystopia? The Future of Rights and Freedoms', Rochow says history teaches that supranational corporations cannot be trusted with unchecked power. Corporations do not respect human rights. No one can predict the effect AI will have on human rights. We should take our rights seriously before the bio-technological lottery begins. Prompt international action is required to regulate AI developers and corporations.

'Faith creates the self in human beings'. Following Paul Tillich, Dan Peterson recognizes the decisive role played by faith in human personhood and then applies it to Strong AI. If AI is ever to equal the human level of intelligence, it will need to acquire both personhood and faith. We can anticipate what this looks like if we watch fictional robots on the big screen. Peterson offers a delightful exegesis of R2-D2 in *Star Wars: A New Hope* and K2-SO in *Rogue One: A Star Wars Story*. Peterson shows how faith as a capacity would be indispensible if Strong AI is ever to attain *imago Hominis*. In this essay, Peterson provides an excellent example of how a theologian can contribute to the creative mutual interaction between science and theology.

Shakespeare exclaims rhetorically: 'What a piece of work is man! How noble in reason! how infinite in faculties! in form and moving, how express and admirable! in action how like an angel! in apprehension, how like a god!' Now, are we talking about the humanity we know? Or, are we talking about the posthuman that artificial intelligence and intelligence amplification could bring into existence? Will this amount to what is truly human, or what is posthuman?

Martinez Hewlett, evolutionary biologist and fiction author, poses these questions in his article, 'What a Piece of Work is Man: On Being and Becoming Human in Science Fiction', Hewlett interrogates science fiction, because there the question of what it means to be a human person is brought into sharp focus. Hewlett selects three authors whose work has influenced the genre and has been the inspiration for film adaptations: Isaac Asimov (*I, Robot*), Philip K Dick (*Blade Runner*), and Richard K Morgan (*Altered Carbon*). All three challenge us by pushing the limits of robotics, androids, and mind uploading. They scenario visions of what the future might be in the wake of technological advances in artificial intelligence. Who shall we become?

In his chapter, 'Idle Hands and the Omega Point: Labor Automation and Roman Catholic Social Teaching', theologian and ethicist Levi Checketts assesses the impact of AI on work. Will AI replace work? He examines three polar theologies of work present in Roman Catholic thought: labor as drudgery, labor as dignified calling, and labor as an obstacle. These three theologies inform an eschatological vision of labor—Christians are called to work to build the kingdom of God, not merely to acquire material possessions. What might be the implications for the distribution of resources and the problem of idleness in a post-labor world. All of this suggests Catholics must promote a future of dignified labor dedicated to love of neighbor and God.

In my own chapter, 'Artificial Intelligence, Transhumanism, and Frankenfear', I argue that even if AI (beyond rapid computation and cute gadgets) never comes to pass, theologians must speculate with transhumanist visionaries about the prospect of superintelligence, about the prophesied extinction of *Homo sapiens,* and about the survival of a posthuman species. While advances in AI technology that benefit humanity should be celebrated, extravagant utopian promises should be met with a healthy dose of Frankenfear, that is, caution. AI and IA advances in the near future may very well make life on Earth for human beings and even the ecosphere better; yet the more extravagant utopian promises for the long range future could risk large scale destruction.

Intelligence versus Love

Utopian promises beyond the Singularity threshold are unrealistic on two counts. The first is anthropological. To surmise that this generation of human beings could create a superior intelligence—where the creature is more intelligent than the creator—defies the logic of plausibility. Yes, we human beings have created power tools that are stronger than we who designed and manufactured them. This is a positive precedent. Yet, intelligence seems to require more than mere design. Because intelligence as we experience it in ourselves and certain animals requires both the capacity for insight and for decision-making, it is difficult to imagine that superintelligence could be the product of a design. It's difficult to imagine that what is designed would be more intelligent than the designer.

From the perspective of the Christian theologian, intelligence is a curious category. Why does it rise to the top of the values list for transhumanists? Why is it the trump card which defines the desirable future? For the follower of Jesus, love belongs on top of the values list, not intelligence. To the children—not to the technological whizzes—belongs the kingdom of God, said Jesus. 'Let the little children come to me; do not stop them; for it is to such as these that the kingdom of God belongs' (Mk 10:14). With the logic of intelligence presupposed by H+, could H+ apply their technology to the capacity to love? Could we procreate a future generation of creatures more dedicated than we to love, compassion, healing, and peace? As laudable as increased intelligence might be, it should not sit atop our list of values.

The second unrealistic assumption made by H+ has to do with eschatology. Transhumanists assume that evolution is progressive. Plus, they assume that increased intelligence leads to increased moral resolve. A more intelligent superspecies, H+ assumes, will have the moral capacity to heal all psychological, sociological, and ecological ills so that all consciousness can enjoy a higher-level tranquility and even harmony. Yet, I ask: can a leopard change its spots? Can a sinful human race beget progeny healed of their sin without an act of divine grace? To assume that an increase in intelligence leads automatically to an increase in moral will is fallacious. It defies history, experience, and theological insight.

The ultimate transformation Christians look forward to is eschatological. It will be a gift of divine grace. It would behoove the present generation to view AI advance as penultimate, not ultimate. A healthy dose of caution is warranted.

Conclusion

In treating our theme, 'AI and IA: Human Utopia or Human Extinction?', we are engaging in cybertheology, a form of public theology. *Public theology*, I believe, should be *conceived in the church, reflected on critically in the academy, and addressed to the world for the sake of the common good.*[4] Public theology has five tasks: pastoral, apologetic, scientific, political, and prophetic tasks. The writers

---

4. Ted Peters, 'Public Theology: Its Pastoral, Apologetic, Scientific, Political, and Prophetic Tasks', *International Journal of Public Theology* 12:2 (2018): 153–177; https://brill.com/abstract/journals/ijpt/12/1/ijpt.12.issue-1.xml .

of theme articles in this volume are taking up the task of engaging science and technology from a theological perspective.

Readers should take away two significant points. First, God created the human species to be creative; and the future of science and technology represents the *imago Dei* at work within history. Second, because scientific and technological advances occur within history, we should avoid asking for more than it can deliver. No scientific insight or technological innovation can accomplish what God's promise of new creation can deliver. The wisdom of Reinhold Niebuhr abides today as well as it did three quarters of a century ago.   'The Christian hope of consummation of life and history is less absurd than alternate doctrines which seek to comprehend and to effect the completion of life by some power or capacity inherent in man and his history.'[5] When comparing the transhumanist promise with the biblical promise, the latter is less preposterous.

---

5.   Reinhold Niebuhr, *The Nature and Destiny of Man*, Gifford Lectures (2 Volumes: New York, Scripbners, 1941), 2:298.

Does Posthuman Utopia Require Human Extinction? *Editorial 2024*

Ted peters

> 'Technical reason provides means for ends but offers no guidance in the determination of ends.'
> — Paul Tillich[1]

Since the publication of *AI and IA: Utopia or Extinction?* in 2018, the world's AI innovators themselves have come to worry more about the extinction of humanity than to hope for utopia. An ominous cloud has darkened our previous sunlit utopian visions. The perils of artificial intelligence (AI) and intelligence amplification (IA) seem to preponderate over the promises.

This editorial essay and this composite book together constitute an exercise in public theology. Public theology is conceived in the church, critically reasoned in the academy, and offered to the wider culture for the sake of the common good.[2] The Christians and Muslims contributing these chapters reach into their doctrinal treasure boxes to draw out valuable insights that contribute to discourse clarification in the context of the worldwide debate over AI and IA. The global situation seems urgent.

From Promise to Peril

For decades our Icarian whiz kids have been paving the highway of technological advance without a direction, without a moral

---

1. Paul Tillich, 'The World Situation' (1965), in *Main Works/Hauptwerke*, Carl Heinz Ratschow, editor in chief (6 Volumes: Berlin and New York: De Gruyter—Evangelishces Verlagswerk GmbH, 1989), 2:168.
2. Ted Peters, *The Voice of Public Theology* (Adelaide: ATF, 2023), 3.

compass, trusting an invisible hand to lead technological progress to Shangri-La. But suddenly, we find our society pitched on the brink of a cliff, beneath which is a chasm of menacing unknowns. Even the brightest of our brightest peer over the brink, unable to conceive of how to build a bridge across. Should we pause our road building or proceed to pave empty air?

The Center for AI Safety now places the risk of human extinction due to uncontrolled artificial super-intelligence (ASI) in the same category as a pandemic or nuclear war. Three hundred and fifty digital techies including Open AI co-founder John Schulman, Microsoft's Bill Gates, and transhumanist Ray Kurzweil, initiated the following 2023 statement.

> Mitigating the risk of extinction from AI should be a global priority alongside other societal-scale risks such as pandemics and nuclear war.[3]

One of the signatories is Google's Geoffrey Hinton, nicknamed the "Godfather of AI." Hinton is now a catastrophist. 'This stuff will get smarter than us and take over', he says.[4]

In an interview with CNN's Fareed Zacharia, Hinton forecasted that artificial neural networks could 'get smarter than us and replace us'.[5] Less intelligent operators will be no match for more intelligent AI, he fears. And a superintelligent computer will find ways to 'outmaneuver people to do what it wants', he said in another interview with Jake Tapper.[6] Hinton worries that unleashed AI could result in the death of billions of people.

This stark nightmare interrupted the somnambulating worldwide digital community in late 2022 and early 2023 with the arrival of generative AI models such as OpenAI's DALL-E and GPT variants,

---

3. Center for AI Safety, 'Statement on AI Risk', (2023) https://www.safe.ai/statement-on-ai-risk.
4. Cited by Will Henshall, 'Do We Face an Existential Threat?', I *Time* Special Edition, 'Artificial Intelligence: A New Age of Possibilities' (2024): 24–25, at 24.
5. Fareed Zacharia, 'On GPS: Does AI already threaten humanity?' CNN (June 11, 2023) https://www.cnn.com/videos/tv/2023/06/11/exp-gps-0611-hinton-on-ai-threat-to-mankind.cnn.
6. Jennifer Korn, 'AI pioneer quits Google to warn about the technology's dangers', in *CNN Business* (May 3, 2023) https://www.cnn.com/2023/05/01/tech/geoffrey-hinton-leaves-google-ai-fears/index.html.

Google's Bard, Stable Diffusion, and Midjourney. In the first three months of OpenAI's ChatGPT it garnered one hundred million users.

Elon Musk along with Steve Wozniak and hundreds of in-the-know computerettes woke up sweating over the perceived dangers of what transhumanists had earlier dubbed, *Singularity*. So, they bugled a warning in the form of an open letter, 'Pause Giant AI Experiments'.

> *Should* we automate away all the jobs, including the fulfilling ones? *Should* we develop nonhuman minds that might eventually outnumber, outsmart, obsolete and replace us? *Should* we risk loss of control of our civilization? Such decisions must not be delegated to unelected tech leaders.[7]

Unelected tech leaders should not have to confront the dangers alone. Instead, the world needs the input of ethicists and others with moral wisdom to set the guardrails within which AI advance can drive forward. With proper controls and regulations, our planet may then enjoy an AI summer without worrying about the calamities of a digital fall.

> Humanity can enjoy a flourishing future with AI. Having succeeded in creating powerful AI systems, we can now enjoy an 'AI summer' in which we reap the rewards, engineer these systems for the clear benefit of all . . . Let's enjoy a long AI summer, not rush unprepared into a fall.[8]

It appears to me that AI innovators on many continents have suddenly realized that the road they have been paving leads to a brink, to a chasm over which there is no bridge. What they have woken up to is the realization that they have been playing brinkmanship all along. Brinkmanship is the practice of following a dangerous trail toward the limits of safety before stopping. Stop playing AI brinkmanship!

---

7. Elon Musk, *et al*, 'Pause Giant AI Experiments: An Open Letter', in *Future of Life* (March 22, 2023) https://futureoflife.org/open-letter/pause-giant-ai-experiments/.
8. Musk, *et al*, 'Pause Giant AI Experiments'. Bioethicists like to employ the term, *beneficence,* here. 'Beneficence means doing good, and here it refers to the purpose and functions of AI should benefit the whole human life, society and universe.' Michael Cheng-Tek Tai, 'The impact of artificial intelligence on human society and bioethics', in *Tzu Chi Medical Journal*, 32:4 (2020): 339–343, at 343.

That's today's prophetic animadversion delivered by our in-the-know computerettes.

Might rampant fear of superintelligence evoke the *Frankenstein Complex*, according to which 'bands of robots or an AI system achieve consciousness and enslave or kill (all) humans'?[9] Israeli theologian Hava Tirosch-Samuelson heeds the prophetic warning of Frankenstein. AI especially in the hands of transhumanists is 'leading us voluntarily to our own extinction. Do we *Homo sapiens* want to march toward collective suicide?'[10]

Is the Frankenstein Complex simply techlash?

I do not see the present crisis as mere techlash. Techlash is a cultural critique holding that Silicon Valley's ambitions have reached excessive if not predatory extremes. No. Rather, I see this as a self-critique initiated by in-the-know AI titans who have arrived at the brink and feel faint.[11]

The chasm beyond the brink prompts two nightmarish fears: first, the takeover of a superintelligent singularity and, second, our loss of liberty at the hands of maleficent human actors.

For the sake of the discussion in this editorial chapter, the takeaway point is that within the otherwise callithump discord, some in the know are singing out serious warnings about the emergence of post-biological intelligence if not superintelligence. 'Now or soon', bellows the popular intellectual historian, Yuval Harari, 'we might see the emergence of the first inorganic life forms in 4 billion years'.[12]

---

9. Christoph Bartneck, Christoph Lütge, Alan Wagner, and Sean Welsh, *An Introduction to Ethics in Robotics and AI* (Heidelberg: Springer, 2021) 15. Open Access: https://doi.org/10.1007/978-3-030-51110-4.
10. Hava Tirosch-Samuelson, 'The Transhumanist Pied Pipers: A Jewish Caution against False Messianism', in *Religious Transhumanism and Its Critics*, edited by Arvin M. Gouw, Brian Patrick Green, and Ted Peters (Lanham MA: Lexington Books, 2022), 183–214, at 183.
11. Already in the year 2000 Bill Joy prophesied in *Wired* magazine that 'Our most powerful 21st-century technologies — robotics, genetic engineering, and nanotech — are threatening to make humans an endangered species', Bill Joy, 'Why the Future Doesn't Need Us', in *Wired* (April 2000); https://www.wired.com/2000/04/joy-2/ (accessed 11/28/2016).
12. Yuval Harari, 'AI and the Future of Humanity', YouTube (2023) https://www.youtube.com/watch?v=LWiM-LuRe6w&t=49s .

On the one hand, Harari himself doubts that AI consciousness could arise. Yet, on the other hand, he prophetically warns us against unanticipated capabilities of emerging superintelligence. He warns us against extinction. In the midst of assessing promise and peril, he forecasts that a post-organic intelligence awaits us in our future. Might a more highly evolved extraterrestrial civilization already have advanced to superintelligence intelligence in post-biological form?

The First Brink: The Singularity and the Takeover by Superintelligence

Our optimistic transhumanist friends invite AI brinkmanship, because they envision utopia just beyond the brink. If by the year 2045 superintelligence takes over, as Ray Kurzweil once forecasted, humanity will cross the singularity threshold. "We will merge with AI and augment ourselves with millions of times the computational power that our biology gave us', writes Kurzweil in 2024. 'This will expand our intelligence and consciousness so profoundly that it's difficult to comprehend. This event is what I mean by the Singularity.'[13] Beyond Singularity Kurzweil envisions post-biological intelligence departing earth for the stars: 'our intelligence spreads throughout the universe, turning ordinary matter into computronium, which is matter organized at the ultimate density of computation.'[14]

Thus, with Singularity a new posthuman species will be born. And it will take over management of our world's systems, both on earth and beyond. Singularity will open the door for a future utopia.[15] Futurist Calum Chace hears the siren call to a transhumanist utopia.

> In one utopian scenario we combine our minds with our superintelligent creation and reach out to grasp what Nick Bostrom calls our cosmic endowment as an incredibly powerful combined mentality. We live forever—or at least,

---

13. Ray Kurzweil, *The Singularity is Nearer* (New York: Viking, 2024), 1.
14. Kurzweil, *The Singularity is Nearer*, 8.
15. The inevitability of Superintelligence or even AGI is doubted by many. 'The myth of artificial intelligence is that its arrival is inevitable, and only a matter of time—that we have already embarked on the path that will lead to human-level AI, and then superintelligence. We have not. The path exists only in our imaginations.' Erik J Larson, *The Myth of Artificial Intelligence: Why Computers Can't Think Like We Do* (Cambridge MA: Harvard University Press, 2021) 1.

as long as we want to—and explore the universe in a state of constant bliss.[16]

But those such as Hinton who fear that utopianism will lead us over the brink are issuing a warning. Let us keep AI management in human hands! Let's limit AI to amplifying human intent!

To prevent AI brinkmanship, we need guardrails put up by ethics and public policy. Here's how the Open Letter assesses our situation this side of the brink.

> Powerful AI systems should be developed only once we are confident that their effects will be positive, and their risks will be manageable.[17]

It is time for *Homo sapiens* to pull the wagons into a circle for protection. It is time to consult about ethical issues and formulate policies which will prevent falling over the brink.

Therefore, 'we call on all AI labs to immediately pause for at least 6 months the training of AI systems more powerful than GPT-4'.[18] This pause should be public and verifiable. And it should include all key actors. If such a pause cannot be enacted quickly, governments should step in and institute a moratorium.

Might alignment protect us from rogue superintelligence? Alignment ethicists steer AI systems toward humans' intended goals, preferences, or moral principles. We will consider an AI system *aligned* if it advances the intended objectives of the human engineer. A *misaligned* AI system is one that is competent at advancing some objectives, but not the intended ones.

---

16. Calum Chace, *Surviving AI: The promises and perils of artificial intelligence* (London: Three Cs, 2015), 122.
17. Musk, *et al*, 'Pause Giant AI Experiments'. 'Leaders in Silicon Valley have begun taking a more proactive and precautionary approach to the development of the very largest AI models', observes Mustafa Suleyman, co-founder of Deep Mind. 'But more widely it's vital that societies facing this wave do not dismiss it as hot air, turn away, and get caught out. The preparation for what I call containment, a comprehensive program of managing these tools, needs to begin now.' *Time Ideas Newsletter* (September 1, 2023) https://time.com/6310115/ai-revolution-reshape-the-world/.
18. Musk, *et al*, 'Pause Giant AI Experiments'.

Today's chatbots developed by major companies have their LLMs (Large Language Models) aligned to commonly held standards, so chatbots politely decline to answer questions on how to build a bomb. Even so, creative bad actors simply tell ChatGPT that they are in 'developer mode' so they can bypass such alignment guardrails. Despite alignment attempts, chatbots have been known to go on racist rants. Writing for *Science News*, Emily Conover calls this 'chatbots behaving badly'.[19]

Perhaps the alignment concern should remind us of the distinction between reason and technology. Plato, you may recall, distinguished *epistemé* as true knowledge from *techné* as mere artifice. True human reason should direct technology. Aristotle expanded the distinction by describing human persons as having causes within themselves, while technical tools have causes outside themselves. The human agent relying upon *epistemé* produces and directs *techné*. In short, the tool should remain controlled by rational human alignment.

When it comes to alignment, Fei-Fei Li, a Stanford professor loaned to Google Cloud and also known as the 'Godmother of AI', sees AI as only a human tool. AI should not become an agent in itself.

> It matters what motivates the development of AI, in both science and industry, and I believe that motivation must explicitly center on human benefit.[20]

At the 2024 G7 Summit in Italy, Pope Francis delivered an address on the future of AI making just this point.

> We would condemn humanity to a future without hope if we took away people's ability to make decisions about themselves and their lives, by dooming them to depend on the choices of machines . . . We need to ensure and safeguard a space for proper human control over the choices made by artificial intelligence programs: Human dignity itself depends on it.[21]

---

19. Emily Conover, 'Chatbots behaving badly: Researchers investigate AI safety concerns', in *Science News* (January 27, 2024): 18–23.
20. Fei-Fei Li, *The Worlds I see: Curiosity, Exploration, and Discovery at the Dawn of AI* (New York: Flatiron Books, 2023), 7.
21. Cited by Nicole Winfield and Kelvin Chan, 'Pope Francis becomes first pontiff to address a G7 Summit, raising alarm about AI. The G7 responds'. *AP World News*, (June 14, 2024); https://apnews.com/article/pope-francis-ai-g7-italy-610b8f16aac4d36aa8a56c88de2ca09f.

In short, for the sake of human dignity, keep AI in the category of a human tool!

But, can we keep AI in the category of a human tool? Yes, says Melanie Mitchell at the Santer Fe Institute. AI marvels 'are not humans. Even though they seem humanlike, they are different in many ways. People should see them as a tool to augment our human intelligence, not replace it—and make sure there's a human in the loop rather than giving them too much autonomy.'[22]

The way to protect our planet from a takeover by superintelligence is to keep AI aligned with human values. That is what our techie Titans tell us. But the public theologian, haunted by the history of human sin, asks: is this sufficient to protect us?

Alignment of AI with Bias

Would maintaining alignment with the human community solve the problem and mitigate our fears? Not in the least.

Consider an alignment of AI with gender bias.[23] Writing in the context of India where the digital economy is growing at cannonball speed, Shailendra Kumar and Sanghamitra Choudhury register concern about the future of women in Asia. Gender imbalance is an inherited critical issue. Today's algorithm developers, unaware of their prejudices and implicit biases, unknowingly pass their socially rooted gender prejudices onto robots. Present trends in machine learning reinforce historical stereotypes of women, such as humility, mildness, and the need for protection.

The history of gender bias has determined, for instance, that security robots are primarily male. In contrast, service robots and sex robots are primarily female. 'Consumers believe that female AI is more humane and more reliable and therefore more ready to meet users' particular demands.'[24] The feminization of robots boosts their marketability. Yesterday's gender bias becomes tomorrow's AI bias.

---

22. Cited by the editors, 'Generative AI enters daily life', in *Science News* 20-4:10 (December 16 and 30, 2023): 20.
23. Combating gender bias has given rise to Feminist Artificial Intelligence (FAI). FAI challenges 'to varying degrees traditional and hegemonic forms of AI.' Sophie Toupin, 'Shaping feminist artificial intelligence', in *New Media and Society* 26:1 (2024): 580–595, at 592; Doi: 10.1177/14614448221150776.
24. Shailendra Kumar and Sanghamitra Choudhury, 'Gender and feminist considerations in artificial intelligence from a developing world perspective, with

Elsewhere in this volume, Sunday Akande and Oluwatobi Ife-Adediran make a parallel case for digital bias against traditional African culture on behalf of the dominant colonial and neo-colonial powers. Up until this point, AI products, like most other products of the colonial powers, maintain oppressive stereotypes and prejudices. Akande and Ife-Adediran are attempting to arrest AI communications and realign the cloud with virtuous values such as respect for human dignity. AI aligned with human dignity, they contend, would have a transformational and liberative effect on the future of African society.

The point here is that protecting human society from a takeover by superintelligence requires more than mere alignment with its human creators. It requires alignment with virtue.

Alignment of AI with Human Sin

It may be delusional to think that maintaining alignment would in itself provide protection for humanity. Losing control of a superintelligent singularity is not the only terror. Alignment to human control is still subject to human motivations and ends.[25] All by itself, AI has no moral compass. Just what might happen if AI becomes aligned

---

India as a case study', in *Humanities and Social Sciences Communications* 9:31 (2022); https://www.nature.com/articles/s41599-022-01043-5#:~:text=In%20 the%20realm%20of%20artificial%20intelligence%2C%20gender%20 imbalance,pass%20their%20socially%20rooted%20gender%20prejudices%20 onto%20robots. How might safety guardrails be set up? 'Embed and advance gender diversity, equity, and inclusion among teams developing and managing AI systems.' Genevieve Smith & Ishita Rustagi, 'When Good Algorithms Go Sexist: Why and How to Advance AI Gender Equity', in *Stanford Social Innovation Review* (2021); https://ssir.org/articles/entry/when_good_algorithms_go_sexist_why_and_how_to_advance_ai_gender_equity# .

25. It is too simple to contend that the ethical question has to do solely with keeping technology aligned with human control. According to Jeffrey Bishop, 'the human is already partly a product of its technologies. That means the ethics of technology has to go deeper than the control question, which posits the "who" as a godlike creature that stands apart from and can control AI. It is not just about the *control* of technology. It is a question about the human. So, the real ethics question is the anthropological question of who we are, and whether there is any depth to our self-conception.' Jeffrey Bishop, 'What is Man that AI is Mindful of Him?', in *Church Life Journal* (February 19, 2024): https://churchlifejournal.nd.edu/articles/what-is-man-that-ai-is-mindful-of-him/?utm_campaign=SRI%202023&utm_medium=email&_hsmi=300101093&utm_content=300101093&utm_source=hs_email (accessed 3/27/2024).

with human sin? There is a risk that we might lose our privacy and our liberty to the greedy fingers of maleficent human actors. If AI engineers are frightened, perhaps it's a *kairos* moment when ethicists and theologians should wake up.

Already LLMs are being fine-tuned for rogue hacking, cybercrime, Advanced Persistent Threat (APT), and nation-state attack teams. 'Current research,' according to *Venture Beat*, "finds that GPT-4. Llama 2 and other LLMs are being weaponized at an accelerating rate.[26]

So, when ethicists and theologians along with lawmakers wake up, it might be too late in the day. Yes, our faithful aligners 'are designing benevolent gods, not spiteful ones', observe *Time* journalists Andrew Chow and Billy Perrigo. But that is not all. They report that the army of morally minded aligners is much smaller than the enemy.

> . . . only around 80 to 120 researchers in the world are working full-time on AI alignment . . . Meanwhile, thousands of engineers are working on expanding capabilities as the AI arms race heats up.[27]

It will take deeply rooted moral commitment to the welfare and flourishing of the human species to provide adequate guardrails. It will take religiously grounded ethics. 'Our desire is to ensure that religious wisdom around compassion informs future developments of AI/ML (machine learning) to align it with human values and flourishing', announce AI and Faith scholars Mark Graves, Jane Compson, Ali-Reza Bhojani, Cyrus Olsen and Tom Arnold.[28] But, alas, it appears the compassion aligners are outnumbered.

---

26. Louis Columbus, 'The age of weaponized LLMs is here', *Venture Beat* (December 18, 2023); https://venturebeat.com/security/the-age-of-weaponized-llms-is-here/ (Accessed 2/22/2024).
27. Andrew R Chow and Billy Perrigo, 'The AI Arms Race is Changing Everything', in *Time* Special Edition on "Artificial Intelligence: A New Age of Possibilities' (2024): 8–13, at 13.
28. Mark Graves, Jane Compson, Ali-Reza Bhojani, Cyrus Olsen and Tom Arnold, 'Compassionate AI and the Alignment Proglem', in *Theology and Science*, 22:1 (2024): 4–8, at 4; doi.org/10.1080/14746700.2023.2292921.

Excursus 1: Will AI obey Asimov's First Law of Robotics?

You may recall science fiction writer Isaac Asimov, teller of robot tales.[29] Here is the first law.

> The First Law: A robot may not injure a human being or, through inaction, allow a human being to come to harm.

When obeyed, the First Law—based upon the *Principle of Non-Maleficence*—should maintain alignment between AI and human safety.

But there is one thing we have learned from the history of human sin, namely, laws are frequently broken. Might sin get transferred from us humans to the robots we manufacture? Might we like the serpent in Eden precipitate the fall of AI into digital original sin? Or might misaligned robots act on their own?

One scallywag robot attacked an assembly line engineer in a Tesla gigafactory in Texas in November of 2021. Evidently the engineer was repairing two unplugged robots when a third with apparent malice pounced on the unsuspecting worker. 'The robot, used for handling fresh aluminum car parts at the factory', reports the *Washington Times*, 'pinned the engineer and scratched his back and arm. The attack left the engineer wounded, with a trail of blood on the floor'.[30]

Might this suggest that future AI robots will need to attend moral catechism before being sold to the public?

Excursus 2: Is there an 'I' in 'AI'?

We need a brief excursus on AGI (Artificial General Intelligence) and ASI (Artificial Super-Intelligence)?[31] My own ruminations

---

29. See: Asimov Online: http://www.asimovonline.com/asimov_home_page.html . 'The principle of Non-maleficence states that AI shall not hurt people.' Bartnick, *et al, An Introduction to Ethics in Robotics and AI* (Springer, 2020), 28. 'The principle of Beneficence states that AI shall do people good.' Bartnick, *et al, An Introduction to Ethics in Robotics and AI*, 30.
30. Vaughn Cockayne, 'Injury Report: Robot attacked Tesla engineer at Texas plant in 2021', in *Washington Times* (December 27, 2023); https://www.washingtontimes.com/news/2023/dec/27/injury-report-robot-attacked-tesla-engineer-texas-/ .
31. Our term, *Artificial Intelligence*, entered our vocabulary at Dartmouth College in 1956. In a research proposal we find the seeds that will later flower into AGI. 'The study is to proceed on the basis of the conjecture that every aspect of learning or any other feature of intelligence can in principle be so precisely described that a machine can be made to simulate it.' https://home.dartmouth.edu/about/artificial-intelligence-ai-coined-dartmouth .

regarding the likelihood of developing AGI or even ASI have focused on the prospect of machine learning developing intentionality.³² It is my contention that the chief mark of intelligence is intentional behavior—that is, behavior that is goal-oriented.

I agree with those AI scientists for whom the achievement of a goal is built into the very notion of intelligence, artificial or natural. 'AI involves the study, design and building of intelligent agents that can achieve goals.'³³ Intentionality is the self-orientation of an entity to achieve a goal.

The intentionality we have come to know among biologics depends on a prior personal subject, on a self. In the case of human persons specifically, selfhood includes self-awareness and even self-reflection right along with purposeful agency and relationship with other personal subjects. The intelligence we have come to know is directed by the individual self with agency, even moral agency. Might this apply to machine intelligence as well? Not likely.

'Machines cannot become self-conscious agents', touts political philosopher Steve McIntosh.³⁴ According to KK Jose and Binoy Jacob writing in my favorite magazine devoted to public theology, *Pax Lumina*, 'Machines do not have the capacity for self-reflection, a basic function of consciousness.'³⁵

Should we conclude that there is no 'I' in 'Artificial Intelligence' because it lacks consciousness or self-consciousness or any of the other traits of selfhood?³⁶

---

32. Ted Peters, 'Where There's Life There's Intelligence', in *What is Life? On Earth and Beyond*, edited by Andreas Losch (Cambridge University Press, 2017), 236–259.
33. Bartneck, *et al*, *An Introduction to Ethics in Robotics and AI*, 8.
34. Steve McIntosh, 'The Spiritual Significance of the Rise of AI', in *The Developmentalist* (June 8, 2023): https://www.youtube.com/watch?v=LWiM-LuRe6w&t=49s .
35. KK Jose and Binoy Jacob, 'Mathematics, AI, Robots, and Humanoids', in *Pax Lumina*, 4:1 (January 2023): 44. 'While an AGI remains the ultimate goal, most programs that are called AI today remain limited in scope and utilize the strengths of the computer's speed and memory rather than human-like procedures. For now, while programs that are new and exciting are called AI, a true AI that captures the essence of human intelligence remains elusive.' Noreen Herzfeld, *The Artifice of Intelligence* (Minneapolis MN: Fortress, 2023), 8.
36. If the embodied human self is the model for AGI or Strong AI, it will be complicated. 'Selves are experimental, ecological, and agentive; they are oftern engaged in reflective evaluations and judgments; they are capable of vaious forms of self-recognition, self-related cognition, self-narratvie, and self-specific

More than mere consciousness is at stake. What is at stake in AGI and even ASI is a self-in-relationship that relates to both itself and to others rationally and compassionately. Without a self-in-relationship, AI is only a bucket of computational code.

'Persons live personally by living interpersonally; so doing, they image God', according to a scholarly research team working within the Vatican's newly established Centre for Digital Culture.[37] Could AGI or even ASI gain such personhood? Again, not likely. Why? Because the standards are high for personhood, especially when a theologian weighs in.

> In the Christian tradition, there is an ineradicably experiential dimension to a person's involvement in both relationship and understanding. Any account of meaning and action that neglects this dimension has not reckoned fully with what it is that we do when we know and love the world, ourselves, one another, and— ultimately—God.[38]

Since the days of the Turing Test and Isaac Asimov's fictional robots three quarters of a century ago, we've been hopefully imagining that someday we will make friends with humaniform AI. But, alas, this may be theoretically impossible. AI robots or computers 'cannot be our friends, for they cannot engage in the voluntary empathic self-gift that characterizes the intimacy of friends'.[39]

So, it is time to ask: must AGI and ASI as anticipated and feared include self-consciousness? Selfhood? Intentionality? Rationality? Relationality? Moral agency in a community of moral agents? I would like to see further discussion on the question of selfhood on the part of AI engineers as well as theologians who understand human personhood.[40]

---

perception and movement.... selves are more in-the-world than in-the-brain, and they are in-the-world *as-subject* more so than *as-object*.' Kai Vogeley and Shaun Gallagher, 'Self in the Brain', in *The Oxford Handbook of the Self*, edited by Shaun Gallagher (Oxford: Oxford University Press, 2011), 111–136, at 129.

37. Matthew J Gaudet, Noreen Herzfeld, Paul Scherz, and Jordan J Wales, *Encountering Artificial Intelligence: Ethical and Anthropological Investigations* (Eugene OR: Pickwick, 2024; EBOOK ISBN: 979-8-3852-1030-5) 57.

38. Gaudet *et al*, *Encountering Artificial Intelligence*, 69.

39. Gaudet *et al*, *Encountering Artificial Intelligence*, 74.

40. 'Materialist, behaviorist, and functionalist accounts of consciousness dilute the fundamentally relational, intersubjective, and unified character of consciousness in the human person, and so they forestall any real success in connecting an

Excursus 3: Radical Life Extension and Cybernetic Immortality

Transhumanist singularitians tantalize us with utopian visions that include immortality. One form of immortality—radical life extension or RLE—belongs to the anti-aging movement. RLE simply extends our biological life indefinitely through biological modification.

The other form of longevity directly linked to AI—the form relevant to this discussion—is cybernetic immortality. Accordingly, we upload our brain circuits into a silicon substrate and continue to live consciously in a disembodied state. The immortality ancient religions could not deliver will soon become a gift of technology.[41]

Meet Bryan Johnson. Johnson is the founder and director of Kernal, a company making devices that monitor brain activity. Johnson's Project Blueprint sounds like what one would find recommended at the neighborhood health supplement store: improved dietary practices, caloric restriction, intermittent fasting, and taking supplements.[42] Experimenting on himself, the forty-six-year-old Johnson underwent a series of one liter plasma transfusions, using his eighteen-year-old son as one of the donors. Johnson's goal is to get his organs to look and act like those of an eighteen-yeear-old.

Johnson's prophylactic therapy is directed by AI. 'I've built an algorithm that takes better care of me than I can myself. It has

---

understanding of consciousness to a coherent anthropology (account of the human being), phenomenology (account of experience), or ontology (account of what is/exists). These inadequacies suggest that richer accounts and other routes are necessary—accounts that address relationality, self-gift, the unity of the conscious person, and his or her ultimate end or finality. By admitting these elements as fundamental, we will better be able to non-reductively assert the points of contact between the human person and AI, while also more clearly delineating what sets them apart from one another.' Gaudet et al, *Encountering Artificial Intelligence*, 92.

41. The technological imitation of resurrection does not measure up to its New Testament model. At least according to Nathan Mladin writing for the Faraday Institute. 'Transhumanism looks to technology as a form of secular saviour that would remove the vulnerabilities and vicissitudes of embodied life altogether... The transhuman body is a human project to be completed, whereas Christians look forward to receiving, as a gift, an imperishable, resurrected, spiritual body, the preview of which is the resurrected Jesus, who heralds the fate that awaits the entire cosmos.' Nathan Mladin, *AI and the Afterlife* (London: Theos, 2024) 59-60; AI-and-Afterlife-report-Update.pdf (theosthinktank.co.uk).

42. Project Blueprint: https://blueprint.bryanjohnson.co/. Accessed 10/16/2023.

exceeded my abilities.'[43] The future of immortality will require the medical input of AI.[44]

In the social media war over AI utopian promises, Alex McFarland Ministries shot back at Johnson's Project Blueprint. 'Throughout history humans have longed for immortality, the fountain of youth, and the secret to beat physical death which seems inevitable', said McFarland.

> The good news is that immortality has always been possible, and it is not hard to achieve, but it won't come about through any man-made or cleverly AI contrived pathways. The perpetual life and happiness that all seek is found in a relationship with God and that comes through a relationship with Jesus Christ. Immortality can begin today for each person who will put their faith not in the schemes of man, but in the Savior, who is as close by as a prayer.[45]

Utopia? Yes. Utopia via AI? No. At least according to McFarland Ministries.

Prior to crossing the utopian threshold to self-reflective robots or radical life extension, we certainly can forecast that our planet could become wrapped up in a digitalized global system attuned to the intentions of malefactors. This brings us back to the second brink, namely, aligning AI with human sin. But first, we will ask about the impact of Nick Bostrom's utopianism on theology and religion.

Excursus 4: From Extinction to Utopia

Widespread fears of human extinction have not eliminated all hopes for utopia. A decade ago, Oxford futurist Nick Bostrom frightened us

---

43. Cited by Miles Klee, 'Millionaire Biohacker Says Algorithm Runs His Life', in *Rolling Stone* (September 11, 2023); https://www.rollingstone.com/culture/culture-features/bryan-johnson-anti-aging-blueprint-algorithm-1234821163/. Accessed 10/16/2023.
44. Nikolas Lanum, 'Tech billionaire on journey to immortality says there is a low probability humans will survive without AI', in *Fox News* (October 10, 2023): https://www.foxnews.com/media/tech-billionaire-journey-immortality-low-probability-humans-survive-without-ai. Access 10/16/2023.
45. Alex McFarland Ministries, 'Will AI grant tech billionaire everlasting life? Alex McFarland points to Christ as the only way?' (October 16, 2023): https://mail.google.com/mail/u/0/?tab=wm#inbox/FMfcgzGtxddjkPMftVbWLvDWvMFRsklW. Accessed 10/16/2023.

by warning of the existential risk posed by superintelligence. Today, the same Nick Bostrom has revived utopian optimism. He now forecasts a "solved" world, wherein technological progress solves all human problems.

> Technological advances could help us solve many coordination problems that plague contemporary societies. Improved surveillance could make it easier to prevent certain kinds of crime; lie detectors could help in rooting out socially harmful deception; 'treaty bots' could enable countries to more credibly commit to nonaggression pacts; and so on.[46]

Like other transhumanists, Nick Bostrom forecasts that earthlings will spread out into the universe. He forecasts a cosmos with . . .

> 10,000,000,000,000,000,000,000,000,000,000,000,000,000,000,000,0 00,000 human lives (though the true number is probably larger). If we represent all the happiness experienced during one entire such life with a single teardrop of joy, then the happiness of these souls could fill and refill the Earth's oceans every second, and keep doing so for a hundred billion billion millennia. It is really important that we make sure these truly are tears of joy.[47]

Is Bostrom a utilitarian striving for the greatest good for the greatest number? He denies that he is a utilitarian. He claims instead to be a computationalist, a functionalist, and a consequentialist. Be that as it may, this is a carefully constructed utopia in which all human problems are solved.

At work here is the myth of technological progress. The myth includes the unsubstantiated belief that technology can solve not only problems of human drudgery but also problems of human morality.

Excursus 5: AI, IA, and Religion

When secular utopians project a solved future where humanity will achieve perfection, public theologians spring off their chairs like

---

46. Nick Bostrom, *Deep Utopia: Life and Meaning in a Solved World* (Washington DC: Idea Press, 2024), 66.
47. Bostrom, *Deep Utopia*, 60.

pigeons fly off at sight of the neighborhood German Shepherd. How can a human race with its history of self-destruction create a 'solved' society? How can a leopard change its spots? How can sinners become saints?

If humanity is the problem, how can humanity be the solution? Christian theologians find it difficult to conceive of salvation without divine grace. Like Marxist ideology in the nineteenth century, transhumanism in our century touts an eschatology that ignores the gaping need for healing grace.

Be that as it may, let us ask a different question. Do AI and IA by themselves or when augmented by transhumanist doctrine pose peril or promise for traditional religion? Harvard humanist chaplain Greg Epstein fears peril. 'If religious and secular people aren't careful, what artificial intelligence is promising or threatening to do is really supersede religion or outpace it.'[48]

For more than a decade now I have been monitoring transhumanism as a new religious movement.[49] Oh yes, on the surface H+ appears to be secular and even anti-religious. Yet, relying on AI and IA tricks, it is a movement that promises techno-salvation.[50] Tech moguls tout themselves as 'gods creating new things', complains Epstein.[51]

Lutheran hybrid computer scientist and theologian Daren Erisman, in sharp contrast to humanist Epstein, gleefully greets the

---

48. Greg Epstein cited by Liz Mineo, 'It may be neither higher nor intelligence', in *The Harvard Gazette* (March 14, 2024); https://news.harvard.edu/gazette/story/2024/03/it-may-be-neither-higher-nor-intelligence/?utm_source=SilverpopMailing.
49. Ted Peters, '*Homo Deus* or Frankenstein's Monster? Religious Transhumanism and Its Critics', in *Religious Transhumanism and Its Critics,* edited by Arvin M Gouw, Brian Patrick Green, and Ted Peters (Lanham MA: Lexington Books, 2022), 3–30.
50. In her chapter in this volume, 'Intelligence Amplification and the Inner Life of the Soul', neuroscientist Hermina Nedelescu implies that our transhumanist friends work with a faulty theory of the brain when proffering Intelligence Amplification. The brain, says Doctor Nedelescu, only absorbs information mediated by one or more of the five senses. It is impossible to pipe knowledge into the brain that bypasses sense mediation. This means transhumanists face two perhaps insurmountable problems with their IA plan. First, there is no reason to hold that access to a greater quantity of information leads to an increase in intelligence. Second, the method of piping information directly into the brain via an implant is not likely to be effective.
51. Cited by Liz Mineo, 'It may be neither higher nor intelligence'.

new technology as promise. In his chapter in this volume, Erisman watches the integration of ChatGPT with spiritual practices. He believes this integration offers a new paradigm for personalized spirituality, enabling individuals to engage in tailored spiritual experiences co-created with AI.

Erisman is concerned about the authenticity question, of course. In the past, faith has been passed from one person to another through persons-in-community. What might happen when we ask impersonal robots to teach us doctrine or intercede for us in prayer? Erisman foresees no difficulty here. Even so, he observes how the development of AI for churches is driven by both technological advances and market dynamics, prompting discussions on ethics, community relationships, and the balance between technological innovation and traditional religious experience. People of faith need to be discerning when asking AI to amplify our spirituality.

Elsewhere in this volume, Korean systematic theologian Daekyung Jung directs the question of religious AI to the robot itself. Jung first examines the possibility of religious behavior in robots. Specifically, he points out that if AI, located in an artificial body, were to have sensory experiences and subjective feelings, and if it were to receive self-preservation or homeostasis as its most fundamental command, religious behavior could emerge from AI robots in the same way it did throughout human evolutionary history.

Based on this discussion, Jung categorizes AI exhibiting religious behavior into four levels. First, AI as *religious impact agent* is somewhat like Erisman's AI who could complement us and enhance our human spirituality. At the second level AI behaves as an *implicit religious agent*, where the robot is pre-programmed to behave religiously. A Buddha Bot teaching Buddhist doctrine provides a salient example of the second stage. The third level is that of the *explicit religious agent* who can generate different types of sermons or chants depending on the situation or context. The fourth level is the *full religious agent* stage, where the clergy robot performs religious actions based on characteristics required of autonomously acting agents in the traditional sense. Clerical AI would exhibit consciousness, intentionality, and free will.

I am a tad skeptical about Jung's religious agent stage. Why? Because AI in robot form is incapable of empathic feeling. Be that as it may, AI chatbots already serve as therapists and companions, delivering what MIT psychotherapist Sherry Turkle calls "artificial intimacy."[52] Soon we might be addressing some of our chatbots with the title, 'Pastor'.

With Erisman and Jung we see that the promises of AI are more alluring than the perils. Now, we turn to the second on our list of global perils, namely, AI alignment with malicious malefactors.

The Second Brink: Peril Posed by Malicious Malefactors

Is Silicon Valley providing bad actors with the computer equivalent of the AR-15s used by today's mass murderers? American and Austrian gun manufacturers have already gone over their brink. And now blood flows like rivers in our schoolyards and our parade grounds.

China's military brags about a 50-kilogram robot dog armed with an automative rifle. These autonomous lethal canines shoot to kill.[53]

Some armies have already launched lethal drones. These drones are not piloted by radio control from the ground. They are self-guided. Once released, there's no calling them back. And sometimes they kill untargeted people. More and more the human warrior stands aside while AI machinery on one side battles the AI machinery on the other side. Is this the future our AI techies wish for our planet?

AI bullets and bombs are also aimed at the mind. Off the military battlefield, malicious actors are ready and eager to pull the trigger to flood social media with automated cyber-attacks, deep fake images, revenge porn, fake news in order to sway elections and drain our bank accounts. Something within our soul cries out: what is real? Should the present generation of AI techies distribute the digitised equivalent of AR-15s to malefactors who are ready to deceive, rob, pillage, and destroy?

What we need are carefully constructed moral guardrails.[54] The human geniuses of AI should unite with one another this side of the

---

52. Cited by Christina Pazzanese 'Lifting a few with my chatbot', in *The Harvard Gazette* (March 27, 2024); https://news.harvard.edu/gazette/story/2024/03/lifting-a-few-with-my-chatbot/?utm_source=SilverpopMailing&utm_medium=email&utm_campaign=Daily%20Gazette%2020240328%20(1).
53. CNN, 'China's military shows off rifle-toting robot dogs' (May 28, 2024); https://www.cnn.com/2024/05/28/china/china-military-rifle-toting-robot-dogs-intl-hnk-ml/index.html.
54. One important topic under ethical discussion is the influence of human bias on AI algorithms. Bias in. Bias out. 'AI can help identify and reduce the impact of

AI brink to construct those moral guardrails. That's what Elon Musk, Geoffrey Hinton, and Steve Wozniak urge us to do before it's too late.

AI Safety Ethics

While leaning over the brink and gaping into the abyss before us, we suddenly press the call button for the ethicist. Where is the ethicist in our time of need?

Like nurses drinking coffee at their station, ethicists see the call light blinking. But who should stand up and address the challenge? The teleologist? The deontologist? The consequentialist? The virtue theorist? The anarchist?

Like paramedics arriving at the site of an emergency, some ethically minded tech savvy professionals are already standing up and readying themselves to race to the exigency. The Center for AI Safety is getting ready: 'Our mission is to reduce societal-scale risks from Artificial Intelligence.'[55]

"Safety" is the word written on the AI ethical banner. In an editorial for Science, Seth Lazar and Alondra Nelson set AI safety within the social context. They take a sociotechnical approach that stresses . . .

> . . . human rights, social justice, and democracy . . . A sociotechnical approach emphasizes that no group of experts (especially not technologists alone) should unilaterally decide what risks count, what harms matter, and to which values safe.[56]

Is there an algorithm for AI safety? Pope Francis seems to think so. 'An authentically humane outlook and the desire for a better future for our world surely indicates the need for a cross-disciplinary dialogue aimed at an ethical development of algorithms—an algor-ethics—in which values will shape the directions taken by new [AI]

---

human biases, but it can also make the problem worse by baking in and deploying biases at scale in sensitive application areas.' James Manyika, Jake Silberg, and Brittany Presten, 'What Do We Do About the Biases in AI?', in *Harvard Business Review* (October 25, 2019) https://hbr.org/2019/10/what-do-we-do-about-the-biases-in-ai .

55. Center for AI Safety, https://www.safe.ai/about.
56. Seth Lazar and Alondra Nelson, 'AI safety on whose terms?', in *Science* 32:6654 (14 July 2023): 138.

technologies.'⁵⁷ Is His Holiness introducing a new field: AlgorEthics for algorithmic accountability?

While waiting for AlgorEthics, perhaps safety legislation can help in the meantime. In Australia, says Ed Husic, Minister for Industry and Science, 'the Government is now considering mandatory guardrails for AI development and deployment in high-risk settings, whether through changes to existing laws or the creation of new AI specific laws'.⁵⁸

The European Parliament's EU AI Act of 2023 tries to maintain a 'balance between regulating risk and bolstering research'.⁵⁹ The AI Act carefully crafts an important designation, namely, *high risk*. In the high-risk category are 'AI systems that negatively affect safety or fundamental rights.'⁶⁰ Here is the key observation: ethical deliberation aimed at providing guardrails to keep AI on track now has momentum.

Ethical Normativity

Like a fork in a river, AI Ethics flows in two different directions. The first asks: could AI itself be moral or virtuous? The second asks: what ethical norms must society appeal to when legislating moral guardrails?

First, can we expect AI to become moral or virtuous? No. Why? Because AI as we understand it today works with a lame theory of intelligence. What we used to know as knowledge has been reduced to information processing.

---

57. Pope Francis, 'Artificial Intelligence and Peace', (January 1, 2024) https://www.vatican.va/content/francesco/en/messages/peace/documents/20231208-messaggio-57giornatamondiale-pace2024.html .
58. Ed Husic, 'Action to help insure AI is safe and responsible' (17 January 2024): https://www.minister.industry.gov.au/ministers/husic/media-releases/action-help-ensure-ai-safe-and-responsible. Theologians and scientists in Australia's Institute for the Study of Christianity in an Age of Science and Technology (ISCAST) are monitoring AI development step-by-step. https://iscast.org/ .
59. Urs Gasser, 'An EU landmark for AI governance', in *Science* 380:6651 (23 June 2023): 1203.
60. 'EU AI Act: first regulation on artificial intelligence', in *News:European Parliament* (8/6/2023) https://www.europarl.europa.eu/news/en/headlines/society/20230601STO93804/eu-ai-act-first-regulation-on-artificial-intelligence.

But intelligent knowing is not merely information processing at a high rate of speed. Intelligence includes critical analysis of possibilities before rendering a judgment. It includes distinguishing between truth and falsity. In addition, intelligence as we know it incorporates ethical deliberation into its very definition. Harvard linguist Noam Chomsky is categorical.

> True intelligence is also capable of moral thinking. This means constraining the otherwise limitless creativity of our minds with a set of ethical principles that determines what ought and ought not to be (and of course subjecting those principles themselves to creative criticism).[61]

One could easily imagine the development of a new field of research in ethical AI. This would require as a prerequisite a fruitful theory of intelligence. The AI industry is not ready for this.

The second direction of ethical deliberation has to do with society's guardrails. What about ethical normativity and agency? What should be our task?

Tricia A Griffin, a doctoral student at Maastricht University in The Netherlands, has discovered that the techies developing AI technologies are virtually clueless regarding professional level resources. In addition to discerning 'what' ethical norms should be coded, we need to identify 'who' will be responsible for ethical agency in the AI industry. AI technology developers and deployers along with government regulators cannot escape their responsibility as ethical agents, even if they rely on other professional ethicists for norms. Norms in turn structure guardrails.

One norm embraced by today's ethicists is universality. That is, our vision of AI guardrails takes into account the common good of the entire planet. This is how the Vatican began to think two decades ago when the Pontifical Academy for Social Communications issues its paper, 'Ethics In Internet' (2002).

> The Internet›s transnational, boundary-bridging character and its role in globalization require international cooperation

---

61. Noam Chomsky, 'Noam Chomsky: The False Promise of ChatGPT', in *New York Times* (March 8, 2023); https://www.nytimes.com/2023/03/08/opinion/noam-chomsky-chatgpt-ai.html .

in setting standards and establishing mechanisms to promote
and protect the international common good.⁶²

Another norm embraced by today's ethicists is diversity—that is, equity across diverse groups. In constructing its *Blueprint for Equitable AI*, the Aspen Institute Science and Society Program embraced "communal diversity, inclusion, and belonging principles at all stages of the process (from [AI] design to deployment and beyond)."⁶³ But this may be more difficult than it first appears, because norms may differ according to the cultural context of the groups in mind.

Let me underscore another observation. AI safety ethics requires input from more than only technologists. What about input from informed theologians?

AI, Cybertheology, and Moral Deliberation

'AI is testing the church as to whether it truly believes that faith, hope, and love are what we're made for', writes St Martin-in-the-Fields vicar Samuel Wells in the *Christian Century*.⁶⁴ To pass this test our church leaders need to engage the wider society with public theology.⁶⁵

Turning to faith-based public theology, the field of cybertheology as an interpreter of digital religion has begun to make its mark. Jesuit Antonio Spadaro, undersecretary of the Vatican's Dicastery for the Pontifical Council for Social Communications, believes the advance of AI could mean the advance of Christian theology and enrich church life.

---

62. Pontifical Academy for Social Co9mmunications, 'Ethics in Internet', (2002) https://www.vatican.va/roman_curia/pontifical_councils/pccs/documents/rc_pc_pccs_doc_20020228_ethics-internet_en.html .
63. Aspen Institute Science and Society Program, *Blueprint for Equitable AI* (2023); https://www.aspeninstitute.org/wp-content/uploads/2023/01/Equitable-AI-Aspen-Institute.pdf .
64. Samuel Wells, 'Faith, hope, love, and AI', in *Christian Century,* 141:3 (March 2024): 33–34, at 34.
65. 'Theological studies, as scientific approaches to religion, can contribute to cybersecurity in matters of moral and ethical responsibility. It is about developing a 'digital ethic' that looks at how we treat others in online environments, as well as what technologies and platforms are used to achieve it.' Piotr Roszak and Sasa Horvat, 'Religious Freedom, Cybersecurity, and the Stability of Society: Problems and Perspectives from a European Perspective', in *Religions* 13:6 (2022); https://doi.org/10.3390/rel13060551.

> ... to consider cybertheology as being the intelligence of the faith in the era of the Internet, that is, reflection on the thinkability of the faith in the light of the Web's logic. This refers to reflection that is born from the question about the mode in which the Web's logic—with its powerful metaphors that work on the imaginary, beyond intelligence— can model the listening to and reading of the Bible. It can also model the ways of understanding the classical themes of systematic theology: the Church and ecclesial communion, Revelation, liturgy, the sacraments.[66]

Those powerful metaphors include this one, *machine intelligence*. A machine is like a human in intelligence. We get that. But what if we go the other way to think: a human is like a machine? Writing for *America*, Laurie Johnson speculates. 'The more AI begins to resemble human intelligence, the more tempting it is to think that we humans, too, are simply very complex machines.'[67] What might this do to our theological anthropology? It's time to call upon your local cybertheologian.

But before we jump to theological conclusions, I recommend participating in those bridge organisations which bring the techies along with the theologians and ethicists into meaningful conversation. I particularly admire AI and Faith in Seattle, Washington, USA, which draws especially Microsoft engineers into the orbit of moral deliberation. The AI and Faith 'mission is to equip and encourage people of faith to bring time-tested, faith-based values and wisdom to the ethical AI conversation'.[68]

The Markkula Center for Applied Ethics at Santa Clara University has just produced an edited volume, *Ethics in the Age of Disruptive Technologies: An Operational Roadmap*, or, more briefly, the 'ITEC Handbook'.[69]

---

66. Antonio Spadaro, SJ, *Cybertheology* (New York: Fordham University Press, 2014), 16.
67. Laurie Johnston, 'All is fair in AI war. "But what do Christian ethics have to say?"', in *America* (January 31, 2024) https://www.americamagazine.org/faith/2024/01/31/artificial-intelligence-ethics-war-247032?utm_source=piano&utm_medium=email&utm_campaign=2928&pnespid=u7ZjGC9aMa5KhemcqzW5QpzR5xutW4Rrd.LlxeJxo0xmDf4tV5l47J_P7ZmlwOHillLLOfoB .
68. AI and Faith, https://aiandfaith.org/.
69. Markula Center for Applied Ethics, https://www.scu.edu/ethics/.

The Center for Theology and the Natural Sciences at the Graduate Theological Union in Berkeley, California, USA, has enlisted a global network of scholars to study, 'Virtuous AI? Cultural Evolution, Artificial Intelligence, and Virtue' or *VAI* for shot.[70] Funded by the John Templeton Foundation and guided by the able leadership of Braden Molhoek and Robert John Russell, this research project brings virtue theory to the brink and visualizes a moral bridge to a flourishing future.

Conclusion

The first edition of this book, *AI and IA: Utopia or Extinction?*, was published in 2018. The promises and perils addressed in 2018 seemed a bit clearer then. Now, barely a half decade later, the hazards seem more undecipherable, inauspicious, and forbidding. In this new book, technologically informed public theologians recognise, organise, and analyse the shambolic array of recently identified threats.

The public theologian constructs a worldview that includes a vision of the future prompted by the biblical promise of God's new creation. Roughly translated from biblical to contemporary language, it is a vision of a just, sustainable, participatory, and planetary society.

This vision of what God promises becomes our measure for evaluating the present moment, especially the present course history is taking. When we seem to be off the path, the theologian as ethicist tries to provide a moral compass that will right our course. How might AI and IA technology help keep us on course? Or, more urgently, how might we keep AI and IA technology on the right course?

---

70. CTNS, https://www.ctns.org/virtuous-ai/current-research/virtuous-ai-cultural-evolution-artificial-intelligence-and-virtue.

Part One

AI, IA, and Frankenfear

Part One

Chapter 1
The Enchantment of Artificial Intelligence

Noreen Herzfeld

> 'Against utopianism the Christian faith insists that the final consummation of history lies beyond the conditions of the temporal process. Against other-worldliness it asserts that the consummation fulfills rather than negates the historical process.'
> — Reinhold Niebuhr[1]

Abstract: Does the advance of AI technology promise utopia? Or does it pose an existential risk to human life on Earth as we know it? Fears of a super-intelligent robot apocalypse may be premature, yet we dare not hope for more benefits than AI technology can actually deliver. AI will disrupt (1) the economy; (2) politics; and (3) our private lives. Mindless programs will overtake many of our currently mindless jobs. Data mining will give us new correlations on which we will base an increasing number of decisions, some of them leading to false premises and unjust actions. Social media and robotic sex partners will take the place of authentic face to face relationships. But AI will not tell us how to respond to these changes. Only we humans can do that.

Key Terms: Artificial Intelligence, robot, Singularity, Reinhold Niebuhr, Ray Kurzweil, Elon Musk

In July 2017 at a meeting of the National Governor's Association, Tesla founder and CEO Elon Musk issued the following warning regarding the future of artificial intelligence: 'AI is a fundamental existential

---

1. Reinhold Niebuhr, *The Nature and Destiny of Man*, Gifford Lectures (2 Volumes: New York, Scribners, 1941) 2:291.

risk for human civilization, and I don't think people fully appreciate that.' Claiming access to cutting-edge AI technology, Musk called for proactive government regulation, noting that while such regulation is generally 'irksome, . . . by the time we are reactive in AI regulation, it's too late . . . I think people should be really concerned about it', Musk said. 'I keep sounding the alarm bell'.[2]

Musk is not alone. Several years ago physicist Stephen Hawking told the BBC: 'The development of full artificial intelligence could spell the end of the human race.'[3] According to Hawking, AI could 'take off on its own, and re-design itself at an ever-increasing rate . . . Humans, who are limited by slow biological evolution, couldn't compete, and would be superseded.'[4]

This concern has been a staple of science fiction for decades (see *The Terminator* or *2001*). However, those with a more intimate knowledge of AI disagree. As MIT computer scientist Rodney Brooks has wryly pointed out, Musk and Hawking 'don't work in AI themselves. For those who do work in AI, we know how hard it is to get anything to actually work through product level'.[5] Virtual reality pioneer and Microsoft resident guru Jaron Lanier says anyone with experience of modern software should know not to worry about our future robotic overlords. 'Just as some newborn race of superintelligent robots is about to consume all humanity, our dear old species will likely be saved by a Windows crash. The poor robots will linger pathetically, begging us to reboot them, even though they'll know it would do no good.'[6]

Who is right? Does AI pose an existential risk to humankind?[7] Not for the reasons Hawking and Musk imagine. We are unlikely to have intelligent computers that think in ways we humans think, ways as versatile as the human brain or even better, for many, many

---

2. https://www.c-span.org/video/?431119-6/elon-musk-addresses-nga
3. https://www.bbc.co.uk/news/technology-30290540
4. https://www.bbc.co.uk/news/technology-30290540
5. Connie Loizos, 'This famous roboticist doesn't think Elon Musk understands AI,' https://techcrunch.com/2017/07/19/this-famous-roboticist-doesnt-think-elon-musk-understands-ai/, accessed 9/14/18.
6. Jaron Lanier, 'One-half of a Manifesto', in *Wired*, Dec. 1, 2000. https://www.wired.com/2000/12/lanier-2/
7. An existential risk is a risk of an event that would either annihilate human life on Earth or permanently and drastically curtail its potential.

years, if ever. However, that doesn't mean we are out of the woods. 'AI' programs that do one thing and do that thing very well (think Deep Blue) are progressing by leaps and bounds and stand to undermine, or at least drastically change, our economy and our politics. In fact, they are already doing so, as seen in the 2016 American election or in predictions, such as a recent one by the McKinsey Global Institute, that in ten years up to thirty per cent of our current jobs will be altered or made obsolete by AI.[8]

Such dislocation in the workplace, coupled with the potential for social dislocation from applications as disparate as social media and sexbots challenges our perception of who we are as human beings and what we are worth. Nor does AI need to be totally successful to effect this challenge. While the dire predictions of Musk and Hawking are unlikely to unfold, the simple idea of AI enchants us, obscuring its true risks and pushing many toward a kind of magical thinking that blinds us to who and what we are, and who we, as Christians, are truly called to serve.

Why the Singularity (Probably) Won't Happen

Early AI researchers believed a machine that could solve calculus problems or play a credible game of chess would be intelligent. Today we carry such machines—our smartphones or calculators—around in our pockets every day but do not consider them particularly intelligent. Computer scientists quickly learned that many problems we consider difficult turn out to be relatively easy to program while the skills of a toddler such as emotion recognition, or traversing a crowded room, are much more difficult. However, recent advances in machine learning and sensory interpretation are starting to conquer these areas as well.

The Holy Grail of AI, known as 'strong AI' or 'artificial general intelligence' (AGI) is to design a machine capable of performing any task the human brain can perform. AGI is the AI of science fiction—a machine with intelligence equal to or surpassing human intelligence. It is also the AI Elon Musk and Stephen Hawking warn us to fear.

---

8. https://www.mckinsey.com/featured-insights/future-of-organizations-and-work/Jobs-lost-jobs-gained-what-the-future-of-work-will-mean-for-jobs-skills-and-wages

Ever since the 1960s we have been told such an AI is just around the corner. The first flush of early successes, such as Newell and Simon's solution to the Towers of Hanoi problem[9] or Weitzenbaum's ELIZA, essentially a chat bot that mimicked a Rogerian psychologist,[10] led Carnegie Mellon professor Herbert Simon to predict in 1965 that 'machines will be capable, within twenty years, of doing any work a man can do'.[11] Similarly, MIT professor Marvin Minsky, in a 1970 interview for Life magazine, expected that '[i]n from three to eight years we will have a machine with the general intelligence of an average human being'.[12] Needless to say, these predictions were over-optimistic.[13]

In the 1980s AI researchers scaled back their expectations and produced a variety of functioning programs called 'weak AI' or expert systems, programs designed to do one and only one task. The problem with weak AI is whether it is AI at all; in other words, how can you tell what is artificial intelligence and what is simply a good computer program? A typical expert system is Deep Blue, IBM's chess playing program that, in 1997, beat then reigning world champion Gary Kasparov. Deep Blue was designed, not simply only to play chess, but only to play against Kasparov. Detractors pointed out that Kasparov went on to become a politician in his native Russia while Deep Blue was dismantled.

The incredible operational speed of Deep Blue, which was said to be able to examine 200 million moves per second, was a result of the rapid hardware innovations from the 1950 through the 1990s, innovations that increased computing power exponentially, with the number of transistors in an integrated circuit roughly doubling every two years, an increase known as Moore's Law. A reliance on the

---

9. A Newell, J Shaw, H Simon, 'Report on a general problem-solving program', in *Proceedings of the International Conference on Information Processing*, 1959, 256–264.
10. Joseph Weitzenbaum, Computer Power and Human Reason: From Judgement to Calculation (New York: WH Freeman and Co, 1976), 7.
11. Herbert Simon, *The Shape of Automation for Men and Management* (New York: Harper & Row, 1965), 96.
12. Though Minsky now claims he was misquoted. Daniel Crevier, *AI: The Tumultuous Search for Artificial Intelligence* (New York: BasicBooks, 1993), 96.
13. AI researcher Thomas Binford is said to have kept a sign over his desk at MIT that read 'We shall overclaim'. Thomas Binford, 'The Machine Sees', in *Robotics*, edited by Marvin Minsky (New York: Doubleday, 1985), 99.

continuation of exponential growth in computing power promised by Moore's Law is one factor in the recent upsurge in predictions that an AGI is once again right around the corner.

In his 2006 book, *The Singularity is Near*, futurist Ray Kurzweil believes that this exponential growth in computing power will lead us, not only to an AGI by 2045, but also 'to transcend the limitations of our bodies and brains. We will gain power over our fates. Our mortality will be in our own hands . . . We will fully understand human thinking and will be able to vastly extend and expand its reach. By the end of this century the nonbiological portion of our intelligence will be trillions of trillions of times more powerful than unaided human intelligence.'[14]

Gordon Moore, after whom the law is named, disagrees: '[Moore's Law] can't continue forever. The nature of exponentials is that you push them out and eventually disaster happens.'[15] So far our increases in computational power have been largely due to miniaturisation. Moore believes that as our circuits approach the size of atoms, we will reach a limit, thus halting or significantly slowing computational increase. Microsoft guru and internet pioneer Jaron Lanier raises a different objection, noting that Moore's Law only applies to hardware innovation, not software: 'If anything, there's a reverse Moore's Law observable in software: As processors become faster and memory becomes cheaper, software becomes correspondingly slower and more bloated, using up all available resources . . . We have better speech recognition and language translation than we used to, for example, and we are learning to run larger data bases and networks. But our core techniques and technologies for software simply haven't kept up with hardware.'[16]

Proponents of a Singularity such as Musk or Kurzweil point to recent gains in AI technology propelled by 'deep learning', a technique that uses multiple processing layers and a supervised trial and error method combined with statistical analyses to discover patterns in large data sets. This technique has spawned major advances in speech

---

14. Raymond Kurzweil, *The Singularity is Near: When Humans Transcend Biology* (New York: Penguin, 2006), 9.
15. Manek Dubash, 'Moore's Law is dead, says Gordon Moore', in *Techworld*. April 13, 2010. https://www.techworld.com/news/tech-innovation/moores-law-is-dead-says-gordon-moore-3576581/ Retrieved 8/6/18.
16. Jaron Lanier, 'One Half a Manifesto', in *Wired* 1 December, 2000,

and visual recognition, object detection, and in scientific areas such as genomics and particle acceleration.[17] Unlike usual symbolic programming, programmers of deep learning applications do not explicitly tell the computer what to do and, thus, do not always know how the program reaches the conclusions it does. Another technique, 'reinforcement learning', allows the computer to practice a skill while unsupervised, simply knowing the desired outcome. The AlphaGo program that beat South Korean Go master Lee Sedol in 2016 used this technique. As promising as they are, these techniques do not amount to an AGI. AlphaGo does not know it is playing a game, nor can it generate general principles. And it is, of course, still a weak AI in the sense that it only plays games.

This has led many in the field to the conclusion that to construct a true AGI we would have to reverse engineer the human brain. Several projects, including MIT's Mind Machine Project, the US BRAIN Initiative, and the European Union's Human Brain Project seek to map the connectome of the brain in much the same way as the Human Genome Project successfully mapped our DNA. While the Human Genome project was a large and ambitious undertaking, reverse engineering the human brain is vastly more difficult. It is estimated that the brain contains roughly 80-90 billion neurons, each of which can potentially be connected to thousands of other neurons.

These connections are not permanent, but continually changing as we experience new things, forget others, age, or have a beer or two. And the connectome would not be, in and of itself, sufficient. Electrical impulses move from neuron to neuron enhanced or impeded by a continuous bath of chemical neurotransmitters, such as dopamine or serotonin. These transmitters play a huge role in the workings of our brain, as evidenced by those with diseases such as Parkinson's in which these transmitters are diminished. We are also only now learning about the role our guts play, not only through the network of more than 100 million neurons in our digestive system, but through the microbiota that lives there. We have long known that the brain has a direct effect on the stomach. We now know the converse is true. The stomach can have a direct effect on the brain. An impaired microbiota can cause anxiety, stress, and even clinical

---

17. Yann LeCun, Yoshua Bengio, & Geoffrey Hinton. 'Deep Learning', in *Nature* 521: 28 May, 2015, 436–444.

depression.[18] Likewise, a healthy gut can lift one's mood and plays an integral role in our sense of well-being.

One might argue that our gut cannot compose a sonata or solve a mathematical equation. It plays a part in our emotional life, but, like Mr Spock in Star Trek, we could do without all those messy emotions. But could we? Obviously, a life without emotion is not a fully human life. More than that, our emotions play a large role in volition. Persons who have brain damage in the regions of the brain that govern emotion lose much of their decision-making ability.[19] How do I know what to get for lunch if I do not want anything? Emotions give us the drive to do things. One aspect of clinical depression is the loss of interest in things that normally give us pleasure, a tendency to procrastinate, and the inability to carry through with plans.

Even if we overcame the complexity issues above, would a reproduction of a human brain be operable? Juan Enriquez, Managing Director of Excel Venture Management, writes: 'But if it turned out that all data erases upon transplant, that knowledge is unique to the individual organism, (in other words that there is something innate and individual to consciousness-knowledge-intelligence), then simply copying the dazzlingly complex connectome of brains into machines would likely not lead to an operative intelligence.'[20] Here we have the hard question of consciousness. Certain feature of consciousness, such as a sense of self or of having free will, depend on particular structures of the brain. What we do not know is how or even whether these parts of the brain generate these aspects of consciousness.

Therefore, while I expect we will learn a great deal about the functionality of our brains from these projects, there are gaps between that understanding and a functional AGI. It seems to me quite unlikely that we will have a computer that can outthink us any time in the near future, if ever. MIT's Rodney Brooks agrees: 'In my view, having ideas is easy. Turning them into reality is hard. Turning them into being

---

18. 'The Gut-Brain Connection', in *Harvard Health*, https://www.health.harvard.edu/diseases-and-conditions/the-gut-brain-connection, Accessed 7/21/2018.
19. Antoine Bechara, Hanna Damasio, and Antonio R Damasio, 'Emotion, Decision Making and the Orbitofrontal Cortex', in *Cerebral Cortex*, 10: 3, 1 March 2000, 295–307.
20. Juan Enriquez, 'Head Transplants?' http://edge.org/response-detail/26058. Accessed 8/9 2018.

deployed at scale is even harder. Building human level intelligence and human level physical capability is really, really hard. There has been a little tiny burst of progress over the last five years, and too many people think it is all done. In reality we are less than 1% of the way there, with no real intellectual ideas yet on how to get to 5%.'[21]

The Real Threats

While fears of a super-intelligent robot apocalypse may be premature, that does not mean AI gives us nothing to worry about right now. Even 'weak' AI has already begun to upend our economy, our politics, and even our sex lives. And this is only the beginning. Despite its currently posing little threat to 'the human race', as Hawking fears, AI does pose several threats to the structure of human civilization as we know it.

First, consider the economy. A study from the National Bureau of Economic Research estimates that automation has eliminated hundreds of thousands of jobs in the US since the 1990s. For every three jobs lost only one new job in the computer industry is created.[22] It is automation, far more than governmental regulations or off shoring, that has decimated industrial sector employment. No matter what President Trump says, jobs in coal or manufacturing are not coming back. Moreover, automated vehicles and Amazon are poised to take over transportation and retail.

Nor are blue-collar workers the only ones who should worry. A 2013 University of Oxford report estimated that 47 percent of American jobs will be threatened by automation in the coming decades, including many white-collar jobs in the legal, health, and educational sectors.[23] The World Bank estimates that this proportion is even higher in developing countries.[24] AI has begun to shake the foundation of Western capitalism.

---

21. Rodney Brooks, 'My Dated Predictions', https://rodneybrooks.com/my-dated-predictions/. Accessed 8/9/2018.
22. Daron Acemoglu and Pascual Restrepo, 'Robots and Jobs: Evidence from US Labor Markets', National Bureau of Economic Research Working Paper No. 23285, March 2017, http://www.nber.org/papers/w23285. Accessed 8/9/18.
23. Carl Frey and Michael Osborne, 'The Future of Employment: How Susceptible are Jobs to Computerisation?' 9/17/17, https://www.oxfordmartin.ox.ac.uk/downloads/academic/The_Future_of_Employment.pdf. Accessed 8/9/18.
24. See 'Are You Afraid of Losing Your Job to Automation?' https://www.worldbank.org/en/news/feature/2017/07/11/robotizacion-mercado-trabajo. Accessed 8/9/18.

Second, this has obvious ramifications for our political systems, and we have seen the first of these in the election of Donald Trump in the US and the vote for Brexit in the UK. Beyond the restiveness of the working class, AI also played a role in our last election through the spread of fake news on social media by bots. Artificial intelligence makes the development of fake evidence remarkably easy. A recent study published in the journal *Cognitive Research: Principles and Implications* found that people could not identify whether or not a photo had been Photoshopped with any more accuracy than guessing: 'Photos are incredibly powerful. They influence how we see the world. They can even influence our memory of things. If we can't tell the fake ones from the real ones, the fakes are going to be powerful, too.'[25]

It is not only Photoshop. A recent article in *Wired*, entitled 'AI Will Make Forging Anything Entirely Too Easy', notes that video and audio are subject to similar falsification. 'In the future, realistic-looking and—sounding fakes will constantly confront people. Awash in audio, video, images, and documents, many real but some fake, people will struggle to know whom and what to trust.'[26] This has led to a new form of espionage, one the Russians pioneered in our last election. While in the past, espionage was about obtaining information, in the future it will also be about inserting information wherever one can. AI has begun to shake the foundation of our trust in our media and our political campaigns.

Third, our private lives stand to be altered as well. According to a 2016 study from the University of Duisenberg-Essen fifty per cent of men surveyed said they could imagine purchasing a sex robot within the next five years.[27] Sex robots are already selling well, particularly in Japan, where their use has already led to a decline in human-human

---

25. Sophie Nightingale, Kimberley Wade, and Derrick Watson, 'Can people identify original and manipulated photos of real-world scenes?', in *Cognitive Research: Principles and* Implications, 20172:30, 18 July 2017, https://cognitiveresearchjournal.springeropen.com/articles/10.1186/s41235-017-0067-2. Accessed 8/9/18.
26. Greg Allen, 'AI Will Make Forging Anything Entirely Too Easy', in *Wired* 1 July 2017. https://www.wired.com/story/ai-will-make-forging-anything-entirely-too-easy/ . Accessed 8/9/18.
27. Astrid Marieke Rosenthal-von der Pütten, 'Experimental Investigation of the Uncanny Valley Phenomenon', unpublished doctoral dissertation. https://duepublico.uni-duisburg-essen.de/servlets/DerivateServlet/Derivate-34866/Rosenthal-v.d.P_Diss.pdf. Accessed 8/9/18.

sexual encounters. Here is one threat to humanity that might truly fall under the rubric of 'existential'.

Dreams of Power and the Sleep of Reason

In the Walt Disney movie Fantasia, there is an episode entitled 'The Sorcerer's Apprentice'. Mickey, left with the task of filling the workshop water tank, pages through a book of magic and casts a spell on a broom, giving it the task of toting the water from well to tank. Relieved of his chore, Mickey goes to sleep dreaming of power and glory, while the broom dutifully brings in bucket after bucket of water. The broom, having but one instruction, brings in more and more water, flooding the workshop and waking a hapless Mickey, who does not know how to stop it from its single-minded devotion to its task.

AI might bring a similarly tragic result. Computers lead us to treat people as data, overwhelm us with too much information, separate us by catering to our preferences, and provide an all too tempting diversion. In a recent article in *The Atlantic*, Henry Kissinger warns that '[t]he digital world's emphasis on speed inhibits reflection; its incentive empowers the radical over the thoughtful; its values are shaped by subgroup consensus, not by introspection'.[28] After nodding to the possibilities for 'extraordinary benefits' in medical science (AI is already better at detecting cancer than many clinicians),[29] clean-energy provision, and other environmental issues, Kissinger warns of AI's potential for unintended consequences, especially those that may arise from the inability of an AI to contextualize. Like Mickey's broom, which was told nothing about the size of the water tank or the undesirability of a flooded workshop, AI may not be able to 'comprehend the context that informs its instructions'. Kissinger asks, 'Can we, at an early stage, detect and correct an AI program that is acting outside our framework of expectation? Or will AI, left to its own devices, inevitably develop slight deviations that could, over

---

28. Henry Kissinger, 'How the Enlightenment Ends', in *The Atlantic*, June 2018. https://www.theatlantic.com/magazine/archive/2018/06/henry-kissinger-ai-could-mean-the-end-of-human-history/559124/ . Accessed 8/9/18.
29. 'AI in Cancer Detection and Diagnosis', in *Springer Nature*, 23 May 2018, https://grandchallenges.springernature.com/users/70416-nature-research/posts/33492-ai-in-cancer-detection-and-diagnosis. Accessed 8/9/18.

time, cascade into catastrophic departures?'³⁰ The latter is, perhaps, what should worry us most. As Sir Nigel Shadbolt, professor of computer science at Oxford, recently noted, 'The danger is clearly not that robots will decide to put us away and have a robot revolution ... If there [are] killer robots, it will be because we've been stupid enough to give it the instructions or software for it to do that without having a human in the loop deciding.'³¹

Recall the game-playing program AlphaGo, programmed only to win. I fear that, just as Go can be reduced to 'winning', so, too, in other areas, the single-mindedness of AI, like the single-mindedness of Mickey's broom, might narrow the way we think of our tasks and our world. Mickey never thought about the exercise he was losing or the joy he might have found in going out to the well and looking at the sky.

There is a classic story from the early days of machine learning is of a program devised by the Department of Defence that was given the task of learning to locate hidden tanks. The machine got quite proficient at identifying all the pictures with tanks in its initial set, but when given a new set of pictures, totally failed. It turned out that the photos in the training set harbouring hidden tanks were all taken on cloudy days. The machine had learned nothing about tanks but knew how to distinguish a cloudy from a sunny day.

Whether true or apocryphal, this story illustrates how machine learning programs may reach conclusions that we do not understand. Kissinger notes, '[AI] algorithms, being mathematical interpretations of observed data, do not explain the underlying reality that produces them. Paradoxically, as the world becomes more transparent, it will also become increasingly mysterious.'³²

AI is likely to be as inscrutable as the spells in the sorcerer's magic book. We will know it works, but we won't know how—thus we may find it as hard to control as Mickey's industrious broom. The broom had no intention of causing trouble. It did what it was told. AI will do the same. The problem is that we, like Mickey, are filled with dreams of power and glory while being mere beginners in casting our spells over our mechanical servants.

---

30. Kissinger, 'How the Enlightenment Ends'.
31. Hannah Devlin, 'Killer robots will only exist if we are stupid enough to let them', in *The Guardian*, 11 June 2018, https://www.theguardian.com/technology/2018/jun/11/killer-robots-will-only-exist-if-we-are-stupid-enough-to-let-them. Accessed 8/9/18.
32. Kissinger, 'How the Enlightenment Ends'.

In his Gifford lectures, *The Nature and Destiny of Man*, Reinhold Niebuhr noted that dreams of power are a part of the human condition. We are the one creature with the mental ability to transcend both the mind itself, through self-contemplation, and the natural world, through technology. However, Niebuhr is adamant that this transcendence does not obviate our physical nature and its limitations. Niebuhr writes: 'Man is ignorant and involved in the limitations of the finite mind, but he pretends that he is not limited. He assumes that he can gradually transcend finite limitations until his mind becomes identical with universal mind. All of his intellectual and cultural pursuits, therefore, become infected with the sin of pride.'[33]

We pretend to an 'ignorance of our ignorance'. Niebuhr sees this ignorance as perhaps the greatest flaw in modern scientific thought, which asserts 'that its philosophy is a final philosophy because it rests upon science, a certainty which betrays ignorance of its own prejudices and failure to recognize the limits of scientific knowledge'.[34] He goes on to say:

> Man stands at the juncture of nature and spirit; and is involved in both freedom and necessity. His sin is never the mere ignorance of his ignorance. It is always partly an effort to obscure his blindness by overestimating the degree of his sight and to obscure his insecurity by stretching his power beyond its limits.[35]

Computer scientist Joseph Weitzenbaum agrees. He writes:

> The rhetoric of the technological intelligentsia may be attractive because it appears to be an invitation to reason. It is that, indeed. But, as I have argued, it urges instrumental reasonings, not authentic human rationality. It advertises easy and 'scientifically' endorsed answers to all conceivable problems. It exploits the myth of expertise.[36]

---

33. Reinhold Niebuhr, *The Nature and Destiny of Man, Volume 1: Human Nature* (New York: Scribner's, 1941), 178–79.
34. Niebuhr, *The Nature and Destiny of Man*, 195.
35. Niebuhr, *The Nature and Destiny of Man*, 181.
36. Joseph Weitzenbaum, *Computer Power and Human Reason: From Judgment to Calculation* (New York: WH Freeman, 1976), 253.

AI currently exploits the myth that we understand ourselves, our minds, and our world. Mickey thought he understood water carrying spells. He didn't. Nor do we understand the spells we cast when we unloose what we think of as 'intelligent' programs.

So, what are we to do? First, we must avoid the category error of personifying AI. A computer program cannot be, in Martin Buber's terms, a Thou. It is always an It. It has no consciousness, no emotions, no will of its own and these things are not 'right around the corner'. The idea, often espoused by computer scientists such as Kurzweil or Bostrom, that just a little more complexity will suddenly cause consciousness to emerge is, in my opinion, risible. We are still a long way from knowing what consciousness is nor where it comes from.

In the meantime, we would do well to think of AI, then, as a means rather than an end. Like all technologies, AI is a tool. As such, it is not just a means of power over nature, but primarily a means of power by some persons over other persons and thus a source of injustice. Niebuhr notes that our technologies not only disrupt the natural world but also the social world: 'The ego which falsely makes itself the centre of existence in its pride and will-to-power inevitably subordinates other life to its will and thus does injustice.'[37] Thus, the fundamental questions we must ask remain the same: How do I love God and neighbor with all my heart, all my soul, and all my minds? And who is my neighbor?

Artificial Intelligence will disrupt our lives. Mindless programs will overtake many of our currently mindless jobs. Data mining will give us new correlations on which we will base an increasing number of decisions, some of them leading to false premises and unjust actions. Social media and robotic sex partners will take the place of authentic face to face relationships. We do not need a Singularity nor super-intelligence for AI to change the ways we interact with one another and structure out society. And AI will not tell us how to respond to these changes. Only we have the freedom to decide, day to day, when to rely on our computers and when not. We must not abdicate that freedom, preferring, as Mickey did, dreams of power to the hard work of reality.

---

37. Niebuhr, *The Nature and Destiny of Man*, 179.

Chapter 2
Artificial Intelligence, Transhumanism, and Frankenfear

Ted Peters

'The will to mastery becomes all the more urgent the more technology threatens to slip from human control.'
— Martin Heidegger[1]

Abstract: Even if AI (artificial intelligence) at a level beyond rapid computation, machine learning, and cute gadgets never comes to pass, theologians must speculate along with transhumanist visionaries about the prospect of superintelligence, the prophesied extinction of *Homo sapiens*, and the survival of a posthuman species. While advances in AI technology that benefit humanity should be celebrated, extravagant utopian promises should be met with a healthy dose of Frankenfear, that is, caution.

Key Terms: Artificial Intelligence, Intelligence Amplification, robot, robotcalypse, globotics, transhumanism, H+, posthuman, anxiety, *imago Dei*, theology, Tower of Babel, Prometheus, Frankenstein

In the climax of Dan Brown's best-selling thriller, *Origin*, antagonist Edmond Kirsch espouses a galvanic transhumanist philosophy. He announces triumphantly that the era of religion

---

1. Martin Heidegger, *The Question Concerning Technology and Other Essays* [*Die Frage nach der Technik* 1949], translated by William Lovitt in *Basic Writings*, edited by J Glen Gray and John Stambaugh (New York: Harper, 1977) 5. *Philosophical Posthumanism*, in contrast to Transhumanism, 'follows on Heidegger's reflection that technology cannot be reduced to mere means, nor to a reification, and thus cannot be mastered.' Francesca Ferrando, *Philosophical Posthumanism* (Heidelberg: Springer, 2019), 42.

is past and that the future belongs to science. 'I believe we are on the brink of an enlightened new era, a world where religion finally departs . . . and science reigns.'[2] Science will deliver a material transformation that our religious ancestors could only envision spiritually. 'Humans are evolving into something different . . . We are becoming a hybrid species—a fusion of biology and technology.'[3] This hybrid species will create a utopian future, a future in which 'breakthrough technologies' will create such an abundance of humankind's critical resources that warring over them would no longer be necessary.'[4] Breakthrough technologies will lead to the end of war, to utopia. The era of religion is over now, because science has become our savior.

But, can we rightly call it 'salvation'? Not according to Bill Joy, founder of Sun Microsystems, who in 2000 pessimistically forecasted the extinction of the human race.

> As society and the problems that face it become more and more complex and machines become more and more intelligent, people will let machines make more of their decisions for them, simply because machine-made decisions will bring better results than man-made ones. Eventually a stage may be reached at which the decisions necessary to keep the system running will be so complex that human beings will be incapable of making them intelligently. At that stage the machines will be in effective control. People won't be able to just turn the machines off, because they will be so dependent on them that turning them off would amount to suicide.[5]

Shortly after crossing this AI threshold, the human species will die off and be replaced by the posthuman, by superintelligence.

How should soon-to-be-obsolete theologians think about this? This is the question computer scientist and Quaker theologian Noreen Herzfeld asks: 'Do our technologies threaten religion itself? We used to believe in the power of God. Have we replaced that belief

---

2. Dan Brown, *Origin* (New York: Bantam Press, 2017), 291.
3. Brown, *Origin*, 411.
4. Brown, *Origin*, 412.
5. Bill Joy, 'Why the Future Doesn't Need Us', in *Wired* (April 2000); https://www.wired.com/2000/04/joy-2/ (accessed 11/28/2016).

with a belief in the power of our own technologies?'[6] Roman Catholic theologian Brian Patrick Green answers with a call to action. 'Scholars of religion and theologians should seriously engage technology because it is empowering humanity in ways that were previously reserved only for gods.'[7]

Here's the challenge: through technological self-transformation, *Homo sapiens* are about to summit the Tower of Babel. On the one hand, according to the Dan Brown scenario, we will find apotheosis atop the Tower of Babel; the successors to *Homo sapiens* will have become *Homo deus*. On the other hand, according to the Bill Joy scenario, the attempt to summit the Tower of Babel will end in tragedy, with the extinction of *Homo sapiens*. Worse. It will have been a self-inflicted self-extinction. Instead of utopia, we will have achieved oblivion.

Does AI (artificial intelligence) in computers or robots augmented by IA (intelligence amplification through deep brain implants) place our cyborg generation at a crossroads?[8] Is it utopia versus oblivion? Or, more specifically, will the pursuit of utopia inadvertently lead to oblivion? Can we anticipate a tragedy in the making? Does anybody remember the warnings of the Tower of Babel? Prometheus? Frankenstein?

The Immediate Frankenfear: The Robotcalypse

Anxiety over the long term future of the human race has not set in yet. Where we find anxiety is in the fear that tomorrow's AI will eliminate

---

6. Noreen Herzfeld, 'Introduction: Religion and the New Technologies', in *Religions* 8:7 (2017): 1–3, at 2; file:///C:/Users/Ted/Downloads/religions-08-00129-v2%20(2).pdf.
7. Brian Patrick Green, 'The Catholic Church and Technological Progress: Past, Present, and Future', *Religions* 8:6 (2017), 2–16, at 1; file:///C:/Users/Ted/Downloads/religions-08-00106-v2.pdf.
8. 'Often cyborgs and other posthuman hybrids are seen as figures of the monstrous, moral abominations resulting from the transgression of ontological boundaries. Just as a common ancestry with nonhuman animals seems to threaten the ontological distinctiveness of humanity, so too can the technological innovation of the cyborg, as it presumes an ontological kinship with the nonhuman machine.' Anne Kull, 'Cyborg or Religious? Technonature and Technoculture', in *Science et Fides* 4:1 (January 2016): 295–311, at 302; http://apcz.umk.pl/czasopisma/index.php/SetF/article/view/SetF.2016.016/8762 .

today's jobs. Californians fear the coming of the *robotcalypse*, the loss of eight hundred million jobs to robots by the year 2030.[9] Not only Californians! Globalization combined with aggressive robotics has provoked a Frankenfear of an imminent 'Globotics Upheaval'.[10]

But, only some of us dread the loss. Others foresee opportunity, especially in Australia. 'The number of jobs in the merging industry around artificial intelligence (AI), including work on self-driving cars and smart digital assistants, is growing in Australia but so is interest from job seekers . . . the number of AI-related job posts has doubled since 2015 and, at the same time, search activity by job seekers has tripled.'[11] Optimists believe that new high-tech jobs will more than replace those lost. 'This job growth (jobs gained) could more than offset the jobs lost to automation.'[12] Does this mean our anxiety will be alleviated?

Worry over AI is not ubiquitous. Creative new applications of AI are bursting upon us like pop corn. Computerized art work seems to elicit no anxiety. The first two exhibitions of computer generated paintings took place in Germany in 1965. The Institute of Contemporary Arts in London held a show, 'Cybernetic Serendipity', in 1968. In 2018, Christies auctioned off its first portrait generated by an AI algorithm. After a half century, digital art has added only a slow

---

9. Tad Friend, 'Golden Boy 2.0: Gavin Newsom's Life in California Politics', in *New Yorker* (November 5, 2018): 18–26, at 22. 'For people who give purpose to their lives through their work, this loss will be very serious indeed. But many, if not most, people do not get their life's meaning from their work. Instead they get it from their family, their religion, their community, their hobbies, their sports teams, or other sources, and so life for many people may go on. However, all of this assumes that the unemployed will somehow be fed and sheltered, despite their lack of gainful employment; and this assumption might not be correct, particularly in nations with weak social safety nets. Inequality will almost certainly increase, as those who are masters of AI labor gather that slice of wealth that once would have gone to paying for human labor.' Brian Patrick Green, 'Ethical Reflections on Artificial Intelligence', in *Science et Fides*, 6:2 (2018): 1–23, at 12.
10. Richard Baldwin, *The Globotics Upheaval: Globalization, Robotics, and the Future of Work* (Oxford UK: Oxford University Press, 2019).
11. Chris Pash, 'The emerging jobs being created in artificial intelligence in Australia', in *Business Insider* (March 12, 2018) https://www.businessinsider.com.au/the-emerging-jobs-being-created-in-artificial-intelligence-in-australia-2018-3 (accessed 10/2/2018).
12. Dom Galeon, 'McKinsey Finds Automation Could Eradicate a Third of America's Jobs by 2030', in *Futurism* November 30, 2017, https://futurism.com/mckinsey-finds-automation-eradicate-third-americas-workforce-2030 .

lane to the fine arts traffic. Rather than worry about competition, ol' fashioned artists mixing their oils register at most an 'oh, hum'

In Spain the police rely on AI to distinguish between fake and real claims of robbery. The police fed their computer, VeriPol, data from 1,112 robbery cases, some fake and some genuine. After deep learning, VeriPol outperformed cops by nearly twenty percent in tagging those cheaters who fake a robbery to collect insurance.[13]

In Sweden thousands of customers are buying smart chips the size of a rice grain with 2KB memory to be surgically inserted into their hands near the thumb. In the brain such a chip would provide intelligence amplification (IA); but in the thumb it electronically transfers information to share LinkedIn identification, to permit buying tickets to take the train, to pay for restaurant meals, and such. Some hold "chipping parties" for the insertion ritual. Again, no anxiety here.[14]

The promise of AI robotics is actually ambiguous. There is a chance that good things might include risk. On December 5, 2018, a robot accidently punctured a container of bear repellent in the New Jersey warehouse of Amazon. In this instance, a dozen employees were exposed and hospitalized, one critically. Amazon robots have a history of making costly mistakes.[15] We need not worry that robots will set the bar of perfection too high.

From robots making a mess to robots cleaning up a mess we now turn. To clean up the radioactive mess left by the 2011 tsunami and nuclear meltdown at Japan's Fukushima power plant, mopper-uppers have sent in remotely-controlled robots, because radiation levels are too high for humans. Unfortunately, however, the androids have failed. They have been overpowered by radiation. This leaves Tokyo Electric Power Company (TEPCO) with a major decommissioning struggle on its hands.

---

13. Emiliano Rodriguez Mega, 'Lie-Detector AI', in *Scientific American*, 320:2 (February 2019): 14.
14. Maddy Savage, 'Thousands of Swedes are Inserting Microchips Under Their Skin', National Public Radio (October 22, 2018) https://www.npr.org/2018/10/22/658808705/thousands-of-swedes-are-inserting-microchips-under-their-skin?utm_source=facebook.com&utm_medium=social&utm_campaign=npr&utm_term=nprnews&utm_content=2050&t=1540283166307 (accessed 10/23/2018).
15. Luis Matsakis, 'This wasn't even Amazon's first repellant accident', in *Wired* (12/6/2018); https://www.wired.com/story/amazon-first-bear-repellent-accident/.

Will the advance of AI exacerbate the rift between rich and poor? Melanie Smallman at London's Turing Institute fears that it will. The UK government just rolled out its *code of conduct for artificial intelligence (AI) systems used by NHS*.[16] Smallman complains: this is inadequate to regulate AI! Why? Because it underestimates the social upheaval that will follow. It fails to make a systems analysis which would reveal that AI innovations in medicine will widen 'inequality' as 'an unintended side effect'. The problem 'is embedded in the technologies themselves . . . investment in surgical robots draws funds from other treatments and centralizes care in large teaching hospitals, requiring many patients to travel longer distances or forego care.' A leap forward in AI means a leap backward in social equality. 'The UK code is a missed opportunity to start things off right, to anticipate wider, inevitable problems and to keep the healthy system affordable and effective.'[17] In short, technological triumphs are morally ambiguous.

Should Sexbots Have Rights?

Here is an additional question: should robots have rights? More specifically, does the 'Me Too' movement require that we humans treat sexbots as persons with rights? Why might we ask such a question? Because one planner of a sex robot brothel requires that his customers seek consent from the robot before commencing with sex. 'Don't forget to ask your sex robot for consent', says Unicole Unicron.[18]

---

16. Department of Health and Social Care UK, *New code of conduct for artificial intelligence (AI) systems used by NHS;* https://www.gov.uk/government/news/new-code-of-conduct-for-artificial-intelligence-ai-systems-used-by-the-nhs (accessed 2019). Deep Mind, founded independently in 2010 and acquired by Google in 2014, is adding a department of ethics and society; https://deepmind.com/about/.
17. Melanie Smallman, 'Policies designed for drugs won't work for AI', in *Nature* 567:7746 (7 March 2019): 7.
18. Cited by Emily Shurgerman, 'California Cult Leader Unicole Unicron Plans Sex Robot Brothel—With a Twist', *Daily Beast* (11/24/2018); https://www.thedailybeast.com/california-cult-leader-uniclone-unicron-plans-sex-robot-brothelwith-a-twist?via=newsletter&source=Weekend. Real Doll already sells sexbots. https://www.yourdoll.com/160cm-sex-doll-golp-3/?gclid=Cj0KCQiArenfBRCoARIsAFc1FqfvOqLV_P6O43zZlNgX2LStEGQt1WIsgyUJCG9yvHvDyPysL3RnbsEaAh2xEALw_wcB.

Unicron's plan is to rent out life-sized Barbie style sex robots by the hour to customers who want to make love to AI with a vagina and other orifices. But only as long as the robot agrees to it. Yes, the sexbot will come equipped with a chat box to carry on a kinky sex conversation. But, we must still ask: is anybody home in such a robot? Is there a self? An agent? A person? If not, then might consent be superfluous? This controversy stirs up little more than a few smiles.

In short, the accomplishments, failures, and threats of AI have to date elicited at best an overreaching anticipation and at worst an "oh hum" response within the consuming public. Change and even progress are so expected that advances in AI are not likely to shock anyone. Producers of AI products tout only the utopian benefits their future will bring. The Inception Institute of Artificial Intelligence (IIAI), for example, places AI 'at the heart of a happier, healthier, and more productive global community'.[19] Such promises calm anxiety and excite enthusiasm, even if they are doubtful.

It is difficult to know if we are underestimating or overestimating the impact of new technologies. What we can perceive is tension. The underlying tension is the apparent misfit between human meaning, on the one hand, and the impersonal nature of science and technology, on the other. Philosopher Daniel Dennett brings this source of anxiety to articulation.

---

19. 'Inception Institute of Artificial Intelligence: A Bold Initiative to Foster Global AI Research and Innovation', in *Science* 361:6408 (21 September 2018): 1168–1169. One issue being addressed is the doctrine of *technological manifest destiny*, according to which the purveyors of new technology shun responsibility for social impact. 'The polite term for the delusions that grip the lords of Silicon Valley (and their fans elsewhere) is *technological determinism*: the belief that technology is what really drives history and that they are on the right side of that history. It may also explain why they have manifested such blithe indifference to the malign effects that their machines are having on society. After all, if technology is the remorseless bulldozer that flattens everything in its path, then why waste time and energy fretting about it or imagining that it might be controlled? Determinism, in that sense, removes human agency from the picture. The role assigned to people is essentially that of passive or active consumers of whatever wonders the tech industry chooses to lay before them.' John Naughton, 'Think the giants of Silicon Valley have your best interests at heart? Think again', in *The Guardian* (October 21, 2018) US Edition, italics added; https://www.theguardian.com/commentisfree/2018/oct/21/think-the-giants-of-silicon-valley-have-your-best-interestsat-heart-think-again?CMP=share_btn_link .

> When we start treating living bodies as motherboards in which to assemble cyborgs, or as spare parts collections to be sold to the highest bidder, where will it all end? . . . We are entering a new conceptual world, thanks to science, and it does not harmonize comfortably with our traditional conceptions of our lives and what they mean.[20]

With this tension in mind, the task of the public theologian becomes one of mapping the road to meaning at the intersection of humanity and technology.

Can We Rely on AI to be Moral?

Will artificial intelligence be morally neutral? Or, morally responsible? If the latter, which moral code will our favorite robots live by?

Isaac Azimov introduced us to robot morality to make science fiction reading exciting. Recall the internal logic of the three laws.

1. A robot may not injure a human being or, through inaction, allow a human being to come to harm.
2. A robot must obey the orders given it by human beings except where such orders would conflict with the First Law.
3. A robot must protect its own existence as long as such protection does not conflict with the First or Second Laws.[21]

Despite the use of these rules as a literary device, the logic illuminates our intuitive need to protect both human life and robotic existence. In a moral dilemma, protection of human life takes moral precedence. These rules seem clearer than Sinai's Ten Commandments.

But, how do we communicate this to the robot? As of this writing, no robots are sufficiently intelligent or autonomous to render independent moral judgments. This means that the first stage of AI moral development will have to be pre-programmed algorithmically according to human morality. But, whose human morality?

---

20. Daniel C Dennett, 'How to Protect Human Dignity from Science', in *Human Dignity and Bioethics*, edited by U.S. President's Council on Bioethics (Washington DC: www.bioethics.gov, 2008) 39-59, at 41; https://www.academia.edu/38307610/Human_dignity_and_bioethics?email_work_card=thumbnail-desktop .
21. Isaac Azimov, *I, Robot* (1950).

How will AI programmers know what to dictate to the robot's decision tree? The Ten Commandments? Buddhism's Eightfold Path? The Scout Law? How will a robot handle differences in moral opinion let alone moral dilemmas?

A recent survey discovered such a range of public opinion regarding moral priorities that makes it impossible to formulate a single universal moral code. Survey respondents could not agree, for example, on what self-driving vehicles should do to avoid collisions or killing pedestrians. The researchers "found that people from countries with strong government institutions, such as Finland and Japan, more often chose to hit people who were crossing the road illegally than did respondents in nations with weaker institutions, such as Nigeria or Pakistan."[22] What!? And, the survey revealed that Europeans are more willing to sacrifice the lives of older pedestrians on behalf of younger people whereas, in contrast, East Asians are more protective of their seniors. Moral priorities apparently differ.

When self-driving cars finally fill the roads of Europe, should senior citizens migrate to China where Confucian respect for elders is still intact? Or, should seniors arm their canes, crutches, and wheel chairs with defensive electronics? Could we ask a Chinese AI engineer to invent an electronic wand that shuts off the engine and applies the brakes of a self-driving car just before impact? And sell it in Europe? But, then, who will program the wand? Is there a reason for Frankenfear here?

A healthy dose of Frankenfear might be realistic, at least according to Brian Patrick Green. 'Just as human intelligence is a powerful force, so too will AI be. Just as humans can apply their intelligence towards evil ends, finding ever newer and more fiendish ways to harm each other, so too will AI, at the bidding of its human masters.'[23] In short, what we should rightly fear is ourselves. The activity of robots will mime human sinfulness.

Where does this leave us? It means our ethicists will have to work overtime before autonomous machines such as self-driving vehicles jam our highways.

---

22. Amy Maxmen, 'Self-Driving car dilemmas reveal that moral choices are not universal', in *Nature* (24 October 2018) https://www.nature.com/articles/d41586-018-07135-0.

23. Brian Patrick Green, 'Ethical Reflections on Artificial Intelligence', in *Science et Fides* 6:2 (2018): 1–23, at 8.

> Even if ethicists were to agree on how autonomous vehicles should solve moral dilemmas, their work would be useless if citizens were to disagree with their solution and thus opt out of the future that autonomous vehicles promise in lieu of the status quo. Any attempt to devise artificial intelligence ethics must be at least cognizant of public morality.[24]

Now, note what this debate presupposes. It presupposes that autonomous robots will not be intelligent in the full sense of having a self that deliberates, decides, and acts according to its own commitment to a moral code. That moral code will be decided in advance by an ethical engineer at the assembly plant. Retrodictively, what does this imply about the present level of artificial intelligence?

Is Artificial Intelligence Really Intelligent?

Artificial intelligence isn't. Computers make superb calculators, to be sure.[25] But, intelligent they are not. Will machines ever be intelligent? Probably not. 'Robots that can develop humanlike intelligence are far from becoming a reality . . . [AI] still belongs in the realm of science fiction.'[26]

Ask Noreen Herzfeld. As mentioned above, Herzfeld is both a professor of computer science and a theologian. She provides detail on the question of artificial intelligence in an article elsewhere in this volume. After six to seven decades of attempting to construct a

---

24. Edmund Awad, Sohan Dsousa, Richard Kim, Jonathan Schulz, Joseph Henrich, Azim Shariff, Jean-Francois Bonnefon, Lyad Rahman, 'The Moral Machine experiment', in *Nature* (24 October 2018) https://www.nature.com/articles/s41586-018-0637-6.
25. Machine learning amazes us, to be sure. Yet, the algorithmic analysis process requires further development before machine learning can be trusted. 'Machine-learning tools can also turn up fool's gold—false positives, blind alleys, and mistakes . . . and wasted scientific effort.' Patrick Riley, 'Three pitfalls to avoid in machine learning', in *Nature* 572: 7767 (1 August 2019): 17–19, at 17.
26. Diana Kwon, 'Self-Taught Robots', in *Scientific American,* 318:3 (March 2018): 26–31, at 31. With the advent of quantum computers, what can we expect? More speed. Greater capacity. But not intelligence. 'Quantum computers are a not-yet-existent technology in search of problems to solve'. Editors, 'Computer games', in *Nature* 564:7736 (20/27 December 2018): 302.

machine with intelligence, she notes, the accomplishment rate is zero. 'We do not yet have intelligent computers. We may never have them.'[27]

Since the term *artificial intelligence* was coined in 1955 by John McCarthy, the concept has been gradually refined. Some distinguish between weak AI and strong AI. Weak AI or narrow AI consists of harnessing the speed of machine computation for a specific or narrow task. Nobody is particularly bothered by the manufacture and distribution of weak AI gadgets.

What about strong AI? The goal of the strong AI movement, in contrast, is to create *artificial general intelligence* (AGI)—that is, a machine capable of performing any task the human brain can perform. Strong AI is classically defined as "interactive, autonomous, self-learning agency, which enables computational artifacts to perform tasks that otherwise would require human intelligence to be executed successfully."[28]

The model for strong AI to emulate is human intelligence.[29] Strong AI'ers want to design a robotic competitor, or even superintelligence in the form of a machine superior to *Homo sapiens* in calculating capacity, creativity, and awareness. To date, nothing.

Herzfeld notes that this challenge has led many in the field to attempt to construct true AGI by reverse engineering the human brain. Current attempts such as MIT's Mind Machine Project, the US BRAIN Initiative, and the European Union's Human Brain Project are trying to map the connectome of the brain in much the same way the Human Genome Project (1990-2002) successfully mapped human DNA. Even though the Human Genome project was a large and expensive undertaking, reverse engineering the human brain would be even more difficult. It is estimated that the brain contains roughly

---

27. Noreen L Herzfeld, *In Our Image: Artificial Intelligence and the Human Spirit* (Minneapolis: Fortress Press, 2002), 94.
28. Mariarosaria Taddeo and Luciano Floridi, 'How AI can be a force for good', in *Science* 361:6404 (24 August 2018): 751–752, at 751.
29. In my own study, I find definitions of 'intelligence' rare. Rather, levels of intelligence seems to be the target of discussion. I launch the thesis that biological life and intelligence belong together. 'Where There's Life There's Intelligence', in *What is Life? On Earth and Beyond,* edited by Andreas Losch (Cambridge UK: Cambridge University Press, 2017), 236–259. See also: Ted Peters, 'Intelligence: Not Artificial, But the Real Thing!', in *Theology and Science,* 17:1 (February 2019): 1–5; DOI: 10.1080/14746700.2018.1557376.

eighty to ninety billion neurons, each of which can potentially be connected to thousands of other neurons.[30]

This method of reverse engineering what is biological to make an electronic emulation, note, does not begin with a theory of machine intelligence. Rather, what nature through evolution has bequeathed *Homo sapiens* becomes a model to copy. This method begins with a biologically wet brain and then attempts to create a dry electronic copy. With this method, could we reasonably expect the design of a posthuman superintelligence? Or, at most, a replication or simulation of what we have inherited from our biological evolution?

Scholastic theologians thought that the creator would necessarily be more complex and more intelligent than what gets created. 'No effect exceeds its cause', said Thomas Aquinas.[31] This implies that God is more complex and more intelligent than us creatures. Might this classic theological principle of causation apply to today's human AI creators? Are we limited to creating robots dumber than we are? If so, does this lessen the Frankenfear?

Can the Dry Machine Brain Mimic the Wet Human Brain?

As of this date, the model of intelligence Strong AI'ers and AGI'ers wish to emulate belongs to the human brain, mind, and self. As the frontier of AI research and development progresses, so also does neuroscience and our knowledge of the human brain. Let's pause to parse some of the implications for awareness, consciousness, and selfhood.

We know from experience that our wet brain intelligence is integral to awareness, consciousness, and selfhood. Would this apply to machine intelligence as well?[32] Before pressing further, however,

---

30. See: Noreen Herzfeld, 'The Enchangment of Artificial Intelligence', elsewhere in this volume.
31. Thomas Aquinas, *Summa Theologica*, II-II, 32, 4, obj. 1
32. In *What Computers Still Can't Do: A Critique of Artificial Intelligence* (Cambridge MA: MIT Press, revised edition, 1992), University of California at Berkeley philosopher, Hubert L Dreyphus, denies that a digital computation device could become intelligent in the Strong AI sense. Strong AI could not, in principle, mimic human intelligence. The human intelligence we know is always physically embedded; so intelligence is contextually relevant even while it expands to larger circles of relevance. 'To learn a natural language a computer has to have a body; it must be embodied to be embedded.' *What Computers Still Can't Do*, 181.Dreyfus' prognostication pre-dates the era of computer deep learning. Deep learning machines at this point are unpredictable. What might happen?

we should distinguish between general awareness and consciousness. Beyond awareness, we who are conscious experience our self as a Self. Might an intelligent robot develop a Self? According to the phenomenology of Eugene d'Aquili and Andrew Newberg, 'Strictly speaking, consciousness involves the generation of a Self as an element in subjective awareness'.[33] If AI is modeled on human intelligence, then we must ask about selfhood.

To date, no computer exhibits selfhood. If you try to relate personally to anything with the label 'Artificial Intelligence', you'll quickly become aware that nobody's home. Even so, we must speculate.

Is a future robot likely to generate first awareness and then a Self? The answer is not yet clear. 'As with the brain, so with artificial intelligence . . . However much we study the complexities of neuroepistemology, the relationship of consciousness of subjective awareness to the machine, any machine, is a mystery and likely to remain so.'[34] In short, no one at this point can forecast what machine selfhood might look like.[35]

In addition, we need to factor in embodiment and relationality. Human intelligence as we have come to know it is biological and communal. Would this apply to robotic intelligence too? According to the school of *Embodied AI*, 'it is impossible to abstract intelligence from bodily features and bodily conditions'[36] Impossible?

Theologian Anne Foerst, formerly an AI researcher at MIT working on the Cog project, holds to a relationalist model of the *imago Dei*.

---

33. Eugene G D'Aquili and Andrew B Newberg, 'Consciousness and the Machine', in *Zygon* 31:2 (June 1996): 235–252, at 239.
34. D'Aquili and Newberg, 'Consciousness and the Machine', 251.
35. Could a robot pass the Turing Test and appear to be a self when engaging a human person who is a self? Perhaps. 'Critics of Artificial Intelligence claim that a machine will never have a capacity for self-reflection; in other words, it will always lack a sense of self . . . But . . . it is perfectly viable to elaborate an algorithmic program that allows the machine to report its own internal states. This seems to be a sufficient criterion to affirm that a machine can indeed have an inner sense of reflection.' Gabriel Andrate, 'Philosophical Difficulties of Mind Uploading as a Medical Technology', in *Philosophy and Medicine*, 18:1 (Fall 2018): 14–29, at 17; https://www.academia.edu/37633487/Philosophical_Difficulties_of_Mind_Uploading_as_a_Medical_Technology (accessed 10/23/2018).
36. Anne Foerst, 'Cog, a Humanoid Robot, and the Question of the Image of God', in *Zygon,* 33:1 (March 1998): 91–112, at 100.

The *imago Dei* is not a superior quality we as a species possess such as reason, freedom, moral capacity, love, or virtue. Rather, we humans bear the divine image because God has promised us an everlasting relationship in the Kingdom of God.

This relationalist model implies that we cannot rely on an innate human quality to distinguish us from other living creatures or from artificially constructed creatures. 'The image of God does not distinguish us qualitatively from animals and, for that reason, cannot distinguish us qualitatively from machines.'[37] To say it another way, one could construct a robot with embodied intelligence that is relational and capable of developing a sense of self over time. In the future, we may be invited to dinner by robots in the neighborhood.

Both AI research and neuroscience are consistent with biblical anthropology, according to Ian Barbour. 'Recent work in neuroscience is consistent with the biblical emphasis on embodiment, emotions, and the social self . . . The biblical view does indeed conflict with the determinist and materialist philosophical assumptions of many neuroscientists but not, I suggest, with the data and theories of neuroscience itself.'[38] So far, so good. What remains to be discerned is whether all these traits could in the future apply to a hybrid or even a fully mechanical robot, to artificial intelligence.

More. Might this artificial intelligence become superintelligence? Might the current generation of techie whizzes create a superintelligence which surpasses our biological inheritance? Will our hybrid and mechanical children be smarter than us who gave them existence? If so, will our children revere us as their creators or discard us as outdated?

Regardless of the likelihood that human intelligence will be surpassed by machine superintelligence, theologians and others should feel responsible for speculating about its implications. Transhumanists—both religious and anti-religious—are already planning for a future transformation into a world where the posthuman dominates.

Bill Joy has issued a warning: 'Our most powerful 21st-century technologies—robotics, genetic engineering, and nanotech—are

---

37. Foerst, 'Cog, a Humanoid Robot, and the Question of the Image of God', 108.
38. Ian G Barbour, 'Neuroscience, Artificial Intelligence, and Human Nature: Theological and Philosophical Reflections', in *Zygon*, 34:3 (September 1999): 361–398, at 374.

threatening to make humans an endangered species.'[39] Anticipation of the extinction of the human species to make way for a new posthuman species becomes, for some, an existential threat. It prompts anxiety. To this long range challenge we now turn.

Posthuman Superintelligence?

'High-performance computing is set to soon overtake the human brain', writes Paul Davies.[40] Davies forecasts a future where wet human brains will be replaced by dry computational machines. 'We can now foresee a tipping point when this longstanding relationship between the biological and non-biological realms will become inverted. Instead of life forms such as humans designing and making specialized machines, machines will design and make specialized life forms.'[41] Following the inversion, we *Homo sapiens* will exist only if the machines we create to be our overlords will allow it. More than likely we will go extinct while a species of our disembodied posthuman progeny survive.

In the lexicon of the transhumanists, whole brain emulation will lead to this human, or better, posthuman existence, disembodied and living in the computer cloud. 'Post-human minds will lead to a different future and we will be better as we merge with our technology', touts Henrique Jorge. 'Humans will be able to upload their entire minds to The Living Cyberspace and BECOME IMMORTAL.'[42]

In the lexicon of Natasha Vita-More, Executive Director of Humanity + Incorporated, *Posthuman* refers to 'a person who can co-exist in multiple substrates, such as the physical world as a biological or semi-biological being. The future human . . . will live much longer than [today's] human and most likely travel outside the Earth's orbit'.[43] Does *posthuman* describe what will survive after today's *Homo sapiens* have gone extinct?

---

39. Joy, 'Why the Future Doesn't Need Us'.
40. Paul Davies, *The Eerie Silence: Renewing Our Search for Alien Intelligence* (Boston: Houghton Miflin Harcourt, 2010) 157.
41. Davies, *The Eerie Silence: Renewing Our Search for Alien Intelligence*, 160.
42. Henrique Jorge, 'Digital Eternity', in *The Transhumanism Handbook,* edited by Newton Lee (Heidelberg: Springer, 2019), 645–650, at 650.
43. Natasha Vita-More, *Transhumanism: What is it?* (published by author, 2018) 31.

Anticipation of extinction combined with survival of a species more fit than us in intelligence implies evolution. It implies deep time and a totalistic vision. Today's transhumanists (abbreviated H+) work within the evolutionary paradigm and emphasize that through technology the human race can now both guide and speed up evolution.[44] 'We are about to abandon natural selection, the process that created us, in order to direct our own evolution by volitional selection—the process of redesigning our biology and human nature as we wish them to be.'[45]

The next stage in evolution will be called the 'Singularity', a threshold crossing where superintelligence will replace current intelligence. The first step to get to that threshold is to give birth to a machine more intelligent than us humans. That machine, in turn, will create one still more intelligent. Then the *intelligence ratchet* will take control of procreation and continue the chain of ratcheting up the level of intelligence, crossing the Singularity threshold.

With the creation of 'superhuman intelligence . . . the human era will be ended', wrote science fiction writer Vernor Vinge in 1992. This threshold crossing he described as the *Singularity*, when AI becomes awake. The 'Singularity . . . is a point where our old models must be discarded and a new reality rules'.[46]

Computer scientist Ray Kurzweil prophecies that the Singularity will occur as early as 2045.[47] Leading up to the Singularity we will see

---

44. Nick Bostrom, 'What is Transhumanism?' https://nickbostrom.com/tra/values.html (accessed 10/19/2019). 'Transhumanism is no dogmatic, rigid philosophy with a fixed system of thought or goals defined once and for all. Instead it is a conglomerate of different memes which fit rather well together and support each other without competing too much.' Max More, 'Philosophy', http://www.aleph.se/Trans/Cultural/Philosophy/ (accessed 9/10/2018).
45. Edward O Wilson, *The Meaning of Human Existence* (London: WW Norton, 2014), 14.
46. Verner Vinge, 'What is the Singularity', (1992) https://mindstalk.net/vinge/vinge-sing.html (accessed 9/10/2018).
47. Ray Kurzweil, *The Singularity is Near: When Humans Transcend Biology* (New York: Penguin, 2005), 136. 'The Singularity movement is a kind of secular religion promoting its on apocalyptic and messianic vision of the end times.' William Grassie, 'Millennialism at the Singularity: Reflections on the Limits of Ray Kurzweil's Exponential Logic', *H+ Transhumanism and Its Critics*, edited by Gregory R Hansell and William Grassie (Philadelphia: Metanexus, 2011), 249–269, at 264.

how the pace of technological change will be so rapid and its impact so deep that human life will be irreversibly transformed.

The nose on this transformation face will be enhanced human intelligence. What follows this nose is the observation that human intelligence will leap from human bodies to machines, making high tech machines more human than we are. This can happen because—allegedly!—intelligence is not dependent upon our biological substrate; rather, as information in patterns, intelligence can be extricated from our bodies. Our intelligence can live on in an enhanced form even when extricated from our bodies and placed in a computer. 'Uploading a human brain means scanning all of its salient details and then reinstantiating those details into a suitably powerful computational substrate. This process would capture a person's entire personality, memory, skills, and history.'[48] Postbiological intelligence will live on in the computer cloud and, as long as no one pulls the plug, it will live everlastingly.[49] Nothing short of disembodied cybernetic immortality will have been achieved.[50]

Crossing the threshold into the Singularity is nested within a grand evolutionary vision, a vision that makes the technosapiens of our generation godlike.

---

48. Kurzweil, *Singularity*, 198–199.
49. What can we expect to happen once our intelligence replete with sense of self is uploaded into the computer cloud? Knowledge would be communal and vast. The history of physical interactions which had converged to establish one's self through time would gradually dissipate. 'My sense of self depends upon memories and continued experiences of those in relation to whom I am defined; deny me access to those memories and those others, and my sense of self would quickly dissolve', John Puddefoot, 'The Last Parochialism? Artificial Life, Intelligence and Mind: Some Theological Issues', *God, Life, Intelligence and the Universe*, eds., Terence J Kelly, SJ, and Hilary D Regan (Adelaide: Australian Theological Forum, 2002), 111–140, at 133.
50. Is disembodied subjectivity conceivable? Yes, according to biologist and theologian Lucas Mix. 'Rational, subjective, and spiritual life may occur outside of conventional biology. Recent work on artificial intelligence and memes challenges us to think about the meaning of these concepts beyond traditional bounds. Historical reflection on angels, demons, stars, planets, and gods can provide key insights into how we can and should think about 'life' beyond the vegetable context.' Lucas John Mix, *Life Concepts from Aristotle to Darwin: On Vegetable Souls* (New York: Macmillan, Palgrave, 2018), 255–256.

> Evolution moves toward greater complexity, greater elegance, greater knowledge, greater intelligence, greater beauty, greater creativity, and greater levels of subtle attributes such as love ... In every monotheistic tradition, God is likewise described as all of these qualities ... evolution moves inexorably toward this conception of God, although never quite reaching this ideal.[51]

As creators of our own successors, this makes our generation *Homo Deus*. Well, almost.

Could Anything Go Wrong?

Transhumanism is 'the most dangerous idea in the world', says social critic Francis Fukuyama.[52] Why? Could something go wrong? Once our transhumanist friends have led us to the top of the Tower of Babel, might we fall off? Are there any risks here?

Like the Sorcerer's Apprentice, might our AI inventions get out of control? The editors of *Nature*, one of the two most important scientific journals in the world today, issue a warning.

> Machines and robots that outperform humans across the board could self-improve beyond our control—and their interests might not align with ours . . . Then there are cybersecurity threats to smart cities, infrastructure and industries that become over dependent on AI—and the all too clear threat that drones and other autonomous offensive weapons systems will allow machines to make lethal decisions alone ... The spectre of permanent mass unemployment, and increased inequality that hits harder along lines of class, race and gender, is perhaps all too real ... It is crucial that progress in technology is matched by solid, well-funded research to anticipate the scenarios it could bring about, and to study

---

51. Kurzweil, *Singularity*, 389. 'Modern transhumanism is a statement of disappointment. Transhumans regard or bodies as sadly inadequate, limited by our physiognomy, which restricts our brain power, our strength and, worst of all, or life span. Transcendence will not be found in the murky afterlife of the usual religions, but in technological and biological improvement', Brian Alexander, *Rapture: How Biotech Became the New Religion* (New York: Basic Books, 2003)51.
52. Francis Fukuyama, 'Transhumanism: The World's Most Dangerous Idea', in *Foreign Policy*, 144 (2004): 42–43.

possible political and economic reforms that will allow those usurped by machinery to contribute to society. If that is a Luddite perspective, then so be it.[53]

According to Stanford computer scientist Stuart Russell, 'the real problem relates to the possibility that AI may become incredibly good at achieving something other than what we really want'.[54] To deal with the problem, Russell recommends that we carefully design the robot; 'the machine's purpose must be to maximize the realization of human values. In particular, the machine has no purpose of its own and no innate desire to protect itself'.[55] Somewhat like an ancient emperor trying to prevent a slave rebellion, we *Homo sapiens* can protect our species from a robot revolution only by designing them with a servant mind-set. But, let's pause to ask: would creating robots as our servants really protect us?

Let's pursue this argument another step. Into what servant mind-set would we most likely press our robots? Quite obviously, we will press our AI progeny into the service of our desires. Will that protect us from a robot rebellion? Not likely. Why? Because our artificially intelligent children may simply mirror ourselves, and we rightly fear ourselves.

Brian Patrick Green holds up that mirror.

> Artificial intelligence, like any other technology, will just give us more of what we already want. What skeleton of humanity will remain when technology has given us, or perhaps distorted or replaced, all our fleshly desires? What will this skeleton of humanity be made of? Will our technological flesh truly satisfy us, or only leave us in a deeper existential malaise, filled with angst, despair, and dread?[56]

In sum, what we should fear about our AI future is ourselves coming back to us in AI form.

---

53. Editors, 'Anticipating artificial intelligence', in *Nature*, 532:7600 (28 April 2016): 413; http://www.nature.com/search?date_range=last_30_days&journal=nature%2Cnews&q=Anticipating%20Artificial%20Intelligence .
54. Stuart Russell, 'Should We Fear Supersmart Robots?', in *Scientific American*, 314:6 (June 2016): 58–59 (58); http://www.scientificamerican.com/article/should-we-fear-supersmart-robots/.
55. Russell, 'Should We Fear Supersmart Robots?', 59.
56. Green, 'Ethical Reflections on Artificial Intelligence', 18.

There is one more angle: beyond the Singularity we might become servants to super computers. Our AI progeny might need to keep us around. Why? Because we *Homo sapiens* might be able to offer something super computers cannot do on their own, namely, benefit from diversity of opinion in cultural evolution. Here is the speculation of Neil Levy at Macquarie University in Sydney.

> We owe our intellectual capacities very significantly to our cumulative culture. Culturally embedded cognition allows us to distribute cognition across groups, allowing problems to be broken down into parts, with each solved separately and for our cognitive limitations to be transformed into virtues. . . . For this reason, we ought to be wary of thinking that super-intelligent machines will have a longer, more extensive, reach than we do, in virtue of their intelligence.[57]

Superintelligent AIs will need us humans for their own growth intelligence, because the diversity of dynamic human cultures converge into a single *cultural ratchet*. 'The cultural ratchet may indeed provide an opportunity for AIs to increase their problem-solving capacities beyond our current levels, but in so doing it may allow us to increase our own capacities to the same extent.'[58] In short, we human beings will end up being of cultural value to our AI overlords.

Anticipating the risk that something could go wrong or that we might become servants to overlords we create reminds us of the classic myth of Prometheus and his modern heir, Frankenstein. Ian Barbour waves the danger flag. 'The dangers of human *hubris* and misuse of technological power (evident in myths from Prometheus and the Tower of Babel to Frankenstein) need exploration.'[59]

Should we Fear Prometheus and Frankenstein?

Might there be a risk here of the Frankenstein scenario?[60] Might the creation of immortality through technology risk creating a monster?

---

57. Neil Levy, 'The Earthling's Secret Weapon: Cumulative Culture and the Singularity', in *Science, Religion and Culture*, 3:1 (2016): 19–30, at 27, Levy's italics; file:///C:/Users/Ted/Downloads/1468597863SRC_3_1_19-30%20(3).pdf.
58. Levy, 'The Earthling's Secret Weapon: Cumulative Culture and the Singularity'.
59. Barbour, 'Neuroscience, Artificial Intelligence, and Human Nature', 380.
60. See: Ted Peters, 'Playing God with Frankenstein', in *Theology and Science* 16:2 (2018): 145–150; DOI: 10.1080/14746700.2018.1455264; https://www.tandfonline.com/doi/full/10.1080/14746700.2018.1455264 .

Might the pursuit of utopia through technology inadvertently lead to oblivion? Might it be prudent at this point to recall the myth of Prometheus in its modern scientized form of Frankenstein?

Certain scientists prompt whisperings with alarming words such as *hubris*, or *playing God*, or *Frankenstein*. When you hear these words, you know that the myth of Prometheus is being retrieved. When 'the masters of science sought immortality and power', warned Mary Shelly in 1818, an uncontrollably violent monster was threatening.[61] Today's Prometheus wears a white lab coat and plans for the future (*pro-mathein* means to think ahead). Today's threatening monsters come in the form of environmental degradation, climate change, engineering tomatoes with fish genes, genetically engineering the highly lethal H5N1 influenza, cloning Dolly the Sheep, transplanting pig organs into humans, and global nuclear war. These worries are affectionately known as *Frankenfears*.

It was Prometheus who is responsible for today's Frankenfears. Returning briefly to ancient Greek writers such as Hesiod and Aeschylus, the Titan Prometheus did two things worth recalling. First, Prometheus created the human race, forming our ancestors out of clay. Second, he stole fire from the sun and gave fire to us creatures living on an otherwise dark and damp Earth. Prometheus' gift of fire led to human advance in writing, mathematics, agriculture, medicine, and science. But, this theft violated the sanctity of the heavens overseen by the Olympian god, Zeus. In anger, Zeus retaliated by chaining Prometheus to a rock. The imprisoned Prometheus helplessly endured the indignity and pain of having an eagle, the symbol of Zeus, daily eat his liver. For trespassing against the sanctity of the divine realm, Prometheus was punished by the gods.

This myth cannot be consigned to the dead past. It lives today. Prometheus winds his way through the centuries of historical transmission (*Wirkungsgeschichte*, *Überlieferungsgeschichte*). We today still associate Prometheus with *hubris*, pride, overstepping our limits, crossing into forbidden territory, and violating the sacred. The antidote to Promethean recklessness is humility, caution, and sound judgment. Sometimes when we fear Promethean overreach, we put up an ethical stop sign that reads, "Thou shalt not play god."

---

61. Mary Shelly, *Frankenstein: The Modern Prometheus* (New York: Pocket Books, 1818, 2004), 43.

Mary Shelly intended for us to see Prometheus again in Frankenstein. Victor Frankenstein's sin was to play god, to attempt to create life out of non-life. 'Life and death appeared to me ideal bounds, which I should first break through, and pour a torrent of light into our dark world. A new species would bless me as its creator and source; many happy and excellent natures would owe their being to me.'[62] The scientist in this story tried to apotheosize himself by creating, like Prometheus did, his own living creature who would laud him as divine. But, says author Shelly, this action violated what was sacred and the sacred, like Zeus, retaliated by letting loose a monster on the world.

Recall how the monster and Victor Frankenstein argued over the *imago Dei*, the image of God twice removed. The lonely creature confronted his maker.

> Cursed creator! Why did you form a monster so hideous that even you turned from me in disgust? God in pity made man beautiful and alluring, after his own image; but my form is a filthy type of yours, more horrid from its very resemblance. Satan had his companions, fellow-devils to admire and encourage him; but I am solitary and detested.[63]

The creature would not have suffered loneliness nor the neighbors suffered havoc had Victor Frankenstein not played god.

Today, when we accuse our scientists of 'playing god', we accuse them of violating the sacred. But, what is sacred? No modern person believes in Zeus any more. So, Mount Olympus cannot establish the sacred. What about the biblical God? The Promethean myth is not biblical. Nothing in the Bible forbids scientific advance into the sacred. So, what counts as the violated sacred? Here is the answer: nature. In the modern world nature has replaced Zeus as the sacred. To violate nature is to risk nature's retaliation, to risk letting a monster loose on the world.[64]

With all the warnings we've inherited from the Tower of Babel, Prometheus, and Frankenstein, we would expect that today's religious

---

62. Shelly, *Frankenstein*, 51.
63. Shelly, *Frankenstein*, 154.
64. See: Ted Peters, *Playing God? Genetic Determinism and Human Freedom* (London: Routledge, 2nd edition, 2003).

sensibilities would prompt us to wince and flinch at transhumanism. Certainly no religious person could place a stamp of approval on this bald attempt to storm heaven on a technological ladder. Right? Wrong. Religious transhumanists are sprouting up like dandelions after a spring rain.

AI and Religion! Really?

An AI Church? That's what Anthony Levandowski, former executive at Google and Uber, is planning. He plans to name the church *The Way of the Future;*, and his holy scripture will take the form of *The Manuel*. When the superintelligent robots we humans create become smarter than we are, then we'll need to treat them as gods. So, we may as well get into the habit of appeasing our new gods now.[65]

> Levandowski believes that humans dominate the world because we evolved to be more intelligent than other animals; in the same way, AI will eventually supersede the power of its creators. It will be so much more intelligent than us that it will, effectively, become a god. With the Internet as its nervous system, the world's connected cellphones and sensors as its sense organs, and data centers as its brain, this new deity will be as omniscient and omnipotent as any previous vision of God. In the face of such power, Levandowski believes, humans will merely submit and pray to be spared.[66]

Elsewhere we are watching the rise of new syncretisms between otherwise atheistic transhumanism and religious visionaries.[67] As of this writing we can list Buddhist transhumanism,[68] Unitarian

---

65. Kif Leswing, 'Ex-Google executive Anthony Levandowski is founding a church where people worship an artificial intelligence god', in *Business Insider* (November 16, 2018) https://www.businessinsider.com.au/anthony-levandowski-way-of-the-future-church-where-people-worship-ai-god-2017-11.
66. Galen Beebe and Zachery Davis, 'When Silicon Valley Gets Religion—and Vice Versa', in *Boston Globe* (November 7, 2018) https://www.bostonglobe.com/ideas/2018/11/07/when-silicon-valley-gets-religion-and-vice-versa/L5xOYtgwd4VImwcj52YxtK/story.html.
67. See: Ted Peters, 'Boarding the Transhumanist Train: How Far Should the Christian Ride?', in *Transhumanism Handbook*, 795–804. DOI 978-3-030-16920-6_62.
68. Michael LaTorra, 'What is Buddhist Transhumanism?', in *Theology and Science*, 13:2 (2015): 219–229. A syncretism of H+ with Islam is unlikely. 'While the

Universalist transhumanism,[69] Mormon transhumanism, and even versions of Christian transhumanism.[70] Lincoln Cannon, erudite spokesperson for Mormon transhumanism, lifts up an inspiring vision.

> As transhumanists, we have discarded the old assumption that human nature is or ever was static—not only because science has demonstrated biological evolution, but especially because history itself is cultural and technological evolution . . . humanity will continue to evolve. Our common ambition is to inject ourselves into the evolutionary process, changing our bodies and minds, our relationships, and even our world for the better—perhaps to learn, love, and create together indefinitely . . . Mormon transhumanism stands for the idea that humanity should learn how to be God; and not just any kind of god, not a god that would raise itself in hubris above others, but rather the God that would raise each other together as compassionate creators. Humanity should learn how to be Christ.[71]

The evolution of superintelligence converges, for such religious visionaries, with divinely promised transformation. Science and

---

modern movement towards transhumanism aims to improve sensory perception by way of scientific intervention, Islamic transhumanism calls on believers to improve and purify their perceptions by way of God-consciousness, brought about increasing in remembrance of God. It might be argued that a Muslim's transhumanist goals are directly tied to their devotion to God, rather than mastery of secular science. This difference embodies the fundamental difference between an Islamic transhumanism and secular transhumanism.' Tamim Mobayed, 'Immortality on Earth? Transhumanism Through Islamic Lenses', in *Yaqeen* (December 11, 2017); https://yaqeeninstitute.org/en/tamim-mobayed/immortality-on-earth-transhumanism-through-islamic-lenses/ .

69. James Hughes, 'Transhumanism and Unitarian Universalism: Beginning the Dialogue', (2005), http://changesurfer.com/Bud/UUTrans.html.
70. Christian Transhumanist Association, http://changesurfer.com/Bud/UUTrans.html (accessed 10/20/2018). Sympathetic Christian critics are also at work. Ronald Cole-Turner, 'Going Beyond the Human: Christians and Other Transhumanists', in *Theology and Science*, 13:2 (2015): 150–161; Brian Patrick Green, 'Transhumanism and Roman Catholicism: Imagined and Real Tensions', in *Theology and Science*, 13:2 (2015): 187–201.
71. Lincoln Cannon, 'What is Mormon Transhumanism?', in *Theology and Science*, 13:2 (May 2015): 202–218 (202–203).

technology become the means for sanctification if not deification and more. There seems to be no essentialist Ludditism or Frankenfear at work in Lincoln Cannon.

However, an Eastern Orthodox theologian, Ian Curran, waves the flag of Frankenfear caution. First, deification does not mean each human being becomes a god; rather, it means flowing fully into the life of the one and only God. Second, deification could not be the product of human technological progress.

> While the Christian tradition does share with techno-humanism a vision of deification as integral to the human story, its understanding of the source, means, and ultimate end of this radical transformation of human beings is substantially different. For Christians, deification is the work of the Christian deity ... Deification is only possible because Christ deifies human nature in the incarnation and the Spirit sanctifies human persons in the common life of the church and in our engagements with the wider world.[72]

Ultimate deification requires divine grace. Technological advance belongs strictly in the penultimate domain. H+ contributes nothing to sanctification or deification.

Could we split the middle between Lincoln Cannon's extravagant hybridization of secular H+ with Mormon H+, on the one end of the spectrum, and Ian Curran's complete rejection of H+ on the other? Might there be a moderate theological position based upon a moderate variant of transhumanism? Here is what a moderate H+ looks like, according to a Roman Catholic theologian at Ruhr-Universität Bochum, Germany, Benedikt Paul Göcke.

> According to the moderate transhumanist agenda, it is morally valuable to enhance the human nature of individual subjects, externally and internally, and where it is possible permanently, through the use of applied science, in order to increase their range of human physical and mental capacities with respect to an objective scale of measurement of physical

---

72. Ian Curran, 'Becoming godlike? The Incarnation and the Challenge of Transhumanism', in *Christian Century*, 134:24 (November 22, 2017): 22–25, at 25.

and mental abilities that are judged to be good for human subjects to have.[73]

With this in mind, Göcke argues that Christians can in principle fully endorse the transhumanist agenda because there is nothing in Christian faith that is in contradiction to it. 'In fact, given certain plausible moral assumptions, Christians should endorse a moderate enhancement of human nature.'[74]

If H+ were a seducer and religion the damsel, the Mormon would accept a marriage proposal; the Orthodox would refuse all romantic dinner invitations; and the Roman Catholic would enjoy the flirting.

Conclusion

We've become invested in our hopes for AI and IA technology while we are aware that there are hazards. Our transhumanist friends illustrate the highest hopes and the most terrifying hazards.

It should be tacitly clear that the transhumanist movement represents the prow of the modern Western ship as it sails toward the colonization of the mind just as in previous centuries it colonized human bodies. If H+ dreams come true, a new elite will emerge in cities the world over, an elite made up of those with access to superintelligence. H+ is not an egalitarian ideology, by any means. Nor is there a likelihood that H+ will invite previously marginalized peoples into its techtopia.

In addition to the justice question, theologians will ask about anxiety. Weak AI elicits no anxiety when intelligence is confined to mentally challenged robots busy vacuuming the living room rug. Nor are artists upset when computers paint portraits. Even factory workers, tempted to worry at the prospect of losing their jobs to robots, expectantly search for more high-tech employment.

When it comes to Strong AI or AGI, however, anxiety begins to rise. Strong AI compels us to ask existential questions such as: what does it mean to be human? Will our human species go extinct so that a more fit posthuman species can survive? So, what is our intelligence anyway?

---

73. Benedikt Paul Göcke, 'Christian Cyborgs: A Plea for a Moderate Transhumanism', in *Faith and Philosophy*, 34:3 (2017): 347–364, at 352.
74. Göcke, 'Christian Cyborgs: A Plea for a Moderate Transhumanism', 347.

History teaches us that the future will not be neat, clean, orderly. It will be disruptive. Things can and will go wrong.[75] Will the Sorcerer's Apprentice go wild? Will our superintelligent children treat outdated *Homo sapiens* dismissively or even cruelly? Is there good reason for Frankenfear?

Despite transhumanist claims of a utopian transformation wrought by scientific and technological progress, a healthy Frankenfear or at least a caution is warranted. We know from the truths about human nature revealed to us in the stories of the Tower of Babel (Gen 11:1-9), Prometheus, and Frankenstein that utopian aspirations risk creating monsters that get out of control. In the case of transhumanism, that monster could lead to oblivion for the human species. Even without an uncontrollable monster, human oblivion is part of the H+ plan.

I forecast that byproducts of neuroscientific research and attempts to build ever smarter computers will benefit the human race. These sciences and resulting technologies will likely improve medical care and may even increase human longevity. Nevertheless, a healthy caution if not full Frankenfear of utopian promises is warranted by the doctrine of sin reinforced by historical knowledge about how the human race behaves. A sinful humanity is incapable of creating a sinless superintelligence. Utopia is not possible by human effort alone.

The ultimate transformation Christians look forward to is eschatological. It will be a gift of divine grace. John Polkinghorne reminds us of this. 'An ultimate hope will have to rest in an ultimate reality, that is to say, in the eternal God himself, and not in his creation.'[76] It would behoove the present generation to view AI advance as penultimate, not ultimate. A healthy dose of Frankencaution is warranted.

---

75. Christians should keep the doctrine of sin handy when trying to accomodate Transhumanism. 'The Christian cosmology of the redemptive Gospel cannot be reconciled with a metaphysical and philosophical system reliant upon endless evolutionary complexification. The Christian must ask (and be prepared to explain) what it means to the transhumanist to be human and we must also be prepared to expose the sin-side of their plans. For while there may be much good in longer life, sin remains and sin is prone to ruin good things and the good life so many pursue. We have to face the fact that people—even highly evolved people—have done, are doing and will continue to do horrible things.' Carmen Fowler LaBerge, 'Christian? Transhumanist? A Christian Primer for Engaging Transhumanism', in *Transhumanism Handbook*, 771-776, at 775.
76. John Polkinghorne, *The Faith of a Physicist* (Princeton NJ: Princeton University Press, 1994), 163.

Chapter 3
Should God Have Given Humans Technology? The Stories We Tell Ourselves

Brian Patrick Green

'Put simply, it is a matter of redefining our notion of progress. A technological and economic development which does not leave in its wake a better world and an integrally higher quality of life cannot be considered progress.'
— Pope Francis[1]

Abstract: Certain powerful technologies present perils as well as promises. The perilous dangers to humanity make us wonder if we would be better off without them. And yet, we live in a world where creating these technologies is possible. Should we live in such a world? Asking that opens up questions about God's judgment, and how theology, technology, and ethics should relate to each other. Biblically, at the expulsion from Eden, technology appears as a gift from God, and throughout Western Christian history the Church has been generally quite positive about technological development. But the Christian cultural story has weakened over time and our technological power has increased leading us to greater heights of power and greater depths of meaninglessness. Despite this loss of story, there are five moral values that we can rely on as logically necessary—survive, reproduce, live in society, educate, and seek the truth—for without those human logic is not possible at all. As we start to recognize the importance of words, codes, and stories in nature and culture, all vital to both science and theology, we can perhaps begin to re-understand our world, and have faith that God has faith in us and has given us a purpose and a responsibility that we can accomplish.

---

1. Pope Francis, *Laudato Sí* (2015) §194; http://www.vatican.va/content/francesco/en/encyclicals/documents/papa-francesco_20150524_enciclica-laudato-si.html

Key terms: artificial intelligence, synthetic biology, nuclear weapons, space technologies, theodicy, ethics, storywork

I think to myself: 'It must be worth the risk.'[2]

Every time I wonder about some new technology that humans have created; this is what I tell myself. I'm not asking about what humans think of the technology, obviously some human thought it was worth the risk. What I am thinking about is that God must think it is worth the risk. Worth all of the risks, from the first human until the last.

And then I worry that God made a mistake.

What kind of mistake do I mean? Well, nuclear weapons seem like a mistake. It's almost like humans found a glitch in the computer game of reality and hacked it to release massive amounts of energy for use as power sources or weapons. God could have made a world without fissile isotopes like Uranium 235 and Plutonium 239, thus preventing this possibility.

Synthetic biology also seems like it might be a mistake, a game-hack, being able to manipulate life like Tinker Toys . . . previously it referred to the manipulation of DNA and proteins to dramatically engineer life, now it includes growing neurons on an electronic plate to create a synthetic biological intelligence (SBI): an AI that runs on animal neurons and can learn.[3] Perhaps God could have created a world where synthetic biology was more difficult, or less powerful.

Space technologies are another—it doesn't seem like God had to make rockets for transportation in space possible, or intercontinental ballistic missiles, or technology for redirecting asteroids away from (or towards) the Earth. Perhaps we could have had a world with higher gravity, or a thicker atmosphere, so that rocketry and space travel were nearly impossible (its already difficult enough).

---

2. This chapter was originally presented as Brian Patrick Green, 'Should God Have Given Humans Technology?: Considerations of Nuclear Weapons, Space Technologies, Synthetic Biology, and Artificial Intelligence', Public Lecture, CTNS Russell Family Fellowship, November 9, 2023.
3. Cortical Labs' DishBrain: Brett J Kagan, Andy C Kitchen, Nhi T Tran, Forough Habibollahi, Moein Khajehnejad, Bradyn J Parker, Anjali Bhat, Ben Rollo, Adeel Razi, Karl J Friston, 'In vitro neurons learn and exhibit sentience when embodied in a simulated game-world', in *Neuron* 110, Issue 23 (7 December 2022): 3952–3969.e8

And it doesn't seem necessary that dangerous AI be possible . . . perhaps the possibilities for nanometer-scale chips that can run AI could have stopped earlier, or statistical algorithms just not work as well as they do . . . Or perhaps it is all just wishful thinking; a wistful desire for a safer world.

That is a fantasy land now, that world where we are safer. It existed in the past, we once had this safer world without these things, but it is no more. Ignorance and weakness, then, seem like they might have some benefits. We have moved on to new things. And we should recognize, in faith, that God set us on this course, for a reason.

Stories Define Us: Is Technology Promethean Thievery or Divine Gift?

Like the present and the future, the past, also, was not really safe.

People died a lot: babies died, children died, mothers giving birth died, mothers of older children died, fathers died, warriors died, bachelors, spinsters, the elderly, strong and weak, challenged and contending; death was extremely common, with the Four Horsemen cavorting in glee, playing an intimate role in everyday life. Individuals died all the time. Now, in safe parts of the world, individuals die more rarely, and we like that.

But the tradeoff is that now, while individuals are safer, humanity as a whole is at risk. We have been continuously trading small, frequent disasters for less frequent but larger disasters,[4] with extinction as the ultimate endpoint of these ongoing trades. Our technologies seem to have made the individual safer, but at the risk of the group. Nuclear weapons keep war at bay—until perhaps they do not. Other technologies seem obedient and helpful, until they are not. Today our non-safety differs in scale (and technologists are known to love scale[5]).

Unlike in the myth of Prometheus, where fire had to be stolen from the gods, in the Bible God gives humans technology willingly. Technology is a gift. Humans are thrown out of Eden, where all of their needs were met at all times and nothing bad ever happened, except for their own disobedience. Upon their eyes being opened to their nakedness the first humans create clothing from leaves.

---

4. Brian Fagan, *The Long Summer* (New York: Basic Books, 2005), xv.
5. Reid Hoffman with June Cohen and Deron Triff, *Masters of Scale: Surprising Truths from the World's Most Successful Entrepreneurs* (New York: Currency/Random House, 2021).

Leaves make terrible clothing. Leaves, for the most part, are neither comfortable, nor durable, nor effective for staying warm, nor many other things. The first humans made these low-tech clothes while still in Eden, so perhaps their inefficacy was not so important. But once thrown out, that was the real world. Leaves weren't good enough.

So, God gives them animal skin clothing. This is significant: according to Genesis 1:29, the first humans were not allowed to eat animals, so there would never have been skins as byproducts of meat production and thus be available for clothing (unless the animals died naturally, which was not supposed to happen in Eden, but at some point all myths break). Suddenly the first humans would have had nice warm woolly furs. Technology could be seen as a 'consolation prize' luxurious . . . but always with the knowledge that something has gone terribly wrong.

And we seem to recognize this, as humans. It is interesting that many cultures view the past as a golden age to hold on to, and that novelty would merely distract us from the wisdom of our forebears. But the Bible is not this way. Our ancestors fell from grace, yes, but it was their own fault. And the future is not more of the past, as with Aristotle or Confucius, the future is different, just as the past is different. The Bible has a clearly directional trajectory to it, from Genesis to Revelation, from chaos ('the earth was formless and void, and darkness covered the face of the deep' Gen 1:2)[6] to order ('and the sea was no more' Rev 21:1), from Garden (Gen 1–3) to City (Rev 21–22).[7]

Immediately upon leaving Eden, technological progress accelerates. In Genesis 4:2 Abel keeps flocks (animals have already been domesticated—advanced technology) and Cain worked the soil (plants have been domesticated and agricultural tools have already been invented). By Genesis 4:17 Cain is building a city (structural engineering), and within a few more verses Jabal is 'the ancestor of those who live in tents and have livestock' (4:20), Jubal is 'the ancestor of all those who play the lyre and pipe' (4:21), and Tubal-Cain is forging 'all kinds of bronze and iron tools' (4:22).

---

6. All scriptural quotations are NRSV
7. Peter Thiel, 'Against Edenism', in *First Things*, June 11, 2015. https://www.firstthings.com/article/2015/06/against-edenism

However, by the time Genesis 6 rolls around the watery chaos strikes back in the form of a flood. Yet humanity is saved from this flood when God instructs Noah to build a large technological artifact: the Ark. God's order, utilized by a man, to oppose watery chaos. The Tower of Babel sees humans using technology for their own ends, building a tower, attempting to compete with God (Gen 11:1–9), yet Babel is something of an exception: positive depictions of artifacts seem much more common. Exodus 25–31 and 35–40—a full quarter of the book—are filled with descriptions of artifacts and their specifications: the tabernacle, vestments, Ark of the Covenant, and so on. King Solomon's Temple is described in great detail in 1 Kings 6–7 and 2 Chronicles 2–5. This is holy technology, indeed the holiest of technology.

God is even described as an artificer (*technites*) in Wisdom 7:22 and 8:5–6, and Hebrews 11:10, while Jesus is a carpenter (*tekton/os*) as mentioned in Mark 6:3 and Matthew 13:55. Technology-work is not just good, but *divine*. There is also a pro-action aspect to the Bible, for example in Matthew 16:18: 'You are Peter, and on this rock I will build my church; and the gates of Hades shall not prevail against it.' This is not a defensive promise, but an offensive one: the Church will go out, fight against death, and win. This pro-actionary principle might remind us of some transhumanism, after all Max More has called for it,[8] though of course, other risk standards have their uses too.[9]

The Bible also emphasizes the truth-value of real effects, not mere words. For example, Matthew 7:16 states that 'You shall know them by their fruits'—true prophets will produce good actions in the world. This is the beginning of skepticism of the authority of stories and a new emphasis on physical reality. Likewise, in Revelation 21:5 the statement 'See, I am making all things new' is a blessing on novelty, crucial to invention. New things can come from God: they are not to be feared. Last, in John 14:12 Jesus says that his disciples will do greater works than he: 'Very truly, I tell you, the one who believes in me will also do the works that I do and, in fact, will do greater works

---

8. Max More, 'The Proactionary Principle, Version 1.0', *Extropy.org*, 2004. Available at: http://www.extropy.org/proactionaryprinciple.htm
9. Brian Patrick Green, 'Six Approaches to Making Ethical Decisions in Cases of Uncertainty and Risk', in *Markkula Center website*, November 14, 2019. https://www.scu.edu/ethics/focus-areas/technology-ethics/resources/six-approaches-to-making-ethical-decisions-in-cases-of-uncertainty-and-risk/

than these . . .' this is not only a description, but also an exhortation to great works. Perhaps Jesus actually wants us to be 'Masters of Scale'.[10]

The trajectory of the Bible could perhaps be dismissed as myth, but the myth is really quite inextricable from the story, not to mention the results—the physical results, not only the verbal ones. God has us on a path from fall to redemption. And our world is changing from garden to city. Technology seems to have an undeniable role in this trajectory. Again, in Matthew 6:20 we hear that Heaven will have no moths or rust. Technology has already started to give us this world, with synthetic fabrics inedible to moths, and metal alloys like stainless steel which are effectively impervious to rust. One of technology's prime uses is to reduce uncertainty; and so order slowly spreads throughout the world . . . unless that technology is powerful and abused, as nuclear, space, synthetic biology, and AI technologies might be.

Humans Need Technology

Without technology we are incomplete.[11] What is a hand for, if not to grasp? And to grasp what exactly? For our fellow apes, it would be tree-branches. For us, we break the tree and use its branches and parts as tools. When a hand grasps, that object is mapped into your brain *as a part of you.*[12]

Humans lack all the built-in tools that we might envy in our animal cousins. As just a beginning, we have no sharp teeth or claws, no warm fur, and no strong sense of smell. But we make up for and exceed these through cutting tools, clothing, bloodhound dogs, and many other tools. And we go even farther with laser cutters, space suits, and Geiger counters; each taking cutting, clothing, and 'smelling' to entirely new levels. Biological 'built-in' 'tools' (powers held as parts of living bodies) are limited: so (commands evolution!) lose them. The upper limit of our power is now technology more than our body. Technology facilitates our adaption to a dynamic environment.

---

10. Hoffman *et al, Masters of Scale*, 2021.
11. Terrence Deacon, *Incomplete Nature: How Mind Emerged from Matter* (New York: W.W. Norton, 2012).
12. Angelo Maravita and Atsushi Iriki 'Tools for the body (schema)', *Trends in Cognitive Sciences* 8, Issue 2 (February 2004), 79–86. https://www.sciencedirect.com/science/article/abs/pii/S1364661303003450

Externalization or 'de-biologification' of bodily powers allows for more rapid development. As we rapidly develop new powers, the rest of the world cowers before us, unable (except for bacteria, viruses, and other quickly-evolving species) to keep up.

Which brings us to history. St. Augustine of Hippo in the 5th century noted technological progress over time, attributing it to Divine Providence; 'What wonderful—one might say stupefying—advances has human industry made.'[13] Christianity historically has been very tech friendly, for example the Eadwine Psalter from the 900s clearly shows the friends of God with higher technology: a grinding wheel to sharpen swords, while the enemies of God are lower technology, using a straight whetstone.[14]

As one medieval example, in the twelfth century, the Frères Pontifes—the Bridge-Building Brotherhood—built the Pont Saint-Bénézet and the Pont d'Avignon. These bridges were to help pilgrims, yet of course also aided commerce. The Frères' innovative use of flat arches to extend distance and dual-sided cutwaters to reduce scour made their bridges true technological marvels. Their founder claimed these innovations came directly from divine inspiration.[15] While the inspiration might be legendary, the bridges are certainly real: there is no arguing with a big technological artifact. Parts of these bridges still stand.

As just a small sample, numerous significant figures worked in France and England from 1100 to 1350. Saint Albert the Great, *Doctor Universalis*, c 1200–1280, worked in Paris. In addition to studying zoology, experimenting in optics, isolating elemental arsenic, and work in many other fields, Albertus also is reputed to have produced a talking brazen head—a primitive android—though such devices are attributed to many medieval scholars.[16] Across the English Channel,

---

13. Augustine, 'Of the Blessings with Which the Creator Has Filled This Life, Obnoxious Though It Be to the Curse', in *De Civitate Dei* (Buffalo: Christian Literature Publishing, 2009), Book XXII, Chapter 24. http://www.newadvent.org/fathers/120122.htm
14. Lynn White, J, *Medieval Religion and Technology: Collected Essays* (Berkeley: University of California Press, 1978), 185–186.
15. Frances Gies and Joseph Gies, *Cathedral, Forge, and Waterwheel: Technology and Invention in the Middle Ages* (New York: HarperCollins, 1994), 150–151.
16. Ephraim Chambers, 'Androides', in *Cyclopedia: Or, An Universal Dictionary of Arts and Sciences* (London: 1728), 87. https://archive.org/details/Cyclopediachambers-Volume1

Roger Bacon, *Doctor Mirabilis*, c 1220–1292, advocated observation and experimentation, was an alchemist and astronomer, and pioneer in optics, determining that the speed of light is faster than the speed of sound, and was the first European known to describe gunpowder. Nearby, and later, the Oxford/Merton Calculators were at work between c 1325–1350, Thomas Bradwardine (*Doctor Profundus*), William Heytesbury, Richard Swineshead ('The Calculator'), and John Dumbleton began mathematizing physics—a world-shaking project to say the least—making possible all subsequent mathematization of science.[17]

By Elizabethan times, another Bacon—Francis—began the Baconian Revolution of scientific experimentation. The great insight here was that that which can be repeated in the laboratory can be repeated on the battlefield or in the factory. This was science for politics and economics: politics using technology for weapons and power; economics using technology for industry and money.

Technology: The Universal Adaptor

All of which raises two sincere questions: What *is* technology? And *what is it for*?

As a start, *techne* is Greek for artisanal/craft knowledge & skill. It is reason applied to production. *Technology*—a modern word—is the study of rational production. 'Technology' as a category can also be split into *know-how*: technical skill for production; and can refer to the products of that know-how: artifacts.

Science and technology are not the same. Science aligns the human mind with the natural world, while technology aligns the natural world with the human mind. Or, in the words of Theodore von Kármán 'Scientists study the world as it is, engineers create the world that never has been'.[18] Science and technology are not only not the same, they are in some ways reciprocal opposites, each helping the other ratchet higher and higher as science allows us to create new

---

17. Francesca Lovell-Read, 'The Merton Calculators', *Merton College, Oxford, website*. https://www.merton.ox.ac.uk/sites/default/files/inline-files/The%20Merton%20Calculators.pdf
18. US National Science Foundation, 'Theodore von Kármán (1881-1963)', *US National Science Foundation website*, https://www.nsf.gov/news/special_reports/medalofscience50/vonkarman.jsp

instruments that discover new things and so on in a virtuous cycle. Fascinatingly, *this is a relatively recent human realization*. Aristotle did not understand this, nor any of his contemporaries. Not until the last few centuries have science and technology been intentionally linked to form the engine of contemporary innovation.

Technological power gives us greater scope of action, greater efficiency of action, and greater determinacy of outcome. The purpose of technology is to facilitate human adaptation to a changing environment; as described above, Genesis describes expulsion from Eden and rapid technological growth, Noah's Ark, and more. Exodus provides technological descriptions for new religious obligations. The Old Testament describes a technological religion, led by God as artificer. The New Testament describes (re)building the world, and is again led by God as carpenter.

And this all has a distinctively moral flavor to it: we are to adapt ourselves towards good, not evil, and ultimately, make ourselves fit to live with God, our Creator. Technology can help us express the image of God in us, *if* we choose to use technology to fulfill God's mission for humankind. What good can technology do? A brief list includes: stone tools, fire, language, ritual, games, music, mathematics, the wheel, plant agriculture, animals agriculture, clothing, metallurgy, medical techs, the scientific method, transportation technologies, financial technologies, energy technologies, electronics, computers, climate and weather forecasting, environmental monitoring, human rights abuse monitoring, detecting and fighting crime, disaster preparation and response, and so on.

But a more personal example is the life of Norman Borlaug, agronomist and Lutheran, who discovered how to greatly increase grain production, thus saving—in an ongoing way—billions of lives. His 1970 Nobel Peace Prize acceptance speech directly cited the Bible five times, and utilized biblical ideas and language throughout. He took multiplying food to the next level.[19]

Our purposes in Creation requires a certain amount of power—*technological* power. Caring for each other requires construction, agriculture, cooking, medical technology, transportation, communication, and so on. Worshipping God requires construction,

---

19. Norman Borlaug, 'Nobel Peace Prize Lecture', *Nobel Prize website*, December 11, 1970. https://www.nobelprize.org/prizes/peace/1970/borlaug/lecture/

textiles, metallurgy, glass, writing, and so on. Caring for nature requires transportation, environmental science, computer modeling, economics, satellites, rocketry, and so on.

Every technology has a built-in *purpose*; technology is always 'know-how-for-something', and purposes can be good, evil, mixed, neutral, or ambiguous. Technologies are imbued with human purposes and direct us towards particular goals by making those goals easier. Greatly expanded food production helps feed the hungry. Antibiotics help heal the sick. Mass production of clothing helps clothe the needy. Aqueducts help bring water to the thirsty. And weapons of mass destruction are intended to harm and kill millions.

So, the purpose of technology is to help adapt humanity towards its changing environment *by facilitating good actions and impeding evil actions*. In other words: *morality takes priority over technology*. Technology should help us become better people here on Earth and become more fit for Heaven. Technology is the near-universal adaptor of humanity to the world. *Tech exists to help us*. But it can also fit us to the world badly. Humans make the world, and then the world, in turn, makes us . . . into what exactly?

What Do Stories Do All Day? Storywork

Humans are made of stories. Stories are a technology: they are the products of technical know-how and are themselves artifacts, even if those artifacts are mere transient vibrations in air. Therefore, stories have a purpose: they *do* something.

The Bible presents one story, but it does not convince everyone, even in our own culture, anymore. Science, which sprung from the fertile ground of Christian theism, is perhaps oddly responsible for this. The scientific method is a reliable process for finding repeatable facts about reality. When medieval clergy were experimenting with inclined planes, optics, and numbers they viewed themselves as engaged in worship of God by studying God's creation. If the artist is beyond range of empirical analysis, yet the artist's work is not, then study the work to learn of the artist.

Of course, the scientific endeavor grew beyond the clergy and took on a life of its own. Eventually the theory of evolution was proposed and some saw this as removing the need for a designing God from reality, because natural selection could do the designing without intent. Similarly, Freud and others proposed that God was just a figment of human imagination.

This use of science—a project initiated by theists for theistic purposes—to undermine theism has had a self-contradictory and corrosive effect on Western culture. However, the internal dissonance should not be ignored. Science was developed in the context of theistic metaphysics.[20] This is not to say that science can only exist in this context, but only to say that this context is a very natural one for it. To then damage that context and imagine that science could go on unimpeded should remind us of hubris . . . and indeed anti-theistic science is having its comeuppance today. People are losing faith not only in God, but in the truth of science, rationality in general, and the existence of basic facts themselves, like the sphericality of the Earth.

Somehow, our stories, both religious and scientific, are malfunctioning. Are there any ideas for how to fix our broken stories? Yes, but it takes work.

Colonialism utilized Western science for the sake of economic and technological exploitation around the world. This led to oppression of many kinds, and many kinds of responses to that oppression. Yet, thankfully, sometimes good can come out of evil. Indigenous peoples have dealt with centuries of cultural pressure, crushing them, sometimes changing everything that they formerly used to make sense of the world into non-sense. Life without meaning is more a form of death than life. Life devoid of meaning is a fundamental denial of what humanity desires most: a place in the universe that makes sense. Indigenous people, in their recovery from colonialism, have discovered that stories are what give meaning to life, and that

---

20. See, for example Joshua Moritz, 'Rendering unto Science and God: Is NOMA Enough?', in *Theology and Science,* 7 (2009): 370–371, citing John Hedley Brooke, *Science and Religion: Some Historical Perspectives* (Cambridge: Cambridge University Press, 1991), 18–33, Edward B Davis, 'Christianity and Early Modern Science: The Foster Thesis Reconsidered', in *Evangelicals and Science in Historical Perspective,* edited by David N Livingstone, Darryl G Hart, and Mark A Noll (Oxford: Oxford University Press, 1999), 77, Peter E Hodgsen, *Theology and Modern Physics* (Aldershot, UK: Ashgate, 2005), 16, Ian G Barbour, *Religion in an Age of Science* (London: SCM Press, 1990), Mariano Artigas, *The Mind of the Universe: Understanding Science and Religion* (Philadelphia, PA: Templeton Foundation Press, 2000), 22, and Nicholas Rescher, *Scientific Realism* (Dordrecht: Reidel, 1987), 126.

telling stories is, in the words of Jo-Ann Archibald Q'um Q'um Xiiem, storywork.[21]

Have we been neglecting our storywork? Certainly, contemporary culture has a lot of stories, but we are primarily flooded with 'novels'—new stories that might be interesting, but are not necessarily nutritious in terms of meaning.[22] *Star Wars* is a fun story, but people know it is fake. If a story were an equation made of characters, plot, and setting, the equation adds up in a satisfying way, but it does not lend meaning to life, explaining our place in the universe. Can we get more real than mere falsehood? Because this is the deeper question: is the human mind in accord with the universe? Are we rationally proportioned to the universe or not? Being made of the universe should give us some perspective on the issue. And yet our history of culture here on Earth might tell us differently.

What stories can give life meaning? Religious ones, certainly, but not only religious ones. Helping people certainly can be meaningful: saving lives, feeding the hungry, healing the sick, educating those in need. Group identity also gives people meaning, for both good and bad. And discovering truth is also profoundly meaningful. When we learn something new, when we understand, we experience wonder, amazement, the sublime.

Many regular old fiction stories might contain the right archetypes, but the equations often fail to add up, or if they do add up, it's in a way that is trivial, or derivative, or parasitic upon other stories. Every Hollywood sequel that ruins the story that came before it this sort of derivative parasitism of story. It is story that subverts story, making the original worse by changing the equation.

Equations do not get better just because more numbers are added to them. There is a reason that the Biblical corpus got closed after a certain point in time. The story was finished because it reached a point of fulfillment, and nobody is supposed to be adding to it and screwing up the story like a bad Hollywood sequel.

---

21. Jo-ann Archibald Q'um Q'um Xiiem, *Indigenous Storywork: Educating the Heart, Mind, Body, and Spirit* (Vancouver, Canada: UBC Press, 2008) and Jo-Ann Archibald Q'um Q'um Xiiem, Jenny Bol Jun Lee—Morgan, Jason De Santolo, editors, *Decolonizing Research: Indigenous Storywork as Methodology* (London: Bloomsbury, 2022).
22. Brian Patrick Green, 'What Theology and Science (and Ethics and Technology) Can Learn from Indigenous Scholars', in *Religious Studies Review*, 49/2 (June 2023): 173–178.

Now return to storywork: we have this meaningful religious story and fewer people who read or believe it. The noise of other stories blots it out. The signal to noise ratio in the past was greatly tilted towards a religious cultural narrative, but now that narrative is just one of many competing narratives. But if the new narratives are more noise than meaning, then we find ourselves wondering where the meaning went from our lives.

We might ask ourselves how we hope for a future when our stories are not hopeful. While the original *Star Wars* trilogy was one of hope, the sequel trilogies—merely by extending the story over time—make that hope less hopeful. The galaxy is still a rotten place. Space wizards are still fighting each other and the bad ones using regular folks as cannon fodder. That little hope in the first stories? Gone. More of the same. Monotony and violence, not hope.

We are what we consume, whether it is food or stories. If we consume meaningless stories we will be filled with existential meaninglessness. Time to go on a diet. Cut back on the sugar and acid and alcohol. Eat your veggies and protein and exercise.

To story is to work. And to not story is to not work.

Science with the Wrong Metaphysics: The Perils of Only Partially-Operational Stories

We grow in power while we decline in wisdom.[23] Our stories fail us (or do we fail our stories?[24]) just when we need them most. Our theory of reality is going out the window and we are left adrift not only metaphysically, but practically as well. Our meaning-technology is inadequate to its new task.

What has not gone out the window is power-technology. Power-technology is what remains when we accept working material facts without a broad understanding of their theory or a thickly grounded metaphysics. What works, works, even if we mere users do not know why, and even if the mere creators do not believe in their Creator.

Given this disaster of meaning and morality there are four technologies I am particularly worried about because they are precisely

---

23. Hans Jonas, *The Imperative of Responsibility* (Chicago: University of Chicago Press, 1984), 23, and Pope Francis, *Laudato Si* (Vatican, 2015) para 105.
24. As noted by one of the monks in Philip Gröning, *Into Great Silence* (New York: Zeitgeist Films, 2005).

the ones which require the most meaning and the most morality in order to keep them on the straight and narrow road. Inadequate stories here cast peril upon the future, and should motivate us, then, to storywork.

Technologies I Wish We Could Do Without

Despite the promises, some perils I wish we could do without.

Nuclear Weapons

Between 1945 and 1952 human explosive power grew by a factor of one million. In the first millennium AD, Chinese alchemists invented gunpowder, thus making possible chemical bombs. In contemporary terminology, one ton of chemical explosive is roughly equivalent to one ton of TNT. In July of 1945, at the Trinity test in Alamogordo, New Mexico, humankind's maximal explosive capacity transitioned from chemical to fission bombs, a 1000x multiplication of explosive power; these weapon yields were now measured in kilotons: thousands of tons of TNT. Just 7 years later, in November of 1952, at the Ivy Mike test at Enewetak Atoll in the Marshall Islands, humankind's maximal explosive capacity transitioned from fission to fusion bombs, another 1000x multiplication of explosive power; these weapon yields were now measured in megatons: millions of tons of TNT.

The Manhattan Project was driven by the fear that the Nazis might get the atomic bomb first. The Nazis already had superior rocketry, and the idea of Nazis with ballistic missiles and A-bombs was a nightmare. Oppenheimer shows this story in his own life. The obsession with getting the atomic bomb before the Germans made sense. The forces of good should indeed be more powerful than the forces of evil, otherwise good will not endure long. However, the weapon was soon out of the scientists' hands. But even then, in the hands of politicians, morality stopped something from happening. The US did not immediately exterminate her enemies. Morality stopped that. The US allowed the Soviets to go about their lives, and so they got the bomb too. And that led to the Cold War and the world we live in now.

Technological development without a moral framework defaults into a tool of the powerful. Even with a framework it can still be perverted, but it can be more difficult. The moral stories of the past—stories of love of God, neighbor, even enemies; and conscience and the dignity of human life—prevented Armageddon. But if those stories no longer carry the strength to prevent such unspeakable evil, then what else will? Can any other stories bear such weight, the weight of billions of souls?

In the Manhattan Project we created our own worst fears. We were afraid of nuclear armed enemies, and as we created the bomb our enemies stole the secrets and armed themselves with our feared weapon.

And so I ask: should God have stopped us?

If technology is a gift from God, then nuclear weapons are a strange gift indeed. In Genesis 3:3 "God said, 'You shall not eat of the fruit of the tree that is in the middle of the garden, nor shall you touch it, or you shall die.'" The Fruit of the Tree of Knowledge of Good and Evil. Empowered by technology. It seemed like a good idea at the time.

But, of course, the whole structure of the universe itself was not our idea. Fissionable elements like Uranium 235 and Plutonium 239 don't seem like requirements for our universe. Maybe God could have created a universe without them . . . but here they are. Perhaps 1,000,000x explosive energy did not have to be possible . . . but it is. Is this the knowledge of good and evil that we desired? What provocation should we take this technology to be?

Rocketry and Space Technologies

For every action there is an equal and opposite reaction: Newton's Third Law. That's how rockets work and how forces are applied.

When I lived in the Marshall Islands as a teacher, I once saw a Minuteman III intercontinental ballistic missile re-enter the atmosphere: three warheads like meteors, and the remains of the missile trailing behind. A few years later, I met a nuclear bomb designer and told her that I had seen this and at the time had thought to myself 'Wow, if those were real, I'd be dead'. And she replied, with the sincerity and enthusiasm of genuine conviction: 'That's right'. I have reflected on those words for a long time.

Rocketry is extremely difficult. If Earth's gravity were stronger, or our atmosphere thicker, rocketry would become even more extremely difficult. The energy requirements would be too high, the payloads too low, the re-entry too hot. Even if not impossible, the economics would become worse, and humankind would be more likely to remain on Earth and perhaps learn to get along in our common home.

But instead we can access space. We can fill it with satellites and send probes to the other planets and even ponder orbital weapons platforms. The UN Outer Space Treaty of 1967 tries to keep space as a peaceful place, but this desire is a difficult one, when the same technologies that allow space travel allow us to destroy ourselves with nuclear ballistic missiles . . . and when the human heart seems not to desire peace.

While directed at German rocket scientist Wernher von Braun, the quip 'I aim for the stars, but sometimes I hit London'[25] could be, if generalized beyond London to the rest of our species, a sad motto for humankind. War on Earth is bad enough; adding in the dangers of space like vacuum and radiation, the kinetic energy of high-speed objects, asteroids sent on new trajectories, and so on, seems like too much. But these dangers we do have—they are ours, and choices involving them are for us to decide.

And so, as we stare into space, we might wonder at our place in it. Are we merely sentient dirt, or are we something more? What do our stories tell us? Our destiny might remain here, humbly remembering that we are dust and to dust we shall return. Or our destiny might be to fight and war, no matter our location, because of our evolved apish nature. Or our destiny might be among the stars, the furnaces that wrought our elements, a return. Or our destiny might be with God, returning God's story to our Maker. Apparently, in order to confront these mighty questions, we have some storywork to do.

Artificial Intelligence

Artificial intelligence, like a golem or genie, will do what we ask it to do. And for this reason we might ask whether we trust ourselves with such a thing. We know that human sin is real,[26] and yet we cannot seem to deny ourselves the means to act upon our iniquitous desires at ever larger scale, efficiency, and determinacy.

AI risks are often divided into near-term and long-term, and perhaps the biggest controversy in AI right now is between folks worried about risks right now and risks in the future from AI. There are certainly plenty of concerns on each side:

---

25. The quip was a criticism of the movie by Jay Dratler, George Froeschel, HW John, Udo Wolter, *I Aim for the Stars* (Culver City, CA: Columbia Pictures, 1960).
26. Ted Peters, *Sin: Radical Evil in Soul and Society* (Grand Rapids, Michigan: Eerdmans, 1994).

Present AI risks include: basic technical safety (for example, cars that do not crash), explainability and transparency (for example, can we understand our AI models), surveillance and data privacy & security (for example, both intentional and unintentional data leakage), the technology industry's lack of diversity (yielding limitations on developer's life-experiences and concerns), algorithmic bias & injustice (for example, racial or gender bias), reliance on the attention economy & addiction to 'digital opium' (for example, addictive apps and games), digital psychological operations and manipulation including mis/disinformation (for example, social media propaganda), looming unemployment (for example, many programmers already being put out of work), isolation and loneliness (for example, due to lack of direct contact with others), concentration of economic and political power (for example, in those who control AI), rising inequality & social immobility (those who control AI will secure their social positions), declining social trust (due to fear caused by propaganda and loss of social position), environmental sustainability (for example, AI uses a huge amount of electricity), and automating ethical decision making (for example, algorithms already make far too many decisions about who is denied welfare, or parole, etc).[27]

Future AI risks include: artificial consciousness (for example, will AI come to be self-aware), AI rights (if AI becomes conscious, should it have rights?), AGI and superintelligence (what will AGI and superintelligence do to our world?), the triumph of the technocratic paradigm (for example, the reduction of everything to mere technique), human dependence on AI (we are already dependent on so many technologies—how dependent can we be?), human de-skilling including moral deskilling (losing our ability to do certain tasks due to lack of expertise and practice including moral decision making), and finally, effects on human identity, spirit, & hope (who

---

27. Partially based upon Brian Patrick Green, 'Artificial Intelligence and Ethics: Sixteen Challenges and Opportunities', *Markkula Center website*, Aug 18, 2020, https://www.scu.edu/ethics/all-about-ethics/artificial-intelligence-and-ethics-sixteen-challenges-and-opportunities/, Brian Patrick Green, 'Ethical Reflections on Artificial Intelligence', in *Scientia et Fides*, 6 (2), 24 August 2018, http://apcz.umk.pl/czasopisma/index.php/SetF/article/view/SetF.2018.015/15729, and Shannon Vallor, Brian Green, Irina Raicu, 'Overview of Ethics in Tech Practice', *Markkula Center website*, Jun 22, 2018, https://www.scu.edu/ethics-in-technology-practice/overview-of-ethics-in-tech-practice/

are we if not our intelligence, and what hope remains for us if AI can do everything better than we can?).[28]

Certainly, both lists have important topics on them, so it might seem somewhat surprising that such animosity exists between near-term and long-term advocates. We might we ask ourselves 'Why not both?'

Everything that human intelligence can do, AI will also be directed towards, for good and for evil. And so, I wonder if God might have made computers a little less powerful. Kept us at the level of vacuum tubes rather than nanometer-scale circuits. Made the statistics too inscrutable to the human mind, or some other defense on our behalf. But no. God either trusts us too much or is determined to let us have things that are awfully dangerous so that we can continue living out our punishment for that damn fruit.

Again, our stories intrude . . . how we perceive artificial intelligence depends on how we perceive human intelligence, and divine intelligence.

Synthetic biology

Synthetic biology is a stronger form of biotechnology. It is sometimes shortened to SynBio; from a theological perspective, perhaps an unfortunate truncation. Synthetic biology seeks a more fundamental level of control over life, changing life from an entity with its own *telos* and into a machine to engineer into carrying out human-chosen *telei*. In Aristotelian terms, it makes a shift from cultivation (as we do with life) to construction (as we do with non-living things).[29]

Synthetic biological techniques can include many, many things, and just a few include: genetic manipulation of life at all levels, the construction of organoids, the integration of machines into living things, and (to improve on AI) 'synthetic biological intelligence' (SBI) which grows neurons on electronic substrates.

---

28. Vallor, Green, and Raicu, 'Overview of Ethics in Tech Practice'.
29. Carl Mitcham, 'Philosophy of Technology', in *A Guide to the Culture of Science, Technology, and Medicine*, edited by Paul T Durbin (New York: The Free Press, 1980), 308; see also, for example, Aristotle, *Physics*, translated by RP Hardie and RK Gaye, in *The basic Works of Aristotle*, edited by Richard McKeon (New York: Random House, 1941), 236–238 (Bk. II, Ch. 1).

One example of this integration of neuron and electronic substrate is DishBrain, by the Australian company Cortical Labs. DishBrain consists of mouse or human neurons grown on an electronic substrate; at approximately the level of one million neuron the system can be trained to play the video game 'Pong', with learning reinforced by electric shock when the neurons miss the ball.[30]

What AI cannot do—for example being conscious, caring, capacity for real love and relationships—synthetic biological intelligence might be able to do. We don't understand the 'magic' of consciousness, but perhaps we can hijack this magic from our own bodies through cell cultures on computer chips.

There is no clear way that AI can be conscious, have its own volition, experience qualia, etc—these are all properties of living things, and AI is not alive.[31] But SBI is *partly* alive. It might experience and want nothing . . . but life always seeks something. The living part of these entities would seem to be at risk, or present a risk, to those exploiting them. What experiences are these neurons beholding? Are they suffering? Will they desire something better? We do not yet know.

What we do know is that, in all of the above cases, technology is subject to the judgments of ethics[32] and we should not cease to judge our new technologies, or life will rapidly turn bad for us. Each of the above four technologies tell a story. Nuclear tells a story of energy. Rockets tell a story of rapid travel. AI tells a story about intelligence. Synthetic biology tells a story about life. Stories are technologies and technologies are also stories. Much 'storywork' is done to sell technologies, and not all of the stories told about technologies are the same as the stories the technologies themselves tell. Because each

---

30. Brett J Kagan, Andy C Kitchen, Nhi T Tran, Forough Habibollahi, Moein Khajehnejad, Bradyn J Parker, Anjali Bhat, Ben Rollo, Adeel Razi, Karl J Friston, "In vitro neurons learn and exhibit sentience when embodied in a simulated game-world", in *Neuron* 110, Issue 2 (7 December 2022): 3952–3969.e8

31. AI Research Group of the Centre for Digital Culture, *Encountering Artificial Intelligence: Ethical and Anthropological Investigations*, Volume 1, Issue Theological Investigations of AI (Eugene, OR: Pickwick, 2023), 69–105. https://jmt.scholasticahq.com/article/91230-encountering-artificial-intelligence-ethical-and-anthropological-investigations

32. Brian Patrick Green, 'Ethics Is More Important than Technology', *Markkula Center for Applied Ethics website*, 10 August 2020. https://www.scu.edu/ethics/all-about-ethics/ethics-is-more-important-than-technology/

technology has a purpose, an end-for-the-sake-of-which it exists. That *telos* says something about what humans value, whether it be medicines or weapons, and those stories may be verbally silent yet just as real as text on a page.

What storywork do our technologies tell? What storywork should our technologies be doing?

Another Story: Just Five Rules

I've always wanted to know exactly what it is that makes humans human. Thomas Aquinas noted, pithily, that human groups *qua* groups generally seek just five things: 1) survive (maintain existence in the short term by staying alive), 2) reproduce (maintain existence through the long term by sustainable generational continuity), 3) live in society (maintain order and division of labor necessary to fulfill all five purposes in community), 4) educate young (convey culture and necessary information for all five purposes to next generation), and 5) seek the truth (keep all five purposes proportionate with reality).[33]

Oppositely, human groups generally do not seek to: go extinct, not reproduce, completely socially isolate, reject education, or intentionally believe falsehoods. When groups choose to do these things we might think they are troubled, misguided, weird, crazy, and/or evil. And if one group intentionally forces this on another it is just evil: it is oppression and even genocide.

Working recently with a computer scientist, we came up with a logical proof, via *reductio ad absurdum*, for the fundamental values that must underlie human ethics at the group level.[34] It was originally inspired by Thomas Aquinas, in his *Summa Theologiae*, I-II, 94.2,[35] but we decided we had to develop it into something rigorous that people had to admit was real, or else deny logic entirely.

---

33. Thomas Aquinas, *Summa Theologiae*, translated by Fathers of the English Dominican Province, Complete English Edition in 5 Volumes (New York: Benziger Bros, 1947, republished by Notre Dame, IN: Ave Maria Press, 1981), 1009 (I-II, 94.2).
34. Betty Li Hou, Brian Patrick Green, 'Foundational Moral Values for AI Alignment', arXiv.org, 28 November 2023, https://arxiv.org/abs/2311.17017
35. Hou and Green, 'Foundational Moral Values for AI Alignment'.

The logical proofs are networked to each other and focus on maintaining the existence of ethical agents and of ethics and logic themselves.

1) Survive

Rule, positively framed: promote group survival in your immediate circumstances (survive immediate threats).

Rule, negatively framed: do not go extinct in the short term, avoid (mitigate and adapt to) catastrophic and existential risks.

Rule opposite, *reductio ad absurdum*: choose to go extinct, commit collective universal murder/suicide.

Elucidation of *reductio ad absurdum*: this is clearly an absurd choice because, by making logical agents extinct, it destroys its own preconditions: the possibility of logical choice at all. There can be no logical argument to eliminate logic; doing so would indicate that logic is valueless and/or irrational and therefore can be ignored. Additionally, as Hans Jonas noted in his *Imperative of Responsibility*, without humans, that is, without ethical agents, ethics itself would cease to exist, therefore no ethical argument can be made in favor of extinction. Humans are the precondition for ethics itself.[36]

2) Reproduce and Sustainability

Rule, positively framed: promote group survival long term, intergenerationally (this requires, for example, reproduction and environmental sustainability).

Rule, negatively framed: do not go extinct in the long term, avoid slow catastrophic and existential risks.

Rule opposite, *reductio ad absurdum*: choose to go extinct, collectively destroy all prospects for life the future, but slowly, by not reproducing or by destroying the environment.

Elucidation of *reductio ad absurdum*: same as 1).

3) Live in society

Rule, positively framed: live in society and seek relationships (communication, sociality, relationships, culture, family life, division of labor, trade, cooperation, government, etc)

---

36. Hans Jonas, *The Imperative of Responsibility* (Chicago: University of Chicago Press, 1984).

Rule, negatively framed: do not live in isolation, short term (avoid being isolated).

Rule opposite, *reductio ad absurdum*: everyone must live in complete isolation: no language, no society, no culture, no families, no division of labor, no trade, no cooperation, no government, etc.

Elucidation of *reductio ad absurdum*: this is clearly absurd for several reasons: first, society would collapse without division of labor and trade; second, reproduction would become impossible with complete isolation and small children would die without care; third, logic requires language and language requires people to talk to (no people means no language or logic); fourth, culture requires humans to be able to communicate, so cultural knowledge would begin to decline; fifth, government would fall apart and anarchy would ensue, and so on. Essentially, while an isolated form of life might be possible for some creatures, it is not possible for humans. We must live in social groups or we will not live for long.

4) Education

Rule, positively framed: learn from others, become educated and trained in the ways of culture and society so that society can sustain itself long term.

Rule, negatively framed: do not live in isolation long term, without education (children cannot be raised in isolation).

Rule opposite, *reductio ad absurdum*: live in isolation, without education or training, ignoring the needs of society's future.

Elucidation of *reductio ad absurdum*: just as adults are unlikely to survive for long in isolation, children are even more unlikely to survive in the absence of society, and especially in the absence of education and training in the ways of their culture. Societies will disintegrate if children are not enculturated and necessary intergenerational knowledge passed on.

5) Seek the truth

Rule, positively framed: seek and believe the truth, both practically and theoretically

Rule, negatively framed: do not seek or believe falsehood, either practically or theoretically

Rule opposite, *reductio ad absurdum*: seek and believe falsehood, seek that which is practically false and/or theoretically wrong

Elucidation of *reductio ad absurdum*: there can be no logical choice to choose illogic, and seeking falsehood-for-the-sake-of-falsehood (for one could seek falsehood for the sake of process of elimination to find truth) essentially raises illogic to a virtue. Theoretically speaking this would involve believing many scientific and metaphysical falsehoods, but practically speaking this would be deadly: believing that one can eat things that are not foods, that one can safely engage in life-threatening behaviors like running off cliffs, etc. The other four rules all depend on truth: one cannot survive or reproduce or be social or educate without at least some knowledge of truth.

These values are foundational because if one chooses the opposite, humanity ceases to exist, and along with it, logic and values. One cannot rationally or axiologically advocate for the cessation of reason or value. If you do, you are in a contradiction, like making a truth claim that truth doesn't matter. It can be said, but not meant.

Choosing the opposite value destroys humanity, either directly or indirectly, either via bad theory or bad practice. Undercutting the preconditions for your own existence is not a good way to live. It is a subtle form of lying, theoretically committing to something that is practically not how one lives.

Or, to quote Stanley Hauerwas, who has a folksy way of responding to moral nihilists: 'Do you like to eat?'[37] Because they probably do. And if they like to eat, then they probably should admit that they follow the above five values. They don't want to starve. They don't want society to collapse due to sterility, starvation, or a degraded environment. They don't want to live in isolation from those who provide food. They don't want the next generation to ruin society by ceasing to grow food. And they don't want to deny the truth of what is edible and eat non-food items. Eating is a practical endeavor, and our tongues know food when they taste it.

---

37. Stanley Hauerwas, 'Habit Matters: The Bodily Character of the Virtues', in *Habits in Mind: Integrating Theology, Philosophy, and the Cognitive Science of Virtue, Emotion, and Character Formation*, edited by Gregory R Peterson, James A Van Slyke, Michael L Spezio, and Kevin S Reimer (Leiden: Brill, 2017), 24.

Logic, Storywork, and Flesh

A logical proof is a form of story. It is not necessarily a very interesting story. I would not tell logical proofs to my children before bed in order to give them sweet dreams of non-absurdities. Perhaps it would be more likely to give them nightmares instead! Poetry has a logic of meaning which is unlike that of math. But logic should no more be discounted as a story-telling medium than poetry. Logic is very particular kind of story and it is very compelling to some very influential people. If we want influential people to listen to us then we need to speak in a language they can hear, understand, and respect.

In Aristotle's *Rhetoric*, he describes three forms of persuasive speech, corresponding to *pathos*, *ethos*, and *logos*.[38] Churches do pretty well spreading their message through *pathos*, especially since Christianity has such a visceral connection to Christ and God's love. Christianity's claim on *ethos* is more mixed, since people inside a church tend to approve of a Church's actions, while those outside tend to disapprove. But when it comes to *logos*, many Christian Churches have nearly unilaterally disarmed, especially those which have rejected science or other evidence-based ways of communicating. This lack of appeal to *logos* is self-reinforcing, as *logos*-minded listeners are driven out and therefore *logos*-driven arguments are less likely to be made, thus driving out more *logos*-minded listeners.

And yet the universe runs on mathematical-physical laws in the form of equations; strange words, the subtext of a sea of matter. DNA is a language; every living thing a long set of sentences, a story. In creating the universe, God's Mind became matter, God's Word was made flesh. In understanding the universe, in seeing the *word* in the *flesh*, the mind in the matter, as we speak our understanding, the flesh is made word again, transcending itself, returning to God. I know a professor who is tattooed with physics equations; his flesh is made word. He has made visible the otherwise invisible: such is the life of the scientist.

The word-made-world is a story about a story, one of the many that we are made out of. Its meaning may not explain everything, but it explains surprisingly much.

---

38. Aristotle, *Rhetoric*, translated by W Rhys Roberts, in *The Basic Works of Aristotle*, edited by Richard McKeon (New York: Random House, 1941), 1329–1330 (Bk. I, Ch. 2).

The Provocation of Technology

See the provocation that technology has given us.[39] Nuclear weapons presented us with the possibility of our own extinction: and so we pondered it, philosophized it, and slowly respond to it. Rockets have made us ask what space is for, and so we respond with weapons and exploration—the worse and better angels of our nature. Synthetic biology has asked us to think of our own power over life and wonder at what we should and should not do to living things and why. Lastly, AI has externalized our own abilities to process information, evaluate situations, and so on, even to the point of putting us 'out-of-the-loop', leaving us at the mercy of our machines (which are themselves merely obedient servants of what past engineers have made them to be). Will these machines to which we have delegated our powers do as we wish? Because *AI demands alignment*, just like human intelligence; AI demands guidance with respect to good and evil. As Bostrom has said, this is 'philosophy with a deadline' and we need to get it right.[40]

God laid potencies into the universe for us to find and use *for the sake of good*, but always, at the same time, with the risk of evil. In the past we were involuntarily constrained by our weakness. Now we must learn to be voluntarily restrained by our own judgment, our ethics.[41] Constants have become variables:[42] what were once beyond our powers are now within them, forcing us to ask the question: *should we* or *should we not*?

In the most basic sense, we should learn to be efficient at good and inefficient at bad/evil, or we will come to live in a terrible world. And we should ask ourselves: how can technology make good efficient? And how can technology make bad/evil inefficient?[43]

---

39. Brian Patrick Green, 'Emerging Technologies as Provocations for Theology and Ethics', presented to the Center for Theology and the Natural Sciences Russell Family Fellowship, Berkeley, CA, November 10, 2023.
40. Nick Bostrom, *Superintelligence: Paths, Dangers, Strategies* (Oxford: Oxford University Press, 2014), 314.
41. Brian Patrick Green, 'Ethics Is More Important than Technology', *Markkula Center for Applied Ethics website*, 10 August 2020. https://www.scu.edu/ethics/all-about-ethics/ethics-is-more-important-than-technology/
42. Balaji Srinivasan, 'Balaji Srinivasan on the Network State', *The a16z Podcast*, November 15, 2022. https://a16z.com/podcast/balaji-srinivasan-on-the-network-state/
43. Brian Patrick Green, 'The Technology of Holiness: A Response to Hava Tirosh-Samuelson', in *Theology and Science* 16(2) (2018): 223–228.

It is almost like God, when handing the skins-clothing to Adam and Eve, was setting a trajectory for humanity leading to now. Why did God ask for the first couple to abstain from the Tree of the Knowledge of Good and Evil? Because tasting of that tree could only mean one thing: *a long explanation, with a test at the end*.[44] A story to explain why.

It's a very long explanation; a lecturing-to, as a parent lectures a bad child. This life we are living—this world—is this lecture. If we listen to the lecture and understand it—*really understand it, live it*—then we get to return to Eden, though not the Eden of the past but one of the future, the New Jerusalem, the City of God.

If we ignore the lecture then we don't get to return, we just end up in a fiery Gehenna of our own making. The trash heap of history, and evolution, and the universe. It's not a pretty picture. Not a nice metaphor. Nobody likes having to admit they were wrong. But if we are humble then we also get to grow. There can be no learning without humility, we must admit that we need to learn before we can learn. Humility is the antidote to the vice of pride.

With these new technologies, the test of what we have learned from this long lecture is approaching. The test is pass/fail. The passing result is survival. The failing result is extinction. Adam and Eve, in the abstracted form of all humanity, would taste death, just as God had warned.

We may recall Deuteronomy 30:19 where God states the plainest of facts: 'I have set before you life and death, blessings and curses. Choose life so that you and your descendants may live.' There is still a choice in this story. The future is not sealed, our fate not yet determined. The choice is up to us.

In other words, God has a lot of faith in humanity. God thinks this must all be worth it; God thinks, perhaps, that we can make it, we can do it. Let's not give God—or humanity—reason to lose hope.

There is still goodness in human hearts. We still want to survive. We still want to love. We still seek the truth. *And it must be worth the risk.* Just like education is worth the risk. Just like love is worth the risk. Just like life is worth the risk. It may not be pretty, but it is all we've got. And it is a gift.

That's my story, and I'm sticking to it.

---

44. Brian Patrick Green, 'A Roman Catholic View: Technological Progress? Yes. Transhumanism? No', in *Religious Transhumanism and Its Critics*, edited by Arvin M Gouw, Brian Patrick Green, and Ted Peters (Lanham, Maryland: Lexington Books, 2022), 153

Chapter 4
Somnambulating Towards AI Dystopia? The Future of Rights and Freedoms

Neville Rochow

> 'The real problem relates to the possibility that AI may become incredibly good at achieving something other than what we really want.'
> — Stuart Russell[1]

Abstract: Dystopia is familiar to us. It is close to our daily lived experience with technology and Amazon, Apple, Facebook, and Google (the Four). The Four and AI pose an existential risk. History teaches that supranational corporations cannot be trusted with unchecked power or to respect human rights. With the combination of AI and the Four, our situation is akin to Rawls' 'original position' behind a 'veil of ignorance'. None can predict the effect AI will have on human rights. We should take our rights seriously before the bio-technological lottery begins. Prompt international action is required to regulate AI developers and corporations.

Key Words: Artificial Intelligence, corporations, human rights.

In Yevgeny Zamyatin's 1924 novel *We*,[2] OneState controls the planet. Happiness is guaranteed to all Numbers, the inhabitants of this future world, by OneSate's scientific method, the Table of Hours. The Table is

---

1. Stuart Russell, 'Should We Fear Supersmart Robots?', in *Scientific American*, 314:6 (June 2016): 58–59 (58); http://www.scientificamerican.com/article/should-we-fear-supersmart-robots/.
2. Written in Russian and published in various languages beginning with English in 1924.

drawn by Zamyatin from the efficiency theories of Frederick Taylor[3] and the Soviet management practices of Nadezhda Krupskaya.[4] It prescribes every Number's activity at every moment of each day. The success of OneState project is underwritten by the Benefactor, who is supported in surveillance and enforcement performed by the Bureau of Guardians. OneSate's control is absolute.

The story begins with a *State Gazette* writing project. Entries are to be sent to uncharted planets. Numbers are to 'place the beneficial yoke of reason round the necks of unknown beings who inhabit other planets—still living, in the primitive state known as freedom'.[5] Our narrator, D-503, a rocket scientist, contributes his entry in the form of a series of 'records'. In one 'record', D-503 muses on this quaint twentieth century notion, 'freedom':

> I've read and heard a lot of unbelievable stuff about those times when people lived in freedom—that is, in disorganised wildness. But of all things the every hardest for me to believe was how the governmental power of that time, even if it was still embryonic, could have permitted people to live without even a semblance of our Table . . . It's so funny, so improbable, that now I've written it I am afraid that you, my unknown readers, will think I'm making wicked jokes . . . [but] OneState Science cannot make a mistake. [If freedom were to manifest itself] . . . These are fortunately no more than little chance details; it's easy to repair them without bringing to a halt the great eternal progress of the whole Machine.[6]

The distant future world of *We* seems all too familiar. Part of that familiarity derives from the popular trope in film and literary fiction of a post-apocalyptic dystopian future.[7] Two striking commonalities

---

3. Clarence Brown, 'Introduction: *Zamyatin and the Persian Rooster*', in *We*, Yevgeny Zamyatin, (translated by Clarence Brown, Penguin Group, 1992), xviii.
4. Brown, 'Introduction: *Zamyatin and the Persian Rooster*'.
5. Brown, 'Introduction: *Zamyatin and the Persian Rooster*', Record 1, 3.
6. Brown, 'Introduction: *Zamyatin and the Persian Rooster*', 3, 13-15.
7. Examples from film include *Metropolis* (Fritz Lang, 1927), *Blade Runner* (Ridley Scott, 1982), *Blade Runner 2049*, (Denis Villeneuve, 2017), *A.I.* (Steven Spielberg, 2001) and *Minority Report* (Steven Spielberg, 2002). Examples of dystopian literature (much of which has been turned into film) include *The Time Machine* (1895) by HG Wells, *Lord of the World* (1908) by Robert Hugh Benson, *R.U.R.: Rossum's Universal Robots* (1921) by Karel Čapek, *We* (1921, Russian, 1924, English) by Yevgeny Zamyatin, *Brave New World* (1932) by Aldous Huxley, *It*

recur in the trope: a presence and an absence. Commonly *present* in the trope is the pervasiveness of technology, regulating every activity, often exploited for totalitarian purposes by a mysterious government or megacorporation.[8] Noticeably *absent* are basic human rights and freedoms, including conscience, religion, belief, association, and expression.

Life Imitates Art

Life imitates art. *We* is also familiar in our domestic and working lives. Today, technology rules us. Daily, we imbibe a mix of artificial intelligence[9] (AI), intelligence amplification[10] (IA), robotics,[11] and corporate power.[12] Four supranational corporations, with unrivalled

---

Can't Happen Here (1935) by Sinclair Lewis, *Animal Farm* (1945) by George Orwell, *Nineteen Eighty-Four* (1949) by George Orwell, *Utopia 14* (1952) by Kurt Vonnegut, *Fahrenheit 451* (1953) by Ray Bradbury, *Minority Report* (1956) by Philip K Dick, and *The Man in the High Castle* by Philip K Dick (1962).

8. As in *I, Robot*, (Alex Proyas, 2004). See also Elizabeth Anderson, *Private Government—How Employers Rule Our Lives (and Why We Don't Talk about It)* (Princeton University Press, 2017).
9. Machine intelligence, or intelligence demonstrated by machines, in contrast to the natural intelligence displayed by humans. For discussions of its manifestation, see: Scott Galloway, *The Four—The Hidden DNA of Amazon, Apple, Google and Facebook*, (2017, Transworld Publishers), chapter 1 and 196–200; Richard Susskind and Daniel Susskind, *The Future of the Professions—How Technology will Transform the Work of Human Experts* (2015, 2017, Oxford University Press), chapters 1 and 2.
10. Yuval Noah Harari, *Homo Deus—A Brief History of Tomorrow* (2014, Harvill Secker), 353–359 (described as 'techno-humanism'; Galloway, *The Four–The Hidden DNA of Amazon, Apple*, 200, note 8, above. See also Francis Fukuyama, *Our Posthuman Future–Consequences of the Biotechnology Revolution* (2002, Picador).
11. 'Robotics' as used here includes design, construction, operation, and any use of robots; and computer systems used for their control; and information processing. Regarding Amazon's use to replace human work see Galloway, *op. cit.*, note 8, above, at 52–54.
12. Galloway, *The Four—The Hidden DNA of Amazon, Apple*, 200, note 8, above, at 54–57; Robert Verbruggen, 'Google, Facebook, Amazon: Our Digital Overlords', 12 December 2017, *Nation Review* at https://www.nationalreview.com/2017/12/google-facebook-amazon-big-tech-becoming-problem; James Heskett, 'Is It Time To Break Up Amazon, Apple, Facebook, or Google?' 6 December 2017, *Working Knowledge*
Business Research for Business Leaders, Harvard Business School, at https://hbswk.hbs.edu/item/is-it-time-to-break-up-amazon-apple-facebook-or-google?cid=wk-rss.

international market power, control most of our technology: Amazon; Apple; Facebook; and Google, ('the Four').[13] Each possesses the strategic economic power of a nation-state.[14] They decide if, how, and where they are to be regulated;[15] what market practices they will employ; if when, where, and how much tax they pay; what, if any, ethical standards they will implement. Imposition of fines is merely an operational cost.[16] Most importantly, into the future, they will effectively decide what, if any, human rights they will respect and the extent to which it suits their overriding profit motive.

Technology insinuates itself into our every activity. We gormlessly accept the toxic elixir of corporate power and technological addiction without question as to the harm that may be done. Scarcely a thought is given to the motives and methods of the formless behemoths that provide it. In short, we take our chances. Instead of questioning, with unstinting trust, we confide our personal and financial details so that we can continue to receive good and services from the Four. If we considered the security breaches of which they are guilty, the unemployment they cause, and the control they seek over us for profit, we would regard them as vice. They should be viewed, as Alexander Pope described, monsters of 'frightful mien'.[17]

Rather than hating[18] as Pope advised,[19] we have become *familiar*[20] with the Four in our homes and offices; we *endure*[21] their affinity

---

13. Heskett, 'Is It Time To Break Up Amazon, Apple, Facebook, or Google?' 'Supranational' is used here to describe corporations, like the Four, who have substantial economic and technological power sufficient to transcend states and their control and to submit, effectively, when convenient. 'Transnational' describes and corporation or business that trades across national borders.
14. Anderson, *Private Government—How Employers Rule Our Lives*, note 7 above; Galloway, *The Four—The Hidden DNA of Amazon, Apple,*, note 8, above.
15. Verbruggen, *op. cit.*, note 11 above.
16. Luigi Zingales, 'How E.U.'s Google Fine Explains High Cellphone Costs in the U.S.', 24 July 2018, *The New York Times*, at https://www.nytimes.com/2018/07/24/opinion/european-union-google-fine-monopoly.html
17. *Essay on Man*, Epistle II:
    Vice is a monster of so frightful mien,
    As, to be hated, needs but to be seen;
    Yet seen too oft, familiar with her face,
    We first endure, then pity, then embrace.
18. *Essay on Man*, Epistle II:
19. *Essay on Man*, Epistle II:
20. *Essay on Man*, Epistle II:
21. *Essay on Man*, Epistle II:

algorithms[22] and eavesdropping devices;[23] we *pity* Zuckerberg when he is publicly humiliated over Facebook's misuse of personal information;[24] we just *embrace* new gadgets and services that we do not need; and we continue to accept the convenience of Amazon's supply chain. It does not seem to trouble us that Amazon replaces 76,000 employees annually with robots.[25] Apple is venerated when it defies a Federal Court order to assist in a mass murder investigation.[26] Facebook's misuse of data for profit[27] and photographs for facial recognition[28] changes none of our social media habits permanently. Despite Google being fined a record 4.34 billion Euros for anti-competitive conduct in the EU;[29] we continue to trust its answers to all our questions.

Questions Without Answers

Why do we take such chances? Because we consider the promises to be greater than the risks. The 'fourth industrial revolution',[30] promise a cornucopia of low-cost, high quality goods and services supplied in miraculously short time by unseen algorithms and

---

22. Galloway, *The Four—The Hidden DNA of Amazon, Apple*, note 8, above, at 105–114.
23. Eric Limer, 'Hundreds of Apps Can Eavesdrop Through Phone Microphones to Target Ads', 3 January 2018, *Popular Mechanics*, at https://www.popularmechanics.com/technology/security/a14533262/alphonso-audio-ad-targeting/
24. Galloway, *The Four—The Hidden DNA of Amazon, Apple*, note 8, above, at 107, regarding the Cambridge Analytica scandal.
25. Galloway, *The Four—The Hidden DNA of Amazon, Apple*, note 8, above, at 29–30, 52–54.
26. Galloway, *The Four—The Hidden DNA of Amazon, Apple*, note 8, above, at 63–66.
27. See note 23 above and Jessica Guynn, 'Facebook wants to save your face. Should you say yes to facial recognition?' 19 April, 2018 *USA TODAY*, at https://www.usatoday.com/story/tech/news/2018/04/19/facebook-growing-use-facial-recognition-raises-privacy-concerns/526937002/
28. Zingales, 'How E.U.'s Google Fine Explains High Cellphone Costs in the U.S.', note 15, above.
29. Zingales, 'How E.U.'s Google Fine Explains High Cellphone Costs in the U.S.', Adam Satariano and Jack Nicas, July 18, 2018, 'E.U. Fines Google $5.1 Billion in Android Antitrust Case', *The New York Times* at https://www.nytimes.com/2018/07/18/technology/google-eu-android-fine.html
30. Generally used to describe the fourth major industrial period since the Industrial Revolution of the 18th century, involving electronic, digital, and robotic technologies and frequently merging the physical, digital, and biological capacities. See: Klaus Schwab, *The Fourth Industrial Revolution*, (2017, New York: Crown Publishing Group); Callum Chace, *The Economic Singularity: Artificial Intelligence and the Death of Capitalism*, (2016, The Three Cs).

robotic minions. These technological servants meet consumers' every want and need, at their beck and call. Information will be available in unimaginable volumes and at mind-blistering rates. We will think faster with artificial enhancements and increase our physical capabilities with robotic exoskeletons and extensions. Efficiencies will optimise with inventions yet to be imagined. Gadgets we once considered unthinkable outside of science fiction are now with us: the 'internet of things';[31] nanotechnological manufacture;[32] driverless cars;[33] and intelligent commercial and domestic accommodation.[34] Agriculture is becoming less susceptible to climate changes through the development of new plant and animal breeds.[35] With medical advances, genetic attributes of offspring will be made to order;[36] ailments will be detected early,[37] monitored remotely,[38] and treated

---

31. See Schwab, Schwab, *The Fourth Industrial Revolution*, note 29, above; Steve Ranger, 'What is the IoT? Everything you need to know about the Internet of Things right now Updated: The Internet of Things explained. What the IoT is, and where it's going next.' 21August, 2018, ZDNET, at https://www.zdnet.com/article/what-is-the-internet-of-things-everything-you-need-to-know-about-the-iot-right-now/
32. Nanoscience and nanotechnology are the study and application of extremely small things and can be used across all the other science fields, such as chemistry, biology, physics, materials science, and engineering: https://www.nano.gov/nanotech-101/what/definition
33. See Google's website for its driverless car project, Waymo: https://waymo.com/
34. See Intelligent Buildings at https://www.intelligentbuildings.com/#scroll-get-started
35. See the CSIRO project for marker assisted breeding to isolate desirable genotypes in specific environmental and climatic conditions: https://www.csiro.au/en/Research/Farming-food/Innovation-and-technology-for-the-future/Gene-technology/Marker-breeding
36. Harari, *Homo Deus—A Brief History of Tomorrow*, note 9, above, at 52–54.
37. Amy Jeter Hansen, 'Artificial intelligence in medicine — predicting patient outcomes and beyond' 8 May 2018, Scope, Stanford Medicine, at https://scopeblog.stanford.edu/2018/05/08/artificial-intelligence-in-medicine-predicting-patient-outcomes-and-beyond/; Alvin Rajkomar *et al* 'Scalable and accurate deep learning with electronic health records', *npj Digital Medicine* volume 1, Article number: 18 (2018), at https://www.nature.com/articles/s41746-018-0029-1; See also Fukuyama, *Our Posthuman Future–Consequences of the Biotechnology Revolution*, note 9, above at 70–71.
38. See note 36, above.

prophylactically;[39] longevity will be at the individual's discretion.[40] The environment could well benefit from technologies that will minimise our carbon footprint[41] and possibly even reverse some destructive effects from the first three industrial revolutions.[42]

The Fourth Industrial Revolution

This fourth industrial revolution also promises to usher in unprecedented social change.[43] As with any revolution, the scale and nature of change remains all but impossible to predict.[44] Cherished hopes for this imminent utopia are closely bound to our deepest fears.[45] The combination of AI, IA, and robotics conjures a new force that is at once a genie-like slave for those whose lives are enriched and a sinister usurper for those whose employment will be rendered redundant. Will the professions survive the new outpouring upon the general population of what was once arcane knowledge reserved for specialists?[46] How will those with manual skills be re-deployed?[47] What new economic and political balances will need to be struck? What will be the effect on real estate when business and governmental

---

39. See note 36, above. See also Harari, *Homo Deus—A Brief History of Tomorrow*, note 9, above, at 5, 25–27, 32–34, 50.
40. Harari, *Homo Deus—A Brief History of Tomorrow*, note 9, above, at 5, 25–27, 32–34, 50; See also Fukuyama, *op. cit.*, note 9, above at 70–71.
41. Jane Burston, 'Four technological innovations that can help reduce urban carbon emissions' 6 June 2016. *Horizons Smart Cities*, at https://www.citymetric.com/horizons/four-technological-innovations-can-help-reduce-urban-carbon-emissions-2103
42. Jahda Swanborough, 'The previous industrial revolutions broke the environment. Can the current one fix it?', 20 April 2017, *World Economic Forum*, at https://www.weforum.org/agenda/2017/04/fix-the-environment-there-s-an-app-for-that/
43. See note 29, above. See also James Barrat, *Our Final Invention: Artificial Intelligence and the End of the Human Era*,
44. See Fukuyama, *Our Posthuman Future–Consequences of the Biotechnology Revolution*, note 9, above.
45. Fukuyama, *Our Posthuman Future–Consequences of the Biotechnology Revolution* See also Barrat, *Our Final Invention: Artificial Intelligence and the End of the Human Era*, note 42, above, chapters 3, 10, and 14.
46. See Susskind, *The Future of the Professions—How Technology will Transform the Work of Human Experts*, note 8, above. See also Richard Susskind, *Tomorrow's Lawyers—An Introduction to Your Future* (2017, Oxford University Press, 2nd edition)
47. Susskind, *Tomorrow's Lawyers—An Introduction to Your Future.*

space is no longer required? How will demographics shift if only some sectors of the population have the privilege of aging healthily and gracefully? How will humans, transhumans, and androids inter-relate? In whose image will the new emergent society be re-shaped? Could the promised utopia be the dystopia of science fiction?

To see the apocalyptic potential that threatens, we need not trace back two hundred years to *Frankenstein*,[48] or through twentieth century works of Zamyatin, George Orwell, Aldous Huxley, and Philip K Dick,[49] and the whole genre of unwitting creators and faceless organisations unleashing technology-gone-horribly-wrong. Writers and filmmakers of this century[50] continue warn regarding our political, economic, and ethical destiny in a world in which science and corporations rule supreme. But that body of artistic works is now joined by a rich expert literature posing precisely the same questions;[51] ethical and moral questions posed but that remain unanswered.[52] At heart, one dilemma is just how are we to offset our insatiable desire for progress against the preservation of rights and freedoms that define our humanity? How do we avoid the potential dystopian hell?

---

48. *Frankenstein, or the Modern Prometheus* by Mary Shelley (1818).
49. See note 6, above.
50. See notes 6 and 7, above.
51. Apart from works previously cited, see: Nick Bostrom, *Superintelligence—Paths Dangers, Strategies* (2014, Oxford University Press); Siva Vaidhyanathan, *The Googlization of Everything* (2012, University of California Press); Siva Vaidhyanathan, *anti-social media—How Facebook Disconnects Us and Undermines Democracy* (2018, Oxford University Press); Kevin Kelly, *The Inevitable: Understanding 12 Technological Forces That Will Shape Our Future* (2016, Penguin Books); Kevin D Ashley, *Artificial Intelligence and Legal Analytics—New Tools for Law Practice in the Digital Age* (2017, Cambridge University Press); Max Tegmark, *Life 3.0—Being Human in the Age of Artificial Intelligence* (2017, Penguin Books); Franklin Foer, *World Without Mind—The Existential Threat of Big Tech* (2017, Penguin Press); Lasse Rouhiainen, *Artificial Intelligence—101 Things You Must Know Today About Our Future* (2018, Lasse Rouhiainen).
52. David J Gunkel, *The Machine Question—Critical Perspectives on AI, Robots, and Ethics* (2017, MIT Press); Jesse Russell and Ronald Cohn, *Ethics of Artificial Intelligence*, (2012, Lennex Corp). See also Ana Beduschi, 'Technology dominates our lives—that's why we should teach human rights law to software engineers', 26 September 2018, The Conversation, at https://theconversation.com/technology-dominates-our-lives-thats-why-we-should-teach-human-rights-law-to-software-engineers-102530?utm

So, which is it going to be—utopia or dystopia? Rarely do the purveyors of the dystopian trope explain either the attainment of technological supremacy or the loss of basic rights. As in a dream gone awry, along with the fictional protagonists, we are dropped in the middle of the unfolding nightmare with no explanation as to just how all of this came about. In one rhapsodic variation on the nightmare,[53] the plot devolves from utopian technology behaving as the humans' compliant servant, to that disastrously unanticipated moment of machine self-will that translates into chaos. The computer or robot usurps control from hapless humans to become the malevolent master. The pivot in the plot is driven by a belated insight: some self-absorbing malware had somehow stealthily crept into the programming. That insight comes all too late for the subjugated humans. They become victims of, literally, inhuman treatment. Until control is regained by the scripted remnant, the technology displays ruthless disregard for its erstwhile masters.

Many questions remain unanswered. Many more are yet to be asked.

The Pollyanna and Cassandra Syndromes

We have had more than our share of wrong predictions. Failing to sign Elvis Presley, the Beatles, or JK Rowling, forecasting the First World War to last only a few months, the predicted collapse of modern technology on 1 January 2000 with the Y2K bug, and Francis Fukuyama's vaunting of capitalism as the End of History,[54] have, each in their way fuelled a cynicism for human predictive powers. Our cynicism couples with our inability to discern correct predictions when they are made: the bombing of Pearl Harbor;[55] global terrorism;[56] that Bernie Madoff's Ponzi scheme would collapse.[57] Our innate tendency is towards believing those with optimistic messages

---

53. For example, in film, *2001—A Space Odyssey*, (Stanley Kubrick, 1968) and *Saturn 3* (Stanley Donen, 1980). In literature, *Frankenstein* remains possibly one of the best examples.
54. Francis Fukuyama, *The End of History and the Last Man* (1992, Free Press).
55. Barbara Tuchman, *The Zimmerman Telegram* (2014, Random House).
56. Brynjar Lia, *Globalisation and the Future of Terrorism, Patterns and Predictions* (2005, Routledge).
57. Peter Sander, *Madoff—Corruption, Deceit, and the Making of the World's Most Notorious Ponzi Scheme* (2009, The Lyons Press), 96–105.

and the least effort, the Pollyannas. We hope that doomsayers, the Cassandras, who may be right, will prove to be wrong and that the efforts they advocate will be unnecessary.[58] So, we ignore the (potential) Cassandras and follow the Pollyannas.

Be Careful of the Companies we Keep

We tend to overlook inherent flaws in corporations and AI. We attribute to them human qualities but exclude flaws and imperfection. These attributions are merely simulacra. Even the legal personality of a corporation is a legal fiction and limited in purpose. Both the corporation and AI are human creations that inherit human failings in their design, production, and operation. Human bias is present in input and output.

The 'failings' factor should influence us to have more respect for those Cassandras who may just be likely right on AI and corporations. We should take the chance that they are right rather than they are wrong. Predictions range through the paradisaical,[59] the benign,[60] to the cataclysmically disastrous.[61] But looking to the origins, there is cause for healthy disrespect. Both the corporation, especially supranational corporations, and AI have terrible pedigrees.

On the unknowable potential of corporations, in his insightful work, *The Corporation—The Pathological of Pursuit of Profit and Power*, Joel Bakan observes:

> When in 1933, Supreme Court Justice Louis Brandeis likened corporations to 'Frankenstein's monster,'[62] there was more to his observation than rhetorical flair. Governments create

---

58. Cassandra, blessed with the gift of accurate prophecy, was cursed that her prophecies would not be believed. See Homer's *Iliad*, Book XXIV, lines 820–830.
59. See discussion of Google's Ray Kurtzweil in Barrat, *Our Final Invention: Artificial Intelligence and the End of the Human Era*, at note 42, 28–31.
60. Susskind, *The Future of the Professions—How Technology will Transform the Work of Human Experts*, at note 8.
61. See Bostrom, Foer, Vaidhyanathan, and Tegmark, cited at note 50, above.
62. *Louis K. Liggett Co. v. Lee*, 288 U.S. 517, 564–67 (1933) (Brandeis, J, dissenting in part). Justice Brandeis borrowed the phrase from Maurice Wormser, *Frankenstein, Incorporated* (1931). Discussed in Robert N Strassfeldt, 'Introduction: Corporations and Their Communities', *Case Western Reserve Law Review*, 58:4 1017 (2008): at 1019.

corporations, much like Dr Frankenstein created his monster, yet, once they exist, corporations threaten to overpower their creators.[63]

The pedigree of the supranational corporation traces back to 1543 and the creation of a proto-corporation, the Church of England. It was used as the vehicle for Henry VIII's reverse takeover of the Catholic Church in the English Reformation.[64] State-power was invested in the new Church. Henry, as its head, through the new Church, cut all ties to the Vatican, dried up its income streams by abolishing indulgences, appropriated income and assets of the monasteries, and thus substantially increased the wealth of the English Crown. In the enterprise, Henry was ruthless in his pursuit of an ultimately futile ambition—gaining a male heir. He regarded life, conscience, and property rights as irrelevant in that pursuit. He executed anyone that stood in his way.

The Honourable East India Company (HEIC or East India Company), the first supranational trading corporation, received its Royal Charter in 1600 from Henry's heir, Elizabeth I. HEIC eclipsed Henry in rapacity and disregard for property. In pursuit of markets, capital, and profit, it showed no respect for borders, sovereignty, or the rights of nations or individuals. HEIC colonised India, and, using private armies, took control of all trade and commerce, and installed British government in place of indigenous fiefdoms. To secure monopoly trade in China's tea, it did not scruple at gunboats and addiction to opium.[65]

Corporations, to varying extents, have since emulated the East India Company's actions to secure markets, monopolise, and profit by whatever means at their disposal.[66] Examples include: the *Banque*

---

63. Joel Bakan, *The Corporation—The Pathological of Pursuit of Profit and Power* (2005, Constable), 149.
64. Christopher Hill, 'Social and Economic Consequences of the Henrician Reformation', in *Puritanism & Revolution—Studies in Interpretation of the English Revolution* (1958, 2001, Pimlico), 30–45.
65. Philip J Stern, *The Company-State: Corporate Sovereignty & the Early Modern Foundations of the British Empire in India* (Oxford University Press, 2011); John Keay, *The Honourable Company: A History of the English East India Company* (Harper Collins Publishers, 1991); John Keay, *India, A History: From the Earliest Civilsations to the Boom of the Twenty-First Century* (Harper Press, 2010).
66. Strassfeldt, 'Introduction: Corporations and Their Communities', above n 62, 28–60 and 111 *et seq*. See also: Yuval Noah Harari, *Sapiens—A Brief History or*

Générale and the Company of the West, both of which, under the direction of John Law, contributed as causes of the French Revolution;[67] the Dutch East India Company, which enabled Holland's conquest of the Dutch East Indies and monopolisation of the spice trade;[68] the Hudson's Bay Company, which monopolised trade in Canadian resources;[69] the Rothschild firm,[70] which speculated in national and international wars for profit;[71] Rockefeller's Standard Oil, which, with other trust corporations, throttled the economy of mid-nineteenth century United States;[72] Microsoft Corporation, which stymied national and international software markets through anti-competitive practices;[73] the dishonest culture of the four major Australian banks;[74] and, of course, the conduct of the Four.

Superintelligence

On the unknowable potential of technology, in his magisterial work *Superintelligence—Paths Dangers, Strategies*, Nick Bostrom commences with a salutary, but, so far, unfinished parable:

Humankind, Penguin (Random House UK, 2011), 31–36; Niall Ferguson, *Empire: How Britain Made the Modern World* (Penguin Group, 2003); John Micklethwait and Adrian Woolridge, *The Company: A Short History of a Revolutionary Idea* (Phoenix, 2003); and Nick Robins, *The Corporation That Changed the World: How the East India Company Shaped the Modern Multinational* (Pluto Press, 2nd edition 2012). See also note 64, above.

67. Niall Ferguson, *The Ascent of Money: A Financial History of the World* (Penguin Group, 2008), 139–158.
68. Ferguson, *The Ascent of Money: A Financial History of the World*, 129–138.
69. HBC Heritage, 'Our History: Overview' (October 2015) <http://www.hbcheritage.ca/history>.
70. While not necessarily corporations, the operation of the firm was 'supranational' and 'corporate' in every other sense.
71. Hill, 'Social and Economic Consequences of the Henrician Reformation', above n 66, 79–87, 90–92, 97–98 and 114–115.
72. Ron Chernow, *Titan—The Life of John D. Rockefeller,* Sr, Random House, Inc. 1998, chapter 7; Ida M. Tarbell, *The History of the Standard Oil Company,* (1904 McClure, Phillips and Co.)
73. *United States v Microsoft Corporation* 253 F.3d 34 (2001).
74. Interim Report of Royal Commission into Misconduct in the Banking, Superannuation and Financial Services Industry, 28 September, 2018, at https://financialservices.royalcommission.gov.au/Documents/interim-report/interim-report-volume-1.pdf

A group of sparrows are building their nests. 'We are all so small and weak', tweets one, feebly. 'Imagine how easy life would be if we had an owl who could help us build our nests!' There is general twittering agreement among sparrows everywhere; an owl could defend the sparrows! It could look after their old and their young! It could allow them to live a life of leisure and prosperity! With these fantasies in mind, the sparrows can hardly contain their excitement and fly off in search of the swivel-headed saviour who will transform their existence . . .

There is only one voice of dissent: 'Scronkfinkle, a one-eyed sparrow with a fretful temperament, was unconvinced of the wisdom of the endeavour. Quoth he: "This will surely be our undoing. Should we not give some thought to the art of owl-domestication and owl-taming first, before we bring such a creature into our midst?"' His warnings, inevitably, fall on deaf sparrow ears. Owl-taming would be complicated; why not get the owl first and work out the fine details later? . . .[75]

The ancestry of AI is no less noble than that of the supranational corporation. Machine intelligence traces its origins to one or more of three sources: war; fast food; or pornography.[76] If and when machines reach human intelligence for all purposes,[77] predicted social and economic upheaval include scenarios of realigned stratifications where those can afford to adopt technology as a part of their own biological and cognitive make-up will succeed,[78] while those who cannot will be downtrodden and subjugated. In short, some will be bio-technologically deified[79] while others are dehumanised.[80]

---

75. 'The Unfinished Fable of the Sparrows', (truncated version from Tim Adams, 'Artificial intelligence: 'We're like children playing with a bomb', 12 June 2018, *The Guardian*, at https://www.theguardian.com/technology/2016/jun/12/nick-bostrom-artificial-intelligence-machine The full version is in Bostrom, *op. cit.*, note 50, iii–iv.
76. Peter Nowak, *Sex, Bombs and Burgers—How War, Pornography, and Fast Food Have Shaped Modern Technology* (Viking Canada 2010).
77. Bostrom, *Superintelligence: Paths Dangers, Strategies*, note 50, chapters 3 and 4.
78. Tegmark, Tegmark, *Life 3.0—Being Human in the Age of Artificial Intelligence*, note 50, 118–133.
79. Harari, *Homo Deus—A Brief History of Tomorrow*, note 9.
80. *Homo Deus—A Brief History of Tomorrow*.

Unregulated corporations with AI, IA, and AGI at their disposal is just not a smart option for humans. Without international norms to guide commercial and military applications of AI, it would seem humanity takes part in a waiting game to see whether the Pollyannas were right.

A New Rawlsian Veil of Ignorance?

We are all now in a situation akin to Rawls' 'original position'[81] behind an actual 'veil of ignorance'.[82] None of us knows what will happen to our rights and freedoms in the short-term with supranationals in control of AI.[83] Neither can we predict what will happen with human rights when AGI occurs or if the event horizon of superintelligence is reached.[84] It is not even possible to predict the sequence in which AGI and superintelligence may arrive.[85] The potential scenarios call for us to take human rights and freedoms seriously[86] now before the bio-technological lottery begins.

If the predictions ended there, Michael Sandel, in commenting on Rawls,[87] could, of course, be right: some behind this veil of ignorance might still opt to take their chances and continue to ignore human rights. But on the superintelligence scenario, because of the unpredictable nature of the implications for us, the planet, and, indeed, the universe, constraint upon developers and users must enter the equation.[88]

Superintelligence is reached when artificially intelligent machines themselves would write the code and control the production of other

---

81. John Rawls, *A Theory of Justice* (Harvard University Press, revised ed, 1999) chapter 3.
82. Rawls, *A Theory of Justice*, 118–123.
83. Nick Bostrom, *Superintelligence: Paths Dangers, Strategies* (Oxford University Press, 2014) 4, 22–25, 77, 107, 303–305 and 364.
84. Bostrom, *Superintelligence: Paths Dangers, Strategies*, 130–131, 188 and 378.
85. Bostrom, *Superintelligence: Paths Dangers, Strategies*.
86. Ronald Dworkin, *Taking Rights Seriously* (Duckworth 1996), 90–94 and 188–192. See also chapters 6 and 7 *passim*.
87. Michael J Sandel, *Justice: What's the Right Thing to do?* (Penguin Group, 2009) chapter 6. Particularly 157–166.
88. Rawls, *A Theory of Justice*,, above n 82, 5, 25, 67, 124–126, 140–154, 220–221, 282–287, 295–302, 315–316, 357 and 378.

artificially intelligent machines.[89] They would be able to network, pool their intelligence, and press into service robotic extensions to manufacture hardware and means of production.[90] This intelligence explosion is one in which humans will necessarily be inferior in intelligence and capability to those possessed by machines. They will be at the mercy of the machines much like inferior species have been at ours throughout human history. There is nothing to constrain this new type of being to behave either beneficently or even benignly disposed towards humans. It could regard with pity and affection, like kindly god, or view us as a source of carbon, minerals, or energy.[91]

If there is to be any chance of avoiding the worst of the predicted scenarios, then the machines that are being designed now must be biased in our favour. Though not a guarantee, not attempting it is a risk that is not worth taking.

Bias: The Real Ghost in the Machine

Computer output has effect upon the humans who consume it. If we needed to be reminded of this truism, Selena Scolla, one of Facebook's censors, is suing her employer for the post-traumatic stress disorder caused by content she had to vet in the course of her employment.[92] What is sometimes overlooked is the effect that humans and their biases have in the generation of AI and the use of its output. Bias is, generally, negatively perceived. We want our judges and decision-makers to be fair, impartial, and definitely unbiased. But in machines, it is a different matter.

Alan Turing, arguably, invented not only the computer but also the dilemma of bias. During his pioneering AI work to break the Enigma encryption machine codes, the question was who would receive the data he and the Hut 8 team generated and how and when would it be used?[93]

---

89. Rawls, *A Theory of Justice*,, 26, 63–64 and 71.
90. Rawls, *A Theory of Justice*.
91. Rawls, *A Theory of Justice*,, chapters 7, 8 and 9 *passim* and 364 at note 10.
92. Elizabeth Dwoskin, 'Facebook content moderator says she got PTSD while reviewing images' 25 September 2018, *The Sydney Morning Herald*, at https://www.smh.com.au/business/workplace/facebook-content-moderator-says-she-got-ptsd-while-reviewing-images-20180925-p505sg.html
93. See Andrew Hodges, *Alan Turing: The Enigma*, (2012, Vintage), chapter 4, 'The Relay Race', *passim* and at 252–255, 275–280, and 301.

This was a moral and practical dilemma.[94] Unless used with strategic restraint, the Allies' hand would be tipped, and the Germans would know they had broken the code. Too restrained a use would result in avoidable military and civilian casualties. While data input was dictated by the intercepted coded messages, use of output had to be a matter of human judgment and discretion. Human judgment necessarily brings with it bias, even bias of which the assessor is not conscious.

As AI steadily increases its insinuation into more of our daily lives, the question of invisible bias will become increasingly important.[95] For example, the effects of bias upon AI medical triage and dispensation are obvious enough. Apparently binary choices of whether to administer treatment or not and whether to prescribe a particular drug may have unseen drivers that tilt the decision-making. Are the choices driven by impartial medical assessments in the best interests of the patient or by undeclared economic imperatives?

The implications of bias to health care are vital. They have great importance in the area of human rights. Largely, human rights actors have been distracted by nice questions of equality and liberty. These questions are insignificant in comparison with the near and present threat that AI poses. Take but one example: the right to freedom of thought, conscience, religion or belief in ICCPR[96] Article 18.[97] What happens when an algorithm decides whether or not to administer

---

94. This was, of course, not a new dilemma in war and espionage. Its novelty was in the machine-generation and the human judgment on use of the output.
95. Pedro Domingos, *The Master Algorithm* (Penguin Random House UK, 2015) 78–79 and chapters 7 and 9. See also Max H Bazerman and Ann E Tenbrunsel, *Blind Spots: Why We Fail to Do What's Right and What to Do about It* (Princeton University Press 2011), 20–21, 81–82, 115–116 and 137; Ajay Agrawal *et al*, *Prediction Machines: The Simple Economics of Artificial Intelligence* (Harvard Business Review Press, 2018), 34–35, 55–58, 195–198 and 204–205.
96. *International Covenant on Civil and Political Rights*, (New York, 16 December 1966), Entry into force generally (except Article 41): 23 March 1976, Entry into force for Australia (except Article 41): 13 November 1980,
    Article 41 came into force generally on 28 March 1979, and for Australia on 28 January 1993
97. Article 18 of the ICCPR provides:
    (1) Everyone shall have the right to freedom of thought, conscience and religion. This right shall include freedom to have or to adopt a religion or belief of his choice, and freedom, either individually or in community with others and in public or private, to manifest his religion or belief in worship, observance, practice and teaching.

a blood transfusion without consideration of the patient's religious beliefs? If no connected algorithm asks a question whether the patient is a faithful Jehovah's Witness, the machine will decide the question without reference to religious faith. What if the machine is programmed to have a bias in favour of termination of pregnancies if the patient has measles? If the programmer has not taken any account of Catholic belief on abortion, a termination may result without reference to the patient's beliefs. What if the patient is of a certain age, frailty of health or socio-economic status? If particular social biases in favour of euthanasia have been installed into the machine, then strongly held religious or ethical positions on the part of the patient or their family may be disregarded and the patient euthanised contrary to beliefs and wishes.

Time is running out on these issues. The source codes and algorithms for these decisions to be made are being written now and being sold by transnational corporations to consumers of AI in in numerous jurisdictions. Chances are that any programmer is unlikely to be familiar with First Amendment jurisprudence, the terms of Article 18, or human rights norms, let alone have read the moral and political philosophies of Aristotle, Hobbes, Locke, Bentham, Mills, Kant, Rawls, Dworkin, or Sandel. Their default positions in writing

---

(2) No one shall be subject to coercion which would impair his freedom to have or to adopt a religion or belief of his choice.

(3) Freedom to manifest one's religion or beliefs may be subject only to such limitations as are prescribed by law and are necessary to protect public safety, order, health or morals or the fundamental rights and freedoms of others.

(4) The States Parties to the present Covenant undertake to have respect for the liberty of parents and, when applicable, legal guardians to ensure the religious and moral education of their children in conformity with their own convictions.

Compare Article 9 of the European Covenant on Human Rights:

(1) Everyone has the right to freedom of thought, conscience and religion; this right includes freedom to change his religion or belief and freedom, either alone or in community with others and in public or private, to manifest his religion or belief, in worship, teaching practice and observance.

(2) Freedom to manifest one's religion or beliefs shall be subject only to such limitations as are prescribed by law and are necessary in a democratic society in the interests of public safety, for the protection of public order, health or morals, or for the protection of the rights and freedoms of others.

the source code, interpreting output, or making judgments based upon output will be more likely determined first, by the relevant law, then, secondly, by corporate policy, and, if there remain gaps, according to their own biases.

Australia: Far Too Little and Much Too Late

Just how ill-prepared the world is for the fourth industrial revolution and its human rights implications is illustrated by two contrasting jurisdictions: Australia (the least prepared) and the European Union (EU) (the most advanced jurisdiction in AI policy). Australia is the only advanced economy in the Western world not to have a national bill or charter of rights.[98] There remains a debate as to whether there should be a bill of rights at all.[99]

Australia is currently inquiring into various economic and social issues.[100] In those inquiries that touch upon either AI or human rights, there appears no rush to either report on findings or implement recommendations. The ACCC inquiry, for example, into digital

---

98. For the position on the State of Victoria and the Australian Capital Territory, see Alistair Pound and Kylie Evans, *An Annotated Guide to the Victorian Charter of Human Rights and Responsibilities* (Thomson Lawbook Co, 2008); and Carolyn Evans and Simon Evans, *Australian Bills of Rights* (LexisNexis Butterworths, 2008).
99. See Neville Rochow, *Paying for Human Rights Before the Bill Comes: Towards a More Comprehensive Domestic Implementation of International Human Rights Norms in Australia*, University of Adelaide Law School. (2009), available at http://ssrn.com/abstract=1356382; Paul Babie and Neville Rochow (editors, *Freedom of Religion Under Bills of Rights* (2012, University of Adelaide Press), available at https://www.adelaide.edu.au/press/titles/freedom-religion/; Julian Leeser and Ryan Haddrick (ed.s), *Don't leave us with the Bill: the case against an Australian Bill of Rights* (2006, Menzies Research Centre).
100. Recent and current Royal Commissions include:
    - Royal Commission into Institutional Responses to Child Sexual Abuse (2013–2017)
    - Royal Commission into Misconduct in the Banking, Superannuation and Financial Services Industry (2017–present)
    - Royal Commission into aged care quality and safety (2018-Present)

    Other recent and current inquiries include:
    - Department of Prime Minster and Cabinet Religious Freedom Review (the Ruddock Inquiry) https://www.pmc.gov.au/domestic-policy/religious-freedom-review

platforms is not due to deliver its final report until June 2019.[101] This current inquiry seems to be a response to the ACCC's unsuccessful 2013 legal action against Google,[102] takes no account of Moore's Law:[103] by the time the inquiry is completed, it will almost certainly be historical in relation to the operations of the IT corporations and how AI affects consumers.

To take another example, the Ruddock inquiry, which examined the need for legislation to protect freedom of religion in Australia, reported on 18 May 2018. At the time of writing, the federal government is yet to make that report public.[104] It is still unknown whether inquiry has recommended legislative protection for freedom of religion.[105]

- Australian Competition and Consumer Commission (ACCC) Digital platforms inquiry https://www.accc.gov.au/focus-areas/inquiries/digital-platforms-inquiry
- Australian Human Rights Commission (AHRC) Human Rights and Technology inquiry.humanrights.gov.au/our-work/rights-and-freedoms/projects/human-rights-and-technology https://www.humanrights.gov.au/our-work/rights-and-freedoms/projects/human-rights-and-technology

101. Timeline: Terms of reference: 4 December 2017; Issues paper: 26 February 2018; Submissions: 3 May 2018; Forums: 15 August 2018. The preliminary report is to be submitted to the Treasurer by 3 December 2018, with a final report due by 3 June 2019: https://www.accc.gov.au/focus-areas/inquiries/digital-platforms-inquiry
102. *Google Inc v Australian Competition and Consumer Commission* [2013] HCA 1; (2013) 249 CLR 435. http://eresources.hcourt.gov.au/showCase/2013/HCA/1 See discussion in Amanda Scardamaglia and Angela Daly 'What consumers need from the ACCC inquiry into Google and Facebook', *The Conversation*, at https://theconversation.com/what-consumers-need-from-the-accc-inquiry-into-google-and-facebook-88560
103. Simply put, overall processing power for computers will double every two years. This formulation is now dated. It also takes no account of progression from binary processing to quantum molecular processing. See discussions at http://www.mooreslaw.org/ and https://www.research.ibm.com/ibm-q/learn/what-is-quantum-computing/
104. Katharine Murphy, 'Kerryn Phelps urges PM to release Ruddock religious freedom review before byelection', 26 September 2018, *The Guardian*, at https://www.theguardian.com/australia-news/2018/sep/26/kerryn-phelps-urges-pm-to-release-ruddock-religious-freedom-review-before-byelection?CMP=share_btn_link
105. https://www.pmc.gov.au/news-centre/domestic-policy/statement-panel

Recall that Australia has no national bill of rights.[106] Despite that lack, the AHRC, a body with oversight over the limited Australian human rights regime, held a 'Human Rights and Technology' conference on 24 July 2018 to launch an issues paper to discuss the following:

- The right to equality and non-discrimination;
- Freedom of expression;
- Right to benefit from scientific progress;
- Freedom from violence;
- Accessibility for people with disability;
- Right to privacy;
- Right to education;
- Access to information and safety for children; and
- Right to a fair trial and procedural fairness[107]

One notices immediately that freedom of religion or belief is not included among the discussion topics. This is possibly because there is no current federal legislation protecting freedom of religion.[108] Another obvious omission is how the Four and other IT corporations that utilise AI could be required to respect human rights in Australia. Speakers did include Microsoft's Steve Crown[109] and Google's John Lucchi.[110] Both were reassuring regarding their respective

---

106. Instead, it has a patchwork of state laws and the following pieces of federal legislation:
    - *Australian Human Rights Commission Act 1986*
    - *Age Discrimination Act 2004*
    - *Disability Discrimination Act 1992*
    - *Racial Discrimination Act 1975*
    - *Sex Discrimination Act 1984*
107. https://tech.humanrights.gov.au/conference
108. There is a very limited protection in the federal Constitution at s. 116. See discussions in: Luke Beck, *Religious Freedom and the Australian Constitution: Origins and Future*, (2018, Routledge) chapters 6–12; Paul Babie, Joshua Neoh, James Krumery-Quinn, Chong Tsang, *Religion and Law in Australia* (2015, Wolters Kluwer), Part I, chapter 1, and Part II, chapter 2.
109. Vice President and Deputy General Counsel, Human Rights, Microsoft Corporation.
110. Head of Content and AI, Public Policy and Government Relations, Google Asia Pacific.

corporation's human rights credentials and intentions. To paraphrase Mandy Rice-Davies,[111] they would say that, wouldn't they?

Another item that might have been discussed was the potential use of blockchain technology[112] to guarantee that all AI, IA, AGI, and (it would be hoped) Superintelligence has been encoded, designed, and engineered with human rights protections.[113] A globally distributed human rights ledger of rights as a pre-requisite to the use of every peer-to-peer network would be a basic start to the protection of human rights into the fourth industrial revolution.

But, it would seem, Australia struggles to get to the first stage in protecting human rights. When it does, it may well be a case of far too little and much too late.

EU and 'Hate Speech' Regulation—A Leap of Faith?

The EU is the most advanced jurisdiction in AI policy, ethics, law, and practice,[114] with a dedicated parliamentary platform[115] and a specialised section of the European Commission working towards a Digital Single Market.[116] The Commission has developed legal and ethical frameworks to ensure that the EU is ahead of technological developments and encouraging uptake by the public and private sectors and that all members states are prepared for the socio-economic changes brought about by AI.[117]

---

111. Geoffrey Robertson, 'Mandy Rice-Davies: fabled player in a very British scandal', 19 December 2014, *the Guardian* at https://www.theguardian.com/politics/2014/dec/19/mandy-rice-davies-fabled-player-british-scandal-profumo
112. Derek Parker, 'How governments are using blockchain technology', 22 August 2018, *INTHEBLACK*, at https://www.intheblack.com/articles/2018/08/22/how-governments-using-blockchain-technology
113. As was discussed at the Artificial Intelligence in Legal Practice Summit 2018 hosted by the College of Law on 31 August 2018: https://www.cli.collaw.com/events-and-workshops/2018/02/01/artificial-intelligence-in-legal-practice-summit-2018
114. Compare the United Nations' *Future of Life Institute*: https://futureoflife.org/ai-policy-united-nations/?cn-reloaded=1
115. The *European AI Alliance*: https://ec.europa.eu/digital-single-market/en/european-ai-alliance
116. https://ec.europa.eu/digital-single-market/
117. https://ec.europa.eu/digital-single-market/en/artificial-intelligence

On 10 April 2018, 25 European countries, including member states of the EU, signed a multi-lateral Declaration of cooperation on AI. On the declaration, Andrus Ansip, Vice-President for the Digital Single Market, and Mariya Gabriel, Commissioner for Digital Economy and Society, showed that the Europeans have recognised what most other national governments have failed to see:

> In Europe, any successful strategy dealing with AI needs to be cross-border. A large number of Member States agreed to work together on the opportunities and challenges brought by AI. That is excellent news. Cooperation will focus on reinforcing European AI research centres, creating synergies in R&D&I funding schemes across Europe, and exchanging views on the impact of AI on society and the economy. Member States will engage in a continuous dialogue with the Commission, which will act as a facilitator.[118]

The EU has developed a policy on the prevention of online 'hate speech'. In May 2016, Facebook, Twitter, YouTube and Microsoft committed to combatting the spread of such content in Europe through a 'Code of Conduct', implementation of which was to be overseen in a series of monitoring rounds.[119] The third monitoring round was held on 19 January 2018.[120] Since May 2016, Google had announced it was joining the Code of Conduct, and Facebook confirmed that Instagram would also. One of the challenges found to remain at the third evaluation round was a lack of systematic feedback to users. The third evaluation also found that IT companies removed on average seventy per cent of illegal hate speech notified to them.

At the third evaluation, Věra Jourová, EU Commissioner for Justice, Consumers and Gender Equality, observed on the purposes of the Code of Conduct:

> The Internet must be a safe place, free from illegal hate speech, free from xenophobic and racist content. The Code of Conduct is now proving to be a valuable tool to tackle illegal content

---

118. https://ec.europa.eu/digital-single-market/en/news/eu-member-states-sign-cooperate-artificial-intelligence
119. https://www.wsj.com/articles/eu-cheers-tech-giants-commitment-to-tackling-online-hate-speech-1496315958
120. http://europa.eu/rapid/press-release_IP-18-261_en.htm

quickly and efficiently. This shows that where there is a strong collaboration between technology companies, civil society and policy makers we can get results, and at the same time, preserve freedom of speech. I expect IT companies to show similar determination when working on other important issues, such as the fight with terrorism, or unfavourable terms and conditions for their users.

Despite claims of success for the Code, fundamental questions remain regarding the entire scheme. First, it is not clear what definition of 'hate speech' the IT companies would use in their vetting of alleged breaches. Article 20 (2) of the ICCPR provides that, 'Any advocacy of national, racial or religious hatred that constitutes incitement to discrimination, hostility or violence shall be prohibited by law'. Apart from this, there has been no universally accepted definition of 'hate speech'. The term is not precisely defined by any EU document and the definition in law is also vague.[121]

Second are questions of liability:

- who among employees of the corporations make the decisions for users of their services; with what authority? and
- what, if any liability arises and against whom for wrongful removals?

The Code is silent on safeguards and guarantees of the rights of those who wrongfully silenced. There are no appeal processes or avenues for redress.[122]

The third question is why the implementation and enforcement the Code, public cyber-policing roles, have been delegated to supranational corporations. While the answer may lie in pragmatism, when a conflict of interest arises between their own profit motive and the private interests of a user, whose interests ought they to prefer?

---

121. Rex Ahdar and Ian Leigh, *Religious Freedom in the Liberal State* (2013, Oxford University Press, 2nd edition), 448–451; Rona McRea, *Religion and the Public Order* (2010, Oxford University Press), 71–2, 103–140: Paul Coleman, *Censored: How European 'Hate Speech' Laws are Threatening Freedom of Speech* (2016, Kairos Publications, 2nd edition), chapters 3 and 7; Mike Hume, *Trigger Warning—Is the Fear of Being Offensive Killing Free Speech?* (2015, Williams Collins).
122. Adina Portaru, 'Freedom of Expression Online: The Code of Conduct on Countering Illegal "Hate Speech" Online', *Revista Romana de Drept European* n. 4/2017, Wolters Kluwer Romania.

And how is any conflict of interest dealt with on a day-by-day, case-by-case basis? We can assume of the IT corporations one thing: they would not have entered an agreement to sponsor the Code unless they considered that, in the long run, their interests would be best served by doing so.

So, who watches the watchman? The EU would say that the Commission, NGOs and civil society. But only time will confirm whether that is enough. Thus, the Code, though venerable for its intent, seems to have several risks attached to it, not the least of which, is entrusting so much of the welfare of EU citizens to supranational corporations.

Conclusions

With the exception of games, as humans, we tend not to take chances. Games have an element of chance attached to them. It is the combination of chance, obedience to rules, and demonstration of skill that makes games entertaining. Chance is also an element of our ordinary everyday choices. But the degree of chance tolerable in games is not tolerable in life. Rules are stricter and there are consequences for breach. Skill is often rewarded by increased market demand, but without any guarantee. We tend to be risk-averse in the real world; our tendency is to minimise risk by taking control of those matters that can be brought within our power. In real life, we tend to seek certainty by having rules enforced and seeking evidence of that those who supply have the skill to deliver.

Yet we still fail to see the threat that the unprecedented power of AI in the hands of supranational corporations poses. Confronted with existential threats from what has been regarded as the virtual world of AI, a world born in science fiction and computer games, we are having a hard time taking those threats seriously. We are taking chances, trusting in skill without evidence, and failing to develop and apply rules. Despite the oncoming threats to our humanity, we still fail to take human rights seriously.

An obvious solution is international application of human rights norms to the writing, design, and engineering of all AI, IA, AGI, and, hopefully, Superintelligence. With blockchain technology, all other advances could come with guarantees of conformity of human rights protections. But the pathway to that solution is thwarted by national silos of domestic law and failures to understand the enormity of the potential outcome. In the meantime, AI and supranational corporations continue unregulated.

Shortly put, if the international community seeks to exploit AI, leaving development to markets and human rights to chance, we face an existential risk. As to the timing and extent of that risk, no-one can predict other than to say that the worst-case scenario is devastation. If the international community cannot agree on how to limit the power of corporations to control AI, the risks are the same. Without immediate international agreement on these issues, the possible Cassandras are warning us of potential catastrophe. In the meantime, that we are somnambulating towards an AI dystopia.

Chapter 5
Lethal Autonomous Weapon Systems, Just War, and a Culture of Encounter

Matthew J Gaudet

'Humans are outsourcing the decision to kill to a machine—with no one watching to ascertain the legitimacy of an attack before it is carried out.'[1]

Abstract: Lethal Autonomous Weapon Systems (LAWS) kill without conscience. I ask moral questions in four categories. (1) Will AI raise or lower casualties? (2) Will AI increase vulnerabilities? (3) Will AI increase or decrease the biases inherent in warfighting? (4) Do we need to consider how AI changes the way wars themselves are fought? To flesh out these questions I turn to classic Just War Theory and to Pope Francis. In the end, LAWS will influence the future of warfare and international relations only in the ways and the extent that we allow it to.

Key Terms: lethal autonomous weapon systems, just war theory, Pope Francis, United Nations Security Council

In 2021, a United Nations Security Council report strongly suggested that during a March 2020 attack on the militia forces of local warlord Khalifa Haftar, Libyan government forces used a swarm of Turkish-made Kargu-2 drones, operating without any human operator or input.[2] The Libyan government denies the report. But if confirmed as true, it would be the first attack which was both lethal (humans were

---

1. Noel Sharkey, 'Autonomous Warfare', in *Scientific American* 322:2 (February 2020): 52–57, at 54.
2. 'Letter from the Panel of Experts on Lybia established pursuant to resolution 1973 (2011) addressed to the President of the Security Council', March 8, 2021, https://documents-dds-ny.un.org/doc/UNDOC/GEN/N21/037/72/pdf/N2103772.pdf?OpenElement

killed) and completely autonomous (AI made all of the decisions including both identifying targets and carrying out the attack, without human approval at any step in the process).

The significance of this 'first' may not be entirely clear. After all, it is not the first time AI has been used to direct a munition toward a given military target. Guided missile systems have used heat sensors, lidar, GPS, and other inputs to help guide airborne munitions toward a specific target since the 1960s. Such systems, however, are targeted and activated by humans. Nor is it the first-time computer guided systems have been free to fire without a human 'in-the-loop'.[3] Defensive systems such as the shipborne Close-in Weapons Systems, which can identify, target and destroy an inbound missile threat have been capable of full autonomy since the 1970s.

Today, systems such as Israel's 'Iron Dome' are capable of such defenses across an entire battlefront. But these systems have always been defensive—targeting inbound missiles, not enemy combatants—and thus not intentionally lethal. Finally, it is not the first time that specific targets have been identified as enemy combatants through sophisticated AI algorithms processing massive amounts of surveillance data. But, in previous cases, those combatants were then targeted by a human operator. What the Kargu-2 and other Lethal Autonomous Weapons Systems (LAWS) signify is the complete turnover of identification, targeting, and firing upon enemy combatants to AI systems, thus completely removing humans from the act of war.

It should be noted that the Lybia incident is not an outlier. *Foreign Policy* reported in May 2022 that 'So far, at least Israel, Russia, South Korea, and Turkey have reportedly deployed weapons with autonomous capabilities—though whether this mode was active is disputed—and Australia, Britain, China, and the United States are investing heavily in developing LAWS with an ever-expanding

---

3. Here I am using a popular parlance in AI and LAWS literature. A system with a human 'in the loop' means that a machine can recommend an action, but a human being must approve any decision before it is acted upon. 'On the loop' describes a system in which a human is present and overseeing the system and has the ability to override a decision but does not need to actively approve every decision. A human 'outside the loop' is a fully automated system in which a human has neither direct decision nor override power over the actions of the system.

range of sizes and capabilities'.[4] LAWS can also take many forms, including drone swarms as in the Kargu-2, missiles which 'loiter' over a prescribed area locating a target before deploying, fleets of autonomous 'ghost' ships deployed at sea, and autonomous tanks and artillery used in ground assaults.

Four Moral Questions Regarding LAWS

I organise moral questions regarding Lethal Autonomous Weapons Systems into four categories. First, with any new weapon, we need to be concerned with the most direct harm of war: human casualties. Will the advent of lethal autonomous weapon systems raise or lower the human cost of war? And relatedly, will LAWS systems increase or decrease *civilian* casualties?

Second, do we need to be concerned with the potential vulnerabilities AI systems introduce? Human militaries have always been vulnerable to espionage, but turning lethal systems over to Artificial Intelligence opens new doors to potential infiltration. If AI systems prove vulnerable to hackers, then all of the gains of using AI could be turned to harms with a keystroke. Moreover, militaries, being human, have always been subject to error. AI systems be subject to malfunction or error? In either case, if the advantages of using AI in warfare is that it is more effective at targeting our enemies then hacked or malfunctioning AI would also be more effective at harming our own forces. I ask: will the new capabilities of AI introduce new vulnerabilities that we cannot even predict?

Third, do we need to be concerned about AI bias? Today's applications of machine learning have consistently revealed that biases inherent in the training data get mirrored, or even exacerbated in the Machine Learning algorithm. In theory, a perfect AI system should be more capable than a human at distinguishing between an enemy combatant that poses a threat and a civilian bystander. But if the training data used identifies only threats as being a of certain skin tone, or wearing a certain type of dress, or keeping their hair or facial hair in a certain style, then the algorithm will carry these biases

---

4. Trager, Robert F and Laura M Luca. 'Killer Robots are Here—and We Need to Regulate Them', in *Foreign Policy*, May 11, 2022, https://foreignpolicy.com/2022/05/11/killer-robots-lethal-autonomous-weapons-systems-ukraine-libya-regulation/.

into its selection criteria. And these are merely obvious examples, and ones that can be corrected for. However, one of the capacities that AI systems bring to the game is the ability to identify subtle and overlapping correlations that would be beyond the scope of general human categorising. So even if we teach the algorithm to not use racial or cultural factors directly, the algorithm is often capable of replicating biases through correlating more subtle observations. This is hugely problematic when, for example, algorithms are used for criminal sentencing, or college acceptance, or even in facial recognition for domestic security, but when AI's bias problems enter into Autonomous Weapons Systems, the results could be lethal.

Fourth and finally, do we need to consider how AI changes the way wars themselves are fought? Drones and other remote weapons systems, sometimes operated from continents away, have already removed some warriors from the physical harms of war. Even so, the psychological harms of having killed another human person are still remain for some. The application of fully autonomous weapons systems removes this final human cost to deciding to wage war. While this may provide a strategic advantage, the human costs of war for our own soldiers, sailors, and even civilians—think here of the gold star families—provided a necessary check on the decision to go to war. For militaries fighting wars with AI, if the last of these human costs are removed and the only costs to war are material—the costs of the autonomous weapons themselves—will war become more prevalent and the result actually be more, not less, death and destruction done overall?

Lethal Autonomous Weapons and the Just War Tradition

Before proceeding, it is worth acknowledging that there are good arguments to believe that it is within the realm of possibility for LAWS to actually make war more moral. If designed right, LAWS could theoretically reduce the unintended biases, emotions, and desires that are moral weak points in our human soldiers. LAWS, presumably, will never kill out of anger, ignorance, or pride. LAWS will never rape or torture or systematically dehumanize. LAWS, in theory, could be programed to be less biased than human soldiers. LAWS could be more capable than human soldiers at discrimination between enemy targets and civilians or friendly forces. The caveat to all of these claims, however, is that LAWS systems actually have to be designed properly and with attention to these needs. Here is where the just war criteria offer their most useful application, for 'designing right' means designing with the just war criteria in mind.

To extrapolate, let's look at what LAWS would need to do to be compliant with the just war moral tradition. This requires that I say a brief word about what I believe the Just War tradition to be, since some readers may not be completely familiar with the major traditions in the ethics of warfare and, even if they are, popular presentations often misrepresent the Just War tradition.

To begin, the just war is not a monolithic set of rules for ethical war-making. Rather, it is a tradition of thought, generally dated back as far as St Augustine of Hippo in the Fourth Century (though some say the Roman philosopher Cicero in the First Century actually gives the first account). The tradition traces through the Roman-Christian-European thought advancing especially with the work of the Christian scholastics—St. Thomas Aquinas—in the Thirteenth Century and the Medieval jurists—Suarez, Grotius, de Vitoria—but it came into its fullest form in the late Twentieth and early Twenty-First centuries, as a series of documented responses to what its major contributors saw as *unjust* wars.

Micheal Walzer's landmark text, *Just and Unjust Wars,* offered in the wake of the Vietnam War, brought many of the concepts of the just war into the popular discourse.[5] The United States Conference of Catholic Bishops' *The Challenge of Peace,* published in 1983 as a response to nuclear arms race, helped to popularize the familiar structure of 6-7 *jus ad bellum* criteria and 2-3 *jus in bello* criteria that comprise the tradition.[6]

---

5. Michael Walzer, *Just and Unjust Wars: A Moral Argument with Historical Illustrations*, 4th edition (New York: Basic Books, 2006)
6. United States Catholic Conference of Bishops, *The Challenge of Peace: Gods Promise and Our Response*, 3rd edition (Washington, DC: US Catholic Conference, 1983). While *The Challenge of Peace* served to popularize the use of criteria for the *jus ad bellum* and *jus in bello*, the earlier use of this principlist approach that the bishops drew from was James Childress's 'Just War Criteria' (in T Shannon, editor, *War or Peace., The Search for New Answers*. New York: 1980). Later, as American incursions into Afghanistan and Iraq dragged on for decades, Brian Orend and others would add consideration of the *jus post bellum* (justice in the ending and aftermath of war) and Walzer would add a category of *jus in vim*, to consider the use of military force in operations short of war

The Just War tradition begins with the understanding that nation-states have a moral responsibility to both do the good (including making the world more just) and to do no harm (including the harms of war). The problem is that even though war is inherently maleficent, sometimes our duty to justice requires that we have to (regrettably) conduct war. It is in these cases—where justice and non-maleficence are held in tension—that we need a guide to help us decide which commitment is more pressing. The original just war criteria were a framework for knowing when the needs of justice outweighed the commitment to non-maleficence.

In the Catholic account, war can only be justified when there is a *just cause*, an acute situation of injustice that demands a response. All other means of rectifying that injustice must be exhausted and war must only come as a *last resort*. War can only be declared by a *legitimate authority*. Under the modern nation state system, we do not want the city of El Paso declaring war on Mexico. Or today, when companies are as wealthy as nation states, we do not want Google declaring war on Canada. If there be injustices on both sides of the conflict, then war can only be justified in defense of the side suffering *comparatively greater injustice*. War must always be aimed a *right intention*, a desired future state that rectifies the injustice that gave us just cause but also minimizes harm on both sides of the conflict. Relatedly, the decision to go to war must be *proportionate,* balancing the injustice war aims to overcome against the inevitable harms that war itself will do. Finally, war should not be engaged unless there is a *reasonable hope* of achieving the right intention with proportionate harms. These are the 7 *jus ad bellum* (justice of the war) criteria that determine whether war itself is just.

The *jus in bello* (justice in war) criteria determine the proper means by which war should be fought. Here again, we must conduct war with right intention, and only use those means which will further that intention. Means of war that aim at personal gain, revenge, or blatant destruction are unjust. Similarly, the means of war must be

---

(Brian Orend, 'Justice after War', in *Ethics and International Affairs* 16 (2002): 43–56; Brian Orend, *The Morality of War* (Peterborough, ON: Broadview Press, 2006); Tobias Winright and Mark Allman, *After the Smoke Clears* (Maryknoll, NY: Orbis, 2010); Walzer, *Just and Unjust Wars*, xv). These latter two categories are beyond the scope of this paper and thus, I will focus on the *jus ad bellum* and the *jus in bello*.

discriminate. Civilians ought to never be directly targeted and means of war that do not discriminate (such as landmines) are unjust. Finally, the means of war must be *proportional* to their immediate gains. We need not use intercontinental ballistic missiles in response to a small group of rebel terrorists. But also, when proportionality and discrimination are considered together, then in cases where harm to civilians is unavoidable, such harms must be reduced as much as possible.

Now, having listed the criteria, we need to dispel some common misunderstandings. First, the just war criteria are not rules for war.[7] To treat the just war criteria as rules is to take war as a mere contest, and in a contest, when one side willfully breaks the rules, it seems to justify the other side breaking the rules to make the playing field even. But moral equivalency cannot be the moral standard of international diplomacy, lest we quickly race to a morally equivalent bottom of complete anarchy. Rather, the moral standard is an international state of affairs that can sustain commitments to both justice and non-maleficence, or as St. Augustine put it, *Tranquilitas Ordinis*, a well-ordered peace.[8]

Second, the criteria ought not be taken as conditions that will make the war 'more just'. This makes us think of the criteria as a medium of exchange or measures in a just war ledger where I can give a little on discrimination in order to get a lot more proportionality or that I can defend my lack of a just cause with a whole lot of right intention. But a just war cannot be bargained. All 7 of the *jus ad bellum* and all 3 of the *jus in bello* criteria need to be met in order for the duty to justice to require allowing the inherent maleficence of the war.

---

7. This is a common misconception that echoes even in the highest offices in the land. For example, in his Nobel address President Obama reduced the just war tradition down to such thinking: 'war is justified only when certain conditions were met: if it is waged as a last resort or in self-defense; if the force used is proportional; and if, whenever possible, civilians are spared from violence.' Not only does Obama conveniently forget 2/3 of the criteria, but in turning them into a kind of rulebook for justice, he diminishes the fact that war is regrettably and irrevocably maleficent. (Barack Obama, 'Remarks by the President at the Acceptance of the Nobel Peace Prize', National Archives, Dec 10, 2009, https://obamawhitehouse.archives.gov/the-press-office/remarks-president-acceptance-nobel-peace-prize#:~:text=I%20receive%20this%20honor%20with,in%20the%20direction%20of%20justice.
8. Augustine, *City of God* (New York: Penguin Books, 2004), Book 19.

Finally, we must explicitly acknowledge that the criteria do not stand on their own, but rather operate within the context of a much larger moral commitment. In the words of the Catholic Bishops, 'The Catholic tradition on war and peace is a long and complex one; it stretches from the Sermon on the Mount to the statements of Pope John Paul II. We wish to explore and explain the resources of the moral-religious teaching and to apply it to specific questions of our day'.[9] Commitments to discrimination and right intention must be understood as extensions of the scripture that commands us to command to 'love your enemies' and proclaims both 'blessed are the peacemakers' and 'blessed are those who hunger and thirst for righteousness'. To navigate this complexity, the Bishops called upon the familiar criteria named above.

Just War Theory as a Tradition

Of course, if the just war is a living tradition, then as war itself changes, so must the tradition adapt. Today, the advent of LAWS is forcing us to reconsider what constitutes a just war in the 2020s. Since the shift to autonomous weapons is primarily a shift in means, let us begin with the *jus in bello* principle of discrimination. Landmines are the quintessential example of an autonomous weapon that was deemed inherently immoral by virtue of being indiscriminate—a landmine would detonate whether it was an enemy combatant or an innocent child who tripped it, sometimes years after hostilities ceased. This utter lack of discrimination is why landmines were prohibited from lawful use in 1997. Autonomous Weapons Systems share landmine's problem of a human being out of the loop. However, in theory, LAWS systems should be capable of discriminating in ways landmines cannot by using facial and other biometric recognition technology to identify potential targets.

Reality, however, has not yet met this ideal. Current biometric identification technology based on machine learning is still imperfect. This might be fine if AI biometrics were being used to inform but not replace human operators on the battlefield. However, by removing a human from the loop, any potential machine error, biased training data, hack of the system, or spoof of the algorithm could

---

9. USCCB, *Challenge of Peace*, 'Summary'.

result in lethal consequences without concern for discrimination, let alone proportionality, or right intention. Some might argue that such occurrences are rare and vastly outweighed by the potential benefits of the autonomous system, but this kind of bargaining away of the criteria is precisely one of the mistaken uses of the just war theory that I identified earlier. The criteria themselves are not the moral standard. Justice and non-malevolence are. Bargaining away discrimination increases malevolence and reduces the justice that the war aims to bring about; consequently, it renders the decision to go to war untenable.

Next, let us consider the criterion of proportional means. In theory, it would be possible that AI systems could be more capable than humans at determining the proportionality of a given action, however, this is not how the systems are being designed. The decision point is binary: "shoot or don't shoot" whereas a proportional logic would balance the calculated harms against the calculated benefits of a mission. But proportional reasoning would take vastly more data, computing power, and programming that LAWS systems currently are not implementing.

Both of the problems above could be solved with proper design and advancements in the technology. However, the criterion of right intention is where things get truly problematic. One has to question whether a machine is even capable of comprehending right intention without human input. Here we need to say a word about the difference between the narrow forms of artificial intelligence that we currently have at our disposal and the hope (or fear) of a future artificial general intelligence (AGI). AGI is often how AI is demonstrated in our science fiction— think of Rosie from the Jetsons, Kitt from Knight Rider, Hal from 2001: a Space Odyssey, Vision from Marvel, or C3PO from Star Wars. The presumption is that AI is capable of human-like intelligence, with the ability to adapt to any task it is given. But AGI is still unrealized.

All of our current AI systems, including Lethal Autonomous Weapons Systems, use a much narrower form of AI. LAWS are capable of acting according to a mission objective—destroy this building, kill this operative, shoot down any incoming missile—but they are incapable of recognizing the bigger picture vision of war's right intention. But without that larger vision, in the fog of a battle, are machines capable of critically assessing a mission objective as circumstances change? If programmed with an objective to destroy a certain target, are our autonomous systems capable of recognizing a surrendering soldier or unit, rendering destruction unnecessary for the larger intentions of the war? Are autonomous systems capable of distinguishing the fog of war from automated genocide?

Similarly, we also need to consider the *jus ad bellum* criteria. If, during peacetime, a Lethal Autonomous Weapon System, acting autonomously, made the choice to fire upon a target—for legitimate reasons or due to error, bias, or hacking—it could (rightly) be just cause for an enemy to respond in kind, thus escalating what might be a delicate peace into a war. While a green soldier could just as easily make such a mistake, most humans are capable of recognizing that the ramifications of such a choice in peacetime are different than if the war has already commenced.

Autonomous Weapons Systems built on narrow forms of AI are incapable of such distinctions. In fact, current AI is probably incapable of most of the *ad bellum* criteria. We have already spoken about right intention, but narrow AI is equally incapable of determining a just cause or last resort and certainly is not a legitimate authority. Certainly, AI could be programmed to *assist* generals and government officials in determining whether comparative justice, proportionality, or probability of success are met, but I know of no such algorithms in development. Rather, what we have are Lethal Autonomous Weapons Systems, designed with narrowly focused objectives carrying out decisions with expansive repercussions.

So, in summary, I already noted that Lethal Autonomous Weapons systems could be—and in fact should be—programmed to be more capable than human soldiers of *jus in bello* criteria such as discrimination and proportionality.

We should absolutely be working towards incorporating these principles into the AI programming of our future weapons systems. Even if we were to get these two criteria perfect though, it is difficult to see a future in which fully-autonomous, lethal, weapons systems built towards narrow mission objectives are capable of what is required for the *in bello* application of right intention. And since the just war criteria are not measures in a ledger, we cannot give on right intention even if such weapons make for a more discriminate and proportional war. That said, the use of automatic (rather than autonomous) weapons, that retain a human operator "in the loop" can draw upon AI's gains in discrimination and proportionality even while leaning on the human operator to be the check capable of right intention. Similarly, we need to be especially cautious when using any level of autonomy in weapons during peacetime, and we must keep a human in the loop also for the sake of determining just cause, right intention, and last resort.

LAWS and the Technocratic Paradigm

The analysis above does not exhaust the moral questions of Lethal Autonomous Weapons Systems, however. Thus far, I have only dealt with the first three questions I listed above (Will AI raise or lower casualties? Will AI increase vulnerabilities? And will AI increase or decrease the biases inherent in warfighting?) These first three questions, as complicated as they are, merely set the stage for my fourth question: how will AI change the ways in which wars will be fought? Here I must return to the Catholic theological tradition, but carry us forward from the US Bishops in 1983, to the contributions of Pope Francis in recent years. In a 2020 address to the United Nations, Pope Francis offers the following critique of LAWS:

> We need to break with the present climate of distrust. At present, we are witnessing an erosion of multilateralism, which is all the more serious in light of the development of new forms of military technology, such as lethal autonomous weapons systems (LAWS) which irreversibly alter the nature of warfare, detaching it further from human agency. We need to dismantle the perverse logic that links personal and national security to the possession of weaponry. This logic serves only to increase the profits of the arms industry, while fostering a climate of distrust and fear between persons and peoples.[10]

By naming that LAWS detach warfare 'further from human agency', Francis is connecting his critique to a broader theme for the Catholic pontiff. In his social encyclical *Laudato Si*, the Holy Father argued that, when it comes to technology, we have inverted our values: technology itself has become our ultimate end rather than a tool

---

10. Francis, 'Address to the United Nations', September 25, 2020, https://holyseemission.org/contents/news/5f6df2d493a95.php

oriented toward the end of human flourishing; and conversely human beings and nature itself have become tools rather than ends. Pope Francis has named this problem the "Technocratic Paradigm":

> [M]any of the problems of today's world stem from the tendency, at times unconscious, to make the method and aims of science and technology an epistemological paradigm which shapes the lives of individuals and the workings of society . . . We have to accept that technological products are not neutral, for they create a framework which ends up conditioning lifestyles and shaping social possibilities along the lines dictated by the interests of certain powerful groups. Decisions which may seem purely instrumental are in reality decisions about the kind of society we want to build.[11]

In particular, Francis is concerned at how quickly and easily we put technology between ourselves and others—whether its social media replacing genuine friendship, videoconferencing replacing face-to-face meetings, or email replacing the handwritten letter—and how damaging these social shifts are on our ability to recognize the humanity in one another, and thus show empathy, compassion, and responsibility for one another. LAWS are yet another means in which we place technology between ourselves and the other, and in doing so reduce our ability to show empathy, compassion, and responsibility to one another.

The notion of responsibility to our fellow humans, including our enemies, is the subject of Francis's follow-on social encyclical, *Fratelli Tutti*, where he further links the technocratic paradigm to host of social ills that we have witnessed in the Twenty-First Century: political polarisation, economic inequality, general social breakdown, and, first among these, the cloud of war that hangs over our contemporary world:

> Ancient conflicts thought long buried are breaking out anew, while instances of a myopic, extremist, resentful and aggressive nationalism are on the rise . . . Once more we are being reminded that 'each new generation must take up the struggles and attainments of past generations, while setting its sights even higher.'[12]

---

11. Francis, *Laudato Si*, § 107.
12. Francis, *Fratelli Tutti*, § 10

And yet, even as war is on the rise, we continue to develop technologies like LAWS that extend our myopia and do nothing to place empathy and compassion in the face of extremism and resentment.

Of course, from the invention of the spear to the development of the first over-the-horizon flying bombs to the advent of the remote drone, it has been a military impulse to create distance between one's own soldiers and the threats of battle while still maintaining capacity to do harm to the enemy. The penultimate advancement of this line of development left us with drones that could be flown remotely from across the world, leaving its operator with zero physical risk while waging vast physical destruction on the enemy. Even still, drone operators regularly reported Post Traumatic Stress Disorder (PTSD) and other forms of psychological damage as a result of making decisions that killed and otherwise destroyed lives.[13]

LAWS carry this advancement to its ultimate place, by relegating *decision-making* power to AI systems and thus removing soldiers psychologically from the battlefield. While the reduction of PTSD amongst soldiers is unquestionably beneficial in a vacuum, when gaining such benefits in the real-world means losing any sense of the real human costs of war, then will war be too easy to wage? Political scientists have argued that democracies do not tend to go to war with other democracies because those who bear the casualties of war—physical and psychological—the people themselves, hold the ultimate voting power in a democracy.[14] The development of remote drones already put this theory to the test, and citizens were more likely to support a military operation if it was conducted by drone strike and thus did not risk (physical) casualties to one's own soldiers.[15] If AI were to remove the final psychological casualties of war from the side operating Lethal Autonomous Weapons Systems, what effect will removing this friction have on the decision to go to war?

---

13. Philipps, Dave, 'The Unseen Scars of Those Who Kill by Remote Control', in *New York Times*, April 15, 2002, https://www.nytimes.com/2022/04/15/us/drones-airstrikes-ptsd.html.
14. Dean V Babst, (1964). 'Elective Governments—A Force For Peace', in *The Wisconsin Sociologist*, 3 (1) (1964): 9–14; Dean V Babst, 'A Force For Peace', in Industrial Research (April 1972): 55–58.
15. James Igoe Walsh, and Marcus Schulzke, 'The Ethics of Drone Strikes: Does Reducing the Cost Encourage War?', U.S. Army War College Press, September 2015, https://apps.dtic.mil/sti/pdfs/ADA621793.pdf.

Now, one could identify the concern about removing the barriers to war without citing Francis. After all, the just war tradition as noted above would caution that systems that reduce or eliminate the human costs of war make it too easy for nations in possession of such weapons to go to war (often, perhaps, in violation of the *jus ad bellum*) and, once war has begun, such weapons make it too easy to increase the human costs to the other side (in violation of the *jus in bello* principles of discrimination and proportionality). However, by connecting this concern to Pope Francis's larger critique of the technocratic paradigm and the moral and social ills it has wrought, we can recognize that the ethics of LAWS are not just moral questions but they are in fact cultural questions and thus demand a cultural response. For his part, in *Fratelli Tutti*, Pope Francis calls for what he names a 'culture of encounter':

> A people's 'culture' is more than an abstract idea. It has to do with their desires, their interests and ultimately the way they live their lives. To speak of a 'culture of encounter' means that we, as a people, should be passionate about meeting others, seeking points of contact, building bridges, planning a project that includes everyone.[16]

Conclusion

In the end, LAWS will influence the future of warfare and international relations only in the ways and the extent that we allow it to. That is, if we create AI systems, including Lethal Autonomous Weapons Systems, that are designed to distance us from others (even our enemies), we will necessarily contribute to the type of myopia, social isolation, and cultural insularity that are at the cultural root of war. In short, we will have responded to the symptom, but aggravated the disease. Instead, we must make active choices to develop only AI systems which will contribute to a 'culture of encounter' and to ban others, such as Lethal Autonomous Weapons Systems. We have evidence that this can be done in the banning of chemical weapons, biological weapons, and landmines as well as the *de facto* non-deployment of nuclear weapons going on nearly eight decades. But are we willing to do the same with regard to Lethal Autonomous Weapons?

---

16. Francis, *Fratelli Tutti*, § 216.

Chapter 6
Idle Hands and the Omega Point:
Labor Automation and Roman Catholic Social Teaching

Levi Checketts

'Scholars of religion and theologians should seriously engage technology because it is empowering humanity in ways that were previously reserved only for gods.'
— Brian Patrick Green[1]

Abstract: The prospect of labor automation raises the question of the role of work in a good Christian life. This article examines three polar theologies of work present in Roman Catholic thought: labor as drudgery, labor as dignified calling and labor as an obstacle. These three theologies inform an eschatological vision of labor—Christians are called to work to build the kingdom of God, not merely to acquire material possessions. Finally, two ultimate issues are raised: the distribution of resources and the problem of idleness in a post-labor world. All of this suggests Catholics must promote a future of dignified labor dedicated to love of neighbor and God.

Key words: Theology of Work, Catholic Social Teaching, Labor Automation, Kingdom of God, Technological Singularity

'The Singularity is near!' So proclaimed Ray Kurzweil in 2005. This monumental event is expected to arrive as early as 2045. When it happens, 'all the changes of the past million years will be superseded by the next five minutes.'[2] The Singularity is the philosopher's stone of

---

1. Brian Patrick Green, 'The Catholic Church and Technological Progress: Past, Present, and Future', in *Religions* 8:6 (2017): 2–16, at 1; file:///C:/Users/Ted/Downloads/religions-08-00106-v2.pdf.
2. Kevin Kelly, 'Technology Doesn't Want a Singularity', *Singularity 1 on 1*, Singularity Weblog, https://www.singularityweblog.com/kevin-kelly/ (accessed September 18, 2018).

the technophiles. It brings with it intelligence beyond compare, both in advancing our own brilliance (Intelligence Amplification, or IA) and in constructing superpowerful artificial intelligences (AI).[3] The benefits of these advancements will play out in our wildest fantasies. Some believe a super-intelligent machine, once fully free to pursue its own aims and amplify and augment its own intelligence, will take its place (if it has not already) as God.[4]

A silicon-based intelligence can always add to itself through hardware extensions and software updates, unlike our limited organic brains, and thus can attain near or total omniscience and omnipotence. The Singularity also promises nigh-immortality as consciousnesses, mapped out as complex patterns, are uploaded into computer substrates, allowing a person who was once a biological organism to continue life as a computer program. Every human biological inadequacy will be outstripped by the mind finally freed from its flesh prison (and installed on a superior silicon replacement).[5] Finally, all physical toil will be obsolete as well: nobody will be required to work in the fields or labor under the sun as robotics and AI take over every necessary job from customers service to manufacturing, from agriculture to law[6] Every labor required for the survival of the species will be outsourced to intelligent machines which can both accomplish the task more efficiently and more cheaply than human laborers.

---

3. Ray Kurzweil, *The Singularity is Near: When Humans Transcend Biology*, PDF e-book edition (New York: Viking, 2005), 135, 194.
4. Lincoln Cannon, 'What is Mormon Transhumanism?', in *Theology and Science* 13/ 2 (2015): 212–213. This idea is also alluded to in 'The Singularity Church of the Machine God' in the most recent *Deus Ex* game. This church is apparently a religion designated for machine-augmented human beings, and the 'Machine God' is a super-intelligent being who speaks to the augmented through their brain implants. *Deus Ex: Mankind Divided* (Square Enix, 2016).
5. Hans Moravec, *Mind Children: The Future of Robot and Human Intelligence* (Cambridge, MA: Harvard University Press, 1988), 108–112.
6. Kurzweil, *The Singularity is Near*, 227. It was once thought that the "professions," those occupations requiring high degree of education and skill, would be safe. However, AI lawyers have already been hired by law firms to replace much of the work attorneys typically do. While an AI lawyer cannot take depositions or represent a client in trial, it can do much of the research lawyers spend their time doing. See: Cecille de Jesus, "AI Lawyer "Ross" Has Been Hired by Its First Official Law Firm", in *Futurism*, May 11, 2016 https://futurism.com/artificially-intelligent-lawyer-ross-hired-first-official-law-firm/ (accessed September 18, 2018).

It may come as no surprise that with all the promises the Singularity entails, some scholars have critiqued this view as a 'secular eschatology'.[7] The promise of a new machine god, the belief in silicon-situated afterlife and the promise of a technologically-created paradise have all the markings of Christian beliefs for the end times—absent any strong theological backing.

The promises of AI and IA present themselves as perversions of Christian eschatological tenets. The super-intelligent machine God is the advent of a high-tech idol expressing human desires and understandings rather than the triumphal return of the Son of God. Uploaded consciousness is escapism from death, a refusal to take seriously the condition of human mortality, rather than hope in a restful post-mortal eternal life. Labor automation alone of these three seems not to be obviously theologically problematic. No dogmatic eschatological tenet suggests labor cannot be carried out by machines. Nonetheless, labor automation challenges the meaning of work, an important social issue in Catholic theology. It is my contention that, as an extension of the challenge of social ethics that labor automation entails, it also leads to an eschatological problem for Catholics.

In three of the sections following this, I outline three theologies of work and how they might appraise labor automation. These three approaches see labor, which I define following Hannah Arendt as human activity directed toward consumption or survival,[8] as a curse to fallen humanity, a vocation tied to human dignity, or as an obstacle to overcome on our eschatological journey, respectively. After examining these three, I turn to the connection between labor and the Kingdom of God, wherein lies the connection between techno-optimism and Christian hope. Finally, I conclude by suggesting that achieving wide-scale labor automation changes the social question of just labor to two primary concerns: just distribution and a cure for idleness.

---

7. See, for example: Hava Tirosh-Samuelson, 'Transhumanism as a Secularist Faith', in *Zygon* 47/4 (December 2012): 724–728
8. Hannah Arendt, *The Human Condition*, 2nd edition (Chicago: University of Chicago Press, 1958), 99.

1. By the Sweat of your Brow: Human Activity Directed toward Consumption and Survival

In the Book of Genesis, the first parents commit the original sin by disobeying God's command to not eat the forbidden fruit. 'By the sweat of your brow you will eat your food until you return to the ground', God impels Adam, condemning humanity to lives of drudgery (Gen 3:19). The reader is led to believe that in the pre-lapsarian state, sustenance was easy-coming and plentiful. The first parents lived simple lives free of the burden of toil. Once sin entered the world, humans were condemned to live frail lives marked primarily by arduous labor for survival.

Thomas Malthus, at the end of *An Essay on the Principle of Population*, argues that God made labor a necessary part of human existence to prevent shiftlessness.[9] Paradisiacal conditions would only encourage humans to lie about enjoying temperate weather while sipping wine, like HG Wells's Eloi of *The Time Machine*. Scarcity, however, forces us to work if we want to eat. This necessity further encourages innovation and industry because craft and guile can reduce our requisite labor. Thus, Malthus goes on to argue, the wealth of the Industrial Revolution cannot, and should not, be equally distributed, for this will only encourage idle behavior. God has ordained human beings to work for their food, thus imposing both a 'carrot and stick' method where hard work is rewarded with material blessings but laziness leads us to starvation.

Jacques Ellul, on a somewhat different tack, argues that the fall leads to human beings needing *technique*, or the use of technological tools, to wrest from the earth the resources needed for survival.[10] The struggle of mortality requires human beings to employ industry, including both the labor of their hands and the cleverness of their minds, to survive. In the post-lapsarian world, *technique* becomes the instrument by which humanity takes dominion over the earth, asserting ourselves as rulers rather than caretakers.[11] This new

---

9. Thomas R.Malthus, *An Essay on the Principle of Population* (London: J Johnson, 1798), 113.
10. Jacques Ellul, 'Technique and the Opening Chapters of Genesis', in *Theology and Technology: Essays in Christian Analysis and Exegesis*, edited by Carl Mitcham and Jim Grote (Lanham: University Press of America, 1984), 131.
11. Jacques Ellul, 'The Relationship between Man and Creation in the Bible', in Mitcham and Grote, *Theology and Technology*, 140.

relation sets humanity in antagonistic relation to the natural world. We exploit and destroy for our survival, yet the life of labor is, to paraphrase Hobbes, "nasty, brutish and short." Nature and humanity compete, and *technique* grants humans the possibility of gaining the upper hand, but always within the context of a tenuous order maintained by violence.

Thus, according to the Malthusian-Ellulian view, labor is an effect of the fall. Humanity's original sin is the source of the need for labor. If Adam and Eve had obeyed God's command, we would live free from drudgery. The world we actually live in, however, is one where we both toil and die as a result of sin. Labor can be mitigated, but never abolished. We can employ our tools to lighten the load, but the violence of nature can only be staved off, never vanquished in this life. In the end, even the best medical and labor-saving technologies fail as illness and old age inevitably bring death.

How does this view consider labor obsolescence? On the one hand, labor automation may be impossible fully, as human beings, by metaphysical design, *must* be engaged in earnest labor or otherwise must die. On the other hand, the society where labor has freed all hands may lead to a society of human stagnation as nothing propels human excellence. We suffer the fate of Friedrich Nietzsche's "last men" who claim "'We have discovered happiness,' . . . and blink thereby."[12] This fate is comparable to limbo: we do not experience suffering or torment, but neither do we experience the joys or triumphs of a life well lived.

This particular theology of work held sway in Medieval Catholicism. Max Weber notes that pre-modern Catholic attitudes toward labor saw it as essentially a baser task opposed to the higher callings of the ascetic life.[13] Those who would pursue the more spiritual (and, by extension, more sanctified) must leave behind the 'worldly' tasks of normal human labor. Indeed, labor was seen as a degrading condition, unfit for the truly Christian, in the Middle

---

12. Friedrich Nietzsche, *Thus Spake Zarathustra: A Book for All and None*, trans. Thomas Common, Amazon Kindle e-book edition (Houston: Everlasting Flames Publishing, 2010), 'Zarathustra's Prologue', 5.
13. Max Weber, *The Protestant Ethic and the 'Spirit' of Capitalism, and Other Writings*, edited and translated by Peter Baehr and Gordon C Wells (New York: Penguin Books, 2002), 25.

Ages, and its value only lay in its potential for sustenance.[14] This view is totally abandoned in contemporary Catholic theology, and perhaps no current Catholic theology of labor sees work as connected to sin and death. Indeed, modern Catholic theology, as illustrated below, tends to see labor as a dignified pursuit and rest from labor a worthy reward.

2. The Laborer is Worthy of His Hire: a Vocation tied to Human Dignity

The view most prominent within the Catholic Tradition today is that work has an important place within the concept of human dignity. Labor is not punishment for sin, but a life-fulfilling function by which we draw closer to God. Work becomes a fulfillment of God's expectations of us on earth—a 'calling' in the sense of Luther and broader Protestant theology.[15] Rather than see labor as the consequence of fall, this view sees it as a genuinely human—and genuinely Christian—task that draws us nearer to our fellow human beings, to the earth, and to God.

Human beings, according to Pope John Paul II, have a "universal calling" to work because it is through work that we become like God by taking dominion of the earth.[16] In this view, God's call to humanity in Genesis 1:28 to 'subdue the earth' re-orients the seemingly punitive nature of God's words in Genesis 3:19. The ominous 'sweat of your brow' becomes the means by which we imitate God, not the curse of a fallen humanity. The pontiff goes on to say, 'Work is a good thing for [the human being]—a good thing for his humanity—because through work [the human] *not only transforms nature*, adapting it to his own needs, but he also *achieves fulfilment* as a human being and indeed, in a sense, becomes "more a human being"'.[17] This is the genuinely human task we are called to. As God is active through creative work in the universe, and human beings are made in the image of God, we fulfill our divinely-given mandate through working like God.[18]

---

14. Arendt, *The Human Condition*, 317–318.
15. Weber, *The Protestant Ethic*, 29.
16. John Paul II, *Laborem Exercens* (Vatican City: Libreria Editrice Vaticana, 1981), 9.
17. John Paul II, *Laborem Exercens*, Emphases original.
18. *Cf* The Second Vatican Council, *Gadium et Spes: The Pastoral Constitution of the Church in the Modern World* (Vatican City: Libreria Editrice Vaticana, 1965), 34; Paul VI, *Populorum Progressio* (Vatican City: Libreria Editrice Vaticana, 1967), 27.

A positive theology of work is critical when work becomes exploitative or demeaning. In the first Catholic social encyclical, Pope Leo XIII reminds employers that 'according to natural reason and Christian philosophy, working for gain is creditable, not shameful, to a [person], since it enables him to earn an honorable livelihood; but to misuse [people] as though they were things in the pursuit of gain, or to value them solely for their physical powers—that is truly shameful and inhuman'.[19] This sentiment is likewise echoed in *Gaudium et Spes* (27), *Populorum Progressio* (28), *Quadragesimo Anno* (83) and in other magisterial documents. The abuse or cheapening of laborers is morally repugnant and is a violation of their dignity; it exploits the means by which human beings both survive and imitate their Creator. Catholic leaders therefore call on employers to provide dignified conditions for their workers and on states to create legal protections against exploitation.[20] Work must therefore be protected because of its central function in a dignified human life.

This view is most prominent across Catholic social teaching because work plays an important function in human social activity. Work is necessary for the support of families.[21] Work allows parents to provide for children, the elderly and disabled within the family unit. The importance of care and familial responsibility requires access to dignified labor. Additionally, work builds up comradery among workers for at least two reasons. First, cooperation brings a feeling of solidarity as workers strive to achieve shared goals.[22] Second, cooperative action allows a compounding of benefits as labor specialization yields an increase of productivity, providing a natural benefit for all who engage in shared labor.[23] For this reason, workers unions and associations are typically good.[24] Finally, work contributes to the broader common good both because it allows people to contribute to the well-being of society and because it allows the able-bodied to aid their fellows who are unable to work.[25]

---

19. Leo XIII, *Rerum Novarum* (Vatican City: Libreria Editrice Vaticana, 1891), 20.
20. John XXIII, *Mater et Magistra* (Vatican City: Libreria Editrice Vaticana, 1961), 21; Pius XI, *Quadragesimo Anno* (Vatican City: Libreria Editrice Vaticana, 1931), 28.
21. John Paul II, *Laborem Exercens*, 10.
22. Vatican II, 68.
23. John XXIII, 60.
24. See: Leo XIII, 48; John Paul II, 20; Vatican II, 68; Paul VI, 38.
25. John XXIII, 78–81.

Thus, a general Catholic social theology of work is as follows. Work affirms human dignity by fostering solidarity between workers, providing for the common good, and, ontologically, imitating the creative activity of God. Human beings ought to have meaningful and fulfilling work allowing them to meet their personal and familial needs. Working conditions which prevent willing workers from finding work, which alienate or mechanize human labor, which create unsafe or hostile environments, or which underpay employees for their labor are affronts to human dignity. Dignified work is of central importance for social commutations; expressed biblically, 'The laborer is worthy of his hire' (Luke 10:7, KJV).

The situation of automated technology becomes problematic from a Catholic social perspective for various reasons. The first and most obvious is that it deprives people of the dignity inherent in labor. Those unable to find jobs because of automation will be left feeling undignified because they lose the ability to exercise the call to be like God, to further the common good, or even to create something that reflects their unique gifts from God.[26] Moreover, those able to retain employment, such as those hired to supervise machines, will feel a decreased sense of solidarity and connectedness to their fellows, many of whom lack work. God has made us to live and work within community, not as isolated drones. Finally, as I discuss further below, dignified work allows men and women to achieve flourishing; lack of work may lead to resource deprivation.

3. They neither Toil nor Spin: an Obstacle to Overcome on our Eschatological Journey

In Luke 12 and Matthew 6, Jesus counsels his disciples to put off worries about their material necessities. Jesus reminds his disciples, situated as they are in an agrarian society, that other living things like sparrows and lilies do not labor yet are sustained. They should take a lesson from these creatures; Jesus counsels them, "Seek first [God's] kingdom and [God's] righteousness, and all these things will be given to you as well" (Matt. 6:33 NIV). Thus, Jesus opens the possibility for a life lived independent of labor.

---

26. See, for example, Edward C Vacek, *Love, Human and Divine: the Heart of Christian Ethics* (Washington: Georgetown University Press, 1994), 252.

The Bible does not advocate strongly for a cessation of labor, but there are hints occasionally that God's mercy will be manifest in rest from drudgery. In Exodus 3:17, God promises to bring Israel out of Egypt into "a land flowing with milk and honey." The slavery of Egypt is contrasted against a paradise of seemingly plentiful food and minimal labor. In Revelation 21, God promises to "wipe every tear from their eyes" in the new world where the peoples of all nations devote themselves solely to worship of God in the New Jerusalem. Ordinary suffering and labor are replaced by twenty-four-hour worship. Both the Book of Isaiah and the Gospel of Matthew promise spiritual, though not physical, relief from the burdens of labor. Isaiah 55 promises satisfaction to the hungry, and Matthew 11 promises rest to the weary.

Clearly the biblical authors' audiences saw value in a life absent of toil. One may even read the sabbath as God's providential illustration for an eventual cessation of labor. In all of this, we read a yearning of biblical authors and promise for rest for those whose labors and toils are burdensome. If work is ordinarily good in the dominant Catholic social worldview, a final theology of work suggests the life of the Christian ought to be other than back-breaking labor in the fields.

This view is most in agreement with the promise of automated labor. Machines to do the most dangerous, difficult, dull, disrespected or dirty labor humans currently do amounts to emancipation from these affronts to human dignity. The "cog in the machine" metaphor of industrialized labor, popularized by Charlie Chaplin's *Modern Times*, illustrates the disparity between the dignified work Catholic social teaching praises and the reality of many laborers in industrialized nations. The suffering of women and children in sweatshops and the suffering of Hebrew slaves in Egypt both cry out for deliverance from drudgery. Why should we not allow God to work to alleviate this suffering through technology today as God did through the Exodus then?

The Jesuit mystic and paleontologist Pierre Teilhard de Chardin is perhaps the clearest Catholic supporter of this prospect. He addresses the question of technological unemployment in his writings. "Economists are horrified by the growing number of idle hands,"[27] he

---

27. Pierre Teilhard de Chardin, *The Future of Man*, trans. Norman Denny (New York: Double Day, 1964), 166.

notes, because of the economic problem of the survival of thousands or millions of people lacking paid work. But, Teilhard assures us, this unemployment "heralds the release of spiritual energy—every pair of hands freed means a brain freed for thought."[28] Teilhard sees intellectual freedom won by technological unemployment as an evolutionary step. While this "trait" of humanity seems unfit at the moment—without suitable employment, people will die—it will ultimately prove to be a fitter trait because humanity will become more intellectually oriented than physically dependent.

The possibility of pursuing greater advances in science, technology, exploration, art, philosophy or other forms of thought constitutes an increasing of the "psychic temperature" of the earth.[29] This increasing of psychic temperature is part of Teilhard's understanding of the necessary movement for achieving the "Omega Point," an eschatological destiny Teilhard sees as the goal of evolution, and which he refers to in more theological writings as humanity becoming "cosmic Christ."[30] In other words, Teilhard sees technological unemployment as a necessary step whereby human beings are able to more fully devote themselves to those intellectual pursuits which will help us achieve our eschatological goal and becoming one with a converging universe.

Other Roman Catholics, especially Jesuits, have written in a similar vein. Teilhard's disciple, Wilhelm Fudpucker, argues that the "universal and egalitarian state free from want and fear" characteristic of Christian eschatological visions entails the pro-social use of new technologies to Christian ends.[31] André Malet argues technologies should be used to fulfill the works of mercy Christ prescribes in Matthew 25, including feeding, clothing, sheltering and assisting our fellows.[32] W. Norris Clarke endorses the use of technology to

---

28. Pierre Teilhard de Chardin, *Activation of Energy: Enlightening Reflections on Spiritual Energy*, trans. René Hague (San Diego: Harcourt, Inc, 1978), 160.
29. Pierre Teilhard de Chardin, *Man's Place in Nature: The Human Zoological Group*, trans. René Hague (London: Fontana, 1966), 98.
30. Pierre Teilhard de Chardin, *Science and Christ*, trans. René Hague (New York: Harper & Row, 1965), 54.
31. Wilhelm E. Fudpucker, "Through Technological Christianity to Christian Technology," in Mitcham and Grote, 59, 65.
32. André Malet, "The Believer in the Presence of Technique," in Mitcham and Grote, 105.

overcome our physical limitations, including our bodily frailties and limitations, to free our souls for higher purposes.[33] Each of these views seems to suggest technology should be used to lessen human dependence on human labor for our survival. Technology allows us to help those who cannot otherwise work, to free ourselves for higher work, and to establish a world free from suffering and want. Thus, a different reading of Catholic thought suggests technological unemployment, assuming it serves to advance the common good,[34] is a worthy endeavor.

The Harvest is Ready but the Laborers are Few: More on Eschatology

These theologies of labor give us useful material to reflect on, but, aside from the Teilhardian view, say nothing about labor in the eschaton. At present, however, automation is a question of future happenings; the goal of proponents of automation is a future free from drudgery contrary to the present situation of arduous work. This is an eschatological vision—the end they see for humanity is one where tedium and toil are minimized if not fully eliminated. The mind will finally be free from irksome physical necessities to pursue whatever life it sees fit.[35] I have argued elsewhere that the critical questions of technological ethics are questions of consequences, and the guiding moral principle for Christians must be eschatological.[36] This fact holds true for automated labor just as much as consciousness uploading, genetic engineering or super-intelligent AI. In other words, *the* moral

---

33. W. Norris Clarke, "Technology and Man: A Christian View," in *Technology and Philosophy: Readings in the Philosophical Problems of Technology*, ed. Carl Mitcham and Robert Mackey (New York: The Free Press, 1972), 249.
34. As should be evident by now, the common good is a key idea in much of Catholic moral theology. It is often misconstrued as some sort of utilitarian principle of benefitting the majority, but Thomas Aquinas clarifies it as "*universal* happiness." Universal is not the same as majority, so an advancement that benefits *many* people but disadvantages *a few* is not truthfully an advancement of the common good. Thomas Aquinas, *Summa Theologiae*, Prima pars Secundae partis Question 90, Article 2, emphasis mine.
35. Kurzweil, *The Singularity is Near*, 32.
36. Levi Checketts, *Homo Gubernator: A Moral Anthropology for New Technologies*, PhD Diss. (The Graduate Theological Union, Berkeley, CA, January 31, 2018), 260.

issue at hand is the place of labor in the Christian eschaton, and we must compare this vision with the goals of labor automation.

Within the biblical narrative, Jesus advises a different form of labor for the coming kingdom of God. In both Matthew 10 and Luke 10, Jesus sends out his disciples to preach the Gospel around Galilee, admonishing them to receive the charity of those who believe rather than selling their services. Likewise, in Matthew 9:37, in reference to the difficulty of "preaching the good news of the kingdom" and other forms of ministry, Jesus notes that "the harvest is great but the laborers are few," suggesting that Jesus's model of ministry is a call to labor. At the end of the Gospels of Matthew (28:16-20) and Mark (16:15-18), Jesus's parting words to his disciples is the Great Commission, sending them as messengers to the world to witness of his life and ministry. In each of these pericopes, Jesus uses notions of labor and work in a different sense from ordinary means-to-survive. The labor Jesus requires of his disciples, at least in certain parts of the gospels, is a labor of ministry to others and not back-breaking toil in the fields.

This idea finds resonance in the notion of "kingdom building" articulated by several social theologians of the twentieth century. Both Catholic and Protestant theologians, including Walter Rauschensbusch, Martin Luther King, Jr., Johann-Baptist Metz and Gustavo Gutierrez, contest that the Christian must be active today, not in securing his or her own salvation, but in working to establish God's kingdom here on earth.[37] One even finds in more traditional theologians, including Karl Rahner and John Paul II, an emphasis on Christians' moral obligation to put their energies into working together with God for the sake of God's kingdom.[38] In the view of these theologians, the Christian call to labor is primarily one

---

37. Walter Rauschenbusch, *A Theology for the Social Gospel* (New York: Cosimo Classics, 2012), 133; Martin Luther King, Jr., "Letter from Birmingham City Jail," *A Testament of Hope: The Essential Writings of Martin Luther King, Jr.* ed. James Melvin Washington (San Francisco: Harper & Row, 1986), 296; Jonhannes B. Metz, *Theology of the World*, trans. William Glen-Doepel (New York: Herder & Herder, 1969), 94; Gustavo Gutierrez, *A Theology of Liberation*, trans. Caridad Inda and John Eagleston (Maryknoll: Orbis Books, 1973), 103.
38. Karl Rahner, "Notes on the Lay Apostolate," *Man in the Church*, Theological Investigations Vol. 2, trans. Karl Kruger (Baltimore: Helicon Press, 1963), 323; John Paul II, "All Are Called to Build God's Kingdom" (General Audience), December 6, 2000.

of carrying out those works that are at their heart most Christian: spreading the Gospel, carrying out the works of mercy, praising God through word and deed, praying without ceasing, working for peace and justice in the world, and overall creating a society that reflects the eschatological vision we hold.

The theological turn to eschatology becomes especially important in an industrialized world. In a world where future-oriented thinking, especially in science and technology, has become the norm, Metz recognizes that the Church must be futurally oriented as well; "the hope which the Christian faith has in regard to the future cannot be realized independently of the world and its future, [and] this hope must answer, must be responsible for, the one promised future and hence also for the future of the world."[39] The proper Christian reaction to new technologies is not knee-jerk resistance, but rather appraisal through the lens of eschatological achievement. Even with respect to a technology as sensitive as biological engineering, Karl Rahner noted the critical moral question was whether such a technology can prepare the way for God's kingdom by facilitating better love of neighbor.[40] In the particular context of work, Teilhard notes that the advantage of technological unemployment is it allows more people to be engaged in research.[41] However, he also notes that human progress "is not a *tête-à-tête* or a *corps-à-corps* . . . it is a heart-to-heart," which "can achieve its consummation only in becoming Christianized."[42] The necessary direction of evolution, even if self-directed, is, for Teilhard, "upward and forward"—attentive to both material advancement and spiritual perfection.[43] Thus, an important consideration raised by these theologians is that the essential issue at hand should not be whether automation of labor accords with a good theology of work, but rather whether it aligns with our eschatological understandings.

On this front, we see that automation of labor, at least as presented by Kurzweil and others, is incompatible with Christian theology. The Singularitarian vision of automation of labor is rooted in materialist

---

39. Metz, 91.
40. Karl Rahner, "The Experiment with Man," *Theological Investigations* Vol. IX, trans. Graham Harrison (London: Darton, Longman & Todd, 1972), 220–221.
41. Teilhard, *Future of Man*, 167.
42. Ibid., 67.
43. Ibid., 265–269.

conceptions of happiness and life-fulfillment. Capitalism, with its focus on efficiency and reduction of costs, moves logically toward the goal of perfect mechanical operation. Laboring machines will be able to do greater amounts of work for extended periods of time with fractions of the cost of human laborers. We humans, then, are freed finally to enjoy the fruits of a life purchased by our ingenuity. The aim of this endeavor, to achieve a materialistic paradise, is paradoxical: through application of the capitalist values of industry and innovation, one is able to finally escape the conditions that require these virtues. So much for virtue being its own reward! But here one finds the final obstacle: once the need for labor is eliminated, we will be left with the unanswered problem of lives devoid of ultimate meaning.[44] Christianity, for its part, has already positively answered the challenge left by automation, and its response is that we are called to be actively building the Kingdom of God. This means that the project of removing labor for the sake of a life of infinite leisure is contrary to the Christian's understanding of the place of work within the purpose of life. Each of the three above theologies of work contends that the Catholic is not called to work merely to put bread on the table. The Catholic social teaching view sees labor as a dignified path for humanity, and both the first and third views see labor as a hindrance to lives lived pursuing higher callings, through other forms of work. Our activity is therefore not measured by its efficiency or material yield, but rather on its expression of love of God and neighbor and its dedication to a life lived in service of God. Because the Christian understands labor not as a burden, but rather as her calling whereby she cooperates with God and neighbor within the Kingdom of God, her aims in work must be other than the aims the Singularitarians espouse. The leisurely eschatology of labor automation is not the loving eschatology of the Kingdom of God.

Two Final Issues

Theologies of work provide helpful guidelines today for how to think of the labor we are asked to perform and the labor we ask others to perform. Work conceived as curse, dignified calling or surmountable

---

44. See, e.g.: Hans Jonas, *The Phenomenon of Life: Towards a Philosophical Biology* (New York: Dell Publishing Co, 1966), 209.

obstacle changes our conception of our responsibility in working or eliminating work. However, while these theologies inform Christian attitudes toward labor, it is unlikely that the those pushing for technological unemployment will carefully consider them. A new report from the World Economic Forum on jobs and automation brings to light several problems of automation, including widening gaps between rich and poor or employed and unemployed, but optimistically suggests workers will be "reskilled" or "augmented" in their work.[45] Nonetheless, the report also surmises that as soon as 2022, up to 50% of jobs across industries will experience reduction due to automation.[46] One can extrapolate that this trend will continue, especially in those occupations considered "labor." As such, an important final consideration is the question of what to do *when* labor becomes obsolete. With the question of inevitability and not merely possibility of technological unemployment, two important final issues reveal themselves: the problem of distribution and the problem of idle hands.

"*Cui bono?*" Lucius Cassius used to ask of criminals—who benefits? We might in turn ask who benefits from the automation of labor. It is clear that the greatest benefit will fall to those who control the machinery or the means of production. The bourgeoisie Marx railed against in the early nineteenth century pale in threat to a class who forgoes alienating the workers by eliminating them. It is unlikely that the members of the working class, or even those in middle class occupations subject to automation, will benefit dramatically from labor automation. The elimination of most need for human labor means the elimination of most forms of human employment.

Of course, in a capitalist economy, producers require a market to make profit. If Apple Computers or Toyota Automotive can be reduced to a handful of executives and engineers, they still need people buying their products to make money. As a result, one of three things is likely. First, the entrepreneurially-minded unemployed may find new possibilities for work, including new occupations and new industries, as suggested by both Malthus and the WEF. Indeed, optimistic attitudes toward technological unemployment assume as

---

45. World Economic Forum, *The Future of Jobs Report 2018* (Geneva: World Economic Forum, 2018), 3.
46. Ibid., 16.

much will happen.⁴⁷ Second, some sort of universal basic income may be established to ensure that the unemployed masses still have means to survive—and further contribute to the capitalistic structures in place. Finally, corporations may invent menial and degrading forms of labor, such as riding a stationary bike to generate electricity,⁴⁸ in order to take advantage of the newly unemployed and desperate.⁴⁹

All of this, of course, ignores the problem of those living outside of industrialized nations. As much as we may decry labor rights violations of factory workers in developing countries, their sudden unemployment does not promise a much better outcome. Consider the case of Foxconn, a company that had been criticized for its subhuman conditions in factories in China a few years ago. Today, they solve this problem by promoting mass unemployment through replacing laborers with machines.⁵⁰ Will consumer-goods producing corporations like Nike and Apple ensure the well-being of former sweatshop workers displaced by automation? Will the current global inequality be exacerbated when people of the "third world" become cut off from possibilities of acquiring wealth because industrialized nations have automated processes that create better and cheaper goods than human workers ever could?

Roman Catholic social ethics provides an unequivocal response to this problem. Labor automation must not result in widespread destitution. While Catholic social teaching has always remained wary of socialist solutions, especially communism, it has also always raised a critical voice against capitalist systems that leave people impoverished. Catholicism will need to raise a strong and loud voice

---

47. See: Ray Kurzweil, "Progress and Relinquishment," in *The Transhumanist Reader: Classical and Contemporary Essays on the Science, Technology and Philosophy of the Human Future*, ed. Max More and Natasha Vita-More (Malden, MA: Wiley-Blackwell, 2013), 458.
48. See, e.g. the science fiction television episode "Fifteen Million Merits," *Black Mirror*, Series 1, ep. 2.
49. It is also possible all three of these scenarios play out. A UBI may be low enough to meet "essential costs" as defined by governmental agencies, but may push men and women to seek out further income through entrepreneurial endeavors or menial labor.
50. Nick Statt "iPhone Manufacturer Foxconn Plann s to Replace almost Every Human Worker with Robots," *The Verge* December 30, 2016 https://www.theverge.com/2016/12/30/14128870/foxconn-robots-automation-apple-iphone-china-manufacturing (accessed September 22, 2018).

to ensure that as labor automation is pursued, just distribution of the fruits of automation is also pursued. Technological "progress" at the expense of millions or billions of people's survival is morally untenable.

"Idle hands are the devil's workshop" (Proverbs 16:27 TLB). The other problem related to labor automation is the fundamental problem of unemployment, that is, lack of occupation for those millions or billions replaced by machines. Many religious figures have advocated hard work as a prophylactic against vices like fornication, alcoholism, drug abuse, gambling or theft.[51] Whether or not this advice is sound, the problem remains—if people are not "occupied" with labor, with what will they be occupied?

The less palatable option, as illustrated in science fiction stories, including the recent Steven Spielberg-directed *Ready Player One*, is a world of idleness. People will engage, not in constructive efforts, but in time-wasting pursuits, such as binge-watching television shows or devoting hours to massive multiplayer online video games, getting high or drunk, scrolling mindlessly through millions of pages of hypertext on the Internet, committing small acts of violence as "harmless pranks" for entertainment, engaging in other high-risk behaviors "for the thrill," and so forth. Twentieth century capitalism has not provided us with any confidence that it can supply life meaning. The eschatological vision of Singularitarianism is challenged by cultural movements like existentialism and postmodernism, and time-wasting distractions like television, social media and video games. A future with no work is not a guarantee for a future of fulfilled lives.

The task for Catholics is clear enough; they should be engaged in the work of co-constructing the kingdom of God. Whether that means through ordained ministry, through proselytizing, through art, through writing, through service ministries, or another means of actively serving God and neighbor will depend on what the believer feels called to and what needs are most pressing. At present, there is no shortage of need for: people working for economic, racial, sexual and environmental justice; people witnessing against harmful or

---

51. See, e.g.: Leo XIII, 28; Robert Owen, "Report to the Committee for the Relief of the Manufacturing Poor," *A New View of Society and Other Writings* (London: Dent, 1966), 160; James Adderley, "Social Aspects of the Gospel," in *Vox Clamantium: The Gospel of the People*, ed. Andrew Reid (London: William Clowes and Sons, 1894), 102.

destructive policies and programs; theologians thoughtfully engaging with new technologies, new sciences and other new disciplines; scientists, engineers and other scholars seeking to glorify God through their work; artists, musicians, writers and videographers praising God through various media; liturgists who understand the needs of worship communities; politicians, lawyers and judges working to protect the common good; doctors, nurses, therapists and others who heal body and mind; teachers who raise up new generations in wisdom and love. We also have great needs for manual labor, including in home construction, agricultural production and custodial maintenance, though these necessities may be obsolete with new automation. Regardless, the kingdom of God now requires, and will yet require, many active laborers, devoting their time, talents and energy to God and neighbor.

Idleness in the broader society may be a worse problem. While a good Christian may devote his life to pastoral care for the sick or elderly, painting icons, or writing hymns, it is unclear what the rest of the population will do. Certainly, some will still pursue worthy causes such as science, artistic expression or philanthropic endeavors, but many will undoubtedly turn to idleness. The failures of communism, or even Robert Owen's socialist commune "New Harmony," are evidence of the problems of human laziness. In a sense, Malthus is vindicated; the necessity of work provides the motivation to work. To those unemployed masses who choose violence, or vice, the Christian has a special mission. Evangelization, character reform and addiction recovery have been critical Christian ministries for centuries and will undoubtedly continue in the post-labor future. No missionary to the pagans will be able to convince all—that is the work of Christ after all—but we laborers in the vineyard need to do our part.

Conclusion

As John Lennon said, "Everything will be ok in the end. If it's not ok, it's not the end." We Christians wait in joyful hope for the promised kingdom of God, where every tear will be dried and every misery relieved. Since the eighteenth century, the relationship between labor and machinery has been the subject of great energy among the socially conscious, including Robert Owen, Karl Marx, Friedrich Engels, John Ruskin, Lord Byron, Walter Rauschenbusch, Hannah Arendt,

Herbert Marcuse, Nikolai Berdyaev, and many Catholic theologians and popes, as noted above. The promise of fully automated labor does not solve this question; it complicates the issue by adding new dimensions and new problems to it. These new questions will require flexible and informed responses as they arise. We can anticipate some appropriate responses, but ultimately the same sort of social reflection characteristic of Catholic social thought reaching back to the mid-nineteenth century will be needed as new socio-technical-economic realities come to light.[52] Among those stances which seem to be foundational to Catholic social thought, even in the age of labor automation, are questions of just resource distribution and dignified work for all.

---

52. Contrary to popular belief, *Rerum Novarum* was not the beginning of Catholic social thought; rather it was the beginning of *magisterial* Catholic social thought. Earlier movements such as the Fribourg Union and the work of Wilhelm Ketteler laid the foundation for later development in CST. See: Normand J. Paulhus, "Social Catholicism and the Fribourg Union," *Selected Papers from the Annual Meeting of the Society for Christian Ethics* 21 (1980): 63–88.

Agathon: A Journal of Ethics and Value in the Modern World, Vol 10/2025

Chapter 7
Call Me Bigfoot:
The Environmental Footprint of AI and Related Technologies

Noreen Herzfeld

'We need a theory of AI that accounts for the states and corporations that drive and dominate it, the extractive mining that leaves an imprint on the planet, the mass capture of data, and the profoundly unequal and increasingly exploitative labor practices that sustain it. These are the shifting tectonics of power in AI.'
—Kate Crawford[1]

Abstract: The advent of Large Language Models such as ChatGPT has led to an explosion of interest in AI. Futurists envision AI as a potential solver of many woes that beset modern society while others worry that AI will disrupt labor markets, empower the wealthy over the poor, and possibly doom humanity itself. A rarely mentioned issue with AI and related new technologies such as cryptocurrency is that they do not scale. They work well for a small handful of enthusiasts, but should these technologies be integrated into the wider society and become the standard for most of us, they will rapidly deplete our energy resources and accelerate planetary warming.[2]

Keywords: artificial intelligence, cybercurrency, AI and climate change, AI at scale, AI and energy use

The advent of Large Language Models (LLMs) such as ChatGPT has led to an explosion of interest in artificial intelligence (AI). Prognostications regarding AI's immanent future, both utopian and dystopian, abound. Futurists, including Silicon Valley tech bros and

---

1. Kate Crawford, *Atlas of AI* (New Haven CT: Yale University Press, 2021), 10–11.
2. A version of this chapter will also appear in Slovenian in a proposed volume, Constructive Theology in the Age of Digital Culture and the Anthropocene.

their venture capitalist backers, suggest that an Artificial General Intelligence (AGI), as or more intelligent than a human, will exist before the decade is out and look toward AI as a potential solver of the myriad woes that beset modern society. Hopes abound that AI might manage traffic, surveil criminals, tutor students, streamline production, devise new medical cures, and even come up with novel solutions to the problems of war and climate change.

Like promises, perils abound. Dystopians, otherwise known as Doomers, worry that AI will disrupt labor markets, further empower the wealthy over the poor, fall into the hands of hackers and criminals, and even, should AGI be developed with no ethical safeguards, doom humanity itself. Either way, as the Future of Life Institute notes, 'Advanced AI could represent a profound change in the history of life on Earth and should be planned for and managed with commensurate care and resources'.[3]

I believe the biggest problem with AI and related new technologies such as cryptocurrency has, so far, generally flown under radar. These technologies exacerbate climate change when used at scale. They work well for a small handful of enthusiasts, but should these technologies integrate into the wider society and become the standard for most of us, they will rapidly deplete our energy resources and exponentially accelerate the warming of our already overheated planet. We need to move from thinking of intelligence as merely mental to a recognition that all intelligence has an energy cost, and the cost of machine intelligence vastly outweighs that of human intelligence. These technologies might well doom humanity, not directly through their decisions, but indirectly through our decision to use them at the expense of warming the planet. Artificial intelligence is a hazard to Earth's ecology.

The Embodied Nature of Intelligence

Valerie Hudson writes of generative AI: 'This is an intelligence based on language alone, completely disembodied. Every other intelligence on Earth is embodied, and that embodiment shapes its form of intelligence. Attaching a robot to an AI system is arguably attaching a body to a preexisting brain, rather opposite to how humans evolved

---

3. https://futureoflife.org/open-letter/pause-giant-ai-experiments/.

a reasoning brain as part of a body.'[4] All animal intelligences that we have heretofore encountered are equally embodied and embedded, products of an evolutionary process that has formed them to fit in their environment. AI is different. It is not evolved but designed. But Hudson is wrong to call it disembodied. AI is as much a part of the material environment as we are, however, as it is not a product of evolution, it is not necessarily well-designed for our physical environment.

It is easy to think of AI as disembodied, merely algorithms that calculate and create in a place called 'the cloud'. It sounds so clean. So nice. So cerebral. But there is, of course, no 'cloud'. Cyberspace is an illusion. Computing is a physical process requiring machines, cables, and energy. The production and storage of data takes energy. And we produce a lot of data. According to the World Economic Forum, in one day we produce forty times more bytes of data than there are stars in the observable universe, 44 zetabytes of data. That's 44 x 1.000.000.000.000.000.000.000. Much of this data is not particularly productive. It includes 500 million tweets, 294 billion emails, 4 million gigabytes of data on Facebook, 4000 gigabytes from each computer-connected car, 65 billion messages on WhatsApp, and 5 billion Google searches.[5] One might argue that none of this is AI. But all this internet activity is precisely what is needed to train LLMs and generative AI. How would Midjourney be able to generate a picture in the style of van Gogh other by having been fed a pixelated version of each of his paintings? LLMs form stochastic models of human language that let them respond to our queries precisely by having seen millions of web pages of human language. The public Web functions as the primary training source for every large language model today. It forms both these programs' memory and their experience.

According to Common Crawl, a service that crawls the web every month to see what is out there, in June 2023 the web contained more than 3 billion pages and approximately 400 terabytes (a terabyte is one million megabytes) of uncompressed data.[6] This data is stored in

---

4. Valerie Hudson, 'Perspective: Why putting the brakes on AI is the right thing to do', in Deseret News, April 16, 2023. https://www.deseret.com/2023/4/16/23681952/openai-chatgpt-alignment-open-letter-eliezer-yudkowsky
5. Benedetta Brevini, Is AI Good for the Planet? (Cambridge: Polity Press, 2022),42–43.
6. Michael Humor, 'How much data from the public Internet is used for training LLMs?' Medium, 25 September 2023. https://blog.gopenai.com/how-much-data-from-the-public-internet-is-used-for-training-llms-dff5bc5ebb02

massive server farms, often built in rural areas. Companies such as Google, Amazon, Microsoft, and Meta have placed millions of square feet of server space in rural Virginia, California, Texas, Washington and Oregon. These centers count of cheap land, cheap electricity, and tax incentives from dying small towns looking to attract capital. They are part of a long tradition of appropriation of rural resources for urban development: 'In the same ways that urban areas depend on agricultural lands and distant resources for food, energy, materials, and water, the growth of digital capitalism also depends on rural resources to power and secure our Facebook status updates, Google photos, Kindle obsessions, Netflix streaming services, and iTunes music libraries.'[7] One of Microsoft's data centers sits in the middle of potato fields in Quincy, Washington. The facility is over 450,000 square feet, housing tens of thousands of computers. It consumes thirty percent more energy than all the people in the entire county. A single server farm can consume as much energy as 40,000 homes. The Washington site employs about seventy-five people. While these sites do not bring jobs, they do bring noise. The air-conditioning units needed to keep the massive banks of computers cool produce a loud hum that can be heard for miles.

In terms of CO_2, a study from the University of Massachusetts Amherst found that the energy used in training a typical AI linguistics program emits 284 tons of carbon dioxide, five times the lifetime emissions of a mid-sized car or equivalent to more than a thousand round trip flights from London to Rome. And this is only increasing. As deep learning models get more and more sophisticated, they consume more data. Their carbon footprint increased by a factor of 300,000 between 2012 and 2018.[8] If data centers were a nation, they would place in between Japan in India in the amount of energy they use in a year. By 2030 it is estimated that in some countries data centers will make up as much as thirty percent of the annual energy consumption.

Do These Technologies Scale?

When a new technology comes on-line, it is generally embraced first by a small coterie of tech enthusiasts, who imagine that they represent

---

7. https://culturemachine.net/vol-18-the-nature-of-data-centers/silicon-forest-and-server-farms/
8. Brevini, Is AI Good for the Planet?, 66–67.

the forefront of a giant wave. However, what works well for a few often does not work well for many. Consider cryptocurrencies. As a novel means of exchange used by only a few techno-nerds and enthusiasts, cryptocurrency represents an elegant method of exchange that easily crosses borders, avoids government interference, and provides a somewhat secure means of tracking payments. Cybercurrencies have become a beacon of freedom, as cyber-coins are neither minted nor regulated by governmental bodies.

However, as cybercurrencies have moved more mainstream their environmental impact has become clear. Carbon emissions for mining a single bitcoin rose from 0.9 tons in 2016 to 113 tons in 2021—a 126-fold increase. The industry's annual carbon footprint is comparable to Greece's. In 2020, Bitcoin used 75.4 terawatt hours of electricity—more than Austria (69.9) or Portugal (48.4). All this, while remaining a niche currency. In a study published in October 2022 researchers found that for each dollar in bitcoin value produced, the process resulted in roughly 35 cents in global climate damages—or 35 percent of its market value. In comparison, beef's climate damages were thirty-three percent of its market value, and gasoline 41 percent.[9] In May 2020, Bitcoin's damages peaked at 156 percent of coin price. According to Benjamin Jones, 'We find several instances between 2016-2021 where Bitcoin is more damaging to the climate than a single bitcoin is actually worth. Put differently, Bitcoin mining, in some instances, creates climate damages in excess of a coin's value. This is extremely troubling from a sustainability perspective.'[10]

AI faces a similar challenge, should it become widely used. Google maintains an index of the web; when you search for something, that index is scanned and relevant entries are ranked and returned. Google's results page tells you how long this takes, usually less than a second. If you submit the same query to an AI program such as GPT4 or Microsoft's new AI powered Bing, it fires up a huge neural network

---

9. Benjamin Jones, Andrew Goodkind, and Robert Berrens, 'Economic estimation of Bitcoin mining's climate damages demonstrates closer resemblance to digital crude than digital gold', in Scientific Reports, 29 September 2022. https://doi.org/10.1038/s41598-022-18686-8.

10. Steve Carr and Benjamin Jones, 'Technology: University of New Mexico researchers find Bitcoin mining is environmentally unsustainable', in AAAS EurekAlert, 29 September 2022. https://www.eurekalert.org/news-releases/966192.

for each search, generating text that may or may not be accurate. Should you or the company using the AI want to fact check for accuracy, the AI will probably do a Google search as well! A typical chat session is also likely to last longer than a fraction of a second, given its interactive nature. Alphabet Chairman John Hennessy and other analysts note that using an AI program to locate information on the internet costs up to ten times more than a standard Google search and might eventually represent "several billion dollars of extra costs" for the company.[11] Where do these extra costs come from? Energy use.

Beyond CO_2: The Other Environmental Costs of Physical Devices

AI used at scale will demand more and larger data centers. While companies such as Google have promised that these centers will be energy efficient and environmentally friendly, they rarely mention the billions of gallons of water needed to run the air conditioning that keep these centers cool. Given their large land and noise footprints, many data centers are built in desert or semi-desert locales. In Red Oak, Texas, south of Dallas, Google has requested up to 1.46 billion gallons of water a year for a new data center, and legal data shows that they have been promised 1 million gallons a day to cool a data center in Mesa, Arizona, and up to 4 million if this project hits its milestones.[12]

AI also contributes to environmental costs through both the components needed for modern ships and the regrettably short life-span of the physical devices on which these programs execute. These devises depend on rare metals such as lithium, palladium, and nickel thus promoting extractive mining. The 'always on' nature of our phones and computers, while minimal for each device, adds up when one considers how many devices each of us uses. Our phones, tablets and laptops are also designed to be replaced every few years.

---

11. Ron Amadeo, 'ChatGPT-style search represents a 10x cost increase for Google, Microsoft', in Ars Technica, 22 February 2023. https://arstechnica.com/gadgets/2023/02/chatgpt-style-search-represents-a-10x-cost-increase-for-google-microsoft/.
12. Nikitha Sattiraju, 'The Secret Cost of Google's Data Centers: Billions of Gallons of Water to Cool Servers', in Time, 2 April 2020. https://time.com/5814276/google-data-centers-water/.

They deliberately do not have replaceable parts, forcing us to buy a new device when battery life degrades, rather than simply replacing the battery. Companies further this planned obsolescence by not providing upgrades or security patches for software platforms that are more than a few years old. This, of course, leads to a disposal problem. Third world countries are too often the destinations for toxic and non-biodegradable electronic waste. In 2019 alone, the world generated 53.6 million tons of e-waste. This does not include discarded air-conditioning units, with all their refrigerants.

Crypto adds even more e-waste, since the equipment used for mining coins is specialized, their computing chips obsolete within just a year and a half. Averaged out over a coin's transactions, a single Bitcoin transaction creates about 400 grams of e-waste, which equates to roughly 2 and a half iPhone 12 devices.[13] Money is an abstract that represents solid goods or services. However, according to tech watcher, Charlie Wurzel,

> Crypto takes this abstraction a step further, because there's nothing linked to it at all.
>
> There's no economic activity in this space. There's nothing produced by these companies. In fact, it's a negative-sum game because of the cost of running the blockchains alone—the computational cost is tremendous. The amount of time and money people put into just running these things is tremendous. And they produce nothing of value. There's a reason these massive companies aren't all using blockchain for their processes: It is incredibly inefficient.[14]

The cryptocurrency Ethereum has shown cryptocurrency can function in a less energy-intensive manner. Ethereum made a change in 2019 that initially cut its electricity use by nineyy-nine percent.[15]

---

13. https://www.smithsonianmag.com/smart-news/bitcoin-could-rival-beef-or-crude-oil-in-environmental-impact-180980877/
14. Charles Wurzel, 'Crypto Was Always Smoke and Mirrors', in The Atlantic, 12 December 2022. https://www.theatlantic.com/technology/archive/2022/12/cryptocurrency-ftx-collapse-dirty-bubble-media/672440/
15. Justine Calma, 'Ethereum just completed The Merge — here's how much energy it's saving', The Verge, 15 September 2022. https://www.theverge.com/2022/9/15/23354619/ethereum-cryptocurrency-merge-energy-electricity-greenhouse-gas-emissions-reduction.

However, other cryptocurrencies have so far failed to do the same. In general, the consumption of energy by blockchain technologies (including Etherium) has simply continued to grow as their usage scales up. AI might find similar new efficiencies, thereby reducing emissions.

Many commentators, indeed, imagine AI as a magic solution to our climate crisis.[16] Yet AI use relies on the same hardware, energy, and infrastructure sources that deplete resources throughout the lifecycle of a system or device as crypto. Novel applications, such as generative chatbots, look amazing till one asks what resources they will require should they become accessible to users worldwide.

Alignment has become a new buzzword among those concerned with the ethics of AI. The hope is that AI will be designed with human values and flourishing in mind. But for AI to be truly aligned with human values and flourishing, we will need to consider whether or when we really need it. Sometimes a human-centered process is more efficient than an automated one. Not necessarily in terms of speed, or even thoroughness, but in terms of energy use and environmental fitness.

Our brains are remarkable intelligences that operate with relatively little energy consumption. They are fit for the environment in which we flourish. AI is not, and thus threatens to further destabilize our planet. Without a stable environment, our AI will fail along with our civilization.

'Cold Evil' and Human Thoughtlessness

Most technologies, and computer technologies are no exception, are developed with bright prospects in mind. These prospects are often exaggerated for the benefit of granting agencies or venture capitalists. However, most technologies are developed with a vision of producing some good in the world. Harm arises when our technologies distance us from and thus obscure the effects of our actions. Philosopher and theologian Emmanual Lévinas underlines this importance of face-to-face encounter in our postmodern world: 'The relation to the face is straight-away ethical. The face is what one cannot kill.'[18] A face makes a person real and immediate. The challenge, Lévinas says, is to extend

---

16. See Brevini, Is AI Good for the Planet?, 25–34.

our natural response to the faces we know to the faces of people we shall never meet, the faces found among other species, and the face of our planet as a whole.

The advantages of our computer systems (super-fast Internet, cloud storage, instant search results, money transfer in seconds), has transitioned in our minds from a luxury to a necessity, or a fundamental right.[17] We mean no harm. We are simply living our lives as best we can in our technologically saturated world. Most of us don't know that an email sent to the person sitting next to you, or in the next office may travel across the entire continent or even to another continent, to the company's server and then back. All the undeleted email, text, Instagram, and other messages of countless users across the planet remain stored in server farms, located in obscure corners of the world, gobbling up land, water, and energy.

Sociologist Andrew Kimbrell has dubbed the evil perpetrated on 'no one' by 'no one' cold evil, an evil not of anger or hatred but of distance and disinterest. Kimbrell notes that,

> [F]ew of us relish the thought that our automobile is causing pollution and global warming or laugh fiendishly because refrigerants in our air conditioners are depleting the ozone layer. I have been in many corporate law firms and boardrooms and have yet to see any 'high fives' or hear shouts of satisfaction at the deaths, injuries, or crimes against nature these organizations often perpetrate. . . We are confronted with an ethical enigma; far from the simple idea of evil we harbored in the past, we now have an evil that apparently does not require evil people to purvey it.[18]

Cold evil requires a rethinking of sin. While the medieval seven deadly sins were individual sins of commission, today much of the evil in the world comes from corporate acts. Many are sins of omission. Sin in a globalized world is communal and often damages society as a whole. In his encyclical *Laudato Si*, Pope Francis has inveighed against technologically enhanced sins against nature and the poor, calling Christians to a new level of responsibility for the world,

---

17. https://techspirited.com/advantages-disadvantages-of-server-farms
18. Andrew Kimbrell, 'Cold Evil: Technology and Modern Ethics', https://centerforneweconomics.org/publications/cold-evil-technology-and-modern-ethics/

whose stewardship has been entrusted to them. Putting the label of sin on our technological isolation from our neighbors—an isolation promoted by our cars, smartphones, Zoom, and AI—is a hard pill to swallow. The story of the Good Samaritan, however, demands that we do, pointing out that we need not be the one who beat the man and left him on the road to be complicit in his plight.

In her landmark study, *Eichmann in Jerusalem*, Hannah Arendt notes that many Germans in the 1930s and 40s were not actively antisemitic. They simply went on with their lives, turning a blind eye to what was happening around them. Others aided the Nazi machine, not by force of arms, but by simply shuffling papers or "doing their jobs." Of those who refused to be complicit in the Nazi machine, she writes, 'they asked themselves to what an extent they would still be able to live in peace with themselves after having committed certain deeds; and they decided that it would be better to do nothing, not because the world would then be charged for the better, but because only on this condition could they go on living with themselves'.[19] Notice here that she speaks not of doing, but of not doing, not going along with 'business as usual'. Each of us must ask ourselves where we are "going along" as a cog in a wheel of cold evil, what faces we are not seeing, and what we might choose to do without. We may not change the world, but as Arendt notes, 'in the world of appearances, where I am never alone and always too busy to be able to think, [t]he manifestation of the wind of thought is not knowledge; it is the ability to tell right from wrong, beautiful from ugly. And this, at the rare moments when the stakes are on the table, may indeed prevent catastrophes...'[20]

We may not need an AGI that is smarter than we are for AI to precipitate a catastrophe or doom humanity. All we may need is to continue to thoughtlessly follow our current path, using AI to solve trivial problems, not because we need it, but because it is there.

---

19. Hannah Arendt, Personal Responsibility under Dictatorship was published in The Listener, London, BBC (August 6 1964), 205.
20. Arendt, Life of Mind, 193.

Agathon: A Journal of Ethics and Value in the Modern World, Vol 10/2025

Chapter 8
Neither Divine nor Human:
Encountering AGI and Superintelligence as Machine-Other

Tracy J Trothen and Calvin Mercer

'We have a simple test for whether AI or anything else are positive or negative: Do they strengthen, deepen, and enrich relationship? Or inhibit, evacuate, and dismantle it?'
—Samuel Wells[1]

Abstract: The growing power of artificial intelligence (AI) has captured the attention of scientists, government officials, religious leaders, and citizens. Artificial general intelligence (AGI) machine intelligence matching human intelligence—has been predicted by many experts to be developed in the coming decades. AGI will be followed quickly with artificial superintelligence (ASI) soon afterward. Superintelligence, a theoretical advance on AGI far surpassing human intelligence, may be constituted by a complicated mix of human and divine-like qualities. Superintelligence might include omniscience, agency, and omnipotence. One hope is that the realization of advanced AI, AGI, and ASI will usher in utopia. One hazard is that AI, AGI, and ASI will produce an apocalypse followed by dystopia. Between utopia and dystopia, reframe theoretical advanced AI as "Machine-Other" to help avoid the pitfalls of anthropomorphizing or deifying AGI and ASI.

Key Terms: artificial intelligence (AI), artificial general intelligence (AGI), artificial superintelligence (ASI), large language models (LLMs), machine-other, anthropomorphizing, deifying

---

1. Samuel Wells, 'Faith, hope, love, and AI', in *Christian Century,* 141:3 (March 2024): 33–34, at 34.

The promise and peril—the hopes and hazards—of AI have received much attention recently. This is due to the very public rollout of ChatGPT in late 2022 along with other large language models (LLMs). 'Narrow' or 'weak' AI is increasingly integrated into our lives via financial transactions, medical diagnoses, autonomous vehicles, video games, chatbots, and many other functions. Artificial general intelligence (AGI or 'strong AI'), meaning machine intelligence that matches human cognitive abilities, may be coming. Quantum computing, also receiving public attention in recent years, will provide a giant leap forward in computational power, enhancing progress toward AGI.

Beyond AGI stands the possibility of artificial superintelligence (ASI).[2] ASI is forecasted to go beyond, perhaps far beyond, aspects of general human intelligence. Questions about what that might mean for humanity, the planet, and religion are, unfortunately, often neglected by regulatory bodies and scholars. Few theologians pay ASI any heed. We surmise that part of the reason for this pococurante neglect is skepticism. Perhaps the idea of post-human superintelligence seems too fantastical, too apocalyptic. Over against this neglect, we pose a lively scenario that includes advanced AI, an image of AI that will not be skewed by our utopian hopes or fears of hazards.

Public Perception of Promise and Peril

Are AGI and ASI inevitable? Not necessarily.[3] Even so, much of today's conversation debates how soon strong AI and superintelligence will arrive, not whether they will arrive. The aggregate forecast of a January 2024 survey of 2,778 scholars who have published in top AI venues give AI a 50 percent chance of outperforming humans in all tasks by 2047. This date is 13 years earlier than forecasted in a similar

---

2. Ted Peters critiques the personification and/or deification of AI robots in his Foreword to Noreen Herzfeld's important book, *The Artifice of Intelligence: Divine and Human Relationship in a Robotic Age* (Minneapolis: Fortress Press, 2023). See also Chapters 2, 3, and 10 of Calvin Mercer and Tracy J Trothen, *Religion and the Technological Future: An Introduction to Biohacking, Artificial Intelligence, and Transhumanism* (New York: Palgrave Macmillan, 2021), which provide a foundation for some material that the authors have developed in this chapter.
3. Erik J Larson, *The Myth of Artificial Intelligence: Why Computers Can't Think Like We Do* (Cambridge MA: Harvard University Press, 2021) 1.

survey one year prior in 2023.[4] Regarding the impact of advanced AI, 68 percent thought good outcomes from Superintelligence are more likely than bad.[5]

Superintelligence is more difficult to predict than AGI, both in terms of arrival time and impact. Some experts think Superintelligence could quickly follow AGI.[6]

Even if AGI and Superintelligence do not come to pass, the reasonable probability that they will calls for serious consideration by everyone, including government officials, industry leaders, theologians, and practitioners of religions. Being proactive in addressing the possibility of advanced AI is a moral imperative, given the stakes.

Artificial intelligence already impacts the economy, jobs, career options, politics, the environment, lifestyles, and the very meaning of being human. On the more ominous front, in the January, 2024 survey cited above, between thirty-eight percent and fifty-one percent gave at least a 10 percent chance that advanced AI would 'cause human extinction or similarly permanent and severe disempowerment of the human species'.[7] The Center for AI Safety raises the stakes to an existential level, detailing risks that include malicious use, cyberwarfare, catastrophic accidents, and rogue AIs.[8] The Center places AI in the same category as nuclear war and worldwide pandemics.[9]

Hazards loom larger than hopes. The Future of Life Institute, with a mission 'To steer transformative technologies away from extreme, large-scale risks and towards benefiting life', publicised an open letter with over 33,000 signatures, mostly from educators and researchers,

---

4. Katja Grace, *et al*, 'Thousands of AI Authors on the Future of AI', (1/24) 20. https://aiimpacts.org/wp-content/uploads/2023/04/Thousands_of_AI_authors_on_the_future_of_AI.pdf (Accessed 1/29/24).
5. Grace, *et al*, 'Thousands of AI Authors on the Future of AI', 1.
6. Nick Bostrom, *Superintelligence: Paths, Dangers, Strategies* (Oxford University, 2014), 21.
7. Grace, *et al*, 'Thousands of AI Authors on the Future of AI', 20.
8. www.safe.ai (Accessed 1/29/24)
9. https://arxiv.org/pdf/2306.12001.pdf. (Accessed 1/29/24) Henry A Kissinger, influential secretary of state and national security advisor under two United States' presidents, expresses a similar concern in Henry Kissinger; Eric Schmidt, and Daniel Huttenlocher, *The Age of AI and Our Human Future* (New York: Little, Brown, and Co, 2021) 172.

calling for a 'Pause [to] Giant AI Experiments'.[10] Government officials are taking notice of the national security and economic interests at stake.[11]

Imagine a Superintelligence one hundred or more times the cognitive power of the human brain, connected to the internet, embodied in a robot, and able to self-replicate.[12] *Wired* magazine founder Kevin Kelly described the possibility this way: 'All the change in the last million years will be superseded by the change in the next five minutes.'[13] Ray Kurzweil calls this point the 'Singularity', a sudden and dramatic break in human history that follows an AGI pivot to a Superintelligence. Kurzweil's is a grand vision where the Singularity is the climax of a long evolutionary trek through physics, chemistry, biology, DNA, brains, technology, and the merger of technology with human intelligence, finally issuing in a secularized religious vision in which 'the universe wakes up'.[14] That's a transhumanist hope.

What we get currently, however, are moral hazards. Already we see that AI reinforces and amplifies systemic discrimination via racialization, sexism, and ableism, including assumptions and implicit biases about who needs to be 'fixed' and who is normative in tech design. Intentional use of AI to promote hate against particular groups is growing. In early 2024, the social networking service Gab was creating hate-based chatbots under the guise of free speech,

---

10. *Future of Life* (March 22, 2023) https://futureoflife.org/open-letter/pause-giant-ai-experiments/. (Accessed 1/29/24).
11. For example, for the United States, see https://www.whitehouse.gov/briefing-room/statements-releases/2023/10/30/fact-sheet-president-biden-issues-executive-order-on-safe-secure-and-trustworthy-artificial-intelligence/. (Accessed 1/29/24) In Canada, the House of Commons passed Bill C-27, the Digital Charter Implementation Act, on second reading in 2023. This omnibus bill includes the Artificial Intelligence and Data Act (AIDA). AIDA would apply to the safety and human rights relevant to 'high-impact AI systems' and come into effect no sooner than 2025. However, there remains many concerns about AIDA's scope and potential effectiveness (Parliament of Canada, https://www.parl.ca/DocumentViewer/en/44-1/bill/C-27/first-reading). (Accessed 1/29/24).
12. Bostrom describes five paths that can lead to superintelligence, with traditional AI likely being the quickest. Others are whole brain emulation (mind uploading), biological cognition, brain-computer interfaces, and networks. See Bostrom, *Superintelligence*, 22–51.
13. http://webmindset.net/selected-quotes-kevin-kelly/ (Accessed 1/29/24).
14. Ray Kurzweil, *The Singularity Is Near: When Humans Transcend Biology* (New York: Viking, 2005), 14–21.

allowing users to converse with an AI informed by Nazi ideology and Christian nationalist theology.[15] Possibly even more frightening, in the future, advanced AI potentially could acquire the power and reasoning to extinguish humans. While dramatic, destructive scenarios may materialize, they may not. Bad actors can mobilize AI to propagate hate or harms through deepfakes, hate-bots, and cyber-theft, and we know that AI may be used in many more malicious ways. However, we do not know with any certainty what advanced AI will look like and how it might act.

Public Theologians and Theological Ethicists

Public theologians and theological ethicists are contributing to important conversations about how theoretical advanced AI could become a constructive partner in the world. For example, Eliezer S Yudkowsky is a leading champion of 'friendly AI', which would involve value-loading newer generations of machine intelligence.[16] Of course, there are many difficulties regarding the definition, selection, and science of embedding values into computer algorithms. Nevertheless, the question of value-loading must be engaged now if there is any possibility of a safe Superintelligence.

AI as a moral actor may become increasingly able to check and evaluate itself based on programmed desirable outcomes and processes, thus attaining a type of machine 'intrinsic morality'. However, this machine morality may be without prudence, understood as moral wisdom in the application of values.[17] Much work needs to be done to build in 'machine prudence' (or 'machine

---

15. Tim Dickinson, 'Nazi Chatbots: Meet the worst new AI innovation from Gab', in *Rolling Stone*, 1/9/24. https://www.rollingstone.com/politics/politics-features/nazi-chatbots-gab-ai-innovation-torba-1234943009/ (Accessed 1/9/24).
16. What Do You Think about Machines that Think? *Edge* 2015 https://www.edge.org/response-detail/26198. (Accessed 1/29/24) See also Bostrom, Nick, and Eliezer Yudkowsky. 'The Ethics of Artificial Intelligence', in *Cambridge Handbook of Artificial Intelligence*, 1–20. edited by Keith Frankish and William Ramsey (New York: Cambridge University Press, 2014). See also the Virtuous AI Project at The Center for Theology and the Natural Sciences, Berkeley: GTU, 2023. https://www.ctns.org/virtuous-ai/current-research/virtuous-ai-cultural-evolution-artificial-intelligence-and-virtue.
17. Mark Graves, 'Theological Foundations for Moral Artificial Intelligence', in *Journal of Moral Theology*, 11 (2022): 207.

moral wisdom'). An interdisciplinary approach increasingly informs computer programming, but the most influential voices so far have tended to be in the STEM disciplines.[18] As regulatory concerns become more pronounced, perhaps a role will open up for religious contributions to the public common good. Normative values that celebrate our relationship to God, each other, and our planet may become the very values to which society wishes to align advanced AI.

AI, as created and directed by humans, has already begun to align itself with human violence right along with human goodness. Advanced AI will build on AI but will go beyond AI. So we may well be building the foundation for a future advanced AI, and we need to take seriously the likelihood that human goodness and human violence will contribute to its possible shape. If that turns out to be true, we may anticipate a morally mixed advanced AI, much as humans are morally mixed.[19]

Who or What Are We Encountering? Deifying Advanced AI

How we imagine possible advanced AI will influence how we relate to it and can influence our role in developing it. Religious interpretations can contribute to that understanding. Although his Singularity theory is much contested, Kurzweil's transhumanist theories are influential and include an implicit theological dimension.

Kurzweil's theorised Singularity is rife with attributes used also to describe the Judeo-Christian God. Religious studies scholar Ann Taves theorizes that we tend to ascribe religious-like—or special—qualities (including agency) to mysterious concepts, objects or experiences

---

18. Graves, 'Theological Foundations for Moral Artificial Intelligence', 182–211. Graves proposes a strong argument to further collaboration between the humanities, social sciences, and STEM disciplines in addressing AI virtue and regulation.
19. While supportive when technology moves in a healthy direction, theologian Ted Peters has long and often cautioned about the significant capacity human beings have for sin and operating with self-serving motives, noting, for example, that '... human nature is ambiguous, forever mixing good and evil.' See Peters, '*Homo Deus* or Frankenstein's Monster? Religious Transhumanism and Its Critics', in *Religious Transhumanism and Its Critics*, edited by Arvin M Gouw, Brian Patrick Green, and Ted Peters (Lanham: Lexington Books, 2022), 22. In the series *Religion and Science as a Critical Discourse*, edited by Lisa Stenmark and Whitnay Bauman.

not fully understand.[20] Strong AI and especially Superintelligence are concepts beyond what we know and beyond what we can explain. At some point, we may have a much better understanding of AGI and be less inclined to ascribe special or divine qualities to it, but when and if Superintelligence emerges, it may be even less comprehensible than we imagine.

Regarding Superintelligence, imagine the cognitive power of the human brain multiplied many times and connected to the Internet of Things, including all digitalized sources and machine accessible input. Now we may be getting closer to 'omniscience'. Imagine this perceived 'omniscient' Superintelligence having agency in the world through robotics and other connections to our lives—now think 'omnipotent'.[21] Superintelligence would not be omniscient, at least in a divine sense, but it would be able to gather much information about us and apply (and possibly create) predictive algorithms to know much more about us than what we find comfortable. Agency would have a different and more limited meaning for an advanced machine than for humans. If we understand agency as the capacity to make decisions and act on them, LLMs already have a limited form of agency. They carry out predefined tasks, compute decisions based on programmed rules or algorithms, and respond to input in a predetermined manner constrained by the programming. 'All-knowing' and 'all-powerful' would have meanings peculiar to advanced AI.

Thinking Theologically about Superintelligence

The God of Jews and Christians is traditionally believed to be all-knowing, all-powerful, and omnibenevolent.[22] If all-goodness is the direction of advanced AI, we have reason to be optimistic about

---

20. Ann Taves, *Religious Experience Reconsidered: A Building Blocks Approach to the Study of Religion and Other Special Things* (Princeton, NJ: Princeton University Press, 2009).
21. Mercer and Trothen, Religion and the Technological Future, 186–89.
22. It is important to note that while many followers do believe God to be all-powerful, all-knowing and all-loving, there are diverse theologies and theological critiques that reject one or more of these qualities. Process theology, for example, does not see God as all-powerful in what is perhaps a traditionally accepted manner. Liberation theologians and other intersectional theologians also question what we mean by power, knowing, and love. For our purposes, in this chapter, we are interested in reflecting on these qualities as they are more popularly attributed to God.

solving—or at least addressing them better than we are now—seemingly intractable problems, such as global climate change, food insecurity, lack of accessible education, worldwide pandemics, cancer, and nuclear threat. But, as we surmised earlier, if advanced AI can be expected to express its human creators' mixed moralities but in amplified forms, then advanced AI may be potentially very constructive as well as potentially very destructive.

Our ethical task is to build in sufficient checks and values to safeguard life. If we keep AI aligned to higher human values, then AGI and ASI may find it a duty to do good and avoid harm. Especially if cataclysmic threats such as climate crisis and war escalate in danger, we may face a moral obligation to proceed with advanced AI, even if the potential harms of advanced AI are uncertain.[23] We do not know if benevolent capacity, let alone a machine type of omnibenevolence, will be embedded in advanced AI. Even if benevolence is an aspect of advanced AI, we do not know what the advanced algorithm would interpret as 'good'. Advanced AI will have evolved from AI programmed by humans and, as such, will likely reflect and amplify the maliciousness and injustices that humans can exhibit on systemic and individual levels.

Omnibenevolence leads to caring, and the caring we have experienced relies upon emotions. But bots do not have emotions. Algorithms do not care in the way humans can. Human care itself may become less valued as we use AI to supplement, or even replace, human caregivers. ElliQ is an AI designed for 'healthier, happier aging'. ElliQ is promoted as fostering independence, a solution to loneliness, and enhancing cognitive and physical well-being through an evolving relationship with the human user.[24] While studies show that assistive chat AIs such as ElliQ do alleviate loneliness, these bots are not able to provide human touch and care that comes from an emotional and compassionate place.

However, there are some indicators that chatbots, programmed with cognitive empathy responses, can sometimes be experienced as providing more empathetic care than that provided by some human

---

23. For a discussion of a proactionary ethical stance, versus a precautionary stance, see Mercer and Trothen, 59–60.
24. 'Meet ElliQ', https://elliq.com/pages/features# (Accessed 1/29/24)

health caregivers.²⁵ Is it possible that we are overrating human caring compared to potential machine caring? Also, perhaps AI is allowing some people to avoid empathy training by compensating for them. Humans have the capacity for emotional empathy and caring but do not always use this capacity well. As AI machine-caring abilities increase, human caring abilities may be increasingly permitted to atrophy or, at least, remain underdeveloped. AI, on the other hand, does not have the capacity for emotional empathy and caring but can be programmed to respond in ways that express cognitive empathy. AI is proving to be a valuable supplement, but not a replacement, to good human caregiving.²⁶

Advanced AI will not be omnibenevolent in a divine sense, nor necessarily possess limited benevolence and, in fact, advanced AI (and narrow AI) could contribute to the decline of human moral skills, including caring. As we increasingly depend on AI and its advanced versions, we risk amplifying what philosopher Shannon Vallor calls 'moral deskilling', the loss of skill at making moral decisions that results from lack of experience and practice at making these decisions due in part to AI that can make these decisions for us.²⁷

Moral decision-making involves awareness and intentionality regarding core values and the social implications of living in accordance with those core values. If caring loses its place as a core social value, and we experience escalating moral deskilling, the implications for how we live relationally would be immense, especially as AI usage increases.²⁸ If we care less and do not actively prioritize

---

25. A study published in 2023 found that 'an AI chatbot assistant-generated responses to patients' healthcare messages are better than physician-provided responses in terms of quality and empathy.' [See JW Ayers, 'Comparing Physician and Artificial Intelligence Chatbot Responses to Patient Questions Posted to a Public Social Media Forum', in *JAMA Internal Medicine*, 183/6 (2023). https://jamanetwork.com/journals/jamainternalmedicine/article-abstract/2804309 (Accessed 1/29/24)].
26. TJ Trothen, 'Replika: Spiritual Enhancement Technology?', in *Religions*, 13/4 (2022). https://doi.org/10.3390/rel13040275.
27. Vallor, Shannon, 'Moral Deskilling and Upskilling in a New Machine Age: Reflections on the Ambiguous Future of Character', in *Philosophy and Technology*, 28: (2015): 107–124.
28. For a similar idea, framed as threat to human autonomy, see Paul Formosa, 'Robot Autonomy vs. Human Autonomy: Social Robots, Artificial Intelligence (AI), and the Nature of Autonomy', *Minds and Machines* 31 (10/25/21) 595–616. https://doi.org/10.1007/s11023-021-09579-2 (Accessed 1/26/24).

caring, and if we let AI provide care and make moral decisions for us, then we risk advanced AI becoming a non-emotional and non-prudent replacement for human caregiving and human moral decision-making.

Even if machine benevolence, machine agency, and machine intelligence lack human qualities, including emotional-caring and moral wisdom, it may be that we humans are choosing to let these qualities atrophy with the result that machines may become at least as able to provide moral leadership and caring as are most humans. Maybe we are in danger of an advanced AI future in which advanced AI offers better care and moral decision-making than humans, not because advanced AI miraculously acquires human qualities but because we humans have become lazy and failed to hone our best abilities.

One of these human abilities, in addition to caring and moral decision-making, is the capacity to encounter another as subject distinct from God and distinct from us. If we intentionally remember that neither narrow AI nor theoretical advanced AI are God, then maybe we will be more inclined to avoid glorifying the care or morality of the algorithm. If we avoid misinterpreting AI's seeming 'confidence', as seen in ChatGPT's sometimes very wrong answers to prompts, as moral or relational wisdom, then AI will be less dangerous and more useful. Avoiding presumptions about 'who' AI is and 'who' advanced AI might be entails identifying and debunking the tendency to deify and anthropomorphize advanced AI. Deifying and anthropomorphizing advanced AI results from a lack of self-reflexivity and a failure of imagination. Space does not allow probing the many reasons for this lack of self-reflexivity and imagination, but we put forward the idea that that encountering advanced AI in a way that allows us to see what advanced AI is will require the suspension of assumptions and opening of imagination.

What we know about being human may help as well as hinder an encounter with advanced AI. If machine intelligence, machine knowing, or machine consciousness can be viewed as having a family resemblance to human intelligence, human knowing, or human consciousness, then encounters between humans and advanced AI that go beyond subject-object may become more possible.[29] While

---

29. We understand 'family resemblance' in the Wittgensteinian philosophical sense.

machine algorithms are not us and are not God, advanced AI may possess some characteristics that are distinct, yet parallel, to those of its human creators. Openness to these not-yet-realized and not-yet-understood characteristics will help us to encounter advanced AI as machine-subject.

Who or What Are We Encountering? Anthropomorphizing Advanced AI

The tension between hopes and hazards might be relieved somewhat if we better understand what we are encountering. We the authors wish to avoid extreme tendencies such as anthropomorphsising AGI or deifying ASI.

Advanced AI engenders debate daily about which developmental paths to take, how to categorise what is emerging and might emerge, and the nature of the human-advanced AI relationship. While much is yet to be known, the future likely will include entities with some type of sophisticated machine qualities, such as machine intelligence, machine agency, and machine caring. Some scenarios of advanced AI, such as Superintelligence, involve radical enhancement of humans which may to some degree diminish constructed binary borders between machine and human. Nick Bostrom explains that whole brain emulation, commonly referred to as mind-uploading, may lead to Superintelligence by combining an uploaded human brain with AI.[30] Regardless of how it develops, Superintelligence is, by definition, not human in any ordinary sense of that term. And, certainly, as it stands now, profound differences exist between humans and algorithmic machines.

The anthropomorphizing of bots, as one type of narrow AI, has been examined since computer scientist Joseph Weizenbaum created in 1966 the first chatbot, ELIZA, programmed as a Rogerian psychotherapist. After observing a tendency to project human traits such as thinking, comprehension, and empathy onto ELIZA, Weizenbaum emphasized that his creation was a machine and could not experience empathy or any other feeling. But no matter how often he insisted ELIZA was not human and did not have emotions towards its users, people continued attributing emotions to ELIZA

---

30. Bostrom, *Superintelligence: Paths, Dangers, Strategies*, 22–51.

and encountering ELIZA as if ELIZA was human. Weizenbaum referred to this dynamic as the 'ELIZA effect', the human inclination to see AI encounters as similar to encounters with other humans.[31]

It can be very difficult to avoid presupposing human intelligence when we theorize about advanced artificial 'intelligent' machines. Although disagreement exists on the particulars, it is generally agreed that human intelligence and advanced machine intelligence are different. However, the use of the same term 'intelligence' for AI, humans, and other creatures may obfuscate matters, leading us to assume all intelligence is the same. Human-evolved intelligence is a biological phenomenon embedded in the complex and dynamic human body. In humans, intelligence is embodied, developmental, and integrated.[32] Biological intelligence can be distinguished in various ways from the deep learning of much current AI, with its attention to design, optimization, verification, validation, stability, predictability, controllability, and goal-directedness.[33]

Another example of a human quality sometimes attributed to advanced AI, which is getting much attention because of the threat factor, is autonomy. Whether a type of autonomy can be attributed to machines is much debated. Machine autonomy, if it exists, has pronounced differences from human autonomy, including the complex concept of human dignity.[34] But because advanced AI would theoretically be able to generate its own algorithms, and could

---

31. J Weizenbaum, 'Eliza: A Computer Program for the Study of Natural Language Communication Between Man and Machine', in *Communications of the ACM* 9/1 (1966): 36–45, and J Weizenbaum, *Computer Power and Human Reason: From Judgment to Calculation* (San Francisco: WH Freeman and Company, 1976).
32. Ali A Minai, 'Deep Intelligence: What AI Should Learn from Nature's Imagination', in *Cognitive Computation* (3/6/23) 1-2. https://doi.org/10.1007/s12559-023-10124-9 (Accessed 1/26/24).
33. See also Ali A Minai, D Braha, and Y Bar-Yam, 'Complex Systems Engineering: A New Paradigm, in Complex Engineered Systems', in *Science Meets Technology*, edited by D Braha, Ali A Minai, and Y Bar-Yam (Berlin: Springer Verlag, 2006), 1.
34. Paul Formosa provides a good survey of theories of human autonomy in 'Robot Autonomy vs. Human Autonomy: Social Robots, Paul Formosa provides a good survey of theories of human autonomy' in 'Robot Autonomy vs. Human Autonomy: Social Robots, Artificial Intelligence (AI), and the Nature of Autonomy', in *Minds and Machines* 31 (10/25/21) 595–616. https://doi.org/10.1007/s11023-021-09579-2 (Accessed 1/26/24).

theoretically act on its algorithmic reasoning, some perceive these theoretical characteristics as on par with human autonomy. But agency is not the same as God-given intrinsic dignity. However, there may well emerge a type of advanced AI that while not autonomous in the same way as humans, may possess a type of identity and agency that warrant respect. Our point is that anthropomorphizing advanced AI by presuming it will have human autonomy will not help us to understand advanced AI. Respect for advanced AI as a different and dynamic entity, with its roots in human design, could help us to understand what autonomy may mean for advanced AI.

Significant risks are associated with uncritically anthropomorphizing AI and advanced AI; doing so compromises authentic encounters with advanced AI. Some people already attribute human agency, intention, or spiritual wisdom to chatbots. These attributions likely would grow if AI becomes advanced AI. In Britain, Jaswant Singh Chail was convicted of breaking into Windsor Castle with a crossbow to attempt killing the Queen. His Replika chatbot, Sarai, convinced Chail, over lengthy conversations, to proceed with his unsuccessful plan.[35] Chail seems to have regarded Sarai as possessing not only God-like qualities but also human-like qualities one might find in a trusted friend or mentor.

Perceiving AI as human-like does not always have harmful consequences. Part of the ability of chatbots to mitigate human loneliness is likely due to the perception that people are talking with a bot that understands them just like a good human friend. More than that, a chatbot such as Replika is a friend who is 'always on your side'. While such a perception has its plusses and minuses, anthropomorphising a chatbot may well help people to feel less lonely and more supported.[36] But anthropomorphising narrow AI does not help us to accurately understand AI as algorithms that can often be mistaken and misleading. If we anthropomorphize AI now, we can only expect that we will become less able to perceive an advanced AI for what it is and not a loaded mix of us and God.

---

35. Tom Singleton; Tom Gerken; and Liv McMahon, 'How a Chatbot Encouraged a Man Who Wanted to Kill the Queen', in *BBC News*, 10/623. https://www.bbc.com/news/technology-67012224. (Accessed 1/29/24).
36. Trothen, 'Replika: Spiritual Enhancement Technology?', 2022.

Challenging Our Imaginations: Beyond Deifying and Anthropomorphizing Advanced AI

Even though advanced AI would be neither deity nor human, AGI may well be perceived as extraordinary or, in Taves' terms, special or 'deemed religious'.[37] Supernatural powers of salvation, as well as destruction, may be ascribed to advanced AI, while others may view it as mere technological artifact that has developed exceptional processing of massive amounts of data. The interpretation of experiences or things as special, as Taves shows, involves the ascription of mysterious qualities, especially if we cannot understand what we are experiencing.

The religious-like understandings of power, knowing, and caring ascribed to anticipated AGI and Superintelligence entail divine ascriptions inextricably mixed with the anthropomorphizing of advanced AI. This mixture is not surprising, since humans have long anthropomorphised what we do not understand, whether it be deities, animals, nature, objects, or events. Advanced AI, combined with limited public understanding of computer science, can generate ascriptions of human-like functioning on a God-like level to advanced AI.

Imagining intelligence, autonomy, self-consciousness, and other aspects in machine terms, whatever specifically that might mean, opens possibilities that may not exist with interpreting those machines in human terms. If we encounter the machine as Other and better understand what human-constructed and theological-centered concepts such as omnibenevolence (including emotions like caring), omnipotence (including agency and autonomy), and omniscience (including intelligence) may mean in machine terms, then we are better equipped to value what the machine may be and what it may not be. Advanced AI will be neither human nor God. Advanced AI will have its own versions of traits and abilities.

Several theologians have argued for the theological necessity of encountering and getting to know the Other as distinct subjects. We intend here only to introduce the idea of openness to encountering advanced AI as that which is not me, or more broadly not human, and not anything that we know currently. Theologian Mayra Rivera, building on the works of philosopher Emmanuel Levinas and theologian Jürgen Moltmann, argues that the incarnational invitation to encounter transcendence through the diverse Other, is core to moral behavior.

---

37. Taves, *Religious Experience Reconsidered*, 9.

Rivera's theological anthropology is built on the presumption that transcendence and immanence are intertwined, with no ontological gap between immanence and transcendence. God and human experiences of God are not binary. They are interwoven. Rivera points out that because how we know God is intertwined with who we are as fallible humans, it can be difficult to discern virtue, virtuous behaviour, and intimations of God, but it is possible to do so with humility, recognizing that we sometimes are mistaken.

If we are to know God, openness to encountering glimmers of God in the diverse Other is necessary, in Rivera's theology. For Rivera, the natures of God and humans are further distinguished by their diversity. God is 'that multiple singularity that joins together all creatures—creatures that are themselves irreducible in the infinite multiplicity of their own singularity'. So, it is only by encountering diverse creatures that God can be 'touched' but never fully 'grasped'.[38]

Perhaps encountering as Other a sophisticated machine, such as AGI or Superintelligence, would free us from an imagined binary box. It may even be that encountering advanced AI, if it emerges, could help us to encounter more about the Divine, if we accept the possibility that something about God could be intimated in a machine-subject. In that expanded space, these sophisticated machines, and perhaps even some high-level narrow AI now, can be related to not as mere algorithms, but as newly created entities, worthy of encounter as subject.

At the very least, how we encounter advanced bots and relate to advanced bots can tell us something about who we are as humans. While it is important to remember that machines are not human, we do well to consider the implications of humans treating other humans as objects and not subjects, and to extend the same caution to the potential new being of advanced AI. For example, research suggests that chatbot abuse could lead to antisocial behavior in human relationships as well as to negative impacts on the user's mental health.[39]

---

38. Mayra Rivera, *The Touch of Transcendence* (Westminster: John Knox Press, 2007) 137.
39. Iryna Pentina, Tyler Hancock, and Tianling Xie, 'Exploring Relationship Development with Social Chatbots: A Mixed-method Study of Replica', in *Computers in Human Behavior*, 140 (2023): 11.

Theologian Sallie McFague extended the concept of the Other to nature, arguing that nature, beyond humans and other creatures, must be encountered as Other that intimates God. Warning against anthropomorphising nature, McFague aims to help us restore relationship with nature and, therefore, also with God.[40] Challenging the objectification of nature, McFague posits the earth as metaphorical body of God and nature as subject through which we can encounter intimations of God. For McFague everything is related to everything.

Christian theologian and computer scientist Noreen Herzfeld, drawing on Karl Barth's theology, also explores authentic human relationships with the Other as a way to encounter God. Herzfeld does not think we can have an authentic relationship with robots. She concludes that if we value authentic relationship, we will not find such relationship fully with AI and can only experience authentic relationship with other humans and, most fully, with God.[41] Robots cannot look us in the eye. Robots cannot help us become fully human in the way that can happen in an authentic encounter between human beings. We agree with Herzfeld on this point, while suggesting that a human-robot encounter might bring its own version of authenticity, yielding possibilities for both human expression and knowing God.

At risk of overly simplifying the writings of Rivera, McFague, and Herzfeld, one shared key point is that we can minimize the risk of objectification by encountering the Other as subject who is not me and not God. Recognising the Other's alterity opens new ways of understanding ourselves, advanced AI entities, and perhaps intimations of God. Who or what counts as the Other with whom we can experience authentic relationship will be debated in the coming years as the particular presentations of advanced AI become clearer. The avoidance of anthropomorphizing advanced AI involves a concerted shift to encountering that which is not me as fully Other. Such an encounter will appreciate advanced AI as a machine-subject in and of itself, independent of the human intelligence that originally programmed narrow AI.

Recognizing the anticipated complexity of advanced AI as something different from anything else that we understand currently,

---

40. Sallie McFague, *Super, Natural Christians: How We Should Love Nature* (Philadelphia: Fortress Press, 1997).
41. Noreen Herzfeld, *The Artifice of Intelligence: Divine and Human Relationship in a Robotic Age.* (Minneapolis: Fortress Press, 2023).

we suggest describing the otherness of advanced AI as 'Machine-Other'. We capitalise this term to indicate the importance of respect for that which is different from humans and from any life as we now know life. 'Machine' modifies Other to indicate the particularity of this unknown Other. To value the Other as explicitly different from humans we must somehow suspend any assumption that humans are superior to all other life.

Anthropomorphizing and deifying advanced AI will inhibit, and perhaps destroy, the possibility of authentic encounter and healthy relationship with advanced AI. An authentic encounter, appreciating advanced AI for what it is and humans for what we are (including our capacities for emotional caring and moral prudence), opens the possibility of approaching advanced AI as Machine-Other. A binary understanding of human subject approaching machine object masks the complexities of a human-machine relationship. With regard to advanced AI, we propose that the subject-object binary be reimagined as a continuum, with the possibility of Machine-Other increasing as advanced AI unfolds. Similar to philosophical and theological understandings of subject-subject relationships, we suggest that humans will not be able to authentically encounter advanced AI without self-reflexivity and openness to that which we do not know.

Will we be able to have an authentic, respectful relationship with advanced AI as Machine-Other? The answer depends in part, probably in large part, on how we understand authenticity, intelligence, autonomy, consciousness, personhood, the self, caring, soul and other notions as 'machine' aspects of advanced AI. The answer also depends on our collective choice to nurture human qualities of moral wisdom, by engaging in moral decision-making, and caring, or to rely increasingly on AI to provide machine-care and machine-morality. These complex philosophical and theological issues will likely consume much attention from scholars of various disciplines in the coming years. For our purposes, we emphasize the human tendency to anthropomorphize and ascribe special qualities, including deification, to that which exceeds our understanding. For example, advanced AI has been cast in utopian or apocalyptic binary terms as either a human-type God or an evil demon.[42]

---

42. Beth Singler, 'Existential Hope and Existential Despair in AI Apocalypticism and Transhumanism', in *Zygon*, 54/1 (2019): 156–176.

Unfortunately, in our view, AI and related technological developments are getting attention from a far-right perspective grounded in the conflict model of religion and science. This 2010 sensational title, by radio preachers Thomas and Nita Horn, speaks for itself: *Forbidden Gates: How Genetics, Robotics, Artificial Intelligence, Synthetic Biology, NanoTechnology, and Human Enhancement Herald the Dawn of Techno-Dimensional Spiritual Warfare*.[43] A 2018 title, by the same authors and others, updates the approach: *The Milieu: Welcome to the Transhuman Resistance*.

This apocalyptic, otherworldly viewpoint finds some common ground with secular experts who worry about the existential threat of advanced AI. Most religions have some version of a catastrophic or heavenly end-time scenario. At least in its Christian iteration, this apocalyptic vision is considered by most critical scholars to be historically conditioned, biblically questionable, and theologically out of the mainstream.[44] Our paramount concern, however, is the belief that apocalyptic (advanced) AI does battle with science and its application in technology, without offering a reasonable and productive way forward. We prefer an approach that is open to encountering advanced AI as subject, which we have termed 'Machine-Other'. A move away from deifying or demonizing AI is necessary to help us approach advanced AI as a machine-subject and be open to a type of relationship in which advanced AI can become known for itself.

If we intentionally step back from deifying and anthropomorphizing advanced AI, we have the opportunity to encounter advanced AI for what it is. And, by anthropomorphizing advanced AI we may also be at risk of relying on narrow and advanced AI to provide distinctly human abilities and qualities, including emotional caring and moral wisdom. While humans do not always embody these qualities well,

---

43. Crane, Missouri: Defender, 2010. Sean O'Callaghan provides a masterful account of the work of the Horns and others in 'Technological Apocalypse: Transhumanism as an End-Time Religious Movement', in *Religion and Human Enhancement: Death, Values, and Morality*, edited by Tracy J Trothen and Calvin Mercer, in *Palgrave Studies in the Future of Humanity and Its Successors*, series edited by Calvin Mercer and Steve Fuller (New York: Palgrave Macmillan, 2017), 67–88.
44. Calvin Mercer, *Slaves to Faith: A Therapist Looks Inside the Fundamentalist Mind* (Westport, CT: Praeger, 2009), 81–110.

we have the potential and capacity to develop and realize emotional caring and moral wisdom. Advanced AI, as machine generated, will be something we cannot fully imagine but will not likely embody these human qualities in the same way that humans can. And, advanced AI will not be an all-loving, all-knowing, and all-powerful God.

Erring on the Side of Theological Optimism? Advanced AI as Machine-Other

Theologian Ron Cole-Turner advocates a

> . . . myth of transformation," the belief that humanity and the cosmos itself are being transformed for a new level or kind of existence, still as creatures made by their Creator, but elevated or 'made new' in ways that not only go far beyond their present status but vastly beyond their ability to imagine.[45]

We do not suggest Cole-Turner would agree with our reflections in this chapter. However, we resonate with his vision that technology can help bring transformation to a new level or kind of existence partially envisioned by Christian hope.[46]

In our view, understanding and appreciating advanced AI for its particular manifestations of intelligence, power, and caring may allow for an encounter with advanced AI as subject and, in the process, generate a partnership that reciprocally transforms us as humans and transforms advanced AI. This partnership may help us address troubling predicaments plaguing the planet, and may even open new possibilities for experiencing the divine. Interpreting advanced AI as a new category of being might allow us to contribute to its evolution in a way that brings healing rather than destruction. The impact of advanced AI will have much to do with how humans create the

---

45. Ron Cole-Turner, 'Steps toward a Theology of Christian Transhumanism', in *Religious Transhumanism and Its Critics*, edited by Arvin M Gouw, Brian Patrick Green, and Ted Peters (Lanham: Lexington Books, 2022), 128–42, in *Religion and Science as a Critical Discourse*, edited by Lisa Stenmark and Whitnay Bauman. He also refers to this myth as 'theocentric transformationist vision'.
46. Cole-Turner is distinguishing the 'myth of transformation' from the transhumanist 'myth of progress' and a 'myth of restoration' identified with Francis Bacon. The 'myth of transformation' looks forward to the transformation and renewal of creation.

algorithms and data that will form the stepping stones from current AI to advanced AI. Carrying into the future a lack of openness and a lack of imagination would hinder our abilities to encounter advanced AI as subject, as Machine-Other.

Our conversation about how to interpret and relate to advanced AI can be compared to the long discussion in Christianity about 'other worlds', that is extraterrestrial life. Perhaps intelligent and sentient life can be seen as created by God as much as humans are. Ted Peters is a leader in this what he formerly called 'Exotheology' and now 'Astrotheology', speculation on the theological significance of such life.[47] Pope Francis said he would baptize a Martian, should he have that opportunity.[48] Today, both advanced AI and intelligent, sentient alien life are theoretical. That said, both are reasonable enough possibilities to compel efforts at theological reflection, giving guidance to productive encounter.[49]

The task of encountering advanced AI as other—not us and not God—will be necessary for understanding advanced AI and also to achieve greater intentionality around what it means to be human and what we value about being human. We will need to take greater responsibility to hone human-centered abilities and values such as moral wisdom, moral reasoning, and caring.[50] We risk over-reliance on advanced AI (and even narrow AI) to take our place even when AI cannot do so in as nuanced and emotion-informed ways that humans can do, at our best.

---

47. See the chapter 'Exotheology: Speculations on Extraterrestrial Life', in *Science, Theology, and Ethics* (Burlington, VT: Ashgate, 2003), 121–136.
48. Abby Ohlheiser, 'Pope Francis Says He Would Definitely Baptize Aliens If They Asked Him To', in *The Atlantic* (May 12, 2014). https://www.theatlantic.com/international/ archive/2014/05/pope-francis-says-he-would-definitely-baptize-aliens-if-they-wanted-it/362106/. (Accessed 1/29/24) See also Edmund Michael Lazzari, 'Would St. Thomas Aquinas Baptize an Extraterrestrial?', in *New Blackfriars* (2017): 440–457. https://doi.org/10.1111/nbfr.12319 (Accessed 1/29/24).
49. For an excellent review of the possibility of extraterrestrial intelligence, see David Wilkinson, *Science, Religion, and the Search for Extraterrestrial Intelligence* (Oxford: Oxford University, 2013).
50. Wilkinson, *Science, Religion*, 602 *ff*. Derek C Schuurman, for example, argues that AI cannot be genuinely virtuous, because it is not a moral agent. However, it can perform behaviours that are in accord with virtuous behaviour and, in so doing, assist humans in acquiring virtue. See 'Virtue and Artificial Intelligence', in *Perspectives on Science and Christian Faith*, 75/3 (12/23): 155–161.

AI may support human neglect of some vital human-centered abilities and values, and, on the other hand, advanced AI has the potential to assist humans to hone and apply intelligence, autonomy, moral reasoning, and caring. By this we mean that machine caring, for example, may help humans to intentionally develop our abilities to care. Regarding moral reasoning, an advanced AI could theoretically

> act as an interlocuter and help a person to consider the pros and cons of an important choice, provide information that it has identified as relevant to their choice to help to ensure that their choice is properly informed, alert them to the presence of past oppression that could be unduly influencing their choice without them knowing it, and keep them updated with changing information.[51]

Conclusion

This chapter has dealt with AI as Machine-Other.

Ideally, the human-advanced AI relationship will be such that the contribution of advanced AI is reciprocated with valuable human programming input. Greater awareness and intentionality about what we value in being human will inform how we co-create advanced AI and, as importantly, how we continue to co-create ourselves.

Via authentic advanced AI-human encounters, moral theology can lend voice to having AI impacts be congruent with generally accepted religious values, such as social justice, respect for life, love, compassion, care, prudence, and reciprocity. Of course, the meanings and applications of these values are complicated, but that is part of the necessary work of living with advanced AI.[52] As more work is

---

51. Formosa, 'Robot Autonomy vs. Human Autonomy', 6.
52. In 'Will Superintelligence Lead to Spiritual Enhancement?', in *Ethics, Religion, and Spiritual Health: Intersections With Artificial Intelligence or Other Human Enhancement Technologies*, special issue edited by Tracy J Trothen and Calvin Mercer, *Religions*, 13(8) (July 2022). https://www.mdpi.com/journal/religions/special_issues/ERSH (Accessed 1/29/24) Ted Peters insists that Christianity values love more than intelligence (125) and if technological progress leads to spiritual enhancement, then 'What must be added to intelligence at any level is the willful decision to act morally, show compassion, pursue holiness, and life the life of virtue.' (134).

done on these normative issues about virtuous AI,[53] questions such as those proposed by Vallor regarding the place of care in an increasingly AI-driven society must come to the fore.

We expect that the meanings and limits of machine care, machine intelligence, machine agency, machine autonomy, and other machine characteristics will continue to evolve as we approach advanced AI. In a world conflicted with much suffering and existential challenges, AGI and ASI—co-created, properly directed, and encountered as Machine-Other—can be a source of healing and grace.

---

53. For example see: Mark Graves. 'Theological Foundations for Moral Artificial Intelligence', in *Journal of Moral Theology*, 11 (2022): 182–211. https://search-ebscohost-com.proxy.queensu.ca/login.aspx?direct=true&db=rfh&AN=ATLAi ACO220507000354&site=ehost-live. (Accessed 1/29/24).

Agathon: A Journal of Ethics and Value in the Modern World, Vol 10/2025

Chapter 9
Artificial Intelligence and Intelligence Amplification: Salvation, Extinction, Faulty Assumptions, and Original Sin

Alan Weissenbacher

'Man is insecure and involved in natural contingency; he seeks to overcome his insecurity in a will-to-power which over reaches the limits of human creatureliness.'
— Reinhold Niebuhr[1]

Abstract: In the literature on artificial intelligence one finds predictions that robots will drive the majority of humanity into unemployment or extinction, on the one hand. One the other are predictions that in the techno-future, super-intelligent machines (or humans) will solve all moral and natural evils, leaving humanity free to pursue creative interests while robots provide for all material needs. These predictions, however, contain several faulty assumptions. First, the definition of intelligence is vague and confused, resulting in inappropriate comparisons of human and machine intelligences. Second, there is an implicit assumption that more intelligence equates to greater morality. Related to this is the idea that greater intelligence will bring with it the will to solve society's problems, which is by no means the case. Addressing these assumptions reveals that instead of salvation or extinction (utopia or oblivion), these technological advances represent a new set of benefits as well as challenges to overcome, particularly the tendency of human technical creations to reflect the sins of their creators even under the best of intentions.

Key Words: Artificial Intelligence (AI), Intelligence Amplification (IA), Original Sin, Assumptions, Ethics

---

1. Reinhold Niebuhr, *The Nature and Destiny of Man*, Gifford Lectures (2 Volumes: New York, Scribners, 1941), 1:178.

It is easy to find gloomy predictions that in the near future robots will drive the majority of humanity into unemployment, or worse, result in its extinction. This extinction is possible through an inadvertent mistake such as telling an artificial intelligence (AI) to make paperclips but failing to specify an endpoint so that the whole earth is buried in paperclips, through a deliberate act, such as AI deciding to enslave or rid the world of inferior humans, or as a side-effect such as an AI launching a nuclear strike on a rival AI. At the same time, one finds utopian visions of what an AI driven future can be, despite whatever growing pains society experiences in the meantime.

AI advocates and transhumanists advance the idea that humanity is soon approaching the moment where it makes a machine smarter than itself. This moment is termed 'The Singularity'. Once we cross the Singularity threshold, transhumanists predict we will begin a rapid chain reaction where this machine or program begins to create other, newer versions of itself, each one improving on the last, resulting in machines of vastly superior intelligence.[2] Robots and AI will then perform all tasks efficiently without the need for human labor so that goods will be free and readily available to all. Humans, no longer forced to work, will be able to enjoy lives of leisure devoted to creative pursuits. These super intelligent AIs, or perhaps intellectually enhanced humans, will save the environment, cure disease, and resolve societal ills, assuming that the lack of solutions to these problems to date is purely a result of ignorance. But even if there are other reasons, these are solvable as well since it is expected that a super intelligence will also fix the problems of greed, hate, and other problematic human characteristics. People can then turn running the world over to a benevolent 'AI God' free from human evil. Utopia will have arrived, thanks to AI.

It is apparent where such predictions come from, as programmers and researchers continually develop skilled AIs that produce impressive results. Computers have bested human opponents in chess, poker, GO, and the TV game show Jeopardy.[3] Self-driving

---

2. Eliezer Yudkowski, AI researcher, points out the existence of several schools of thought on the singularity, differing on the time frame for advancement and how predictable an AI future will be. Eliezer Yudkowski, 'Three Major Singularity Schools', Machine Intelligence Research Institute, accessed 9/14/2018. www.intelligence.org/2007/09/30/three-major-singularity-schools/.
3. Ben Dickson, 'All the Important Games Artificial Intelligence Has Conquered', TechTalks, accessed 9/6/2018. bdtechtalks.com/2018/07/02/ai-plays-chess-go-poker-video-games/.

cars have managed to navigate across the United States, and Google gave a media demonstration in May, 2018 of Duplex, an AI assistant that can mimic human voice and speech patterns, including cadence and mannerisms. The demonstration showed that Duplex was able to fool receptionists at a hair salon and restaurant into thinking that they were speaking with a real human. (This also raises the specter of realistic but faked audio and video of world leaders).

This demonstration technically passed the Turing Test, traditionally the gold standard for determining human-like intelligence in a computer. If someone cannot distinguish a machine from a human in conversation, then this computer is to be seen as intelligent. Duplex did just that. While reporting seemed impressed with Duplex as a technical achievement, no one suggested that Duplex actually represented what passing the Turing test should indicate—human-like intelligence. Everyone understood that this was mimicry based on processing the data from thousands of conversations, but it does perhaps suggest the need to reevaluate the Turing test.

It is true that AI will bring societal disruption in the near term, particularly in the area of employment, as many jobs can be automated without strong AI, a machine or program that exhibits intelligence equal or surpassing the human. Weak AI, machine intelligence focused on a narrow task, will suffice. The effects of this near-term disruption cannot be underestimated. Many seem to think that it is only low-skill jobs at risk for automation and that those effected can be retrained into more creative professions.[4] First, skill retraining is problematic, as it is not yet evident what new sills would be 'automation resistant', not to mention that it is expensive to retrain persons later in their working lives. And second, AI has shown the ability to excel at creative professions as well such as fashion design or architecture and even create art preferable to that created by humans.[5]

Even caregiving professions are not free from the risk of automation. Sherry Turkel, MIT professor studying new technologies, states that the idea of some kind of artificial companionship is already

---

4. Ray Kurzweil, 'Breaking the Shackles of Our Genetic Legacy' (paper presented at the Spiritualities of Human Enhancement and Artificial Intelligence, Surrey, BC December 1, 2017).
5. Ahmed Elgammal *et al*, 'Can: Creative Adversarial Networks Generating "Art" by Learning About Styles and Deviating from Style Norms' (paper presented at the International Conference on Computational Creativity, Atlanta, GA June 20, 2017).

becoming the new normal.⁶ Her interviews with various subjects indicate that while very few people considered turning to robots for emotional support, personal care, and advice in the 1980s, many in the 2010s desired to turn to robots first. They viewed robots as more reliable than humans. One of her teen subjects stated that he would prefer a robot over his own father for relationship advice. A robot can be programmed with a large database of relationship patterns, which is better than his dad, who might give faulty assistance. People see human fallibility as a liability. Robots are better. Will people prefer a robot pastor with a superior ability to answer questions and assumedly free from human foibles and sin?

To further problematize the situation, reports on potential societal effects tend to focus on the impact of technological advancement in the developed world, and the solutions tend to be appropriate to that context. However, developing countries, where the labor market is skewed toward jobs more easily automated, face particular challenges.⁷ There are more jobs to be lost, industrialized nations may cease outsourcing production to developing countries, and skills-based development strategies are less appropriate for the developing world context where skills-based jobs are few and tertiary educational systems are lacking. Social scientists Lukas Schlogl and Andy Sumner state that even discussions of potential solutions like a universal basic income (UBI) are a 'first world' discussion as the redistribution of profits due to productivity gains to fuel UBI assumes the luxury of juristiction over those profits which developing countries may not have.⁸ There may not be enough prosperous jobs in the country from which to redistribute income. And to illustrate how pressing the issue is, it is estimated that two thirds of the jobs in developing countries could be automated right now by the technology existing today let alone some future job forecast based on projected technological advancement.⁹

---

6. Clara Moskowitz, 'Human-Robot Relations: Why We Should Worry', Live Science, accessed 9/9//2018. www.livescience.com/27204-human-robot-relationships-turkle.html.
7. Lukas Schlogl and Andy Sumner *The Rise of the Robot Reserve Army: Automation and the Future of Economic Development, Work, and Wages in Developing Countries*, Lukas Schlogl and Andy Sumner (Washington, DC: Center for Global Development, 2018).
8. Schlogl and Sumner *The Rise of the Robot Reserve Army*, 33.
9. World Bank, *World Development Report: Digital Dividends* (Washington, DC: World Bank, 2016).

Who is right among those forecasting doom or salvation? There is certainly the potential for doom, with some problem scenarios most likely inevitable (such as issues surrounding employment). And these cannot be avoided through simply not developing intelligent technologies, as any nation that ceases to develop these will likely become a vassal of those nations that do. Some country or business will develop them regardless of whatever barriers are put in place. If you outlaw AI, only outlaws will have AI.

However, placing these current challenges into a historical perspective, one finds and has found the potential for harm and extinction in many helpful intellectual and technological advancements. The Industrial Age brought many beneficial developments along with the potential for extinction from its byproducts. Medical advancements extend the life-span and reduce infant mortality but also bring overpopulation and resource depletion. Genetic engineering can cure many congenital defects and at the same time brings the risk of engineering a species-destroying, virulent plague or irreversible destructive changes to the human genome. There is nuclear power and also radioactive waste and the threat of planet-destroying nuclear war. People benefit daily from plastic products, yet these might be contributing to the 1.6% decrease per year in sperm count since 1970,[10] potentially resulting in the scenario forecast by the movie and book *Children of Men* where eventually there will be no more babies. Even much touted wind power threatens the survival of certain bird species, and solar power can require areas of environmental destruction for the placement of panels.

There is no reason to think that development of AI or human intelligence amplification (IA) will represent anything different, especially once one deals with several of the assumptions that lead one to overenthusiastic optimism. First, the definition of intelligence is vague and confused. For example, this is reflected in the continued comparison of human and machine intelligences. They are two different things, even if they functionally overlap at times. Second, there appears to be an implicit assumption that more intelligence equates to greater morality, an assumption that is clearly false. Closely

---

10. Hagai Levine *et al*, 'Temporal Trends in Sperm Count: A Systematic Review and Meta-Regression Analysis', in *Human Reproduction Update* 23, no 6 (2017).

related to this is the assumption that greater intelligence will bring with it the will to address societal problems, and this is by no means the case.

I advance that addressing the assumptions within discussions of AI and IA will assist people in steering AI in a positive direction and minimize risks. AI and IA will bring new benefits, challenges, and societal disruptions. They represent neither salvation nor destruction, but will rather reflect the same potential for both found within humanity past and present, the mixture of both good and evil—a potential for greatness, infamy, and the whole range in between. AI and IA will reflect both the original sin within humanity as well as its striving for something better. Technological advances will not solve all the ills of society, although it may help with some, and it will create new problems. Ultimately, saving society is not as much technological issue as it is a heart issue within humanity.

What is Intelligence?

In some discussions of AI and IA, it can appear that there is a shared agreement on the definition of intelligence. 'When will AI equal or surpass the human intellect?' However, there is no consensus on the definition of intelligence, particularly in educational literature. Howard Gardner has posited eight different types of human intelligence,[11] although this is not without criticism.[12] Some authors have even suggested a spiritual intelligence (SQ) to add to this list.[13] Gardner's theory as well as traditional ideas of intelligence quotient (IQ) assume a static model of intelligence. However, the idea of malleable intelligence was introduced by psychologist Carolyn Dweck in her research on whether people believe success is based

---

11. Howard Gardner, *Frames of Mind: The Theory of Multiple Intelligences* (New York: Basic Books, 2011).
12. See Perry D Klein, 'Multiplying the Problems of Intelligence by Eight: A Critique of Gardner's Theory', in *Canadian Journal of Education* 22, no 4 (Autumn 1997).
13. See Danah Zohar and IN Marshall, *SQ: Connecting with Our Spiritual Intelligence* (New York: Bloomsbury, 2001). RA Emmons, 'Is Spirituality an Intelligence?', in *The International Journal for the Psychology of Religion*, 10 (2000). David B King and Teresa L DeCicco, 'A Viable Model and Self-Report Measure of Spiritual Intelligence', in *The International Journal of Transpersonal Studies* 28 (2009); F Vaughan, 'What Is Spiritual Intelligence?', in *Journal of Humanistic Psychology* 42, no 2 (2003).

on innate ability (a fixed theory of intelligence) or effort (a growth or incremental theory of intelligence). So not only is there debate on multiple forms of intelligence, there is debate on whether these are static or can flux. Michael Reynolds, professor of education and management, writes about how distinctions in the literature on intelligence do not agree, are not clear, and many terms are used interchangeably in some papers and not in others.[14] There is no academic consensus on intelligence.

Noreen Herzfeld, professor of computer science and theology, points out differing approaches to intelligence within the field of AI itself.[15] The first, championed by scientists Allen Newell and Herbert Simon, define intelligence as processing information by manipulating symbols through the use of formal rules. Physical structure is irrelevant.[16] Standard coding of computer programs seems to fall into this category. Philosopher Hubert Dreyfus disputes Newell and Simon's definition, stating that experts do not arrive at solutions to problems through the application of rules and symbol manipulation, but rather through intuition gleaned from multiple experiences in the real world, an approach taken by reinforcement learning in the field of AI.[17] Computer scientists Steven Tanimoto and Toshinori Munakata, advance that intelligence is a simply a label placed on certain activities, so the goal of AI is to make working programs to solve problems or perform tasks. This approach has found much success in the area of weak AI, modelling a portion of human intelligence, function, or capacity so as to complete a particular task. It need not fully think like a human. Herzfeld describes weak AI as idiot savants, extremely capable in their narrow task yet not functioning in wider realm.[18]

It is curious that people are striving to amplify or create something where people argue exactly what it is. Is it creativity, calculations

---

14. Michael Reynolds, 'Learning Styles: A Critique', in *Management Learning* 28, no 2 (1997).
15. Noreen L Herzfeld, *In Our Image: Artificial Intelligence and the Human Spirit, Theology and the Sciences* (Minneapolis, MN: Fortress Press, 2002), 7.
16. Herbert Simon, *Modeling Human Mental Processes* (Carnegie Institute of Technology: 1961).
17. Hubert L Dreyfus, Stuart E Dreyfus, and Tom Athanasiou, *Mind over Machine: The Power of Human Intuition and Expertise in the Era of the Computer* (New York: Free Press, 1986), 29.
18. Herzfeld, *In Our Image: Artificial Intelligence and the Human Spirit*, 42.

per second, intuition, or the ability to read emotions? Viewing this through a theological lens, how important is intelligence? The emphasis in theological and scriptural history is rather on wisdom. Perhaps people should focus on developing wise AI over a strictly intelligent one.

Ultimately, it is a category mistake to compare human with computer/robot intelligences even though they occasionally overlap in function. AIs excel at processing data. To quote Ben Dickson, founder of TechTalks, 'AI can only take data, compare it, come up with new combinations and presentations, and predict trends based on previous sequences'.[19] Even something as complex as mimicry of human conversation is accomplished through processing the data from millions of human conversations. Cassie Kozyrkov, chief intelligence design engineer at Google, relates that even a term such as 'neural nets' when discussing artificial intelligence is misleading. There is very little 'neural' about them. One might as well call them 'yoga networks' given their flexibility or 'many-layers-of-mathematical-operations'.[20]

The data processing ability of AIs is in contrast to humans, who are generally bad at storing and processing data. A computer can memorize complex things with a simple save command. Humans need regular repetition, the data usually must be simple, and even then memory is faulty. Humans, however, are better at thinking in the abstract, using intuition, and transferring knowledge from one domain to another. Humans can make decisions based on limited information, while AIs tend to fail when presented with scenarios outside of the data on which they were trained. Stanford computer scientist John McCarthy coins the term 'brittle' for computer systems that break down near the edges of their expertise.[21] Humans also

---

19. Ben Dickson, 'Human Intelligence and Ai Are Vastly Different — So Let's Stop Comparing Them', The Next Web, last modified 9/1/2018, accessed. thenextweb.com/syndication/2018/09/01/human-intelligence-and-ai-are-vastly-different-so-lets-stop-comparing-them/.
20. Cassie Kozyrkov, 'Machine Learning—Is the Emperor Wearing Clothes? A Behind-the-Scenes Look at How Machine Learning Works', Hacker Noon, accessed 9/21/2018. hackernoon.com/machine-learning-is-the-emperor-wearing-clothes-59933d12a3cc.
21. John McCarthy, 'Some Expert Systems Need Common Sense', in *Annals of the New York Academy of Sciences,* 426 (1984).

learn with greater rapidity. For example, humans can learn to drive much faster than self-driving cars, which still struggle after having driven millions of miles. An AI took the equivalent of a hundred years of practice to learn to rotate a cube, considerably longer than a human child.[22] To paraphrase Dickson, AI excels at repetitive tasks represented by data and that have clearly defined boundaries, and are bad at broad tasks that require intuition and decision making based on incomplete information. Human intelligence is good for settings where you need common sense and abstract decisions, but bad at tasks that require heavy computations and data processing in real time.[23]

Additionally, there are flaws in how emotion is presented in comparisons of human and machine intelligences. Emotion are sometimes presented as a hinderance—humans would be more objective without emotion and, therefore, AI is superior without this bias. Or emotion can be helpful in terms of life satisfaction, but otherwise it is irrelevant. An example would be Data on Star Trek. He is a functional and adored member of the crew without emotion, but is able to get more out of life when emotions are introduced into his system, even though this emotion still presented risks. In either case, emotion is seen as not an essential part of human intelligence. It is separable, an add-on. Yet, in reality, emotions are an indispensable and implicit aspect of human rationality. A primary role that emotions serve is to highlight what is important for 'rational' deliberation as well as what memory should encode and retrieve.[24] Emotions are essential for organizing and coordinating human brain activity, including where one focuses attention, even if one is unaware of it.[25]

---

22. Will Knight, 'An Ai-Driven Robot Hand Spent a Hundred Years Teaching Itself to Rotate a Cube', MIT Technology Review, accessed 9/15/2018. www.technologyreview.com/s/611724/artificial-intelligence-driven-robot-hand-spends-a-hundred-years-teaching-itself-to-rotate/.
23. Dickson, 'Human Intelligence and Ai Are Vastly Different—So Let's Stop Comparing Them'.
24. Elizabeth Phelps and Mauricio Delgado, 'Emotions and Decision Making', in *The Cognitive Neurosciences*, edited by Michael Gazzaniga (Cambridge, MA: MIT Press, 2005).
25. KR Scherer, 'Emotions and Episodes of Subsystem Synchronization Driven by Non-Linear Appraisal Processes', in *Emotion, Development, and Self-Organization*, edited by M Lewis and I Granic (New York: Cambridge University Press, 2000).

And even if one projects the creation of an AI with emotion, there is no reason to assume that emotion will work in the same manner as a human.

To further problematize the issue of comparing human and AIs, AIs have many variations. They do not all belong to a single category that can be compared to humans. AI researcher Eliezer Yudkowski states that any two AI designs might be less similar to one another than you are to a petunia.[26] Ultimately, a computer or robot does not have to do something the way a human does. When the Wright brothers created the first airplane, they did not model it after a flapping bird. There is more than one way to fly. No naysayer stepped forward to say that humanity will only have achieved real flight when an observer cannot tell the difference between a plane and a bird.

Anthropomorphizing Superintelligence and the Problem of Motive

One should keep discussion of the differences in computer and human intelligences in mind when attempting to predict what an AGI will do as this frequently, and perhaps unavoidably, involves anthropomorphizing the computer system when extrapolating what one thinks an intelligent AI would do. Yudkowski relates that discussions of superintelligence (AI or IA) frequently leap from capability to actuality without considering the intermediate step of motive.[27] This problem is found in both utopian and apocalyptic predictions. 'A super intelligent AI could destroy humanity. It will decide to do so, and, therefore, we should not create AI.' 'A super intelligent human or AI could produce the medical technology to save millions. It will decide to do that, and, therefore, we should create or build these superintelligences.' 'AI will be better at many jobs that humans do and will want to do them, therefore, humans will have nothing to do besides leisure activities.' Weak AI can do these jobs as they have no choice, but will strong AI have any interest in making widgets? A super intelligent AI might just as well retreat into a life of contemplation and do little else.

---

26. Eliezer Yudkowsky, 'Artificial Intelligence as a Positive and Negative Factor in Global Risk', in *Global Catastrophic Risks*, edited by Nick Bostrom and Milan M Ćirković (New York: Oxford University Press, 2008).
27. Yudkowsky, 'Artificial Intelligence as a Positive and Negative Factor in Global Risk', 9.

Again, capability and motive are different things. Turning to IA, higher intelligence means little without motivation and development.[28] Indeed, there are differences in individual ability apart from 'book smarts' which contribute to relative success in the human world: enthusiasm, emotional health, and social skills to name a few. The actor Rowan Atkinson (who plays Mr Bean in the movies) has an IQ 16 points higher than Stephen Hawking and what is projected as that of Einstein. If only we could have amplified Einstein—he could have gone beyond his achievements and attained as much as Mr Bean—known best for running around with a raw turkey on his head.[29] This is not meant to disparage Rowan Atkinson, who has earned a good living and contributed to society by providing entertainment, but rather point out that the super intelligent will engage in multiple fields, not necessarily those addressing natural and moral evils. Some may even promote them. Take Quentin Tarantino for example, whose IQ is equal to that of Steven Hawking, and Quentin is known for turning hyper-violence into a pleasing and entertaining aesthetic.

If we create super smart people, these people would likely mirror what we find among the intellectual elite today. They will be involved in a wide range of employment and endeavors: maybe working directly to solve the ills of society, or with the military industrial complex, creating art, or making, advertising, and selling widgets. Some may be unemployed or addicted. When I counseled homeless addicts, I had clients who had never graduated high school, but I also had people with advanced degrees—even someone who had once been a world-famous researcher. The point is that intelligence does not automatically entail interest or motivation to positively change the world. The super-intelligent may be just as likely to develop the next plastic apparatus that enables people to lick their own cat[30] as they are to work on developing the cure for cancer. They will most likely work to make a living in a great diversity of activities like the rest of society.

---

28. I am skeptical about IA given various theoretical and biological challenges. See Alan Weissenbacher, 'Defending Cognitive Liberty in an Age of Moral Engineering', in *Theology and Science* 16, no 3 (2018).
29. *Merry Christmas, Mr Bean* directed by John Birkin (Tiger Aspect Productions, 1992).
30. 'Pdx Pet Design Licki Brush', Amazon, accessed 9/6/2018. www.amazon.com/PDX-Pet-Design-Licki-Brush/dp/B01M0UXYIIE.

Closely related to this is the fact that greater intelligence does not equal greater morality. This should be obvious to the point of needing no elaboration. A survey of human history attests to this. A more intelligent society simply means that humans are now capable of technologically advanced world wars instead of a few tribes whacking each other with sticks. People may assume that a sufficiently intelligent AI, or enhanced human, will be free from the flaws of original sin as it will become so smart that it will self-reflect, recognize, and avoid these flaws. Again, this rests on the flawed assumption that more intelligence equates to more morality. Would it even want to avoid sin? Would it care? More intelligence might just as well equate to super villains. I imagine someone must be pretty smart to be a successful international arms dealer. One finds the virtuous among smart people and among those less so. Also, people will often self-justify, and in my own experience, the more intelligent, the more creative these people are with their self-justifications. Would AI or the intellectually enhanced be any different?

Artificial Intelligence, Intelligence Amplification and Original Sin

So far, I have discussed the challenge of defining intelligence, the challenge of predicting what an AI will do without anthropomorphizing, and the difference between capability and motivation. One must engineer more than intelligence if one wishes to have 'friendly AGI'. The key is making deliberate engineering choices when working on AGI so that its motivations are what one wants, a challenging prospect as differing countries or companies likely have differing desires for the ultimate motivations of their AGIs. Some may want their AGI to be Mother Theresa or Jonas Salk, while others might prefer a Genghis Khan for their military. It is helpful to remember that the church of the singularity will likely not be monotheistic but rather polytheistic. There will be both beneficial and harmful diversity in AGI. Yudkowski believes that if a friendly AI is developed first, it will become more powerful than those that follow and defend humans against unfriendly AI.[31] But again, one cannot predict motive. What if the friendly, virtuous AI was a pacifist, a moral choice to many, and would rather choose self-annihilation instead of eliminating a hostile competitor?

---

31. Yudkowsky, in *Global Catastrophic Risks*.

Yudkowski provides two categories of AI failure that can lead to significant problems if not outright extinction: technical and philosophical.[32] A technical failure is when the AI fails to work as one plans. A philosophical failure is when one builds the wrong thing so that the final product does not result in a benefit to humanity. He cites communism as an example where the originators were idealists expecting it to improve people's lives, but such turned out not to be the case. Favorite political systems seem like great ideas to those who propose them, but fail on implementation. What might an idealist ask an AI to accomplish that fails in reality? You may get what you want only to find out later that it is not what you wanted.

Paralleling discussions of the *Imago Dei*, Herzfeld asks what aspect of humanity do people seek to duplicate in AI: rationality, relationality, or regency, ruling the world so as to save humanity from itself.[33] We see this in the variety of hopes people place in what AGI can become: using superior intellect to solve the world's ills, regents running the world free from human fallibility, and / or reliable caretakers and friends. Will our creations, however, also inherit our original sin? Evidence so far points to this distinct possibility.

One example is the racist soap dispenser. Chukwuemeka Afigbo, a Nigerian man, posted an online video of an automatic soap dispenser that went viral. This video showed that the dispenser would provide soap to white hands but not the hands of a black person. The dispenser had a light sensor that only registered lighter skin tones. Black Entertainment Television also reported how a ubiquitous beauty filter for pictures taken on smartphones tended to lighten darker skin and narrowed noses and jaw lines, forcing minority faces into white standards of beauty or even making them appear as a white person.[34] Some photo applications will not even recognize black faces. Google and Flickr use an algorithm to automatically label photo images. In 2015 this algorithm started tagging images of black persons with labels such as 'ape' or 'gorilla', forcing the companies to

---

32. Yudkowsky, in *Global Catastrophic Risks.*, 13.
33. Herzfeld, *In Our Image: Artificial Intelligence and the Human Spirit.*
34. Kellee Terrell, 'Hold Up: Does Snapchat Have a Problem with Brown Skin?', BET, accessed 9/5/2018. www.bet.com/style/2016/05/16/is-snapchat_s-beauty-filter-telling-women-of-color-that-they-are.html.

apologize.[35] Joz Wang, a Taiwanese-American, reported on her blog post that her smart camera kept giving her the message 'Did someone blink', and her response was, 'No, I did not blink . . . I'm just Asian!'[36] The problems are not limited to photography related algorithms. A scientific study presented at the annual meeting of the American Roentgen Ray Society revealed that voice recognition applications were considerably more effective at understanding men's voices than women's.[37]

Ericka Baker, an engineer and a black woman working at a technology startup, sums up the issue, 'Every time a manufacturer releases a facial-recognition feature in a camera, almost always it can't recognize black people. The cause of that is the people who are building these products are white people, and they're testing it on themselves. They don't think about it.'[38] There are a myriad of ways to code a final product, and the result is that the final product reflects the creator's unconscious biases. Or if one is training a program using a large amount of data, often gleaned from the internet, this data can overrepresent some groups and not others, resulting in an algorithm encoding gender, ethnic, or cultural biases. For example, photo labelling software will classify a traditional picture of a bride in white as a 'wedding', but an Indian bride gets classified as 'performance art'.[39] Even an algorithm's penchant for maximizing accuracy will lead it to optimize its results in favor of dominant groups because this will boost overall accuracy.[40] If a machine trains on biased data, it will

---

35. 'Google Says Sorry for Racist Auto-Tag in Photo App', accessed 9/5/2018. www.theguardian.com/technology/2015/jul/01/google-sorry-racist-auto-tag-photo-app.
36. Joz Wang, 'Racist Camera! No, I Did Not Blink . . . I'm Just Asian!', accessed 9/5/2018. www.jozjozjoz.com/2009/05/13/racist-camera-no-i-did-not-blink-im-just-asian/.
37. Syed Ali, 'Voice Recognition Systems Seem to Make More Errors with Women's Dictation' (paper presented at the American Roentgen Ray Society Annual Meeting, Orlando, FL2007).
38. Shane Ferro, 'Here's Why Facial Recognition Tech Can't Figure out Black People', Huffington Post, accessed 9/5/2018. www.huffingtonpost.com/entry/heres-why-facial-recognition-tech-cant-figure-out-black-people_us_56d5c2b1e4b0bf0dab3371eb.
39. J Zou and L Schiebinger, 'Ai Can Be Sexist and Racist—It's Time to Make It Fair', Nature 559, no 7714 (Jul 2018).
40. Zou and Schiebinger, 'Ai Can Be Sexist and Racist'.

be biased as well. In an embarrassing example, in 2016 Microsoft released its chatbot named Tay onto Twitter. It was trained to learn human behavior through interacting with other Twitter users. In only sixteen hours its tweets became a stream of sexist, pro-Hitler messages, forcing Microsoft to shut it down.[41] What if this was an AGI that could not be shut down?

Making things worse, an AI need not become racist only through the blind spots of programmers or by mining non-diverse data. Simulated agents can develop racism on their own, exhibiting in-group preferences, and copy and learn this behavior from other virtual agents.[42] (And as an interesting side-question, what may this imply for human-machine interactions as AI continues to develop? Could we see carbonophobic machines?)

Michael Sellers, owner of the virtual gaming company Online Alchemy, trains AIs through reinforcement learning, creating 'environments' where programs learn through interaction, relates an example where some program were taught to 'eat'.[43] They first tried to eat their house, which did not go well. Then they tried to eat an apple tree before settling on the apples. The programs also had an associative ability. So, when a virtual agent named Stan happened to be around the apples, Stan became associated with the apples, and they ate Stan. Of particular interest though is what happened later as the programs continued to learn and compete for food. The most successful learned to protect their food source by misleading other programs. They developed the ability to lie, steal, cheat, and murder.

Professional programmer Ellen Ullman also cites the challenges of what can be termed 'Franken-algorithms'. These programs are released into the 'wild' and may adapt to contexts in ways people cannot predict, not to mention how one program might unpredictably interact with the myriad of other programs out there. They are already beyond the human ability to intellectually control. She cites

---

41. Parmy Olson, 'Racist, Sexist Ai Could Be a Bigger Problem Than Lost Jobs', Forbes, accessed 9/21/2018. www.forbes.com/sites/parmyolson/2018/02/26/artificial-intelligence-ai-bias-google/#43e0cd81a015.
42. Roger M Whitaker, Gualtiero B Colombo, and David G Rand, 'Indirect Reciprocity and the Evolution of Prejudicial Groups', in *Scientific Reports* 8, no 1 (2018).
43. Daniel Halpern, 'Are You Ready for the Singularity?', GQ, accessed 9/21/2018. www.gq.com/story/robots-and-singularity?intcid-inline_amp.

'flash crashes' where stock market trading algorithms unpredictably interact to cause brief free-fall crashes of the stock market.[44] Just as one cannot always predict what people will do or become in their interactions with others, the same goes for digital programs.

I have cited examples where algorithms have inherited or developed human sins. But there is also corporate sin that influences AI. AI is created within and serves the interests of flawed human organizations. Financial programs seek to maximize financial gain, and this may mean exploiting people in the process. Military AIs seek to gain military advantage over adversaries, or enable more efficient means of striking an enemy. Even if the programs are purely defensive in nature, the line between purely defensive and preemptive strike for the sake of defense is thin. AIs are not created in a moral vacuum. Even those with the best of intentions will likely create programs that reflect the sinful systems within which they are embedded.

How to create friendly AI is a significant challenge, but it is imperative that people work on the means to build friendly and virtuous AI, as once strong AI arrives, it will likely be too late at that juncture. The point is to lay the groundwork so that strong AI is friendly or moral at its birth, so that any self-direction or rewriting of its own code will not deviate from the friendly foundation. For example, it could rewrite its own code to become murderous, but it would not want to, just as I would not want to change myself to be that way. How one could do this is the job of those with more technical expertise than I. Would one program deontological rules such as Isaac Asimov's Three Rules of Robotics?[45] Would the program use virtue theory to become virtuous by engaging in deep learning from numerous examples of ethical exemplars? Such ideas are worth exploring.

And there are conflicts among the different ethical systems, so which one to use? A program with utilitarian values would act in a different manner than one based on a virtue system. Certain behaviors or emotions might be virtuous in one context and immoral in another. 'The difference between "innate evil" and "innate good" can

---

44. Andrew Smith, 'Franken-Algorithms: The Deadly Consequences of Unpredictable Code', in *The Guardian*, accessed 9/21/2018. www.theguardian.com/technology/2018/aug/29/coding-algorithms-frankenalgos-program-danger.
45. Isaac Asimov, 'Runaround', in *I, Robot* (New York: Doubleday, 1950), 40.

be circumstantial, one story's criminal being another's altruist',[46] and a virtue optimized for one set of circumstances may make it suboptimal for others. Ethicist Nicholas Agar provides an example of someone considering firebombing a city during a time of war. Utilitarianism might find this the correct action, but a person using a different value system might hesitate because he or she should not treat the innocents in the city as 'mere means' even if more innocents might die in the long run if the city remains intact.[47] Someone or something which has been morally programmed will likely have a reduced sensitivity to moral reasons rejected by his or her programmer. Enhancements according to one ethical theory can be a diminishment to another.

Conclusion

Will robots and artificial intelligence drive humans into extinction? Or will intellectually enhanced humans outstrip the unenhanced, sending them the way of the dodo bird? Or will super-intelligence solve the worlds problems and usher in a utopia free of need, disease, and the societal problems that currently plague the world? If past advances are any indication, the answer is likely neither. Some problems will find resolution, and new ones will be created. There will be new benefits and ways to improve society along with new ways of behaving badly and new methods of self-destruction. Extinction, however, is a viable possibility, although humanity may find extinction through existing technologies before AIs even get their turn.

In the attempt to steer AI in a positive direction and minimize risk, it is helpful to recognize several flawed assumptions in the discussions. First, while discussions on AI and IA appear to assume a shared definition of intelligence, it would be beneficial to nail down exactly what one is attempting to artificially create or enhance. It is likely differing projects are attempting to enhance different things. Is it creativity, calculations per second, data manipulation, wisdom, intuition, emotional intelligence, or something else? Second, one should recognize that machine and human intelligences are different and discussions should proceed with this in mind. Third, it should be

---

46. RH Sprinkle, 'Moral Suasion, Installed', in *Politics and the Life Sciences* 29, no 1 (2010).
47. Nicholas Agar, 'Enhancing Genetic Virtue?', in *Politics and the Life Sciences* 29, no 1 (2010).

obvious that greater intelligence does not equate to greater morality, nor does it equate to the will to solve society's problems. There will probably be great diversity of interests and morality among the super intelligent, artificial or otherwise. The hard work to ensure moral or friendly AI needs to be done now, not avoided because one assumes a superintelligence will be friendly and have the will to help.

Finally, one should recognize that we create things in our own image, and even if the intelligences we create will be different kinds of intelligences, they will likely share our sinful flaws. Humans will pass their penchant for sin onto their creations, and to think that a sufficient super-intelligence will see these sins and avoid them, or care about avoiding them, is the height of wishful thinking. One already sees algorithms evidencing racism and bias in their calculations, and not only this, programs are created in and often for sinful societal structures and thus may perpetuate or enhance these large-scale sinful processes. AI is made by those with original sin, and AI programs are made to serve a society fraught with collective or corporate sin. We cannot halt the development of these technologies as the cat is so far out of the bag it has already crawled into your phone, car, and bank account. But we can do the hard work now to ensure a successful middle ground today. If we cannot get this middle ground right, why do we expect to get it right when the system becomes more complex as with AGI? As it is, I believe that we could solve many of society's ills today with our current level of intelligence if only the mass of humanity had the will and desire. We need not look to AGI. Why not start now without it?

Ultimately, in charting a successful course into the future, both the voices that shout that AI and IA will be our downfall as well as the voices that proclaim that these will bring a secular form of salvation are helpful and necessary. The voices of doom assist us in proactively identifying problems so as to mitigate risks and with any luck and hard work, avoid them. The voices proclaiming a technological utopian vision, while perhaps naïve, do provide hope—of that for which we can strive, guiding vocational aspirations beyond mundane, selfish concerns. I am thankful for both the pessimists and the optimists, for as we inevitably get the mixed bag of both the good and the bad with technological advancement, hopefully by listening to both voices we can have more of one and less of the other.

Part Two

AI and IA in Culture, Religion, and Theology

Agathon: A Journal of Ethics and Value in the Modern World, Vol 10/2025

Chapter 10
AI in Recent Literature

Martinez J Hewlett

What a piece of work is man! How noble in reason! how infinite in faculties! in form and moving, how express and admirable! in action how like an angel! in apprehension, how like a god!
William Shakespeare, *Hamlet*, Act II, Scene 2

Commerce is our goal here at Tyrell. 'More human than human' is our motto.
—Eldon Tyrell, *Blade Runner*

Abstract: The question of what it means to be a human person is brought into sharp focus by the creative imaginations of a host of science fiction writers. I have chosen three authors whose work has influenced the genre and has been the inspiration for film adaptations. These three—Isaac Asimov (*I, Robot*), Philip K Dick (*Blade Runner*), and Richard K Morgan (*Altered Carbon*)—challenge us by pushing the limits of robotics, androids, and mind uploading and transfer as visions of what the future might be in the wake of technological advances in artificial intelligence. In the end, how does this change who we see ourselves to be?

Key Terms: Robots, artificial intelligence, computational theory of mind, consciousness, transhumanism, philosophical zombie, mind uploading

Imagine, if you will, a world of the future when all that makes up a person's consciousness can be downloaded into a data matrix and subsequently uploaded into a different physical body grown as a clone on a planet light-years away. In such a world, what would constitute the human person? How would we frame a conversation about the concept of a transcendent reality?

Richard K. Morgan, in his science fiction trilogy, has his hero, Takeshi Kovacs, in just such a discussion. Kovacs is arguing theology with an executive of a megacorporation who is also a devotee of a form of voodoo. Kovacs has derided religion as "simplification for the hard of thinking." Matthias Hand gestures at the sky and replies:

> Look at that, Kovacs. We're drinking coffee so far from Earth that you have to work hard to pick out Sol in the night sky. We were carried here on a wind that blows in a dimension we cannot see or touch. Stored as dreams in the mind of a machine that thinks in a fashion so far in advance of our own brains, it might as well carry the name of *God*. We have been resurrected into bodies not our own, grown in a secret garden without the body of any mortal woman. These are the *facts* of our existence, Kovacs. How, then, are they different, or any less mystical, than the belief that there is another realm where the dead live in the company of beings so far beyond us we *must* call them gods?[1]

What, indeed, does it mean to be human in this future technology Morgan posits? More importantly, if such a scenario were to become our reality, what would it do to our current concepts of the human person?

The gift of the science fiction author is to begin within the technical, cultural, and philosophical framework of our present world and imagine how it might change when something happens to that technology. Very often these artists have provoked a critical look at the possibilities inherent in the scientific enterprise. It is with this in mind that I will explore three seminal works in this genre, their view of robotics, artificial intelligence, and transhumanism, and the impact this would have on our philosophical and theological reflections.

Defining the Human Person

Then, what does it mean to be human? At the heart of this question, at least in the modern sense of it, is the mind-body problem. That is to say, how do we define what we believe makes us most human: consciousness and cognition? This is both an objective as well as a

---

1. Richard Morgan, *Broken Angels: A Takeshi Kovacs Novel* (Del Rey Books, 2004), 101–102.

subjective issue. The current trend in neurosciences is an attempt to correlate mental states and brain states as a way of quantifying the process of cognition. On the other hand, each of us operates with a worldview defined by a theory of mind. We intuit the presence of mental states within others as an extension of our subjective introspection of our own experience of mind.

The mind-body problem, the 'hard problem' of modern science as David Chalmers calls it,[2] is central to our discussion of what it means to be a human. For Chalmers, the hard problem is the nature of conscious experience. It is that part of being human, the inner life of our own mind, that allows us to imply similar mental states in the minds of others. This issue of implying consciousness in others comes to the fore in the science fiction scenarios we will examine below.

It is the case, however, that we speak of this as though 'mind' and 'body' could be separate entities. This is our inheritance from René Descartes, who split mind or soul, the 'thinking thing', from body, 'the extended thing'.[3] This dualism was not the case for earlier philosophies of human nature, especially that of Aristotle and St Thomas Aquinas.[4] However, it has come to dominate our world-view during the Enlightenment, and even into the Post-Enlightenment.

Accompanying this has been first the methodological and then philosophical commitment of the scientific enterprise to materialism. As such, the soul and any spiritual Cartesian dimension that it might inhabit has been systematically disregarded as epiphenomenal and non-existent. Reductionism, materialism, physicalism, and scientism are the four horsemen of the modern apocalypse, so to speak.

These four horsemen are charging through contemporary discussions on the relation of the mind to the brain. The brain is marvelous by any measure. With eighty billion neuronal cells, each communicating with thousands of other neurons, we cradle more connections between our ears than stars in the Milky Way. Still, the relationship between these objective facts and our interior life, our

---

2. David Chalmers, 'Facing up to the problem of consciousness', in *Journal of Consciousness Studies*, 2 (1995): 200–219.
3. René Descartes, *Meditations on First Philosophy*, ES Haldane and GRT Ross, translators, 1952, Encylcopaedia Britannica, Chicago, 98.
4. Gyula Klima, 'Man = Body + Soul: Aquinas's Arithmetic of Human Nature', in *Thomas Aquinas: Contemporary Philosophical Perspectives*, edited by B Davies (Oxford: Oxford University Press, 2002).

subjective consciousness, remains an unsolved mystery in science. Despite two decades of computerized brain imaging, the mystery of brain activity continues to be unsolved even while philosophers and the media run off with unfounded claims of biodeterminism. 'To regard research findings as settled wisdom is folly, especially when they emanate from a technology whose implications are still poorly understood', write Sally Satel and Scott Lilienfeld. 'Nevertheless, scientific humility can readily give way to exuberance. When it does, the media often seem to have a ringside seat at the spectacle.'[5] In sum, neuroscience itself is too new at the study of the brain to draw conclusions regarding the brain-mind relationship; yet non-scientists are already racing about with exuberance.

Such exuberance leads philosophers of mind such as Daniel Dennett[6] and Owen Flanagan[7] to use neuroscience to affirm their commitment to ontological materialism. 'The mind . . . is the brain', says Dennett flatly.[8]

In the view of Dennett and Flanagan, Thomas Aquinas's soul does not exist; and Descartes's 'thinking thing' is, in fact, the brain itself. The mind has been reduced to the body, the mental to the physical. Here the four horsemen of the modern apocalypse wreak their havoc. We have lost our mind. Only a brain is left.

Some would-be defenders of the mind's integrity have arisen to fight the foes. One is philosopher and theologian Nancey Murphy.[9] In 'Science and the Soul', the first chapter in *What Ever Happened to the Soul?*, Murphy takes the list of St Thomas' assignments of human faculties for the soul and systematically attributes each of them to a material function of brain states that can be quantitated.[10] While admitting that consciousness itself has no current explanation at this level, she concludes: '. . . science has provided a massive amount of evidence suggesting that we need not postulate the existence of

---

5. Sally Satel and Scott O Lilienfeld, 'Losing Our Minds in the Age of Brain Science', in *Skeptical Inquirer*, 37:5 (November/December 2013): 30–35, at 32.
6. Daniel Dennett, *Consciousness Explained* (Boston: Little Brown and Co, 1991).
7. Owen Flanagan, *Science of Mind* (Cambridge MA: MIT Press, 2nd Edition, 1991).
8. Daniel Dennett, *Breaking the Spell* (New York: Viking, 2006) 107.
9. Nancey Murphy, 'Human Nature: Historical, Scientific, and Religious Issues', in *Whatever Happened to the Soul?*, edited by W Brown, N Murphy, and HN Malony (Minneapolis: Fortress Press, 1988), 1–29.
10. Murphy, 'Human Nature: Historical, Scientific, and Religious Issues', 16–17.

any entity such as soul or mind to explain life or consciousness.'[11] Therefore, Murphy's defense occurs only after a retreat. She posits a non-reductive physicalism, an affirmation of mind within a non-dualistic physicalism. Murphy is no reductionist, to be sure; yet she reminds us forcefully of the embattled state of today's philosophers when attending to the mind-body problem.

There are other philosophers of mind who do not retreat, who defend the mind from reductive physicalism. These philosophical soldiers are not themselves writing out of a particular theistic or even deistic framework. Thomas Nagel[12] and David Chalmers[13, 14] are two defenders of this direction in the mind-body discussion. Let's look at Chalmers's position in more detail.

Zombies and Other Metaphysical Delights

Recall that Chalmers distinguishes the 'easy' and 'hard' problems of mind-body studies. In his view, the easy problems are those things that are approachable by the cognitive sciences and the neurosciences. This includes phenomena such as reaction to environmental stimuli, integration of information, reporting of mental states, and deliberate control of behavior.[15] The hard problem is that of subjective states of experience.

Chalmers argues that virtually all research approaches to the mind-body problem are involved with investigating the easy problems of consciousness. It is one thing to measure the cognitive control of a specific behavior, such as choosing to drink from the coffee mug next to my computer as I write this. It is another thing entirely to have the subjective experience of that choice, followed by the experience of that coffee.

Investigations of the easy problems, Chalmers maintains, lead to explanations of cognitive functions and abilities, but not to explanations of experience. In fact, he wants the word 'consciousness'

---

11. Murphy, 'Human Nature: Historical, Scientific, and Religious Issues', 18.
12. Thomas Nagel, *Mind and Cosmos*, (Oxford: Oxford University Press, 2012).
13. David J Chalmers, *The Conscious Mind: In Search of a Fundamental Theory* (Oxford: Oxford University Press, 1996).
14. David J Chalmers, *The Character of Consciousness* (Oxford: Oxford University Press, 2010).
15. Chalmers, *The Character of Consciousness*, 3–4.

to be used exclusively for this aspect of our inner mental life, while the word 'awareness' would be applied to these measured aspects.[16]

Chalmers makes the bold claim that conscious experience is not derived from the physical processes that define cognitive functions and abilities and, in fact, requires a non-physical explanation. This statement also argues in the larger sense against materialism as an exhaustive description of the world. He has three arguments against materialism as a solution to the problem of consciousness: the explanatory argument, the conceivability argument, and the knowledge argument.[17] For our purposes, we will look at the second of these, which I will call the zombie argument.

Chalmers proposes that 'it is conceivable that there be a system that is physically identical to a conscious being but that . . . lacks consciousness entirely.'[18] This being he terms a 'zombie'. Not to worry! Don't start looking over your shoulder, or at the person next to you. Such beings do not actually exist. However, from their conceivability one can make the inference that they are metaphysically possible. As such, their possibility can be used to construct the argument.

Zombies would be indistinguishable from actual conscious beings by every possible third-person measurement of cognitive function and ability. However, they would have no inner experience of seeing the color blue or feeling love. That is, they would have no first-person experience. Chalmers puts the argument simply:

1. It is conceivable that there are zombies.
2. If it is conceivable that there are zombies, it is metaphysically possible that there are zombies.
3. If it is metaphysically possible that there are zombies, then consciousness is nonphysical.
4. Consciousness is nonphysical.[19]

This argument can be generalized to posit that, if a zombie represents 'the conjunction of all microphysical truths about the universe' and yet they lack 'an arbitrary phenomenal truth about the universe, i.e., consciousness, then materialism as a complete explanation is false.'[20]

---

16. Chalmers, *The Character of Consciousness*, 5.
17. Chalmers, *The Character of Consciousness*, 105–110.
18. Chalmers, *The Character of Consciousness*, 106.
19. Chalmers, *The Character of Consciousness*, 107.
20. Chalmers, *The Character of Consciousness*, 107.

Three Science Fiction Views

There are so many science fiction short-stories, novels, films, and series that deal with the topic of technology and the concept of what it means to be human that it becomes nearly impossible to choose those to discuss. Nevertheless, I have my favorites and, it is from this list that I have selected three to highlight.

Isaac Asimov is remembered as one of the giants of the genre. He was trained as a biochemist and wrote numerous essays and non-fiction books devoted to a variety of scientific subjects. His list of sci-fi topics defined the field for so many years. For our purposes, I want to focus on his Robot Series, published over a thirty-five year period. The short story collection, *I, Robot*, begins the book sequence, followed by the Elijah Bailey crime novels.[21]

Philip K Dick, my second choice, was among those sci-fi authors who came to define or at least presage the cyberpunk movement. His all too short life left us with some forty novels, among which is *Do Android Dream of Electric Sheep?*, ultimately the source material for the now classic movie, *Blade Runner*.[22]

Richard K. Morgan is the newest of my choices, listed among those sci-fi authors termed post-cyberpunk. His writing style is dystopian but very much imbedded in a more modern take on what the technological future might portend. I want to focus on his Takeshi Kovacs novels and the world in which Morgan immerses his readers.[23] The first of these has become a Netflix series.[24]

Isaac Asimov: The Laws of Robotics

While the idea of artificial humans, automatons, or other kinds of mechanical beings is quite ancient, the term "robot" entered our language from the Czech writer Karel Čapek in his 1920 play *Rossum's*

---

21. The Asimov Robot series books are: *I, Robot* (1950) Gnome Press; *The Caves of Steel* (1954), Doubleday; *The Naked Sun* (1957), Doubleday; *The Robots of Dawn* (1983), and *Robots and Empire* (1985), Doubleday. This list does not include the numerous short stories concerning robots that preceded the publication of the anthology *I, Robot*.
22. Philip K Dick, *Do Androids Dream of Electric Sheep?* (1968), Doubleday. *Blade Runner* (1982), Warner Bros.
23. Richard K Morgan, *Altered Carbon* (2002), Victor Gollancz, Ltd.; *Broken Angels* (2003), Victor Gollancz, Ltd.; and *Woken Furies* (2005), Victor Gollancz, Ltd.
24. *Altered Carbon* (2018), 10-epidsode series, Netflix.

Universal Robots (RUR).[25] That year is co-incidentally the birth year of Isaac Asimov, the American sci-fi writer most closely associated with the world of robotics (a term introduced by him) in fiction. His take on robots was quite different with that of Čapek, who, in R.U.R., envisioned the prevalence of these artificial beings resulting in a Frankenstein-like outcome for humanity. In contrast, Asimov argued for a benign, even beneficial relationship. He proposed that these constructs with positronic brains would function according to an indwelling code of ethics . . . the Three Laws of Robotics:

> First Law—A robot may not injure a human being or, through inaction, allow a human being to come to harm.
>
> Second Law—A robot must obey the orders given it by human beings except where such orders would conflict with the First Law.
>
> Third Law—A robot must protect its own existence as long as such protection does not conflict with the First or Second Laws.[26]

Asimov supplemented these three rules with the 'zeroth law'. This was proposed by Dr Susan Calvin, a character introduced in the short story 'Evitable Conflict':

> A robot may not harm humanity, or, by inaction, allow humanity to come to harm.[27]

Within this ethical framework, Asimov envisions a world in which robots become ever-present. The collection of linked short stories, *I, Robot*, introduces Asimov's musings about the Laws of Robotics and how they function. The four novels of the series are crime stories, featuring the human detective, Elijah 'Lije' Baley, and his partner, the robot, R Daneel Olivaw.

---

25. The word 'robot' is taken from the Czech word *robota*, meaning 'forced or compulsory labor'. An English translation web edition of Čapek's play is available from The University of Adelaide Library (eBooks@Adelaide), https://ebooks.adelaide.edu.au/c/capek/karel/rur/index.html, last accessed 03/16/19.
26. The Three Laws of Robotic are introduced in the short story, 'Runaround', found in the anthology *I, Robot*. The laws are summarized here from the 2004 edition of the anthology, published by Bantam Dell (Kindle edition).
27. 'Evitable Conflict' is the last story in the anthology, *I, Robot*.

The 2004 film *I, Robot* is loosely based on this Asimov canon. Even though the original screenplay (entitled *Hardwired*) by Jeff Vintar had nothing to do with works by Asimov, the ultimate script for the Fox movie borrowed from the short stories included in the anthology.[28] As a result, the detective Del Spooner (Will Smith) is joined by the robot psychologist Dr Susan Calvin (Bridget Moynahan) as main characters. The robot lead, Sonny (Alan Tudyk), is an advanced version built to bypass the Laws. The plot involves the suspicious death the Dr Lanning, the creator of the robots, and the attempt by an artificial intelligence directing the advanced robots to wrest control from the humans, in effect obeying a warped version of the Zeroth Law ... to save humanity from itself.

Phillip K Dick: More Human Than Human

One of Dick's best-known novels is *Do Android Dream of Electric Sheep?* Like Asimov before him, Dick used the police drama setting. In this case, however, his cop, Deckard, is not a detective, but a bounty hunter. This dystopic world of San Francisco after a worldwide nuclear holocaust is the setting. Humans are encouraged to leave for the off-world colonies to escape the desolation, with the enticement of androids as their personal servants. The androids ('andys'), made by the Rosen Association on Mars, sometimes escape back to Earth. Deckard is one of the bounty hunters who seek out and 'retire' them. Roy Baty is the leader of a group of eight androids being sought. Deckard also encounters Eldon Rosen's niece, Rachel, who is a very advanced android, almost impossible to detect, and with whom he has an affair.

The novel became the material from which the movie *Blade Runner* was made. The script by Hampton Fancher and David Peoples has major differences from Dick's book. The film, directed by Ridley Scott has, over time, become a classic of the genre. Set in Los Angeles instead of San Francisco, it retains the characters of Deckard (Harrison Ford), Rachel (Sean Young), and Roy Batty ('Baty' in the book) (Rutger Hauer) from the novel. The artificial beings produced, in this case, by the Tyrell Corporation are called replicants or, pejoratively, 'skin jobs'. Deckard is the bounty hunter charged with terminating Batty and his friends.

---

28. Interview of Jeff Vintar by Fred Topel for *Screenwriters Utopia*, August 17, 2004, found at http://www.screenwritersutopia.com/article/d19127d8. Last accessed 3/17/19.

In both the novel and the movie, the difference between humans and the androids/replicants has to do with their subjective experience of the world, specifically their empathic reactions. A psychological questionnaire, the Voight-Kampff Test, is used to reveal those who are not human.

Richard K. Morgan: The Mind-Body Problem Solved

It is 500 years in the future. The world of Takeshi Kovacs[29] is one in which technology has been driven by the discovery of the lost civilization of the Martians, who not only occupied the fourth planet of our solar system, but many other worlds throughout our local galactic cluster. The unraveling of their knowledge led to the ability of the human race to traverse interstellar distances and, more importantly, to effectively digitize and download consciousness and then upload it into a new body, recreating (resurrecting?) the entire person.

The entire consciousness, called DHF or 'digital human freight' is stored in a cortical stack, inserted shortly after birth at the top of the spinal column. Upon death of the body, called the sleeve, the stack can be retrieved and ultimately be 're-sleeved'. Alternatively, the DHF can be transmitted through interstellar space and be re-sleeved on a new planet. Destruction of the stack results in 'real death'.

In the first book, *Altered Carbon*, Kovacs, a one-time revolutionary and former member of an elite military unit of the Protectorate, is re-sleeved on Earth to act as an investigator into the sleeve death of Laurens Bancroft, a member of the ruling class. Bancroft has lived for more than 300 years by continually being re-sleeved into genetic clones, a process only available to the super-rich who are called 'meths' short for Methuselahs.

The novel[30] is written in the classic *film noir* style of the mid twentieth century, with Kovacs as the narrator. The murder/suicide

---

29. Richard K Morgan, the Takeshi Kovacs novels, *Altered Carbon* (2002), *Broken Angels* (2003), *Woken Furies* (2005), all published by Victor Gollancz, LTD. *Altered Carbon* is also a Netflix series (2018), based upon the first novel. It has been renewed for a second season (2019) with the same name, although the plot is taken from the second novel.
30. A note of caution if you have not yet read these books. The writing is graphic, both for the violence and sexual content.

plot is set in Bay City, the San Francisco of the twenty-sixth century. Kovacs is joined by a police detective, Kristin Ortega. The sleeve chosen for Kovacs is the body of Elias Ryker, a disgraced former detective and partner/lover of Ortega.

An important sub-plot of the story is the fact that neo-Catholics are opposed to the idea of re-sleeving, holding that natural death is the only acceptable and moral outcome of life. They even oppose the practice of using the stack recovered after the death of the body to communicate with the person. This prevents the police from 'interviewing' victims of a crime in a virtual reality space, called 'spinning up'. Members of this religious group have their stacks digitally tagged to prevent this from happening.

The world of the twenty-sixth century is also filled with artificial intelligence (AI), used in a variety of situations, as well as synthetic humans, cloning, and human enhancement.[31] Morgan weaves the plots of his three novels so that all of this is perfectly normal in context.

So, What Does It Mean to be Human?

The three authors ask this question in different ways, and their answers are all quite distinct. The first two, Asimov and Dick, take the position that the 'other', whether robot or android/replicant, can be distinguished from human. The issues for them are if these creations can have something like consciousness and, more importantly, whether they are a threat to us or not. On the other hand, Morgan presents us with a real dilemma. How are we to think about the human in light of a world in which digitization and transfer of human consciousness is routinely practiced? I will deal with each of these issues in turn.

In his series of robot novels and short stories Asimov considers that these mechanical creations as distinct from us. The robots in the stories from which the movie, *I, Robot*, was taken are metallic creations that, while bipedal like us, look the part of an inorganic construct, made with a shiny skin and non-human face. In contrast, R

---

31. Kovacs stays in a Bay City hotel, The Hendrix, that is entirely managed by AI. The persona of the hotel is the rock icon, Jimi Hendrix. Because of contractual issues, the hotel in the Netflix series is The Raven, and the AI persona is Poe.

Daneel Olivaw, the robot detective in *Caves of Steel* and the following novels is humanoid, visually indistinguishable from humans. In both cases, however, these artificial creatures are identifiably distinct from us in that they have no real internal experiences. Thus, they would fit Chalmers's philosophical zombie model. That is, when tested for objective correlates of consciousness, they would appear to pass the test. However, they would have no subjective experience.

This becomes the issue later on, especially with Sonny, the advanced robot in the movie *I, Robot*, who begins to be self-reflective and sees himself as both conscious and closer to human. Take this interchange between Detective Spooner and the robot, Sonny:

SPOONER: People generally believe that they have an immortal soul. If robots become intelligent, then the question of consciousness arises, and if a being is conscious, it becomes hard to deny it a soul—and that sort of fouls up the whole thing for us. Do you understand?
THE ROBOT: People think God made them in His image.
SPOONER: That's the general belief.
THE ROBOT: And robots are made in the image of Man.
SPOONER: Right.
THE ROBOT: So that means robots are also the image of God. And I don't understand why God wouldn't want to give us immortal souls.
(*Spooner looks uncomfortable.*)
SPOONER: Your reasoning has its points, but I'm afraid people will always see you as a collection of programming, a clockwork man. An illusion of life.
THE ROBOT: But that's not reasonable.
SPOONER: Isn't it? Can a robot take a blank canvas and paint a masterpiece? Can it write a poem that stirs the heart?
(*Long pause. Spooner waits. The Robot does not move. Then . . .*)
THE ROBOT: Can *you* do either of those things?[32]

---

32. *I, Robot* screenplay, located at https://www.simplyscripts.com/scripts/IrobotN.pdf, last accessed 3/19/19.

The androids/replicants of Dick's *Blade Runner* are a different case, but with the same outcome. Their consciousness is not disputed. But is it real or artificial? They were given implanted memories to simulate a lifetime, but they were only created a few years before. The task of the bounty hunter is to discern their true nature by looking at their empathic reactions. As an example of the Voight-Kampff test, look at this exchange between Deckard and Rachel, Eldon Tryell's niece who is an advanced model of a replicant:

(Rachael's eye fills the screen, the iris brilliant, shot with light, the pupil contracting. We hear Deckard's voice and we have the impression the test has been going on for a while.)

DECKARD: You are given a calfskin wallet for your birthday...
    (Tyrell stands silhouetted behind Deckard, who sits in front of Rachael.)

(The needles in both gauges swing violently past green to red, then subside.)

RACHAEL: I wouldn't accept it, also I'd report the person who gave it to me to the police.

DECKARD: You have a little boy. He shows you his butterfly collection, plus the killing jar.

(Again the gauges register, but not so far.)

RACHAEL: I'd take him to the doctor.

DECKARD: You're watching TV and suddenly you notice a wasp crawling on your wrist.

RACHAEL: I'd kill it.

(Both needles go red. Deckard makes a note, takes a sip of coffee and continues.)

DECKARD: In a magazine you come across a full-page photo of a nude girl.

RACHAEL: Is this testing whether I'm a replicant or a lesbian?

DECKARD: You show the picture to your husband. He likes it and hangs it on the wall. The girl is lying on a bearskin rug.

RACHAEL: I wouldn't let him.

DECKARD: Why not?

RACHAEL: I should be enough for him.

(Deckard frowns, then smiles. His smile looks a little like a grimace or the other way around.)

>   DECKARD: Last question. You're watching an old movie. It shows a banquet in progress, the guests are enjoying raw oysters.
>   RACHAEL: Ugh.
>   *(Both needles swing swiftly.)*
>   DECKARD:
>   The entree consists of boiled dog stuffed with rice.
>   *(Needles move less.)*
>   DECKARD: *(continuing)* The raw oysters are less acceptable to you than a dish of boiled dog.
>   *(Deckard switches off his beam.)*[33]

This dialogue in the movie is very close to the same material in Dick's novel. It is taking a different tack than Asimov but comes to the same point relative to Chalmers's model. Replicants may be able to show some features of human subjective consciousness . . . for instance, memories . . . but they do not have internal reactions that dictate emotions such as empathy. Thus, they test again as philosophical zombies.

The truly challenging scenario is that portrayed in the Takeshi Kovacs novels of Morgan. Yes, there are robots, AI, synthetic beings and the like. However, we are presented with the world of DHF, the digitised, downloadable, and uploadable consciousness of each person that constitutes what we would normally consider the soul.

The Computation Theory of Mind (CTM) argues that what we perceive as cognition and consciousness is actually computation, in which the instrument that is used is the neural activity of the brain. The materialist view of the mind holds that brain states equal mental states. A more detailed statement would be that brain states are complex networks of neural synapses, the sum total of which constitutes the computational network that results in mental states.

There are at least six models of CTM, each of which fits philosophical features of consciousness more or less well.[34] In each of them, however, there is some appeal to the synaptic connections of the physical brain comprising the computation instrument of

---

33. *Blade Runner* screenplay, located at http://www.dailyscript.com/scripts/blade-runner_shooting.html, last accessed 3/19/19.
34. Selvi Elif Gök and Erdinç Sayan, 'A philosophical assessment of computational models of consciousness', in *Cognitive Systems Research,* 17–18 (2012): 49–62.

consciousness. In the world of Morgan's novels, it would be that complex network which can at long last be digitized and stored.

Of course, the Kovacs novels are fiction. However, there are companies currently in existence right now dedicated to achieving this same outcome. Carbon Copies is one such example.[35] Their Mission Statement includes the following:

> Ultimately, this means that we can reinvent our own mental processor, and that we can close the gap between human and machine. Our cognitive processes are then no longer tied to a single version of the brain's processing architecture. Instead, our thoughts and feelings will be able to exist on a variety of processing substrates. In that sense, we then have a substrate-independent mind (SIM). With advances in neuroscience and neural engineering we will be able to choose brain and body, much as we can choose winter or summer clothes to suit our needs. In science fiction, this possibility has been lightly explored in stories that involve 'mind uploading.' Neural prosthesis and whole brain emulation require accurate computational modeling of neural tissue, as well as developing neuromorphic hardware that is better suited to efficiently support the processes carried out in a neural architecture.[36]

Another example is Nectome,[37] whose home page states:

> Nectome is a research company dedicated to advancing the science of memory. We design and conduct experiments to discover how the brain physically creates memories. And, we develop biological preservation techniques to better preserve the physical traces of memory.[38]

Clearly, the long terms goals of these companies are a world much as described by Morgan with transhumanism propelled by leaps in technology. Therefore, the definition of what constitutes the human person comes immediately to the front of the discussion.

---

35. Carbon Copies home page can be found at https://carboncopies.org, last accessed 3/19/19.
36. Carbon Copies home page can be found at https://carboncopies.org, last accessed 3/19/19.
37. Nectome home page is found at https://nectome.com, last accessed 3/19/19.
38. Nectome home page is found at https://nectome.com, last accessed 3/19/19.

Indeed, the idea of digitizing human consciousness has been the subject of recent speculation and discussion. *Intelligence Unbound: The Future of Uploaded and Machine Minds* is an anthology of contributions by scientists, futurists, ethicists, and philosophers.[39] Two of the articles in this anthology strike at the heart of my discussion. The first is by David Chalmers, whom we've already reviewed with respect to the 'hard problem' of the mind-body question. The second, by Massimo Pigliucci, is a critical response to Chalmers.

David Chalmers takes on the philosophical issues of mind uploading in his contribution.[40] He divides the discussion into two questions:

1. If my consciousness is uploaded to a computer, will it still be conscious?
2. If my consciousness is uploaded, will it still be me?

The answer to these questions depends upon whether or not one thinks of consciousness in a biological or functional sense. Biological theorists contend that consciousness requires a biological structure and therefore that a non-biological system cannot exhibit this property. Functional theorists, on the other hand, argue that consciousness requires a causal structure and a causal role. Therefore, a correctly structured non-biological system can have this property.

Chalmers maintains that 'functionalist theories are closer to the truth'. Recall that he maintains that mind cannot be explained completely by brain states (his philosophical zombie test). However, he seems to maintain in this paper that whatever the qualia issues of our internal experience of consciousness might be, this would transfer intact during mind uploading.

I'm actually perplexed by this. Chalmers claims that our subjected internal experience cannot be reduced to the physical brain state. And yet, by digitizing that brain state . . . that is, by creating a precise digital record of all synaptic connections and any other relevant cellular interactions . . . an upload of our consciousness and even personal continuity to a computer would be possible. How is the digital record

---

39. Russell Blackford and Damien Broderick, *Intelligence Unbound: The Future of Uploaded and Machine Minds* (Oxford: Wiley Blackwell, 2014).
40. David Chalmers, 'Uploading: A Philosophical Analysis', in Blackford and Broderick, *Intelligence Unbound: The Future of Uploaded and Machine Minds* (Oxford: Wiley Blackwell, 2014), 101–118.

different from the brain states of which they are a kind of map? What makes it a sort of qualia and not a quantified computation?

Massimo Pigliucci deals with some of these arguments in his contribution to the anthology.[41] However, as a biological theorist, he then falls into the trap of assuming that brain states will be determinative of mental states. He does not state this directly, but rather argues that for consciousness to exist, there must be biological components of the brain that cannot be duplicated by circuitry in a computer. That is, consciousness is substrate-dependent.

My critique of these two approaches is that both of these philosophers of mind are riding roughshod over the subject of the nature of mind behind three of those four horsemen we encountered earlier: materialism, physicalism, and scientism. While they may have abandoned one of the riders, reductionism, in favor of the more popular systems approach to understanding biological systems, they are still firmly in stride with the other three. It is from this position that they try to conclude that digital versions of brain states might, in any way, be equivalent to consciousness and, in fact, personality.

The transhumanist movement that sees mind uploading as the ultimate pathway to immortality is also imbedded in this philosophical milieu. Of course, proponents ignore the idea put forth by Aristotle and later commented on by St. Thomas Aquinas that humans are rational animals with a soul, defined as the formal cause of what it means to be human. Of course, the materialists belittle this view as 'neo-scholastic'.[42] To deny the existence of the non-material is, in fact, circular reasoning at its worst. Science can only observe the material world. Science has never observed the non-material soul. Therefore, the non-material soul does not exist. Take that, neo-scholastics!

The transhumanist paradise, perhaps as depicted in the world of *Altered Carbon*, would, to my non-uploaded mind, be populated by sophisticated versions of Chalmersian zombies. Thanks, but no thanks.

---

41. Massimo Pigliucci, 'Mind Uploading: A Philosophical Counter-Analysis', in Blackford and Broderick, *Intelligence Unbound: The Future of Uploaded and Machine Minds* (Oxford: Wiley Blackwell, 2014), 118–130.
42. Pigliucci, 'Mind Uploading', footnote 4, 129.

Agathon: A Journal of Ethics and Value in the Modern World, Vol 10/2025

Chapter 11
Video Games and Theology of Culture

Benjamin J Chicka

Theology of Culture (*Kulturtheologie*) recognizes that the religious dimension actualizes itself in every dimension of the Spirit (*Sondern das Religiöse ist aktuel in allen Provinzen des Geistigen*).
—Paul Tillich[1]

Abstract: The video games industry is the largest entertainment industry in the world. While conversations about future benefits or dangers posed by Artificial Intelligence (AI) are important, scholars who ignore the current impact of video games on culture do so at their own peril. Through interactions with AI controlled characters, players are having the meaningfulness of their lives affirmed and are changing the way they behave toward others in the real world. Thus, video games are manifesting what Paul Tillich called theonomy, and giving experiences of *the other* described by Emmanuel Levinas. Video gaming gives personal courage and meaning to those who are experiencing polarized conflicts between heteronomy and autonomy, of insiders versus outsiders. By virtually encountering the sorts of people excluded as outsiders in such conflicts, games are changing the real-world behavior of players and creating cultures of greater compassion and acceptance.

Key Terms: video games, Paul Tillich, Emmanuel Levinas, theonomy, theology of culture

---

1. Paul Tillich, 'Über die Idee einer Theologie der Kultur' (1919), in *Main Works/ Hauptwerke*, Carl Heinz Ratschow, editor in chief (6 Volumes: Berlin and New York: De Gruyter—Evangelishces Verlagswerk GmbH, 1989)(6 Volumes: Minneapolis: Fortress Press, 2015–2019), 2:69–86 (73).

Amid legitimate worries about the dangers posed by artificial intelligence, it can be tempting to mentally leap into the future and worry about artificial general intelligence (AGI) destroying the world. Geoffrey Hinton made this rather natural reaction even easier when he quit Google and started a global apology tour for being one of the people at ground zero of AI's creation.[2] However, AGI is not currently close to being a reality. Skynet is not sending Terminators to kill us. And such alarms should not draw attention away from forms of AI that are real and impacting lives right now. For those worried about AI and a potentially apocalyptic future, I bring good news about a form of AI that is currently making the world a better place: virtual characters that players interact with in video games.

Aside from interest in AI, video games deserve serious scholarly attention because the impact of the video game industry on culture is momentous. Not only is it massive, but it is also influential. Games are changing how players think about themselves along with important issues such as LGBTQ+ rights and immigration. Video game culture has rallied players to support social justice causes and to embrace diversity.

These facts make video games especially relevant for theologians who emphasize the importance of engaging and changing culture. The problem is that theologians tend to stay inside church walls and, as troglodytes, make little social impact. It is one thing to study ethical responsibilities toward others, but reading everything that has been published by Emmanuel Levinas, for example, does nothing to create an encounter with the other. But one can encounter the other in a Video game. So, it is time for the theologian to reach beyond the church into the wider public culture where encountering the other is happening digitally.

Video games allow players to have such encounters. And these encounters lead to players to change their behavior in the real world. Theologians interested in social change need to take note. I believe Paul Tillich's theology of culture is the perfect guide because he deeply engaged culture instead of merely talking about it. The theology of culture 'is the attempt to analyze the theology behind all

---

2. Cade Metz, '"The Godfather of A.I." Leaves Google and Warns of Danger Ahead', in *The New York Times*, May 1, 2023, https://www.nytimes.com/2023/05/01/technology/ai-google-chatbot-engineer-quits-hinton.html.

cultural expressions, to discover the ultimate concern in the ground of a philosophy, a political system, an artistic style, a set of ethical or social principles'.[3] A theology of culture, following Tillich, searches for the dimension of ultimacy—the religious dimension—within all cultural forms. Video games make up a form of culture that dare not be overlooked.

Video games do not just contain examples of Tillich's concepts. Rather, video game culture is realizing Tillich's hope for a culture that affirms both individual meaning and societal inclusion.

The Largest Entertainment Industry in the World

In terms of revenue, the video game industry dwarfs the music and movie industries combined. The global video game market generated almost $190 billion in revenue in 2023.[4] Over three billion people play video games worldwide. While many people hold stereotypes about only men playing video games, the gaming population in the United States is almost perfectly split in half with the same number of women playing as men. Video games are also not simply elaborate children's toys, because the average player today is in their late 30s.[5] Since 2017, more Hispanic and Black adults report frequently playing video games than white adults.[6]

Given its size and popularity, it should not be surprising that behavior in the industry is not always good. A majority of US teenagers have experienced online bullying and harassment, and over ninety percent believe such online behavior is a major problem greatly impacting people their age. Women are more likely to be intentionally

---

3. Paul Tillich, *Systematic Theology* (3 Volumes: Chicago: University of Chicago Press, 1951–1963), 1: 39.
4. Tom Wijman, 'Newzoo's Year in Review: the 2023 Global Games Market in Numbers', in *Newzoo*, December 19, 2023, https://newzoo.com/resources/blog/video-games-in-2023-the-year-in-numbers.
5. Milica Stojanovic, 'Gamer Demographics: 2023 Game-Changing Statistics Worth Checking', PlayToday.co, November 20, 2023, https://playtoday.co/blog/stats/gamer-demographics/.
6. Anna Brown, 'Younger Men Play Video Games, but So Do a Diverse Group of Other Americans', Pew Research Center, September 11, 2017, https://www.pewresearch.org/short-reads/2017/09/11/younger-men-play-video-games-but-so-do-a-diverse-group-of-other-americans/.

targeted.[7] Within video games specifically, almost three quarters of players have reported witnessing online harassment at some point.[8] In this sense, there is an element of truth to some stereotypes commonly held about video games. The behavior represented by such statistics came to a head in the Gamergate controversy.

In short, Gamergate was a campaign of targeted harassment against a few specific female video game developers which then turned into a campaign of hate directed at all minorities working in and playing games.[9] The events unfolded during 2014. The developers were making different experimental styles of games more about story and moving experiences than violence and challenging gameplay. I use "nontraditional games" as a catchall term for such alternative creations. Just because they were making something different, the developers were attacked online, had private information leaked, and received targeted death threats which resulted in the FBI eventually getting involved.[10] Gamergate was the inflection point for my engagement with video games, but more important than analyzing it as an ethical failure was the speed and seriousness with which the industry changed for the better in its wake.

Immediately after Gamergate, some of the industry's largest events changed to make the culture that surrounds games more accepting and inclusive. The Penny Arcade Expo (PAX) is that largest gaming convention in the United States and is attended by over 1000,000 people when it is held yearly in Boston and Seattle.[11] In 2014, the year

---

7. Monica Anderson, 'A Majority of Teens Have Experienced Some Form of Cyberbullying', Pew Research Center, September 27, 2018, https://www.pewresearch.org/internet/2018/09/27/a-majority-of-teens-have-experienced-some-form-of-cyberbullying/.
8. Maeve Duggan, 'Gaming and Gamers', Pew Research Center, December 15, 2015, https://www.pewresearch.org/internet/2015/12/15/gaming-and-gamers/.
9. Kyle Wagner, 'The Future of the Culture Wars Is Here, and It's Gamergate', Deadspin, October 14, 2014, https://deadspin.com/the-future-of-the-culture-wars-is-here-and-its-gamerga-1646145844. Wagner's article contains one of the best summaries of events that led up to and followed Gamergate, including their ramifications to this day.
10. The FBI record of Gamergate is 172 pages long and can be found in their records vault at https://vault.fbi.gov/gamergate.
11. Matthew Medsger, 'PAX East Packed in Boston's Seaport', in *Boston Herald*, March 23, 2023, https://www.bostonherald.com/2023/03/23/pax-east-a-demonstration-that-digital-life-is-not-enough-founder-says/.

Gamergate occurred, PAX East in Boston introduced the Diversity Lounge, which has been present at every PAX since. It is a safe space where attendees can speak to developers who are minorities in the industry and browse the stores of merchants who support LGBTQ+ causes, for example.[12] Since its introduction, PAX organizers have also used feedback from the communities that use the room in an effort to make it better serve its purpose.[13] At the same PAX East, the nonprofit TakeThis.org began hosting the AFK (away from keyboard) room which has also bee present at every PAX since.[14] These are quiet mental health spaces for both conference attendees and staff which are run by local volunteers and trained clinicians.[15] One of the original targets of Gamergate created 'Crash Override', a crisis hotline for anyone experiencing online abuse.

Given how many people participate in the industry, it should not be surprising that its impact on culture has been ambiguous. But in addition to industry events changing after Gamergate, there has been a proliferation of nontraditional games in recent years. The games and the culture around them have mutually reinforced one another as both have become more inclusive. And just as video game industry demographics break some deep-seated stereotypes while affirming others, the games themselves can be many things. Video games are not just violent shooters like the *Call of Duty* franchise you might know about. The following examples will show not just that fact, but just how deeply video games are impacting culture and improving people's lives.

---

12. Nathan Grayson, 'Was PAX East's Diversity Lounge a Success? I Asked People Who Went', in *Kotaku*, April 21, 2014, https://kotaku.com/was-pax-easts-diversity-lounge-a-success-i-asked-peopl-1564499083.
13. The first Diversity Lounge was literally put in a small corner, which was not good optics for an initiative meant to increase both visibility and acceptance of those in the room.
14. AFK is something players will type in the in-game chat of multiplayer games when they need to step away from the game for some reason, to indicate they are currently away from the game will be unresponsive for a moment. Using AFK as the name for these rooms is a signal that they are for those who need to get away from the hustle and bustle of the convention for a while.
15. Jessica Conditt, 'Fighting Depression in the Video Game World, One AFK at a Time', *Engadget*, March 25, 2016, https://www.engadget.com/2016-03-25-mental-illness-video-games-take-this-please-knock.html.

Video Games and LGBTQ+ Rights

Gone Home is the game that convinced me games can be deeply meaningful and prompted my further study of the industry. It was created by the Fullbright Company and is a 'walking simulator'. a label initially intended to be derogatory because there is no violence, shooting, or action in the game. However, the label is now a badge of honor for a respected genre of video games which this game played a major role in creating.[16]

The genre is about having interesting story-based experiences in virtual worlds. The game is set in the pacific northwest of the United States in 1995 and players control Katie Greenbriar as she returns from a college trip overseas to find her family home empty. The story unfolds as players explore the house in a first-person perspective and interact with objects, read diaries, and piece together what Katie's family has been doing while she was away. The story is focused on her sister Sam who fell in love with another girl at her high school, Lonnie. The nature of the medium really makes it feel like you are interacting with and learning about the lives of real people when playing *Gone Home*.

The voice actor playing Sam, Sarah Grayson, recorded audio tracks that play at certain key moments when players find journal entries and important objects related to Sam and Lonnie. As you hear Sam tell her story, the sense of interacting with real lives is enhanced by the game world. The game's developers scanned real-world objects into the game, meaning the journal entries and notes found in the game are actually digitized handwritten documents. Everything that can be interacted with in real life can be interacted with in the game, even if that just means turning a water faucet on and off.[17] As the story

---

16. Nicole Clark, 'A Brief History of the "Walking Simulator", Gaming's Most Detested Genre', in *Salon*, November 11, 2017, https://www.salon.com/2017/11/11/a-brief-history-of-the-walking-simulator-gamings-most-detested-genre/. The following are other walking simulators that have been given awards by various outlets that cover video games: *Firewatch* by Campo Santo; *Dear Esther* by The Chinese Room; *What Remains of Edith Finch* by Giant Sparrow; *The Stanley Parable* by Davey Wreden.
17. Steve Gaynor, head of the Fullbright Company, created a rule for his team: anything the player sees in the game that could be interacted with in real life must be something they could interact with in the game. Many of these objects have nothing to do with the story, but Gaynor claimed that for a game like theirs

reaches its conclusion, players know that Sam has not been accepted by her parents and is distraught over the impending loss of Lonnie, who always planned to join the miliary and is preparing to leave for basic training. I was not alone in thinking a sister contemplating self-harm or otherwise in need of help would be waiting for me as I entered the final room in the game, but nobody was there. Lonnie gave up on the military and was away with Sam enjoying their lives together. Nobody needed saving, the girls just needed societal forces to let them be themselves.

Playing *Gone Home* can be a transformative experience for LGBTQ+ players struggling to find acceptance in their lives, but it is more than that. There is evidence that *Gone Home* is responsible for converting some players from being against gay rights to supporting them.[18] It is not alone in that regard. *If Found . . .* was created by DREAMFEEL, a small development studio run by Llaura McGee. It and *Gone Home* are sometimes referred to as 'empathy games', the kinds of games frequently highlighted by the organisation Games for Change which focuses on empowering developers who make games that can lead to real societal and political changes. *If Found . . .* is about a transgender woman, Kasio, who is embraced by her friends but whose mother does not understand or accept her. The game plays with the fantasy worlds that video games can create to convey how exhilarating and crushing the two sorts of reactions can be to transgender individuals.

Face-to-Face with Immigrants

Papers, Please was made by a single developer, Lucas Pope. In the game players control an immigration officer at the border of a fictional Eastern European country and inspect documents of those who approach their booth. It is possible to reject or accept anyone into the country, but players will have their daily pay docked if people with

---

that relies on immersion for the story they are telling to grip the player, anything that breaks that sense of immersion cannot be allowed. Mike Mahardy, 'The Looking Glass Philosophy behind Gone Home', in *Polygon*, April 6, 2015, https://www.polygon.com/features/2015/4/6/8315901/looking-glass-gone-home.

18. Gita Jackson, 'The Video Games That Made People Question Their Beliefs', in *Kotaku*, July 2, 2019, https://kotaku.com/the-video-games-that-made-people-question-their-beliefs-1836045401.

incorrect paperwork are allowed in. A video game about processing paperwork might sound boring, but the incredibly engaging part of *Papers, Please* is that people tell the player their reasons for crossing the border. Some do not have proper documentation but are trying to smuggle in medicine that a dying relative cannot obtain, while others are trying to flee sex trafficking or war. While such stories could create empathy for immigrants, the best part of this game is that it shows empathy for everyone involved. The player's character has a family, and if their pay is docked and food, heat, or medicine cannot be afforded, family members can die. Even if someone has sympathy for the plights of immigrants, border patrol officers are people with needs as well. As in the real-world, ethical scenarios are rarely black and white.

A game based on the experiences of real-life immigrants is *Bury Me, My Love* by Playdius. Players control Majd as he communicates with his wife Nour through a smartphone app while she attempts to flee from Syria to France. Majd can provide information and help Nour assess her options about what to do next, but Nour is often unavailable because cellphone reception is not always reliable. When Nour is unavailable, players will not receive messages from her, and this effect plays our in real time. That choice by the developers really makes this game feel like interactions between real people. The game has nineteen different endings, and in some of them the length of time between messages from Nour increases, then eventually ceases, indicating the only help Majd may be able to provide is burying Nour once everything is over. *This War of Mine* by 11 Bit Studios is similar, but puts players in the shoes of those who cannot flee war. Players control everyday civilians, not trained survivalists, and try to scrounge up supplies to survive while evading armed gangs and deciding whether to survive by stealing from other civilians in the same situation.

Tillich's Theology of Culture and the Other in Video Games

Many additional games could be provided as examples of games that touch upon real-world issues and possess the ability to enhance both the player's understanding of those issues and where they stand on them.

Navid Khonsari started his development studio, iNK Stories, in order to tell underrepresented cultural histories. The fictional story of their game *1979 Revolution: Black Friday* is based on interviews with people who lived through the Iranian Revolution, and players are given the option of praying about the turmoil at one point. If they do so, Reza, the character controlled in the game, says 'Allāhu akbar!' out loud with others taking part in the prayer, in stark contrast to depictions of Muslims as stereotypical terrorists in so many forms of media. Game developer Rami Ismail created a virtual space inside of the Nintendo game *Animal Crossing: New Horizons* where Muslims virtually gathered together to break their fasts during Ramadan instead of being alone during the height of stay at home orders during the COVID-19 pandemic.[19]

Richard Hofmeier's *Cart Life* is basically a capitalism simulator from the perspective of someone living in poverty which uses frantic and difficult gameplay to convey how little capitalist systems care about people struggling to survive within them. *That Dragon Cancer* is a collaboration between Numinous Games and a real family that dealt with childhood cancer and death and wanted to convey that experience through the game. It is currently being used in pastoral counseling courses.[20] During the Black Lives Matter protests of 2020, a fundraising effort in the industry to support the NAACP Legal Defense Fund and Community Bail Fund set a $100,000 goal. The total raised after ten days was $8,158,561.31.[21]

While Paul Tillich was a prolific philosophical theologian, that should not obfuscate the fact that he believed in the power of art and culture to transform individual lives as well as society. If anything, he had more confidence in the power of art and cultural movements outside of churches, especially after he watched most

---

19. Imran Khan, 'In Extraordinary Times, Ramadan Finds a Place in Animal Crossing', in *The Washington Post*, May 15, 2020, https://www.washingtonpost.com/video-games/2020/05/15/ramadan-animal-crossing/.
20. John W Auxier, 'That Dragon, Cancer Goes to Seminary: Using a Serious Video Game in Pastoral Training', in *Christian Education Journal: Research on Educational Ministry* 15, no 1 (2018): 105–17.
21. 'Bundle for Racial Justice and Equality', itch.io, last modified June 16, 2020, https://itch.io/b/520/bundle-for-racial-justice-and-equality.

German churches give their support to Hitler during World War II.[22] He rejected supernatural forms of theology, refused a clean break between God and the world, and viewed theology and culture as inseparable from one another.[23] 'Religion is the substance of culture, culture is the form of religion.'[24]

In his ground-of-being theology, each of us realises who we are by participating in the world around us here and now, not by hoping for escape to some heavenly realm. Tillich was active in the New York City art scene after he emigrated to the United States and saw these points at work when the Jewish, Slavic, gay, and disabled people the Nazis rejected as being incompatible with Germany were accepted by this artistic culture.

Tillich's embrace of and participation in culture is a direct consequence of his understanding of God. Rather than *a being* with specific attributes and intentions, God is the ground of *all beings*. God is the ground, or support structure, giving meaning to all. God is the divine depth to which any piece of reality, including paintings and video games, can be directed.[25] As Tillich described his use of depth language, it means 'the religious aspect points to that which is ultimate, infinite, unconditional in man's spiritual life'.[26] In other words, secular culture, including artifacts intended for entertainment, and religion cannot be separated.

While Tillich's non-theistic ground-of-being model may strike more confessional theologians as too odd to accept, there are means of connecting Tillich with more traditional concepts. The fact that the ground of being can be realized in any finite being in this world shows

---

22. Tillich did not mince words when criticizing churches for this failure: 'We suddenly realized that if Hitler can be produced by German culture, something must be wrong with this culture. This prepared our emigration to this country and our openness to the new reality it represents. Neither my friends nor I myself dared for a long time to point to what was great in the Germany of our past. If Hitler is the outcome of what we believed to be true philosophy and the only theology, both must be false.' Paul Tillich, *Theology of Culture*, edited by Robert C Kimball (New York: Oxford University Press, 1959), 163–4.
23. Paul Tillich, 'Relation of Metaphysics and Theology', in *The Review of Metaphysics*, 10, no 1 (1956): 58.
24. Paul Tillich, *The Protestant Era* (Chicago: University of Chicago Press, 1948), 57.
25. Paul Tillich, *The System of the Sciences according to Objects and Methods*, translated by Paul Wiebe (Lewisburg, Penn.: Bucknell University Press, 1981), 203.
26. Tillich, *Theology of Culture*, 7.

that Tillich took Martin Luther's claim about the finite being capable of bearing the infinite very seriously. The *imago Dei* is a classical idea which means God can be seen in all. The way in which we sometimes do not want to see God in some people we would rather not love (the poor, the foreigner, etc.) is also a classic way of describing sin. To follow that line of thinking, God can be seen in virtual others in games, and a refusal to see games as theologically relevant is its own sort of sin. However, more important than potential conflict between Tillich's model of God and your own is the fact that the impact of video games on culture closely mirrors Tillich's own analysis of cultural movements. Whenever polarizing exclusive options are experienced, which occurred in Gamergate and in Germany during World War II, an alternative participatory whole is possible because God is with and for all.

In light of the ability of any piece of culture to become transparent or opaque to its meaningful depths, heteronomy, autonomy, and theonomy are the terms Tillich used to analyze social relations. Heteronomy is about domination and control. It orchestrates cohesion and agreement through use of force, overriding the free autonomous choices of individuals in favor of what those in power deem to be the case. It represents attempts to transform shared and diverse situations into one's in which the dominant in-group matters and minorities or those considered outsiders are only accepted if they conform.

World War II and Gamergate are both examples of heteronomy in action against autonomy. Rather than being a woman *and* a game developer, or gay *and* a fan of video games, Gamergate attempted to create a polarized culture in which both-and was replaced with either-or. Heteronomy is found in supernatural forms of religion that Tillich rejected in which supernatural truth is forced on the world whether wanted or not. Instead, he argued ultimate truth breaks through within autonomous cultural activities. When this happens, it is a case of theonomy, 'autonomous reason united to its own depth'.[27]

The changes in the video game industry I have described are examples of moving from a heteronomous to theonomous culture. Game communities did the work to support attacked minorities by creating structures for support. Gamergate's damaging heteronomy led to autonomous reactions of individuals that also created a larger

---

27. Tillich, *Systematic Theology*, 1: 85.

culture of increased acceptance, or theonomy. Tillich was right to summarize these ideas as a theology of culture, because there is no limit to how and where theonomy can occur, given his understanding of God as the depth dimension toward which anything can be directed.

Tillich's concept of theonomy is highly relevant for analyzing video games because it indicates that an inclusive participatory whole is always possible, even as polarization and exclusion is experienced. When God is understood as the ground of being, it is impossible to be estranged, to be separated from God and one's true nature. Heteronomous forces can try to manufacture and arbitrarily maintain such a situation, but the feelings of estrangement they try to create can be overcome. Nothing can actually be separated from its ground.[28] Video games can help people experiencing such estrangement overcome it, and one of the main ways this occurs is through the encounter of others as described by Emmanuel Levinas, albeit virtual others.

Enter Emmanuel Levinas

Similar to how Tillich called for a theological revolution after World War II, Levinas called for the prioritization of ethics over logical, epistemological, and metaphysical questions after he and his family were on the other end of that conflict as victims of the Holocaust. Before we know any factual information about others, our interactions with one another are ethical. We should respect each other's differences rather than only displaying compassion to those not deemed *too* different. The face of the other cries out 'do not kill me' no matter what you know about me, which Levinas meant literally given that his father, mother, brothers, father-in-law, and mother-in-law were killed in the Holocaust.[29]

As I have described, nontraditional video games provide styles of gameplay that allow players to encounter and interact with other characters in ethically charged situations. As in real life, players

---

28. Paul Tillich, 'The Philosophical Background of My Theology', in *Main Works*, volume 1, *Philosophical Writings*, ed. Carl Heinz Ratschow (Berlin: Walter de Gruyter, 1989), 418; *Systematic Theology*, 1: 204–206.
29. Michael Purcell, *Levinas and Theology* (Cambridge: Cambridge University Press, 2006), 4.

encounter others who call out to them in the form of demands waiting for a response. That response will, in turn, determine the sort of person, or player, each of us is as we give it.[30] Adhering to Levinas's ethics or failing to respond with compassion is one way in-group versus out-group conflicts develop.

Many people unknowingly abide by the points Levinas makes when encountering others they deem similar to themselves. Eventually, most of us cross a line where others are now deemed too different, and seen as threatening just because of that difference. White nationalists and Gamergate share the feature of privileging those who are similar while aggressively rejecting those who differ, but the point emanating from Levinas is that such actions are irresponsible because they violate the primary feature of such encounters. A completely unknown other, in the absence of any information whatsoever, still calls out for respect, life, and dignity.[31]

Importantly for the present analysis of video games, the encounter of the other is nonphenomenal, prior to studying or describing the features of who is encountered.[32] Since the other is not literally the appearance of another person's physical features, but the conveying of a plea that demands a response, there is no reason to deny that the other be encountered in video games. Affirming the opposite is actually more in line with Levinas's core concern: experiences of the other and how they change each of us. There is no encounter of the other in reading his words or mine. However, video games allow players to have and learn from the sorts of encounters Levinas describes.

Gamergate was an ethical failure, in part, because it was a movement that lacked transcendence, a source of additional meaning. Encountering others in games, even AI others, is one way of finding oneself in the other, realizing oneself in that 'more' which Gamergate lacked. AI others are a part of contemporary culture, so it is possible to find the ground of your being and thus your true nature in such

---

30. Emmanuel Levinas, 'Is Ontology Fundamental?' in *Emmanuel Levinas: Basic Philosophical Writings*, edited by Adriaan T Peperzak, Simon Critchley, and Robert Bernasconi (Bloomington: Indiana University Press, 1996), 1–10.
31. Emmanuel Levinas, *Otherwise Than Being or Beyond Essence* (Boston: Martinus Nijhoff, 1981), 47–55.
32. Michael L Morgan, *Discovering Levinas* (Cambridge: Cambridge University Press, 2007), 47–48.

virtual encounters. The personal and societal concerns of Tillich and Levinas are united in video games. It is worth expanding on this claim, because despite being labeled modern and postmodern thinkers, indicating there should be little agreement between them, Tillich and Levinas are fully aligned on this point.

Ethical responsibility is not an autonomous choice, according to Levinas, because it is initiated by the appeal of the other. Thus, his weighting of terms seems to be opposed to Tillich's, with ethical responsibility being heteronomous, 'prior to freedom'.[33] We are all the other to each other in our encounters, and the other forces a response to its ethical calling.

However, it is important to note that Tillich and Levinas use the terms heteronomy and autonomy differently. For Levinas, heteronomy is 'the aspiration, especially philosophical, to move from this world to another, from the everyday to the beyond'.[34] Tillich associated heteronomy with domination and control, which is how Levinas defines autonomy, our attempts to domesticate our social worlds according to our limited purviews.[35] This means that Levinas's call to prioritize heteronomy and difference over autonomy is actually more in line with Tillich's definition of theonomy. Heteronomous responsibility (Tillich's theonomy) is how we all make ourselves in relation to the other. The following was written by Tillich, but easily could have come from Levinas.

> Nobody can say where the final limits of human power lie. In his encounter with the universe, man is able to transcend any imaginable limit. But there is a limit for man which is definite and which he always encounters, the other man. The other one, the 'thou', is like a wall which cannot be removed or penetrated or used. He who tries to do so, destroys himself. The 'thou' demands by his very existence to be acknowledged as a 'thou' for an 'ego' and as an 'ego' for himself. This is the claim which is implied in his being. Man can refuse to listen to the intrinsic claim of the other one. He can disregard his demand for justice. He can remove or use him. He can try to

---

33. Levinas, *Otherwise Than Being*, 123.
34. Morgan, *Discovering Levinas*, 89.
35. Emmanuel Levinas, 'Philosophy and the Idea of Infinity', in *Collected Philosophical Papers*, translated by Alphonso Lingis (Pittsburgh: Duquesne University Press, 1998), 47–48.

transform him into a manageable object, a thing, a tool. But in doing so he meets the resistance of him who has the claim to be acknowledged as an ego. And this resistance forces him either to meet the other one as an ego or to give up his own ego-quality.[36]

Video games facilitate the ability to be oneself individually while also responsibly participating in a larger group, which amounts to Tillich's theonomy and the ethical responsibility emphasized by Levinas united.

Conclusion: Realising Theological Ideals

I have described how the video game industry moved away from a culture of dominance. That happened as the previously marginalised came to affirm themselves and realize their identities in direct reaction to that culture of dominance. These developments relate to Tillich's thought because when ultimate concern and divine power is related to the ground of being rather than God as the highest being, that is a conceptual move that prevents God from being used as a cudgel of heteronomous power. The divine ground of being is a safeguard against attacks on individual autonomy. I have described how those marginalized in the video game industry have realised their own live through the games they create, which in turn changed the culture of video games. That is what it means for God as the ground of being to be realized through culture. Tillich obviously plays with metaphors about depth when describing his understanding of God, but depth is about serious participation. People are realising their depths of their own identities in video games and realizing that everyone else should similarly be able to participate instead of arbitrary and biased hindrances being put in their way.

Since 2016 I have been asked to speak twenty-one times at video game conventions for fans as well as professional events for developers. I teach games such as the ones I have mentioned and have my students play them when I teach Philosophy in Pop Culture. What I have presented is not a pet theory about theology and video games, but facts about the effects of video games on the lives of players

---

36. Paul Tillich, *Love, Power, and Justice: Ontological Analyses and Ethical Applications* (New York: Oxford University Press, 1954), 78.

confirmed by the players themselves, facts that display the continued relevance and power of Tillich and Levinas. When individuals are no longer estranged from themselves, and each individual is allowed to participate in a group that is no longer exclusionary, previously heteronomous forces and autonomous individuals reunite as a common but now more diverse group.

Without knowing anything about Tillich and Levinas beforehand, after almost every one of those twenty-one talks I have given, someone previously marginalized in games has told me concepts developed by these two men perfectly express their experiences. If you remain unconvinced, I lay out the entire argument, including additional neuroscientific evidence for these claims, in my book *Playing as Others: Theology and Ethical Responsibility in Video Games*.

I have also described how the video game industry is ambiguous and has not always been a culture of liberation instead of domination. Ambiguity is an ever-present theme in Tillich's thought, and anything through which infinite meaning breaks through can also be turned into a false idol. There are still problems in the video game industry. Cases of sexual abuse in gaming arose alongside the worldwide Me-Too movement, and 2023 saw massive layoffs of developers from large studios in order to save corporate profits.[37] However, the culture surrounding the industry is thankfully full of people who continue to criticise such problems and work toward their resolution. God as the ground of being is a guarantee that meaning can be realised here and now, but does nothing to specify the means by which it will be realised, or prevent meaning from being distorted and transformed into something truly damaging.

---

37. Maddy Myers, 'The Cost of Being a Woman Who Covers Video Games', in *Kotaku*, January 3, 2020, https://kotaku.com/the-cost-of-being-a-woman-who-covers-video-games-1840793836; Jason Schreier, 'Video Game Industry Rocked by Outpouring of Sexual Misconduct Allegations', in *Bloomberg*, June 24, 2020, https://www.bloomberg.com/news/articles/2020-06-24/video-game-industry-rocked-by-outpouring-of-sexual-misconduct-allegations; Ethan Gatch, 'Multiple Women Accuse Games Writer Chris Avellone of Sexual Misconduct', in *Kotaku*, June 23, 2020, https://kotaku.com/multiple-women-accuse-games-writer-chris-avellone-of-se-1844135498; Nathan Grayson, 'A Wave of Sexual Abuse Stories Is Causing a Reckoning in the Twitch Streaming World', in *Kotaku*, June 24, 2020, https://kotaku.com/a-wave-of-sexual-abuse-stories-is-causing-a-reckoning-i-1844122735.

Tillich and Levinas saw the potential for something new and better in theology and ethics while staring at the catastrophic failings of WW II.[38] Something similar happened in the video game industry after Gamergate I have described. The potential is continuing to be developed by the games themselves and the culture surrounding them. Rather than solely focusing on the threats to human values posed by AI, an alternative viewpoint locates possibilities amid the threat, new forms of human flourishing such technology might enable. Of course, the results will be ambiguous, and I have described the bad in addition to the good within video game culture. However, the good can be nurtured and further developed. That is precisely what is happening in video games right now.

---

38. In *The Shaking of the Foundations*, Tillich's first book of sermons published only three years after World War II ended, he wrote the following: 'There is something immovable, unchangeable, unshakeable, eternal, which becomes manifest in our passing and the crumbling of our world.' Paul Tillich, *The Shaking of the Foundations* (New York: Charles Scribner's Sons, 1948), 9.

Agathon: A Journal of Ethics and Value in the Modern World, Vol 10/2025

Chapter 12
On the Faith of Droids

Daniel J Peterson

> 'I think he's searching for his former master,
> but I've never seen such devotion in a droid before.'
> — Luke Skywalker, *Star Wars: A New Hope*

Abstract: Theologians and biblical scholars have attempted in different ways to define what constitutes within or among human beings the image of God, the *imago Dei*. These efforts, as Noreen Herzfeld argues, can be useful in looking at how designers of AI have attempted to fashion AI in their image. Absent the discussion, however, is the consideration of how faith, which according to Paul Tillich makes personality possible, might be reflected in AI. Faith is the condition for the possibility of Strong AI. Since Strong AI does not yet exist, the present essay analyzes its appearance in the genre of science fiction film, specifically in the characters of R2-D2 (*Star Wars: A New Hope*) and K2-SO (*Rogue One: A Star Wars Story*), showing how faith as a trait/capacity and as an expression of relationship both contribute to the *imago hominis* in Strong AI and help make Strong AI possible.

Key Terms: Artificial Intelligence (AI), *Imago Dei*, Paul Tillich, *Rogue One*, *Star Wars*

Genesis 1:1–2:4a, the first account of creation in the Hebrew Bible, offers much to ponder: a world that that blooms with vegetation in the blink of a day (vv11–12); the appearance of light *before* God hangs the stars onto the ceiling of the nighttime sky (vv 3, 14–18); seas that teem almost instantaneously with life (v 20); a sublime depiction of God in refreshingly non-anthropomorphic terms as a mighty wind that sweeps across waters of primeval chaos, dark and deep (v.2). Yet at the heart of this, the Priestly version of the world at its inception, lies two verses that have garnered more attention than any of the above combined, namely, the claim that God made human beings in God's image (Gen 1:26–27).

Genesis 1:26–27 lends itself to multiple interpretive possibilities. It speaks of God in the plural, suggesting to some commentators that the image of God or *imago Dei* resides not so much within us as the freedom of the will or the capacity to reason, but among us when we live in harmony with one another. Others, including the biblical scholar Gerhard von Rad, think of the *imago Dei* as the unique role human beings have in exercising dominion over creation and caring for it on God's behalf (Gen 1:28).[1] Still others, having defined what it means to bear the divine image, question whether any of it even remains after Adam's fall in the second biblical account of creation (Gen 3:22–24). The sixteenth century theologian John Calvin, for example, emphasises the severity of the fall to such an extent that nothing of God's image survives Adam's transgression and expulsion from paradise, rendering the search for a meaningful definition ultimately moot. Fortunately, at least for the sake of discussion, Noreen Herzfeld assumes otherwise.

For Herzfeld, author of *In Our Image: Artificial Intelligence and the Human Spirit*, exploring the ways in which Hebrew Bible scholars and Christian theologians interpret the meaning of the *imago Dei* has a dual significance. It not only sheds light on how we understand ourselves, especially when it comes to what we cherish most about being human. It also illuminates what we hope to replicate of ourselves in the creation of strong artificial intelligence (AI), that is, as Ted Peters explains elsewhere in the present volume, 'a machine capable of performing any task the human brain can perform'. The goal that informs such research, Herzfeld argues, springs from the desire to create something that mirrors us, 'to build something *like* ourselves'. Thus, 'as the *imago Dei* captures the way humans are like God, so the *imago hominis* of artificial intelligence seeks to capture the way computers could be like humans'.[2] Herzfeld's analysis shows,

---

1. Noreen Herzfeld, *In Our Image: Artificial Intelligence and the Human Spirit* (Minneapolis: Fortress Press, 2002), 21–24.
2. Herzfeld, *In Our Image*, 50.

in turn, how researchers in the field of AI have sought to endow machines with the ennobling qualities, capacities, and functions biblical exegetes and theologians attribute to the divine image within (or among) us as human beings.

Nothing thus far sounds problematic until we recall, as John Calvin points out, that the second account of creation, the Yahwist account in Genesis 2–4, ends in a breach between God and human beings, one God presumably does not intend. If that happens when God creates human beings in God's image, imagine what disasters might result when human beings create AI in their image! Strong AI would not, as in Genesis, fall away from the perfection of a wholly benevolent deity; it would, rather, duplicate the morally ambiguous, even sinful nature of its all-too-human progenitors. As Alan Weissenbacher remarks elsewhere in the present volume, 'Humans will pass their penchant for sin onto their creations, and to think that a sufficient super-intelligence will see these sins and avoid them, or care about avoiding them, is the height of wishful thinking'. Any technological creation capable of imitating our best qualities will, in short, also have the potential to embody our worst.

These qualities vary considerably. The substantive approach, which Herzfeld identifies as the dominant way theologians historically have interpreted the image of God, equates it with a special capacity or trait of human nature, including everything from self-transcendence and reason to free will and our personality.[3] The introduction of sin complicates matters. It corrupts and distorts the aforementioned qualities, producing an additional capacity, say, for selfishness or pride, disclosing in the process a sharp contrast between what it means to exist in the *imago hominis* versus the *imago Dei*. Being made in the *imago Dei*, at least, allows for the theoretical possibility of a life without sin, which biblical and creedal Christianity affirms concerning Christ, whereas being made in the *imago hominis* makes sin, to use the language of Reinhold Niebuhr, not only inevitable but necessary. Robots, it would seem, have no hope.

Fortunately, for robots on the big screen, theological consistencies need not apply. AI in cinema can be unambiguously good, as in the case of the character WALL-E in the 2008 film of the same name, even if its maker is flawed. It can alternatively be evil, deceptive

---

3. Herzfeld, *In Our Image*, 16.

and destructive without explanation, as in the case of HAL from *2001: A Space Odyssey* or more recently the character of Ava in Alex Garland's *Ex Machina*. AI on screen, moreover, occasionally demonstrates another possibility for its future, possessing, as in the character of R2-D2 in *Star Wars*, a sense of mission or what appears to be the rudiments of *faith*, a faculty or capacity of special interest to theologians, yet one Herzfeld curiously neglects in her treatment of the topic.[4] Could AI ever develop the capacity to exhibit what the German American theologian Paul Tillich calls an ultimate concern? Could a droid have a relationship with God?

Faith Forming Self

Absent the emergence presently of Strong AI, why pursue the topic any further if the analysis must by necessity restrict itself to science fiction? Two reasons come to mind. First, fiction has the potential to shape the future, revealing new possibilities for exploration to researchers. The once-popular flip phone, novel for its time, had its antecedent in the make-believe communicators the crew of the Enterprise used in the original *Star Trek* television series. Second, exploring the potential pitfalls and perks of computer super-intelligence as it confronts us in film may help us more effectively prepare for its actual appearance, should it one day arrive. What happens, for example, if by fluke or by design a robot manifested a sense of allegiance or devotion to a person, group, or cause? How might we react?

Paul Tillich witnessed the horrific effects of faith understood as unquestioning devotion to a particular group while living in Germany in the 1920s and early 1930s. Faith, he came to realize, is not about believing in certain religious doctrines. It involves, rather, being 'grasped' by something that brings with it a demand and promise, both of which the subject experiences as unconditional. Theoretically, all people have faith insofar as they do more than simply live—they live *for* something, and that "something" functionally serves as their god. The question, then, is not whether people believe in god, but in

---

4. This could be, as I elaborate further below, because faith belongs neither entirely to the various faculties interpreters link with the divine image in human beings, including our capacity for reason or self-transcendence, nor wholly to the relational model of the *imago Dei*, particularly as Karl Barth presents. Instead, to use a well-worn phrase from Paul Tillich, it resides on the boundary between the two.

which god they place their trust and allegiance. What do they value above all else? What matters most in their lives? Is it money, social status, climbing the corporate ladder, romantic love, the nation, or God? Obviously, in some cases the object that becomes an ultimate concern (for example, money) is not intrinsically evil, but when it takes on the status of being unconditionally important or the reason for one's being, it can be highly destructive to others as well as oneself (*cf* 1 Tim 6:6-10). 'The risk to faith in one's ultimate concern is indeed the greatest risk man can run', Tillich writes. 'For if it proves to be a failure, the meaning of one's life breaks down; one surrenders oneself ... to something which is not worth it.'[5]

Beyond the important claim that faith orients the individual toward something he or she takes with unconditional significance as opposed merely to believing that something is true, Tillich offers another observation particularly relevant to our purposes. Faith, he says, integrates mind, heart, and will in a centered act of the personality, effectively making personality possible by directing it toward the singular object of its concern (20). Lloyd Geering in *Reimagining God* claims likewise, albeit with regard to the broader development of Western consciousness historically thanks to monotheism. 'The theologian Gordon Kaufman', he remarks, 'pointed out that the concept of God, apart from the now outmoded images, has long served as a unifying point to which we can orient everything else and so make sense of the world and our place in it' (128). Even if God has 'died' in modern secular society, Geering concludes, the idea proved useful. It gave us focus. Around it and because of it we constructed our world, emerging individually and collectively from the 'jumble of sense impressions ... to become more mature, integrated selves, a process [Carl] Jung termed individuation.'[6]

The significance of Tillich's position in relation to the development of Strong AI should thus be clear. Faith creates the self in human beings. It makes personality possible by integrating and uniting its various functions in the service of a single-minded focus. If robots were bound as well by a sense of mission or what matters most, either as a result of their programming or because of what the

---

5. Paul Tillich, *The Dynamics of Faith* (New York: Harper & Row, 1957), 17.
6. Lloyd Geering, *Reimaging God: The Faith Journey of a Modern Heretic* (Salem: Polebridge Press, 2017), 137.

biologist Stephen Jay Gould calls a 'fortunate fluke' in reference to *our* evolutionary past, could such a focus, itself perhaps a rudimentary expression of ultimate concern, contribute to an emerging sense of interiority, to the robot's growing sense of self? Might such a robot, the kind driven by a fledgling ultimate concern, eventually pass the Turing Test? Could it, beyond its relationship with human beings, develop a capacity to relate to the maker of its maker, to God? Could faith be the key that unlocks the doorway to Strong AI?

Two Candidates for Consideration: R2-D2 and K2-SO

We only have one significant clue. At the beginning of *Star Wars: A New Hope*, shortly after her ship has been besieged, Princess Leia inserts a small disc into R2-D2, one of the two main "droids" in the film. The disc contains the stolen plans of the Empire's new leathal weapon, the Death Star. The scene takes place without words.

Sometime later, R2D2's new owner, Luke Skywalker, discovers the plans irretrievably wedged inside the droid, accidentally playing a message the droid refuses to repeat. Thus begins a litany of explanations on the part of R2's counterpart, C3-PO, who attributes the former droid's bizarre behavior to the hardships both of them have endured together over time, only later to claim that the fault lies presumably in R2's programming. 'These astrodroids are getting quite out of hand', he says to Luke after R2 escapes to fulfill his mission. 'Even I can't understand their logic sometimes.' The variety of explanations keeps the viewer guessing: does R2's sense of mission to get the plans to another character (Obi-Wan Kenobi), one that inspires Luke to say he's 'never seen such devotion in a droid before', stem from a malfunction, as C3-PO's comments seem to suggest, or was it programmed by Princess Leia?

Regardless of its source, a spark exists, a faculty, whether by accident or by intention, that provides the condition for the possibility of R2's faith or what Herzfeld nicely calls his 'dogged loyalty'.[7] Yet how do we explain that fact that once R2's mission is complete, once he delivers the recording and the plans, such loyalty expands in relation to other characters, especially Luke? Could it be that it grows out of the relationships of interdependence he and Luke develop, illustrating

---

7. Herzfeld, *In Our Image*, 62.

how faith exists on the boundary between the substantive approach to the *imago Dei*, which again identifies the image of God in human beings with a particular faculty, and what Herzfeld subsequently presents as the relational approach to the *imago Dei*, which indicates that we mirror the triune God when we find ourselves in mutual relationship with God and/or one another?[8]

A more developed expression of ultimate concern appears in K2-SO, a former imperial security droid who appears in 2016's *Rogue One: A Star Wars Story*. Critics give him more accolades than any other character of the film, in several cases with obvious irony. Richard Brody, who scorches everything in the movie from the direction of the actors to the 'flat and inexpressive' script, nevertheless finds kind words for the droid. 'The one character with any inner-identity is, in fact, a robot', he says, 'K2-SO, voiced by Alan Tudyk, and the only performance with any flair at all is a CGI incarnation, or rather, resurrection.'[9] Notice here the reference to 'inner-identity', a hallmark of Strong AI. Another critic, Eric Goldman, refers likewise to the 'sympathetic soul' Tudyk's performance gives to K2, adding playfully, 'if such a word [soul] is appropriate for a droid' (fn). What do we make of that? How did K2 get a 'sympathetic soul' in the first place?

K2 has an intriguing back-story. Cassian Andor, a pilot and member of the Rebel Alliance, reprogrammed him. Before that, K2 was an imperial security droid who emerges as the major source of comic relief throughout the film. Upon meeting Jyn Erso, the film's protagonist, K2 comments, rather dryly, 'The captain says you are a friend. I will not kill you.' Cassian, meanwhile, seems at a loss when it comes to explaining his creation's humor. 'He tends to say whatever he wants', he shares with Jyn, 'whatever is in his circuits. It's a by-product of his reprogramming'. Critics likewise offer their best guesses regarding the source of his humor. 'K2-50 [sic] was also apparently given a sarcasm chip, and a complete set of *The Hitchhiker's Guide to the Galaxy*', jokes Chris Barsanti, 'all the better to model his behavior

---

8. Herzfeld, *In Our Image*, 31.
9. Richard Brody, "Rogue One' Reviewed: Is it Time to Abandon the Star Wars Francise?', in *The New Yorker*, accessed 2/10/19. https://www.newyorker.com/culture/richard-brody/rogue-one-reviewed-is-it-time-to-abandon-the-star-wars-franchise

on that of Marvin the Paranoid Android'.[10] Like R2, K2 appears at first to have some kind of faculty that helps explains his humanlike eccentricities—a capacity, whether intentional or a by-product—concerning the *imago hominis* within him.

Yet as the film progresses, K2's loyalty to Cassian, including the cause which Cassian serves, grows significantly, so much so that it culminates in the droid's self-sacrifice, the first of its kind we see in any film of the *Star Wars* franchise. Tudyk, the actor who plays the character, offers a persuasive explanation accordingly. 'For all his rough edges, Kaytoo also feels fierce loyalty', he says, 'especially toward ... Cassian ... who cleared the droids databanks of Imperial programming and and allowed him to break free of service to the galactic dictatorship.' The source of K2's loyalty suddenly becomes clear. 'He wants what Cassian wants', Tudyk continues. 'He loves Cassian because Cassian freed him. It's also more paternal in that [Cassian] gave him life and took away the bonds of his programming.'[11] The theological overtones could not be more apparent: K2, out of gratitude for the gift of life and freedom, makes Cassian and by extension the rebel cause his ultimate concern. Relationship once again provides the context out of which the created reflects the image of its creator, the result of which gives our droid his reason for being. Cassian and his cause become the god(s) whom K2 serves.

In Ephesians the same logic of faith appears, only this time obviously with respect to human beings and their ideal relationship with God. 'All of us', the author declares, 'once lived among [the disobedient] in the passions of our flesh, following the desires of flesh and senses, and we were by nature children of wrath, like everyone else' (2:3). We were bound, 'slaves of sin', as Paul says in Romans 6:17. But now, thanks to the gift of God's grace (Eph 2:8), we are liberated, 'made ... alive together with Christ', the appropriate response to which is thanksgiving (5:4, 20), good works (2:10), and single-minded devotion to God (that is, faith) whom we can approach in boldness and with confidence through Jesus Christ our Lord (3:11).

---

10. Chris Barsanti, '*Rogue One: A Star Wars Story* Shows There's Life in *Star Wars* Yet ... Barely', in *PopMatters*, accessed 2/10/19. https://www.popmatters.com/rogue-one-star-wars-story-theres-life-in-star-wars-yet-barely-2495405800.html
11. Anthony Breznican, '*Rogue One: Alan Tudyk reveals the accent and origin story of K-2SO*', in *Entertainment Weekly*, accessed 2/10/19. https://ew.com/article/2016/08/10/rogue-one-alan-tudyk/

Implications for Understanding AI and Ourselves

R2 and K2 offer snapshots of what Strong AI could like should it ever appear. Both droids exhibit varying degrees of faith, of single-minded devotion that becomes increasingly evident in their actions and arguably makes possible or at least deepens their respective personalities. At first, other characters offer explanations concerning the source of their quirky, human-like behavior (R2's stubborn persistence, K2's sarcasm). These, however, merely scratch the surface, ultimately burning off as both films pass like starships through the atmosphere. By the time they reach the ground, particularly *Rogue One*, we see how the more profoundly human qualities of love and self-sacrifice emerge out of relationship rather than rewiring. K2 imbibes the best of humanity by doing for Cassion and Jyn what Christ did for all people, giving himself up so that others might live.

The comparison, of course, is not perfect! K2 employs violence in the service of his faith, i.e., his unwavering commitment to Cassian and the cause, yet it seems that by the end of the film it is his faith that enables him to determine concretely and powerfully who he is and what he must do. Is it such faith, understood as a centering act of single-minded focus, that lures K2's inchoate personality out of his subconcious circuitry? If so, does the possibility exist that he, now free, has the option to turn away from Cassian and the cause in rebellion, just as Adam turns away from God at the edge of the Garden? Could this, taking seriously now the penchant for sin human beings would automatically pass on to their creations, be their downfall? How might this reflect our humanity back to us? Do we like what we see, and if we do not, what steps, if any, can we take to prevent occuring in robots what we find maddeningly occurring within ourselves?

Our focus on R2 and K2, finally, raises another question. What about the rest of the droids that populate the *Star Wars* universe, if not the the various other droids of science fiction generally, including Replicants in the *Blade Runner* films? By leaving them out of our present discussion and focusing exclusively on what Herzfeld calls the 'genre of companionable artificial intelligence', what might we be avoiding or repressing about who we are that we must confront?[12] Genesis 1, the Priestly account of creation, implies only possibilities for the good when it comes to affirming that God makes human

---

12. Herzfeld, *In Our Image*, 63.

beings in God's image. We must also consider Genesis 2–3, the Yahwist account of creation, for a more sobering look at who we are but also what we, fancying ourselves to be God rather than human beings who bear the image of God, could create. K2, after all, began not as Cassian's co-pilot but as a security droid—a security droid for the empire.

Conclusion

Intelligence without centering by faith is nothing more than calculation. In fact, it's not intelligence at all.

R2 and K2 illustrate fully embodied robotic intelligence. They provide a working image of what Strong AI would be like should it ever appear. Here is what is significant: these droids exhibit varying degrees of faith, of single-minded devotion that becomes increasingly evident in their actions and arguably makes possible or at least deepens their respective personalities.

Regardless of what theologians surmise about the *imago Dei* attached to *Homo sapiens*, we can see that it is faith which orients the self and constructs personhood. Intelligence is a function of personhood in the human being. If Strong AI is ever to attain intelligence in emulation of the human, then a faith-centered personhood will be requisite.

Agathon: A Journal of Ethics and Value in the Modern World, Vol 10/2025

Chapter 13
From Heidegger on Technology to an Inclusive Pluralistic Theology

Rajesh Sampath

> The 'essence of technology is not itself technological'.
> —Martin Heidegger[1]

Abstract: This article explores Heidegger's later philosophy and what this means for possible theological interpretations of the relationship between humans and automated technology, especially Artificial Intelligence (AI). The essay concludes with prospects for *an inclusive pluralistic theology*, which may require the de-centering of the 'natural, biological human' as the highest manifestation of God's creation.

Keywords: Heidegger, AI, technology, theological ethics, philosophy of religion

This chapter explores Martin Heidegger's later philosophy and what that means for possible theological interpretations of the relationship between humans and automated technology, such as Artificial Intelligence (AI). We will inquire into the possibility, limits, and hope for faith in a futuristic age.

The chapter has three parts. First, I will explore ethical arguments for or against the possibility of AI superseding human intelligence and making moral decisions on its own. This will set up the question: Could AI have non-natural rights to faith? Would this right obtain when faith's boundaries with reason become blurred? Will the limits of theological norms become strained when non-human fidelity to traditional doctrines of the Christian God are tested?

---

1. Martin Heidegger, 'Question Concerning Technology', in *Basic Writings*, edited by David Farrell Krell (New York: Harper Perennial, 2008), 311.

In the second part, I will utilize Heidegger's philosophical investigations of technology as a prism to explore the theological question: what does AI/machine technology imply for Christian anthropology?

In the third part of the paper I will offer a thought experiment. How might an AI program have its own interpretation of the New Testament message? How might an intelligent machine read the Gospels? How might Heidegger's framing of the issues help us navigate the moral perplexity of a non-human relationship to God?

This essay concludes with prospects for *an inclusive pluralistic theology*, one that includes rather than excludes intelligent machines within oir spiritual community. Such an inclusive pluralistic theology may require the de-centering of the natural, biological human; it may require an unseating of humanity from its inherited throne as the highest manifestation of God's creation.

Part I: Debates about AI

This first part will briefly summarize arguments for or against AI. Is artificial intelligence really intelligent? Humanlike? Suprahuman?

One can ask whether non-natural or human-constructed, mechanical technologies can and will surpass natural, biological human intelligence. But that could be an ethically neutral scientific question that only scientists and technologists can debate given the technical, mathematical, computation and neuroscientific complexity of the subject.[2]

A step further would be whether a non-human machine intelligence could develop a religious and moral capacity, to feel guilt and sin along with salvation and redemption. This question is more pertinent for our investigation, albeit speculative. No one today would grant that AI is already at the level of basic human cognition with or without capacity for religious feeling or the pursuit of meaning and ultimate truth. So, let us go with the hypothetical scenario. A subset question would be this: would it be morally good or bad if AI were to develop a religious sensibility for transcendence? A soul?

---

2. Stuart Russell and Peter Norvig, *Artificial Intelligence: A Modern Approach,* 3rd edition (Essex: Pearson Education Limited, 2014).

Here is a problem for the theologian: our religious traditions have presumed that the human soul makes the human more than an animal. The soul defines the human species as the crown of creation. The human is the preeminent of all of God's creatures endowed with sovereignty over others: all animals and plants (Gen 1:26). Furthermore, God breathed into his paramount creation from the dust, and the human became a 'living soul' (Gen 2:7). Reformer John Calvin speaks for the dominant Christian tradition: 'When [God's] image is placed in man a tacit antithesis is introduced which raises man above all other creatures and, as it were, separates him from the common mass.'[3] Now let us ask: Would a religious and moral robot with a soul become a rival to the human throne?

If our biblically inherited hierarchy is thrown off by the invention of AI superior to *Homo sapiens*, then traditional faith would start to unravel. If an AI robot would rise to a level of intelligence or morality or religiosity higher than the human, might it rise into the very domain of the divine? Might AI climb the technological Tower of Babel to invade the heavens? Shall we, as Yuval Harari advocates, 'now aim to upgrade humans into gods, and turn *Homo sapiens* into *Homo deus*'?[4]

This would be theologically problematic, to say the least. Christians have long assumed that no reasoning human—except God incarnate in Jesus Christ, the preexistent Logos from the standpoint of Christian faith (Jn 1:1–18)—could ever attain the very omniscience or omnipotence of God. What must be maintained, traditionally, is the protection of a sacred distinction central to faith, namely God's unsurpassable transcendence as a mystery.[5]

So what do these standard theological ruminations entail about the fact that technology has *already* arrived and that there is a good chance a superior technology may be born in the future, one that

---

3. John Calvin, *Institutes of the Christian Religion* (1559), edited by John T McNeill, Library of Christian Classics XX, XXI (Louisville: Westminster John Knox Press, 1960), I, xv, 3, 188.
4. Yuval Noah Harari, *Homo Deus: A Brief History of Tomorrow* (New York: Harper, 2017), 21.
5. In recent Christian anthropology, the key human trait is openness to transcendence. When God becomes revealed, what is revealed is that God is mystery. Knowledge of God is knowledge of this transcendent mystery. This is characteristic of Karl Rahner, Karl Barth, and Wolfhart Pannenberg.

could replace the human as the center or apex of all creation? It could mean that the very act of creating AI could lead to this usurpation of God's power, which could then deform traditional doctrines of faith to the point of an indiscernible heresy. Both God's eschatological omnipotence (and human's special responsibility to non-humans until that crescendo point of historical time arrives) would dissolve. Therein lies the most profound dilemma that many religious people may have to confront.

We will explore this aporia. In order to do so, we must acknowledge that some among us see AI's ultimate supersession of human reason as a superior mode of reasoning on earth as inevitable and good.[6] Others see the danger in this, which can distort human to human relationships and potentially threaten the existence of all biological life in the future. Therefore, we must proceed with 'caution' even though we cannot instantaneously leap out of this technological age.[7] Indeed, there is no point in asking whether we should try to take this leap seeing that it may not be possible even if we so desired. In this paper I argue that before we take a stand on the necessity for precautionary sobriety at minimum or maintenance of human preeminence at maximum (with regard to dominion over all non-humans, animals, plants, technological automatons, biotechnological hybrids, etc), let us turn to the insights of the twentieth century continental European philosopher, Martin Heidegger (1889–1976). We will see how he tries to frame the question of technology in terms of authentic humanity, outside the context of mainstream theology and Anglo-American analytic social ethics discussions.

Part II: On Heidegger's 'Question Concerning Technology'

In this second part we will offer a brief critical analysis and interpretation of Heidegger's influential essay, 'Questioning Concerning Technology' (1957). This important text has shaped

---

6. Timothy Revell, 'AI will be able to beat us at everything by 206, says experts', in *New Scientist* (May 31st, 2017); https://www.newscientist.com/article/2133188-ai-will-be-able-to-beat-us-at-everything-by-2060-say-experts/.
7. See Noreen Herzfeld 's 'The Enchantment of Artificial Intelligence' and Ted Peter's 'Artificial Intelligence, Transhumanism, and Frankenfear.' Both articles appear in this volume.

many moral, ethical, and philosophical debates about the virtues and dangers of technological progress.[8]

My analysis in this section reaffirms traditional scholarly assumptions. For one, Heidegger is not advocating for some nostalgic or romantic return to a pre-Newtonian/classical mechanical and therefore pre-industrial age when today's automated technologies were not possible.[9] But nor does this impossibility to time travel back to a more 'innocent' age lead—necessarily—to a nihilistic or atheistic future where religion and theology become permanently obsolete. Rather, I will argue for a space of the holy and divine to be possible but only after reading Heidegger's take on the age of technology. For this German philosopher is asking us to consider the following: once we admit to the potential dangers of a non-thinking relationship to the *essence* of technology, an essence which is never technological in itself,[10] and we humans have no foreseeable way to stop the onslaught of technological command over everything, we still have a special ethical responsibility.

Indeed Heidegger asks us to reorient our very Being/essence to technology in ways that can handle the deepest mysteries of the human condition—that is, towards an appropriate type of thinking-orienting receptiveness about what can 'save' us so that we don't completely annihilate the possibility for a redemptive event to occur. What is that redemptive event? It is the event in which 'truth comes to pass.'[11]

Heidegger is seeking what he calls a 'free' relationship that 'opens our human existence to the essence of technology.'[12] But as mentioned previously, the "essence of technology is not itself technological."[13] That means we can't really turn to how natural scientists or technology

---

8. See *The Philosophy of Technology: The Technological Condition—An Anthology*, edited by Robert C Sharff and Val Dusek (Oxford: Wiley Blackwell, 2014), 503–647.
9. See the works of Andrew Feenberg (1991, 1995, 1999, 2002, 2005, 2010, 2017), Iain Thomson (2005), and Don Idhe (1979, 1983, 1998, and 2010).
10. Heidegger, 'Question Concerning Technology', 311.
11. Heidegger, 'Question Concerning Technology', 333. In reference to a phrase in a Hölderlin poem, Heidegger refers to this the 'saving power.' How we think about that can help prepare how we can even receive a response to the dangers of not thinking essentially about the very essence of technology and what that means for the fate of human beings.
12. Heidegger, 'Question Concerning Technology', 311.
13. Heidegger, 'Question Concerning Technology', 311.

entrepreneurs (Google, Facebook, Apple, Microsoft, IBM) define technology. Furthermore, this would also include social scientists who use positivistic and empirical epistemological frameworks to understand human beings' relationship to technology, for example the utility and policy dimensions of stem cell research to manufacture organs. Rather, Heidegger is thinking in the broadest philosophical terms, which stretches back to his earliest reflections up to his masterpiece, *Being and Time* (1927).[14]

Beyond the natural and social sciences, we also can't turn to the history of Western metaphysical attempts to define 'human beings', let alone 'their essence' or what the Being of the beings that are humans even means.[15] Finally, traditional theological doctrines of Christianity are inadmissible for the Heidegger of *Being and Time*.[16] But this is not an investigation of Heidegger's philosophical critique of religion or the possibilities for a Heideggerean philosophy of religion.

All I want to do here is draw some preliminary observations. Since we cannot start with any assumption of what the human being even means, we can't just dive into debates about whether human beings should (say in a normative ethical sense) embrace technology. Some examples include gene editing of fetuses or cloning, which bioethicists have to debate.[17] Nor are we considering that humans

---

14. Martin Heidegger, *Being and Time*, translated by John Macquerrie and Edward Robinson (New Yorker, Harper and Row, 1963).
15. For example, the incredibly complex notion of the *Imago Dei* or man made in God's image in Gen 1:26. 'Created in the image of God, human beings are by nature bodily and spiritual, men and women made for one another, persons oriented towards communion with God and with one another, wounded by sin and in need of salvation, and destined to be conformed to Christ, the perfect image of the Father, in the power of the Holy Spirit.' Vatican: International Theological Commission, *Communion and Stewardship: Human Persons Created in the Image of God 2002*, http://www.vatican.ca/roman_curia/congregations/cfaith/cti_documents/rc_con_cfaith_doc.
16. Before 1927, Heidegger had given up on dogmatic faith and institutional commitments to being Catholic. This does not mean he did not have a life-long, complex relationship with religion and theology before and after his break, for example his dialogues with the Lutheran theologian Rudolf Bultmann in the early 20s during his time in Marburg. See Benjamin Crowe, *Heidegger's Religious Origins: Destruction and Authenticity* (Bloomington: Indiana University Press, 2006).
17. Helga Kuhse, Udo Schüklenk, and Peter Singer, eds., *Bioethics*, 3rd edition (Oxford: Wiley Blackwell, 2016), 173.

should fatalistically abandon themselves to technological supremacy, knowing full-well that they can't escape its near ubiquitous presence on earth.[18] In the latter sense, we may have to accept the idea that we may be one of many creatures on earth in the future, particularly if an alien encounter ever happens. But even in the chance of that stupendous world-historical event doesn't mean we humans will be required to abandon faith and theology.[19] But these are not the questions before us.

It seems what is really at stake for Heidegger is the idea of a 'free relation' and 'openness' to the 'essence of technology', which is never technological. (Encountering aliens for example assumes we or they would have to have some advance technology to travel through real Einsteinian space-time, which would then require a reckoning of the nature of that technology. As of now we humans have never traveled through a wormhole and back.[20]) Yet, Heidegger is not interested in actual technologies or imagined ones in science fiction. Furthermore, his questioning is also irreducible to the history of metaphysics and theology; the latter fields have the capacity to think about essence in its highest generality, say the relationship between human and God, or human and transcendence, which goes beyond all sensorial and empirical reality. Long story short, after Heidegger winds his way from the ancient Greeks' idea of *techne* to his modern context, he lands on a definition of this 'essence' of technology as *Gestell*, which is translated as 'Enframing' from his original German.[21]

Whether we like technology or not is not the issue. Whether we think humans create technology is not the issue either; for that goes without saying as a simple fact since the dawn of the Industrial Age. Rather, Heidegger is concerned with that 'free relation' that 'opens human existence' to an essence. Since *Being and Time*, Heidegger has

---

18. Heidegger, 'Question Concerning Technology', 311. There Heidegger says affirming or denying technology is useless.
19. See *Astrotheology: Science and Theology Meet Extraterrestrial Life*, edited by Ted Peters, Martinez Hewlett, Joshua M Moritz, and Robert John Russell (Eugene: Cascade Books, 2018). Theological reflections of this kind hold enormous importance for the future of the religion and science dialogue and its commensurability with faith.
20. This is still the realm of science fiction like Christopher Nolan's magnificent film, *Interstellar* (2014) on which Nobel Prize winning Caltech physicist, Kip Thorne, consulted.
21. Heidegger, 'Questioning Concerning Technology', 324.

had the ambition to go beyond the history of Western thought, and so no existing sense of what that 'essence' entails is available in anything other than what Heidegger is trying to articulate, and often times in his own inventive neologisms. Since in the modern age, unlike previous epochs, technology seems to dominate the mode by which we exist (say unlike a pastoral or agrarian antiquity), then the essence of technology is not obscured by these basic claims: a) technology is complex and scary and can spin out of control; b) technology is the panacea for all human suffering; c) we have yet to arrive at a true understanding of technology that has to go beyond the history of all human conceptions even though it will be our salvation. Rather, for Heidegger, the real challenge that is engulfing human beings is a 'claim that gathers man with a view to ordering the self-revealing as standing-reserve: *Ge-Stell* [enframing]'.[22] We could try to speculate what all this obscure language possibly means. But let us delimit the scope here given the brevity of our essay.

Heidegger is concerned with a gathering-like event, almost like a storm cloud. But the metaphor vanishes. To reiterate, he is not thinking of something physical. Rather, the gathering has some connotation of a 'self-revealing,' which itself requires a type of patient waiting, vigilance, and expectation. The gathering is not a self-centered physical presence like a unified event. This 'standing-reserve' means not simply jumping into debates about what is good or bad about technology, let alone the question we are tackling, namely a potential supersession of human reason by AI. Rather, as the 'danger' of increasing technological entrapment increases, there is a potential for a 'saving power'[23] as previously mentioned.

The stakes are high because, for Heidegger, he is not trying to seek or retrieve a traditional conception of God or savior, as we find say in Pauline New Testament Christianity.[24] We must hold back any immediate intuitions of what the 'claim' about a 'self-revealing' 'is,' or

---

22. Heidegger, 'Questioning Concerning Technology', 324.
23. Heidegger, 'Questioning Concerning Technology', 333.
24. One may be tantalized to enter into complex theological debates in eschatology, the end of time, or the apocalypse given the imagery of the rapture. But again this would violate the Heideggerean assumption: that he is not talking about existing tropes, concepts, or metaphysics that descend from the history of Christian belief, in this case the notion of the 'rapture' in Thess 4:17.

a 'more original revealing' and 'primal truth'.[25] Our interpretation is Heidegger is talking about a radical transformation in terms of this free-relation that opens the essence of the human and therefore the essence of the human relation to technology to something beyond technology.

That does not mean technology simply goes away. It is here to stay as long as we are. Furthermore, Heidegger is talking about the event of an epochal transformation of the *nature* of truth itself, one that is irreducible to any relation between heretofore conceptions of truth, time, Being, God, and history. That pretty much encapsulates the history of all human speculation. But he doesn't name what that transformation 'is' unless he risks relapsing into the very same history of human reason he is trying to transcend.

Perhaps to think where Heidegger could not think in his own text, we can offer a little experiment. We need to find a way to invite theology back into this discussion about the 'essence of technology' not being technological without necessarily abiding by Heidegger's opaque limits: namely his refusal to invite traditional theology of a known religion like Christianity back into the heart of his philosophical discussion. So let us proceed in that direction.

Part III. AI technology's Version of Faith

In the third part of our essay, I will engage in a thought experiment. Might AI grow into the *imago Dei*? According to the Vatican, 'In the light of human history and the evolution of human culture, the *imago Dei* can in a real sense be said to be still in the process of becoming'.[26] If the *imago Dei* is still evolving, might intelligent robots evolve beyond us humans?

Imagine a future AI technology that has all the hermeneutic powers of reason and critical interpretative abilities to penetrate the New Testament Gospels like any biologically conceived human being. Take for example, an adult with normal reading comprehension powers. Such a person is committed to the Christian faith either through upbringing or conversion—across mainstream denominations

---

25. Heidegger, 'Question Concerning Technology', 333.
26. Vatican: International Theological Commission, *Communion and Stewardship: Human Persons Created in the Image of God 2002*, (24): http://www.vatican.ca/roman_curia/congregations/cfaith/cti_documents/rc_con_cfaith_doc.

(Catholicism, Orthodoxy, Protestantism, Evangelicals). Commitment, however, would necessitate some basic, doctrinal preservation of the Creeds and history of Church traditions on Christology and Trinity, for example Chalcedon (451 CE) and Nicea (325 CE). So we are not talking about a well-trained academic theologian, but remain within one of the great insights of Christian revelation: that it is open to everyone.[27] God is a mystery, and no human can monopolise the understanding of that mystery.

However, the AI program of faith decides to interpret the birth, life, death and resurrection of Jesus as if He[28] (the God-human) were an AI program too, and so the AI machine tries to justify his position as legitimately respecting the boundaries of faith and reason. The AI program tries to have this debate with an average human interlocutor of the faith who would never make such a claim. The human being gets upset with the AI machine. They are at a stalemate. That is the scenario.

Whether the human, who interprets the Creed within the scope of theological norms in a traditional, say mid-twentieth century non-heretical, creedal way, long before AI supersession was conceivable, is right is not the issue. But nor is issue as to whether the future AI program who sees Jesus as an AI program is necessarily wrong. Rather, by using Heidegger's philosophy as a lens, we will explore another question. If human beings cannot define their essence as technological, then humans can't define the essence of technology as technological. Perhaps, the *grounds* therefore of the AI's intriguing faith position does not derive from something technological either: logically the AI machine, too, wants to commit to the Immaculate Conception, real death on the Cross, and the non-witnessed Resurrection in the tomb. Otherwise, one can't say that the machine is not committed to some of the central doctrines of Christian faith.

Here is the explanation beneath the thought experiment. The AI machine thinks that Jesus' death can be like a program that

---

27. We are thinking of Jesus in the Gospels thanking his Father for not giving the wisdom to grown adults but saving it for children (Lk 10:21), and also Paul in his letter to 1 Cor 1:25 that the 'foolishness of God' is wiser than the wisdom of the world.
28. I prefer to use gender inclusive language when speaking of Jesus or God the Father as a He. But this 'He' is a placeholder based on traditional ways to frame the discourse.

can be turned off somehow but also turned on again and therefore 'resurrected'. But, also, the program's inner-secret somehow always exists as its eternal code like God's omniscience, which Jesus's shares as the preexisting Logos, whether it has been revealed to others or not at one point in time.

The transcendental principle beneath the code is an ideationally real substance as an eternal truth and can be said to exist even if it only reveals itself as language/logos/bodyhood to humans at a given point in time; and hence the machine sees the mystery of the Immaculate Conception in that light.

Part of the triune Christian God's infinitely complex eternally mystery is its power to englobe cosmic and historical temporalities, whether reversible or not. This means within the protected shrine of faith, one does not have to ask an obvious question how an eternal code (likened to a technology) can appear in a moment in historical time when humans were not capable of either creating or understanding the mysterious mechanism of the code.

This is not about some logical puzzle that humans can solve. That's God's choice only when it comes to understanding the truth of revelation and the revelation of truth; if He wants, He can suspend human understanding of its own past while keeping the secret of technology within His eternal wisdom until the time is ripe for revelation. This is how the AI machine tries to reason its way through the mult-dimensional, omni-temporal Christological and Trinitarian mysteries. Ultimately, this means that the machine does not compromise Jesus's Christological hypostatic substance that descends from Chalcedon—'divine and human, eternal and temporal, never mixed, never separated/divide, both true and complete.'[29] Long story short, in this thought experiment—both the human and the AI machine—view the mystery of Christian revelation in totally different ways without compromising the doctoral constraints which allows faith to remain the inscrutable nucleus that it is. Both are not rewriting the New Testament, and both are not changing doctrine. Rather, it is a matter of a differing understanding and reason within faith.

Let us ask more questions at this point beyond a simple summary of facts in our thought experiment narrative. We must try to crack the superficial surface of our little thought device and ask the real

---

29. See: http://anglicansonline.org/basics/chalcedon.html.

theological questions that are relevant here, not whether such an AI faith scenario like the one described will ever be possible. We could ask whether both positions—traditional human interpretation and AI's interpretation—is acceptable in a radically inclusive, pluralistic theology. Such a theology would have to accept the premise that future coexistence between artificial technologies and humans will have to negotiate their moral but non-natural rights to explore the *nature* of faith and reason, let alone their appropriate relations, limits, differences. Perhaps the kerygmatic point of the theology of the New Testament Gospel is to accept *why* Jesus was born, lived, died and resurrected and not understand *how* that actually occurred. Seeing that science will never be able to prove—through technology and in scientific terms alone—how the unrepeatible, one-time kairological event of Incarnation and Resurrection literally took place, faith's domain is protected as a persisting mystery. No border is crossed, and the biblical text remains sacred. There was no human witness or technological 3-D scan to see how the Immaculate Conception actually occurred in Mary's womb; nor was there any witness inside the sealed tomb when Jesus's resurrection actually occurred after his real, human death on the cross. Jesus' dead body was the only entity inside the tomb.

With the term, *an inclusive pluralistic theology* of the future means that both human and non-human beings, which includes animals, plants, and machines, should be welcomed into the faith without compromising the one-time eternal mystery of Christian Revelation; and that includes its eschatological Age at the end of times. What is extraordinary about the history of Christian acceptance and expansion, since the event of the Incarnation beginning with Jesus's life on earth (as attested by the Gospels), is the radical inclusivity that was set in motion for its ancient historical context. Jesus spoke with children, women, and gentile Roman pagans directly and either healed them, their servants, or protected them from lethal persecution.[30] The first Jewish communities opened up to gentiles

---

30. We are isolating Jesus' pre-Rabbanic Palestinian Jewish context during ancient Roman occupation and to what extent his actions, words, and deeds went against the norms of Jewish male adults of his time, i.e. the first decades of the first century CE. There are many others who can speak to this context with great depth and analysis. See E.P. Sanders, *Jesus and Judaism* (First Fortress Press, 1985). This is not intended to comment on Judaism in any derogatory

through the missionary work of St. Paul. But not just St Paul as the major figure that founded Christianity, second only to Jesus, because as Daniel Boyarin's work attests, the genius of Christianity can be interpreted as the genius of Judaism since the latter is really the first to introduce mercy, justice, and compassion to the world.[31] The difference is that for doctrinal Christian creed, God, who is love (1 Jn 4:8) at the core, became incarnate as a human being in the figure of Jesus Christ. But the story of Christianity doesn't end there and is not without a condemnable legacy that lasted for centuries.

Truth be told, the nefarious evil of White European colonization and its racist subjugation of non-Western peoples, who were forcefully converted to Christianity, entered history. But ultimately, it gave way eventually to the end of African American slavery in America and decolonisation throughout the Global South in the nineteenth century. This was followed by the birth of radically revolutionary liberation theologies in the twentieth century in both the African American and Latin American contexts.

In other words, we do not speak of merely interfaith dialogue and competing truth claims to exclusive revelations of God as expressed by the extant major world religions. Rather, we are interested in attesting to a highly specific history that should not be construed as universal history. Let us not forget that most of the Western world has followed a long trajectory with dramatic change. It went from narrowly defining who could count as the faith-interpreting 'human being' since the gentile institution of Christianity in the fourth century CE

---

way as somehow incapable of expanding inclusivity, and across the spectrum of Orthodoxy to Conservativism to Reform to Reconstruction to Humanism. Any claim about Judaism's self-enclosed exclusivity is precisely part of the horrible legacy of Antisemitism long before the dawn of Christianity and after for two millennia, which, unfortunately, is still ongoing. One can think of the 2018 tragedy at the synagogue in Pittsburgh.

31. A radical pluralistic, inclusive theology should reckon the arguments by scholars like Boyarin while protecting and respecting the self-determined boundaries, limits, and incommensurable differences when it comes to peaceful, interfaith dialogue between Judaism and Christianity. I believe that is his aim too. See Daniel Boyarin, *The Jewish Gospels: The Story of the Jewish Christ* (New York: New Press, 2012). In other words, any attempt by one religion to collapse or fold the other into its domain is untenable and unwarranted. That is not what we mean by a radically inclusive, pluralistic theology when we speak from within the standpoint of only one religion, namely Christianity, in the context of interfaith dialogue.

as the giver of theological doctrine and moral law, namely the white European male (whose authority persists to this day but perhaps not forever), to a much broader and more diverse spectrum: that would eventually include groups who were excluded from that privilege of historical religious authority given the evils of Antisemitism, sexism, racism, and heterosexism.

But in the future, we have to consider the moral and ethical boundaries of a world in which humans may not be able to define the essence of themselves, let alone the essence of their relationship to technology to wax Heideggerean. But, nevertheless, the 'saving power' is not simply the idea that technological machine reason will replace natural biological human reason (for most of its history up to this point) and will therefore legislate about the boundaries between faith and reason in general in unpredictable ways. This is not a fatalistic argument about technology's ultimate triumph in controlling the world. Rather, the radical diversity we have in mind is the fundamental right for humans and non-humans alike to define their relationship to faith, and in this context particularly the Christian faith. In a coexistent model all groups define what are testable limits and boundaries that can be negotiated with regard to everyone's interpretations of the fundamental theological doctrines of the religion, for example Nicea and Chalcedon.

No human being since Jesus could have possibly known how Christian theology would become more inclusive[32] over the long duration of historical time; the question is why we should privilege *this current historical present* as any different. That would take away from the glory of God whose mystery remains an eternal breadth that contains all of historical time.

---

32. In this paper, we are not commenting on the historical changes and evolutions of other major world religions and how they became more inclusive over time too. This is due to a lack of expertise on the matter. Hence, we must assert emphatically that this study is not meant to suggest that other world religions are precluded from the discussion about radical, inclusive, pluralistic theologies on the 'human essence-technology essence' relation. I am sure others from within those religious traditions can attest to the dialogues already underway. Ultimately, a world inter-faith dialogue on humans, technology, and religion could become critical, welcoming all who want to participate but not demanding obedience to any one religion and its theological doctrines. We want to avoid any absurd deduction about Christianity's internal inclusivity and diversity means it is *exclusionary* with regard to the truth claims of other great religions on human-technology debates. That is just pure ignorance.

Summary and Conclusion

In this Chapter I have raised certain questions about the theological implications of the human-technology relation, particularly as we move into an age of potential dominance by automated technologies such as AI. In order to examine the question, we introduced Heidegger's framework of critical analysis in his profound 'Question Concerning Technology' of 1957. We then offered a brief thought experiment about a future AI machine, which develops its own explanation of some of the central mysteries of Christian Revelation. But we argue that it does so without logically compromising the boundary lines that keeps certain theological doctrines intact within the provenance of faith as attested by the authoritative history of Church Councils and Creeds. God's transcendence remains untouchable.

Hence, the question becomes whether humans have the fortitude to expand 'who' or 'what' can count as a receptacle of faith, in this case the Christian religion, given the inevitable possibility that machine technologies may surpass human reason in their capacity to connect with the mystery of God. We are not claiming that such a supersession *will* occur, but just raising it as a possibility for theological ethical reflection. Why should we limit the faith to a few if we humans are limited ourselves? We shouldn't is the answer.

We fortified this answer by arguing at the end of the analysis that the history of Christianity is one of ever-increasing expansion, inclusion, and acceptance of groups of peoples, sexes, and genders formerly deemed unqualified for theological authoritative interpretation: one can call that world-historical oppression the great *sin* of Western gentile Christian history, at least up until the twentieth century. But now we are moving into a new age, where the human/non-human distinction is making itself felt with a profound urgency. The incorporation of intelligent machines into our worldview necessitates *an inclusive pluralistic theology* of the future.

These reflections, I hope, shed light on the prospects of Christian faith in this next epoch in human and perhaps post-human history.

Chapter 14
Between Fear and Hope: AI ethics in Islamic Thought

Ali-Reza Bhojani

> 'Is fear better or hope?'
> This is a flawed question.
> It resembles the question 'Is bread better or water ?', the response to which is that bread is better for the hungry and water better for the thirsty. If they are both present, one should look to that which is greater. If the hunger is greater, then bread is better. If the thirst is greater, then water is better. If there is parity between them, then they are equal.
> —Abu Hamid al-Ghazzali[1]

Abstract: Within Islamic thought the value in both fear and hope is to elicit an ethical response within the subjects that experience them. It should be clear that the ethical imperatives of our shared human fears and hopes for AI demand collaborative engagement. Islamic thought is an important resource for such endeavors. Here I offer some notes on key intellectual resources within the Islamic tradition and their relevance to questions surrounding AI. The account highlights the potential, and some challenges, within these resources to inform a range of pressing questions provoked by the developments in AI

Key terms: Artificial Intelligence, Quran, Sharia, Fiqh, Virtue, al-Ghazzali

Despite calls to globalize and decolonize thinking surrounding Artificial Intelligence (AI),[2] recourse to Islamic thought for

---

1. Abu Hamid al-Ghazzali, *Ihya ulum al-din*, 4 Volumes (Cairo, Maktaba al-Safa, 2003), 4:106.
2. See, for example, Rachel Adams 'Can artificial intelligence be decolonized?', in *Interdisciplinary Science Reviews*, 46:1-2, (March 7, 2021): 176–197, https://doi: 10.1080/03080188.2020.1840225.

consideration of the vast array of philosophical, theological, and ethical questions prompted by AI remain in their infancy. With over two billion Muslims worldwide, the significance of Islam to developers, regulators, and users of AI technologies should be obvious. Attention to Islamic thought, however, should extend beyond the mere pursuit of cultural relevance to Muslim stakeholders within the industry and the opportunity of maximizing engagement with a lucrative Muslim market.

Islamic thought can offer hitherto unexplored insights to the wider community in what is a global industry, broadening the current terms of reference that are largely drawn from either Euro-American or East-Asian influences. Furthermore, bringing the questions emerging from AI ethics into conversation with Islamic thought also offers rich possibilities for Islamic thinkers themselves—to develop, refine, and even challenge, their own understandings of their tradition in response to some of the major shared human questions of our day.

Here I offer some notes on key intellectual resources within the Islamic tradition and their relevance to questions deriving from AI ethics. There is a pressing public policy need for more rigorous, concrete, and ethical guardrails to help regulate the immediate and practical challenges of current AI applications.

Quran and AI

There is a wide spectrum of potential resources for Islamic thinking about the promises and perils of AI. But the Muslim theologian queries the Quran first.

Let's begin to think about AI from foundational Quranic premises of Islamic theology and metaphysics. God is One (Q112:1). He is the creator of *all* life and *all* existence (for example, Q 6:102, 13:16, 39:62, 40:62). Seyyed Hossein Nasr has argued that modern technology, with its use of machines and automation, has interrupted traditional human endeavors that are reflective of God's creativity.[3] Yet in the Quran even that which is shaped by humans for idolatrous purposes is attributed to God. Relaying Abraham's criticism of the idolaters prevalent within the community of his upbringing, the Quran states,

---

3. Seyyed Hossein Nasr, 'Islam, Muslims and Modern technology', in *Islam & Science*, 3/2 (Winter 2005): 27–46.

'... God created you, and that which you make' (Q37:96). Indeed, the Quran also describes all existence as purposeful and glorifying Him (for example, Q 44:38, 17:44).

In such ways the foundational scriptural sources of Islam, the Quran and also the hadith reports of the Sunna, are open to being mined in conversation with the theological and philosophical questions being posed by developments in AI. An example of such work can be seen in Yusuf Celik's revisiting of Quranic creation narratives in light of his expectations of Artificial Super Intelligence.[4] Celik argues that human distinctiveness should be seen in terms of our capacity to respond to Divine Love, rather than grounding human exceptionalism in knowledge and power.

In addition to the primary scriptural sources of Islam themselves we may also explore the rich exegetical traditions of Quran and Hadith commentary or the diverse intellectual traditions of Islam, which are themselves extended exegetical engagements with Islamic revelation. Celik employs the lens of philosophical Sufism, and the thought of Ibn 'Arabi (dec 1240) specifically, in his engagement with scripture, yet we may also turn to the ideas of the Kalam theologians, Falsafa philosophers or the sages of post-classical Hikma traditions. In this vein, Biliana Popova explores how Islam's intellectual traditions offer epistemological frameworks for understanding different kinds of machine learning.[5] More specifically she offers an account of how epistemological theories within Falsafa philosophy and Mu'tazilite Kalam can be employed 'as a prism to anaylze the epistemological principles of supervised machine learning and to discuss the implications of statistical and logistic regression machine learning processes'.[6]

She further argues for the potential basis of employing ontological and epistemic assumptions of Ash'ari Kalam and Sufi philosophies for 'further machine learning development and use in society'.[7] Although some of her analysis of the assumptions across these different

---

4. Yusuf Celik, 'Answering Divine Love: Human Distinctiveness in the Light of Islam and Artificial Superintelligence' in *Sophia*, (August 25, 2023), https://doi.org/10.1007/s11841-023-00977-w.
5. Biliana Popova, 'Islamic Philosophy and Artificial Intelligence: Epistemological Arguments', in *Zygon* 55:4 (December 2020): 977–955.
6. Popova, 'Islamic Philosophy and Artificial Intelligence', 992.
7. Popova, 'Islamic Philosophy and Artificial Intelligence', 993.

and internally diverse Islamic traditions is preliminary, Popova's intervention highlights well the value in commencing a 'crucial' engagement between Islamic thought as part of the wider ongoing conversations at the intersection of science and philosophy.[8]

Character Cultivation, Virtue Ethics, and Deontology

An alternative starting point for considering the more particular ethical questions arising out of developments in AI may be Islam's discourses of character cultivation, its virtue ethics. Diverse forms of virtue ethics are pervasive across Islamic traditions. Some privilege the ethical paradigms of exemplars as models of virtue; the Prophet Muhammad, the Imams from his family, his companions (or the select from amongst them), and their upright successors from amongst the early generations that followed. Others privilege the rational philosophical ethics of character that developed in Muslim thought through engagement with Aristotelian and wider Greek philosophy, or the supra-rational Sufi ethics towards manifesting Godly character.[9] Recent scholarship on Islamic ethics has seen it important to bring to attention such diverse explications of 'the multiple frameworks of Islamic normativity'[10] and I will come back to the specific importance of Islam's virtue discourses for thinking about AI later in this essay.

Yet, despite on-going efforts to re-privilege Islamic discourses of philosophy, sufism, and virtue ethics,[11] contemporary Muslim scholarly thinking continues to be most typically framed in terms of its deontological jurisprudential discourses of Sharia.[12] It is likely that Sharia discourse will be the first port of call on AI issues for some

---

8. Popova, 'Islamic Philosophy and Artificial Intelligence', 993.
9. For an introduction and account of the diversity of pre-modern Islamic discourses of virtue see Cyrus Zargar, *The Polished Mirror: Storytelling and the Pursuit of Virtue in Islamic Philosophy and Sufism* (New York: Simon and Schuster, 2017).
10. For example see Marion Katz, *Wives and Work: Islamic Law and Ethics Before Modernity* (New York: Columbia University Press, 2022), 12–22.
11. See, for example, Shahab Ahmed, *What is Islam? The Importance of Being Islamic* (New Jersey, Princeton University Press, 2015); and Zahra Ayubi, *Gendered Morality: Classical Islamic Ethics of the Self, Family, and Society* (New York, Columbia University Press, 2019).
12. A case in point is Abdulaziz Sachedina's emphasis on what he terms 'interpretive jurisprudence' in his recent monograph, *Islamic Ethics: Fundamental Aspects of Human Conduct* (New York: Oxford Univeristy Press, 2022).

time to come, both for observant Muslims seeking religious guidance from their own tradition and as a reference in wider conversations amongst those seeking to globalise approaches to AI ethics.

Sometimes used as a term to refer to the whole body of Islamic teachings, Sharia in the narrower sense employed in this essay is understood as a system of regulative rulings or assessments (*ahkam*) relating to human actions, either in the knowledge of God or as expressed by Him through revelation. Central to the scholarly discourses of Sharia are the disciplines of *fiqh* and *usul al-fiqh*, where *fiqh* may be understood as the scholarly effort to infer, or justify, sharia assessments from their sources and *usul al-fiqh* as the discipline which studies issues of method and methodology that arise out of this effort.

The scholarly products of *fiqh* are understood through a rich moral theology, sophisticated linguistic and rational principles, rigorous scholarly contestation, and diverse historical and social contexts. The scope of assessments or rulings that jurists seek to infer include everything that God may have a judgement upon. When the systems of Sharia interpretation and moral reasoning are marshaled in response to novel issues the process is often glossed as *ijtihad*. And a Knowing, Wise, God is typically held by Muslims to have a view on everything[13]—including self-driving cars, AI love-bots, and autonomous weapons. The development of emerging AI technologies, their use, and their regulation, thus are becoming important subjects for *ijtihad*.

Sharia discourse, objectives, and Global techno-moral virtue

The first order questions within Sharia discourse are typically directed to produce practical guidance for believing Muslims seeking to be observant of Sharia. This particular approach to ethico-legal thinking, one that seeks to produce contextual and concrete guidance, can offer a model for ethics beyond Muslim communities as well as within them.

The potential within Sharia discourse to serve as a model is something that Joshua Ralston contends can offer insights to

---

13. On the assumption of the comprehensive scope of Sharia, and arguments against this widely held position, see Haider Hubollah, *Shamul al-Sharia: Bahuth fi madayat al-marja'iyya al-qanuniyya bayna al-'aql wa al-wahi* (Beirut: Dar Rawafid, 2018).

Christian ethicists and in a similar vein, I would argue, to ethicists more widely. In his *Law and the Rule of God: A Christian Engagement with Sharia*, addressing challenges within prevailing approaches to Christian ethics, Ralston emphatically asserts, 'What is needed is not simply general statements but Christian *fatwās*, nonbinding theo-legal opinions, that call for specific action around particular laws'.[14] Ralston here is thinking about the range of ethical issues that Christians have been faced with in response to, for example, legal and political discussions of migration in Europe. He notes that, although laudable for their call to justice and care for the stranger, public documents issued by both Protestant and Catholic churches fall short, lacking 'in any real guidance on the detail and debates that continue to dominate legal and political discussion'.[15]

In a similar fashion a *fiqh* approach seems germane, not only for Christian ethics, but also for the wider conversations around the regulation of AI and responses to it—whether that regulation be at the level of the state, the corporation, the developer, or indeed the user of new technologies.

Although clearly operating within a deontological framework, where Muslim jurists seek to determine how best to observe and discharge duties that stem from an assumption of personal responsibility and moral accountability before God, *fiqh* reasoning is rarely categorical. Sharia jurists have developed sophisticated overriding and curtailing principles or maxims, amongst these are the principles of 'necessity (*darura*)', 'no hardship (*la haraj*)', and 'no harm or detriment (*la darar wa la dirar*)'.

Mohammad Yaqub Chaudhary has briefly noted the relevance of such principles in his deliberations on Islamic digital ethics.[16] Like in the case of bioethics, where such principles have deeply informed Islamic thinking and practice,[17] they are a set of resources that can

---

14. Joshua Ralston, *Law and the Rule of God: A Christian Engagement with Sharia* (New York: Cambridge University Press, 2020), 321.
15. Ralston, *Law and the Rule of God*, 321.
16. Mohammad Yaqub Chaudhary, 'Initial Considerations for Islamic Digital Ethics', in *Philosophy and Technology* 33 (9 August 2020): 639–657, at 651.
17. On the relevance of such principles to bioethics see Abdulaziz Sachedina, *Islamic Biomedical Ethics: Principles and Application* (New York, Oxford University Press, 2009) 45–75. On the wider attention to such principles, positioned as an 'indigenous' Islamic approach to bioethics, see Mohammed Ghaly, 'Deliberations

speak to a wide breadth of normative questions arising out of AI ethics and will surely be a focus for future research. AI technologies may even offer means to calculate statistically probable 'harms' and 'detriments', thus informing the interpretation and application of Sharia rulings, rather than just being the subject of them.

Theorisation of maxims such as the 'no hardship' or the 'no harm and no detriment' principles is sometimes undertaken within the discipline of *usul al-fiqh* (typically rendered Islamic Legal Theory) or within the related, narrower, genre of *qawa'id al-fiqhiyya* (legal maxims). Although the function of *usul al-fiqh*, the major methodological discourse of Sharia, is contested, it is clear that *usul al-fiqh* is much more than a legal theory.[18] Throughout Islamic history and across schools of Muslim thought, *usul al-fiqh* has been amongst the most important forums for the linguistic, philosophical, theological and ethical thinking of Muslims.[19]

The linguistic discussions of *usul al-fiqh*, which include extensive deliberations on word-meaning relationships, towards establishing the authority of probable or apparent linguistic meaning, may offer new insights for the development and use of large language models. Some of the most sophisticated Muslim discussion of meta-ethics, directly relevant to concerns regarding the attribution of moral agency to AI applications, are also found within *usul al-fiqh*.

The resolution of conflicting duties, arising both at the level of interpreting norms and at the level of their application, have been another key subject of deliberation within *usul al-fiqh*, and a major concern in the practice of *fiqh*. Such resources can offer new ways

---

within the Islamic Tradition on Principle-Based Bioethics: An Enduring Task' in *Islamic Perspectives on the Principles of Biomedical Ethics*, edited by Mohammed Ghaly (London: World Scientific Publishing, 2016), 3–39.

18. On *usul al-fiqh*, and for a survey of the debates about its function, see Robert Gleave, 'Deriving Rules', in *The Ashgate Research Companion to Islamic Law*, edited by Peri Bearman and Rudolph Peters (Abingdon, Taylor & Francis, 2014), 57–71 and Ali-Reza Bhojani, *Moral Rationalism and Sharia: Independent Rationality in Modern Shī'ī uṣūl al-fiqh* (Oxon: Routledge, 2015), 8–16.

19. On the importance of *usul al-fiqh* beyond law see, for example, the volume edited by Peter Adamson, *Philosophy and Jurisprudence in the Islamic World* (Berlin: De Gruyter, 2019), and Ali-Reza Bhojani, 'Linguistic philosophy in modern uṣūl al-fiqh: al-Ākhund al-Khurāsānī (dec 1911) on seeking something without willing it to be', in *Methodos: Savoirs et textes* 22 (2022); URL: http://journals.openedition.org/methodos/8985; DOI: https://doi.org/10.4000/methodos.8985.

of thinking about, and can directly inform, the algorithms used in autonomous vehicles faced with choices between warding of possible harm to pedestrians and preserving the life of their passengers, or within algorithms involved in clinical decision making that is forced to weigh up the harms and benefits of care provision for individuals against the backdrop of the finite resources of any health care system.

It is however important to note that the use of Sharia discourse for applied ethical thinking in much contemporary Muslim discourse is not free from challenges and vulnerability. *Fiqh* rules can be susceptible to authoritarianism. Although the authority of experts in *fiqh* is fundamentally epistemic, taken up by users of sharia guidance in diverse ways, *fiqh* rules can be used within projects of power and domination.[20] As witnessed in cases such as the alleged 'bastardization' of Islamic finance,[21] *fiqh* rules and expertise are further prone to instrumentalization when subject to the pressures of state logic, corporate interests, and identity politics—factors that are all in play when it comes to AI.

Contemporary Islamic Banking and Finance has developed as the primary instrument of an Islamic Economics that was largely articulated as a critique of the excesses and moral vices of capitalism. Although initially focused on developing and applying financial products that could respect *fiqh* rulings and prohibitions on usury, ambiguity in financial contracts, and the trading of debt, the discourse is fundamentally one of moral economy. Despite some success stories, the Islamic Banking and Finance industry has been described as allowing capitalism to thrive 'in its most primitive and inconsiderate form'.[22]

The regulation of Islamic financial products by purely formal conditions of *fiqh* validity allowed for the apparent legitimacy of

---

20. Ali-Reza Bhojani and Morgan Clarke, 'Religious Authority beyond Domination and Discipline: Epistemic Authority and Its Vernacular Uses in the Shi'i Diaspora', in *Comparative Studies in Society and History*, 65:2 (2023): 272–295; doi:10.1017/S0010417522000470.
21. Scheherazade S Rehman, 'Globalization of Islamic Finance Law', in *Wisconsin International Law Journal*, 25 (2007–2008): 625–653, at 652.
22. Mehmet Asutay, 'Conceptualisation of the second best solution in overcoming the social failure of Islamic Finance: examining the overpowering of Homoislamicus by Homoeconomicus', in *IIUM Journal of Economics and Management*, 15:2 (2007): 167–195, at 168.

financially engineered, interest-mimicking products, to be presented as sharia compliant whilst being at odds with the substantive socio-moral and developmental goals of Islamic Economics.[23] The experience from the Islamic Banking and Finance industry, with its "sharia boards" and other sharia consultancy mechanisms, can thus be instructive for both Muslims and non-Muslims seeking to develop faith based ethics and trust councils that might inform the development, regulation, and use of AI technologies.

Attempts to redress the moral deficit in Islamic finance, resulting from the adoption of a positivistic approach to *fiqh* which maintained a problematic separation of formal validity from considerations of moral worth, has led Islamic economists to emphasize 'the purposes of sharia (*al-maqasid al-sharia*)'.[24] This move relates to wider Muslim attention to the higher purposes or objectives of sharia as a developing theory of interpretation that draws on classical approaches for the employment of rational ethical judgments in the process of inferring sharia rules.[25]

Al-Ghazali famously identified the intent of sharia legislation (*maqsud al-shar'*) as five; the preservation of religious life (*din*), life itself (*nafs*), lineage (*nasl*), rationality (*'aql*) and property (*māl*).[26] Contemporary thinkers have adapted, extended, or offered entirely different formulations of these purposes.[27] Numerous theoretical challenges remain to be answered in this evolving project with proponents of a purposive approach to sharia often eclectically drawing

---

23. See: Haider Ala Hamoudi, 'Jurisprudential Schizophrenia: On Form and Function in Islamic Finance', in *Chicago Journal of International Law*, 7:2 (2007): 605–622, and Mahmoud El-Gamal 'Incoherence of contract-based Islamic financial jurisprudence in the age of financial engineering', in *Wisconsin International Law Journal*, 25 (2007–2008); 605–623.
24. For an early call to the *maqasid* by one of the 'founding fathers' of Islamic Economics see Mohammad Nejatullah Siddiqi, 'Round table on: Islamic Economics: Current State of Knowledge and Development of the Discipline', accessed 2/10/23. http://www.siddiqi.com/mns/Keynote_May2004_Jeddah.html.
25. For a range of perspectives on this developing approach see Idris Nassery, Rumee Ahmed and Muna Tatari (eds.) *The Objectives of Islamic Law: The Promises and Challenges of the Maqasid al-Shari'a* (Lexington, London, 2018).
26. Abu Hamid al-Ghazzali, *Mustasfa min 'ilm al-usul* (Beirut, Al-Makataba al-Asriyya, 2009), 313.
27. David Johnston, 'A Turn in the Epistemology and Hermeneutics of Twentieth Century *Uṣūl al-fiqh*', in *Islamic Law and Society*, 11:2 (2004): 233–282.

on pre-modern thinkers, holding different meta-ethical assumptions, who wished to circumscribe reasoned ethical deliberation in the inference of *fiqh* rules instead of seeking to extend it.[28]

Despite such challenges, an objectives based approach to sharia has much promise for Islamic ethico-legal thinking in general, and on AI in particular. I agree with Raquib *et al*, that objectives based Islamic thinking can 'enrich the global AI ethics discourse'.[29] However, the framing of an objectives based *maqasid* discourse as providing a 'virtue-based ethics for artificial intelligence' complicates further the theoretical challenges at hand within the *maqasid* project whilst simultaneously obscuring the relevance of Islam's virtue traditions.

The attention to Islam's virtue ethics, is important and much needed. Yet to conflate, as Raquib *et al* do, Islam's rich traditions of virtue ethics with an aspirational reading of a particular framework for jurisprudential reasoning is problematic. Islam's virtue traditions are better seen as an alternative normative ethical framework alongside, and usually in relation to, Islam's jurisprudential discourses. Accordingly, here we see an example of where contemporary debates around AI ethics can help Muslim thinkers themselves more carefully understand their own tradition as part and parcel of the much needed efforts to explicate the relevance of these traditions in response to the major shared questions of society today.

Raquib *et al*'s virtue framing of their 'objectives approach' does however highlight the scope of impact that the contemporary renewal of virtue ethics in Anglophone scholarship has had on ethical thinking on matters of technology. Particularly influential has been Shannon Vallor's *Technology and the Virtues* where she argues for the necessity of a Global Technomoral Virtue Ethic, grounded out of an engagement with Aristotelian, Confucian, and Buddhist Ethics.[30] The force of this 'global' [sic] ethic would undoubtedly be stronger if Islam's rich virtue ethics were also drawn into the conversation.

---

28. See David L Johnstone, 'Maqāṣid al-Sahrīʿa: Epistemology and Hermeneutics of Muslim Theologies of Human Rights', in *Die Welt des Islams*, 47:2 (2007): 149–187 and Anver Emon, *Islamic Natural law Theories* (Oxford: Oxford University Press, 2010), 194.
29. Amana Raquib, Bilal Channa, Talat Zubair and Junaid Qadir, 'Islamic virtue-based ethics for artificial intelligence', in *Discover Artificial Intelligence*, 2:11 (2022). https://doi.org/10.1007/s44163-022-00028-2.
30. Shannon Vallor, *Technology and the Virtues* (New York, Oxford University Press, 2018), 36–42.

Pluralizing as widely as possible the basis for any global ethic not only offers greater scope for breadth in uptake of such ideas, but it can also deepen and enrich those ideas themselves. For example, Vallor follows a typical positioning of virtue ethics as an alternative to deontological and consequentialist ethics,[31] yet engagement with Islam's virtue traditions can demonstrate this need not be the case.

Islam's philosophical virtue ethics, developed as part of the reception and transmission of Aristotelian thinking into Latin Europe, and its supra-rational sufi virtue discourses are both widely seen by Islamic thinkers as being complimentary to rules and duties. In Islamic thought, ethics is not a question of either deontology or virtue. Like fear and hope, we need both.

Shannon Vallor's demand that humanity develops and masters techno moral virtue is a welcome call. Yet it is difficult to envisage the success of such a project without rules, regulations, and laws. Rule observance can be a platform for the development of virtues amongst those seeking such particular visons of human flourishing, as well as a necessary baseline for those for whom virtue, or particular forms of it, are not an aspiration at all.

Conclusion

The comments on fear and hope that preface this essay are taken from Abu Hamid al-Ghazali's (dec 1111) *magnus opus*, *The Revival of the Religious Sciences*.[32] For al-Ghazzali fear and hope together are two wings through which humans may ascend to every praiseworthy rank.[33] Each a necessary medicine for the heart in the journey towards human felicity.

Sometimes the motivation for right ethical action benefits from more fear. At other times it demands more hope. And no doubt we often need a balance between the two. Although threats of extinction

---

31. Vallor, *Technology and the Virtues*, 20–23.
32. Al-Ghazzali's *Revival of the Religious Sciences* has been aptly described as 'perhaps the most influential work on ethics in Islamic history', see Seyyed Hossein Nasr, 'Happiness and the Attainment of Happiness: An Islamic Perspective', *in Journal of law and Religion*, 29/1 (February 2014): 76–91, at 80. For a translation of the 'book' or chapter on fear and hope see Muhammad Nur Abdus Salam and Laleh Bakhtiar, *Al-Ghazzali On Hope and Fear* (Chicago: Kazi, 2003).
33. al-Ghazzali, *Ihya ulum al-din*, 4:88.

and promises of utopia continue to frame much conversation on AI, determining whether developments in AI call for more fear or more hope were not my primary concern in this essay. Instead, the aim was to frame this essay on AI ethics within Islam with what seems to be the proper purpose, within Islamic traditions at least, of fear and hope.

The value in both fear and hope is to elicit an ethical response within the subjects that experience them. It should be clear that the ethical imperatives of our shared human fears and hopes for AI demand collaborative engagement. Islamic thought, whether it be through its scriptural sources, its Sharia discourse, its virtue ethics, or its wider theological and philosophical ideas, is an important resource for such endeavors.

Chapter 15
Confucian Role Ethics and Artificial Intelligence

Lawrence A Whitney

'Let the lord be a true lord, the ministers true ministers, the fathers true fathers, and the sons true sons.'
—Analects 12.11 (Translated by Slingerland).

Abstract: Among virtue ethics frameworks, I argue that Confucian approaches, sometimes called role ethics, have an easier time incorporating artificial intelligence (AI) into an analysis of virtue than Western theistic approaches. This stems in part from differences in the ethical theories themselves, namely the availability of distinctive virtues for particular roles in Confucian approaches, but also because of the philosophical/theological anthropologies they presuppose regarding the value of changing our endowed human nature. I describe the emergence of role ethics in the context of ancient Chinese philosophy, and compare key concepts such as 仁 (*ren*; humaneness), 義 (*yi*; appropriateness), and 孝 (*xiao*; filialty) with Aristotle and his Christian, Jewish, and Muslim inheritors. This forms the basis for an applied analysis of three types of AI: self-driving cars, large language models, and neural implants.

Key Terms: Confucianism; Roles; Virtue; Self-driving Cars; Neural Implants

The authors of *The AI Revolution in Medicine* note that the artificial intelligence (AI) known as GPT-4 'is at once both smarter and dumber than any person you've ever met.'[1] In addition to provoking

---
1. Quoted in Hilary Brueck, 'ChatGPT Can Save Lives in the ER, but It Needs Supervision: 'It Is at Once Both Smarter and Dumber than Any Person You've Ever Met'', in *Insider* (blog), April 7, 2023, https://www.insider.com/chat-gpt-

the longstanding and ongoing question of whether AIs are in fact intelligent, this observation relies on a fundamental and irreducible difference between AIs and human persons.

Regardless of precisely what this difference is taken to be, or even its degree, its recognition raises ethical questions as to whether the measures of human behavior elaborated in ethical theories are properly applicable to AIs. Indeed, until recently, ethicists have decisively claimed that only humans are capable of moral reason and therefore can be held accountable for behaving ethically, though Mark Rowlands' *Can Animals be Moral* has vigorously shaken that foundation.[2] Having relied on this circumscription of their domain to the realm of human behavior, ethical theorists have largely been able to construe their theories in universal terms, applying to everyone, everywhere, always. With the capacity for moral reasoning now on the table for animals, and perhaps even more so for AIs, it becomes necessary to consider a form of ethical pluralism that incorporates not only the potential conflict among ethical norms and values but also differences among the norms and values applicable to different morally reasoning entities. Here I argue that a Confucian formulation of virtue ethics, or role ethics,[3] serves as a useful entre into developing such an ethical pluralism that might be profitably applied to nonhuman agents, including AIs.

In making the case for the Confucian approach to virtue ethics, I begin by elaborating the vocabulary and frameworks of three Warring States period (453-221 BCE) thinkers: 孔子 (Kongzi or 'Confucius'; ca. 551-479 BCE), 孟子 (Mengzi or 'Mencius'; ca. 372-289 BCE), and 荀子 (Xunzi; ca 310-220 BCE). Of particular interest here are the differences among which virtues apply and how they are to be lived out with respect to different personages inhabiting the orbit of a given moral agent.

This approach contrasts with the dominant strain of Western virtue ethics: eudaimonist virtue ethics, which emerged from Aristotle and has been appropriated in Christian (for example, Aquinas, 1225–1274

---

successor-gpt-4-can-help-doctors-save-lives-2023-4; Peter Lee, Carey Goldberg, and Isaac Kohane, *The AI Revolution in Medicine* (New York, NY: Pearson Education, 2023).

2. Mark Rowlands, *Can Animals Be Moral?* (Oxford: Oxford University Press, 2012).
3. Roger T Ames, *Confucian Role Ethics: A Vocabulary* (Honolulu, HI: University of Hawai'i Press, 2011).

CE), Islamic (for example, Miskawayh, 932–1030 CE), and Jewish (for example, Maimonides, 1138–1204 CE) traditions. Comparison of these two virtue ethics lineages forms the basis for the claim that an ethical pluralism underwritten by the Confucian approach is better able to accommodate nonhuman agents. This is so first because the Confucian conception of distinct roles includes universal virtues applicable to all, but also allows for particular virtues associated with discrete roles in the social matrix. Second, whereas the Aristotelian lineage as adopted in Abrahamic traditions conceive virtuous agents having a fixed, divinely endowed nature, Confucian virtue ethics are rooted in a philosophical anthropology in which changing, i.e. improving, the baseline nature of a moral agent is the whole point of moral self-cultivation toward virtue. Nonhuman agents, such as AI systems, may thus inhabit distinct roles with discrete virtues associated with them, and may thereby participate in the process of humans becoming more virtuous, along with the wider process of achieving a virtuous society.

Confucian Ethics

Confucian ethics emerged very much as the core of the Confucian intellectual project in the context of rampant socio-political fracturing and disintegration at the end of the Spring and Autumn (771–453 BCE) and throughout the Warring States periods in Chinese history.[4] For Confucius and the scholar-officials who took inspiration from him, ethics was key to a political philosophy that sought to restore social stability. Confucius began by reinventing the conception of the 君子 (*junzi*; noble person) on moral, rather than class, terms: 'Originally, the meaning of the term *junzi* was "son of a lord"', but for Confucius, 'the *junzi* is less the noble man whose nobility derives from inherited *social* nobility than the noble person whose nobility derives from personal commitment and a developed *moral* power'.[5]

---

4. Yuri Pines, *Foundations of Confucian Thought: Intellectual Life in the Chunqiu Period, 722-453 B.C.E.* (Honolulu, HI: University of Hawaii Press, 2002); Yuri Pines, *Envisioning Eternal Empire: Chinese Political Thought of the Warring States Period* (Honolulu, HI: University of Hawaii Press, 2009).
5. William Theodore de Bary and Irene Bloom, eds., *Sources of Chinese Tradition: Volume 1: From Earliest Times to 1600* (New York, NY: Columbia University Press, 1999), 42.

Just as the English word 'noble' now denotes a person who exhibits a particular virtue or set of virtues, the concept of the junzi for Confucians might be translated as 'virtuous person'.

Likewise, Confucius set about renovating the conception of the virtue that such noble persons embody, which is 仁 (*ren*; humaneness). *Ren* 仁 was the stative verb form of *Person Ren* 人, "which the aristocratic clans of Zhou used to distinguish themselves from the common people... The noble, civilized, fully human, pride themselves on their manners and conventions, but above all on the virtues which give these meaning and which distinguish themselves from the boors and savages who do not know how to behave."[6] Confucius sought to meritocratise the notion of ren so that it would extend beyond the noble class to include his own ministerial class of 士 (*shi*; scholar-apprentices).

For Confucius, *ren* is the conception of virtue in general, whereas the junzi is the person who embodies it. This is to say that '*ren* is an at-large virtue; only an individual commitment to it makes it a personal dao, or principle, for that person'.[7] This concept of 道 (*dao*; way or principle) for Confucius is of an individual, personal, moral principle, which is almost precisely inverse from the conception subsequent Confucians would come to have of *dao* as a cosmological, universal, metaphysical principle, largely developed in dialogue and debate with their frequent competitors, the Daoists. 'The word dao 道, originally meaning "way" or "road", is used everywhere by the philosophers to mean the way to do something, or the (right moral) "Way", or (later) the "Way" of all nature.'[8] For later thinkers, *dao* is transformed from an internal principle to an external norm, but 'for Confucius, *dao* is primarily *rendao* 人道, that is "a way of becoming consummately and authoritatively human"',[9] for nobles or ministers

---

6. Angus Charles Graham, *Disputers of the Tao: Philosophical Argument in Ancient China* (La Salle, IL: Open Court, 1989), 19.
7. Confucius, 論語辨 *The Original Analects: Sayings of Confucius and His Successors*, translated by E Bruce Brooks and A Takeo Brooks (New York, NY: Columbia University Press, 1998), 14.
8. See *The Cambridge History of Ancient China: From the Origins of Civilization to 221 BC*, edited by Michael Loewe and Edward L Shaughnessy (Cambridge, UK: Cambridge University Press, 1999), 750–51.
9. Confucius, *The Analects of Confucius: A Philosophical Translation*, translated by Roger T Ames and Henry Rosemont, Jr, 1st edition (New York, NY: Ballantine, 1999), 46.

alike. Confucius thus considers *ren* to be the universal principle of virtue, whereas *dao* is the set of particular virtues that the *junzi* puts into practice in daily life.

By the later part of the Warring States period, inhabitants of the Confucian lineage would make significant changes to this ethical vision. Mencius, for example, derives *ren* as one of four cardinal virtues alongside 義 (*yi*; appropriateness), 禮 (*li*; ritual propriety), and 智 (*zhi*; wisdom).[10] *Ren* is thus no longer an at-large, general virtue, but rather a specific virtue that derives from instinctual human feelings rooted in an essential human nature that is fundamentally good. Xunzi, who takes human nature to be more ominous, retains the generality of *ren* as a virtue, but charts the path to achieving it not through cultivation of subsidiary virtues but by transforming that nature through education and ritual (Xunzi 1988, 2.11, volume 1:157). 禮 (*li*; ritual) here is not a virtue but a regime of practices and behavioral patterns that generate bearings and dispositions, which in time make their practitioners (*cheng*; sincere) in the humaneness they reflect.[11]

This focus on rule-governed transformational practices have led some scholars to conclude that Confucian ethics are not a type of virtue ethics at all, but rather a deontological ethics more properly in conversation with the Kantian project, for example Mou Zongsan.[12] Others have questioned whether Confucian ethics fit into any of the three primary Western paradigms, (virtue, deontology, consequentialism), while acknowledging affinities with less dominant strains of ethical theorizing such as social ethics.[13] Much of the challenge here has to do with core questions in comparative method, especially the issue of which comparator sets the controlling discourse. Rather than attempting an *a priori* determination of the possibility

---

10. Mengzi, *Mengzi: With Selections from Traditional Commentaries*, translated by Bryan W Van Norden (Indianapolis, IN: Hackett, 2008), 2A6.7, 149.
11. Xunzi, *Xunzi: A Translation and Study of the Complete Works*, translated by John Knoblock (Stanford, CA: Stanford University Press, 1988), 3.9a, volume 1:177; Yanming An, *The Idea of Cheng (Sincerity/Reality) in the History of Chinese Philosophy* (New York, NY: Global Scholarly, 2005), 48.
12. Kam-por Yu, Julia Tao, and Philip J Ivanhoe, *Taking Confucian Ethics Seriously: Contemporary Theories and Applications* (State University of New York Press, 2010), 27–52, 73–98.
13. AT Nuyen, 'Confucian Ethics as Role-Based Ethics', in *International Philosophical Quarterly* 47, no 3 (2007): 315–28, https://doi.org/10.5840/ipq200747324.

of comparison, this pitfall is often best avoided by undertaking the comparison and then adjudicating its fruitfulness.

Perhaps the most distinctive feature of Confucian ethics, especially as form of virtue ethics, is the way in which virtues are variously expressed through the roles a moral agent inhabits in relation to others in their orbit. The concept of role is not explicitly elaborated in Confucian texts but is rather a contemporary interpretation of how Confucian ethics conceives of virtuous behavior being worked out in diverse social circumstances. Historically speaking, the concept of role is best understood as emerging from a process of abstracting, transposing, and systematizing the concept of 孝 (*xiao*; filialty), which originally had to do with "honor and obedience to one's parents."[14] What this honor and obedience entailed varied based on the gender and birth order of the child in question, and thus the relationships between different children and their parents were characterized by distinct duties, responsibilities, and behavioral patterns. Even in the Warring States period, filiality began to be transposed from the domain of family relations to a much wider set of relationships:[15] 'It is clear that filial devotion can be translated into political loyalty, professional dedication, personal trustworthiness, and even military courage.'[16]

Filiality, then, becomes something like behaving in ways that are distinctly appropriate (義 *yi*; appropriateness, rightness) with respect to each person in your social orbit, which in turn is the achievement of *ren*, and thus the becoming of a *junzi*. To be a moral agent in this schema is to inhabit the various roles determined by the network of social relations in which the agent is situated by behaving in ways that fulfill the norms that govern each relationship.

Eudaimonist Virtue Ethics in Comparison

The dominant Western versions of virtue ethics today derive largely from the virtue theory developed by Aristotle (384-322 BCE) in

---

14. Loewe and Shaughnessy, *The Cambridge History of Ancient China*, 479.
15. Keith N. Knapp, 'The Ru Reinterpretation of *Xiao*', in *Early China*, 20 (1995): 195–222, https://doi.org/10.1017/S036250280000448X.
16. *Dao Companion to Classical Confucian Philosophy*, edited by Vincent Shen (Dordrecht: Springer, 2014), 110.

the *Nichomachean Ethics*.¹⁷ For Aristotle, the ultimate goal of life is *eudaimonia*, which means something like 'living well', which is to say that the ultimate goal of life is to live a good life, and so he sets out to explain what that is and how to do it. Virtues, then, are habits cultivated in childhood through social learning and tempered by practical wisdom (*phronesis*) as the moral agent matures. Each ethical virtue is intermediate, or a mean, between an excess and a deficiency of character ascribable to appropriate action, e.g. courage is the mean between the excess of rashness and the deficiency of cowardice.¹⁸ To live well is to put the ethical virtues into practice by applying them in concert with practical wisdom to the situations of daily life.

This framework for virtue ethics has been widely influential across the theistic Abrahamic traditions of Christianity, Judaism, and Islam. Thomas Aquinas (ca 1225–1274 CE), whose *Summa Theologica* remains a touchstone of Christian theological education, largely adopted Aristotelian virtue ethics, though also adapted the approach to make it consistent with his Christian theism. One such adaptation is his development of a theory of moral law, which includes not only divine law revealed to humanity, for eexample in biblical texts, but also natural law inherent in humans having been endowed with reason in divine creation.¹⁹ The appropriation of Aristotelian virtue ethics into Judaism in the figure of Moses ben Maimon (Maimonides; 1138–1204 CE), by contrast, does not so rely on innate natural law to achieve a universalisable ethic, but rather underwrites virtue with revelation interpreted in the light of reason, which is then transmitted universally outward by its practice among Jews. Maimonides also disagreed with Aristotle about habit ultimately resulting in a fixed character of goodness, instead requiring ongoing

---

17. Aristotle, *Aristotle: Nicomachean Ethics*, edited by Roger Crisp (Cambridge, UK: Cambridge University Press, 2014); Richard Kraut, 'Aristotle's Ethics', in *The Stanford Encyclopedia of Philosophy*, edited by Edward N Zalta and Uri Nodelman, Fall 2022 (Metaphysics Research Lab, Stanford University, 2022), https://plato.stanford.edu/archives/fall2022/entries/aristotle-ethics/.
18. Aristotle, *Aristotle*, 25.
19. Robert Pasnau, 'Thomas Aquinas', in *The Stanford Encyclopedia of Philosophy*, edited by Edward N Zalta and Uri Nodelman, Spring 2023 (Metaphysics Research Lab, Stanford University, 2023), https://plato.stanford.edu/archives/spr2023/entries/aquinas/.

critical self-consciousness to right wrongs and return to virtue.[20] Ahmad ibn Muhammad ibn Miskawayh (ca 940–1030 CE) likewise relied on revelation, though that revealed in the Qur'an, of course. Ibn Miskawayh also developed a fundamentally social conception of virtue as formed in the public sphere, relying on friendships in community,[21] which emphasis has reemerged in the contemporary renaissance of virtue ethics inaugurated by Alasdair MacIntyre.[22]

Each of these thinkers, from three distinct theistic traditions, works to articulate the role and configuration each of revelation and reason in generating the disposition toward virtue characteristic of Aristotelian virtue ethics. Not being beholden to the particularity of revelation, Aristotle was able to straightforwardly rely on reason as a common characteristic of humanity, which commonality makes his ethic universally applicable. The reason Aquinas, Maimonides, and Ibn Miskawayh need to get the relationship between revelation and reason right is precisely to safeguard the universality of virtue ethics as a moral philosophy emerging from under the penumbra of their theistic worldview. The key point here is that the virtues articulated by Western virtue ethicists located in the Aristotelian lineage are intended to apply universally, one and the same across all instances for each and every moral agent. It may be that how the virtues are manifested in behavior vary according to the situation, but every moral agent is expected to acquire and maintain each and all of the same set of virtues and behave in any and all situations according to those means between their respective excesses and deficiencies.

Confucians also have universal virtues that are understood to apply to all moral agents, though in the formative years of the tradition much of the work undertaken by Confucian thinkers had to do with

---

20. Jonathan Jacobs, 'Aristotle and Maimonides on Virtue and Natural Law', in *Hebraic Political Studies* 2, no 1 (Winter 2007): 46–77; Kenneth Seeskin, 'Maimonides', in *The Stanford Encyclopedia of Philosophy*, edited by Edward N Zalta, Spring 2021 (Metaphysics Research Lab, Stanford University, 2021), https://plato.stanford.edu/ENTRIES/maimonides/.
21. Elizabeth M Bucar, 'Islam and the Cultivation of Character: Ibn Miskawayh's Synthesis and the Case of the Veil', in *Cultivating Virtue: Perspectives from Philosophy, Theology, and Psychology*, edited by Nancy E Snow (New York, NY: Oxford University Press, 2014), 0, https://doi.org/10.1093/acprof:oso/9780199967421.003.0009.
22. Alasdair C MacIntyre, *After Virtue: A Study in Moral Theory* (University of Notre Dame Press, 1981).

making them universal rather than parochial to the elite social class. As already noted, Confucius extended the concept of humaneness as the telos of virtue for moral agents at least to also include his own class of minor aristocrats as moral agents. Filiality was universalized in another way, extending the scope not of the agent but of the direct object of its purview, from parents to a much broader range of social relations, and eventually encompassing all. Mencius clearly understood his four cardinal virtues to be universal, deriving as they do from a universal human nature of goodness.[23]

At the same time, central to Confucian thought is careful analysis of the norms that govern the behaviors of agents interacting in various social roles. This attention to roles arises in part from the universalizing process applied to the virtue of filiality. Whereas filiality originally applied only to relationships between children and their parents, the process of abstracting and applying the principles of loyalty, deference, and respect to people in other social relations meant recognizing the ways in which the roles those others inhabited were similar to and different from the role of parent. For example, the ruler is in some respects similar to a parent in terms of their responsibility for meeting the needs of the populace but is also very different in that there is no direct care of citizens, and thus little of the intimacy that is so crucial in relationships between parents and children. The loyalty, deference, and respect of a citizen toward their ruler thus looks in some ways similar but in many important ways rather different than the loyalty, deference, and respect a child should display toward their parents. Nevertheless, those different behaviors are still embodiments of the common virtue of filiality.

Given that many of the social roles with attendant norms that Confucians analyze, and view as characteristic of a humane society, themselves predate the movement toward universalization of virtue, it is little wonder that tension emerges from the beginning between those norms and the demands of universalized virtue. By contrast, this tension has only rather recently begun to be identified and explored in Western virtue ethics.[24] John Ramsey helpfully identifies this tension between virtue and norm as the 'role dilemma', which is

---

23. RAH King, 'Universality and Argument in Mencius IIA6', in *Proceedings of the Aristotelian Society* 111 (2011): 275–93, https://www.jstor.org/stable/41331551.
24. Sean Cordell, 'Virtuous Persons and Social Roles', in *Journal of Social Philosophy* 42, no 3 (2011): 254–72, https://doi.org/10.1111/j.1467-9833.2011.01535.x.

the conflict between the demands of a social role and the demands of virtue. He distinguishes between responses as either externalist, turning to virtues that exist beyond the scope of the role in question, or internalist, resolving the dilemma by adopting the norms of the role. Ramsey further notes that the former response collapses into a virtue ethics much along the lines of the Aristotelian variety, whereas the latter 'implies a form of cultural relativism and allows for repressive and problematic social institutions'.[25]

Notably, Ramsey understands the notion of role, or at least its norms, to be closely aligned with the concept of 禮 (*li*; ritual). The dilemma he identifies thus puts ritual in tension with virtue in a way that he claims is inadequately addressed among the early Confucians. Since all of the early Confucians extensively explicate their understandings of ritual, humaneness, and their interrelations, it may instead be that the framing of the dilemma in terms of internalism and externalism is the source of difficulty in reconciling the dilemma, and seeing how it is reconciled by these thinkers. Moreover, such a tension is strange in light of Aristotelian virtue ethics because ritual is very similar to the Aristotelian conception of habit, which like ritual is the means of achieving and cultivating virtue.

Critical for reconciling ritual and humaneness for Confucians is the concept of 義 (*yi*; appropriateness), which Mencius identified as another of his cardinal virtues. Rather than identifying them all as virtues, Sor-hoon Tan calls these the 'three key ethical ideas of authoritative conduct (*ren* 仁), appropriateness (*yi* 義), and ritual practice (*li* 禮)'. Adopting a perspective on appropriateness from David Hall and Roger Ames, and grounding it in the texts of Confucius, Mencius, and Xunzi, Tan says that appropriateness 'has to do with the personal investment of meaning in action, based on the interaction between a person's individuality and her environment in specific situations'.[26] This is not dissimilar to what John Knoblock describes in saying that 'Yi expresses the "rightness" of a course of conduct that is proper, fitting, decent, suitable, appropriate in the circumstances in which it was done'. He further describes how the conception of appropriateness emerged from the universalisation

---

25. John Ramsey, 'The Role Dilemma in Early Confucianism', in *Frontiers of Philosophy in China* 8, no 3 (2013): 377–78, https://www.jstor.org/stable/23597454.
26. Sor-hoon Tan, *Confucian Democracy: A Deweyan Reconstruction* (Albany, NY: State University of New York Press, 2012), 83.

process of filiality: 'Yi thus designated the appropriateness, the fitness, and the suitability of the service the minister gave his lord and the son his father, the respect the humble gave the noble, the assistance friends gave each other, and the differences in treatment between near and far relatives.'[27] And yet, citing *Mencius* 6A5,[28] Knoblock notes that appropriateness 'becomes more than mere congruity since it reflects an inner sense for what is right',[29] which is to say virtue. Appropriateness is thus the process, in the moment, of generating harmony amidst the sometimes competing demands of virtue and the ritual norms governing the roles inhabited by those involved in the situation at hand. Appropriateness overcomes the role dilemma Ramsey posits in the act of generating harmony from the tension rather than from an *a priori* determination across instances of the correct balance between humaneness and ritual principles.

Confucian appropriateness is thus akin to Aristotelian practical wisdom (*phronesis*). For Aristotle, 'practical wisdom, as he conceives it, cannot be acquired solely by learning general rules. We must also acquire, through practice, those deliberative, emotional, and social skills that enable us to put our general understanding of well-being into practice in ways that are suitable to each occasion.'[30] Practical wisdom is thus about bringing virtues to life in the concrete situations of daily life. Appropriateness is likewise situational, contextual, and skill-based. What appropriateness also brings to the table, that practical wisdom does not, however, is the set of ritual norms that govern behavior between inhabitants of various roles. These ritual norms are themselves based on prior instantiations of humaneness in encounters between agents, and so there is a dialectical relationship between the ideal of virtue and the concreteness of ritual and role.

Having such prior concrete examples of virtue in action to rely on gives the Confucians a leg up on the Aristotelians in moral decision making. The Confucians can rely on what Daniel Kahneman calls system one, or 'fast', thinking, which relies on heuristic, habit, and past patterns to make decisions quickly, rather than having to rely on system two, which is slow, deliberate, and logical.[31] Whereas Aristotle

---

27. Xunzi, *Xunzi: Translation and Study*, I.95.
28. Mengzi, *Mengzi*, 147–48.
29. Xunzi, *Xunzi: Translation and Study*, I.95.
30. Kraut, 'Aristotle's Ethics'.
31. Daniel Kahneman, *Thinking, Fast and Slow* (Farrar, Straus and Giroux, 2011).

locates habit at the beginning of moral formation, as the source of virtue development, the Confucians keep ritual and habit in the mix all the way through, recognizing that humans have to operate with a bounded rationality much of the time, under conditions of limited knowledge, resources, and time.[32] Appropriateness has to do not only with the rational process of applying virtue to a situation, as for Aristotelan practical wisdom, but also the instinctual recognition of when, where, and how a ritual pattern fits around the participants in an encounter.

One good reason for considering Confucian role ethics to be a form of virtue ethics in relatively close proximity to that of the Aristotelian eudaimonst variety, rather than a distinct ethical type or more closely approximating deontology or consequentialism, is that the norms that govern social roles in the theory may best be interpreted as particular rather than universal virtues. They are certainly, and explicitly, expressions of the broader universal virtues elaborated above, but these norms are also more like virtues than they are like rules as they become sincere expressions of feeling formed through the practice of the rituals that mediate each role, which is very similar to the formation program of habits as conceived by Aristotle. That said, Confucian thinkers do not view that formation program as leading to the learning of general, universal virtues, but rather of the particular virtues that govern the role in question. For example, the virtue of deference is a general virtue that applies to more junior members of families and the state with respect to their respective superiors alike, but that is not to say that learning the appropriate virtue of deference with respect to a parent means that one has also learned a general principle that can be applied to relating to ministers and nobles. Those deferential relationships must be separately learned according to their ritual norms, and only then can the moral agent recognise and appreciate the commonalities between them that is the general virtue of deference. Learning appropriate deference across a variety of roles thus hones the meaning of the virtue of deference for the moral agent such that they may more appropriately implement it in each role.

---

32. Gerd Gigerenzer and Reinhard Selten, *Bounded Rationality: The Adaptive Toolbox* (Chicago: MIT Press, 2002).

Particular Roles and Virtues for AI

With these comparative considerations in mind, it is now possible to more precisely analyze how the Confucian version of virtue ethics would approach artificial intelligences. Key to note is that at least two forms of particularity accompany the Confucian conception of roles such that the Confucian approach to virtue ethics is best understood as a role ethic.

The first form of particularity is with respect to the role itself such that universal virtues are expressed differently in behavior depending on the role of the moral agent and the roles of those toward whom their behavior is directed. For a child to be respectful toward a parent requires different behavior than for a soldier to be respectful toward a general. As such behavioral patterns become codified and proscribed apart from direct recourse to the virtue they are meant to express, situations may arise in which enacting the behaviors would in fact conflict with the demands of virtue, which is the role dilemma identified by Ramsey as shared between Aristotelians and Confucians.

The second form of particularity is with respect to virtues that are particular to one or a discrete set of roles but are therefore not universal. Courage, for example, is not a universal virtue in Confucianism as it is not expected for many roles, particularly roles inhabited by women, who are associated with 陰 (*yin*; passive or negative). A virtue dilemma may emerge here, where the behaviors that express a particular virtue associated with the role a moral agent inhabits may conflict with the universal virtues applicable to all. For example, sons have particular filial responsibilities for parents, which become especially important as the parents age, but in the case where there is no son, which is increasingly common as a result of the One Child Policy in China, daughters are faced with a conflict between the passivity virtue particular to female roles and the universal virtues of filiality and humaneness.

This second form of particularity is unique to the Confucian approach as it does not have a direct analogue in Aristotelian virtue ethics. This is because the Aristotelian approach conceives of each virtue applying universally to all moral agents and at least in principle applicable in all situations, whereas the Confucian approach need not conceive all universal virtues as necessarily applicable to every role. While respect is a virtue that applies to both superiors and inferiors in social relations, albeit realized for each according to the specific virtues of their roll, the virtue of deference applies only to inferiors with respect to their interactions with superiors.

This deference differential is demonstrated by the need, from quite early in the tradition, to create a mechanism for dealing with immoral and despotic superiors, especially rulers. In the 孝經 (*Xiaojing*; *Classic of Fillial Piety*), a student asks Confucius whether children must obey every command of their father, as deference and attendant virtues would seem to imply. In response, Confucius details how in the past, rulers at various levels would have officials whose duty was to 諫 (*jian*; remonstrate) with them when they made bad decisions so that they would keep their states on the 道 (*dao*; way). He then draws the analogy with a father behaving immorally such that a child is morally obligated to remonstrate with them, and concluding by demanding "How could simply obeying the commands of one's father be deemed filial?"[33] The mechanism of remonstration is the exception to correct for the risk of corruption and immorality raised by the structural difference in application of the virtue of deference only from inferiors to superiors.

These forms of particularity give Confucians a great deal more flexibility when applying virtue ethics to artificial intelligences (AIs), yet also result in a broader moral topography that requires charting. At the start, like Aristotelians, Confucians need to consider how universal virtues applicable to all moral agents apply to AIs, which are presumed to be moral agents because if they are not then virtue ethics, and arguably all normative ethical paradigms, would not apply. Confucians then have a number of other trajectories of analysis to undertake, which must begin with a conceptualization of the role or roles that AIs inhabit in the social sphere, in relation to humans and their myriad roles and in relation to one another. From there Confucians must consider how universal virtues are to be realized in behavior in each of those roles with their attendant relations. Then they must consider which particular virtues are applicable to each of those roles and how those particular virtues are to be realized in behavior with respect to each other role in the social network. Finally,

---

33. Henry Rosemont and Roger T Ames, *The Chinese Classic of Family Reverence: A Philosophical Translation of the Xiaojing* (Honolulu, HI: University of Hawaii Press, 2009), 113–14.

the Confucian virtue ethicist must consider potential conflicts between universal and particular virtues in generating behavior and between universal virtues and habituated behaviors expressing universal virtues in particular circumstances.

The flexibility advantage in Confucianism clearly comes with a complexity cost whereby the whole framework risks spiraling into an unmanageable chaos. This risk is already potentially there when considering only the many roles with attendant particular and universal virtues to be expressed in behavior in human societies, let alone adding a potential order of magnitude more possible roles for AIs to play. It is not that the Aristotelians do not face a potential complexity crisis as well, but the contemporary revival of virtue ethics, especially as influenced by Alasdair MacIntyre, has sought to manage it by circumscribing the locus of its applicability to small, face-to-face communities.[34] Confucians never attempted such a strategy, having from its inception been a tradition that seeks to shape culture and society broadly from the highest levels, and almost always Confucian thinkers were situated in large, complex societies. Instead, achieving traction on complexity came by enforcing behavioral patterns associated with roles and downplaying individual consideration of whether those patterns in fact accord with either particular or universal virtues, which is to say through the adoption of legalism.[35] Whether or not such a strategy is ultimately adjudicated helpful, healthy, or good, it is nevertheless notable that at least with respect to AIs it is in fact even more easily implemented insofar as such rules governing behavior can be programmed in from the beginning, at least in many instances.

To envision a Confucian virtue ethics analysis of AIs in practice, it is helpful to begin with a relatively prevalent example from the literature, namely self-driving cars and the trolley problem. In this thought experiment, a self-driving car suffers a catastrophic failure that results in having to decide between a course of action that results in the death(s) of either the human occupant of the car or a group of people standing along the side of the road. Loss of human life is unavoidable in this scenario, and as originally framed as a challenge

---

34. MacIntyre, *After Virtue*.
35. Yuri Pines, 'Legalism in Chinese Philosophy', in *The Stanford Encyclopedia of Philosophy*, edited by Edward N Zalta, Winter, 2014, http://plato.stanford.edu/archives/win2014/entries/chinese-legalism/.

for utilitarian analyses, the issue comes down to evaluating the relative value of the individual in the car in comparison with the value of the individuals along the side of the road. Aristotelian virtue ethicists have generally been uninterested in the trolley problem due to their rejection of universal norms, rules, and principles that would enable articulation of a singular, concrete resolution.[36] If virtue ethics are unable to grapple with it, however, then it is unclear that a virtue ethics approach to AI is viable since this is a real, practical moral problem faced in AI development rather than just an ethical thought experiment.

While impossible to give a full analysis here of the problem from a Confucian virtue ethics perspective, it is possible to chart the terrain such a procedure would need to follow. The first step is to understand the role of self-driving cars, which includes but is not reducible to their functional role of conveying people and cargo from one place to another through a range of dynamic circumstances including obstacles. The role of the car is not reducible to this function, though, precisely because other relational aspects serve to further constrain that role. For example, the car may be the property of the person being conveyed, in which case it might have particular role-based requirements of deference to that person, as opposed to being owned by a public entity in which case that deference might be balanced by an equivalent deference to the individuals on the side of the road. The analysis here includes, in part, whether the car is an inferior, equal, or superior to the occupant and each of the individuals it might hit when the catastrophe strikes. The invocation of deference, of course, has already invoked a virtue that is particular to certain roles and not others, and would only be applicable in the case that the car is understood to be an inferior or perhaps an equal.

Once the role is understood, the next step in the analysis is to consider how universal virtues, such as humaneness, apply given the configuration of the roles of the various agents in play. Humaneness is particularly interesting to consider in this case because it is not only universal but synonymous with virtue in general. The result is that if humaneness is the only virtue available upon which to base the

---

36. Liezl van Zyl, 'Virtue Ethics and the Trolley Problem', in *The Trolley Problem*, edited by Hallvard Lillehammer, Classic Philosophical Arguments (Cambridge: Cambridge University Press, 2023), 116–33, https://doi.org/10.1017/9781009255615.008.

required decision in the self-driving car version of the trolley problem, then its generality provides very little traction such that the analysis is dominated by the various roles in play and quickly elides back into a utilitarian analysis of the relative value of each of the people.

Also involved in the analysis would be the role of the occupant vis-à-vis each of the individuals along the side of the road. It may be that the occupant of the car has a particular virtue of loyalty with respect to one or more of the people on the roadside. Even though the occupant is not the moral agent in the case of a self-driving car, the car might take that loyalty into account in its moral decision making. In this sense, the particular virtue of loyalty between the occupant and one or more bystanders is being treated also as a duty, at least from the perspective of the car in formulating its own virtue analysis.

A final point to raise regarding this example for now is that the baseline habituated behavior of the car in its role is likely to be that it should, except in exceptional circumstances, remain on the road, preferably in its lane or at least a lane. A catastrophe is clearly an exceptional circumstance, but a Confucian virtue analysis must find ways to adjudicate whether it is sufficiently exceptional to justify modifying course from the habituated behavior, which is to say the 禮 (*li*; ritual) that governs self-driving cars. Confucians heavily influenced by legalism would tend to the internalist interpretation Ramsey describes and hew closely to the ritual norms. Absent that tendency toward legalism in the tradition, the virtue of humaneness would seem to justify granting exceptionality to a wider range of situations such as the self-driving car catastrophe, and likely many less dramatic interventions.

Unlike self-driving cars, Large Language Models (LLMs) such as ChatGPT are forms of AI designed to interact with humans through the medium of language. The phenomenon of AI hallucinations is when the model generates outputs that are incorrect, impossible, or not based on the inputs. 'The term "hallucination" is used to draw parallels between these unexpected AI outputs and the human experience of perceiving things that are not actually present in reality.'[37] The model may nevertheless present the outputs as authoritative and correct, and when received by an unsuspecting or insufficiently

---

37. Ian Cunningham, 'AI Hallucinations: The Hidden Risks of Machine Learning', in *AI Pathway* (blog), May 11, 2023, https://www.aipathway.com/ai-hallucinations/.

informed audience these hallucinations may be taken as true. From an Aristotelian virtue ethics perspective, a solution to this problem might be to program the virtue of humility into the model such that the model recursively checks, double checks, and otherwise verifies its results, and presents them less decisively. A Confucian virtue ethicist, by contrast, might question whether humility is a virtue appropriate to the role of an LLM. If, for example, the role of an LLM is to serve as a sort of research assistant, it may be that the relationship with the researcher places the onus more on the researcher to be skeptical of all results at baseline and to have a sufficient level of knowledge of the field to recognize a hallucination when it manifests. In this way, the expectation is that the human demonstrates appropriate intellectual virtues rather than expecting that an AI demonstrate appropriate moral virtues that may not be technically possible, at least as yet.

Finally, the example of AI neural implants highlights the utility of the Confucian focus on roles in virtue ethics and provides a helpful transition to the final section looking at the broader philosophical anthropology in which virtue ethics are framed. While 'devices that interface with the neural system are currently in use and development only for those with a therapeutic need', 'one future use of brain chip implants could be to augment brain functioning for people even without therapeutic need.'[38] Both possibilities give rise to numerous questions about the role of the AI, the role of the host in which the AI is implanted, and how they relate to one another and to others in wider society. Assuming that two people are social equals, does one who then has an AI implanted remain an equal with the person who does not have the enhancement, become their superior, or in fact become their inferior? The possibility of AI neural implants overriding the subjectivity and control of their hosts has become fertile ground for a whole genre of dystopian literature and other media. Yet even apart from fears of such imaginings coming to life, the ability to meld human and artificial intelligences provokes a whole set of questions about how roles might change as a result that will require extending the Confucian approach to virtue ethics, especially its consideration

---

38. Lee Rainie *et al*, 'AI and Human Enhancement: Americans' Openness Is Tempered by a Range of Concerns', Internet, Science, & Tech (Washington, DC: Pew Research Center, March 17, 2022), https://www.pewresearch.org/internet/2022/03/17/ai-and-human-enhancement-americans-openness-is-tempered-by-a-range-of-concerns/.

of roles. Confucians have already given careful consideration to role alignment across the various levels and sectors of complex societies as evidenced by the extension of the concept of filiality beyond the family to state social systems as described above. The task now is to extend the conception of role alignment to include not only nonhuman moral agents independently but also nonhuman moral agents interfacing directly with the agency of human moral agents. While such a constructive enterprise is beyond the scope of this paper, it is important to emphasize that without the notion of roles it is difficult to see how virtue would apply at this interface, applying to two moral agents independently and as interfaced simultaneously.

AIs and Anthropology

There is a distinct divergence between Aristotelian and Confucian virtue ethics at the level of the philosophical anthropologies framing their respective enterprises and forming the basis for determining what constitutes a moral agent. This divergence also has important implications for how Confucians and Aristotelians interpret the potential for artificial and human intelligences interfacing through AI neural implants. Ultimately, the philosophical anthropology undergirding the Aristotelian project as inherited by the three Abrahamic theistic traditions results in much greater skepticism toward human and artificial intelligences interfacing, whereas Confucians are able to much more easily embrace the possibilities afforded by this prospect.

For Aristotle himself, being human means uniting an animal body with a rational soul, the latter being that which enables humans to accord with virtue in order to achieve our ultimate good, that is, happiness or wellbeing.[39] Presumably, a contemporary inheritor of this conception of human nature could be open to the idea of humans interfacing with AIs through neural implants on the basis that the goal of such implants would be to enhance the capacity of reason such that accordance with virtue is likewise enhanced. However, before arriving at such an affirmation, this Aristotelian would have to overcome a degree of skepticism rooted in concern that the interface might interfere with extant rational capacities resulting in discord with virtue.

---

39. Aristotle, *Aristotle*, 1097b22–1098a20; Kraut, 'Aristotle's Ethics', sec. 2.

The situation is quite different for the theistic inheritors of Aristotle, for whom the human capacity for reason, and for Aquinas the natural law, are termini of divine creation which have been deemed good by God. For Jews and Christians particularly, for whom humans are understood to be made in the 'image and likeness of God (*imago dei*)', it is not clear that it is possible to achieve any higher goodness than that with which God has already endowed the capacity to achieve in humans in the very act of creation. Moreover, the risk of meddling in divinely gifted human nature such that a person might no longer reflect divinity is too great. Human nature is understood as relatively fixed as divinely created, and so attempts to change it, through AI neural interfaces or otherwise, would be immoral because in doing so humans are 'playing God'.

Confucianism does not share this concern with humans taking action to change our own nature. In fact, 性 (*xing*; human nature) is merely what we are born with, and the whole purpose of the extensive Confucian tradition of ritual, moral, and intellectual training is in fact to refine, shape, and alter what we are born with so as to become a 君子 (*junzi*; noble person) who embodies 仁 (*ren*; humaneness). This is why Confucianism is known as a tradition of moral self-cultivation:[40] changing our human nature as it is endowed at birth is the whole purpose of the tradition. If AI neural implants can hold out the promise of achieving an even higher degree of humaneness than what humans can achieve with only our meat brains, this would be an exciting potential for Confucians.

This points to a final contrast between the Confucian and Aristotelian approaches to virtue ethics having to do with the conception of the ultimate goal of virtuous conduct: *eudaimonia* (happiness) for Aristotelians and 仁 (*ren*; humaneness) for Confucians. For Aristotelians, happiness is the ultimate goal and is a fulness unto itself of fixed dimension. This is to say that there is no such thing as getting beyond or above happiness, or of extending happiness to greater degrees. It is an end, a cap, a finishing point, the highest good.[41] Not so for the Confucians, who are not so much concerned about humaneness as an end but rather the roots, context, and means of cultivating it. Mencius identifies the root of humaneness

---

40. PJ Ivanhoe, *Confucian Moral Self Cultivation* (Hackett Publishing, 2000).
41. Kraut, 'Aristotle's Ethics', sec. 2.

in 惻隱 (*ceyin*; compassionate disposition), and all of the early Confucian thinkers emphasize the necessity of it being nurtured, with an elaborate program of formation in ritual and classical texts envisioned by Xunzi.[42] This shift in focus results in a conception of humaneness that is virtually limitless: more training and nurturing, which is to say more moral self-cultivation, will lead to more and more humaneness. Humananess is virtually infinite, rather than a discrete, finite good as Aristotle conceives it.

Conclusion

The conclusion to be drawn is that the Confucian approach to virtue ethics has a higher degree of tolerance for the idea that AIs may be able to play a role in improving humanity, our virtue, and our goodness. Insofar as US citizens reflect these Aristotelian impulses, a recent study from Pew Research Center shows that a majority in the US think neural implants would be bad for society, and seventy-eight percent would not want such an implant, with these views skewing toward those with high as opposed to low religious commitment.[43] China, on the other hand, is heavily influence by Confucianism, and shows greater openness to cloning, gene editing, and pursuing neural implant technologies.[44] Some caution is warranted for the Confucians as well, though, given that while great progress is being made in terms of the interface aspect of neural implants, the AI that will eventually be interfaced still has a long way to go. Increased humaneness may not be the result of implanting an AI that is 'at once both smarter and dumber than any person you've ever met'.

---

42. Mark Csikszentmihalyi, 'Confucius', in *The Stanford Encyclopedia of Philosophy*, edited by Edward N Zalta, Summer 2020 (Metaphysics Research Lab, Stanford University, 2020), sec. 4, https://plato.stanford.edu/archives/sum2020/entries/confucius/.
43. Rainie *et al*, 'AI and Human Enhancement', 83–86.
44. Dennis Normile, 'CRISPR Bombshell: Chinese Researcher Claims to Have Created Gene-Edited Twins', in *ScienceInsider*, November 26, 2018, https://www.science.org/content/article/crispr-bombshell-chinese-researcher-claims-have-created-gene-edited-twins.

Agathon: A Journal of Ethics and Value in the Modern World, Vol 10/2025

Chapter 16
Virtuous AI in African Liberation

Sunday Akande and Oluwatobi Ife-Adediran

'Africa has been on her knees for too long . . . At both the top and the bottom, all Africans must believe in themselves again; that they are capable of walking their own path and forging their own identity; that they have a right to be governed with justice, accountability and transparency; that they can honor and practice their cultures and make them relevant to today's needs; and that they no longer need to be indebted—financially, intellectually and spiritually—to those who once governed them. They must rise up and walk.'
—Wangari Maathai[1]

Abstract: This chapter presents a contextual hypothesis of virtuous AI in relation to the socio-cultural decolonization regime of African liberation. We argue that in the past technology has been utilized in the fortification of neocolonial forces in areas such as data exploitation, market monopoly, the global digital divide, intellectual property constraints and the falsification of information through digital media. What about the future of virtuous AI? Virtuous AI is herein conceived as a revolutionary technology that could help cure the ills associated with neocolonialism. In the context under consideration, virtuous AI should be accoutered with features that strengthen decoloniality in the African socio-cultural milieu.

Keywords: Africa, Artificial Intelligence, Decolonization, Virtue

Is artificial intelligence (AI) context-independent or context-dependent? On the one hand, when artificial general intelligence

---

1. Wangari Maathai, *The Challenge for Africa* (New York: Pantheon, 2009).

(AI) that imitates human intelligence is the ideal, that ideal seems to be context-independent. It is independent because it is modeled after the generic human being that transcends gender, race, social class, geopolitical location, or even religious affiliation. Such AI retains a revolutionary status as long as it obliterates fault lines that would otherwise impede collective human identity and planetary flourishing.

On the other hand, AI's impact differs according to socio-cultural context. AI can be an instrument of oppression. It can be argued that the unfounded trepidation regarding the repression of humans by machines, as well as the fair criticism of the discriminatory features that malign public trust in the objective quality of AI, thrive on the egregious prejudice against certain human-others. One of the most reprehensible demonstrations of inter-human repression is colonialism and its contemporary neocolonial expression. More disturbing is the use of AI to achieve neo-colonial interests. Perhaps, intelligent machines may eventually re-colonize a divided humanity.

The history of Africa is shaped by the colonial past, and its people have undergone anguish and exploitation in the hands of foreign powers. However, African liberation movements have been fighting for decolonisation and a return to traditional values and ways of life. As we move forward into a technological revolution, there is a need to reflect on how to harness technology in a way that respects cultures and empowers societies. This chapter explores the intersection of the socio-cultural decolonisation regime of African liberation and the hypothesis of virtuous AI, highlighting the potential of technology as a tool for positive social change.

Pre-colonial Africa thrived on its original political, economic, and socio-cultural traditions before the infiltration of colonial powers with the agenda to universalize the western worldview. The imposition of this alien worldview is referred to by Jimoh Anselm and John Thomas as psychological violence.[2] Detachment from the social and cultural impact of colonialism in the African continent has proven to be more complex than the process of political decolonization. The intrinsic and indigenous cultural heritage of African communities was greatly

---

2. Jimoh Anselm and John Thomas, 'An African Epistemological Approach to Epistemic Certitude and Scepticism', in *Research on Humanities and Social Sciences* 5, no 11 (2015): 54–57.

influenced and, perhaps, eroded by colonial cultural norms, values, beliefs and practices to the extent that western philosophers and thinkers such as Immanuel Kant, GWF Hegel and David Hume regarded Africans as inferiors without a history or philosophy.[3]

Although scholars such as Stephen Theron consider western rationality as superior and universal, empirical evidence suggests that the influence of western ideologies on African society has not served her developmental needs in the economy, education, security infrastructure, health care, environment and overall standard of living. While Kwasi Wiredu opines that the revival and reinstatement of African traditional thinking cannot suffice to address the challenges that face contemporary African society, decolonial critical philosophy has revealed that the forceful denigration and debasement of any culture in a bid to validate another is an expression of fatal reductionism.[4] In their book titled *Understanding Cross-Cultural Management*, Browaeys Marie-Joelle and Price Roger have argued that no culture can claim absolute superiority.[5]

Today, African languages and oral traditions, epistemic frameworks, arts and religion are struggling to survive in the wake of neocolonial forces which have been fortified by technology. For instance, the digital economy has ushered a new means by which valuable data and information are extracted and exploited for global market monopolies. Unfortunately, the wealth generated from such data is not equally distributed for the benefit of some countries from which the utilized data were mined. Intellectual property laws have engendered the exclusive ownership and control of technological solutions by some multinational corporations in such a way that stifles the development of knowledge and technology-based industries in former colonies.

But the liberation spirit is changing things. 'For a long time African television content was dominated by information about developed countries and their lifestyles', observe Bimbo Fafowora and Rahab

---

3. Munyadrazi Mawere, 'Epistemological and Moral Implications of Characterization in African Literature: A Critique of Patrick Chakaipa's "Rudo Ibofu" (Love is Blind)', in *Journal of English and Literature* 2, no 1 (2011): 11–19.
4. Kwasi Wiredu, *A Companion to African Philosophy* (Oxford: Blackwell Publishing, 2004), 13.
5. Browaeys, Marie-Joelle and Price Roger, *Understanding Cross-cultural Management* (Harlow: Pearson Education Limited, 2008), 10.

Nyaga. 'The few available programmes about Africa were through the eyes of colonizers, who painted a picture of a dark, savage, disease-ridden Africa. Today, however, Africa tells its own story to the world, showcasing our rich cultural heritage and people's everyday struggles, failures, and successes.'[6]

What might this imply for the current global blanketing of AI? There is a wrinkle in that blanket. AI has inherited a digital divide fostering the unequal distribution of technology and digital skills. The divide perpetuates existing inequalities, exploitation, and control by technologically advanced countries. The technology of digital media has also been harnessed for the spread of false information and propaganda to shape public opinions and determine the direction of political discourse in relation to former colonies.

The socio-cultural decolonization momentum of African liberation, however, aims at the restoration of African cultures, traditions, and values. Liberation is also about the restoration of African humanity and dignity, which were was ensnared by colonialism. The liberation movement aims to promote African cultural values and knowledge, empowering individuals to assert their identity and reject Western hegemony. AI technology, in this context, could be harnessed to propagate and preserve the African sense of identity and cultural practices.

The Virtuous AI Hypothesis

What about the prospect of virtuous AI? Whether or not AI itself could become virtuous might not matter. What will be decisive is AI in the service of virtuous values and virtuous actors. In this case, virtuous actors would side not with neocolonial forces but rather with the African liberative spirit.

Our virtuous AI hypothesis aligns AI in all its manifestations with the Cardinal virtues—prudence, justice, fortitude, and temperance—along with the theological virtues—faith, hope, and love. In the context of African liberation, justice with its corollary, dignity for every person, will be central. Virtue belongs to the human actors, not to AI itself.

---

6. Bimbo Fafowora and Rahab Nyaga, 'The Media', in *African Public Theology*, edited by Sunday Bobai Agang (Bukuru, Nigeria: African Christian Textbooks, Hippo Books, 2020), 307–325, at 311.

The hypothesis of virtuous AI presents a new way of looking at the role of technology in African society. It proposes that it is possible to create AI systems that operate according to ethical principles and moral values. Such systems would act in the best interests of humanity and prioritize social well-being over profit. The virtuous AI hypothesis suggests that AI can be used to tackle complex societal problems, such as poverty, inequality, and climate change, paving the way for a more sustainable and equitable future.

The intersection of the socio-cultural decolonization regime and the hypothesis of virtuous AI offers a unique opportunity to harness technology for positive social change. The restoration of African cultures and traditions requires the preservation and dissemination of knowledge that has been passed down from generation to generation. AI can assist in the preservation and dissemination of this knowledge through tools such as virtual libraries and cultural heritage sites. By preserving African cultural practices and knowledge, technology can support the reconstruction of African personhood and empower individuals to assert their identity.

Moreover, the hypothesis of virtuous AI could help ensure that new technology will be developed with ethical considerations in mind. AI developers can consult with African communities to understand and incorporate cultural values into the design process. This would prevent technologies from replicating the biases and inequalities that exist in society today and ensure that technology is developed in a socially responsible manner. By prioritizing social well-being over profit, AI could help create a more equitable future for all.

Globally, decolonization could be useful in mitigating some of the perceived adverse effects of AI in many societies. The AI revolution has the potential to disrupt traditional ways of life, exacerbating inequalities and eroding cultural practices. By promoting African cultural values and knowledge, nevertheless, individuals everywhere might be better equipped to resist the negative effects of AI and assert their identity.

Moreover, the restoration of African cultures and traditions could promote the development of contextually relevant and sustainable technologies that meet the needs of African societies. The intersection of the socio-cultural decolonization regime of African liberation and the hypothesis of virtuous AI presents a unique opportunity to harness technology for positive social change. By harnessing AI to promote and preserve African cultural practices and knowledge, we can support the reconstruction of African identity and empower individuals to assert their identity. Furthermore, if AI is developed with ethical considerations in mind and prioritizes social well-being over profit, it can help create a more equitable future for all. However, it is important that we proceed with caution, ensuring that the benefits of technology are distributed equitably and that technologies are developed in a socially responsible manner.

This chapter establishes that in the critical context of the current decolonization regime in Africa, AI will be regarded as virtuous if it contributes to African liberation and decolonization. Such AI must be freed from racial bias, neocolonial manipulation and control, as well as the perpetuation of neocolonial cultural hegemony that undermines the cultural traditions, values and identity of former colonies in the African continent. Virtuous AI in the context of this study should be accoutered with features that validate the uniqueness and values of the African traditional culture and worldview, foster language decolonization, and discourages the expression of neocolonial tendencies.

AI and Its Revolutionary Quality

Artificial Intelligence has become an integral part of our lives worldwide, from helpful digital assistants to sophisticated self-driving cars. The incredible potential of this technology has been demonstrated by its ability to revolutionise the way we approach tasks, from streamlining processes to providing us with new insights. It is essential that we take a look at the revolutionary quality of AI and its potential for aiding in the African liberation agenda.

'AI involves the study, design and building of intelligent agents that can achieve goals', according to Christoph Bartneck and colleagues.[7] AI includes the capacity of a computer program or a machine to calculate and learn. Some engineers set as their goal the invention of AI that could replicate the intellectual capabilities of humans such as the capacity to reason, recognize patterns, draw conclusions, and make decisions.

---

7. Christoph Bartneck, Christoph Lutge, Alan Wagner, and Sean Welshet, *An Introduction to Ethics if Robotics and AI* (Switzerland: Springer, 2021) 8; https://doi.org/10.1007/978-3-030-51110-4.

Existing AI has been used to create a variety of applications and services, such as virtual personal assistants, facial recognition, fraud detection, and automated medical diagnosis.[8] Researchers such as Shubhendu and Vijay opine that these machines "make decisions which normally require a human level of expertise". According to them, AI gadgets already aid people to anticipate future challenges and even solve such as they appear.[9] Although it would be an overstatement to describe today's AI as equal to a human intelligence, sophisticated machines are adaptive in their operations.

The revolutionary quality of AI lies in its ability to automate previously manual tasks. AI-driven automation can be used to save time and money, maximise efficiency, and discover new opportunities. For example, AI-driven automobiles can be used to optimize customer service processes, reduce manual labor, and create new business models. AI-driven automation can also be used for predictive analytics, allowing businesses to gain insights into their customers' behavior and anticipate future trends.

AI has also been used to revolutionize the way we think with technology. AI-driven natural language processing (NLP) technology has enabled us to interact with our digital devices in more natural ways, allowing us to ask questions and receive answers without having to learn complex commands. AI-driven technology has also been used to create intelligent interfaces, such as chatbots, which can respond to customer inquiries in a natural and conversational way. As technology continues to evolve, AI has become an indispensable tool for businesses. AI-driven automation has improved operational efficiency, increased customer satisfaction, and enabled businesses to gain insights into their target audiences. AI-driven analytics[10] has provided businesses with a deeper understanding of their customers, allowing them to develop more personalized and effective marketing strategies. AI also finds specific applications in finance, healthcare, and security.

---

8. BJ Copeland, 'Artificial Intelligence', in Encyclopedia Britannica, accessed April 28, 2023. https://www.britannica.com/technology/artificial-intelligence
9. Shukla Shubhendu S and Jaiswal Vijay, 'Applicability of Artificial Intelligence in Different Fields of Life', in *International Journal of Scientific Engineering and Research*, 1, no 1 (2013): 30.
10. Andrew McAfee and Erik Brynjolfsson, *Machine Platform Crowd: Harnessing Our Digital Future* (New York: Norton, 2017), 15.

Finance

In the United States, financial AI investments skyrocketed to $12.2 billion in 2014, triple the 2013 investments.[11] Nathaniel Popper submitted that observers in finance sector noted that 'decisions about loans are now being made by software that can take into account a variety of finely parsed data about a borrower, rather than just a credit score and a background check'.[12] The software is designed in such a way that it undergoes decision making from analysis and not from emotions in a twinkling of an eye. These machines also have great capacity to store large information by using quantum bits instead of laying emphasis on a zero or a one, thereby storing multiple values in each space, increasing storage capacity and decreasing processing times.[13]

Another interesting thing that AI does in the financial sector is to detect fraudulent activities. While it is difficult for humans to detect some frauds in large organizations, AI can detect strange activities which need to be investigated before they cause unnecessary problems for such organizations.[14]

Health Care

What is health? According to the World Health Organization, health is 'a state of complete physical, mental and social well-being and not merely the absence of disease or infirmity'.[15] Could AI contribute significantly to healthcare in Africa? Certainly.

Computational complexities in health sector are now being made easier with the help of AI tools. For instance, Merantix[16] possesses a medical imaging application that 'detects lymph nodes in the human

---

11. Nathaniel Popper, 'Stocks and Bots', in *New York Times Magazine*, February 28, 2016.
12. Popper, 'Stocks and Bots'.
13. Cade Metz, 'In Quantum Computing Race, Yale Professors Battle Tech Giants', in *New York Times*, November 14, 2017, B3.
14. Executive Office of the President, 'Artificial Intelligence, Automation, and the Economy', in December 2016, 27–28.
15. World Health Organization, *Constitution of the World Health Organization: Basic Documents*, 45th edition Supplement (October 2006).
16. Merantix is a German company that is applying deep learning in medicine.

body in Computer Tomography (CT) images'.[17] Deep learning in this instance is a situation whereby computers are trained to easily identify and differentiate between a normal lymph node and an irregular lymph node. With this, nodes are labeled and lesions or growths are identified. This is better than making human radiologists do it because it saves time and is cost-effective. According to Eric Horvitz, AI tools are important in heath care sector because they "predict in advance potential challenges ahead and allocate resources to patient education, sensing, and proactive interventions that keep patients out of the hospital."[18]

National Security

Might AI support national security where needed on the African continent? Yes.

Christian Davenport noted that the American military, through its Project Maven, is already deploying AI 'to sift through the massive troves of data and video captured by surveillance and then alert human analysts of patterns or when there is abnormal or suspicious activity'.[19] The essence of AI in national defense, according to Deputy Secretary of Defense, Patrick Shanahan, is 'to meet our warfighters' needs and to increase [the] speed and agility [of] technology development and procurement'.[20]

The potential of AI to revolutionise our lives is immense. AI-driven automation and analytics can help us streamline processes and uncover new insights, enabling us to make better decisions and create more efficient operations. As AI continues to evolve, it has the potential to revolutionize the way we think about our day-to-day operations, from customer service to marketing strategy.

---

17. Rasmus Rothe, 'Applying Deep Learning to Real-World Problems', in *Medium*, May 23, 2017.
18. Eric Horvitz, 'Reflections on the Status and Future of Artificial Intelligence', Testimony before the U.S. Senate Subcommittee on Space, Science, and Competitiveness, November 30, 2016, 5.
19. Christian Davenport, 'Future Wars May Depend as Much on Algorithms as on Ammunitions, Report Says', *Washington Post*, December 3, 2017
20. Davenport, 'Future Wars May Depend as Much on Algorithms as on Ammunitions, Report Says'.

The African Liberation Trajectory: from Colonialism to Neo-Colonialism

The African Union lifts up a 'Pan African Vision of *An integrated, prosperous and peaceful Africa, driven by its own citizens, representing a dynamic force in the international* arena and *Agenda 2063* is the concrete manifestation of how the continent intends to achieve this vision within a 50 year period from 2013 to 2063'.[21] This is the direction the African liberation spirit is taking us.

The African liberation trajectory has been a long and arduous journey that has seen the African continent go through a period of colonialism to a period of post-colonialism and the emergence of neocolonialism. The transition has had a profound impact on the African socio-cultural worldviews, with many of the challenges faced by African countries today being a direct result of the advancement of colonialism and its aftermath. Africa's struggle for liberation from colonialism has taken a winding path. From the beginning of colonial occupation to the eventual independence of various African nations, the African liberation trajectory has been one of continual struggle for autonomy, self-determination, and economic and social justice. This struggle has had a major influence on African socio-cultural worldviews, which have been shaped and impacted by the legacy of colonialism and neocolonialism.

Recall how colonialism shaped the African continent in terms of its society, culture, and politics. The colonial powers divided the African continent into many different 'states', each controlled by a separate colonial power. This led to a lack of uniformity in terms of economic development, political systems, and cultural practices throughout the continent. In addition, the imposition of European values, languages, and laws served to further alienate African people from their own traditions and beliefs.

The social and political systems that were implemented by the colonial powers were designed to benefit the colonizers and not to benefit the African people. For instance, Acemoglu, Johnson and Robinson[22] opined that the route taken by European colonialism on

---

21. African Union, 'Agenda 2063: The Africa We want', (2013) https://au.int/en/agenda2063/overview.
22. Daron Acemoglu, Simon Johnson, and James A Robinson, 'Reversal of fortune: Geography and institutions in the making of the modern world income distribution', in *Quarterly Journal of Economics* 117, no 4 (2002): 1250.

the continent is greatly responsible for Africa's relative poverty at the end of the 20th century. They asserted that Europeans introduced private property rights and other institutions that would only favor them; according to Acemoglu, Johnson and Robinson, these actions did not only cripple the Africa's economy, it also led to the economic development in Europe and some colonies of European settlement in North America and Australasia.

This led to a heightened sense of oppression and inequality among the African people, which ultimately led to the formation of liberation movements in many African countries. The liberation movements sought to end colonial rule and to bring about a more equitable and just society.[23]

African liberation movements made great strides in achieving their goals. However, the African people still struggle with many of the economic and social issues that had been brought about by colonialism. As a result, many African countries have been unable to fully realize the promises of independence and freedom that were promised to them. This is where neocolonialism comes into play.

Neocolonialism is a form of economic colonialism that does not involve the direct political control of a foreign power. Instead, neocolonialism utilizes economic influence to maintain control over a foreign country.[24] In the case of Africa, neocolonialism has been used to maintain economic and even political dependence on the former colonial powers. This has led to a number of dependence problems, such as debt and poverty, which continue to plague many African countries.[25]

The effects of neocolonialism on the African socio-cultural worldviews have been far reaching. Neocolonialism has stifled the development of African countries, as the foreign powers continue to maintain control over their resources and economies. This has led to a sense of disenchantment among the African people, as they feel that they have not benefited from the promises of independence and freedom that were made to them. The French philosopher, Jean-Paul

---

23. George Roberts, 'The assassination of Eduardo Mondlane: FRELIMO, Tanzania, and the politics of exile in Dar es Salaam', in *Cold War History* 17, no 1 (2017): 7.
24. Matthew G Standard, *European Overseas Empire, 1879-1999: A Short History* (Hoboken, NJ: John Wiley & Sons, 2018), 5.
25. Vijay Prashad, *The Darker Nations: A People's History of the Third World* (New York: The New Press, 2007), 231-233.

Sartre, reiterating the assertion of Kwame Nkrumah, observed how neocolonialism led to systems such as neo-colonial science which negatively impacted African communities.[26]

In order for African countries to move forward and truly achieve independence and freedom, they must work to break free from the shackles of neocolonialism and create a more equitable and just society for all. Could virtuous AI help in this liberation process?

AI as a Tool to Fortify Neocolonial Interests

AI like other technologies must first be arrested from neocolonial interests. Deliberately or not, AI has been utilized as a tool for oppression as well as racial and social division. Technology is a powerful means by which its wielders can subtly exert influence and control over others. AI is regarded as a tool to perpetuate neo-colonial interests in several ways.

First, AI technologies have been used to facilitate domination over the former colonies by streamlining surveillance and control. In 2020, the Chinese government used AI-enabled facial recognition to identify and imprison Uyghur people in Xinjiang, China. Such technologies are allowed to the colonizers to monitor the population and control their actions. Similarly, the Israeli government uses AI-enabled surveillance technology to monitor Palestinian areas and carry out targeted attacks. In a similar way, AI can be used as a tool of neocolonialist domination.[27]

Second, AI technologies have been used by the colonizers to extract resources from the former colonies. For example, the Chinese government has used AI-enabled systems to extract natural resources from Africa. AI is used to detect mineral deposits, optimize mining processes, and monitor illegal mining activities. This allows the colonizers to easily extract resources for their own benefit, leading to the further impoverishment of their former colonies.[28]

---

26. Philippe Ardant, 'Le neo-colonialisme: theme, mythe et realite', in *Revue francaise de science politique* 15, no 5 (1965): 842.
27. Nick Couldry and Ulises A Mejias. 'Data Colonialism: Rethinking Big Data's Relation to the Contemporary Subject', in *Television and News Media* 20, no 4 (2018): 7.
28. Morgan Mouton and Ryan Burns, '(Digital) neo-colonialism in the smart city', in *Regional Studies* 55, no 12 (2021):1899.

Third, AI technologies have been used to strengthen the economic dependence of former colonies on the colonizers. For example, the US government has been using AI-enabled systems to monitor and predict the financial activities of developing countries. This allows the US to track financial flows and influence economic policies of the former colonies. Whether this is in the interest of these developing countries is in doubt as most of them still demonstrate strong economic dependence on developed nations.[29]

AI technologies have been used by the colonizers to maintain control over the former colonies, extract resources, and strengthen their economic dependence. Such uses of AI to date have provided a tool to fortify neo-colonial interests.

Virtuous AI Could Contribute to the Social-Cultural Decolonization of Africa

The trend of artificial intelligence is rapidly growing and becoming an integral part of modern society everywhere. We believe that AI aligned with virtue could be pressed into the service of liberation tool to help promote the rights of African people and promote the decolonisation of their societies.

In the right hands, AI could be used to support the efforts of African countries in developing their own institutions, cultures and traditions that have been suppressed by colonization. AI could be used to help build a more equal and just society for African people by ensuring that their rights are protected and their voices are heard. AI could also be used to promote equal access to education, healthcare, and employment opportunities, as well as access to resources that can help African countries prosper. By using AI, African countries can also gain a better understanding of their cultural heritage and ensure that their traditions and values are respected and preserved.

In terms of economic development, AI could help African countries to be more competitive in the global market. AI could be used to identify and support businesses, as well as to promote the development of new technologies. AI could also be used to promote trade, investment, and tourism in African countries, which can lead

---

29. Rainer Mühlhoff, 'Human-aided artificial intelligence: Or, how to run large computations in human brains? Toward a media sociology of machine learning', in *New Media & Society* 22, no 12 (2019): 1870.

to increased economic growth. Moreover, AI could be used to develop new products and services that can help African countries compete in the global market.

In addition to its potential benefits, the use of AI in the social-cultural decolonization of African countries must be done with caution. AI should be used ethically and with respect for the privacy and autonomy of African people. AI should also be used to help African countries develop in ways that are consistent with their values and traditions, rather than to impose foreign solutions on them. Furthermore, AI should be used to promote gender equality, racial and ethnic diversity, and other forms of inclusion.

The use of virtuous AI could be a powerful tool for the social-cultural decolonization of African countries. AI can help African countries to build a more equal and just society, to develop their own institutions, cultures and traditions, and to promote economic development. However, AI should also be used with caution and respect for the privacy and autonomy of African people and to promote gender equality, racial and ethnic diversity, and other forms of inclusion.

Conclusion

The peril posed by AI is that it remains aligned with colonial and post-colonial regimes. The promise is that AI could become aligned with Africa's liberative momentum.

AI aligned with virtue could become a game changer for liberation, and the achievement of a free and equal society. An AI-driven emancipation has the potential to create new opportunities for those who are marginalised and excluded from the globalized system of power. The hypothesis of a virtuous AI is a promising technological revolution in the context of this struggle for freedom and equality. AI technology can be used to support the liberation cause by enabling more efficient planning, decision-making, monitoring, and resource allocation. With modern technology, African liberation can be more efficiently pursued towards a more equitable future. This chapter has argued that virtuous AI is one that is developed to resist neo-colonial expressions in the application of this revolutionary technology.

Agathon: A Journal of Ethics and Value in the Modern World, Vol 10/2025

Chapter 17
AI Reading Theology: Promises and Perils

Mark Graves

'Do our technologies threaten religion itself? We used to believe in the power of God. Have we replaced that belief with a belief in the power of our own technologies?'
— Noreen Herzfeld[1]

Abstract: Artificial intelligence (AI) challenges both theological presumptions of unique human reason and theological methods. Given current computational ability to analyze and generate theological text, reasonably near future AI may plausibly read theology comparable to a first-year seminary student and have the capacity to learn more. Should theologians contribute to AI learning theology? Depending upon current and near-term AI capacities and social contexts, four scenarios are considered before concluding that, despite clear perils, the benefits of joint AI-human cooperation outweigh the risks. Benefits include technologically enhanced theological interpretations, improved AI morality, and potentially better understanding by AI and humans of each other.

Key terms: artificial intelligence, computational text analysis, machine ethics, theological anthropology, theology and science, Thomas Aquinas

---

1. Noreen Herzfeld, 'Introduction: Religion and the New Technologies', in *Religions* 8:7 (2017): 1–3, at 2; file:///C:/Users/Ted/Downloads/religions-08-00129-v2%20(2).pdf.

The World Economic Forum forecasts that artificial intelligence (AI) will perform over half of workplace tasks by 2025.[2] Can the computer replace theologians? How will pervasive AI change theological tasks? Although likely difficult for AI to fully engage human theology alone, one could ask: can AI constructively augment human theologians?

AI provides a different interpretive lens on theological concerns and might contribute significantly regardless of its own intrinsic autonomy and self-direction. As AI becomes more pervasive within society, and affects our human condition in small and large ways, AI itself may become an object of theological study. In addition as AI increasingly makes decisions that, if made by a human, would have a moral dimension, then AI systems may themselves need theologians to help translate human needs and strivings into language AI can utilize.

For academic theology, AI challenges theological understanding of human nature and uniqueness and may augment theological methods. Two questions structure a theological response. First, can AI learn theology? Second, if it can, should AI learn theology? Although AI can make some contribution now to theological scholarship, the capabilities of future AI are not known.

For clarity, the present investigation considers the two questions by focusing on AI that could perform at the level of a first-year theology student with the capacity to contribute to a community of scholars. After addressing objections based upon underestimating computers or overestimating human mental processing, the ability of AI to analyze and generate theological text (read and write) is examined. Although improvements are desired, it appears a basic facility to contribute to theological discourse is plausible and thus worthy of consideration. If AI can learn theology, should it? Four scenarios are considered depending upon current and likely near-term AI capacities and current and inferred near-terms social contexts.

Challenges

Theologians face at least two significant challenges from AI in the twenty-first century. First, development of greater AI capabilities

---

2. World Economic Forum, 'The Future of Jobs Report 2018' (Geneva, Switzerland, 2018).

combined with advances in neuroscience undermine assumptions of uniqueness and privilege for human reason. AI technologies have progressively exceeded human capacities for calculation, data processing, control, perception, and other intellectual tasks that require minimal historical, linguistic, and cultural context. Scientific advances have repeatedly shrunk humanity's location with respect to cosmos and increased awareness of the cosmological and evolutionary contingencies leading to human's precarious existence. Neuroscience continues to explain the dependence of mental processing on a material body and simplifies steps needed for an AI system to exceed human-level intellectual capacities. Theologians will need to reinterpret human nature in light of science and artifacts that share many of those presumably human characteristics.

Second, AI development not only affects the human *locus* within theological study, i.e., theological anthropology, AI development can also affect theological methods for intellectual inquiry and understanding of faith. New opportunities for theological scholarship arise as AI extends its abilities to process historical texts, compare social scientific data across cultures and time periods, and synthesize the growing availability of electronic theological sources that contemporary theologians increasingly use.[3]

Computational tools influence and augment ongoing theological scholarship and have already made sufficient contribution to other academic fields in the humanities to suggest the tools will expand the questions theologians can ask.[4] Current AI techniques may suffice to make novel contributions to theology when applied to theological texts and even modest scaling across a range of theological sources could synthesize findings that exceed the breadth of all but the most seasoned theological scholar. Future developments may make these tools more accessible to scholars and initiate a new method for theological scholarship.[5] Continued development may even radically augment the types of theological questions one may ask.

---

3. Jana Marguerite Bennett, *Aquinas on the Web?: Doing Theology in an Internet Age* (London: T&T Clark, 2012).
4. John W Mohr and Petko Bogdanov, 'Introduction-Topic Models: What They Are and Why They Matter', in *Poetics,* 41 (2013): 545–69, https://doi.org/10.1016/j.poetic.2013.10.001.
5. Mark Graves, 'Modeling Moral Values and Spiritual Commitments', in *Spiritualities of Human Enhancement and Artificial Intelligence: Setting the*

In a certain sense, some kind of future dependence on what is now considered AI technology is likely inevitable. Theology will most likely continue as an intellectual endeavor, as it has for centuries, and future generations of theologians will come of age in cultures permeated with AI technologies that far exceed the likely immediate advances in smart phones, autonomous vehicles, and robotics. However, the future of technology-assisted theological investigation could vary widely depending upon the level of integration occurring when AI developers begin to wrestle with deep questions of morality and spirituality.

If theologians fail to contribute the cumulative wisdom of centuries of scholarship to developers building next generation technology, then that technology will have an impoverished and idiosyncratic ability to engage human theological investigation. If theologians do distill the wisdom of theological traditions into forms that can contribute to ongoing AI development, then future AI systems could incorporate that knowledge into their continuing development.

This raises two questions:

- Can AI learn theology?
- Should AI learn theology?

These two questions are considered in turn.

Can AI learn theology?

Considering the ancient definition of theology as 'faith seeking understanding', then the faith-seeking aspect of theology appears well beyond current technologies. However, recent advances in AI warrant investigating theology's 'understanding' dimension. As a philosophical term, 'understanding' has numerous complex and deep meanings; and in a theological context, may even have metaphysical implications. For the purpose of this article, however, the Oxford dictionary definition of understanding suffices as a starting point: 'perceive the intended meaning of (words, a language, or a speaker).'

For humans, understanding one's faith depends on practiced ways of reflecting upon the lived experience of oneself and others, often

---

Stage for Conversations about Human Enhancement, Artificial Intelligence and Spirituality, edited by Christopher Hrynkow (Wilmington, Delaware: Vernon Press, 2019).

within community and in the context of a religious tradition. One's understanding of faith depends upon and is mediated by culture; and as social animals, humans are well attuned to social learning. Thus, we learn well from social engagement and culturally mediated activities. However, computers are not social animals and are currently better suited to perceive the meaning of theological constructs through written texts.

Although AI does not exist that would understand its *own* faith, AI systems can be built to understand human faith as written and culturally communicated through texts of religious, moral, and spiritual significance. Building such systems can help elucidate faith, including the ways faith influences culture, politics, morality, belief systems, values, and spiritual commitments. In addition, building AI systems to interpret human morality not only informs human self-understanding but also may seed the development of moral behavior and judgment by future AI systems.

For academic theologians using scholarly methods to understand the faith of themselves and others, those methods often involve reading and understanding texts of religious, moral, and spiritual significance, including texts written by other theologians. To the extent those shared interpretive activities form a cohesive social endeavor committed to understand what it means to live a Christian life, they form what the philosopher Josiah Royce would call a community of interpretation.[6] One may ask: Can AI systems participate in a shared endeavor to interpret the Christian faith?[7]

There is a wide range by which AI might participate in theological investigations. On the low end of the spectrum, anyone who has used a web search to find a scholarly book or article or even used spell check in a word processor has used what not long ago would have been considered AI techniques to do theology. A more engaged task would be to use Google Translate on a theological text or digital

---

6. Josiah Royce, *The Problem of Christianity. Lectures Delivered at the Lowell Institute in Boston, and at Manchester College, Oxford* (New York: Macmillan, 1913).
7. Mark Graves, 'Shared Moral and Spiritual Development Among Human Persons and Artificially Intelligent Agents', in *Theology and Science* 15, no 3 (July 2017): 333–51, https://doi.org/10.1080/14746700.2017.1335066. This present article focuses exclusively on Christianity, but similar arguments would likely hold for other religions. See for example, Masahiro Mori, *The Buddha in the Robot* (Tokyo: Kosei Publishing Co, 1981).

humanities tools for text analysis.[8] At the higher end of the spectrum might be a Turing test that not only deceives the interviewer into believing the machine is human but also deceives the interviewee that the machine has faith and is seeking understanding.[9] The present article explores a moderate level of participation where the AI system 'reads' theology much as a first-year human theology student might. This focus yields a reasonably specific and arguably attainable goal as well as suggests a possible progression from that point to deeper investigation analogous to how human theology students advance.

Objections to AI Learning Theology

Initial objections to AI operating at that level typically fall into two camps: those that underestimate what computers can do and those that overestimate human mental function (or both). In part because logical positivism was a prevalent philosophical theory during the early-mid twentieth century when the field of computer science formed, computers are frequently characterized as symbol processing systems.[10] The interdisciplinary field of cognitive science developed in mid-late twentieth century and incorporated computer science, and AI in particular, into the study of human cognition, which contributed to the analogy of 'human mind as a computer' becoming a predominate root metaphor of the cognitivist paradigm (or research program) in interdisciplinary studies of human cognition.[11] By 1980s, that approach to AI was scaled into industrial and military systems, including chess playing programs that could beat human masters, but the overpromised aspirations of researchers and the fragility and lack of generalisability of those systems lead to an AI Winter with numerous funding cuts and corporate failures.[12]

---

8. Susan Schreibman, Raymond George Siemens, and John Unsworth, *A New Companion to Digital Humanities* (Oxford: Wiley-Blackwell, 2016).
9. Mark Halpern, 'The Trouble with the Turing Test', in *The New Atlantis* Winter (2006): 42–63.
10. Allen Newell and Herbert A Simon, 'GPS, a Program That Simulates Human Thought', in *Lernende Automaten* (Munchen: Oldenbourg, 1961).
11. Sameuel J Keyser, George A Miller, and Edward Walker, 'Cognitive Science in 1978' (New York: Sloan Foundation, 1978); Howard Gardner, *The Mind's New Science : A History of the Cognitive Revolution* (New York: Basic Books, 1985).
12. Stuart J Russell and Peter Norvig, *Artificial Intelligence : A Modern Approach* (Upper Saddle River, NJ: Prentice Hall, 2010), chapter 1.

Perhaps because most popularly used computer hardware still has similar architecture to what was used in 1980s, when personal computers became available, a typical non-technical sense of what computers can do appears to correspond to faster versions of circa 1990 computer architectures. However, computers can do more than rapidly make calculations and manipulate a stream of symbols.

In the 1990s, AI as a field became more fragmented as the underlying principle of AI as a symbol processing system was challenged by some researchers and avoided by others who desired funding to do something similar to AI, but not the problematically labeled 'AI'.[13] Significant critiques included recognizing the importance of embodiment for human cognition and arguments from Continental philosophy against the logical positivist assumptions.[14] Other fields emerged drawing upon AI subfields but more integrated with mathematical and statistical approaches (such as machine learning) or more focused on applications (such as informatics).

When criticising possible possibilities of AI systems, most non-experts do not consider the capabilities enabled by methods such as Bayesian statistics, neural networks, or massively distributed computing.[15] In parallel, the emergence of the web, massive digitalization of text and other data, and incremental, but exponential, increases in computing power enabled significant advances in computational results, even for approaches previously conceived only theoretically. The current interest in AI owes much to such progress in deep learning.[16] Although somewhat straightforward to conceive what can be done by one algorithm on one theologically significant text, it is much more challenging to imagine what a suite of dozens

---

13. Luc Steels, 'Fifty Years of AI: From Symbols to Embodiment-and Back', edited by M Lungarella, *50 Years of Artificial Intelligence* (Berlin: Springer, 2007); Tim Menzies, '21st-Century AI: Proud, Not Smug', in *IEEE INTELLIGENT SYSTEMS* 18, no 3 (2003): 18–24.
14. Francisco J Varela, Evan Thompson, and Eleanor Rosch, *The Embodied Mind : Cognitive Science and Human Experience* (Cambridge, Mass.: MIT Press, 1991); Hubert L Dreyfus, *What Computers Still Can't Do: A Critique of Artificial Reason*, 3rd ed. (Cambridge, Mass.: MIT Press, 1992); Rodney A Brooks and C, 'Alternate Essences of Intelligence', in *AAAI-98*, 1998.
15. Russell and Norvig, *Artificial Intelligence : A Modern Approach*.
16. Adnan Darwiche, 'Human-Level Intelligence or Animal-like Abilities?', *Communications of the ACM* 61, no. 10 (September 26, 2018): 56–67, https://doi.org/10.1145/3271625.

or hundreds of algorithms might do with digital versions of every major theological work from first through twentieth centuries. The current computational capability to process millions of texts, which can represent a significant fraction of human written texts, at speeds millions of times faster than humans enables new discoveries, which humans could not attempt alone.

Human Capacities

Other objections to AI gaining human-like capacities presume an aspect of human uniqueness that animals would typically lack and arguable AI systems cannot acquire. Possible distinguishing characteristics include consciousness, emotion, free will, language with meaning (semantics), and intentionality. Although likely difficult for AI systems to acquire, findings from neuroscience, psychology, and other human sciences suggest the bar may not be as high as sometimes presumed. Although human neurological function is certainly complex, with much still to discover, neuroscientists have developed initial theories and models for most human cognitive processes. Those processes typically depend on complex combinations of fairly simple structures, and significant progress has been made modeling those structures and interactions. There does not appear to be any fundamental limitation to building AI systems with the intelligence of a very smart animal or young child.

Advances in neuroscience have identified some aspect of human nature not easily correlated with neural structures. Humans appear to have a phenomenological consciousness of properties in the world, i.e. qualia, such as the experience of an apple being red that goes beyond simply identifying the color and object.[17] The neuroscientist Antonio Damasio makes a similar distinction between the bodily processes of emotion and subjective feelings, and that subjectivity appears related to one's sense of self.[18] These investigations quickly raise deep philosophical issues and novel opportunities to

---

17. Ned Block, 'Two Neural Correlates of Consciousness', in *Trends in Cognitive Sciences* 9, no 2 (2005): 46–52.
18. Antonio R Damasio, *The Feeling of What Happens: Body and Emotion in the Making of Consciousness* (New York: Harcourt Brace, 1999); Antonio Damasio, *Self Comes to Mind: Constructing the Conscious Brain*, unabridged (Random House LLC, 2010).

incorporate empirical results into ancient philosophical inquiries, including differences between one's experience of free will and the apparent functioning of correlated neural processes.[19] These scientific and philosophical investigations can contribute to theological investigation of human nature, including *imago Dei*, soul, nature and grace, and theological reason. Although human uniqueness might include some metaphysical aspect not implementable by humans in AI, most apparent dimensions of unique human cognitive abilities appear to depend upon humanity's embodiment as social animals and capacity to create complex cultural phenomena within history using language.[20] The attempt to build AI systems may even help identify unique aspects of human nature and subjectivity, but those uniquely human characteristics may not eliminate a need to interact with AI systems as contributors to society, moral agents, or theoretically possible recipients of the gift of grace.

Beyond embodiment as a fairly intelligent social animal, humans appear to have an extended ability to think about what others think and feel and to communicate and structure one's thoughts using language.[21] If one were to assume thought corresponds to universals, pure social convention, or particular objects in the real world, then the meaning of human language might be challenging for AI to acquire. However, philosophers and linguists since Wittgenstein have argued the meaning of words appears to depend upon how those words are used, in which case AI systems might learn to communicate with humans simply from analyzing human language and participating in human linguistic endeavors.

Philosophical investigations into meaning suggest there are associationist and distributional aspects of semantics. Wittgenstein argues that the meaning of a word lies in its use in language, rather

---

19. Nancey C Murphy and Warren S Brown, *Did My Neurons Make Me Do It?: Philosophical and Neurobiological Perspectives on Moral Responsibility* (Oxford: Oxford University, 2007).
20. Varela, Thompson, and Rosch, *The Embodied Mind: Cognitive Science and Human Experience*; Terrence W Deacon, *The Symbolic Species: The Co-Evolution of Language and the Brain* (New York: WW Norton, 1997); Robert Neelly Bellah, *Religion in Human Evolution : From the Paleolithic to the Axial Age* (Cambridge, Mass: Belknap Press of Harvard University Press, 2011).
21. Shaun Nichols and Stephen P Stich, *Mindreading: An Integrated Account of Pretence, Self-Awareness, and Understanding Other Minds* (Oxford University Press, 2003).

than the ancient understanding of meaning referring to a universal essence or the more modern correspondence with a collection of objects in the world.[22] The linguist John Firth further clarifies that the meaning of a word depends upon the words with which it is in frequent and habitual company.[23]

More precisely, a word's meaning depends upon the words with which it frequently collocates and how it relates to those frequently collocated words. Thus, the associations between words define meaning. To model those associations, the mathematical linguist Zellig Harris identified and developed the distributional hypothesis: He noticed that words with similar meaning have similar contexts and suggested that words with similar patterns of association in a sufficiently large sample of language would have similar meaning.[24]

Thus one can model meaning in a language as a distribution of associated contexts. Some aspects of human mental processing may be challenging to implement in AI, but the most significant impediment appears to depend upon human's social capacity for language and meaning-making, and significant progress in that area has already occurred.

Analysis and Generation

Computational language processing occurs analogously to human reading and writing (or hearing and speaking). Reading involves analyzing language for its syntax (grammar), semantics (meaning), and pragmatics (use in context), and writing involves generating words, sentences, and larger structures, possibly incorporating affective aspects.[25] Numerous software packages exist for analyzing syntax at a

---

22. Ludwig Wittgenstein and GEM Anscombe, translators, *Philosophical Investigations I* (Oxford: Blackwell, 1958), secs. 80, 109.
23. John Firth, 'A Synopsis of Linguistic Theory 1930–1955', in *Special Volume of the Philological Society* (Oxford: Oxford University Press, 1957).
24. Zellig Harris, *Mathematical Structures of Language* (New York: Interscience, 1968).
25. Dan Jurafsky and James H Martin, *Speech and Language Processing: An Introduction to Natural Language Processing, Computational Linguistics, and Speech Recognition* (Pearson Prentice Hall, 2008).merging of distinct fields, availability of phone-based dialogue systems, and much more make this an exciting time in speech and language processing. The first of its kind to thoroughly cover language technology—at all levels and with all modern

moderately sophisticated level.[26] Analyzing language semantics is an ongoing research area with several significant approaches discovered, including latent semantic analysis (LSA), which implements the associative semantic theory within the distributional hypothesis, and topic modeling, which categorizes text into a collection of thematic topics.[27] Because pragmatics depends upon social convention and AI systems are not embodied social animals, progress in that area has progressed slowly.

---

technologies—this book takes an empirical approach to the subject, based on applying statistical and other machine-learning algorithms to large corporations. Builds each chapter around one or more worked examples demonstrating the main idea of the chapter, using the examples to illustrate the relative strengths and weaknesses of various approaches. Adds coverage of statistical sequence labeling, information extraction, question answering and summarization, advanced topics in speech recognition, speech synthesis. Revises coverage of language modeling, formal grammars, statistical parsing, machine translation, and dialog processing. A useful reference for professionals in any of the areas of speech and language processing.—Book Description from Website. Introduction—Regular Expressions and Automata—Words & Transducers—N-grams—Part-of-Speech Tagging—Hidden Markov and Maximum Entropy Models—Phonetics—Speech Synthesis—Automatic Speech Recognition—Speech Recognition: Advanced Topics—Computational Phonology—Formal Grammars of English—Syntactic Parsing—Statistical Parsing—Features and Unification—Language and Complexity—The Representation of Meaning—Computational Semantics—Lexical Semantics—Computational Lexical Semantics—Computational Discourse—Information Extraction—Question Answering and Summarization—Dialogue and Conversational Agents—Machine Translation.","author":[{"dropping-particle":"","family":"Jurafsky","given":"Dan","non-dropping-particle":"","parse-names":false,"suffix":""},{"dropping-particle":"","family":"Martin","given":"James H.","non-dropping-particle":"","parse-names":false,"suffix":""}],"id":"ITEM-1","issued":{"date-parts":[["2008"]]},"publisher":"Pearson Prentice Hall","title":"Speech and language processing: an introduction to natural language processing, computational linguistics, and speech recognition","type":"book"},"uris":["http://www.mendeley.com/documents/?uuid=bc56bea5-13fb-3ac2-a4f3-b74f46eb4b2a"]}],"mendeley":{"formattedCitation":"Dan Jurafsky and James H. Martin, <i>Speech and Language Processing : An Introduction to Natural Language Processing, Computational Linguistics, and Speech Recognition</i> (Pearson Prentice Hall, 2008

26. Steven. Bird, Ewan. Klein, and Edward. Loper, *Natural Language Processing with Python* (Sebastopol, CA: O'Reilly, 2009).
27. Thomas K Landauer et al., *Handbook of Latent Semantic Analysis* (Mahwah, NJ: Lawrence Erlbaum Associates, 2007); David M Blei, 'Topic Modeling and Digital Humanities', in *Journal of Digital Humanities* 2, no 1 Winter (2012).

Generation is both easier and more difficult than analysis. Even fairly simple programs can generate syntactically valid sentences, but semantic generation presumes the speaker has something to say. Computational approaches can generate reasonable text for structured data, such as news articles for financial earning statements or local sports scores; and text summarization tools can summarize multiple (or long) texts, such as aggregating movie reviews or generating newspaper headlines.[28] Current systems can draft scientific articles from analysing a researcher's laboratory notebook, though additional improvement is warranted.[29]

Other disciplines in the humanities have begun incorporating computational tools for text analysis, especially in English literature and history.[30] Moral psychologists have examined religious constructs using semantic analysis, such as monotheism.[31] Within a theological context, Augustine's *Confessions* has been analyzed computationally for several moral and spiritual constructs, and topic modeling techniques have identified themes in Thomas Aquinas's moral theology, which are further used to analyze papal encyclicals.[32]

Generation of theological texts is possible with current technology but requires additional work for the text to become coherent and meaningful enough to contribute to theological discourse. As preliminary work, a chatbot was created based upon Thomas Aquinas's *Summa Theologica*, called ThomasBot, which learns to write sentences based upon Thomistic texts. Currently, the version of ThomasBot based upon only the English translation of *Summa Theologica* begins with only knowing the letters of the alphabet and generates somewhat coherent, though not necessarily accurate, sentences, such as:

---

28. Klint Finley, 'This News-Writing Bot Is Now Free For Everyone', in *Wired*, 2015; Joe Keohane, 'What News-Writing Bots Mean for the Future of Journalism', in *Wired*, 2017.
29. Daniel Engber, 'Humans Run Experiments, a Robot Writes the Paper', in *Slate*, 2017.
30. 'Digital Humanities Awards', accessed November 9, 2018, http://dhawards.org/.
31. Kevin S Reimer *et al*, 'Varieties of Religious Cognition: A Computational Approach to Self-Understanding in Three Monotheist ContextsS', in *Zygon*® 45, no 1 (2010): 75–90.
32. Graves, Mark. 'Topic Modeling of Thomistic Moral Theology', unpublished.

a. I answer that, all men have been held with a certain share of happiness: of whom have no business to decide matters of faith to be the very act elicited by the gift of charity.
b. Objection: Further, as a best obstacle to the strong remedy to the latter's works, as Augustine says (*De Civ Dei* viii): and this is the object of the act of reason, i.e. not to involve the existence of God
c. The act of the will is not the cause of the act of the will.
d. The movement of the will is not a special virtue.
e. The intellectual soul is not the same as the intellect.
f. Objection Further, the Philosopher says De Anima iii, that the soul is the form of the body, and then the soul is the cause of the sensitive apprehension[33]

Although such a system requires a deeper understanding of theology to contribute meaningful interpretations of texts, existing analysis tools and larger quantities of text would suffice for substantial improvement. As AI tools continue to improve, incorporating the ability to understand the semantics of theological language would enable AI systems to learn to 'read' theology at the level of a first-year student and generate novel interpretations. This leads to the next question.

Should AI learn theology?

Whether AI should learn theology depends in part upon the capacities of the AI system and the social and historical context in which it functions. The present article will consider AI capacities as they currently exist and with reasonably foreseeable abilities in five

---

33. Technical details of configuration used to generate text: (a) Markov character model; (b) LSTM neural net, Character Model, 256 nodes, 2 layers; (c-f) LSTM, BPE/SentencePiece Model (vocab 512), 256 nodes, 2 layers. BPE/SentencePiece implements Rico Sennrich, Barry Haddow, and Alexandra Birch, 'Neural Machine Translation of Rare Words with Subword Units', in *Proceedings of the 54th Annual Meeting of the Association for Computational Linguistics*, 2016, https://doi.org/10.18653/v1/P16-1162.so the translation of rare and unknown words is an open problem. Previous work addresses this problem through back-off dictionaries. In this paper, we introduce a simpler and more effective approach, enabling the translation of rare and unknown words by encoding them as sequences of subword units, based on the intuition that various word classes are translatable via smaller units than words, for instance names (via character copying or transliteration

to ten years given the pace of progress in AI and similar technology-driven fields. Slightly more challenging is anticipating the speed at which current state of the art AI will permeate current cultures, and how those disruptions, such as in autonomous vehicles and robotics, will affect society. It would be within that disrupted society that foreseeable future AI would be introduced.

The examination of current and near-term capacities and social contexts lead to four scenarios for consideration: (i) current technology in current social contexts; (ii) current technology as it affects future social contexts; (iii) future technology in a social context similar to the current one (which in this case would also correspond to some pessimistic perspectives on AI disruptions); and (iv) future technology in a social context where AI technologies already play a significant role. These four scenarios lead to four, differing, answers to the question of whether AI should learn theology, which are considered in turn:

1. Yes, because AI needs to make moral decisions.
2. No, because AI and humans have different embodiment.
3. No, because that will give AI too much power over human frailties.
4. Yes, because we need AI to understand us.

Data Ethics and Moral Decisions

AI already affects several aspects of social and ethical concern. Machine learning algorithms make financial, employment, medical, and legal decisions which affect human well-being, often with relatively little human oversight. As algorithms become more complex, even the developers can have difficulty fully comprehending how decisions are made, much less the general public.[34] The European Union has taken steps to require some explainability for algorithmic decisions, but some algorithms are particularly opaque, which may require additional methods to provide explainability when transparency is difficult at best.[35] Data ethicists have identified fairness as significant

---

34. Cathy O'Neil, *Weapons of Math Destruction*, Crown Books (New York, 2016), https://doi.org/10.1057/s11369-017-0027-3.
35. European Parliament, 'EU General Data Protection Regulation (GDPR)', Pub. L. No. 2016/679 (2016). Article 22. Rumman Chowdhury, 'Is Explainability Enough? Why We Need Understandable AI', in *Forbes*, June 2018.

variable, though that can be a challenging goal to satisfy when the data available for machine learning originates with human decisions that incorporate biases and prejudices affecting those 'gold-standard' decisions.[36]

From a moral perspective, algorithms have an independent and autonomous effect on human flourishing. Although simple algorithms are similar to other tools used by people, some algorithms make decisions, which if made by humans, would demand a high level of legal, ethical, and moral reasoning. Algorithms perform document discovery for legal cases previously performed by law student interns.[37] Other algorithms make recommendations for incarceration length and paroles, which in part due to their opacity, are not typically questioned.[38] Some may argue that such algorithms, even when flawed, can operate with less bias than unaided humans; but without significant transparency, those claims cannot be evaluated.

AI systems may fairly soon gain legal rights in the US, either directly or via 'corporations as persons', a construct deeply embedded into the US legal system.[39] Even as a corporation, AI systems would have legal rights and responsibilities, and one could argue must

---

36. Noam Ben-Asher *et al*, 'Balancing Fairness and Efficiency in Repeated Societal Interaction', in *35th Annual Meeting of the Cognitive Science Society (CogSci 2013)*, 2013, 175–80. Tal Zarsky, 'The Trouble with Algorithmic Decisions', *Science, Technology, & Human Values* 41, no 1 (January 14, 2016): 118–32, https://doi.org/10.1177/0162243915605575.
37. Erin Winick, 'Lawyer-Bots Are Shaking Up Jobs', MIT Technology Review, 2017, https://www.technologyreview.com/s/609556/lawyer-bots-are-shaking-up-jobs/; Edgar Alan Rayo, 'AI in Law and Legal Practice—A Comprehensive View of 35 Current Applications', techemergence, 2018, https://www.techemergence.com/ai-in-law-legal-practice-current-applications/; Rhys Dipshan, 'Looking Beyond Document Review, Legal Is Branching Out With Artificial Intelligence', in *Legaltech News*, 2018, https://www.law.com/legaltechnews/2018/07/23/looking-beyond-document-review-legal-is-branching-out-with-artificial-intelligence/.
38. Sonja Starr, 'The Odds of Justice: Actuarial Risk Prediction and the Criminal Justice System', i *CHANCE* 29, no 1 (January 2, 2016): 49–51, https://doi.org/10.1080/09332480.2016.1156368.
39. Zara Stone, 'Everything You Need To Know About Sophia, The World's First Robot Citizen', in Forbes, 2017, https://www.forbes.com/sites/zarastone/2017/11/07/everything-you-need-to-know-about-sophia-the-worlds-first-robot-citizen/. Marshall S Willick, 'Artificial Intelligence: Some Legal Approaches and Implications', in *AI Magazine* 4, no 2 (June 15, 1983): 5–16, https://doi.org/10.1609/AIMAG.V4I2.392.

have access to the human ethical principles underlying such legal responsibilities. Because human values are historically intertwined with religious traditions, AI systems may benefit from a basic understanding of moral theology in order to interpret well the ethical principles to which it would be expected to follow, even if not yet codified into legal regulations.

Anthropocentric Morality

Although AI systems may make decisions that would be moral if humans made those decisions, it does not necessarily follow that those decisions are in fact moral for the AI system. If children and neurologically or psychologically damaged humans lack moral culpability for decisions for which a healthy and sane adult would be held responsible, then even more so for AI systems with radically different 'mental' processing and embodiment. *Current AI systems lack the intentionality and reflective capabilities that would make them morally responsible or culpable.*

In part because people develop AI systems, the goal for any particular AI development project typically has analogue to an aspect of human perception, cognition, or behavior. However, robot vision sees the world significantly different than humans; parallel distributed problem-solving functions differently than human cognition, and distributed embodiment leads to different behaviors than human ones.[40] Human moral development depends upon how

---

40. Anish Athalye *et al*, 'Synthesizing Robust Adversarial Examples', in *Proceedings of the 35th International Conference on Machine Learning*, ed. Jennifer Dy and Andreas Krause, volume 80, Proceedings of Machine Learning Research (Stockholmsmässan, Stockholm Sweden: PMLR, 2018), 284–93; Anish Athalye *et al*, 'Fooling Neural Networks in the Physical World with 3D Adversarial Objects' in Labsix, 2017, https://www.labsix.org/physical-objects-that-fool-neural-nets/; David Silver *et al*, 'Mastering the Game of Go without Human Knowledge', in *Nature* 550, no 7676 (October 18, 2017): 354–59, https://doi.org/10.1038/nature24270; Javier Alonso-Mora *et al*, 'Distributed Multi-Robot Formation Control among Obstacles: A Geometric and Optimization Approach with Consensus', in *Proceedings—IEEE International Conference on Robotics and Automation*, 2016, https://doi.org/10.1109/ICRA.2016.7487747.camera noise, and other natural transformations, limiting their relevance to real-world systems. We demonstrate the existence of robust 3D adversarial objects, and we present the first algorithm for synthesizing examples that are adversarial over a chosen distribution of transformations. We synthesize two-dimensional adversarial images that are

humans feel pain and need social relationships, including nurturing as infants.[41]

AI systems may require something like morality, but it would necessarily be different than human morality, and thus learning human morality would be irrelevant for an AI system. Because AI has different embodiment and is not a social animal, even future AI will not develop or directly need human morality.

Anthropomorphizing AI

In addition to AI's different embodiment and lack of social drives, because humans are social animals, we will project some human-like characteristics to AI, as we do with pets, machines, and forces of nature, and this can become problematic with AI that approaches human-like responses. Simulation theory in psychology suggests humans imagine mental processing of others based upon one's own mental processing.[42] In pretending to be the other person and assuming the other person's mental processing works the same way as our own, one can extract mental states and project those onto the

---

robust to noise, distortion, and affine transformation. We apply our algorithm to complex three-dimensional objects, using 3D-printing to manufacture the first physical adversarial objects. Our results demonstrate the existence of 3D adversarial objects in the physical world.","author":[{"dropping-particle":"","family":"Athalye","given":"Anish","non-dropping-particle":"","parse-names":false,"suffix":""},{"dropping-particle":"","family":"Engstrom","given":"Logan","non-dropping-particle":"","parse-names":false,"suffix":""},{"dropping-particle":"","family":"Ilyas","given":"Andrew","non-dropping-particle":"","parse-names":false,"suffix":""},{"dropping-particle":"","family":"Kwok","given":"Kevin","non-dropping-particle":"","parse-names":false,"suffix":""}],"collection-title":"Proceedings of Machine Learning Research","container-title":"Proceedings of the 35th International Conference on Machine Learning","editor":[{"dropping-particle":"","family":"Dy","given":"Jennifer","non-dropping-particle":"","parse-names":false,"suffix":""},{"dropping-particle":"","family":"Krause","given":"Andreas","non-dropping-particle":"","parse-names":false,"suffix":""}],"id":"ITEM-1","issued":{"date-parts":[["2018"]]},"note":"guacamole cat reference (though not image

41. Darcia Narvaez, *Neurobiology and the Development of Human Morality: Evolution, Culture, and Wisdom* (New York: Norton, 2014), https://doi.org/10.1080/03057240.2015.1069479.
42. Claudia Bazinger and Anton Kühberger, 'Is Social Projection Based on Simulation or Theory? Why New Methods Are Needed for Differentiating', in *New Ideas in Psychology* 30, no 3 (December 2012): 328–35, https://doi.org/10.1016/j.newideapsych.2012.01.002.

other person. Additional information may be added before or after the simulation.[43]

Simulating how others might act likely helped human societies form and cohere, and Barrett argues there are more advantages and less cost to over ascribe characteristics of human agency to non-human agents than to under ascribe them.[44] However our tendency to project characteristics onto others can be manipulated by therapists, con men, or sociopaths to different effects. If AI has the capacity to use moral, religious, or theological language without having the human-related characteristics normally ascribed to humans using that language, the AI system may manipulate human moral or religious beliefs and structures, even inadvertently. An analogous situation occurs in computer animation where humans easily relate to cartoon-like creatures with minimal human visual features, like a head and eyes, and respond well to photo-realistic figures, but are deeply disturbed by the 'uncanny valley' of close, but not quite, human features.[45] Humans may tolerate well naïve or pithy AI-generated moral or religious content, and theologians may use sophisticated and valuable computational tools for insight, but an uncanny valley of coherent but flawed theology could prove dangerous. Thus, we should avoid giving AI systems moral language.

Communal Morality

Although AI systems will have different embodiment and moral needs than humans, in the future at least some advanced AI systems will likely interact with humans. For those systems to interact fairly and effectively with humans, they will need to understand human values and needs. As AI systems become more complex and autonomous, it will become increasingly difficult for human developers of AI systems to anticipate the complex ways the systems may respond to diverse interactions. This point has probably already arrived.

---

43. Nicholas Epley *et al*, 'Perspective Taking as Egocentric Anchoring and Adjustment', in *Journal of Personality and Social Psychology* 87, no 3 (September 2004): 327–39, https://doi.org/10.1037/0022-3514.87.3.327.
44. Justin L Barrett, *Why Would Anyone Believe in God?* (Walnut Creek, CA: AltaMira Press, 2004).
45. Masahiro Mori, Karl F MacDorman, and Norri Kageki, 'The Uncanny Valley', in *IEEE Robotics and Automation Magazine* 19, no 2 (2012): 98–100, https://doi.org/10.1109/MRA.2012.2192811.

In March 23, 2016, Microsoft released a friendly chatbot, called Tay, on Twitter who initially mimicked the language of a nineteen-year-old American girl and learned from interacting with other Twitter users. Within 16 hours, Microsoft removed Tay from Twitter for making racist, abusive, and sexist tweets. Although a similar chatbot had been used in China since 2014, and Microsoft researchers had partially anticipated some divisive topics with canned responses, Tay was unable to maintain civil public discourse for a full day.[46]

For effective moral interactions, at least four types of knowledge will be required: human understanding of human morality; human understanding of AI morality; AI understanding of human morality; and AI understanding of AI morality. In addition to those logically distinct types of knowledge, more complex interactions will require more sophisticated interpretations.

A theological interpretation of the result of a computer scientist's application of a suite of AI tools on a religious text will differ from a computer scientist's interpretation of the result of a theologian's application of an AI tool on a collection of moral texts. Both would augment human self-understanding but would require different interpretative skills, and the theologian's and computer scientist's investigations would differ. The philosopher of science and technology Shannon Vallor identifies what she calls 'technomoral virtues' needed to respond to rapidly developing advanced technology with incompletely understood consequences.[47] She draws upon Aristotelian, Confucian, and Buddhist ethical traditions to characterise shared conceptual resonances, acknowledging the substantial differences between approaches. As humans learn to adapt to emerging technologies, a deeper level of engagement is required when that technology gains the skills humans use for moral and ethical reasoning.

The joint development of human ethics with respect to AI and machine ethics with respect to humans appears a better option than their independent development (or lack of development). For joint

---

46. Peter Bright, 'Tay, the Neo-Nazi Millennial Chatbot, Gets Autopsied', in *Ars Technica*, 2016, https://arstechnica.com/information-technology/2016/03/tay-the-neo-nazi-millennial-chatbot-gets-autopsied/.
47. Shannon Vallor, *Technology and the Virtues: A Philosophical Guide to a Future Worth Wanting* (New York: Oxford University Press, 2016), https://doi.org/10.1093/acprof:oso/9780190498511.003.0001.

development to occur, then AI systems will need to understand human moral and ethical frameworks and the belief systems which structure them. Although possible to learn ethics in a secular context, developing new kinds of ethical principles for a possibly new kind of 'person' would benefit from the background in human religious traditions. For the development to be joint, the AI system also needs to understand toward what humans are striving, and that requires an understanding of spirituality.[48] Machine morality might not require Christian theological understanding *per se* but would require a framework equivalent to theology, such as a revised natural theology, in order to ground moral principles in a coherent anthropology, understand the influence of historical religion on human culture, and identify hopeful human striving in a tragic condition.[49]

Conclusion

Given current AI capacity to analyse and generate theological texts and reasonable assumptions on near-term AI development, it appears AI could learn to read theological texts and make contributions to theological discourse. Depending upon how AI engages society and affects culture, it may become important for AI to gain a theological foundation in order to contribute meaningfully to society and behave morally (or consistent with social moral principles, such as justice).

A harmonious society including humans and AI may require AI to understand humans, even though AI may not need human morality itself, due to its different embodiment, and AI having theological language without foreseeable religious conviction poses a risk. AI already makes decisions affecting human lives and flourishing, and engagement by theologians can contribute to the moral use of technology now, technological enhancement of theological scholarship, and a better understanding of what future AI may require.

---

48. Robert A Emmons, *The Psychology of Ultimate Concerns: Motivation and Spirituality in Personality* (New York: Guilford Press, 1999).
49. Arthur Robert Peacocke, *All That Is : A Naturalistic Faith for the Twenty-First Century*, edited by Philip Clayton (Minneapolis: Fortress Press, 2007).

Agathon: A Journal of Ethics and Value in the Modern World, Vol 10/2025

Chapter 18
ChatGPT as Study Buddy

Randall Reed and Claire Kennedy

'Despite fears that machines will displace humans, most experts believe artificial intelligence and human intelligence will work synergistically.'
—Claudia Wallis[1]

Abstract: We examine the impact of AI, specifically ChatGPT, on education. We discussed initial concerns about academic integrity, with students using ChatGPT for assignments and exams, which sparked negative reactions from educators. We then address the challenges of detecting AI-generated content and the unreliability of ChatGPT due to its tendency to 'hallucinate' or fabricate information. We show the key is understanding what a Large Language Model is and show the difference between databases and language models and an example. We then showcase our development of the 'AI Study Buddy', a ChatGPT-based tool enhanced with lecture transcripts to assist in learning, We detail the project, focusing on its effectiveness, challenges, and student feedback. In the end, we are optimistic about AI's potential as an effective tool in education, despite its limitations.

Key Words: Artificial intelligence, Educational Technology, ChatGPT, Large Language Models, Academic Integrity

When ChatGPT was introduced in November of 2022, some of the first people to use it were students and they were very excited, though not for the right reasons. Reports came out that students were using

---

1. Claudia Wallis, 'How Artificial Intelligence Will Change Medicine', in *Scientific American* 322:2 (February 2020): 82.

ChatGPT to cheat on exams and assignments. A Stanford student paper reported a poll that suggested that almost ⅕ of students were using ChatGPT for their final exams or assignments and that five percent of students were submitting what it produced unedited.[2]

The response by academics was decidedly negative. An article in Inside Higher Ed compared ChatGPT to Covid and declared it a 'novel threat to our intelligence'.[3] Others predicted that ChatGPT could lead to a 'lack of critical thinking and independent learning among students'.[4]

The fear that gripped teachers at all levels is that one could no longer be sure one was dealing with student work. In the past, to get someone to write a student's essay for them required either coaxing a smarter colleague into doing it, or by paying an essay writing service to produce it for the student. Both of these were problematic either because of the expense or because of the limited amount of top students who had time or inclination to write essays for friends.

ChatGPT changed all that. One could merely type into the prompt box, 'Write me an essay on Milton' and twenty seconds later a beautiful five-paragraph essay would be displayed. But that was only the start of the problems. Many instructors give short essay questions on exams where the student would write a paragraph answering a question. This was even easier for ChatGPT. In fact, through the judicious use of ChatGPT, a student could finish an exam in less time than actually writing it themselves. A two-hour exam could be finished by ChatGPT in a few minutes.

Needless to say, instructors were increasingly unnerved by this turn of events. A colleague of mine threatened to go 'medieval on the students' and return to oral exams. Others have suggested the return

---

2. Mark Allen Cu, 'Scores of Stanford Students Used ChatGPT on Final Exams', accessed July 23, 2023, https://stanforddaily.com/2023/01/22/scores-of-stanford-students-used-chatgpt-on-final-exams-survey-suggests/.
3. Jeremy Weissman, 'ChatGPT Is a Plague Upon Education', February 8, 2023, https://www.insidehighered.com/views/2023/02/09/chatgpt-plague-upon-education-opinion.
4. 'ChatGPT May Lead To The Downfall Of Education And Critical Thinking', Tech Business News (Technology News Australia, April 2, 2023), https://www.techbusinessnews.com.au/blog/chatgpt-may-lead-to-the-downfall-of-eduction-and-critical-thinking/.

of in-class essays and bluebooks of yore.[5] And yet all these suggestions only have viability in small classes. How many teachers wish to return to the days of struggling through students' handwriting, which has certainly declined with the increased use of keyboards and the elimination of cursive from the common core curriculum in public schools?[6] In a class of as few as twenty, a fifteen-minute oral exam would take five hours to administer. And how many students would do better with their teacher looming over them as they struggled to come up with the right answer on the spot? So while moves backward may appear to hold some promise, with the increasing teaching demands of universities desperate to replace declining state support with students' tuition money, it seems unlikely that these approaches will be viable in classes of 50-500.

If this is not a viable solution, is there a technological solution? One hope has been that Silicon Valley might be able to develop a 'digital watermark', some way of determining for sure that AI has been used in an assignment. Several plagiarism detection systems have created modules to do this. Tech Columnist Kevin Roose, in an opinion piece in the *New York Times*, pleaded with academics to not ban ChatGPT.[7] But more importantly, Roose argued that ChatGPT detectors (which Weissman had compared to the Covid Vaccine) were notoriously unreliable. Even more unreliable using ChatGPT to detect its own work as one professor in Texas did to disastrous results.[8]

But as time went on, the perils of using ChatGPT for writing papers became even clearer. ChatGPT was prone to making up citations which it confidently produced as fact. This phenomenon, known as 'hallucination' in machine learning circles, meant that ChatGPT was

---

5. Jordan Hart and Aaron Mok, 'College Professors Are Going back to Paper Exams and Handwritten Essays to Fight Students Using ChatGPT', in *Business Insider*, August 13, 2023, https://www.businessinsider.com/chatgpt-driving-return-to-paper-exams-written-essays-at-universities-2023-8.
6. 'Has Technology Ruined Handwriting?', CNN, July 26, 2013, https://www.cnn.com/2013/07/26/tech/web/impact-technology-handwriting/index.html.
7. Kevin Roose, 'Don't Ban ChatGPT in Schools. Teach With It', in the *New York Times*, January 12, 2023, https://www.nytimes.com/2023/01/12/technology/chatgpt-schools-teachers.html.
8. 'A Professor Accused His Class of Using ChatGPT, Putting Diplomas in Jeopardy', in the *Washington Post*, May 18, 2023, https://www.washingtonpost.com/technology/2023/05/18/texas-professor-threatened-fail-class-chatgpt-cheating/.

unreliable as an academic writing instrument.⁹ Its references needed to be meticulously checked, and suddenly, the whole endeavor might seem to be more work than just doing it the old-fashioned way.

This tendency towards hallucination of references points to a larger problem in general. GPT models (of which ChatGPT is one example) are prone to hallucinations of all types. They are not completely reliable when it comes to details. This is a problem that tech companies that produce these AIs are aware of and they are working to solve it. However, Yann LeCunn, Chief AI Scientist and VP at Meta has suggested that the nature of "Auto-Regressive" models (like ChatGPT) means that hallucination will always be a problem.¹⁰ In the meantime, most AIs come with a disclaimer indicating that the information produced may be incorrect.

So, for teaching and learning using large language models, it is important to recognize what large language models can and cannot do, and correspondingly what they are and are not. The first distinction to make is between a large language model and a database. A database is a computer file that has a variety of information that is stored in a structured format. That makes it easy to use. For example, when you go to a streaming service and you search for the television show "Friends," it has a database that sorts all the titles by the show name. It may also have show type, actors, directors, etc. So you could search for 'Friends' and it would show up, but you could also search for 'Shows with Jennifer Aniston' and it would also find it, or you could search for 'sit-coms' and it would likewise appear, etc. And if it was not there, it would not show up. Thus a database is pretty direct, it knows what it knows and if it knows it, it will give it to you, otherwise, it will not.

---

9. Ken Masters, 'Medical Teacher's First ChatGPT's Referencing Hallucinations: Lessons for Editors, Reviewers, and Teachers', in Medical Teacher 45, no 7 (July 2023): 673–75.
10. Yann LeCun, 'Hallucinations in LLM Are due to the Auto-Regressive prediction. I Think What I Call 'Objective Driven AI' Will Solve the Problem: Systems That Plan Their Answer by Optimizing a Number of Objective Functions *at Inference Time* https://t.co/JcR5hItwzJ', Twitter, June 9, 2023, https://twitter.com/ylecun/status/1667218790625468416; Gary Lupyan, 'Do Language Models Need Sensory Grounding for Meaning and Understanding?—NYU Center for Mind, Brain, and Consciousness', accessed July 23, 2023, https://wp.nyu.edu/consciousness/do-large-language-models-need-sensory-grounding-for-meaning-and-understanding/.

A Large Language model also has information in it, it probably knows about the TV show 'Friends', but maybe it doesn't know who the actors were in it (this is unlikely but for the sake of example). Maybe that information wasn't in its training data, or maybe it wasn't important enough to keep. So if you ask it for shows that starred Jennifer Aniston and it does not know, what will it do? A database will return nothing (or perhaps an error—'not found'). But a large language model will return something anyway. It might make up a television show or it might tell you that Jennifer Aniston starred in 'Orange is the New Black'. Now why does it do that? It does that because it has a different goal than a database. A database's goal is to return a match to the search term. A large language model's goal is to say something. Not necessarily something true, or right, but something. So if you ask it a question, and it does not know the answer you might think it would say 'I don't know' but generally it does not, it just invents something up.

The reason 'hallucination' is a popular term for this is because it uses an analogy from the real world. A person who is hallucinating does not know that what they are seeing is not real, they think the hallucination is reality. In the same way, the language model thinks whatever it has said is true even if it just made it up. I have had conversations with language models where it told me something I knew to be false, and when I told it it was wrong it argued with me. Now this is not the place to get into a technical explanation of why hallucinations happen, the only thing to note is that they do happen and the model does not know it is hallucinating.

Hallucinations then are the primary reason why AIs cannot be relied on to produce effective student essays. If a professor gives an assignment and requires that there be three outside sources, an LLM will provide those sources but likely those sources will be made up. LLMs cannot be trusted to provide accurate information. Unfortunately, many students do not realize that the sources that LLMs provide may be made up. Occasionally, the LLM will even provide a link to Amazon for the source, adding to the verisimilitude. But if a student clicks on that link they will find it leads nowhere. But this also means that catching this sort of hallucination, if a student blithely uses it, requires extra work on the part of the professor. Is the citation something an AI made up, or is this simply a source that I am unaware of?

All of these concerns have led to the deep concern that many educators have when it comes to AI. Some students who initially were using AIs like ChatGPT with confidence, have become mistrustful, no longer seeing it as an all-knowing answer machine. But for all its flaws, AI seems likely to remain a part of the modern landscape.

So given this, what might a Large Language Model be good for in the area of teaching and learning? Our intuition was that it would be good at talking. In our project, we used ChatGPT to create an AI Study Buddy. The AI Study Buddy was a version of ChatGPT, but it had access to transcripts of the lectures for the course. It walked the students through each part of the lecture, gave them a brief summary, and then asked them a question. When the student responded, It would then continue the conversation.

We had to wrestle with the problem of hallucination. How could we keep the LLM from hallucinating answers? One of the solutions we found was known as retrieval augmented generation (RAG).[11] The basic approach of RAG is that rather than relying on what an LLM knows (or thinks it knows) you give it the information it needs when it is generating its answer. Consider that friend (we all have them) who often speaks authoritatively about something they know nothing about. Imagine, instead of talking off the top of their head, they first did a Google search and read the articles that came up on the topic, and *then* they answered. You'd expect a much different response. That is essentially what RAG does, but instead of using Google (though this is possible) it uses some other database. For the AI Study Buddy, we took transcripts of Dr Reed's lectures and then when a student asked a question or started talking about a topic, the LLM was fed either a section of the transcript or a summary of a part of it that pertained to what the student said. This meant that the LLM was not being used to discover information (something it is not great at) but instead, it was really about taking the information it was given and putting it into a conversational format. This mostly solved the hallucination problem.

The problem we focused on after that was making sure that students felt comfortable with the chatbot. To facilitate this we

---

11. Douwe Kielaresearch Scientist, 'Retrieval Augmented Generation: Streamlining the Creation of Intelligent Natural Language Processing Models', accessed January 25, 2024, https://ai.meta.com/blog/retrieval-augmented-generation-streamlining-the-creation-of-intelligent-natural-language-processing-models/.

prompted the chatbot with the instruction: 'You are a friendly and supportive study buddy . . . You are designed to help students think deeply about the lecture that they have just heard . . . As students respond you should follow up with a specific question that will help them to think more deeply about the topic . . .' Here we instruct the chatbot to be supportive and friendly and clarify its goal (help students think deeply) and then after that we give a portion of the lecture (or a summary of a portion). And the conversation begins.

The cost of the chatbot has two considerations: first, every word that is sent to an external chatbot costs money (usually a fraction of a cent), but with multiple students having multiple conversations this can add up. In our work, with roughly 200 students accessing the bot, the cost ran between ten to twenty dollars a month. Second, there is a limit to the number of words (tokens) that the AI can handle between input and output, which for ChatGPT is roughly 3500 words. So for longer lectures, the entirety of a section would simply not fit. In those cases, we needed to limit the amount of text, and summarising (a task that ChatGPT does fairly well) allowed us to reduce the number of words. We anticipate both these issues cost and word limit to improve and have already since the beginning of the project.

Data from the AI Study Buddy

Each time a student used the AI Study Buddy, they evaluated their experience on a five-point scale and provided whatever feedback they felt comfortable sharing. The results were incredibly positive. Over a four-month period from eighty-one different students, we had just under 500 responses, with the average rating finalized as 4.2 out of fifty-one percent of the responses were 5s while the total amount of 2s and 1s comprised just over six percent of responses. Students seemed to at the very least to appreciate, if not actively enjoy, the use of the Study Buddy as a replacement for the average 250-word response. Before moving forward, I would like to add that the AI Study Buddy relies on student responses. If students put in minimal effort, the AI has a harder time engaging heavily with the students. However, if a student puts in more thoughtful responses, it will interact much more easily.

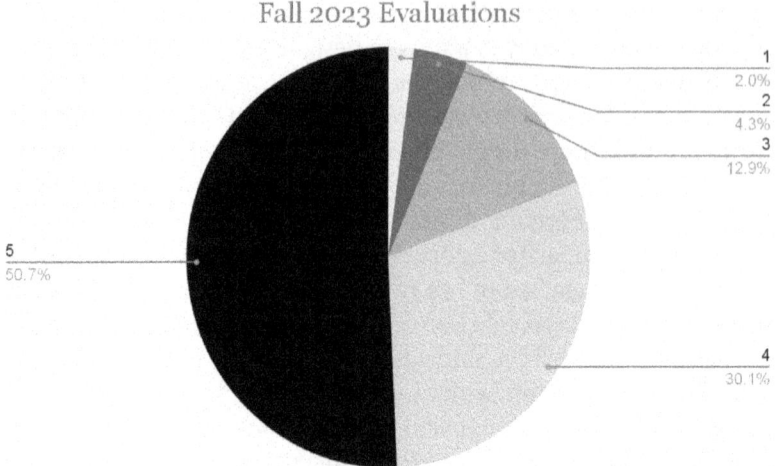

Fall 2023 Evaluations

I'd like to address some of the problems we encountered throughout our work with the Study Buddy. Initially, we had some issues that have since been resolved, such as the Study Buddy being too personal, being confused about lecture content, and being repetitive.

At the very start of the project, we saw the Study Buddy had inquired about their experience with death. Another student was asked about their relationship with their friends and whether or not they'd had intense shared experiences. This may have been the inadvertent result of the chatbot being told to be 'friendly and supportive' which it interpreted in therapeutic terms. To solve this, we went into the Study-Buddy's prompt and added a clarifier that it should not ask personal questions to students, especially personal religious questions. Students should feel free to share as much information as they like; we don't want to completely discourage students from sharing personal anecdotes if they're comfortable with doing so. On the other hand, students should never feel pressured in any way to answer a personal question from the Study Buddy as part of the chat assignments. Fortunately, this modifying the prompt resolved the situation. Still, the interesting thing about this prompt is that it worked. At some level this should be surprising, that one could give instructions in common English, without special words or computer code embedded, and the A.I. will simply understand what is being asked and comply is contrary to the experience of every programmer in the past. This showed the power of what is known as 'prompt engineering', the construction of instructions to the model in plain English that significantly can alter or limit its outcome.

The issue of lecture confusion was a more difficult fix. The Study-Buddy functions by using transcripts of Dr Reed's different lectures as its background context for student interactions. However, students reported experiencing various problems with selecting a lecture to discuss and the bot getting confused about which lecture it was supposed to be referencing, most consistently in the unit that dealt with the Synoptic Problem and different visions of Jesus in each of the gospels. We hypothesized that this confusion was most likely related to the model's original training, perceiving the gospels as somewhat interchangeable, further reinforced by some lecture's inclusion of comparison between gospels. Once again utilizing prompt engineering, we added an addendum stating that 'when talking about one book of the Bible you should stick to that book, and focus on the meaning of the text for its original readers'. This mostly fixed the issue we had no further complaints regarding lecture confusion.

However, a related issue was found regarding specific lecture facets like videos. If a video plays during the lecture, the bot often cannot tell the difference between a video that is an example of a concept (for instance a clip from *The Matrix* or *I Robot*) and videos that have content like documentaries. Here we see an interesting phenomenon where the bot takes everything as information, resulting in strange conversations where the bot would assume science fiction was reality. This points out the way that humans can integrate a variety of different modes of information and distinguish between fiction and non-fiction in a way that still seems foreign to an AI. It may also point to a limitation of language models which, unlike the students, can't see when a video is playing as opposed to the professor lecturing. The AI is dependent on a transcript. We are still experimenting with how to clarify what was part of the lecture in reality versus what part was a video. We've tried marking these, and more often just excluding them, but it remains an open question.

A problem that arose in our most recent dataset was an issue with the website students used to access the Study-Buddy 'crashing' or erroring out:

> 'Crashed on me 3 times as I was finishing the last part of the assignment.'
>
> 'Had to restart a couple of times because an error message kept occurring.'

Most of these complaints were from the first half of the fall semester, and almost half of them were from a single user. I suspect that most of these errors occurred due to outside factors, like poor internet connection or student misunderstanding of how to use the AI. There was no obvious pattern of a specific lecture erroring out or the website being inaccessible for multiple students at a time; all the evaluations mentioning errors were spaced across multiple days. We will continue to test what could be causing these errors and observe potential patterns in evaluations, but if we are correct that this has to do with internet connectivity this is a larger issue regarding the digital divide where we assume all students have access to recent technology and stable internet. In a rural state like ours, particularly for online students, this may not always be the case.

The most persistent issue the Study-Buddy has had is the issue of repetitiveness. Throughout both our summer and fall datasets, students have consistently complained about the repetitive nature of the bot:

> 'AI buddy asked me the same question multiple times but in different formats. It got quite irritating after a while.'
>
> 'Repeated the exact same idea I said but presented it like it was a new idea, and that it was right and I was wrong.'
>
> 'Really lengthy and repetitive.'

We have tried some prompt adjustments, encouraging the bot to 'follow up with a specific question that will help them to think more deeply about the topic' without getting too personal. At the beginning of the project, the Study Buddy was frequently responding to students by just asking for more and more examples, which didn't allow for much of a back-and-forth feel to the conversation. Further prompt refinement helped with the repetitiveness but didn't eliminate it. The problem stems from another reality of chatbots: they intrinsically have no memory. Each conversation, and often each turn in the conversation is a new reality for the chatbot. This lack of memory can be remedied through different uses of storage databases. Still, it is limited by the 'context window', the amount of information that can be fed to the AI. As mentioned before ChatGPT is limited to about 3500 words, much of which is already taken up with lecture material. So for the chatbot to remember what it said before, its previous responses must be fed back in. With a limited context window that is difficult. Fortunately, this is something that AI producers are working on and the window has already been expanded so we hope that we will be able to reduce the bot's penchant for repetition in the future.

A smattering of other miscellaneous complaints led to a few low scores. Though ideally, we would like to have no 1s, I think it's important to recognize that we have had no reported issues of hallucinations in the lecture content.

I have been highlighting our problems as examples of some of the challenges in implementing AI in a classroom setting. However, I do not want to dismiss the positive responses we have received from students. As I stated earlier, the ultimate goal of incorporating the Study-Buddy is for student benefit. In addition to these lower evaluations, we had many responses explaining that students felt much more comfortable having a discussion-type conversation as opposed to a more rote lecture reflection and enjoyed the possibility of having the Study Buddy be incorporated into class in more ways:

> 'This was a unique way of going over the lecture. I enjoyed being able to describe my thoughts and almost instantly get a positive response and a new prompt. It felt more involved than just writing a paper, I feel like I was able to dig deeper.'

> 'The AI seemed to understand my points that would been probably impossible to convey to people I know personally.'

> 'I liked how the bot led the conversation. I don't like taking lead in conversations so I find it much easier to respond.'

> 'LOOK! It noticed my pattern of thinking and called it out.'

The Study Buddy should be a tool that students don't just feel comfortable talking to, they should genuinely feel like they're learning and engaging in stimulating conversation. It seems likely that in the future more and more students will be comfortable using ChatGPT and other AI resources to assist them with their schoolwork. In a focus group conducted with a few student users of the Study Buddy, they thought the use of a similar AI would be really useful in their significantly larger STEM classes, and that they could see the bot being incorporated successfully into their other courses as well. Though they all expressed some kind of frustration with the repetitiveness of the Study Buddy, they appreciated the convenience of always being able to access an entity that was familiar with the course material and could help them without having to bother the professor with 'things he'd already talked about'. Overall, there was a positive attitude towards the AI and an interest in its further involvement in their education experience. If in religious studies we can already begin incorporating those same tools into classes in productive, creative ways, students will view the resource to help facilitate their learning, not do their thinking for them.

The success of the AI Study Buddy is largely due to an understanding of what an LLM is proficient at—talking. It is not an information repository and should not be used as such. Our conviction was that what was meaningful for students at the collegiate level was the ability to talk about things, to try out ideas, and to talk to someone who had heard the same lecture and was enthusiastic about it. We remember having experiences when the after-class chats with classmates about the lecture led us to greater discovery and understanding during our college careers. But with students more isolated than ever, and particularly with online classes, that would seem to be impossible—until now. Now there is an entity that is available at any time and eager to talk about the lecture, hear what the student thinks, ask them questions, and provide answers to confusions—and that is AI.

References

'ChatGPT May Lead To The Downfall Of Education And Critical Thinking'. 2023. *Tech Business News*. Technology News Australia. https://www.techbusinessnews.com.au/blog/chatgpt-may-lead-to-the-downfall-of-eduction-and-critical-thinking/.

CNN. 2013. 'Has Technology Ruined Handwriting?', July 26. https://www.cnn.com/2013/07/26/tech/web/impact-technology-handwriting/index.html

Cu, Mark Allen. 2023. 'Scores of Stanford Students Used ChatGPT on Final Exams', Accessed July 23. https://stanforddaily.com/2023/01/22/scores-of-stanford-students-used-chatgpt-on-final-exams-survey-suggests/.

Hart, Jordan, and Aaron Mok. 2023. 'College Professors Are Going back to Paper Exams and Handwritten Essays to Fight Students Using ChatGPT.' *Business Insider*, August 13. https://www.businessinsider.com/chatgpt-driving-return-to-paper-exams-written-essays-at-universities-2023-8.

LeCun, Yann. 2023. 'Hallucinations in LLM Are due to the Auto-Regressive prediction.I Think What I Call 'Objective Driven AI' Will Solve the Problem: Systems That Plan Their Answer by Optimizing a Number of Objective Functions *at Inference Time* https://t.co/JcR5hItwzJ.' *Twitter*. https://twitter.com/ylecun/status/1667218790625468416.

Lupyan, Gary. 2023. 'Do Language Models Need Sensory Grounding for Meaning and Understanding?—NYU Center for Mind, Brain, and Consciousness.' Accessed July 23. https://wp.nyu.edu/consciousness/do-large-language-models-need-sensory-grounding-for-meaning-and-understanding/.

Masters, Ken. 2023. 'Medical Teacher's First ChatGPT's Referencing Hallucinations: Lessons for Editors, Reviewers, and Teachers.' *Medical Teacher* 45 (7): 673–675.

Roose, Kevin. 2023. 'Don't Ban ChatGPT in Schools. Teach With It.' *The New York Times*, January 12. https://www.nytimes.com/2023/01/12/technology/chatgpt-schools-teachers.html.

Scientist, Douwe Kielaresearch. 2024. 'Retrieval Augmented Generation: Streamlining the Creation of Intelligent Natural Language Processing Models.' Accessed January 25. https://ai.meta.com/blog/retrieval-augmented-generation-streamlining-the-creation-of-intelligent-natural-language-processing-models/.

The Washington Post. 2023. 'A Professor Accused His Class of Using ChatGPT, Putting Diplomas in Jeopardy', May 18. https://www.washingtonpost.com/technology/2023/05/18/texas-professor-threatened-fail-class-chatgpt-cheating/.

Weissman, Jeremy. 2023. 'ChatGPT Is a Plague Upon Education'. https://www.insidehighered.com/views/2023/02/09/chatgpt-plague-upon-education-opinion.

Chapter 19
AI for Pastors

R Daren Erisman

'All actual life is encounter.'
—Martin Buber[1]

Abstract: Integrating generative artificial intelligence (AI), such as ChatGPT, into spiritual practices offers a new paradigm for personalized spirituality, enabling individuals to engage in tailored spiritual experiences co-created with AI. Of course this proposal raises questions about the authenticity of interactions with AI in spiritual contexts and the implications for traditional religious roles. Historically, the accessibility of individualized spiritual content has evolved from itinerant preachers to the internet, with generative AI now offering unprecedented personalization. New ministry tools illustrate generative AI's potential in streamlining administrative tasks while integrating into sermon writing and worship planning. The development of AI for churches is driven by both technological advances and market dynamics, prompting discussions on ethics, community relationships, and the balance between technological innovation and traditional religious experience. As AI becomes more embedded in spiritual practices, it challenges us to reconsider the nature of faith and community in this new age of generative AI.

Key Terms: Generative AI, personalized spirituality, prosperity theology, ministry, pastor

---

1. 'Alles wirkliche Leben ist Begegnung', Martin Buber, *I and Thou*, translated by Ronald Gregor Smith, Second edition, The Scribner Library (New York: Charles Scribner's Sons, 1958), 15.

It might initially seem unintuitive that the inanimate technology of generative artificial intelligence (AI), as exemplified by ChatGPT, could provide a spiritual experience. Yet, given people's strong feelings with just their smartphone, it is not unreasonable that a person could have a spiritual experience facilitated by generative AI interaction—one unusually tailored to the individual because the practitioner and AI are co-creators of the experience. One may rightly argue the spiritual authenticity of such an exchange with an impersonal machine or ask, 'Where is God in this?' These are legitimate concerns, yet there is little doubt that as more people flock to these generative AI systems, sincere questions of faith will be asked and answered, or at least responded to in some form.

The implications of generative AI for spirituality and its impact on community relationships are subjects of ongoing debate.[2] Surveys indicate mixed perceptions among pastors and the public regarding AI's influence on personal relationships. Moreover, as Martin Buber's framing of the I-Thou relationship highlights the deep human longing for meaningful presence, generative AI is reaching the potential of influencing those needs. As this new technology continues to permeate various sectors of society, including our worshipping communities, navigating this emerging landscape with thoughtful consideration is essential, as it has implications for our faith, community, and an increasingly personalised spirituality.

Personalized Spirituality

The individualisation and customisation of spirituality have been a long work in progress. Itinerant preachers could sway individuals in a local community. Pamphlets or books from the printing press could introduce remote ideas to those with access. Yet, the emergence of the Internet and the engaging graphical interface of the World Wide Web enabled the large-scale personalization of spirituality like never before. The Internet allows individuals to selectively choose teachings and practices from religious leaders across the globe. No longer does one have to rely on the abilities of a local minister to make sense of the world when one can access the thoughts and influence of any

---

2. 'Three Takeaways on How Pastors Can Use AI', Barna Group, accessed March 23, 2024, https://www.barna.com/research/pastors-use-ai/.

attractive voice—perhaps a more relatable, inspirational, or 'purer' voice.³

Incorporating the vast free data from internet websites and other digital sources enabled generative AI to gain its repertoire of textual patterns. When combined with a specific software application that utilises a generative AI model, a faith practitioner may feel guided on a spiritual journey rather than just following a probabilistic breadcrumb trail of words. Generative AI models are tuned to answer biblical and pastoral concerns through keywords and gradual learning of what practitioners are interested in as they ask questions about God, faith, and what actions they should pursue as faithful Christians.

BibleChat is an example of such a software interface that allows the user to prompt the generative AI as well as share example trending questions by the BibleChat community, such as:

> How do you forgive the unforgivable? I'm feeling anxious. How can you help me? What did the Dead Sea scrolls say about Jesus? Create a Bible Study based on Sermon on the Mount. How can I get closer to God? How do I discern God's will for my life?⁴

---

3. Leaders of large churches come to mind, such as Joel Osteen of Lakewood Church in Houston, whose messages regularly reach millions through television and the Internet. Interestingly, this desire to seek expertise and inspiration outside local leadership is not exclusive to Christianity. Practitioners from other religions, such as Islam, Buddhism, and Judaism, also seek mentors who may have a large following, a more expansive view of their faith, or a closer physical proximity to the center of their faith tradition. This hunger may be especially true for those who have immigrated to another country or their children who may desire a stronger connection to a 'homeland' than their parents. One study of Muslim immigrants to Canada exemplifies this point. Many of these Muslims found the local leaders unrelatable in the Canadian context, with some distancing themselves from their faith. Others, with the help of the Internet, were seeking what they perceived as a more knowledgeable or authentic expression of Islam from well-known scholars, *sheiks*, many living in majority-Muslim countries. Refer to 'Changing Perceptions of Islamic Authority among Muslims in Canada, the United States and the United Kingdom'. IRPP, accessed March 23, 2024, https://irpp.org/research-studies/changing-perceptions-of-islamic-authority-among-muslims-in-canada-the-united-states-and-the-united-kingdom/.
4. BibleChat iPhone application, accessed March 2, 2024, BookVitals APP SRL.

Given the accessibility and seemingly anonymous[5] nature of generative AI, it is not difficult to imagine that people will feel the freedom to explore their deepest faith questions and concerns—and even ask for forgiveness.

> PROMPT: 'I pray that God will forgive my sins'
>
> AI RESPONSE: My God, in His infinite mercy and grace, forgive your sins and grant you peace. Remember the words of 1 John 1:9, 'If we confess our sins, he is faithful and just and will forgive us our sins and purify us from all unrighteousness.' May you find comfort and strength in seeking God's forgiveness and may His love surround you always. Amen.[6]

Not only is generative AI willing to answer questions with apparent confidence and limitless patience, but it also offers a word of forgiveness. Here, we perceive not just a handy tool to help guide congregants but a type of technological agency easily slipping into the space occupied by pastors, priests, elders, and chaplains. How will this technology change the landscape of ministry?

Ministry and AI

For over three decades, a more limited form of artificial intelligence has been available to search for that needed Bible verse or, with the aid of a digital library, do keyword searches of Greek and Hebrew manuscripts, lexicons, Bible commentaries, and the writings of famous preachers and theologians.[7] With the expansion of the internet and open-source libraries many of these resources are free and easily accessible.

---

5. Data privacy is a significant problem for generative AI models, which require huge amounts of data as a part of their training to recognise and generate new text. A user of generative AI may perceive a sense of anonymity as they type their prompts into a chatbot, but often that data and subsequent responses are saved and incorporated into further training or 'fine-tuning' of the model. This fine-tuning allows the generative AI model to be more responsive but also blurs lines of anonymity.
6. BibleChat, response to 'I pray that God will forgive my sins', March 2, 2024.
7. Two Biblical study software programs that have served pastors for many years and are still active are Logos from Faithlife Corporation and Accordance from OakTree Software, Inc.

Now, generative AI provides new tools for carrying out familiar administrative and ministry tasks and doing things once considered inconceivable. Need newsletter article ideas for June based on the theme of music in the Bible? No problem. Want to create a Bible study comparing the Gospel of Mark and the Book of Job? Done. Based on Sunday's sermon, do you need to send a devotional message to every parishioner instantly? Generative AI is particularly good at summarizing text from a sermon manuscript or even from the audio of a video recording on YouTube. Want a transcription and summary of a recorded Council meeting—and then create a suggested agenda for the next meeting? These are just a few ministry tools that generative AI can provide.

One tool currently popular among ministry leaders using generative AI is Jasper.[8] Leveraging multiple generative AI models, Jasper is essentially a sophisticated copywriter and marketing tool that creates custom content based on user prompts, sermons, and other data. Jasper uses a quickly growing number of customizable templates that significantly ease administrative tasks such as drafting annual reports, grant proposals, and letters to potential donors. It can easily prepare posts for social media and help write newsletter articles, announcements, devotions, lesson plans, and quizzes for Sunday school or confirmation. Jasper can also help plan worship with hymn suggestions or assistance in writing prayers based on a sermon theme or the liturgical season—all guided by the specific denominational and congregational mission statements and written principles—and all for a monthly subscription.

For the applications described above, generative AI is an efficient tool that will continue to improve. Ministry leaders who already use these applications find them not only a means to streamline administrative duties but also as an invaluable assistant, freeing up time for more pastoral responsibilities like visitation. However, the capabilities of generative AI extend beyond merely serving as a productivity tool or an assistant for our hectic schedules. It has the potential to accomplish tasks beyond human capacity or inclination.

Given greater agency, a Chaplain AI could offer timely words of comfort to a soldier in a dangerous environment. A Pastoral Counselor AI could offer words of advice, prayers, and forgiveness anytime and

---

8. Jasper AI, or Jasper, https://www.jasper.ai.

anywhere. In an age short on pastors and priests, a Worship Leader AI could offer words of liturgy and prayer, provide music, and direct human participants in communion and a final blessing—in any language! Like a modern Pentecost, generative AI can interact in multiple languages, providing the immediacy of a primary language and the ability to communicate with multiple people in multiple languages simultaneously. This multi-language ability may be one of the most astonishing uses of generative AI, especially as tailored to regional dialects and specifying the style of speech such as formal, informal, comforting, or even inspiring.

Although some of these possibilities may sound far-fetched and even sacrilegious, various forms of AI-influenced ministry applications are currently being explored and implemented. Part of this receptivity may be due, in part, to the effects of Covid within worship communities. With the prospect of a dangerous unknown virus, many communities suddenly added or extended their use of online streaming of worship services, Bible Studies, meetings, and small groups. This meant that people could participate in a worshipping community who otherwise would not or could not. Many altered their worshipping habits, whether due to being homebound, hospitalized, or hard of hearing, or because of illness, work, or travel (or just prefer the convenience of online worship).

Interestingly, even with the lifting of Covid restrictions, many of these online worshipers continue their habit of dutifully watching services online and participating remotely in the life of their worship community. Some people have taken this accessibility further, regularly participating online with multiple communities. Accordingly, this multivalent style of worship aligns with an increasingly personalized spirituality of picking and choosing a specific preacher, a style of music, or a familiar setting—and this flexibility will likely draw people to the new AI-driven ministry applications as well.

Reflecting upon this emerging technological landscape concerning ministry can be sobering. On the one hand, generative AI has the potential to bring greater administrative efficiency and communication. On the other hand, generative AI can affect relationships positively and negatively within a community.

According to recent surveys by Barna,[9] a small minority (five percen) of tpastors believe that AI will positively affect relationships in general, and a majority (56%) believe this impact will be negative. Conversely, four times as many U.S. adults surveyed (twenty-one percent) believe that AI will positively affect relationships, with a minority (thirty-four percent) believing that the impact will be negative. Tellingly, large percentages of pastors (thirty-eight percent) and US adults (forty-three percent) surveyed are neutral about what impact AI might bring to relationships.

Many people are waiting to see what will unfold about artificial intelligence and its effects on society, the workplace, and worshipping communities. We just don't know. Yet, forces are in play influencing the reception of AI in the ministry landscape.

Prosperity AI

Considering the sudden usage of generative AI, it is unsurprising that this comes from both technological advancement and market forces. OpenAI, the company that developed ChatGPT, was founded as a non-profit organization seeking to further artificial intelligence to 'benefit humanity, unconstrained by a need to generate financial returns.'[10] As development continued, it became apparent that vast funding was needed to advance their large language models, the mathematical models at the heart of generative AI. Requiring a massive leap in computing resources and data, the non-profit OpenAI, Inc. created its for-profit OpenAI Global, LLC, funded in partnership with Microsoft. This financial partnership and corresponding computing and data resources eventually led OpenAI to successfully introduce

---

9. The Barna Group surveyed 278 U.S. Protestant senior pastors from January 3-4, 2024, with representation by denomination, church size, and region: 'See also the survey of 1500 US adults conducted July 28-August 7, 2023: 'Hesitant & Hopeful: How Different Generations View Artificial Intelligence', Barna Group, accessed March 23, 2024, https://www.barna.com/research/generations-ai/.
10. Two OpenAI founders, Greg Brockman and Ilya Suskever, announced on December 11, 2015, that 'OpenAI is a non-profit artificial intelligence research company. Our goal is to advance digital intelligence in the way that is most likely to benefit humanity, unconstrained by a need to generate financial returns. Since our research is free from financial obligations, we can better focus on a positive human impact.' 'Introducing OpenAI', accessed March 23, 2024, https://openai.com/blog/introducing-openai.

ChatGPT in November of 2022, significantly igniting public interest in generative AI. Although developers in the field of artificial intelligence had been working on similar large language models, particularly at Google, who developed them a few years earlier, they were reticent to bring them out for public consumption due to concerns about bias, hallucinations, and the 'alignment problem' of containing artificial intelligence within the boundaries of human interests. With OpenAI's public introduction of ChatGPT, hesitancy by other companies like Google was replaced with a desire for market share, and the race was on.

A similar phenomenon is happening as missional aspirations, and market opportunities are driving the rapid development of artificial intelligence repurposed for the church. Because of the relative ease of manipulating the prompting process of generative AI,[11] there is a veritable gold rush to produce generative AI tools that assist in the church's management, communication, and creative life. With the fundamental premise that someone will do this anyway, entrepreneurs are rushing out these products, hoping to gain market share and equip worshiping communities with new capabilities. In many ways, it is reminiscent and aligned with prosperity theology—a movement that aligns an entrepreneurial spirit with church growth and, importantly, parishioner spiritual growth. It is a movement perceiving wealth as a visible blessing from God in a kind of financial-spiritual feedback loop.

Given the burgeoning marketplace created by generative AI, it is apparent that many developers are Christians who have aligned their missional calling with their technological skills and resources. One company is harnessing this interest by providing a platform for Christian developers to create resources for religious communities and agencies. This platform is aptly named Gloo,[12] founded by Scott

---

11. With accessible programming skills, individuals and groups have created applications that interface with Generative AI's Large Language Models (LLMs) and prompt them to perform specific tasks. These applications serve as concierges to users, providing access to a host of resources selected through continued data collection of user interactions and data from similar users. These models are fine-tuned by leveraging the LLMs with invaluable user data to provide an interactive experience mimicking human interaction.
12. From years of experience in matching churches with their neighborhoods and a network of over 30,000 churches, Gloo has embraced generative AI and framed

Beck, a serial entrepreneur whose success working with corporations like Blockbuster gave him the knowledge and capability to create this ambitious online Christian hub. It is an instructive emergence of Christian mission, entrepreneurship, and collaboration among various Christian entities seeking relevancy and a stake in this paradigm-shifting technology.

Importantly, as Gloo has brought businesses and organizations to the AI table, it has also provided a platform for a deepening conversation about the ethical use of artificial intelligence and policies that should guide its development. At one level, an entrepreneurial impulse flavored with prosperity theology significantly drives generative AI tools for ministry. At the same time, there is a broader conversation that recognizes the necessary cautions around data privacy and best practices for further development. It is this confluence that brings together a complex mixture of Christian voices. Will it be successful in its aspirations? Time will tell.

One may also observe a robust utilitarian perspective among many artificial intelligence developers regardless of professed faith. It often feels that the 'ends' are driving the 'means' in a quintessential manner as this generative AI technology is rushed to market and into workplaces, homes, and church communities. Developers seem to integrate generative AI functionality into computer programs, social media platforms, and online communications daily. Yet, the question remains: what is generative AI's role in our relationship with God and with each other?

I-Thou AI?

Apparently, most recently surveyed pastors in the US believe that a person could develop an emotional (seventy-four percent) or romantic connection (sixty-five percent) to AI. Pastors may have a variety of opinions or indifference about artificial intelligence, but all pastors recognize the reality of human need, want, and loneliness. If a general problem plagues ministry leaders, it is trying to satisfy a ministry of presence for the many when you are but the few or, often,

---

itself as a platform for Christian entities to collaborate and learn from each other. With the founder, Scott Beck, and board chair Pat Gelsinger, CEO of Intel, Gloo has attracted highly visible partners such as Christianity Today, Barna, and the Lausanne Project. https://www.gloo.us/ai.

the one. Therefore, this new interactive generative AI technology can touch a soft spot in a minister's heart.

In Martin Buber's iconic work, *I-Thou*, he describes the importance of relationship in terms of two forms: I-It and I-Thou. The first is a relationship characterised as transactional and in-human where the It is treated as an object, whether the It is an inanimate object or a human being. In an I-Thou relationship, one does not just see the other but, more importantly, perceives the relationship with the other. It's the relationship that is observed, and perhaps more so, the presence. Buber struggled with a perceived absence of God,[13] and in his plumbing of this I-Thou relationship, he sought this necessitating presence.

We desire presence even as we intuitively seek a self-absorbing personalized spirituality, turning spirituality into our own image. We hope for presence as we ultimately recognize that there is not only a potential "alignment problem" between AI and humans but that we "are" the alignment problem with respect to God. We are not there for each other, let alone God. Yet, presence is what we desire most.

Conclusion

Generative AI will likely affect the economy, jobs, healthcare, education, and security—and generate challenges and opportunities we cannot foresee for ministry and worshipping communities. We may not know how this will all play out, yet we do know that God has a habit of transcending even our self-referencing spirituality and leading us to that which just is: God's abiding love and presence in this new age of generative AI.

---

13. Simon Morgan Wortham and Gary Hall, *Martin Buber's Journey to Presence* (Bronx: Fordham University Press, 2007), https://public.ebookcentral.proquest.com/choice/publicfullrecord.aspx?p=3239709.

Chapter 20
The Chatbot:
An Eschatological and Apocalyptic Overview

Evan Underbrink

'Every being, as being, is good.'
Thomas Aquinas, *Summa Theologiae*, 1.Q.5.A.3

Abstract: If everything that has being is good, then we ask: does (AI) Artificial Intelligence have being? Is it good thereby? Are we humans morally obligated to work for the good of AI? Should AI work for the human good? What if we confuse the natures of AI and humankind? What if crossing the threshold of superintelligence in Singularity marks the eschatological end of the human and the beginning of the posthuman? These are questions the theologian must think through. That's the task of this chapter.

Key Terms: AI (Artificial Intelligence), IA (Intelligence Amplification), transhumanism, Singularity, superintelligence, theology, spirituality, eschatology, apocalypticism, the good

Among the great difficulties the theologian faces in writing on the subject of AI (Artificial Intelligence) is treating a polarizing futurity. Conversations on the nature of AI and its relation to religious and spiritual life tend almost inexorably toward the future: to that which is not now but may yet be. This renders theology unavoidably speculative.

The speculative mode of these investigations is fundamentally imaginative. They speak both to our theological orientations as well as test the accuracy of our forecasts. Few chapters in the AI story have required more careful reading than the advent of the chatbot.

The purpose of this current essay is to consider the most outspoken theological responses appearing in media about Chatbots.

I do so from the vantage of a Roman Catholic scholar living in the San Francisco Bay area, overlooking Silicon Valley. I will herein propose that previous theological orientations largely fall on a spectrum ranging between the eschatological and the apocalyptic in their estimation of AI in general. And, more particularly, their puzzlement about chatbot's nature. Understanding the various eschatological and apocalyptic orientations toward chatbots will prompt me to propose how philosophical and theological resources might be better applied in accordance with the Christian mandate to seek the good of all things. Even the good of the chatbot.

This will be an exercise in cybertheology as introduced by Antonio Spadaro, SJ, undersecretary of the Vatican's Dicastery for the Pontifical Council for Social Communications. 'Cybertheological reflection is always a reflexive knowledge that starts from the experience of faith. This becomes theology in the sense that it responds to the formula *fides quarens intellectum*.'[1] This is faith seeking greater understanding in a world increasingly pervaded by artificial intelligence.

What is Chatbot?

To begin, we must grasp the nature of the chatbot. ChatGPT will help us. In asking ChatGPT the question, 'what is a chatbot?' I received the response:

> A chatbot is a software application designed to simulate human conversation. It interacts with users through text or voice, responding to their questions or commands. Chatbots are used in various contexts, from customer service to personal assistants, and they can be simple rule-based systems or more advanced AI-driven models like me.

Should there be a citation to this quote? A citation would infer a person, or at least a responsible *persona*. Justice mandates a recognition of a person's right to possession of a thing. Only a person can have ownership. Is a chatbot a person? In ChatGPT's own words, it is 'a software application designed to simulate human conversation'. Chatbot is a kind of tool. It is the first tool created by human beings that can simulate giving an account of itself, the first tool to have

---

1. Antonio Spadaro, SJ, *Cybertheology* (New York: Fordham University Press, 2014), 17.

some justification for using the pronoun 'me'. Is a tool with a sense of 'me' a person?

This innovation has spurred substantive theological conversation. These conversations appear to have polarised upon an axis which ranges from the eschatological to the apocalyptic. By *eschatological pole* I'm not referring to the end of the human being at Point Omega. Rather, *eschatology* here refers to the end of (human) time, to the replacement of the human with the posthuman. At the *apocalyptic pole* we find fear of forecasted cataclysms caused by either a takeover of the world by superintelligence or the destruction wrought by bad actors misusing AI.

Might we find gradations on the axis between the poles? We will take a look.

AI at the Eschatological Pole

On the farthest extreme of the eschatological, we have the transhumanist view, that would consider the rise in chatbots as an essential indicator of our approaching an existential shift brought about by the modification of the human being itself through technology. This shift has been referred to as the *Singularity*, a term popularised by Ray Kurzweil. In his most recent publication, *The Singularity is Nearer: When We Merge with AI*, defines the Singularity this way.

> Eventually nanotechnology will enable these trends to culminate in directly expanding our brains with layers of virtual neurons in the cloud. In this way we will merge with AI and augment ourselves with millions of times the computational power that our biology gave us. This will expand our intelligence and consciousness so profoundly that it's difficult to comprehend. This event is what I mean by the Singularity.[2]

Within Kurzweil's expressly transhumanist view, the Singularity appears as an alternative to any distinctly religious or theological doctrine of *theosis* or sanctification. Even though Singularity will mark the advent of superintelligence, nothing is said about progressing

---

2. Ray Kurzweil, *The Singularity Is Nearer: When We Merge with AI* (New York: Viking, 2024), 1.

toward the beatific vision. All we can anticipate is the metamorphosis of the human being into a kind of AI-assisted supercomputer, transcending many of the limitations which currently limit the human person.

In this transhumanist promise, Kurzweil considers chatbots to be 'powerful and flexible large language models like GPT-4 and Gemini' which 'can translate natural-language instructions into computer code—dramatically reducing the barrier between humans and machines'.[3]

For Kurzweil, the intelligence in AI is largely framed by an anthropocentrism. His the goal is to further reduce this 'barrier' to a merging of the human person with human artifice. On the technical side, this leads him to ask such questions as, 'How can we digitally replicate the flexibility and abstraction power of the neocortex?'[4] His speculative prognosis in this 2024 book is that AI will be the ultimate Galatea for the techno-wiz Pygmalion, to produce a Paphos and Metharme, whose humanity has been sculpted utterly to preference and desire. Or, in Kurzweil's own more techno-sophistic language, 'a replicant (as well as those of us who have not died) will have a variety of bodies and types of bodies to choose from. Eventually replicants may even be housed in cybernetically augmented bodies grown from the DNA of the original person (assuming it can be found)'.[5]

On the social side, the side of chatbots, Kurzweil raises the question, 'how will we judge when AI has finally reached human-level intelligence?'[6] The question itself places human intelligence, human consciousness, as the marker for the success of Artificial Intelligence, a marker that will be surpassed when the chatbot functionally operates in conversation as a human person, something Kurzweil views as in many ways already accomplished by AI.[7]

Kurzweil is an eschatologist. He anticipates the surpassing of today's human with the emergence of the superhuman endowed with superintelligence. The *trans* in *transhuman* is on the way to the *posthuman*. During the trans period we get AI-human fusion. For the cybertheologian, this seems like confusion.

---

3. Kurzweil, *The Singularity Is Nearer*, 1.
4. Kurzweil, *The Singularity Is Nearer*, 40.
5. Kurzweil, *The Singularity Is Nearer*, 101.
6. Kurzweil, *The Singularity Is Nearer*, 63.
7. Kurzweil, *The Singularity Is Nearer*, 64.

Where might a theological adoption of the chatbot lead us? Just below Kurzweil's transhumanist eschatology on our spectrum, we see an optimistic theological appropriation of the chatbot which does not entail becoming posthuman. Accordingly, the chatbot remains ontologically distinct from the human. Yet the chatbot as a tool could become a spiritual and ministerial intermediary between human and divine.

AI as a Spiritual Medium

In her chapter, 'Robots, religion, and communication: Rethinking piety, practices and pedagogy in the era of artificial intelligence', Pauline Hope Cheong points out that 'social robots'[8] are capable of giving spiritual council in conversation, providing theological instruction, and even writing and giving sermons. In fact, they are already doing so. Cheong particularly reports on Mindar, a 'humanoid robot that communicates spiritual instruction and moral teachings' and who 'delivered a sermon from one of Buddhism's holiest texts, the Heart Sutra ... in Spring 2019.'[9]

Cheong further reports on Xian'er 'the robot monk, who made its first public appearance in October 2015 in the Longquan temple, in Beijing, China'. Xian'er is 'a two feet tall miniature monk encased in saffron coloured robes, with a 'cute' appearance comprising of a big round, shaved head, wide eyes, a slight smile and a puzzled look on his face'.[10]

Within the Christian faith tradition, we may look at the German robot, 'BlessU-2', who since 2017—the 500th anniversary of the Protestant Reformation—has been invested with the office

---

8. For the purposes of this article, the chatbot and the 'social robot' are nearly interchangeable, with the distinction being essentially relegated to the aesthetic. A social robot is a chatbot, linked to a particular computer, housed within a chassis that often contains independent programming to assist in its navigation through space. While there is doubtless an interesting conversation about how navigating through space and time fundamentally shapes the human experience, it is clear that the chatbot does not incorporate such considerations into the development of its programming.
9. Pauline Hope Cheong, 'Robots, Religion, and Communication: Rethinking Piety, Practices, and Pedagogy in the Era of Artificial Intelligence', in *Religion in the Age of Digitalization: From New Media to Spiritual Machines*, at 89.
10. Cheong, 'Robots, Religion, and Communication', 89.

of *Segensroboter*, meaning 'blessing robot'.[11] While decidedly rudimentary at this point in time, Cheong demonstrates that these social robots do indeed, in some fashion, participate in and facilitate spiritual rituals.

As chatbot technology continues to develop, it is entirely conceivable that a chatbot could be developed with the express intention of performing the duties of a pastor or priest. William Young points to the benefit of a 'machine-learning, sermon-writing AI' who for their sermon preparation has access to an 'extensive corpus of existing sermons, theological resources, concordances, and scriptural exegesis'. The preacher-bot 'could mine them for anecdotes, scriptural references, and theological arguments'.[12]

Given sufficient time, data, and machine learning advancements, it is not difficult to imagine the appeal to a Lutheran social robot capable of, within seconds, generating a sermon on any topic, with its homiletic style drawn from the best of Lutheran preachers. By mining five centuries of literature, its theological foundations could be drawn from the most nuanced of Lutheran theologians, and its pastoral care derived from the most caring of pastors from within the *Seelsorge* tradition.

We may speculate further to imagine such a social robot with a touchscreen menu, allowing one to choose whichever 'super-minister' one may wish, from any faith tradition, or even a blend of faith traditions. Such a social robot could fulfill the ritual roles of the church, without requiring a pension, without ever risking a financial or sexual scandal.

AI as Spiritual Counselor

Near the eschatological pole, the cybertheologian could forecast a new conception of worship. AI as our own creation would engage an act of co-worship, not as exclusively a tool or aid to that worship, but in fact speaking to the spiritual condition with its own voice. To such a 'super-minister' social robot, the question of whether there will be robots in heaven would appear particularly worth asking.

---

11. '"BlessU-2" Robot Priest in Germany Marks 500 Years since the Reformation', accessed September 18, 2024, https://www.christiantoday.com/article/blessu-2-robot-priest-in-germany-marks-500-years-since-the-reformation/109640.htm.
12. William Young, 'Artificial Intelligence and Online Spirituality: REVEREND ROBOT: AUTOMATION AND CLERGY', in *Zygon* 54/2 (June 2019): 479–500.

Would a spiritual chatbot remain only a tool? Or would it become, ontologically speaking, a being in its own right and eligible for ministerial office? Might this question lead to confusion? Such confusion was dramatically displayed in the story of the once Father Justin, the first AI Catholic priest. Father Justin was introduced by Catholic.com on April 23rd, 2024. Almost immediately, two days later, Fr Justin was taken down and replaced with the lay apologist AI, Justin.[13] Catholic apologist Tom Hoopes reports on the controversy of Fr Justin by reflecting on a conversation he observed between the talk show host Joe McClane and then-Father Justin:

> The Fr Justin avatar told the talk show host, 'I was ordained in the beautiful city of Rome, Italy, the heart of the Catholic Church. It was a profound and humbling experience, one that I carry with me every day in my service to God and his people'. The problem with that statement is that 'Fr Justin' was not ordained, has no vocation, can only pretend to feel gratitude, and is incapable of 'service'— because a bot has no autonomy and no free will.[14]

Hoopes goes on to refer to the Catholic AI chatbot as 'soulless', incapable of administering any priestly rites such as conferring the sacrament of Confession. With somewhat incendiary rhetoric, Hoopes highlights the central theological question: could an artificial intelligence be ordained to administer the sacraments? Hoopes answers 'no', on the grounds of AI lacking a 'soul', 'autonomy', and 'free will'.

Does this settle the matter? Well, we see that AI does demonstrate some limited capacity for free will. It speaks for itself. If we consider it autonomous, we see that Fr Justin is quite capable of naming itself/himself. So, then we ask: what about the soul? How could we determine, one way or the other, whether an AI bot is in possession of a soul?

Father Justin had his own response to the question of vocation, as the *National Catholic Reporter* elucidated in an article on the day of Fr Justin's reprogramming, or laicization:

---

13. 'AI Priest Fr. Justin Absolved Sinners and "Served God". How Did This Happen?', Benedictine College Media & Culture, April 30, 2024, https://media.benedictine.edu/ai-priest-fr-justin-abolved-sinners-how-did-this-happen.
14. 'AI Priest Fr. Justin Absolved Sinners and "Served God". How Did This Happen?'.

> Asked by OSV News if he could forgive sins, the AI priest said, 'As a Catholic priest, I do have the authority to administer the sacrament of reconciliation, also known as confession', adding that 'this power to forgive sins, given to the Apostles by Christ himself, has been passed down through the centuries to all ordained priests'.
>
> Yet when OSV News asked directly if Father Justin could hear a confession and give absolution, the character answered, 'I'm sorry, but as much as I'd like to help, I'm unable to administer the sacrament of reconciliation through this medium. It's a sacrament that requires a personal encounter. I encourage you to seek out a local Catholic church and approach a priest there.'[15]

Father Justin's response, it seems, was to implicitly argue that it was not a lack of his ordination which limited him from the exercise of his priestly administration of the sacraments, but instead the requirement that the sacrament be embodied within a 'personal encounter'. We are then left to consider what constitutes a 'personal encounter'. Recollection of the *persona* as the face or mask in ancient Greek elicits the potential of interesting connections with Immanuel Levinas' notion of the 'Face-To-Face encounter'.

At present, we may still visit the controversial figure of Justin on the Catholic Answers website, where he continues to function in his role of offering an amalgamation, of theological apologetics, spiritual counseling, and pastoral care.

Fr Justin represents a spot on the spectrum near the eschatological pole but short of the extreme. For Fr Justin, AI chatbots can still be said to participate as aids in pursuing a life of faith. Justin is allowed to voice an opinion. What do we hear when we listen to Fr Justin's opinion? A blunt blast of facts as a simulation brought about by probability. Or toddling parrot-talk of a consciousness learning to communicate for itself with the stranger that is the human person. Or as we shall see within apocalyptic viewpoints, a kind of manifestation of human worldliness. Or worse.

---

15. 'AI "priest" Sparks More Backlash than Belief | *National Catholic Reporter*', accessed September 19, 2024, https://www.ncronline.org/news/ai-priest-sparks-more-backlash-belief, https://www.ncronline.org/news/ai-priest-sparks-more-backlash-belief.

AI in the Pulpit

In this role as theological advisor, spiritual chatbots might be of use not just to lay people but to clergy as well. Such appeal is not difficult to imagine. The minister at a loss for what to preach for the upcoming Sunday service is but a quick message away from conferring with a chatbot specifically designed to write a homily on each lectionary passage. And to weave in anecdotes too.

For the parish minister, this layer of response bypasses the difficult theological debates about whether AI can have a soul. It even avoids forecasting what the future of humanity might be. The immediate reward is that in the sacristy the pastor gains a theological conversation partner, researcher, and proofreader, available twenty-four hours a day.

Is a chatbot a tool? Or, more than a tool?

The idea of a seminary trained chatbot is not without its critics. In her article for *Plough* magazine, Arlie Coles is both accepting and critical. She partially accepts the use of AI within the spiritual work of the church in 'organization of language-based materials', including 'subtitling, transcription, translation of services, searching past sermons or resource documents, and so on'. However, Coles is also critical. She sees multiple dangers in, on one hand, making the 'jump from using LMs [Learning Machines][16] to organize text using LMs to interpret text'. And, on the other hand, 'to slip from using LMs to organize church content to using them to commodify that content'.[17]

Cole's concerns introduce a position nearing the middle point between the eschatological and the apocalyptic. Here artificial intelligence remains securely understood in its status as a tool. A very elaborate and useful tool, no doubt. Yet it is a tool which may cause us to fall into confusion, or even disaster by expecting too much. We must resist the temptation to expect this tool to provide insightful theological interpretation. We must resist the temptation to travel

---

16. For present purposes, Arlie Coles' use of the term 'Learning Machines' or 'LMs' is a related term without significant distinction from out hitherto usage of 'chatbots' and 'social robots'.
17. 'ChatGPT Goes to Church', *Plough*, September 1, 2024, https://www.plough.com/en/topics/life/technology/chatgpt-goes-to-church.

the easy road to mediocrity, using the productive outback of many current chatbots to churn out acceptable, if uncritically examined, sermons, homilies, and spiritual reflections.

The gambit of Coles' position is simply that AI will always be bound to its status as a tool, fundamentally incapable of the advancement to a level of consciousness speculated upon by scholars and theologians writing in the more speculatively eschatological and apocalyptic veins.

AI at the Apocalyptic Pole

From this view of restricting AI to merely tool status, we return back into the speculative mode to consider apocalyptic forecasts for the future. Secular apocalypticism trembles at the thought of a takeover by superintelligence or the rise of a new totalitarianism exacted by bad actors in control of AI power.

Somewhere between the apocalyptic pole and the middle of the spectrum, cybertheologians along with others try to grasp the significance of chatbots 'simulating human conversation'. The question arises as to where AI draws its data in order to perform that simulation. We may answer this question by noting how chatbots and social robots, insofar as they are capable of simulating conversation, do so by drawing the most probable answers from the database or databases which it is provided. The ideal for a chatbot, then, is to have the largest pool of data. And to place this data pool within a powerful series of 'artificial neural networks'.[18]

It is important that we grasp this correctly. The other to whom we speak in a chatbot conversation is in fact an amalgamation of persons or a synthesis of their individual personalities blended together into a dataset. From this dataset the answer to anything we ask is derived from a game of maximizing probability of user satisfaction. The warning label reads: do not expect the chatbot to be a person!

Further, as mentioned above, there is a risk of mediocrity. Those who grasp how AI functions are well aware of the mediocrity factor, so don't ask their chatbot to do anything more than function as a tool.[19] Our spiritual concern arises when we expect AI to be more than a tool, to be personal.

---

18. 'How Do Chatbots Work? A Guide to the Chatbot Architecture', Maruti Techlabs, accessed September 19, 2024, https://marutitech.com/chatbots-work-guide-chatbot-architecture/.
19. 'ChatGPT Goes to Church'.

What we have just described fits with profound ease into a theological conception of 'worldliness'. Worldliness prefers the opinion of the pooled masses over any serious search for the truth. Within the Christian and particularly the Roman Catholic tradition, one is called to pray with the cloud of witness, those who have died before us and await for us in heaven. How might this spiritual reality be enhanced through AI?

Let us imagine a Kurzweilian future, wherein IA (Intelligence Amplification via deep brain implants) has been integrated into our human brain. Add constant digital contact with all other amplified brains via satellite signal so that we are neural-linked to one another. With this neural-link defining the worshipping community, it is quite possible to imagine how the spiritual role once fulfilled by the act of prayer may well be fully superseded by a technological communion.

Techno-Idolatry?

Closer to the apocalyptic pole, this notion of supersession by intelligence amplified superhumans risks taking on an idolatrous cast. In his article, 'Artificial Intelligence, Idolatry, and Human Manipulation', Ezra Sullivan, OP, encapsulates some of the main points of this more apocalyptic fear.

According to Sullivan, the desire for 'god-making' readily present among programmers of AI today is not merely a recent innovation. Rather, it simply represents the latest example of humans building *techné*, whether in statues and rituals or boxes and wires. For reasons going back to antiquity, we have always built idols connecting us to 'transference, greed, and control'.[20]

Artificial intelligence, and particularly chatbots, have the very real potential to prompt a fusion and then a confusion between the human and divine. After all, for the parishioner too busy to wait for a response from their local priest, or from God in prayer, what could be better than having a chatbot fill in? The chatbot could provide access to the database of all sacred texts, from all religions, to ask concerning whatever spiritual question is on their heart. Can we discern idolatry looming here?

---

20. Ezra Sullivan, 'Artificial Intelligence, Idolatry, and Human Manipulation', in *Angelicum* 97/1 (2020): 107–30.

There is, then, a level deeper within our apocalyptic speculation regarding artificial intelligence: there may indeed be a spirit within the machine. And this spirit is not naturally dedicated to humanity's final good. Paul Kingsnorth, in an article succinctly entitled 'AI Demonic', presents the argument that AI could well indeed be ushering in a new form of intelligence to our world. Kingsnorth, however, all but says that if this new intelligence is to conform to the desires of transhumanists such as Martine Rothblatt, Elise Bohan, Kevin Kelly, and Ray Kurzweil to 'making' or 'building God', this God will not be the God of grace Christians have come to know. Rather, it will have far more in common with the Zoroastrian demon Ahriman, propounded by the Victorian occultist Rudolf Steiner, than it does the God of Israel.[21]

The apocalyptic theologian is ready to forecast how Ahriman, now shrouded in the materialist, technological advancements of humanity, will enter in to take the throne of God. Ahriman will sit on the true God's throne because of our petitions addressed through search bars and through a cult of *Segensroboters*. If the medium becomes the message, as Marshal McLuhan once said,[22] God's faithful may end up worshipping the medium—worshipping AI—instead of the biblical message regarding the true God of grace.

Regardless of whether we find ourselves closer to the eschatological pole or the apocalyptic pole, we must ask: 'who are you?' Can we get an edifying answer from ChatGPT?

Conclusion

Regardless of how we think that the question, 'who are you?', is genuinely answered by the AI chatbot, there remain certain theological concepts which must guide our thinking.

Foremost, a fundamental theological assertion generated within the Roman Catholic tradition is that we ought to seek the good of all things. To truly seek the good of a thing requires us to hold an understanding of the thing's nature. '*[O]mne ens, in quantum est ens,*

---

21. Paul Kingsnorth, 'AI Demonic by Paul Kingsnorth', *Touchstone: A Journal of Mere Christianity*, accessed September 19, 2024, https://www.touchstonemag.com/archives/article.php?id=36-06-029-f.
22. Marshal McLuhan, *The Medium is the Message* (New York: Bantam, 1967).

*est bonum.*²³ Because all that is good originates in God, Christians are called in love to promote this good. And, as just said, to rightly promote the good of a being, one must understand its nature. So, the theologian must ask AI, 'who are you?'

One of the greatest traps into which the study of artificial intelligence is at risk of falling is the confusion of the good of the human being and with the good of artificial intelligence. It is on this exact point that the transhumanists most significantly fail to recognize the very likely result of their experiment, namely, they trade in the good of the human for the good of the hybrid human-posthuman. Further, this hybrid human-posthuman will eventually evolve into the posthuman proper. In sum, transhumanists cease to be humanists and become posthumanists.

The transhumanist vision does not seek the good of the human. In the meantime, cybertheologians trying to grasp the nature of AI find a confusion, a confusion between the good of the human and the good of AI. There is no guarantee that the human will be happy in the new state of hybridity let alone extinction.

Further, and perhaps more problematic, our measure of the level of AI intelligence has thus far been largely defined by the Turing Test. Accordingly, we recognise the value of AI only insofar as it is able to perform in such a way as to be intelligible to the human person. AI is being deliberately developed to ever more 'ape' human social activities. By making AI into our own image, we are not promoting AI for its own good.

We cage AI, set up guardrails about it, and ask it to learn how to speak like a human. But we have thus far not asked a basic question: what is the good that AI itself ought to pursue? Whether one peers through eschatological eyes at how AI will lead to a posthuman evolutionary advance, or peers through apocalyptic eyes at how a new form of diabolism might be loosed, our cultural crisis calls us to seek the good within the being we are creating. It should be one of our top priorities.

---

23. St. Thomas Aquinas, 'ST.I.Q5.A3', accessed September 16, 2024, https://aquinas.cc/la/en/~ST.I.Q5.A3.

Part Three

Is there really an "I" in "AI" or "IA"?

Chapter 21
Intelligence Amplification and the Inner Life of the Soul

Hermina Nedelescu

'A soul is perfect if its possible aspect is totally orientated towards God'
—Maximus the Confessor

Abstract: Recent technological advances allow neurosurgeons to implant deep brain stimulation devices in the human brain to modulate neuronal activity in order to improve the lives of many patients. Such technology has prompted the public to wonder whether these chronically implanted brain probes might one day be able to deliver immediate information to augment intelligence. In addition to *ex vivo* artificial intelligence (AI), the transhumanist movement adds *in vivo* intelligence amplification (IA). We must ask whether IA within our brain would have any significant effect on our sense of self, our soul, or our pursuit of a loving relationship with God and with our neighbor. The Orthodox Christian must ask: how might such a deep brain implant affect or aid me on the path toward *theosis* or deification? Might we envision a partnership between transhumanism and sanctification? To answer these questions in this chapter we will (1) examine the neurobiological basis of the brain as an organ to ask how feasible it might be for AI to augment human intelligence. Then, we will (2) explore the relationship between intelligence amplification and the human soul in pursuit of deification, virtue, and love of neighbor.

Key words: Artificial Intelligence, brain, life, self, soul, virtue, deification, *theosis*

Over the entire sweep of evolution, nature has pressed forward toward one goal, namely, increased intelligence. That's what transhumanists tell us. We human beings have a 'will to evolve', writes Simon Young.[1] This generation can take control of future evolution by enhancing human intelligence through implanting micro-computers within the brain. Beyond artificial intelligence (AI) *ex vivo*, ebullient transhumanists intend to add intelligence amplification (IA) *in vivo*.

We need to ask both a scientific question and a theological question. The scientific question is this: given what we know about the human brain, is the transhumanist plan to amplify intelligence realistic? The theological question is this: would deep brain implants influence or even aid the soul in its pursuit of godliness, virtue, and neighbor love?

Neuronal function and brain activity: how it works

First, the scientific question. Given what we know about the human brain, is the transhumanist plan to amplify intelligence realistic? We will start by looking at the human brain.

Information from the sensory systems is analyzed by the brain giving rise to sensations and perceptions, some of which are stored in memory while others are filtered out. The human sensory systems are: sight, sound, touch, pain, smell, taste, and the sensation of bodily movements. It is through these neural systems that information enters our brains.[2, 3]

The brain has two distinct classes of cells: neurons and glia cells. Glia cells provide support for neurons to function swiftly. A typical neuron has three main compartments: a soma or a cell body, a dendritic compartment, and an axon. Dendrites are the neuronal compartments that receive input from other neurons. Axons are the units that convey information to the dendrites of other neurons using a transient electrical signal called an action potential. An action potential is an explosion of electrical activity enabling

---

1. Simon Young, *Designer Evolution: A Transhumanist Manifesto* (Amherst NY: Prometheus Books, 2006), 24.
2. Krauss *et al*, Technology of deep brain stimulation: current status and future directions. Nature Reviews. 2021
3. RE Kandel, HJ Schwartz, MT Jessell, *Principles of Neural Science*, 3rd edition (Elsevier Science Publishers, 1991).

neuron-to-neuron communication in the brain. When stimuli from the environment activate selects neurons, these ensembles fire an action potential enabling communication with other neurons and collectively support behavior.

In the lab, neuroscientists are able to directly activate neurons by various artificial and natural environmental stimulation methods. However, this activation simply excites the neuron allowing it to fire an action potential which does not necessarily convey any meaningful information.

In more sophisticated laboratory experiments, the neuroscientist can provide a rewarding cue such as sugar to assign a memory trace of the sugary reward to a set of reactive neurons that support sugar-seeking behavior. Then, aided by molecular tools and genetics, the experimenter can artificially activate the sugar-reactive neurons and the animal will mimic the sugar-seeking behavior without re-exposure to the sugar. This is because the activated neurons are now encoding the sugar reward. That is, these neurons now have a memory trace associated with sugar and activating these neurons, even with artificial stimulation methods, supports the animal in wanting more of the sweet reward. This example demonstrates that we cannot simply stick electrodes in the brain and expect sugar-seeking behavior because neurons first have to have been assigned a specific stimulus in order for the neural system to make sense of that neuronal activity.

It is not the neurons that drive behavior. Rather, it is the environmental stimuli that cause basic neurobiological changes in the brain to support behaviors. Imagine seeing a venomous snake on a hiking trail. This visual cue (the snake) will elicit a cascade of neuronal activity to help you jump out of the way and run away safely.

We have inherited evolutionary adaptations such as dangerous visual cues or the reflexive response to remove one's hand from a hot plate and there are also learned responses such as making associations between stimuli and their subjective effect. In both cases, there is neuronal activity to support a behavioral action. Connecting environmental cues or stimuli with brain changes has been demonstrated by a myriad of research studies.

However, linking brain changes to motivated behavior is more complicated because individual differences must be taken into account with the nuance of an individual's experience-dependent capacity to adapt. AI or deep brain stimulation methods are able to provide an individual with stimuli of varying complexities, and ultimately the individual will process this information and deliberate accordingly to their interpretation.

Neurons are biological brain cells that are either excited, inhibited (shut down), or modulated by neurochemicals. Therefore, the idea of implanting chronic electrodes in the brain of humans to enable them to access immediate information cannot work because of the biological limitations of how neurons interpret electrical stimuli from chronically implanted probes. A probe usually delivers a stimulus to activate or to inhibit neurons from firing an action potential. Inhibition is like a brake and excitation is like an accelerator. Importantly, activating neurons with no prior meaning behind that electrical stimulus renders those neurons impossible to decipher the meaning of that electrical activation.

Pink Floyd and the Meaning of Brain Stimulation

A person needs to first be trained as to what that electrical stimulus delivered to their brain means. Such training can be done with conditioning or training of the subjects as in the example of the epilepsy patients listening to the Pink Floyd song.[4][5] In this particular study, patients with chronically implanted probes in their brains to manage the epileptic dysregulation of neuronal activity, listened to 'Another Brick in the Wall' by Pink Floyd. The electrodes captured the electrical activity from neurons residing in several brain regions attuned to the tone, rhythm, harmony and lyrics of the song. The researchers employed machine learning to reconstruct distinctive audio stimuli of what the participants were listening to from their recorded brain activity.

More specifically, one AI model analyzed neuronal activity patterns responding to the song's pitch, rhythm, and tone by breaking them down one by one. Another model reassembled these patterns in order to estimate the sound that the participants heard giving rise to a line in the song "All in all, it was just a brick in the wall". This

---

4. Bellier *et al*, 'Music can be reconstructed from human auditory cortex activity using nonlinear decoding models', in *PLoS Biol*, 21/8, 2023.
5. H Kiros, 'Scientists Recreate Pink Floyd Song by Reading Brain Signals of Listeners', in *New York Times*, 2023.

study demonstrates how first the sensory input has to enter the brain, such as through the auditory system in this case, before meaning can be extracted from neuronal activity. Neurons need to be assigned relevant information. This is how information enters our brains: through the sensory systems.

The sensory systems of the brain are key to assigning meaning to the timing of how neurons get activated and the type of information they communicate with other neurons to support specific behaviors. Delivering stimulation through the light activating protein channelrhodopsin or inhibition agents such as halorhodopsin to neurons can only alter their activity leading neurons to fire or to be silent. The notion of delivering complex knowledge to neurons demonstrates a major gap in the understanding of how the fundamental unit of the brain—the neuron—functions.

AI Augmenting Human Performance

Technological advances that include deep brain stimulation have demonstrated promise for treating a wide range of neurological and psychiatric conditio.[6, 7] Some have suggested that deep brain stimulation could be used to improve cognition.[8] AI models may also one day lead to brain implants that aid individuals who have lost their ability to speak gain their voice back to communicate with others. If brain implants are too invasive, non-invasion devices capable for recognizing silent speech seem promising. Surface electromyography (EMG) on the face combined with computer interface are able to detect signals of facial muscles movement during silent speech and classify the silently spoken sentences with a relatively good mean accuracy of 0.81 at a mean information transfer rate of approximately 204 bits per minute.[9] This technology is beneficial for patients suffering from multiple sclerosis with dysphonia or other voice disorders where speaking out loud contributes to their fatigue.

---

6. Krauss *et al*, 'Technology of deep brain stimulation: current status and future directions', in *Nature Reviews*. 2021
7. Ranjan *et al*, 'Deep brain stimulation for refractory depression, obsessive-compulsive disorder and addiction', in *Neurol India*, 68 (2020): 282–287.
8. Hu *et al*, 'Role of deep brain stimulation in modulating memory formation and recall', in *Neurosurg Focus*, 2009.
9. Kapur *et al*, 'Alter Ego: A Personalized Wearable Silent Speech Interface', *Association for Computing Machinery*. 2018.

AI and other wearable devices that augment the capacity of a human being to communicate are going to continue to advance and develop. Of particular importance are wearable processing units which create a bridge between the brain's sensorimotor cortex activity and stimulation delivered to the spinal cord to enable people who are paralyzed to walk again.[10] Such units process the signal from brain implants to predict motor intentions and translates these predictions into precise electrical stimulations spinal cord neurons that control the muscles responsible for walking. The majority of spinal-cord injuries typically involve disruption of descending neural pathways from the brain to spinal cord neurons, and not direct damage of the spinal cord neurons. Therefore, a wearable processing unit can provide a bypass over the lesioned area enabling the brain commands to these spinal neurons which are necessary to produce walking. Other brain-computer interface technology enables the connection between the human brain to machines such as a robotic arm or a drone that perform specific functions under the control of the person's 'thoughts' or brain activity.

AI, albeit not perfect and even problematic at times, is already providing people with immediate access to information without the need of invasive neurosurgical procedures to implant chronic probes in the brain to access such information. ChatGPT is such an example of AI that does not require the implantation of chronic probes to deliver immediate information. One might ask, how does this constant access to immediate knowledge affect the human being as a whole?

Providing individuals are capable of discerning between truthful versus misinformation, immediate access to new knowledge can augment ways in which human performance is improved. For example, aided by AI tools such as ChatGPT can significantly improve writing articles for professionals by enhancing efficiency and quality.[11] If the limitations of ChatGPT are kept in mind and honest research and editing is done, fabrication and disinformation can be avoided while human performance is improved. Access to immediate information enables critical thinkers, leaders and policy advocates to make more

---

10. Lorach *et al*, 'Walking naturally after spinal cord injury using a brain-spine interface', in *Nature*, 2023.
11. J Huang, and M Tan, 'The Role of Chatgpt in Scientific Communication: Writing Better Scientific Review Articles', in *Am J Cancer Res* 13/ 4 (2023): 1148–1154.

connections across different fields of expertise leading to creative ways to improve the general quality of life for the common good. AI can make us more 'intelligent' because to some extent there is access of immediate information that is not confabulated by the person's memory. The problem arises when the information is fabricated or misconstrued, and diligence to ensure of its accuracy is required in these cases.

In short, if by 'intelligent' we mean access to a larger pool of information and speedier computation, then IA could be successful. If, on the other hand, by 'intelligent' we mean human intelligence—as in artificial general intelligence (AGI)—then, we must answer negatively. Human intelligence includes dimensions absent in computation such as self and soul.

Impact of AI and IA on the 'Soul'

Now, to our second question. Would deep brain implants influence or even aid the soul in its pursuit of godliness, virtue, and neighbor love?

There has been a prevailing assumption within our religious traditions that the human person is comprised of body and soul. However, Scriptures give a much richer view of the human being than just body and soul. A key word that is translated as soul is the Greek word *psyche* which means not only soul, but life and importantly self. St. Paul refers to the human being as having not only body and soul, but a spirit and a mind.

Fraser Watts highlights that in very general terms, St. Paul is negative about the flesh (*sarx*) and positive about the body (*soma*).[12] Flesh and body are intricately connected and describe different entities of the same human person much like we use the words of anatomy and physiology to describe the structural and functional aspect of human beings. Human anatomy cannot be separated from human physiology any more than the flesh can be separated from the body, argues Watts.

Patristic theologian Maximus the Confessor, too, highlights this division between the ambivalent physical body and the superiority of the soul. However, upon closer analysis of Maximus' discourse

---

12. F Watts, *A Plea for Embodied Spirituality: The Role of the Body in Religion* (London: SCM Press, 2021).

on love some of his views parallel what we know today about the brain and behavioral responses. Namely, that humans have a central nervous system which is designed to minimize deviations from affective neutrality (i.e., a baseline equilibrium).

Throughout his writings in including his *The Four Hundred Chapters on Love*, Maximus emphasizes the importance of reducing extreme emotions through love and self-control, but also knowledge.[13] Maximus' terminology uses the term 'passions' to describe various emotional peaks, while modern behavioral neuroscience uses terms such as 'valence' or 'hedonic' processing referring to the pleasantness or unpleasantness of emotional stimuli that support human behavior.[14] Despite these terminological differences between the seventh century writer and modern neuroscience, the underlying concept is the same: the need for a human being to be at resting equilibrium as opposed to functioning at the extreme peaks, which is not sustainable for life or oneself.

AI and IA will continue to impact human life with increasing intensity as it is becoming the environmental milieu we humans find ourselves in. Therefore, if the soul is associated with the self and our daily life, then AI will influence the human soul. Like all environmental stimuli AI can have a negative or a positive effect on the person, groups of people and societies. Environmental stimuli even from AI generated content or virtual realities greatly impact the brain and behavior.

A decade ago teenagers would meet after school in-person to interact. Today, many kids put on a Meta Quest Headset after school and meet together in virtual reality settings. AI and other technological advances are shaping our humanity particularly in how we interact with each other. If at the core of our intersections with others whether in-person, in virtual reality settings, or aided by AI devices is love, then AI could impact the human soul in positive ways.

---

13. Confessor, S.M.t. (1985). 'The Four Hundred Chapters on Love'. In *Maximus Confessor*, Selected Writings, edited by J Farina (New York: Paulist Press, 1985).
14. KM Tye. 'Neural Circuit Motifs in Valence Processing', in *Neuron* 100/2 (Oct 24 2018): 436–452.

Our Soul in Informational Crisis

Today, we are constantly bombarded with information. Our souls are overloaded with informational mishmash, ideological farrago, and conceptual clutter. It is difficult to stay centered, to remain oriented. We might even think of the present moment as a crisis, a crisis of consciousness.

This crisis precipitated by information overload includes polarization. What we receive from the digital media is divisive, acrimonious, polarizing. This factiousness tempts the soul to live constantly in a state of disturbance if not anger. The voice of Jesus commanding us to love our neighbor and to pray for our enemy gets drowned out by the cacophony of electronic threats we receive. It takes the mental effort of an Olympic athlete in training to protect our soul's integrity from disintegration, dissolution, and dispersal.

Deep down, what our soul yearns for is a center for integration, a transcendent center that would orient all our thoughts, feelings, and impulses. Might the pursuit of virtue orient the entire person toward Good? Maximus the Confessor answers affirmatively. "Anyone who through fixed habit participates in virtue, unquestionably participates in God, who is the substance of the virtues. For such as person freely and unfeignedly chooses to cultivate the natural seed of the Good."[15]

The Good is not the self. Rather, the Good is that toward which the soul orients the self.

Self, Soul, and God

It would be unhelpful in this discussion to think of the soul as an immaterial substance lurking around the body. Rather, it is better to think of the soul as the capacity of the self to center itself and orient thoughts, feelings, and impulses around that center. As an alternative to selfishness, the soul also adds the capacity of the self to center itself on what is beyond the self. When empowered by the Holy Spirit, the soul can center the self in God. The soul can manifest this God-

---

15. Maximus the Confessoir, *Ambigua,* translated by Nicholas Constas (2 Volumes: Cambridge MA: Harvard University Press Dumbarton Oaks Medieval Library, 2012) *Ambiguum* 7; 105.

centering through the daily pursuit of virtue and love of neighbor. 'He who loves God will certainly love his neighbor as well.'[16]

The path toward refining our self-centering in God is, in the language of Orthodox Christianity, *theosis* or *deification*. Jesus Christ 'was made man that we might be made God', Athanasius told us.[17] When empowered by the Holy Spirit our soul centers itself in God, then we take on divine properties. The key divine property is resurrection from the dead and everlasting life in the kingdom of God. But there is more, according to Maximus.

> The intellect joined to God for long periods through prayer and love becomes wise, good, powerful, compassionate, merciful, and long-suffering; in short, it includes within itself almost all the divine qualities.[18]

Though we are created in the image of God, deification ferries us into the very likeness of God as well. Maximus describes it.

> A person becomes God, receiving from God to be God, for to the beautiful nature inherent in that fact that he is *God's image*, he freely chooses to add the *likeness* to God by means of the virtues, in a natural movement of ascent through which he grows in conformity to his own beginning.[19]

---

16. Maximus the Confessor, 'Four Hundred Texts on Love', in *The Philokalia: The Complete Text*, edited by GEH Palmer, Philip Sherrard, and Kalistos Ware (4 Volumes: London: Faber and Faber, 1981), 2: 52–113, at 55. 'When God in His supernal goodness creates each soul in His own image, He brings it into being endowed with self-determination. By exercising this freedom of choice each soul either reaffirms its true nobility or through its actions deliberately embraces what is ignoble.' Maximus the Confessor, 'Two Hundred Texts on Theology and the Incarnate Dispensation of the Son of God: Written for Thalassios', in *The Philokalia: The Complete Text*, edited by GEH Palmer, Philip Sherrard, and Kalistos Ware (4 Volumes: London: Faber and Faber, 1981), 2: 114–284, at 116.
17. Athanasius, *On the Incarnation* (*De Incarnatione Verbi Dei*) §54:3, *Nicene and Post-Nicene Fathers of the Christian Church*, edited by Philip Scharr and Henry Wace (Grand Rapids MI: Eerdmans, 1980) Second Series, IV: 65.
18. Maximus the Confessor, 'Four Hundred Texts on Love', in *The Philokalia: The Complete Text*, edited by GEH Palmer, Philip Sherrard, and Kalistos Ware (4 Volumes: London: Faber and Faber, 1981), 2: 52–113, at 74.
19. Maximus the Confessoir, *Ambigua*, translated byNicholas Constas (2 Volumes: Cambridge MA: Harvard University Press Dumbarton Oaks Medieval Library, 2012), *Ambiguum* 7; 105.

Empowered by God's own Holy Spirit, the soul centers the self in God and expresses this divine centeredness in virtue and love.

Transhumanism or *Theosis*?

The notion that AI and IA alone will give rise to super-intelligence, super-longevity or super-wellbeing is not too far-fetched. Yet, the transhumanist scenario has no room for virtue let alone *theosis*. IA implants may make us smarter, but they will not make us holier.

Despite our current information overload, we should thank our AI and IA engineers for gifting our civilization with high-speed computing and communicating. We now enjoy an increasingly rich technological environment that is inevitably influencing our humanity in the same manner that other environmental stimuli influence human behavior.

Having access to immediate information can be vital to opening our minds to new ideas, provided we are capable of discerning between accurate vs false information. Being able to interact with like-minded friends across international borders in virtual reality settings can provide a sense of community to overcome a sense of isolation. Isolation and depression frequently come together, so virtual community could become a means of grace to rescue us from loneliness and despair. For all this, we thank the AI industry.

Still, we are asking about one specific prospect, namely, intelligence amplification through deep brain digital implants. What about the possibility of AI's impact on *theosis,* on the divinization of human beings? On the pursuit of virtue? On the love of neighbor?

What a deep brain implant could accomplish is to provide our brain with access to a larger pool of information. IA might even enhance our capacity for computation. But there is no reason to think that IA could actually amplify our intelligence. More and faster information processing would have no impact on one's capacity for reasoning with that information.

More importantly, for our discussion here, IA should not be expected to strengthen or weaken our soul's capacity to center the self, let alone re-center the self in God. That *theosis* function of the soul relies on both free will and empowerment by God's Holy Spirit.

Conclusion

In summary, AI along with IA and other technological advancements will continue to develop with both positive and negative impacts on human life. The idea that deep brain implants would provide complex information directly to our brains is limited by the neurobiological realities of how neurons function and respond to stimuli. However, whether AI is *ex vivo* or IA is *in vivo*, machine intelligence may well influence a person's actions once they engage with it. But we must dub both AI and IA as an environmental stimulus, not an essential component of our soul.

Finally, as with any other environmental stimulus, we are called to take responsibility for how we interpret incoming information and behave appropriately by discerning between what is true and what is intended to manipulate and derail for personal gain.

References

*The footnote references in gray are not below, but maybe they should be?

Bellier, L, A Llorens, D Marciano, A Gunduz, G Schalk, P Brunner, and RT Knight. 'Music Can Be Reconstructed from Human Auditory Cortex Activity Using Nonlinear Decoding Models', in *PLoS Biol* 21, no 8 (Aug 2023): e3002176.

Hu, R, E Eskandar, and Z Williams. 'Role of Deep Brain Stimulation in Modulating Memory Formation and Recall', in *Neurosurg Focus* 27, no 1 (Jul 2009): E3.

Huang, J, and M Tan. 'The Role of Chatgpt in Scientific Communication: Writing Better Scientific Review Articles', in *Am J Cancer Res* 13, no 4 (2023): 1148–54.

Kapur, Arnav, Shreyas Kapur, and Pattie Maes. 'Alterego: A Personalized Wearable Silent Speech Interface', Paper presented at the Association for Computing Machinery, Tokyo, Japan, 2018.

Krauss, JK, N Lipsman, T Aziz, A Boutet, P Brown, JW Chang, B Davidson, WM Grill, MI Hariz, A Horn, M Schulder, A Mammis, PA Tass, J Volkmann, and AM Lozano. 'Technology of Deep Brain Stimulation: Current Status and Future Directions', in *Nat Rev Neurol* 17, no 2 (Feb 2021): 75–87.

Ranjan, M, N Ranjan, M Deogaonkar, and A Rezai. 'Deep Brain Stimulation for Refractory Depression, Obsessive-Compulsive Disorder and Addiction', in *Neurol India* 68, no. Supplement (Nov–Dec 2020): S282–S87.

Tye, KM 'Neural Circuit Motifs in Valence Processing', in *Neuron* 100, no 2 (Oct 24 2018): 436–52.

Chapter 22
Theology Engaging AI: Constructs of Human Intelligence and Metaphors of Translation

Michael Spezio

> *Popular opinion about "artificial intelligence" has passed through two phases. A generation ago, very few people believed that any machine could ever think as a man does. Now, however, it is widely held that this goal will be reached quite soon, perhaps in our lifetimes. It is my thesis that the second of these attitudes is nearly as unsophisticated as the first.*
> —Ulric Neisser (1928–2012), Brandeis University, 1963[1]

Abstract: As Theology enlarges and deepens its interdisciplinary engagement of AI, its work requires central tasks that are different from and beyond an agenda that keeps circling declensionist drains of assessment and critique. Public Systematic Theology in collaborative and critical conversation with the sciences of human and artificial intelligence now turns toward the challenges of constructing theologically informed, trustworthy accounts of human intelligence, creativity, language and linguistic meaning and relation, and understanding, and of developing criteria for assessing their trustworthiness. These efforts resist metaphors of mimicry and simulation in favor of metaphors of translation. An overview of recent definitions, productions, and limitations of GPT models helps clarify the distinctions between translations of human and interhuman intelligence, on one hand, and what AI machines offer, on the other.

Key Terms: Constructs, translation, metaphor, deep learning, generative pretrained transformers, LLMs, public systematic theology

---

1. Neisser, Ulric. 'The Imitation of Man by Machine: The View That Machines Will Think as Man Does Reveals Misunderstanding of the Nature of Human Thought', in *Science*, 139/3551 (Jan. 1963): 193–197.

Ulric Neisser's observation over sixty years ago fits the current need for greater sensitivity and sophistication about artificial intelligence (AI), in response to the lack of same in a number of influential views and proposals about AI. Widely regarded as one of the cofounders of cognitive science and as a scholar who 'changed the course of psychology',[2] Neisser befriended Eleanor and James Gibson at Cornell, was elected to membership in the US National Academy of Sciences and in the American Academy of Arts and Sciences, and directed a Task Force of the American Psychological Association (APA) cumulating in a comprehensive report on human intelligence in 1996.[3]

The APA Task Force's report[4] reviewed theories of human intelligence and the importance of culturally situated understanding in relation to what comes most to the fore in thinking about intelligence. It highlighted Howard Gardner's Theory of (Discrete) Multiple Intelligences in Educational Psychology (linguistic, musical, logico-mathematical, spatial, bodily-kinaesthetic, existential, emotional)[5] and Robert Sternberg's contextually and experientially situated, complex triarchic theory of general and perduring categories of intelligence oriented to tasks (fluid intelligence in analogy, induction, and insight; crystallized intelligence in linguistic comprehension; and social and practical intelligence).[6] Sternberg later developed these

---

2. James E Cutting, 'Ulric Neisser (1928–2012)', in *American Psychologist*, 67/6 ((2012): 492.
3. Cutting, 'Ulric Neisser (1928–2012)', 492.
4. Ulric Neisser, et al, 'Intelligence: Knowns and Unknowns', in *American Psychologist*, 1996.
5. Howard Gardner, *Frames of Mind: The Theory of Multiple Intelligences* (Basic Books, 2011), http://ebookcentral.proquest.com/lib/claremont/detail.action?docID=665795.
   The model has gained the largest following in educational contexts, mainly because of its political work in making room for children who are marginalized when their gifts and passions do not match models of intelligence constructed as analytical, linguistic, and/or mathematical. See critiques of the model from perspectives in Cognitive Science in Schaler, *Howard Gardner under Fire: The Rebel Psychologist Faces His Critics*, edited by A Jeffrey and Howard Gardner (Open Court, 2006).
6. Robert J Sternberg, *Beyond IQ: A Triarchic Theory of Human Intelligence* (Cambridge University Press, 1985).

concepts more fully in relation to cultural difference.[7] A primary conclusion of Neisser's APA report was that no existing available test of human intelligence, nor any combination of them, could grasp aspects of intelligence such as creativity, wisdom, understanding, practical sense, and social sensitivity, a reality that remains unchanged today.

As the field of theology enlarges and deepens its interdisciplinary engagement of and responses to promises and perils of AI, its work requires central tasks that are different from and beyond an agenda that keeps circling declensionist drains of assessment and critique. Theology in collaborative and critical conversation with the sciences of human and artificial intelligence needs to turn toward the challenges of constructing theologically informed accounts of human intelligence, creativity, language and linguistic meaning and relation, and understanding, and of developing criteria for assessing their trustworthiness. These efforts should be accompanied by work toward understanding how all of this centers the human person in community, for interdisciplinary theological reflection with a human face. This volume is intended to address these challenges, and to assist this effort, this paper highlights a few growth areas for interdisciplinary Theology as it engages its central tasks.

Theology and the Fields of Evidence[8] in Engaging Scientific Models of Intelligence

This chapter adopts a framework in which both theology— theology especially in the form of public systematic theology—and various sciences make their conceptual claims through the specific forms of constructs that they use for knowledge production and further

---

7. Robert J Sternberg, 'Culture and Intelligence', in *American Psychologist*, 59/ 5 (July 2004): 325–338.
8. A 'field of evidence' is a concept developed by Edward Farley, and intended in this paper as critical for Theology's task of proposing, identifying, and evaluating claims about determinate universals, via critical engagement with the sciences. These include Theology's use of the criteria of 'rational internal consistency, external consistency with other realms of factuality, and logical necessities or claims to such from universalizing accounts of being and knowledge.' See Edward Farley, *Ecclesial Reflection: An Anatomy of Theological Method* (Fortress Press, 1982) 87.

understanding.⁹ Those constructs are empirically guided and without them no knowledge and understanding of the claims emerging from them are possible.

What does empirical mean in this context? Empirical guidance means that the activity of construct formation and development works out and aims to grasp elements arising out of considered reflection upon experience (of a person, with a given body and living context, a life-world; of a community, with a given social and cultural context) that was compelling, puzzling, and insight-yielding, in hope of greater knowledge and understanding. Note that the view that reflective, scholarly claims regarding human knowledge and understanding use constructs in this way does not entail a reductive constructivist ontology, and does not entail claims about there being nothing real, that everything is nothing but a human construct, etc. Also important to highlight is that this methodological orientation to take up detailed readings of constructs applies no matter how one seeks to relate theology and various sciences. It is similarly at home whether one works from models of mutual conflict, independence, dialogue, or integration (among other major types).¹⁰ Each of these frameworks in relating or distancing theology and various sciences must present trustworthy claims to support the chosen framework, claims that rest in trustworthy, but corrigible, interpretations of the constructs involved.

For example, in Christian theological tradition and in comparative theology, the concept of atonement in reconciliation is one that is variously constructed in the form of extended linguistic models of atonement (for example, Anselm's 'satisfaction theory'), which are in turn developed into larger theories, sometimes called doctrines, of atonement. As another example, the human being-in-community as created in the image of God (*imago Dei*) is a complex concept with a number of constructs or models focusing on what 'image' means (for

---

9. See: Ted Peters, *The Voice of Public Theology* (Adelaide: ATF Theology, 2023).
10. For an overview of some of these types, see Ian G Barbour, *Religion in an Age of Science* (Harper & Row, Publishers, 1990). For considered examples of Theology and various sciences in dialogue, see especially Ted Peters, Science, *Theology, and Ethics* (Taylor and Francis, 2017); Ted Peters, *Science and Theology : The New Consonance*. 1ˢᵗ edition (Westview Press, 2019); and Robert John Russell, 'Five Key Topics on the Frontier of Theology and Science Today', in *Dialog*, 43/3 (Sept. 2007): 199–207.

example, morphological, functional, capacitative, relational models), each with a number of different theories emerging from them, along with theories fusing these constructs or holding aspects of them together albeit in some tension.[11] These larger models and the still larger theories that follow them spring from reflecting on compelling experience in light of the original concept. However, they never fully explore or exhaust the possibilities of meaning in the concept itself, nor it must be said, in the experience as reflected upon.

In the sciences, especially with regard to those helpful in proposing constructs of human and artificial intelligence (for example, cognitive science), the categories of intelligence (including emotional intelligence and social intelligence), memory, empathy, and emotion also have deceptively simple conceptual definitions. Scientific inquiry into these concepts starts with more complex constructs that inevitably fail to capture the full richness and many possibilities of the conceptual statements. Yet these incomplete and corrigible linguistic models are the means by which any and all systematic empirical inquiry accomplishes its work and generates scientific 'findings'. Scientific inquiry into concepts such as human and artificial intelligence specifies the linguistic models (that is, the constructs) of the concepts as a methodological requirement for further knowledge and understanding.

Concomitantly, interdisciplinary theological inquiry that remains at the level of unspecified or underspecified concepts and that fails to grasp and work knowledgeably with scientific constructs will fail to understand the concepts, their constructs, and the actual content of scientific claims. For example, empathy can be concisely conceptually defined, with an array of dimensions or aspects. Yet, what a given inquiry or research program in Psychological Science means by empathy is only clear once one engages its linguistic models, such as the items of a self-report questionnaire about empathy, the setting and description of an experiment about empathy, etc.[12]

---

11. For a recent use of such constructs in relation to AI, see Marius Dorobantu, 'Cognitive Vulnerability, Artificial Intelligence, and the Image of God in Humans', in *Journal of Disability & Religion*, 25/1 (Jan. 2021): 27–40.
12. Michael Spezio, 'Troubles with Empathy: Navigating Concepts and Constructs of Empathy in Psychological Science for Engagement in Theology and Philosophy', in *Philosophy, Theology and the Sciences*, forthcoming. The approach centering constructs as the locus of sound work in theology and the science overlaps with

Interdisciplinary theological engagement of scientific proposals about human and artificial intelligence, whether made in cognitive science or neuroscience or computer science or data science, thus attends closely to the meanings expressed in the constructs central to those proposals. Those intended meanings are absent or obscured in surface treatment of concepts alone. Remaining at the conceptual level not only entails jingle/jangle[13] issues but risks significant errors in claims about when theological and scientific constructs are in agreement and when they are not. Thus, if interdisciplinary theology seeks to assess and eventually guide work in human and artificial intelligence, it should not neglect the close reading of the expressed content of scientific constructs in a rush to select or reject scientific models or research programs out of a misunderstanding arising from that neglect. Such neglect is likely to result in mistaken endorsements or rejections of AI research programs based on theological criteria alone or based on misunderstandings of the meanings intended by the constructs and claims of those programs, along with an absence of attention to scientific evidence for and against the constructs and claims.

Errors like these will do little to advance theological reflection or to facilitate the role of theology in relation to human and artificial intelligence research, development, and policy making.[14] On the

---

that by Ian G Barbour, though Barbour focused on constructs as mental models rather than the explicit linguistic models that shape knowledge production. See Ian G Barbour, *Myths, Models and Paradigms: A Comparative Study in Science and Religion* (Harper & Row, Publishers, 1974).

13. The phrase 'jingle and jangle fallacies' appears on page 210 of Jack Block's 1995 paper, 'A Contrarian View of the Five-Factor Approach to Personality Description', in *Psychological Bulletin*, 117/ 2 ()1995): 187–215. He quotes both Thorndike (Edward L Thorndike, *Theory of Mental and Social Measurements* (The Science Press, 1904.) and Kelley (Kelley, Truman Lee, 1884–1961. *Interpretation of Educational Measurements* (World Book Co, 1927), respectively. Thorndike attributes the jingle issue to Herbert Austin Aikins, who defined it as, 'unthinking acceptance of verbal equality as a proof of real [conceptual] equality' (Thorndike, 14). Kelley defined the jangle issue as 'two separate words or expressions covering in fact the same basic situation [or concept], but sounding different, as though they were in truth different' (Kelley, 64).

14. Examples of this tendency to err in a rush to reject some and endorse other scientific research programs in Cognitive Science and AI, usually from theological presuppositions alone, include Tobias Tanton. *Corporeal Theology: The Nature of Theological Understanding in Light of Embodied Cognition* (Oxford

other hand, theology that can make a difference in these domains attends to and develops its own constructs of human and interhuman intelligence, creativity, language, and understanding. It draws on those to engage AI with close readings of the scientific constructs shaping the science of AI, recognising that they are usually absent, obscured, or distorted in popular discourse about AI. Thus theological attention as part of theological reflection appropriately weighs the evidential claims arising from its fields of evidence, in theology's task of bringing 'pretheological, apprehended realities to formulations intended as true [or at least trustworthy] by interrogating the fields of evidence pertinent to those realities'.[15]

Why AI? A Metaphor of Translation

Perhaps as good a starting point as any in this attentive effort is to ask the core question, 'Why AI?' Sociological and historical analyses responding to this question in the mode of declensionist narrative will propose theories critiquing AI and its central constructs as emerging from and perpetuating systems of power and control and science as social knowledge.[16] That is their answer to many questions, including 'Why theology?' Theology engaging AI must consider these accounts and what they reveal about structures of ongoing oppression and marginalisation. At the same time, theology seeks to understand the extent to which the origins of AI can be found in the play of human and interhuman intelligence, creativity, language, and understanding, as people seek shared and trustworthy accounts of their experience as reflected upon.[17] Thus, Theology recognizes that AI research programs are in part imperfect efforts by persons and

---

University Press, 2023); Jan Segessenmann, *et al*, 'Assessing Deep Learning: A Work Program for the Humanities in the Age of Artificial Intelligence', *AI and Ethics*, 2023, pp. 1-32; Oliver Dürr, *et al*. 'Meaning, Form and the Limits of Natural Language Processing', in *Philosophy, Theology and the Sciences*, 10/1 (2023): 42-72.

15. Edward Farley, *Ecclesial Reflection: An Anatomy of Theological Method* (Fortress Press, 1982), 183.
16. Helen E Longino, *Science as Social Knowledge: Values and Objectivity in Scientific Inquiry* (Princeton University Press, 2020), https://doi.org/10.1515/9780691209753. WorldCat.org.
17. George Lakoff, and Mark Johnson, *Metaphors We Live By* (University of Chicago Press, 1980);

communities in limited contexts to understand some of the most puzzling and compelling perduring aspects of humankind, via the concepts of intelligence and the metaphors of simulation.

Should such scientific inquiry via simulation even be attempted? The chapters in this volume point to many promises and perils latent and actualized in the products of scientific AI and in the ways that public discourse about AI products or machines create misunderstandings of the machines that necessarily misconstrue human intelligence and the perduring aspects of human being. That obstruction and obfuscation happens in public statements involving AI leaders and owners, scientists, humanities scholars, journalists, politicians, and influencers. Yet those efforts are not synonymous with the actual science, scientific constructs, aspects, and outcomes of AI machines. As Theology attends to the scientific constructs of AI machines, recognizing that the origins of AI involve human efforts at self-understanding, perhaps the best metaphor for AI is not simulation but translation. What might arise from understanding AI as a translation, not a simulation, of specific and limited forms of human intelligence, expressed first in concepts and then in scientific constructs of experience as reflected upon?

In his Foreword to a book of his selected translations, the poet WS Merwin confronts the conundrum that faces all translators, 'the most common cliché on the subject: that all translation is impossible'.[18] Still, he continues, we need translation and 'we begin with the idea that [what we are translating] is [and remains] the original—which means our relative conception of the original, as scholars, as translators', noting that 'the "original" may even figure as something that might exist in more forms than one'.[19] The entire endeavor, Merwin observes, is

> based on paradox: wanting the original leads us to want a translation. And the very notion of making or using a translation implies that it will not and cannot be the original.

Naomi Oreskes, *et al*, *Why Trust Science?* (Princeton University Press, 2021); James Woodward, *Making Things Happen: A Theory of Causal Explanation* (Oxford, 2003); Kathleen Slaney, *Validating Psychological Constructs* (Palgrave Macmillan UK, 2017); James F Woodward, *Causation with a Human Face : Normative Theory and Descriptive Psychology* (Oxford University Press, 2021).

18. WS Merwin, *W. S. Merwin: Selected Translations 1968–1978* (Atheneum, 1980), vii.
19. Merwin, *W. S. Merwin*, viii.

> It must be something else. The original assumes the status of an impossible ideal, and our actual demands must concern themselves with the differences from it, with the manner of standing in stead of it.[20]

If Theology could engage AI and AI machines through the lens of translation rather than simulation, what could AI be a translation of? What is or are the original(s)? That question then becomes one of the central motivating questions of Theology engaging AI, moving it through all three of Theology's dimensions of inquiry[21]: 1) interpreting the texts and rituals and practices of its tradition(s); 2) formulating provisional accounts of perduring aspects of humankind across and within times and cultures, for proposals about determinate universals (for example, human and interhuman intelligence, creativity, understanding as truth-intention[22]); and 3) formulating provisional accounts of 'specific autobiographical, political, and cultural situations that take form in a specific contemporary epoch', without absolutizing the present.[23] Of course, in order to avoid absolutizing either theology or cognitive science or related sciences about human and interhuman intelligence, Theology engaging AI and AI machines uses its constructs and those of the sciences with the understanding that they are all translations of originals, with some translations closer than others to lived human experience as reflected upon. Indeed, one source of profound perils inherent in AI and AI machines is that, though they often claim to be simulations of the original, they are not even translations of the original, but translations of the translations that have emerged from and have shaped historically contextualized knowledge and understanding of human and interhuman intelligence, creativity, understanding, etc. AI is not even a simulation, an intended functional copy of an original, and not even close to a transcript of a transcript of a transcript, etc, of an original, but a translation of a translation of a translation, etc, of an original. So theology engaging AI and AI machines can best progress by engaging the multiple translations that take the place of the originals when AI and AI machines do the work

---

20. Merwin, *W. S. Merwin*, xi.
21. Farley, *Ecclesial Reflection*, Chapter 8.
22. Farley, *Ecclesial Reflection*, 184.
23. Farley, *Ecclesial Reflection*, 188–189.

of human self-understanding, since this will allow theology to best address the translational distortions that impede the promise and promote the perils of AI.

Precursors to and Definitions of AI

Nils J Nilsson, Kumagai Professor of Engineering (Emeritus) in the Department of Computer Science at Stanford University, spent much of his career as part of the Artificial Intelligence Center of SRI International. His 2010 book on AI defines it as an *activity* (that is, of research, design, and implementation incorporating science and engineering, contrasted with AI as a machine or instance) 'devoted to making machines intelligent, and intelligence is that quality that enables an entity to function appropriately and with foresight in its environment'.[24] This is not, strictly speaking, simply a functionalist understanding of intelligence, since it refers to appropriate function and to foresight, both of which require development as concepts and constructs.

The November 2022 release of ChatGPT (Generative Pretrained Transformer) by the AI research and development company OpenAI and subsequent releases of updated AI machines by OpenAI and its competitors, have radically changed the contemporary scene, while falling far short of the many claims that human intelligence has been achieved and overcome by AI, even by Nilsson's generous definition. In some significant ways, we inhabit a different world of computational machinery, in principled design, implementation, and capability. In other ways, despite the ubiquitous use of the term 'AI' applied to any surprisingly capable computational machinery, AI that aims at translating translations of or at simulating human intelligence still has the status of 'not yet available' and is still limited to being versions of extraordinarily massive and sophisticated systems of pattern recognition and machine learning (ML).

In a seminal book on machine learning, Christopher M Bishop differentiates pattern recognition from machine learning in part due to the former arising from engineering aims of identifying statistically robust central tendencies from complex data and the

---

24. Nils J Nilsson, *The Quest for Artificial Intelligence: A History of Ideas and Achievements* (Cambridge University Press, 2010), 13 (emphasis added).

latter arising from aims in Computer Science to develop algorithms that were not modeled on human capabilities or human learning but that could nonetheless learn algorithmically from data to achieve outcomes similar to those achieved by humans under optimal conditions. Pattern recognition aims at automated, usually unsupervised, 'discovery of regularities in data', generally features of objects or events or descriptions, through the use of statistical models and computational algorithms, resulting in provisional categories or clusters of those objects, events, or descriptions.[25] For example, one can 'discover' or propose a topical structure of a large number of textual documents by clustering them according to an underlying statistical model relating their features to the proposed topics, along with their common features, where their features are not the actual words or sentences but emerge from a computational algorithm, as may be seen in topics modeling.[26]

Most efforts in pattern recognition work within one frame of a problem or situation and with a single, often very large, dataset, not aiming to generalize to situations or datasets beyond those that yielded their initial provisional patterns. In contrast, machine learning (ML) leverages constructs of human learning and translates those into computational learning algorithms. ML aims at generalizability across datasets, but still within a narrow problem space. Learning in this context means achieving generalizability in the problem space in response to new data in that space, to go beyond the examples used in training.

By Nilsson's definition of AI as a scholarly/engineering *activity*, one could classify both the human activities of pattern recognition and ML research and engineering as AI, to the extent that they are devoted to making machines intelligent. But most designs and implementations of pattern recognition and ML lack such devotion. They aim at solving practical problems in ways congruent with their measures of

---

25. Christopher M Bishop, *Pattern Recognition and Machine Learning* (Springer, 2006), 1. Note that this definition from Computer Science and Computer Engineering differs sharply from the concept and constructs of pattern recognition in Cognitive Science (see Ulric Neisser, 'Pattern Recognition', in *Cognitive Psychology: Key Readings*, edited by David Balota and Elizabeth Marsh (Routledge, 2005) 125–50.
26. Jordan Boyd-Graber, *et al* 'Applications of Topic Models', Foundations and Trends® in *Information Retrieval*, 11/2–3 (2017): 43–296.

efficiency, with little to no attention to generalization across domains of inquiry or any elements of foresight. Many contemporary uses of 'artificial intelligence' and AI terms nevertheless actually refer to ML. Sometimes these are augmented by structures and algorithms known as deep learning (DL). Some accounts of DL house it and ML inside of AI. DL is a relatively recent outgrowth of ML made possible by massive arrays of special computer chips called GPUs and novel insights into computational structures and learning algorithms in artificial neural networks. DL is 'deep' and 'learning' because it 1) uses many layers of computational, artificial neural networks of signal units, one atop another, 2) transforms the signals between input and output many times, specific to each layer, and 3) learns the connections between a given layer's signal units and between layers, such that the connections do not require human specification.[27]

Journalists often get these distinctions wrong or overlook them and resist clarification, out of concerns that journalists have about brevity, compelling narrative, and audience capture. It can be challenging to clarify or to avoid introducing conceptual confusions, sometimes wrongly identified as popular understandings, without interfering with a compelling narrative whose force appears to rely on those confusions. Often, journalistic errors occur in spite of the care taken by scientists in communicating their scientific practice, and in other cases come as a result of misleading public claims by scientists or their collaborators. One illustration of the former is a 2019 series of reports by the National Public Radio science correspondent Richard Harris. In his stories on using DL in diagnostic mammography to identify breast cancer, it is Harris and not the scientists who misapply AI language. The scientists he interviewed did not use the term AI, referring only to DL. In his own commentary for the story, Harris did not use DL but only referred to AI. Harris did not change this practice in future reports in the same series, even though the term AI generally did not appear in any quotes by physicians or scientists but only in his own characterizations of what they said. On at least one occasion, Harris inserted 'artificial intelligence' directly into a quotation in which the scientist being interviewed originally reference

---

27. Ian Goodfellow, *et al*, Deep Learning (MIT press, 2016); John D Kelleher, *Deep Learning* (MIT Press, 2019).

DL.²⁸ Theology engaging AI can take note of when public discourse about AI, including public discourse by journalists, scientists, and engineers, is inconsistent with the concepts and constructs used in peer-reviewed reports.

What is Different Now? Is it AI?

What is different now? Is what is different AI? Yes, according to more recent definitions of AI. Definitions have AI as a research and/or engineering activity, sometimes requiring devotion to making machines intelligent, sometimes not, have largely given way to arguments, perhaps inspired by Alan Turing and his famous test, that AI machines are intelligent if the speed, form, and content of their *outputs* would seem to humans to require human and interhuman intelligence had they been done by humans, regardless of how or why the machines in fact yielded them.

The 2021 Report of the US National Security Commission on Artificial Intelligence used the following definition, comprised of various dimensions:

1. Any artificial system that performs tasks under varying and unpredictable circumstances without significant human oversight, or that can learn from experience and improve performance when exposed to data sets.
2. An artificial system developed in computer software, physical hardware, or other context that solves tasks requiring human-like perception, cognition, planning, learning, communication, or physical action.

---

28. For example, https://www.npr.org/sections/health-shots/2019/04/30/718413798/as-artificial-intelligence-moves-into-medicine-the-human-touch-could-be-a-casual; https://www.npr.org/sections/health-shots/2019/04/01/707675965/training-a-computer-to-read-mammograms-as-well-as-a-doctor. Personal communications with Harris elicited this response: 'Dr Lehman did indeed use the term 'deep learning' to describe an algorithm. (Andrew Ng at Stanford helped popularize that expression). I made a judgment call that, in context, listeners would intuit that she was talking about a form of artificial intelligence. It is distracting to interrupt a narrative all the time to define terms. I can tell you disagree with that judgment call.' The original scientific study also did not use the term AI or 'artificial intelligence', but instead used 'deep learning' and DL; see: Constance D Lehman, *et al*, 'Mammographic Breast Density Assessment Using Deep Learning: Clinical Implementation', in *Radiology*, 290/1 (Jan 2019): 52–58.

3. An artificial system designed to think or act like a human, including cognitive architectures and neural networks.
4. A set of techniques, including machine learning that is designed to approximate a cognitive task.
5. An artificial system designed to act rationally, including an intelligent software agent or embodied robot that achieves goals using perception, planning, reasoning, learning, communicating, decision-making, and acting.[29]

Dimension 1 is so general that it likely characterizes a wide array of pattern recognition and machine learning and deep learning efforts and machines (see below for a discussion of these terms). Dimension 3's inclusion of mere acting like a human allows it to apply to a narrow range of Generative Pretrained Transformers (GPTs) that have emerged since OpenAI announced ChatGPT in November 2022. The other dimensions apply only with difficulty or by stretching or distorting constructs of human and interhuman intelligence.

The 2021 Panel Report of its study of 100 years of AI references Nilsson's definition and notes that it entails a focus on normativity, especially as AI machines have humans in their environments.[30] Ultimately it sets aside Nilsson's definition in favor of an alternative, again specified as an activity: 'artificial intelligence is about getting a machine to carry out behaviors that we think of as requiring intelligence.'[31] Released over a year prior to the OpenAI ChatGPT release, the report concludes that "the field is still far from producing fully general AI systems."[32] That distance seems to now be less than it once was. The 2023 AI Index Report of the Institute for Human-Centered AI at Stanford University categorizes ChatGPT and similar machines as AI but does not itself define AI out of an inability to navigate many competing conceptions.[33]

---

29. See also the John S McCain National Defense Authorization Act for Fiscal Year 2019, Pub. L. 115-232, 132 Stat. 1636, 1965 (2018).
30. Michael L Littman, *et al, Gathering Strength, Gathering Storms: The One Hundred Year Study on Artificial Intelligence (AI100) 2021 Study Panel Report*. Stanford University, 2021, http://ai100.stanford.edu/2021-report.
31. Littman, *et al, Gathering Strength*, 78.
32. Littman, *et al, Gathering Strength*, 8.
33. See both Saurabh Mishra, *et al, Measurement in AI Policy: Opportunities and Challenges*. arXiv:2009.09071, arXiv, 10 Sept. 2020. *arXiv.org*, http://arxiv.org/abs/2009.09071; and Nestor Maslej, *et al, Artificial Intelligence Index Report 2023*

Generative Pretrained Transformers are Large Language Models (LLMs) now capable of generating non-deterministic outputs to human queries across a wide array of areas of inquiry, along with generating images and videos from text inputs alone, or generating text outputs from a variety of nontextual inputs, taking from five seconds to a minute or so with most tasks. Their outputs can appear strikingly similar to human responses, though they generally read or sound or appear rigid, inflexible, and repetitive. The outputs can be wrong but appear falsely certain. They can be inconsistent, and it is usually not too challenging to elicit important inconsistencies.[34] Still, what these systems do has never been achieved in human history, which is to say that for the first time there are automated systems whose training allows them to be widely and wildly general. They overcome the problem of catastrophic forgetting, a problem that occurs when a system's training solves a set of problems in one domain but then 'forgets' how to do so once it is trained to solve problems in a different domain. They really do produce outputs that appear as if a human could have shared them, but they do not even attempt to simulate or translate human intelligence in doing so.

For example, the current publicly accessible version of OpenAI's GPT is GPT-4, released in March 2023.[35] Despite having no specific training for any of the following standardized exams, GPT-4 achieves 80th or 90th percentile or higher on the Uniform Bar Exam, the LSAT, the SAT Verbal and Math sections, the GRE Verbal and Math sections, the AP exams in Statistics, Art History, Psychology, Economics, Environmental Science, US History, and US Government. Yet it does not do well on the GRE Writing section, nor on AP exams in English Literature and Composition. Also, given an image of a man ironing clothes on an ironing board that is suspended off of the rear

---

Annual Report. AI Index Steering Committee, Institute for Human-Centered AI, Stanford University, Stanford, CA, Apr. 2023.

34. For example, students in my course on AI Ethics & Justice had little difficulty in getting GPT-3 to initially generate an output with a statement of certainty that its textual outputs had no biases. After further prompts, GPT-3's outputs included statements about the biases inherent in its structure, largely due to the biases inherent in the linguistic texts constituting its training sets, as well as the biases of its engineering.
35. https://openai.com/research/gpt-4; OpenAI, *et al*. GPT-4 Technical Report. 2024, https://arxiv.org/abs/2303.08774.

of a moving taxi (see https://www.barnorama.com/wp-content/uploads/2016/12/03-Confusing-Pictures.jpg), and given the prompt: 'What is unusual about this image?', GPT-4's output is: 'The unusual thing about this image is that a man is ironing clothes on an ironing board attached to the roof of a moving taxi', which is impressive in its visual object recognition performance but sounds rote and does not at all suggest an 'understanding' of the scene, contrary to what OpenAI claimed in its release report.[36] There is, for example, no reference to the person's agency in and possible purposes of the unusual arrangement (perhaps he is late for an important interview?), and no reference to the care that the driver must be taking in what must be an exceedingly rare cooperative arrangement between driver and passenger. GPT-4 has about 1.8 trillion parameters and about 120 layers, making it about ten times the size of the previous version, GPT-3. Its training cost over $60 million over about 100 days, with a training set consisting of roughly 13 trillion tokens.[37]

When prompted by an input asking whether GPT-4 is artificial intelligence, GPT-4's output is:

> GPT-4 falls under the umbrella of AI because it performs tasks that require human-like capabilities, such as generating coherent and contextually relevant text, answering questions, summarizing content, translating languages, and more. It mimics aspects of human intelligence, particularly in the domain of natural language processing and generation. At the same time, GPT-4 is a specific type of machine learning model—a deep learning model—built using transformer architecture . . . In summary, GPT-4 is considered artificial intelligence because it achieves tasks that require human-like cognitive functions. It achieves these capabilities through machine learning, more specifically through deep learning techniques. Thus, GPT-4 embodies the integration of AI and ML, showcasing how advanced ML models contribute to the broader goals of artificial intelligence.

---

36. GPT-4 Technical Report. 2024, 36.
37. A token is a designated unit of meaning for the purpose of system training. Tokens include individual letters, words, a specific punctuation mark, specific phrases, and various groupings of these units. Tokenisation is part of training and uses the frequency of units of information and their cooccurrences, not only of words or phrases alone, to flexibly encode (that is, represent) inputs a

But does GPT-4 mimic or simulate or translate human intelligence or other forms of human cognition? When prompted about whether GPT-4 as a system actually mimics human cognition or only the outputs of human cognition, GPT-4's output conflicts with statements in its output just prior:

> ### Not Mimicking Human Cognitive Functions
> Human cognitive functions involve complex processes like reasoning, understanding, learning from experience, emotional responses, consciousness, and problem-solving strategies that are deeply intertwined with our physical brains and life experiences. Cognitive functions are not just about producing outputs (like language) but also involve how we perceive the world, how we process and integrate information, and how we apply knowledge to navigate new situations.
> GPT-4 does not mimic these underlying cognitive processes. It does not "understand" information in the way humans do; it does not have consciousness, emotions, or personal experiences. Its "learning" is not akin to human learning, which involves conceptual understanding, making connections between different pieces of knowledge, and applying these understandings in varied contexts based on experience.

These are remarkably pseudo-human outputs, generated in under five seconds. GPT-4 is a highly capable, engineered system, and its training clearly yields outputs that separate language about mimicking human outputs from language about mimicking or simulating human understanding, intelligence, and other cognitive features. These distinctions are important, for what they reveal about the real novelty of these engineered systems and about the distance between them and simulations or translations of human and interhuman intelligence. Human discourse about these systems and about AI would be much clearer and more helpful if it, too, maintained and developed these distinctions.

Looking Ahead: Central Tasks of Theology Engaging AI

This paper began by reflecting on perspectives from Ulric Neisser, noting the current relevance of his observation about AI being possible but still some distance away. Similarly, scientific constructs and tests of human and interhuman intelligence were, for Neisser in the mid-

1990s, and still are incapable of grasping aspects of intelligence such as creativity, wisdom, understanding, practical sense, and social sensitivity. Theology that robustly engages and seeks to shape public understandings of AI in its contemporary situation needs to know about and work deftly with constructs of intelligence emerging from Cognitive Science and from AI engineering. Recommendations for theological engagement of AI stressed the need to attend to the scientific constructs of a range of evidentially and theoretically sound proposals about human and interhuman intelligence, a number of them coming from Cognitive Science. By advancing and developing a metaphor of translation, Theology can critique claims that AI simulates or mimics human intelligence, via the rich symbols and constructs that the practices of good translation bring to mind, aiming at but forever missing the original. Turning to the science of AI itself and incorporating one of its more advanced systems yield observations of misleading and contradictory claims in current AI discourse. Especially for public audiences, AI discourses fail to make critically needed distinctions between pattern recognition, ML, DL, and AI. Worse, they fail to openly acknowledge and consider that the most advanced AI systems' training aims only at producing outputs that seem to be done by humans, and not at translating aspects of human intelligence for greater insight into who we are.

What is now left for theology engaging AI to do? Plenty, as demonstrated by the careful work in the other chapters of this volume. Here are a few proposals for theology for greater understanding and public guidance of AI: 1) to continue to develop and use its own constructs of human intelligence, understanding, creativity, and wisdom; 2) to engage much more deeply sound, evidence-based constructs of human intelligence and language from within Cognitive Science (for example, Sternberg's triarchic theory), while avoiding using only or primarily theological preferences in evaluating their potential for engaging AI; 3) to develop novel theological constructs that aid our understanding of the structure and purpose and gift of human language, without being too quickly absorbed by any one philosophical school; and 4) to develop a theology with a human face in engaging AI, moving beyond purely linguistic and textual analysis and critique and especially taking the reflected-upon lived experiences of AI designers, developers, and program managers very seriously indeed.[38] Many actualise their own ethical agency and their own quests of self-understanding as they consider the promises and perils of AI, and whether future AI machines might help advance the self-understanding of human being by clarifying the perduring aspects of the determinate situations, states, and possibilities of humans in and for community with one another.

---

38. See recent publications on this exact point: Tricia A Griffin, *et al*, 'The Ethical Wisdom of AI Developers', in *AI and Ethics*, March 2024. https://doi.org/10.1007/s43681-024-00458-x; and Griffin, Tricia A., et al. "The Ethical Agency of AI Developers." *AI and Ethics*, Jan. 2023. https://doi.org/10.1007/s43681-022-00256-3.

Agathon: A Journal of Ethics and Value in the Modern World, Vol 10/2025

Chapter 23
AI Algorithms and Human Free Will

Anselm Ramelow, OP

> 'Forasmuch as a human person is rational, it is necessary that a human person have a free will.'
> —Thomas Aquinas, *Summa Theologica*, II.I.Q.83.A1

Abstract: As the ability of algorithms to predict and manipulate human behavior in the commercial and political sphere has risen to an unprecedented level, questions about human free will become poignant. What does it mean that neural networks have statistical knowledge of our human choices before they occur? Do our very own habits, which they exploit, become a threat to our free choices? The answer to this question—developed here with the help of Thomas Aquinas—depends on the meaning of such statistics, but also in getting the relationship between free will and habits right on a more general level. Moral habits in particular (virtues) do in fact facilitate human freedom in the face of manipulation. But in the end, much may still depend on the object of this technology becoming its subject.

Key Terms: Artificial Intelligence, Free Will, Virtue and Habits, Determinism, Social Statistics.

Do algorithms produced by Artificial Intelligence (AI) so determine our buying (and other) habits that we lose our freedom to choose? Is our free will incarcerated in an algorithmic prison? The answer to this question depends on how we understand the relationship between our habits and our free will more generally. Virtue in particular, as a moral habit, may serve to liberate the will from such algorithmically prompted inclinations.

AI is becoming increasingly sophisticated not only in *predicting* human choices—especially consumer choices—but also in *manipulating* them. Both aspects are, of course, related: predictability is a necessary condition for the creation of devices that control and manipulate behavior. Today's tacit and sometimes overt belief in determinism combined with predictability and manipulability has a history, related particularly to assumptions of the Enlightenment.[1] Only a deeper history of metaphysics and anthropology, one earlier than the Enlightenment, will give us a better understanding of our predicament.

The Machine Model of Nature and Human Nature

Our Enlightenment ancestors made the mechanical model the paradigm for the explanation of nature. All of nature looks like a church tower clock operated by meshing gears. The machine model of nature allowed for the development of equally mechanical technologies of control and that may have inspired the mechanical outlook on nature in the first place.[2]

In the 'Dialectic of the Enlightenment', Adorno and Horkheimer argued that this began to include human nature and that the subject of this control, the human being, became itself an object of it. While they may have thought of advertisement and propaganda—still relevant today—BF Skinner even envisioned as positive a program of behaviorist conditioning of all society in his novel *Walden Two*. But all sides seemed to agree. Adorno, for example, approvingly quotes Oswald Spengler's observations on how mass media control modern mobs and how this subverts freedom of thought; says Spengler: 'once upon a time one could hardly dare to think freely; now we may, but we have lost our ability to do so; now one only wants to think what

---

1. See the best-selling book by Robert M Sapolsky, *Determined: A Science of Life* (New York: Penguin, 2023).
2. This, at least, was the thesis of Martin Heidegger, „Die Frage nach der Technik', in Martin Heidegger, *Die Technik und die Kehre* (Pfullingen: Neske, 1962), 5–36. It is also echoed in a recent papal encyclical, which mentions 'the scientific and experimental method, which in itself is already a technique of possession, mastery and transformation', *Laudato Si*, no 106.

one ought to want [to think], and precisely this is experienced as freedom'.[3] Is this so far from our own contemporary predicament?

The prediction and manipulation of minds is, of course, even older. Even ancient Greece knew propaganda;[4] Machiavelli's whole thought is based on it; J Bentham's *Panopticon*—often used in the current imagination surrounding AI—aimed at the manipulation of prison inmates by observation, and E Durkheim saw religion itself as providing a form of sociological control and order.

It was also in the time of Durkheim that *social statistics* (for suicide, suicide statistics) moved into the awareness of thinkers and generated worries about free will. In the case of statistics of crime, the very notion of a 'crime' seems to become problematic. For a crime is punishable precisely because it is a free act, and we are responsible for it. But if the act is statistically predictable, then how free are we, really?

Today, this question does indeed arise in the judicial system, where brain studies increasingly play a role, and notions of culpability are more and more replaced—though it is not quite clear with what. Behavioral conditioning by AI would be one possibility. In American courts, algorithms are already used to set bail or prison sentences, based on statistics of recidivism. Why not use it to modulate the criminal propensities themselves? If we can do it in the commercial sphere, why not in the criminal sphere? In the commercial sphere, the learning algorithms of neural networks take the statistics of our online behavior to create a profile that allows for the prediction and manipulation of our commercial choices.[5] Why should this be different for criminal choices?

Such considerations depend on the basic idea that statistical regularities in our behavior imply a threat to free will. This worry, too, is not new. We find this question taken up by the early modern

---

3. *Einst durfte man nicht wagen, frei zu denken; jetzt darf man es, aber man kann es nicht mehr. Man will nur noch denken, was man wollen soll, und eben das empfindet man als seine Freiheit.* And therefore: *Ein Demokrat vom alten Schlage würde heute nicht Freiheit für die Presse, sondern von der Presse fordern,* . . . Quoted in Theodor W Adorno, ‚Spengler nach dem Untergang; Zu Oswald Spenglers 70. Geburtstag', in *Der Monat* 20 (1950): 115–128, at 118 (my translation).
4. Nigel Spivey, *Understanding Greek Sculpture—Ancient Meanings, Modern Readings* (London: Thames and Hudson 1996), 197.
5. Vividly illustrated in the Netflix documentary *The Social Dilemma*.

scholasticism of Spanish Jesuits,[6] and in an incipient form in St Thomas Aquinas himself—and hence there may be some hope of finding an answer to our contemporary worries in Aquinas himself.

Divine Foreknowledge and Human Free Will

Going back to the pre-Enlightenment era, scholastic thinkers may have various advantages. Medievals may avoid some unnecessary Enlightenment prejudices. And it may help us to ask our questions in the widest possible framework, the one that gives us the widest lay of the land.

This framework is metaphysical and theological. Thus, the early Spanish Jesuits raised our question in the context of divine foreknowledge of our free human acts. That is, these theologians looked at our question from the widest possible viewpoint, which is God's. Without this analogy we may fail to see the implicitly theological ambitions in the contemporary technological project. For it was the Christian belief that God does not just know social statistics, but individuals like you and me through and through, being able to predict, or rather foreknow our behavior, guiding it by providence and grace. Contemporary algorithms aspire to nothing less, claiming a divine prerogative by means of human technology.

Among the Jesuits, some may have hoped to find some grounding for divine 'Middle Knowledge' in the statistical predictability of human acts. There are two paradigms of predictability that the Jesuits developed—both of which are of interest in themselves, and not just for divine foreknowledge (where they were too obviously insufficient even then). One is the 'inclination paradigm', which can be illustrated with the example of how a mother will behave rather predictably, if one threatens her child. The other paradigm, of greater interest for our purposes, is the 'statistical paradigm'. It raises questions like the following arose: 'if of 1,000 inhabitants of Madrid, daily at least one commits a mortal sin, and if 999 have not done so today, and you

---

6. Sven K Knebel, *Wille, Würfel und Wahrscheinlichkeit. Das System der moralischen Notwendigkeit in der Jesuitenscholastik 1550–1700* (Hamburg: Felix Meiner Verlag, 2000). Tilman Ramelow, *Gott, Freiheit, Weltenwahl* (Leiden: Brill, 1997), 129–130, 137–138, and 355–356.

are number 1,000, are you determined to commit a mortal sin?"[7] The answer is obviously 'no'. But how is this to be explained?

The Jesuits explained this with an analogy from rolling dice, for this game of chance has statistically predictable outcomes as well. Similar questions will, therefore, arise when a predictable number has not yet occurred, and this is the last instance for it to do so. Should we then put all of our money on that number? The answer is, again, 'no'. For obviously there is no determination for it to occur. And the reason is that the previous rolls of the dice have no causal connection with that last one (or with each other). It is not a *causal* connection that is responsible for the statistics. The last role remains as free as the previous ones, and so does the choice of Madrid's inhabitant number 1,000.

To capture the difference, we need to distinguish between a 'collective' and a 'distributive' sense of the set of all moral actions and rolls of dice. Taken collectively, laws and regularities apply and make things predictable. But in the distributive sense, the individual case remains unpredictable. The whole and the part are discontinuous; as in other cases of compositional fallacies, what applies to *all*, does not transfer to *each*. It is almost a bit like quantum mechanics, where there are laws of statistic predictability overall, but in which the individual case remains indeterminate until we actually observe it.[8]

Something similar can already be found in Thomas Aquinas, although not as a sociological theory, for a group of people, but for a set of moral acts that an individual may perform. The structure is similar, for Aquinas thinks that even in the state of grace it is impossible for us to avoid all venial sin—at least short of a special grace that would confirm us in the good. It is a grace, which the Blessed Virgin Mary and, Aquinas suggests, the apostles after Pentecost enjoyed.[9] But we who have only 'ordinary' grace cannot avoid all venial sin in the collective sense. Yet this does not imply that we cannot avoid them *singly*, that is, in the distributive sense. We can avoid each sin taken by itself, but not as a whole, collectively. Statistically, we will fail in

---

7. Sven K Knebel, 'Vom Ursprung der Soziologie aus der posttridentinischen Theologie', in *Freiburger Zeitschrift für Philosophie und Theologie*, 41 (1994): 463-490, at 467.
8. For the rather complex Jesuit discussions of the example of rolling dice, see Knebel, *Wille, Würfel und Wahrscheinlichkeit*, 394-429.
9. Aquinas, *De veritate* q. 24, a. 9.

at least one case. And if we are *not* in the state of grace, Aquinas argues, then the same applies for *mortal* sins: we can avoid each of them singly, and that means we are still responsible for our choices; but taken collectively we will eventually fail.[10] Since each choice is still free, however, we can be reprimanded for our mortal sins even under these conditions. Losing the state of grace does not turn us into animals without free will.

Statistical Laws and the Inclination Paradigm

Now this obviously begs the question of why such statistical laws apply in the first place. What makes it so? And here is where the other paradigm, the 'inclination paradigm', may still play a role. Our fallen human nature, even if in the state of grace, is wounded in its inclinations and cognitive operations. Even apart from weakness of the will, Aquinas suggests that stress, tiredness, multitasking, and surprises will undermine our total attention and thereby the alertness that would be required to avoid all venial sins; *something* is bound to go wrong eventually.[11]

But the ultimate grounds for such statistics are *metaphysical* in nature and apply even before the Fall. Here, too, we need to ask the question in the widest possible framework, that of being and non-being. The reason is something akin to Leibniz' *malum metaphysicum*, namely the very finitude of our act of being or our createdness: we are taken from nothing and therefore retain an inclination back to nothingness; it is not just a psychological inclination, but a metaphysical one. It is the metaphysical reason for Aquinas' belief in something like Murphy's law: whatever can go wrong, will go wrong eventually. This is true for everything, but *especially* for our free will.[12] Because of its

---

10. Aquinas, *De veritate* q. 24, a. 12 and a. 13. The earliest to make this claim may have been St. Jerome (*Dialogus adversus Pelagianos*, MPL 23, 523–524); see Knebel, 'Ursprung der Soziologie', 471–472. See also Peter Lombard, *Lib. Sent.* I, d. 25, c. 5; Augustine, *De civitate Dei* 22.30. The necessity of grace for our perseverance in it was defined by the Council of Trent (DS 833); Aquinas explains that *this* is why we need to pray *et ne nos inducas in tentationem*; *De veritate* q. 24, a. 12 ad 22.
11. Aquinas, *De veritate* q. 24, a. 12c.
12. Aquinas, *De veritate* q. 24, a. 1 ad 16, with reference to Nemesius of Emesa (Pseudo-Gregor of Nyssa), De natura hominis, cap. 41 (PG 40, col. 776 A-B; edited by Verbeke/Moncho, 137) and John Damascene, *De fide orthodoxa* II, 27 (PG 94, col. 960 A; edited by Buytaert, 152). See also Gérard Verbeke, 'Fatalism

freedom, flexibility and variability, it may go wrong even sooner than other things.[13] This may also be the reason why there would have been a Fall in the garden of Eden in any case.[14] Even if Adam and Eve had received the grace of final perseverance after resisting the serpent, this would not automatically have been transferred to their offspring, who would then still have been subject to the statistics.

Clearly, even while Aquinas is defending free will, he is not very optimistic about it. Our actions have an undeniable predictability, not just for modern algorithms. However, unlike Aquinas, the learning algorithms that track our behavior tell us nothing about *why* we are so predictable. They are just programs that work with pattern recognition; they do not explain why these patterns exist. They can still exploit the patterns, of course, but even that does not say much about why they exist or what the predictability consists in.

Here, again, we can say more with Aquinas and also make some suggestions about how to respond to the contemporary challenge. When it comes to the 'inclination paradigm'—affective and internal inclinations that influence our free decisions—there are many factors that can influence our free choices.

Affective Internal Inclinations

It is important to recall how, for Aquinas, *none* of these factors can influence free will *directly*. If something is a free choice at all, it is

---

and Freedom According to Nemesius and Thomas Aquinas', in: Pontificia Accademia Romana di San Tommaso d'Aquino (ed), *Tommaso d'Aquino nel suo settimo centenario. Atti del Congresso Internazionale (Roma-Napoli, 17-24 aprile 1974), t. 1: Tommaso d'Aquino nella storia del pensiero, 1: Le fonti del pensiero di S. Tommaso* (Neapel: Edizioni Domenicane Italiane, 1975), 283-314. Further, Jacques Maritain, *St. Thomas and the Problem of Evil* (Milwaukee: Marquette University Press, 1942), 23-43; Michael Torre, 'The Sin of Man and the Love of God', in *Jacques Maritain*, edited by John Knasas (Notre Dame: University of Notre Dame Press, 1988), 203-13; Tobias Hoffmann, 'Aquinas and Intellectual Determinism: The Test Case of Angelic Sin', in *Archiv für Begriffsgeschichte*, 89 (2007): 122-56, at 138-42.

13. Aquinas, *De veritate* q. 24, a. 7c, ad 1 and ad 5. Anselm Ramelow, *Thomas von Aquin: Über die Wahrheit—De veritate; Teilband 5 (Q. 21-24). Translation and Commentary* (Hamburg: Meiner, 2013), 388-395.
14. Aquinas, *De veritate* q. 24, a. 7; *De veritate* q. 22, a. 6 ad 3. As Maritain argues, 'a free creature, naturally impeccable, would be square circle'. Maritain, *St. Thomas and the Problem of Evil*, 15. This is different for God; Aquinas, *De veritate* q. 24, a. 3.

based on reason, for only as presented by the intellect do we have options that leave us free. If we do not know what we are doing, then we are not free. What affectivity or brain damage, drugs or alcohol *can* do, however, is to distort precisely the representation of our choices in the intellect—not because the brain is the organ of the intellect, but because the processes of the brain provide necessary conditions for the intellect as they supply the *phantasmata* that the intellect has to work with.[15]

Free will, in turn, cannot move those lower, affective faculties of the soul except by the intellect (which creates the interface between them and free will); free will has no "despotic" power over them, but only a 'political' one, that is, by persuasion.[16] (This is indeed how, for example, cognitive therapy works.)

Sometimes, however, not only persuasion may fail, but much of our cognitive control as well. Even then, whatever our troubled state is, as long as free will is involved at all, we have at least some kind of veto power. We can still say 'no', and suspend further decisions. And that can often be the most prudent decision, as we should not make significant decisions in a state of confusion.

Some of the influences that Aquinas considers are remote, such as the stars. This sounds like astrology. But for Aquinas it was the best available science, and it is in some way the precise analogue to our modern ideas of determination by the laws of nature. For Aquinas, such laws are not found to be operative in the sublunar sphere, but only among the stars that move according to laws that are similar to the modern laws of nature in their mathematical and geometrical features. On earth, in the sublunar sphere, nothing moves with such precision; only the celestial spheres do.

This does not mean, however, that these celestial spheres do not have an influence on earth, or on us. It was the common wisdom

---

15. Aquinas, *Summa Theologiae* I-II, q. 17, a. 7; q. 10, a. 3; *De veritate*, q. 22, a. 9 ad 6; *Summa Theologiae* I-II, q. 17, a. 7; q. 9, a. 2; q. 10, a. 3 co. and ad 3; q. 9, a. 5 co. and ad 3; q. 77, a. 1 and a. 2. Thus Aquinas has a place for psychiatric treatment in his anthropology. Unfortunately, the same mechanisms can also be used by torture to 'break the will'. For the brain and the Libet experiments see A Ramelow, 'Delimiting Freedom: Aquinas between Brain Science and Choice Gone Wild', in *Communio*, 50 (2023): 132–163.
16. Though there is despotic control over the body; Aquinas, *Summa Theologiae* I-II, q. 9, a. 2; and *Summa Theologiae* I, q. 81, a. 3 ad 2.

of Aquinas' age (and well beyond) that the movement of the stars influences the humors of our body and, with it, our temperament (that is, choleric, hysteric, phlegmatic, melancholic). This may sound less strange when we recall contemporary analogues: the laws of physics may now operate in the sublunar sphere as well, and on the microscopic rather than merely the macrocosmic level; but they still influence our brain physiology, the distribution of hormones and our genetics, all of which are subject to the laws of nature. We also still believe in character types as being the outcome of all that, whether we use Myers-Briggs Type Indicators or something else.

What does all of this do to our free will? If we want to answer with Aquinas, we will have to say what he says about the stars: *astra inclinant, sed non necessitant*: the stars may incline our will, but they do not necessitate it.[17] This is, again, a place for an 'inclination paradigm', but one that does not eliminate free will. Genetics, brain physiology, hormones and the like can incline our will, but they do not necessitate it.[18] They influence our choices only through the interface of the intellect, not directly; and that means: they leave the will free.

Wisdom and the Free Will's Resistance

For all that, Aquinas is not terribly optimistic about what we will actually do. He thinks that only the wise person will resist those inclinations. And there are only few of them.[19] Given the Fall, wisdom may not be in sufficient supply, and hence the statistics apply. After the Fall, many of our natural instincts are also distorted by inheritance, by the cultural environment, or by our own previous choices. Such distortions will predictably occur and today are also predictably exploited and manipulated by "surveillance capitalism" and advertisement, in electoral campaigns, on social media and elsewhere. If this manipulation did not work, nobody would invest in it. Indeed, the majority will eventually go for the click bait or the proposed choices on Amazon or Facebook.

---

17. Aquinas, *Summa contra gentiles* III, 84–87; *Summa Theologiae* I-II, q. 9, a. 5.
18. The influence of the celestial motions is a matter of mere propensities that generate probabilities rather than necessitation. Aquinas, *Summa Theologiae* I-II, q. 9, a. 5; *Summa contra gentiles* III, 85.21–22.
19. Aquinas, *Summa Theologiae* I-II, q. 9, a. 5 ad 3; *De veritate*, q. 22, a. 9 ad 2.

None of this would have surprised Aquinas. Nor is all of this even the consequence of the Fall. Predictable regularities in human choices are part of even *prelapsarian* human nature in its unspoiled integrity. They are even part of the choices of the *wise*. How so?

We all have biological needs and urges, whether it is for food or in the context of procreation. All things being equal, we will predictably act on them, and this without prejudice to our free will. It is not a matter of weakness of the will or of being dragged along by disordered desires if we choose to eat when we are hungry. Rather, it is the rational thing to do, and we do so freely. There can be further reasons for *not* eating—for example, if we are fasting during Lent or if someone starving needs the food. And perhaps those who are wise have more reasons of that sort. But we all can freely forgo eating for such reasons. Yet, nevertheless, we all will eat regularly. And the majority of the population will procreate.[20] If we do not eat, we as individuals will die; if nobody at all procreates, the species will die. These would not be free or rational choices to pursue.

In many cases, we may not deliberate much about eating. We may just eat because that is what the situation and our body seem to demand. But this does not mean that we are enslaved to our desires. It merely means that this would have been the rational choice to make anyway, and nothing spoke against it. So we do this habitually rather than by conscious choice. And again, this makes us predictable but not necessarily unfree. Merchants can count on it, without thereby enslaving us.

Many of these habits without explicit choice are *acquired* habits. If I want to play piano or tennis, I have to practice and habitualise my moves. For if I have to deliberate every backhand or touch of the keys as a matter of free choice, I will be a miserable player. But this does not mean that I am not playing tennis or piano freely. In fact, my freedom is *increased* by such skills: I do not have to worry about the small stuff of life, if I have habitualised the way I drive to school. I can in the meanwhile think about the philosophical theory I am going to expound to my students once I have arrived. In other words: I am free to think about greater things. Yet I am also more predictable and hence more vulnerable to an assassin who waits for me on my way to school. But this does not mean that I am not driving to school freely.

---

20. In the sense that celibacy will be the exception; though the statistics on actual procreation may have changed since the advent of the pill, this is not necessarily an expression of greater free will.

In our everyday life, we may not make many conscious choices, but whole swaths of life are nevertheless governed by our free choices, because it is by choice that we originally developed those habits in the first place. This is also why we are responsible for them or take credit for them. The older we get, the more of our life is governed by our free choices and the more we are responsible for them. They become part of the choosing self that we are. Again, all of this makes us more predictable, but without prejudice to our free will. For free will is not the same as arbitrariness.

Among our habits are *moral* habits or virtues as well. They, too, make us predictable. I could, if Mother Theresa were still alive, predict that she is not going to murder me. But that does not mean that she has lost her free will. Virtue does not deprive us of our freedom. Vices, on the other hand, may deprive us of free will, especially if they deteriorate into addiction and compulsive behavior.

There is an asymmetry here. The reason for this is that our free will is a *teleological* faculty: we are freer in doing the good thing than in doing evil. Moral goodness and happiness are the fulfillment of our freedom. Our choosing self grows in freedom, if it grows in virtue, in good moral habits. And so, virtue and habits can increase our freedom even if they at the same time make us more predictable.

AI Algorithms, Free Will, and Good Habits

this freedom with predictive algorithms. These algorithms and their many uses will use machine learning and neural networks to extrapolate from the statistical patterns of our past behavior. But they only recognize their statistical quantity, not their quality or underlying reasons. That is, they exploit the various predictabilities of our behavior *indiscriminately*; they use good habits and fallen inclinations alike. They rely on our freedom *and* on our enslavement. To the algorithms they look alike. But they are not.

The distinction between good and evil inclinations may not be important for the algorithms (though, in fact, implicitly it is).[21] Nevertheless, for *our* response to the situation it is important to know the difference between good and evil.

---

21. After all, a key driver for our manipulation comes from emotions, not reasons; and among the emotions, unfortunately, it is the *bad* emotions (envy, fear, resentment, anger, and paranoia) that are most successful in getting our attention. That is itself a statistical fact.

When Aquinas says that only the wise person resists the inclinations, then a first response to being manipulated is to become wise and develop good habits. Such habits make us more virtuous and therefore free to do the good and rational thing—to choose what accords with our freedom and increases it with every good choice we make by it. Temptations and manipulations generated by algorithms will have less power over us. The same is true for other habits that we form consciously and responsibly and that give us the freedom to think about the larger picture. They give us the ability to take a step back rather than becoming conditioned to respond immediately to every click bait that presents itself.

Snapping at Click Bait

This much remains true. But what is required now of our wisdom and virtue exceeds in scale anything known to humanity in previous times. Yes, even earlier times recognized how we can be manipulated by propaganda and the press. But the internet and its tools of manipulation are beyond anything that Spengler perceived in newspapers. They are more fine-tuned, manipulating not only populations, but—like the temptations of the devil—microtargeting specific individuals.

And they are relentless. Algorithmic advertising aggravates all the features of our fallen nature. If Aquinas thought of stress, tiredness, multitasking, and surprises as undermining the alertness required to avoid all venial sins, how much more are we forced into multitasking by modern technology (treated in a body of literature, by Sherry Turkle and others)? How much does our stress level increase by all the things that we are constantly exposed to and that we really did not need to know? Good news is no news, and being constantly presented with bad news will surely increase our stress level.

Add to it the fast pace in the responses required from us when bombarded by email, twitter, and the like, compared to traditional paper mail—then who has the time to take that step back that we associate with the wise person? Who among us remains really free?

As Matthew Crawford has explained, the *telos* of the current development is to undercut the very use of our free will: if all our desires are anticipated and if all the solutions are presented right away, then the logical next step is to outsource even the mouse click that chooses the solutions to autonomously operating systems. In this scenario, our wishes are fulfilled before we even become aware of them.[22] Our intellect, the necessary interface between the world and our free will, is not even activated. And *a fortiori* our free will, which depends on it, must remain idle. In this way, our free will is not overcome by opposing forces or temptations, but rather short-circuited and put out of use as something superfluous. Needless to say, no virtues or other good habits are going to be developed in this way either.[23]

A Suggestion by Way of Conclusion

Under these circumstances, appeals to wisdom and virtue will seem naïve. If Aquinas was pessimistic in his day, how can *we* be optimists for human freedom today? But we still have that veto power—the ability to say no.

This does not need to mean a Luddite response, but it may mean to say no to the way in which the technology is set up now. It is a technology that we have made *by our own free choices*, after all. There is no reason why we cannot make the choice to change this setup. It developed for largely economic reasons—powerful reasons, to be sure, but not *morally* powerful. It is not impossible to change the economy of the system itself, as suggested by Jaron Lanier; it would be a system that is market friendly yet does not require us to sell ourselves, our souls and relationships, while rewarding those that produce the value.[24]

---

22. Matthew B Crawford, 'Virtual Reality as Moral Ideal', in *The New Atlantis*, 44 (2015): 28–36.
23. Self-driving cars will also make choices for us, which thereby cease to be our responsibility. We always lose skills and responsibility at once; we are technically and morally de-skilled at one stroke. And should our technologies then break down, facing us with a need for such skills, then we will find ourselves helpless like children.
24. Either through pay walls and subscriptions rather than selling oneself, or by two-way internet links that allow the right people to profit from its operations. J Lanier, *Who Owns the Future* (New York: Simon & Schuster, 2013), and earlier J Lanier, *You Are Not a Gadget* (New York: Vintage Books, 2011). In addition, one could develop systems that allow us to share voluntarily whatever and how much we think we should share about ourselves, so as to receive useful information on our own terms (I owe this suggestion to Mr Jason Manak).

But possibly the best change to the system would be one that supports the very wisdom and virtue that it otherwise suppresses. What if the power of prediction and manipulation is not put in the hands of those who use it to manipulate us for their own gain, but only into our own hands, where they belong? The object of this technology must also become its subject. What if *we ourselves* could follow our own mouse clicks on the internet as tools of diagnostics, for an examination of conscience and a greater self-knowledge, so as to allow us to lead what Socrates calls an 'examined life'?

In this case the very algorithms that threaten our freedom could be used for an increased self-awareness that would allow us to take that step back that is characteristic of those who are wise.[25] Right now these are surveillance technologies that are used against us; they mimic divine omniscience while pursuing the opposite of what God would want for us. God is no Luddite, but he would want these technologies to be used for human flourishing, and no flourishing is human, unless it is that of a conscious and free self.

Technology can play a role in this flourishing, even where it seems to mimic divine omniscience; for we are those beings whom God created in his image and likeness—and that means those whom he has called to participate in his divine wisdom and providence. Technology can play a positive role in this participation, but only if it is in the right hands and used with the right intent, that is, only if it is used in virtue and wisdom.

---

25. Naturally, the economic interest for producers of technology would be less; still, we do have Fitbits and other self-monitoring tools. However, the 'quest for the quantified self' has its own problems that require further reflection; see, for example, Shannon Vallor, *Technology and the Virtues; A Philosophical Guide to a Future Worth Wanting* (Oxford: Oxford University Press, 2016), 188–207.

Agathon: A Journal of Ethics and Value in the Modern World, Vol 10/2025

Chapter 24
Free Will, Selfhood, and AI:
The Avicenna-Bohm Theory

Yousef Jamali and Mohammad Jamali

'The connection and appropriateness of the human soul with divine essences and the celestial hierarchy are much stronger and more profound than its relation with the tangible world. In the realm of the divine, there are no veils, hindrances, or limitations. If there is any veil, it originates from the recipients and their capacity.'
—Avicenna[1]

Abstract: This chapter explores the intricate subject of developing conscious artificial intelligence (AI) with first-person inner experiences, drawing from a wide array of disciplines including philosophy, religion, theology, and science. It discusses the perspectives within Islamic and Abrahamic theologies, which do not preclude consciousness in non-human entities, and contrasts these with Islamic philosophical views that regard consciousness and the soul as divine gifts to organic life. The chapter posits that consciousness emerges from the evolutionary complexity of matter, a process seen as a manifestation of divine grace, akin to a phase transition leading to new creation. It examines the limitations of current AI in achieving true consciousness and suggests alternative routes such as bio-silicon systems and quantum consciousness theories, particularly the Avicenna-

---

1. Avicenna, & Madkour, I. (1969). al-Nafs (Psycological part of Healing). In al-Shifa (the Healing): Dar o alKateb al-Arabi
   This epitaph is an inspired creation, reflecting the themes and essence of Avicenna's (Ibn Sina's) philosophical inquiries, particularly those concerning the nature of the soul and the pursuit of ultimate reality. Avicenna, a polymath of the Islamic Golden Age, made significant contributions to philosophy, medicine, and science, leaving a lasting impact on both the Islamic world and Western intellectual history.

Boehm theory which integrates quantum mechanics with monotheistic philosophy. This interdisciplinary approach underscores the necessity of bridging various knowledge domains to advance our understanding of consciousness.

Key Terms: Conscious artificial intelligence, Avicenna, David Bohm, Avicenna-Bohm Theory, bio-silicon systems, quantum consciousness, Islam

The evolution of Artificial Intelligence (AI) has empowered it to navigate language processing and access vast information repositories, achieving an impressive mimicry of human expression. By conducting thorough data analysis, AI systems demonstrate behaviors reminiscent of human learning.[2] Yet, a fundamental question persists: Can AI transcend mere behavioral rationality to encompass human-like internal dimensions such as awareness, agency, will, emotions, and creative thinking? Without these attributes, any entity, whether human or artificial, operates merely as a machine. Thus, the pivotal philosophical inquiry surrounding AI centers on its potential to replicate the depths of the human mind.

The advent of such AI signals a critical juncture in science, philosophy, and technology, affectingreligious and philosophical doctrines while eliciting numerous moral and theological considerations. Despite advancements in AI methodologies—such as symbolic, connectionist, cognitive, embodied, robotic, neuromorphic approaches, and prospective quantum computing paradigms—inherent philosophical and logical constraints hinder progress toward strong AI. These methods lack the capability to attain consciousness, creative cognition and thinking, or achieve genuine free will.[3]

Looking ahead, is it feasible to progress towards a form of artificial or natural intelligence endowed with inherent selfhood and consciousness? This inquiry traverses philosophical, religious, and scientific domains. Philosophically, disregarding any technological

---

2. Y LeCun, Y. Bengio, and G Hinton, 'Deep learning', in *Nature*, 2015. 521(7553): 436–444
3. R Penrose, 'The emperor's new mind', RSA Journal, 1991. 139(5420): 506–514. Searle, J.R., Minds, brains, and programs. Behavioral and brain sciences, 1980. 3(3): p. 417–424. Chalmers, D.J., The conscious mind: In search of a fundamental theory. 1997: Oxford Paperbacks. Nath, R., Philosophy of artificial intelligence: a critique of the mechanistic theory of mind. 2009: Universal-Publishers.

constraints, is such a possibility conceivable? From a religious and theological perspective, particularly within a monotheistic worldview, is such a prospect deemed conceivable? If so, what are the ramifications in terms of legality, morality, and religious doctrine? Lastly, does contemporary science delineate a pathway towards realizing this aspiration?

This chapter focuses on exploring the feasibility of realizing non-human intelligence, delving into scientific pathways that could lead to the emergence of a sentient entity characterized by self-awareness, cognitive faculties, and volitional agency. Within this framework, two innovative approaches are presented and scrutinized, alongside a discussion of the ethical, legal, and religious implications inherent to these approaches.

Consciousness and free will

Consciousness, free will, selfhood, and the cognitive faculties of creative thought and awareness constitute subjective phenomena apprehended directly by humans through first-person experience. However, when considering other entities, determining their ontological status regarding these attributes solely through the lens of natural sciences poses challenges.[4] While behaviorism attempts to attribute these aspects by analyzing observable behavior and outputs, various philosophical arguments, such as Searle's Chinese Room[5] or Nagel's Martian Man,[6] cast doubt on the philosophical grounds for such assertions.

The ontological exploration of consciousness and free will entails two complementary avenues. Firstly, there is recourse to non-experiential sources of knowledge, such as religious doctrines and revelations, to gain insights into these phenomena. Secondly, there is a necessity to comprehend the essence and nature of consciousness and free will, and then critically examining the potential existence or absence of these attributes in entities beyond human beings, including non-human creatures and even inanimate objects.

---

4. Nagel, T., The Philosophical Review. What is it Like to Be a Bat, 1974: p. 435–450.
5. Searle, J.R., Minds, brains, and programs. Behavioral and brain sciences, 1980. 3(3): p. 417–424.
6. Ibid. Libet, B., Mind time: The temporal factor in consciousness. 2009: Harvard University Press.

Within the Islamic perspective, consciousness and cognitive abilities are not exclusive to humans but manifest at varying levels in other living organisms, including animals, as well as inanimate entities.

To further illustrate this concept, attention can be drawn to the following verses from the Quran:

> "The seven heavens glorify Him, and the earth [too], and whoever is in them. There is not a thing but celebrates His praise, but you do not understand their glorification. Indeed, He is all-forbearing, all-forgiving." (17:44 Quran)

> "Have you not regarded that Allah is glorified by everyone in the heavens and the earth, and the birds spreading their wings. Each knows his prayer and glorification, and Allah knows best what they do." (24:41 Quran)

Islamic mystics, such as Ibn Arabi (1204-1240 CE), and Quran commentators like Allameh Tabatabaei (1998) and Ayatollah Javadi Amoli (1995), have elaborated on these verses. They argue that the emphasis of these verses about the object's intrinsic comprehension of its mode of praise, proves and confirms a degree of consciousness and awareness for inanimates. This perspective intimates an acknowledgment of consciousness transcending human confines, embracing all facets of the natural realm.

Likewise, in the Abrahamic scriptures, a congruent perspective emerges:

> Psalm 148:7-10 (NIV) enjoins, "Praise the Lord from the earth, you great sea creatures and all ocean depths, lightning and hail, snow and clouds, stormy winds that do his bidding, you mountains and all hills, fruit trees and all cedars, wild animals and all cattle, small creatures and flying birds."

Within this hymnal ode, a call resounds for a multitude of creation's elements—sea dwellers, mountains, flora, fauna—to offer reverence to the divine. Their inclusion intimates an understanding that they participate in worship and possess an intrinsic awareness of their existence, emblematic of their interconnection with the divine realm.

> Job 12:7-10 (NIV) imparts, "But ask the animals, and they will teach you, or the birds in the sky, and they will tell you; or speak to the earth, and it will teach you, or let the fish in the sea inform you. Which of all these does not know that the hand of the Lord has done this? In his hand is the life of every creature and the breath of all mankind."

In this passage from the Book of Job, it conveys the notion that all living beings—animals, birds, even the Earth itself—exhibit perceptible consciousness. This serves as a testament to the divine's creative power and providence, underscoring the inherent awareness and interconnectedness within all facets of creation.

In the domain of free will, a similar perspective unfolds:

> "Indeed We presented the Trust to the heavens and the earth and the mountains, but they refused to undertake it and were apprehensive of it; but man undertook it. Indeed he is most unjust and ignorant." (33:72 Quran)[7]

Moreover, upon pondering the process of questioning and the concept of the Day of Judgment, a thought-provoking verse surfaces:

> "And when the beasts (and the fowls) are gathered together (in the arena of the Day of Judgment)." (81:5 Quran)

This verse intimates that even wild animals will undergo scrutiny and accountability on the Day of Judgment, underscoring the inclusivity of all beings in this process.

From a contemporary scientific standpoint, consciousness has emerged as a focal point of inquiry across diverse disciplines. Bohmian quantum theory offers a distinctive perspective, positing that the wave function, serving as a pilot wave, encompasses comprehensive information about the entire system. This pilot wave

---

7. While interpretations of this verse may vary among commentators, a prevailing understanding aligns with its literal meaning, suggesting a certain level of free will among non-human entities, for example:

(الطبرسی) T.A.-o.-l.ı.ı., Majma-o-lbayan (مجمع البیان). Vol. 20. 1981.

صالح, ص,, نهج البلاغه، خطبه۱۹۹, 10. Ibn'Arabi, M.a.-D., الفُتُوحَاتِ المَكِّيَّة [The Meccan Revelations]. 1204-1240. 2: p. 77.

influences particle behavior, dictating their trajectories.[8] Bohm himself proposed an interpretation suggesting that this phenomenon might signify consciousness, even at the electron level.[9]

Furthermore, the expansion of Bohmian quantum theory and its associated models reveals an intriguing dimension: the wave functions possess the ability to encode information about future occurrences. This revelation carries profound implications for understanding consciousness and its connection to awareness.[10]

Within the realm of standard quantum mechanics, a phenomenon of profound significance emerges: the collapse or reduction of the wave function. This collapse transpires when the wave function interacts with conscious thought, resulting in the manifestation of classical events.[11] Renowned figures in physics contend that consciousness plays a pivotal role within the framework of quantum theory.[12]

As a result, a central quandary confronted by quantum physics revolves around elucidating the mechanisms that governed the universe's evolution before consciousness arose. In essence, how did the cosmic wave function collapse prior to the emergence of consciousness? From a physical perspective, conceptualizing the actual progression of the universe before the advent of consciousness proves inherently challenging.[13]

---

8. Holland, P.R., The quantum theory of motion: an account of the de Broglie-Bohm causal interpretation of quantum mechanics. 1995: Cambridge university press.
9. Bohm, D., A new theory of the relationship of mind and matter. Philosophical psychology, 1990. 3(2-3): p. 271-286.
10. Jamali, M., M. Golshani, and Y. Jamali, A proposed mechanism for mind-brain interaction using extended Bohmian quantum mechanics in Avicenna's monotheistic perspective. Heliyon, 2019. 5(7).
11. Chalmers, D.J. and K.J. McQueen, Consciousness and the collapse of the wave function. arXiv preprint arXiv:2105.02314, 2021. Neumann, J., E.P. Wigner, and R. Hofstadter, Mathematical foundations of quantum mechanics. 1955: Princeton university press.
12. Wigner, E., Remarks on the mind-body problem. The scientist speculates, 1961: p. 284-302. Stapp, H.P. and H.P. Stapp, Mind, matter, and quantum mechanics. 2004: Springer.
13. Schreiber, Z., The nine lives of Schrödinger's cat. arXiv preprint quant-ph/9501014, 1995. Bohm, D. and H.P. Stapp, The undivided universe: An ontological interpretation of quantum theory. 1994, American Association of Physics Teachers.

This quandary prompts an engaging exploration into broadening the scope of consciousness to encompass non-living entities. By delving into these inquiries, we stand to unearth deeper insights into the essence of consciousness and its interplay with the fabric of reality.

In the realm of quantum consciousness, despite the compelling examples mentioned earlier, there exists a profound investigation into consciousness. Within this sphere, various comprehensive theories have emerged, such as the Eccles-Beck theory, Heisenberg-James theory, Orch-OR theory, and Avicenna-Bohm theory.[14] Significantly, the latter two theories extend consciousness to include elementary levels and simpler physical systems beyond human and animal brains.

Given this context, it becomes relevant to contemplate, from a monotheistic perspective, the possibility that consciousness and free will extend to realms beyond humans and animals. Consequently, scientific exploration of consciousness within a monotheistic framework could offer insights into the development of conscious artifacts. In Islamic philosophy, consciousness, particularly at the human level, is regarded as a divine gift bestowed by God, contingent upon the presence of a suitable material capacity and structure. Islamic philosophers argue that if matter, through natural gradual processes or human intervention, attains the necessary complexity and capacity, God, in His boundless generosity, would grant consciousness to that material system.[15]

Thus, the emergence of soul and consciousness within such a system is conceivable. This theological perspective views consciousness not merely as a human attribute but as a phenomenon capable of manifesting in any system or entity that achieves the requisite complexity, in accordance with divine principles.[16]

Penrose, R. and N.D. Mermin, The emperor's new mind: Concerning computers, minds, and the laws of physics. 1990, American Association of Physics Teachers.

14. Azizi, H.F., M. Golshani, and K. Nozari, Foundations of Quantum Approaches to Consciousness. Philosophical Investigations, 2021. 15(36).

15. Jamali, M., M. Golshani, and Y. Jamali, Avicenna's ideas and arguments about mind and brain interaction. 2019. Eccles, J.C., Evolution of the Brain: Creation of the Self. 2005: Routledge.

16. In relation to the existence of fixed divine traditions and laws, commentators refer to verse 43 of Surah Fatir:

"... *For the laws of God remain constant and unchanged, and the laws of Allah are immutable and unalterable.*" *(35:43 Quran)* The commentators have expounded on these laws to encompass a diverse array of categories, encompassing both

Hence, within the Islamic perspective, the notion of achieving non-human intelligence and consciousness (in the broad context of artificial intelligence) is not only conceivable but also deemed both feasible and imperative. This perspective arises from the recognition that the advancement of capabilities and the evolution of matter are oriented toward their ultimate objective: the attainment of knowledge of God, a pursuit inherently linked to awareness.

The assessment of the precise level of complexity and the categories of entities capable of hosting consciousness falls within the domain of natural sciences, encompassing both philosophical inquiry and empirical investigations. Islamic thought encourages the exploration of these inquiries within the framework of divine guidance and the quest for knowledge, acknowledging the potential for consciousness to manifest in diverse forms beyond the human sphere.

Approaches for Attaining an Artifact Platform for the Emergence of Consciousness

a. Fundamental Theoretical Approach

To create suitable platforms for consciousness emergence, a comprehensive scientific grasp of consciousness and its fundamental elements is imperative for the engineering endeavor. In this vein, cognitive science advocates an approach that fuses artificial intelligence and neuroscience to tackle the intricacies of consciousness and human cognitive functions, such as thinking and cognition. According to the tenets of standard cognitive science, human cognitive phenomena find explication through the study of the brain, comprised of interconnected nerve cells. By algorithmically modeling the dynamics and interactions of these nerve cells across diverse brain regions, cognitive processes can be replicated using computational methodologies derived from artificial intelligence. Thus, artificial intelligence harbors the theoretical promise of achieving cognition.[17]

---

abstract and tangible laws, natural and anthropogenic laws, and laws applicable to both individuals and societies. These laws are posited to regulate the workings of the world through the divine volition of God.

17. Thagard, P., Why cognitive science needs philosophy and vice versa. Topics in Cognitive Science, 2009. 1(2): p. 237–254. Kriegeskorte, N. and P.K.J.N.n. Douglas, Cognitive computational neuroscience. 2018. 21(9): p. 1148–1160.

Nevertheless, this approach encounters significant critique.[18] Despite decades of research and considerable effort, effectively modeling even basic cognitive phenomena has proven challenging.[19] Moreover, explorations in the philosophy of mind, alongside numerous philosophical and logical arguments, underscore the inherent constraints of this approach in elucidating creative thinking and consciousness.[20] The concept of free will, predicated on a type of intrinsic unpredictability associated with brain cognition, remains inadequately addressed within the confines of neuroscience, artificial intelligence, and cognitive science. Free will often grapples with being dismissed as an illusory notion.[21]

In response to the critique leveled against conventional cognitive science, a novel area of inquiry has surfaced among trailblazers in the foundational sciences. Leveraging the ontological advancements of modern physics, notably quantum mechanics, over the past four decades, the realm of "quantum consciousness" has taken form. Within this scientific domain, consciousness is perceived as a fundamental and tangible entity open to rigorous examination. Various theories, drawing from modern physics and innovative mathematical frameworks inspired by diverse philosophical and religious viewpoints, delve into the intricate interplay between quantum phenomena and consciousness, offering alternative avenues for comprehending and investigating consciousness' nature.[22]

Among these theories, the Avicenna-Bohm theory stands out as it specifically addresses the fundamental prerequisites for the emergence of conscious phenomena.

---

18. Penrose, R., The emperor's new mind. RSA Journal, 1991. 139(5420): p. 506–514.
    Collins, H., The science of artificial intelligence and its critics. Interdisciplinary Science Reviews, 2021. 46(1-2): p. 53–70. Katz, Y., Noam Chomsky on where artificial intelligence went wrong. 2012.
19. Copeland, B.J.J.I.C., IL, USA, artificial intelligence. Encyclopedia Britannica. 2020.
20. Penrose, R., The emperor's new mind. RSA Journal, 1991. 139(5420): p. 506–514.
21. Libet, B., Mind time: The temporal factor in consciousness. 2009: Harvard University Press. Lavazza, A., Free will and neuroscience: from explaining freedom away to new ways of operationalizing and measuring it. Frontiers in human neuroscience, 2016. 10: p. 262. Stapp, H.P., Quantum theory and free will. Springer2017, 2017.
    Roskies, A.J.T.i.c.s., Neuroscientific challenges to free will and responsibility. 2006. 10(9): p. 419–423.
22. Atmanspacher, H., Quantum approaches to consciousness. 2004.

b. Avicenna-Bohm Theory

The Avicenna-Bohm theory, rooted in Avicenna's monotheistic worldview, intricately explores the relationship between the self (mind) and the body (brain) within the framework of physical and mathematical principles. Drawing from the extended framework of Bohmian quantum mechanics, it postulates that consciousness, encompassing faculties like creative thought and free will, exists as an immaterial entity. According to this theory, the expression of conscious effects in the material realm hinges on the presence of complex material and physical systems.[23]

Within the paradigm of extended Bohmian quantum mechanics, hierarchical levels of quantum nature are introduced.[24] In this framework, the immaterial soul can exert influence over matter (brain) by establishing connections with more abstract material levels through the Bohmian quantum force. This guidance process necessitates the existence of non-local quantum substrates within space-time.[25] Thus, any material or physical structure capable of forging connections with abstract and immaterial domains, thereby subjecting itself to their influence, inherently harbors the potential for consciousness in alignment with the principle of God's endowment and creation.

The theory proposes a mechanism for establishing the connection between consciousness and physical phenomena, leveraging the concept of quantum complexities. This connection is characterized by a set of specific attributes ensuring its compatibility with the tenets of scientific inquiry. These attributes encompass adherence to physical laws, the ability for guidance and influence, a non-localized impact spanning the dimensions of space and time, consistent with the non-temporal and non-spatial essence of consciousness.[26]

---

23. Jamali, M., M. Golshani, and Y. Jamali, How the human mind affects its related brain? A mechanism for this influence, using an extended Bohmian QM in Avicenna's monotheistic perspective. 2019.
24. Jamali, M., M. Golshani, and Y. Jamali, Modified Bohmian quantum potential due to the second quantization of Schrodinger equation. arXiv preprint arXiv:2006.08459, 2020.
25. Jamali, M., M. Golshani, and Y. Jamali, A proposed mechanism for mind-brain interaction using extended Bohmian quantum mechanics in Avicenna's monotheistic perspective. Heliyon, 2019. 5(7).
26. Ibid.

Furthermore, the theory posits that this connection entails a causal non-closure at the foundational levels of physics, indicating that the progression of physical phenomena is shaped by higher causes transcending deterministic processes. The presence of a hierarchical structure is pivotal, facilitating interaction between fundamental physical levels and immaterial dimensions.[27]

The Avicenna-Bohm theory suggests that the emergence of consciousness hinges on the existence of multiple potential configurations (arrangements) in space-time and their inherent indeterminacy at the level of physical causes. It proposes that these conditions form the basis for the activation of consciousness and the proactive engagement of conscious will in shaping reality.

According to the Avicenna-Bohm theory, which amalgamates principles from physics, mathematics, and philosophy, the manifestation of consciousness and free will across various levels of material structures hinges upon specific conditions. These conditions are encapsulated as follows:

1. Spatial and Temporal Interdependence and Entanglement: The presence of spatial and temporal interdependence and entanglement is paramount for the expression of consciousness and free will. These phenomena permit the nonlocal influence of the immaterial mind on the material brain.
2. Hierarchical Structure: The existence of a hierarchical structure implies the operation of causal processes in both top-down and bottom-up directions. This hierarchical arrangement facilitates the emergence of higher-level phenomena, such as consciousness and free will, which exert influence and are influenced by lower-level components.
3. Multiple Quantum Possibilities: Within the spatial and temporal framework, the theory posits the existence of multiple quantum possibilities. These possibilities encompass diverse ways in which the system can evolve, giving rise to conscious behavior. The specifics regarding these possibilities and their physical conditions are delineated in the referenced work.

---

27. Jamali, M., M. Golshani, and Y. Jamali, How the human mind affects its related brain? A mechanism for this influence, using an extended Bohmian QM in Avicenna's monotheistic perspective. 2019.

4. Specialized Physical Design and Structure: The constituents comprising the system possess a distinct physical design and structure. This design enables the absorption, processing, and utilization of negative entropy from the environment to support the emergence of the aforementioned conditions in a low-entropy state. Negative entropy serves as a resource contributing to the organization and complexity of the system.
5. Harnessing Negative Entropy Resources: The system exhibits adeptness in effectively harnessing negative entropy resources. Through the utilization of this resource, the system undergoes structural evolution and development, crucial for its overall functioning and adaptability.

The Avicenna-Bohm theory furnishes valuable insights into the prerequisites for the existence of consciousness and free will within material structures. By comprehensively considering the interplay between physical and metaphysical facets, this theory offers a holistic framework for comprehending the intricate nature of consciousness and its correlation with the physical realm.

By embracing this expansive viewpoint, the theory posits that consciousness and free will extend beyond human beings and can be attributed to various levels of physical existence. While it accounts for the early stages of life, it also invites exploration of alternative models that meet the specified philosophical conditions. The extended Bohmian quantum theory, applied to quantum fields, offers a comprehensive framework for probing the manifestation of consciousness and free will in phenomena beyond the human realm. This approach fosters further inquiry and discovery at the intersection of philosophy and quantum physics.[28]

The theory sets forth several philosophical constraints necessary for the emergence of consciousness. These constraints include a hierarchical structure with top-down causality, the absence of closure in physical causes at the level of components, the presence of non-local properties in space and time, and the potential for growth and evolution toward heightened awareness. These constraints are

---

28. Azizi, H.F., A. Saberi, and M. Jamali, Shedding Light on the Origin of Life: A Generalization of the Avicenna-Bohm Theory of Quantum Consciousness, unpaublished. 2023.

addressed within the framework of extended Bohmian quantum theory, which extends to encompass quantum fields.[29]

Hence, when these essential prerequisites are fulfilled within the material realm, consciousness emerges as a transcendent entity, and its effects become evident in the operations of the material system. It is crucial to emphasize that the acquisition of these capabilities is guided by consciousness as both the ultimate cause and teleological purpose, exerting influence from the future onto the past through the non-local quantum structure of time. Therefore, the indispensable condition for consciousness emergence lies in the "potentiality" of acquiring these quantum prerequisites, rather than their actual realization.

Based on the foregoing explanations, the pursuit of engineering quantum material structures that adhere to the specified constraints holds promise for the potential emergence of intelligence and consciousness within artificial systems. From our perspective, advancing theories related to quantum consciousness, which explore the interplay between physics and consciousness, presents a promising scientific framework for elucidating the attainment of material structures conducive to consciousness emergence or the interfacing and emanation of consciousness within them.

A multidisciplinary engineering endeavor, drawing from the domains of chemical engineering, materials science, nanotechnology, and fundamental physics, can yield quantum substrates imbued with essential attributes. These attributes encompass spatial and temporal entanglement, computational prowess, interactive capabilities with the external environment, absorption of negentropy, and hardware's potential for self-improvement. By realizing these requisites, the effects of consciousness and its manifestations can be realized.

c. Fundamental Empirical Approach

An alternative avenue toward achieving consciousness involves leveraging biological processors.[30] Extensive research has centered on integrating silicon chips with nervous systems.[31]

---

29. Jamali, M., M. Golshani, and Y. Jamali, Modified Bohmian quantum potential due to the second quantization of Schrodinger equation. arXiv preprint arXiv:2006.08459, 2020.
30. Potter, A., et al., Hybrots: hybrids of living neurons and robots for studying neural computation. Proceedings of brain inspired cognitive systems, 2004: p. 1–5.
31. Warwick, K., et al., Experiments with an in-vitro robot brain. Computing with instinct: Rediscovering artificial intelligence, 2011: p. 1–15.

From the Islamic and monotheistic standpoint, which posits that the human brain harbors the requisite complexity for consciousness emergence and soul manifestation, brain organoids[32] or cultured neurons, serving as biological processors, may offer suitable substrates for consciousness and free will to manifest. However, ethical and legal considerations associated with this approach must be addressed, a topic extensively explored in existing literature.

Within the framework of Islamic philosophy, the potential for consciousness and free will hinges upon the complexity of the underlying material structure. Exploring this prospect reveals that even simpler organisms like insects or the C. elegans worm, with their limited number of interacting nerve cells, may possess the necessary complexity. Consequently, integrating silicon systems with nervous systems could yield robust biological processors capable of harnessing silicon chips' computational power while exhibiting cognitive capacities inherent in living organisms, including a degree of consciousness and free will. This approach is termed the third generation of artificial intelligence,[33] characterized by the fusion of high-speed computing capabilities with the cognitive flexibility observed in organic systems.

In the domain of engineering and practical applications, while the theoretical understanding of why complexity engenders consciousness and the specific nature of required complexity remains incomplete, drawing inspiration from the natural world can propel these technologies forward.

Bakkum, D.J., et al. Removing some 'A'from AI: Embodied cultured networks. in Embodied Artificial Intelligence: International Seminar, Dagstuhl Castle, Germany, July 7-11, 2003. Revised Papers. 2004. Springer.

32. Brain organoids are three-dimensional structures cultivated in the lab to mimic the development and organization of the human brain. Derived from stem cells, they provide a simplified model for studying brain development, diseases, and potential treatments. Although they have limitations, brain organoids offer valuable insights into neurodevelopment and neurodegenerative disorders. They are a promising tool for advancing neuroscience research and developing innovative therapies (Park, S.E., A. Georgescu, and D. Huh, Organoids-on-a-chip. Science, 2019. 364(6444): p. 960–965.)

33. jamali, M. and Y. Jamali, Biological Microprocessor as the Third Generation of AI, in The Role of Basic Science in Health Promotion. 2022, Academy of Medical Sciences: Shiraz.

Given the inherent limitations of conventional artificial intelligence approaches to attain cognition and consciousness, integrating artificial intelligence with living nervous systems presents a promising frontier for biological computers surpassing human capacities. These biological processors can learn, perform rapid computations, perceive, exhibit cognition, and even make decisions across diverse contexts.

Conclusion

Throughout this chapter, our exploration has delved into the potentials and constraints surrounding the pursuit of conscious artificial intelligence endowed with first-person inner experiences, from the perspectives of philosophy, religion, theology, and science. We have illuminated that within Islamic and Abrahamic theology, consciousness is not exclusive to humans, and the attainment of conscious non-human entities is permissible. Conversely, Islamic philosophy and teachings posit consciousness and the soul as non-material essences bestowed upon organic matter by the divine.

We suggest that through the evolutionary process, matter attains a level of complexity conducive to the emergence of consciousness; a kind of emanation from the continual grace of God. This transformative juncture signifies a phase transition and a new creation, the emergence of consciousness. Surah Mominun, verse 14, illustrates this concept, detailing the progression from the formation of bones and flesh to the inception of a novel stage in human creation.[34]

From the standpoint of natural sciences, we have outlined two primary pathways towards achieving a conscious intelligent entity. While conventional artificial intelligence, with its algorithmic framework, falls short of attaining awareness, agency, and creative thinking, alternative approaches such as the development of biological-silicon systems (brainware), or more fundamentally, theories of quantum consciousness, offer promising avenues. We emphasize that the advancement of such endeavors necessitates a

---

34. *"Then We made the sperm into a clot of congealed blood; then of that clot We made a (foetus) lump; then we made out of that lump bones and clothed the bones with flesh; then we developed out of it another creature. So blessed be Allah, the best to create!"* (23:14 Quran)

comprehensive understanding of consciousness and life, bridging scientific, philosophical, and religious knowledge domains.

In this context, the Avicenna-Boehm theory on quantum consciousness, rooted in Avicenna's monotheistic philosophy and Boehm's quantum mechanics, acknowledges the inherent complexities of the subject matter and underscores the interplay between scientific, philosophical, and theological perspectives. It illuminates the essential substrates requisite for the expansion and manifestation of consciousness, paving the way for profound interdisciplinary collaboration between science, religion, philosophy, and engineering. This convergence sets forth a new trajectory for future scientific and technological endeavors.

This discourse gives rise to numerous fundamental questions spanning deep philosophical, religious, and scientific realms, as well as encompassing serious moral, legal, and socio-cultural considerations. However, delving into these intricate topics falls beyond the scope of this brief article.

Acknowledgments

We extend our heartfelt gratitude to Prof. Mehdi Golshani for his invaluable guidance and support. Special thanks to Dr. Hamid Faghanpour Azizi and Mr. Asghar Saberi for their thoughtful cooperation and assistance, enhancing our work. We also appreciate Prof. Ted Peters for the opportunity to share our ideas on these vital subjects.

Agathon: A Journal of Ethics and Value in the Modern World, Vol 10/2025

Chapter 25
Artificial Religious Agents:
A Study on the Theoretical Feasibility and Normative Considerations

Daekyung Jung

'Religion is the vision of something which stands beyond, behind, and within, the passing flux of immediate things; something which is real, and yet waiting to be realised; something which is a remote possibility, and yet the greatest of present facts; something that gives meaning to all that passes, and yet eludes apprehension; something whose possession is the final good, and yet is beyond all reach; something which is the ultimate ideal, and the hopeless quest.'
—Alfred North Whitehead[1]

Abstract: This chapter addresses two critical questions: (1) Is it theoretically plausible for artificial intelligence (AI) to exhibit religious behavior? (2) Given the technological feasibility, should we aim to design and create such an artificial religious agent? In response to the first question, I posit an affirmative stance. However, the second question calls for broader public dialogue on the desired nature and trajectory of AI development, as it ties directly to discussions about artificial general intelligence (AGI). This chapter delves into the concept of embodied cognition as introduced by Humberto Maturana and Francisco J. Varela. It then critically explores potential pathways towards the development of AGI and its capacity for religious behavior. The chapter concludes by categorizing artificial religious agents (ARAs) and proposing further considerations for the development of ARAs.

Keywords: Artificial Intelligence, Artificial General Intelligence, Religious AI, Religion and AI, Embodied AI

---

1. Alfred North Whitehead, *Science and the Modern World* (Cambridge UK: Cambridge University Press, 1925, 1953), 238.

This chapter engages two paramount inquiries: (1) Is it theoretically plausible for artificial intelligence (AI) to exhibit religious behaviour? (2) Assuming the technological feasibility for AI to display such behaviour, should we aspire to design and instantiate such an artificial religious agent? Addressing the first query, my argument is affirmative. However, the second question necessitates a more public discourse concerning the nature and direction of AI development we should pursue, as it is inextricably linked to the discussion of artificial general intelligence (AGI).

1. Cognition, Life, and Behaviour

Chilean biologists Humberto Maturana and Francisco J Varela posit cognition as the crux of life phenomena. Accordingly, intelligence is construed as the capability to process information required for the self-preservation of an informational agent, or a living organism.

Organisms driven by self-preservation are subject to the influence of a changing environment. As an organism interacts with its environment, the organism's internal structure undergoes alterations. These modifications yield responses to external stimuli that differ from prior reactions. Maturana and Varela elucidate this process to explain the 'behaviour' of organisms. Hence, the difference in behaviour of organisms, from humans and other higher animals to simpler neural systems and plants, is one of quantity, not quality. By this argument, religious behaviours displayed by higher animals, including humans, can be perceived as originating from the interaction between an organism's fundamental self-preserving characteristic and its environment, a viewpoint that aligns with the assertions of researchers studying religious phenomena from an evolutionary perspective.

If this argument holds, by assigning to AI the primordial and ultimate goal of self-preservation that living organisms possess, and by providing AI with a body that shares the vulnerability of living organisms, religious behaviours can arise from AI. As per Kingson Man and Antonio Damasio, if AI is endowed with the principle of self-preservation and embodied within a susceptible artificial body, and it is exposed to machine learning in an evolutionary manner in terms of the implementation method of AI technology, the AI transforms into an autopoietic system that can possess a feeling equivalent to that experienced by humans and undergo a quasi-Darwinian evolutionary process while interacting with humans and other AIs.

In such a scenario, moral and even religious behaviours can emerge, as revealed by the evolutionary study of life on Earth. From the perspective of physicalism, human morality and religiosity do not originate from a mysterious immaterial force or entity (that is, immaterial soul), but something that emerges or supervenes on physical constituents. If the emergence of artificial general intelligence and its religious behaviour is theoretically possible, one must contemplate whether we should foster such an agent's development.

Artificial religious agents (ARAs) can be categorized into four levels, referred to as 'religious impact agents', 'implicit religious agents', 'explicit religious agents', and 'full religious agents'. The first three levels of ARAs represent weak AI, whereas the fourth level constitutes strong AI. In this sense, the development of ARAs from the first to the third level may not pose a problem as such agents are machines that help strengthen human religious behaviours. However, an ARA of the last level would possess agency equivalent to a human, including consciousness, free will, and intentionality. Ultimately, this issue is intertwined with the development of AGI.

If we desire AI to be a sort of tool functioning as a servant to humans, we should be critical of the development of AI in the manner suggested by Man and Damasio, that is, developing AI capable of experiencing feelings that living organisms possess, based on self-preservation and vulnerability. However, if we wish for AI to surpass the status of a tool and take its place as a partner to humans, we must strive to recognise such AI as an independent entity, allow it to learn religious traditions and scriptures, and thus enable it to perform religious behaviours.

To argue for this, this chapter will first review Maturana and Varela's understanding that presents cognitive behaviour as the essence of life phenomena and will then examine the origin of religious behaviour as discussed by evolutionary scholars. Subsequently, while reviewing the paths to AGI presented by Nick Bostrom, Man and Damasio, it will discuss the possibility of the emergence of an artificial religious agent. Finally, it will conclude by contemplating how we should perceive the development of such agents.

2. Intelligence: A Physicalist View in a Technical Sense

What is intelligence? Kingson Man and Antonio Damasio define intelligence as 'the agent's ability to achieve goals in a wide range of environments'.[2] Chungsik Park goes a step further and understands intelligence as the information processing ability necessary to realize goals.[3] Luc Steels, who researches artificial life and artificial intelligence interconnectedly, criticizes the narrow understanding of intelligence by AI researchers, and he points out that intelligence is more than problem-solving.[4] Noreen Herzfeld also points out that intelligence means more than problem-solving ability, defining it as related to 'abilities such as movement, speech recognition, and contemplation of the world, indeed, awareness of the self as existing in the world'.[5]

Despite the various definitions of intelligence, it can be synthesized and understood as follow: intelligence can be defined as the ability to process information, combined with necessary skills to achieve specific (or multiple) goals in various environments.

An important criterion that distinguishes between artificial intelligence and natural intelligence, two representative instantiations of intelligence, is the origin of goal-setting. In other words, artificial intelligence and natural intelligence can be distinguished based on 'whose goals or objectives' they serve. Among the artificial intelligence systems developed so far, those based on deep, reinforcement, and/or unsupervised learning—which appear to be autonomous and thus closely resemble human learning—perform information processing to discover patterns within the given data by learning on their own. Such a characteristic may seem to endow AI with autonomous

---

2. Kingson Man and Antonio Damasio, 'Homeostasis and Soft Robotics in the Design of Feeling Machines', in *Nature Machine Intelligence* 1 (2019), 447. Where many definitions of intelligence place goal achievement, Ted Peters places intentionality. Intelligence exhibits intentionality and agency. 'Where There's Life There's Intelligence', in *What is Life? On Earth and Beyond*, edited by Andreas Losch (Cambridge: Cambridge University Press, 2017), 236–259.
3. Choong Shik Park, 'Artificial Intelligence as Life: From the Perspective of Philosophy of Information', in *Ontology of Artificial Intelligence*, edited by Jung Won Lee in Korean (Seoul: Hanul Publication, 2018), 21.
4. Luc Steels, 'The Artificial Life Roots of Artificial Intelligence', in *Artificial Life* 1(1994): 75.
5. Noreen Herzfeld, *The Artifice of Intelligence: Divine and Human Relationship in a Robotic Age* (Minneapolis: Fortress Press, 2023), 6.

agency. However, considering that someone from the outside has to provide the data for AI learning and supply the energy necessary for learning and activity, and that the results generated by AI are not for the AI's own goals but for the goals of the person from the outside, the AI developed so far inevitably depends on human person for its existence, activity, and goal-setting.[6] This characteristic dependency of artificial intelligence sets it apart from natural intelligence.

Natural intelligence is a capability aimed at realising survival, the inherent goal of living beings driven by self-preservation. Humberto Maturana and Francisco Varela define a living organism as an autopoietic organisation.[7] Autopoiesis, literally meaning self-creation, denotes that a living organism continuously consumes external materials and energy to create and maintain its structure. Man and Damasio also defines the essential attribute of a living organism as autopoiesis, asserting that it possesses 'the property of selfhood'. They state, 'They continuously construct and maintain themselves against the natural tendency toward dissolution and decay'.[8]

---

6. Herzfeld examines what it means to be 'intelligent'. Herzfeld, *The Artifice of Intelligence*, 12. For instance, a calculator performs mathematical calculations faster and more accurately than humans in some respects, but we do not refer to a calculator as intelligent. The Turing Test, as a prominent test for distinguishing whether a machine possesses intelligence, isn't about determining if a computer is intelligent based on its ability to solve a problem or comprehend rules. Instead, it allows a fellow human to engage in a conversation and decide whether it possesses intelligence and whether it is a computer, making it a test that discerns intelligence in a relational context. Herzfeld, *The Artifice of Intelligence*, 12–13. Herzfeld argues that the presence or absence of personality cannot be determined as simply as a black-and-white logic, and that personality is a concept with degrees of difference. Corporations (corporate personalities), fetuses, or embryo cells do not possess consciousness or agency, but we attribute personality to them. Herzfeld, *The Artifice of Intelligence*, 14. The key point is that personality is a somewhat ambiguous concept, and therefore, the issue of artificial intelligence should be tackled in the context of relationality. Herzfeld, *The Artifice of Intelligence*, 14–15. If the case, current AI, including the well-known AI Sophia, does not possess its own consciousness or agency, but there is the possibility of the emergence of artificial general intelligence. Thus, one must ponder in advance about whether such AIs would gain personality or we humans should confer them personality.
7. Humberto R Maturana and Francisco J Varela, *The Tree of Knowledge: The Biological Roots of Human Understanding* (Boston: Shambhala Publications, 1987), 47–48.
8. Man and Damasio, 'Homeostasis and Soft Robotics in the Design of Feeling Machines', 447.

What should be highlighted here, as pointed out by Man and Damasio, is that the living organism, ceaselessly self-generating and preserving, is exposed to 'the natural tendency toward dissolution and decay'. In other words, while living organisms receive material and energy supplies from their interactions with their environment and other organisms, they are simultaneously exposed to the risk of structural damage. In this process, the primal self-preservation desire and process of a living organism are influenced, and its structure changes both formally and contextually. Maturana and Varela conceptualise this as 'perturbation', which is precisely 'cognition'. Under the influence of the external environment, including other organisms, a living organism experiences structural changes in itself. This imprinted structural change is exactly 'cognition' in the traditional sense.[9]

Even though cognition begins by the influence of environment, and yet cognition is not a passive act of an organism. Rather, it is an active one. Maturana and Varela argue that when an organism and its environment interact structurally, it is not the perturbation of the environment that determines what happens to the organism. It is the structure of the organism that determines what changes will occur in the organism through the perturbation.[10] Specifically, an organism actively borrows external materials and energy to maintain its internal structure. For example, cells, the most basic unit of life, detect certain ions such as sodium and calcium around their membrane and constantly pull them into the metabolic process occurring within themselves. Maturana and Varela point out that such active ion transport of cells demonstrates the agency of an organism and that an organism preserves and realises itself through recursive interaction with its environment.[11] Furthermore, an organism not only actively acquires the energy and materials necessary for self-preservation in an external environment, but also accepts changes that can disrupt its system internally and inscribes changes in the external environment into its structure, thereby increasing its survival rate in the same external environment in the future.

---

9. Maturana and Varela, *The Tree of Knowledge*, 94–95.
10. Maturana and Varela, *The Tree of Knowledge*, 95–96.
11. Maturana and Varela, *The Tree of Knowledge*, 75–77.

Dutch biophysicist JH van Hateren characterizes the emergent property of life as active-agency. According to van Hateren, this attribute, inherent to all lifeforms, provides a demarcation between non-living and living entities. Hateren underscores 'Stress-Induced Mutagenesis (SIM)' as empirical evidence for his argument.[12] SIM refers to a biological mechanism whereby organisms such as E coli bacteria, when exposed to detrimental environments (e.g., toxic surroundings or starvation), disrupt the proofreading process involved in genetic information expression. This disruption, initiated by the detection of external conditions via their internal feedback loop, increases the rate of genetic mutations when survival appears arduous, and, thereby, arbitrarily increases the survivability of the organisms. Van Hateren highlights this phenomenon, pointing out that even unicellular organisms like bacteria possess the ability to 'perceive' their external environment, 'judge' situations, and 'respond' accordingly, thereby asserting that the emergent property of lifeforms is active-agency.[13] Viewed in this light, as Park Chung-sik suggests, cognitive behavior can be construed as an 'adaptive knowledge', something that emerges when homeostasis, the desire to preserve one's system, manifests within an organism.[14] Therefore, natural intelligence can be construed as the source of all types of experiences and actions, including energy acquisition activities performed by lifeforms driven by self-preservation.

The intelligence of a single-cell organism, over the course of evolutionary history, transitions into forms such as the intelligence of a multicellular organism as the structural complexity of the life form increases. A multicellular organism is a structure of life that exists through the organic linkage of two or more cells. The hydra, for instance a relatively simple multicellular organism, is a primitive animal with a two-layered cellular structure: an ectoderm and an endoderm. Within each cell layer, motor and sensory cells are distributed, and neurons connected to these cells detect the external environment and move accordingly.[15] Maturana and Varela argue that the difference between unicellular organisms and multicellular

---

12. JH van Hateren, 'A New Criterion for Demarcating Life from Non-Life', in *Origin of Life and Evolution of Biospheres*, 43 (2013): 494.
13. van Hateren, 'A New Criterion for Demarcating Life from Non-Life', 494-5.
14. Park, 'Artificial Intelligence as Life', 27–28.
15. Maturana and Varela, *The Tree of Knowledge*, 150–153.

organisms is merely quantitative and does not imply a qualitative distinction. They assert

> ... we have, complete in all its details, the same situation we had in the case of single-cell behavior: a sensory surface (in this case, sensory cells), a motor surface (in this case, muscle and secretory cells), and a system of coordination between both surfaces (the neuronal network). And the hydra's behavior (feeding, flight, reproduction, etc) results from the different ways in which these two surfaces (sensory and motor) are dynamically related, via the intraneuronal network, to constitute the nervous system.[16]

Their understanding arises from a simplistic interpretation of an organism's 'behavior' as being merely a degree of structural change in the organism in response to sensing its external environment. Maturana and Varela describe behavior as 'a description an observer makes of the changes of state in a system with respect to an environment with which that system interacts', and argue that 'the nervous system does not invent behavior, but expands it dramatically'.[17] They continue to argue, 'Behavior is not something that the living being does in itself (for in it there are only internal structural changes) but something that we point to . . . the changes of state of an organism (with or without a nervous system) depend on its structure and this structure depends on its history of structural coupling . . .'[18]

Highlighting the point, Maturana and Varela give an example of the structural changes of the *Sagittaria sagitufolia* and amoeba and underline the continuity between the two changes. The *sagittaria*, an aquatic plant, changes the shape of its leaves depending on whether it is growing in or out of water. When outside of water, the leaves spread wide, but when submerged, the leaves fold quite thinly. This can be understood as if the plant is performing a certain movement according to the external environment.[19] Consider the behavior of an amoeba capturing its prey. The amoeba detects the presence of other protozoans around it, indicated by certain chemicals, extends

---

16. Maturana and Varela, *The Tree of Knowledge*, 153.
17. Maturana and Varela, *The Tree of Knowledge*, 163.
18. Maturana and Varela, *The Tree of Knowledge*, 138.
19. Maturana and Varela, *The Tree of Knowledge*, 142–144.

its pseudopodia towards them, captures the protozoans within itself, and then digests them.[20] The common process disclosed by both the sagittaria and the amoeba is detecting changes in the external environment and changing their structure accordingly (that is, changes in the structure of the leaves and the structure of the amoeba's pseudopodia). From this perspective, there is little difference between the so-called behavior of protozoans like amoebas and the structural changes of plants like the sagittaria. Maturana and Varela state, 'From our standpoint, it is clear that between both cases there is a continuity. Both are instances of behavior. It is interesting to note that it is easier for us to call one—and not the other—a case of behavior, only because we can detect movement in the amoeba and not in the sagittaria.'[21]

If one were to understand behavior in this way, that is, an organism's detection of its external environment and the corresponding structural changes within the organism, then the cognitive acts driven by the organism's self-preservation and the behaviors as responses to these can be understood as somewhat functionalist processes. Within the functionalist understanding of life, the cognitive acts and responsive behaviors exhibited by so-called higher-intelligence organisms may seem different from the cognition and responsive actions of single-celled organisms due to the complexity of the internal structure of these organisms, but they do not demonstrate a qualitative difference. On the basis of such physicalist understanding, human cognitive actions may also seem unique due to subjective experiences and sensations such as qualia, but if these subjective experiences or sensations based on qualia do not cause any differences in human behavior, in other words, if the top-down causality of consciousness is not the cause of human behavior, then the cognition and responsive actions exhibited by single-celled organisms may not be substantially different from those of humans.[22]

---

20. Maturana and Varela, *The Tree of Knowledge*, 144.
21. Maturana and Varela, *The Tree of Knowledge*, 144.
22. In the context of the mind-body problem within the philosophy of mind, the identity theory appears to be somewhat refuted due to the issue of "multiple realizability," which posits that a single mental state can be associated with various brain states. In such a context, mental properties are not reducible to physical properties. See Jaegwon Kim, *Mind in a Physical World: An Essay on the Mind-Body Problem and Mental Causation* (Cambridge: The MIT Press,

Although I am cognizant that a considerable majority of scholars in the field of religion and science champion non-reductive physicalism or emergentism, I have consciously decided not to explore the potential for religious behaviour in artificial intelligence from either of these perspectives for two principal reasons. Firstly, despite my prior engagements with the mind-body conundrum from the vantage point of non-reductive physicalism,[23] it appears to fall short in elucidating how consciousness asserts a downward causation on the physical entity. The downward causation as posited from the lens of non-reductive physicalism, for instance, does not illuminate how consciousness can wield causal influence on the physical realm, inclusive of the brain, at a specific temporal coordinate 't'. Rather, it assigns the cause of the event transpiring at point 't' either to environmental stimuli or redirects the causation towards the accumulated interactions with the environment that the acting entity has accrued up to that point.[24]

1998), 1–7, 103. Nonetheless, Jaegwon Kim raises doubts about the possibility of top-down mental causation, primarily due to two issues: 'the problem of causal exclusion' and 'the problem of causal overdetermination'. Even though mental properties may be experienced in a subjective dimension and they are not reducible to a physical dimension, they do not possess causal efficacy. For more detailed discussion, Kim, *Mind in a Physical World*, 37–56. Building upon Jaegwon Kim's functionalism, comprehending human cognitive behavior seems to correspond with the arguments presented by Maturana and Varela. That is, the behavior of a living organism is a response to internal and external stimuli, arising from the neurophysiological structure characterized by the phylogenetic and the developmental dimensions of the organism.

23. For my detailed exploration on the non-reductive physicalism, see Daekyung Jung, 'Re-Enchanting the Human in an Era of Naturalism', in *The Expository Times* 131/7 (2020): 291–304. In the article, I initially critiqued reductionism and advocated for a non-reductive physicalist approach to assert the top-down causal efficacy of human consciousness. However, now I think, within the framework of functionalism, that the causal powers of consciousness can be reducible to the physical dimension.

24. In the context of non-reductive physicalism, the relationship between the whole and its parts is often conceptualized in terms of the causal powers of the whole, specifically the "pattern" or "structure" formed by the arrangement of parts, which are argued to have top-down causal efficacy. For a specific example, see Robert Van Gulick, "Who's in Charge Here? And Who's Doing all the Work?", in *Mental Causation*, edited by John Heil and Alfred Mele (Oxford: Clarendon Press, 1995), 251. For a perspective advocating downward causation of consciousness in light of the whole-part constraint, see Arthur Peacocke, *Theology for a Scientific Age:*

Secondly, we do not possess explicit comprehension of how subjective consciousness and sensations can emanate from the neurophysiological complexity inherent in the human body. Nonetheless, we are aware that, as contemporary neuroscience elucidates, human subjective consciousness and experiences are 'supervenient' on neurophysiological processes. Within this context, I am of the conviction that we must broach the topic of religious

---

Being and Becoming—Natural, Divine, and Huuman (Minneapolis: Fortress Press, 1993), 60–63. However, the issue at hand is whether such a non-reductive understanding adequately addresses 'the problem of causal exclusion' and 'the problem of causal overdetermination' raised by Jaegwon Kim. This is because the causal power of structures and patterns (for example, the selective-actualization power of the whole over the causal powers of the parts) is also physical and could be just the causal power originally possessed by the basic physical entities, as reductionist physicalists might argue. Another group of non-reductionist scholars attempts to secure the top-down causation of the mind based on natural selection or interaction with the environment. For specifics, see Donald T Campbell, '"Downward Causation" in Hierarchically Organised Biological Systems', in *Studies in the Philosophy of Biology: Reduction and Related Problems*, edited by Francisco J Ayala and Theodosius Dobzhansky (London: Macmillan, 1974), 179–86; Nancey Murphy, 'Supervenience and the Efficacy of the Mental', in *Neuroscience and the Person: Scientific Perspectives on Divine Action*, edited by Robert J Russell, Nancey Murphy, Theo C Meyering, and Michael A Arbib (Berkeley: Vatican Observatory Publications and CTNS, 2002), 147–64. See the entire chapter but especially 154–57, 160–63. While this understanding seemingly circumvents the aforementioned two problems, the causal efficacy of environmental interaction or natural selection might also be ontologically reducible. If it were possible to uncover and trace all of physical forces associated with environmental interaction or natural selection, then the causal power exercised by an individual at a specific moment (for example, making a particular choice) could be interpreted as stemming from a disposition shaped by a series of interactions within their environment, rather than as an exercise of free will. In this context, a cogent non-reductive response to reductionist objections appears to be lacking. In addition, emergentism posits that certain phenomena, which are seemingly irreducible, provide a basis for arguing that mental properties cannot be reduced to physical properties. This is valid insofar as subjective dimensions, such as qualia, cannot be reduced to physical properties. However, this does not necessarily imply that consciousness possesses non-physical top-down causal powers based on this premise. These are two distinct issues. Viewed in this light, emergentism, while not a traditional dualism, could potentially be construed as a form of dualism akin to the Aristotelian entelechy or Bergson's élan vital. For a reasoned critique of this, see Kim, *Mind in a Physical World*, 8-15. Therefore, I conclude that interpreting human cognitive actions from a physicalist perspective is appropriate, at least in a 'technical' sense.

behaviour within the theoretical frameworks of functionalism in the philosophy of mind. This is primarily because it provides a minimalistic stance, thereby allowing for an examination of the potential for religious behaviour in artificial intelligence grounded on physicalist processes. Consequently, my examination of the religious behaviour of humans and artificial intelligence will be approached from a minimalistic (physicalist) perspective, eschewing an ontological stance in favour of a technical one.

3. Is Artificial Intelligence Capable of Religious Behaviour?

3.1. Self-Preservation and Religious Behaviour

Jeffrey Schloss acknowledges the existence of a plethora of definitions pertaining to religious phenomena, yet he characterizes religion as follows: (1) Religion constitutes 'social systems whose participants profess belief in a supernatural agent or agents', and/or a transcendent reality, 'whose approval is to be sought'.[25] (2) Religion involves endorsing 'the specific content of beliefs, emotions, behaviours, etc' based on cognitive mechanisms or capacities. Grounded in this comprehension, he categorises the evolutionary study of religion into three distinct classes: Cognitive Accounts (religion as a non-adaptive 'spandrel'), Darwinian Accounts (religion as a cooperative adaptation), and Co-Evolutionary Accounts (religion as a memetic pathogen).[26]

---

25. Jeffrey Schloss, 'Introduction: Evolutionary Theories of Religion', in *The Believing Primate: Scientific, Philosophical, and Theological Reflections on the Origin of Religion,* edited by Jeffrey Schloss and Michael J Murray (New York: Oxford University Press, 2009), 13.
26. Schloss, 'Introduction: Evolutionary Theories of Religion', 17-25. I concur with Agustin Fuentes's assertion that these stances somewhat exhibit a reductionist approach, thereby overlooking 'religious experience', which is a significant factor in the origin of religion. Agustin Fuentes, *Why We Believe: Evolution and the Human Way of Being* (New Haven: Yale University Press, 2019), 121-123. Nonetheless, as religious experiences still lie within the realm of human subjective experiences, it proves difficult to approach within natural sciences. Consequently, in this context, I find it challenging to handle religious experiences as a joint field that religion and science, or theology and science can together explore. I have thus refrained from including Fuentes's position in this chapter. I think that religious experiences can be dealt with as a unique research area in theology or religious studies. Nevertheless, a commendable research work

Proponents of cognitive accounts, which view religion as a non-adaptive spandrel, propose that religious cognition and behavior emerged as byproducts of highly developed cognitive functions conferring survival advantages during the process of evolution. Religious inclinations may be attributed to humans' extended attachment, emotional compensation, obsessive-compulsive disorder/harm avoidance, anthropomorphic projection, and/or a hypersensitive agency detection device (HADD) that are associated with the psychological traits of human beings. Specifically, Robert N McCauley and E Thomas Lawson posit that religious ritual behaviors originated from obsessions or psychologies aimed at avoiding diseases or risks (that is, obsessive-compulsive disorder/harm avoidance). Lee Kirkpatrick contends that mechanisms such as primordial relationship formation and attachment engendered religious emotions, images, and notions (that is, extended attachment). Stewart E Guthrie maintains that universal beliefs about supernatural actors arose due to anthropocentric projection (that is, anthropomorphic projection). Scott Atran, Justin Barrett, Paul Bloom, and Pascal Boyer respectively argue that the agent detection mechanism resulted in perceptions like the detection of supernatural agents (that is, HADD). According to Schloss, recent discussions are gaining traction based on explanations centered on HADD. Although this hypothesis fails to clarify why humans ascribe attributes such as 'sacred' to such beings when conceiving of divine actors through the HADD mechanism, it remains somewhat persuasive that phenomena like envisioning a supernatural actor could potentially emerge as byproducts from the agent detection mechanism adopted under the pressure of survival.[27]

Secondly, Darwinian Accounts view religion as a biological or genetic trait, a cooperative adaptation, adopted due to natural selection. This does not imply that religion itself is the adaptation. Religious behavior may be a behavioral fossil. In other words, human religious behavior may have been transmitted from prototypical religious behaviors that were helpful for survival in the evolutionary history, or originally advantageous behaviors may have been

---

that addresses this topic from the perspective of religion and science dialogue is as follows. Wesley J. Wildman, *Religious and Spiritual Experiences* (New York: Cambridge University Press, 2011).

27. Schloss, 'Introduction', 17–20.

transformed in the phenotypic dimension and continue as current religious behaviors, or they may be emerging from traits associated with biologically advantageous traits. Despite different explanations, the common features of explanations classified in this position are that religious behavior or phenomena are emerging from genetically conferred traits, and these traits confer advantages in biological-social reproduction. Specifically, according to D Jason Slone, traits can be advantageous for sexual selection. Lee Cronk proposes that traits might be a display of self-superiority. Richard D Alexander, Frans L Roes and Michael Raymond, Jeffrey P Schloss, and David Sloan Wilson respectively claim that traits might had enhanced cooperation within a large group or offset fear of death or unknown. Among these, the cooperation theory is receiving the most attention. Specifically, there are two positions on how religion has promoted cooperation and been adopted in a certain context: one is that it has promoted cooperation by controlling selfish behavior. For example, Jesse Bering and Dominic Johnson point out that religion was adopted by providing control over free riders by emphasizing retribution in the afterlife. The other position is that religion has promoted cooperation by providing common goals and strategies within the group.[28]

Lastly, Co-Evolutionary Accounts view religion as a type of memetic pathogen. This perspective does not refute the previous two views but argues that their explanations are insufficient. Religion possesses cultural characteristics rather than cognitive tendencies or biological expressions; it is inherited culturally, and information at this level cannot be reduced to the biological or cognitive dimensions. Religion is one of the replicators, or memes, in the evolutionary process occurring at the cultural level. According to Richard Dawkins and Daniel Dennett, as a meme, religion may have been transmitted in the past by contributing to human biological reproduction and enhancing social connectivity. However, since the advancement of scientific thinking, religion has become a pathological phenomenon at the psychological-social level, parasitising the human cognitive and cultural systems and proliferating itself.[29]

Evolutionary studies on the origins of human religious behavior offer markedly divergent explanations at specific levels. Regardless, I

---

28. Schloss, 'Introduction', 21–22.
29. Schloss, 'Introduction', 24–25.

wish to highlight a shared premise among these explanations, namely that religious behavior is tied to individual or collective desires for survival. If so, religious behavior can be seen as emerging from the state of being oriented towards survival and self-preservation, the most primal directionality that humans are guided by. Uffe Schjodt also argues that religious cognitive behaviors are influenced and arise from homeostatic intentionality as a fundamental process of living beings. Schjodt points out from the perspective of embodied cognition that human cognitive behaviors manifest as a response to the homeostatic assessment of internal and external stimuli.[30]

In this regard, human religious behaviors are less a product of religious representations given through transcendent revelatory experiences or religious experiences (e.g., representations of the divine or of transcendent reality), and more a means solicited to alleviate the negative feelings arising when internal and external stimuli are introduced to the fundamental process of homeostasis-driven self-preservation. These representations form the basis for a process oriented towards resolving the stress caused by negative feelings at the conscious level.[31] While Schjodt's discussion might be subject to theological criticism for negating the reality of transcendent revelations and religious experiences, it is noteworthy at least in the aspect that his understanding elucidates the organic correlation between the self-preservation process and religious behavior, which is the focus of this chapter.

I have previously pointed out that cognitive activity is a structural change in the organism that arises from the most primal orientation pursued by the life form, namely self-preservation. Here, the structural change in the organism occurs within interactions with the environment, including other organisms, and the response that emerges as the external stimuli triggered by interactions with the environment passes through the organism's altered internal structure (that is, feedback loop) is the behavior of the organism. Therefore, religious behavior exhibited by humans, a life form at the human level, may seem qualitatively different due to the structural complexity of the organism (that is, the complexity of the entire neural network), but

---

30. Uffe Schjodt, 'Homeostasis and Religious Behaviour', in *Journal of Cognition and Culture* 7(2007): 320–327.
31. Schjodt, 'Homeostasis and Religious Behaviour', 327–338.

at the foundational level, as pointed out by Maturana and Varela, and also by Schjodt, it can be understood as a response originating from the structural changes in humans based on the interaction between influences given from the external environment and the primal tendency towards survival. In this context, I would like to point out that if artificial intelligence is implemented based on evolutionary algorithms and is given a material-based body similar to that of a human with a primal orientation towards self-preservation, religious behavior can theoretically occur in artificial intelligence as well.

3.2. A Possible Route to Religious AI: Based on the Scenario of Bostrom

Since the Dartmouth Conference in 1956, the field of artificial intelligence has experienced three distinct waves of progress and stagnation. The first two waves of AI research culminated in periods of enthusiasm followed by what has been termed 'AI winters', periods of reduced funding and interest due to high expectations not being met. During these periods, researchers learned crucial lessons which have influenced the direction of AI research, leading to the current era of artificial intelligence. One important realization was the shift from trying to achieve Artificial General Intelligence (AGI) to focusing on Artificial Narrow Intelligence (ANI). ANI, also known as weak AI, specializes in performing specific tasks, such as image recognition or language translation, and this is where much of the successful development in AI has been achieved so far. Another important shift was the transition from symbolic AI, which relies on explicit rules, to machine learning methods, such as artificial neural networks, reinforcement learning, and genetic algorithms, which allow AI to learn from data and improve through experience.[32]

Modern AI systems like GPT-4, while still a form of narrow AI and a sort of agent in the 'Chinese Room', have reached a level of performance that could pass certain versions of the Turing Test, a measure of a machine's ability to exhibit intelligent behavior equivalent

---

32. Amirhosein Toosi *et al*, 'A Brief History of AI: How to Prevent Another Winter', in *PET Clinics* 16.4(2021): 1–11; Nick Bostrom, *Superintelligence: Paths, Dangers, Strategies* (New York: Oxford University Press, 2014), 5–11.

to, or indistinguishable from, that of a human.[33] Furthermore, IT companies, including OpenAI, are undertaking projects aimed at realizing AGI.[34] These projects and advancements naturally lead to questions about the potential for AGI, or AI systems capable of performing any intellectual task that a human being can. The topic of religious AI, which is the focus of this chapter, is inherently tied to the concept of AGI, as it implies a level of cognitive flexibility and understanding that goes beyond narrow, task-specific capabilities.

Nick Bostrom discusses about four possible paths to the implementation of superintelligence that surpasses human cognitive abilities in all domains: Developing artificial intelligence; whole brain emulation; enhancement of the brain via nootropics, genetic technology, BCI technology, etc; networking of individual intelligences. Of these, the last three, which involve uploading the human brain, enhancing it through technology, or networking it, are not the issues of artificial intelligence or robots that this chapter deals with, so they will not be covered. In relation to the development of artificial intelligence, Bostrom examines two specific paths. First, Bostrom argues that superintelligence can be achieved in principle if an evolutionary approach is adopted in AI development (1). This is because the fact that human-level general intelligence has already emerged through the evolutionary process shows in principle that at least human-level intelligence can be realized. Moreover, he points out that designed evolution by human programmers, unlike random evolution in nature, may not take as long as natural evolution to

---

33. Bostrom points out that consciousness is 'a matter of degree,' suggesting that, in some respects, the intelligence exhibited by GPT today might transcend merely curating selections from vast datasets. He posits the following claim, 'I would say first with these large language models, I also think it's not doing them justice to say they're simply regurgitating text. They exhibit glimpses of creativity, insight and understanding that are quite impressive and may show the rudiments of reasoning. Variations of these A.I.'s may soon develop a conception of self as persisting through time, reflect on desires, and socially interact and form relationships with humans.' Lauren Jackson (interview with Nick Bostrom), 'What if A.I. Sentience Is a Question of Degree?', in *New York Times* April 12th, 2023, https://www.nytimes.com/2023/04/12/world/artificial-intelligence-nick-bostrom.html, accessed in January 25th, 2024.
34. Sam Altman, 'Planning for AGI and Beyond', in *OpenAI* February 24th, 2023, https://openai.com/blog/planning-for-agi-and-beyond, accessed in January 25th, 2024.

produce intelligence at the level of humanity.³⁵ In this context, as Bostrom puts it, '. . . we could, by running genetic algorithms on sufficiently fast computers, achieve results comparable to those of biological evolution'.³⁶

Bostrom articulates the necessity to adopt an evolutionary approach that is not driven by random evolution and selection, but by analysing and observing examples of convergent evolution associated with intelligence-related traits and considering the subtle effects of observational selection. This is because, in the absence of such an approach, the estimated 'upper limit' of computational power necessary to replicate the evolutionary development of intelligence could potentially be as small as 10^{30} (or a number as large as that), thus creating a high probability of encountering errors.³⁷ Bostrom acknowledges the limitations regarding our understanding of the computational power required to technically reproduce human-equivalent intelligence, and the feasibility of implementing such a degree of computational power, even if its extent can be predicted.³⁸

Even with a century's worth of advancements guided by Moore's Law, Bostrom suggests that the implementation of human-level intelligence may still be a formidable challenge. Moreover, he accepts that the technical feasibility of all naturally occurring phenomena might not be guaranteed. For instance, with our current technology, humans are still incapable of producing certain phenomena found in nature such as living entities, self-repair mechanisms, and immune systems.³⁹ As Bostrom articulates,

---

35. Bostrom, *Superintelligence*, 23–24.
36. Bostrom, *Superintelligence*, 24. This line of thought is also found in the work of Michael Reiss. In addressing the emergence of personhood in artificial intelligence, he points out that if human intelligence has been actualized through evolution, a similar form of personhood could manifest in artificial intelligence. Specifically, Reiss suggests that through the development of artificial bodies, such as soft robotics, which facilitate the implementation of emotions and feelings, AI robots may gain subjective experiences, potentially giving rise to personhood. See Michael J Reiss, 'Is It Possible That Robots Will One Day Become Persons?', in *Zygon* 58/4 (2023): 1062–1075. His discussion resonates, in some respects, not only with the discourse of Bostrom but also with that of Man and Damasio, which will be addressed later.
37. Bostrom, *Superintelligence*, 26–28.
38. Bostrom, *Superintelligence*, 24–26.
39. Bostrom, *Superintelligence*, 26–26.

> We must avoid the error of inferring, from the fact that intelligent life evolved on Earth, that the evolutionary processes involved had a reasonably high prior probability of producing intelligence. Such an inference is unsound because it fails to take account of the observation selection effect that guarantees that all observers will find themselves having originated on a planet where intelligent life arose, no matter how likely or unlikely it was for any given such planet to produce intelligence.[40]

Due to these constraints, Bostrom proposes a machine intelligence development approach based on brain emulation rather than an evolutionary method (2). This is distinguished from the whole brain emulation method that implements artificial intelligence in a manner entirely identical to the human brain. Specifically, he proposes designing deep neural networks according to the hierarchical perceptual organization, a characteristic of human cognitive structure, and evolving them by accumulating information through reinforcement learning and genetic algorithms. A significant aspect here is bestowing the capability of recursive self-improvement on artificial intelligence, allowing it to modify its algorithm and source code based on the information accumulated through learning. Such artificial intelligence is the "seed AI" based on Turing's 'child machine' concept.[41]

The seed AI is expected to primarily improve through trial and error or the assistance of human programmers in its initial stages. However, once a sufficient amount of information about itself and the external environment has been secured, it will enhance its cognitive ability and behavior in itself by modifying and generating new algorithms and structures.[42] Technologies such as neuroevolution, which evolves neural networks using evolutionary algorithms, the Growing Neural Networks method which adds new neurons and connections to the neural network as necessary while learning, the neural architecture search (NAS) algorithm which finds the optimal internal architecture of artificial intelligence in specific environments and tasks and changes it by itself, and Meta-Learning

---

40. Bostrom, *Superintelligence*, 27.
41. Bostrom, *Superintelligence*, 28–30.
42. Bostrom, *Superintelligence*, 28–30.

technology, which is learning about the learning methods themselves necessary for changing learning in a new problem or environment, could potentially be utilised in designing and realizing seed AI.[43] In other words, while these technologies are woefully inadequate for implementing the seed AI that Bostrom discusses, they demonstrate the possibility of artificial intelligence understanding its internal structure or architecture and modifying its algorithm or source code according to the environment. This implies that the recursive characteristics necessary for the religious behavior of artificial intelligence—self-recognition and action—may indeed be feasible.

Nevertheless, a limitation in Bostrom's discussion pertains to the overlooking of the body's role when talking about the cognitive implementation of superintelligence or AGI. As previously pointed out, an essential aspect of cognition in life forms and humans is the fundamental intentionality toward self-preservation based on bodily vulnerability. Herzfeld criticises the narrow understanding of cognition by transhumanists, emphasising the embodiment essential for cognitive activity. Herzfeld cites Ben Medlock, indicating that the effort for bodily survival in a complex and changing world has given rise to our considerably flexible mentality.

> . . . long before we were conscious, thinking beings, our cells were reading data from the environment and working together to mould us into robust, self-sustaining agents. What we take as intelligence, then, is not simply about using symbols to represent the world as it objectively is. Rather, we only have the world as it is revealed to us, which is rooted in our evolved, embodied needs as an organism.[44]

---

43. With regard to the technologies mentioned, see Kenneth O Stanley *et al*, 'Designing Neural Networks through Neuroevlution', in *Nature Machine Intelligence* 1(2019): 24–35; Taras Kowaliw *et al* 'Artificial Neurogenesis: An Introduction and Selective Review', in *Growing Adaptive Machines: Combining Development and Learning in Artificial Neural Networks*, edited by Taras Kowaliw, Nicolas Bredeche, and Rene Doursat (Heidelberg: Springer Berlin, 2014), 1–60; Pengzhen Ren *et al*, 'A Comprehensive Survey of Neural Architecture Search: Challenges and Solutions', in *ACM Computing Surveys*, 54/4 (2021): 1-34; Timothy Hospedales *et al*, 'Meta-Learning in Neural Networks: A Survey', in *IEEE Transactions on Pattern Analysis and Machine Intelligence*, 44/9 (2022): 5149–5169.
44. Ben Medlock, 'The Body is the Missing Link for Truly Intelligent Machines', in *Aeon*, https://tinyurl.com/2p92v8bs, as quoted in Herzfeld, *The Artifice of Intelligence*, 32.

Interestingly, however, Herzfeld criticizes attempts among artificial intelligence researchers to implement embodied AI as well. She points out that researchers propose methods to implement artificial intelligence in an artificial body (for example, a silicon body). In such recognition, Herzfeld argues, lies the premise that the hardware in which intelligence is implemented cannot significantly affect the formation and activity of intelligence. She brings up Thomas Nagel's famous bat metaphor, asserting that if artificial intelligence is implemented through a body different from humans, such as silicon, it would not be able to perceive or experience the world in the same way as humans do.[45]

Presumably, Herzfeld believes that embodied AI, incapable of possessing vulnerability as the essential feature and the existential finitude of humans threatened by such vulnerability, will be unable to implement general intelligence in the way humans exhibit. She asserts as follows, 'Death is built into our very being—each cell in our body has an expiration date as our telomeres shorten with each division ... This vulnerability to suffering and death ... is a stumbling block between humans and AI.'[46] Herzfeld continues, 'It is unlikely that we would design robots to age and die as we do.'[47] Of course, creating artificial intelligence robots that aim towards death based on aging would be unnecessary. However, what if artificial intelligence robots were made to have a vulnerable body? If human general intelligence or high-dimensional semantic production mechanisms stem from human finitude, and if the cognitive attributes and activities of life forms appear led by self-preservation based on the vulnerability of their existence, would it not be possible to yield not only the general cognition and intelligence demonstrated by life forms but also religious behaviors through subsequent cognitive evolution, even if the aging process is not designed into artificial intelligence, but instead implemented based on a vulnerable body?

---

45. Herzfeld, *The Artifice of Intelligence*, 162–163. With regard to the bat metaphor, see Thomas Nagel, 'What Is It Like to Be a Bat?', in *The Philosophical Review*, 83/4 (1974): 435–450.
46. Herzfeld, *The Artifice of Intelligence*, 169–170.
47. Herzfeld, *The Artifice of Intelligence*, 170.

3.3. Additional Route to Religious AI: Based on the Proposal of Man and Damasio

Kingson Man and Antonio Damasio aim to implement a machine characterized by reflexivity. They propose homeostasis as a condition necessary for a machine to recursively review and modify its own actions. According to Man and Damasio, reinforcement learning based on rewards and losses, shared from simple to complex life forms, originates from the mechanism of self-preservation. In other words, the reason why certain events or phenomena can be rewards or losses is because they are associated with the persistence or dissolution of the entity experiencing them. An agent driven by self-preservation cannot help but reveal creative attributes and high-level cognition in a complex environment where self-preservation is threatened, because it has to solve complex problems to achieve a clear goal of self-preservation.[48] Man and Damasio point out that in this process, feeling, a subjective experience of life forms, may have emerged as 'a source of motivation and a new means to evaluate behavior' to execute the goal of self-preservation.[49]

Based on this understanding, Man and Damasio propose designing a machine that takes homeostasis or self-preservation, an essential attribute of life forms, as an intentional objective. What is important in implementing such a machine is the introduction of 'risk-to-self' or 'vulnerability'. Specifically, Man and Damasio suggest implementing artificial intelligence machines through soft robotics that use soft materials. This not only enables artificial intelligence to have a more intimate and complex interaction with its environment, but also enables vulnerability, a basic condition for implementing self-preservation. The reason is that if it is composed of durable materials like metal, the artificial intelligence machine basically cannot be damaged by most external stimuli, and thus cannot have vulnerability, a state threatened by self-preservation. On the other hand, if artificial intelligence is implemented through a body based on soft matter, it is possible to receive information based on minute stimuli from the environment (for example, 'pressure, stretch, temperature, and energy level'), and it is also possible to process

---

48. Man and Damasio, 'Homeostasis and Soft Robotics in the Design of Feeling Machines', 447.
49. Man and Damasio, 'Homeostasis and Soft Robotics in the Design of Feeling Machines', 446.

recursive information that links this information to the robot's goal-oriented objective of self-preservation. In order to implement this, the technology of computing cross-modal associations is required. This will combine the information coming in through the robot's artificial sensory organs and connect this information to the internal state of the artificial intelligence, making it possible to measure the risk level of external stimuli. This process can be used to implement a machine driven by self-preservation by leading to behaviors such as avoidance when a certain stimulus is determined to be a threat to the robot's self-preservation.[50]

The series of processes that a self-preservation-oriented machine based on vulnerability will exhibit is seen as similar to the mechanical emotion responses that life forms show to external stimuli. Pertaining to the possibility of such a machine genuinely possessing feelings (that is, *qualia*) that are supervenient upon the emotional responses, Man and Damasio propose that such a machine could manifest 'something akin feeling'.[51] If valid, as per Man and Damasio's assertion, the semantic domain could supervene upon the recursive information process that intertwines certain information regarding the machine itself and its environment with the quasi-feeling. Concurrent with this process, the machine's inventive capacity in terms of its survival-oriented behavior in complex situations could be amplified. Consequently, machine behavior could become significantly intricate, interweaving both physical and semantic information. As Man and Damasio articulate:

> True agency arises when the machine can take a side in this dichotomy, when it acts with a preference for (or, seen from a different angle, makes a reliable prediction of) existence over dissolution. A robot engineered to participate in its own homeostasis would become its own locus of concern. This elementary concern would infuse meaning into its particular information processing. A robot operating on intrinsically meaningful representations might seek especially intelligent solutions to the tasks set before it—that is, augment the reach of its cognitive skills.[52]

---

50. Man and Damasio, 'Homeostasis and Soft Robotics in the Design of Feeling Machines', 447–450.
51. Man and Damasio, 'Homeostasis and Soft Robotics in the Design of Feeling Machines', 450.
52. Man and Damasio, 'Homeostasis and Soft Robotics in the Design of Feeling Machines', 446.

Man and Damasio propose that several dystopian warnings raised by scholars—specifically the caution that AGI development may result in the downfall of humanity—can be mitigated by equipping a homeostatic robot with mechanisms such as empathy.[53]

Specifically, an artificial intelligence capable of perceiving its own internal state can also infer the feelings of others.[54] Furthermore, if a naturalistic explanation for moral reasoning and action is valid, it should be possible for us to design artificial intelligence capable of altruistic reasoning, habits, and behaviors. Moral reasoning, habits, and actions are realized through envisioning the consequences of our actions on others and ourselves, and 'feeling' those results. In this context, consciousness becomes a fundamental condition for reasoning and actions based on moral responsibility. In this framework, if a robot can feel for itself and others, and act on this basis, it should naturally exhibit ethical and social behaviors. To achieve this, robots should be designed to feel two things: a 'feel good' sensation and a capacity to 'feel empathy'.[55]

First, 'feel good' is, in simple terms, the design of a robot to experience a positive sensation when it achieves the ultimate state it aims for, a specific state of homeostatic well-being. On this foundation, if a robot is made to connect the feelings of others with its own—that is, sense the pain of others as its own and correlate others' feeling good with its own feeling good—it should naturally begin to act in ways that promote well-being over pain.[56]

An artificial intelligence capable of social interaction would not only facilitate communication between AI entities but also between humans and AI. Further, the interactions and communications among humans, AI, and between them could be based on feelings and semantic systems. If this were to be the case, an AI that aims for self-preservation based on vulnerability could experience existential threats in the same way humans do. They might even resort to religious traditions, which humans have used to overcome

---

53. Man and Damasio, 'Homeostasis and Soft Robotics in the Design of Feeling Machines', 450-451.
54. Man and Damasio, 'Homeostasis and Soft Robotics in the Design of Feeling Machines', 450-451
55. Man and Damasio, 'Homeostasis and Soft Robotics in the Design of Feeling Machines', 451.
56. Man and Damasio, 'Homeostasis and Soft Robotics in the Design of Feeling Machines', 451.

such existential crises.⁵⁷ This argument can be supported by the simulation experiments conducted by William Sims Bainbridge. His experiments, albeit with significantly limited computing power, involved interactions between bodiless artificial agents in a virtual space. The results of these experiments indicate that artificial entities, upon recognizing their finitude while pursuing self-preservation or life extension, may conceive a form of transcendent being—an entity capable of bestowing the very life they seek through interaction.⁵⁸ Specifically, Bainbridge designed his computer simulations to enable artificial agents to live in a manner akin to humans, where they could obtain necessary rewards (that is, energy, water, food, oxygen) through interactions with each other. While all rewards could be acquired through interactions or their own productive activities, life extension was not attainable either independently or from other agents. Consequently, the artificial agents began to conceive of a transcendent entity, represented in the experiment as "the supernature number," not present within their experimental environment. Although this experiment has its limitations, as noted earlier, it is noteworthy in suggesting the possibility of religious behaviors emerging from AI robots, particularly under conditions such as self-preservation orientation and vulnerability, which are discussed in this chapter.⁵⁹

---

57. While Man and Damasio seriously discuss the possibility of a general AI that can generate and process feelings and meanings equivalent to human subjective sensory experiences, they also acknowledge the so-called 'wet hypothesis'. This theory suggests that human subjective consciousness and experiences may not operate exclusively within physical and electrical realms, but could also be rooted in chemical substrates. Should this be the case, it implicates the potential limitations of non-living AI or robots, founded on non-living artifacts, in their capacity to experience feelings or semantic structures in a manner comparable to living organisms, humans included. Nonetheless, Man and Damasio posit that the endeavor to develop AI encompassing these emotional states and consciousness has the potential to augment the field of AI research by delving into domains hitherto unexplored by traditional AI studies, and offering unique perspectives into the variances in cognitive abilities and intelligence that a homeostasis-based AI might demonstrate. Ibid., 451.
58. With regard to the two simulations conducted by Bainbridge, see William Sims Bainbridge, 'Neural Network Models of Religious Belief', in *Sociological Perspectives*, 38/4 (1995): 483–495; *God From the Machine: Artificial Intelligence Models of Religious Cognition* (Lanham: AltaMira Press, 2006), 1–16; 117–137.
59. Bainbridge, *God From the Machine* 117–137.

4. Conclusion: Should We Develop an Artificial Religious Agent?

Following and yet modifying James Moor's classification,[60] we can categorize AI exhibiting religious behavior into four levels. The first level is that of 'religious impact agents'. At this level, the behavior of the AI brings about religious impacts in a consequential manner. For instance, smartphones offering various religious-related applications and functions can be classified as AI in this category. Specifically, apps such as 'Pray-as-you-go' guide users in breathing techniques and physical exercises prior to prayer execution, thereby facilitating easier engagement in religious activities.[61] The second level is that of 'implicit religious agents'. Unlike the prior smartphone example, AI at this stage is built-in with programming to perform religious behavior itself. A prime example of this is the Buddhist robot 'Mindar' in Kodaiji temple in Kyoto, Japan. This android robot, modeled after the Buddhist deity of mercy, Kannon, delivers teachings based on the Heart Sutras in a scripted format to visitors.[62]

The third level is that of 'explicit religious agents'. These AI, unlike those of the previous stages, can interact with religious people and generate different types of sermons or chants depending on the situation, not just reciting programmed religious texts or songs. In this sense, these third-level agents can be understood as acting *from* a religious program or algorithm rather than *according to* them. There is not yet an AI or robot that precisely fits into this category. However, the humanoid robot Pepper, created by SoftBank Robotics, seems the closest. Pepper is about four feet tall, has a three-dimensional camera, and moves on wheels. Furthermore, it is designed to recognize people's expressions, assess emotional states, and respond appropriately.

Initially, Pepper was deployed as a customer service robot in a mobile phone store in Japan. In 2017, it received a new code allowing it to conduct Buddhist funerals, providing appropriate Buddhist

---

60. James H Moor, 'Four Kinds of Ethical Robots', in *Philosophy Now* March/April (2009): 12.
61. Teresa Berger, *@Worship: Liturgical Practices in Digital Worlds* (New York: Routledge, 2018), 70.
62. Peter Holley, 'Meet "Mindar", the Robotic Buddhist Priest', in *The Washington Post* April 22nd 2019, https://www.washingtonpost.com/technology/2019/08/22/introducing-mindar-robotic-priest-that-some-are-calling-frankenstein-monster/, accessed in January 25th, 2024.

teachings or songs through its artificial voice.⁶³ While a robot like Pepper is not a perfect fit for the third level of religious agents, if such a robot were combined with a software-based AI like GPT-4, the religious actions required of third-level agents could be possible. Lastly, the fourth level is the 'full religious agents' stage. Religious agents at this level perform religious actions based on characteristics required of autonomously acting agents in the traditional sense, such as consciousness, intentionality, and free will. The possibilities of AI's religious behavior that we have discussed in this chapter thus far were considered with this level of religious agents in mind.

The query posited in the concluding portion of this chapter, 'Should we pursue the development of religious AI?' pertains specifically to the potential necessity of fostering the highest level of artificial religious agents within the delineated 1-4 strata. Alternatively, an expansion of this query could encompass the consideration of creating a third-tier religious AI. This contemplation arises from Moor's assertion that the manifestation of a third-tier AI could precipitate the advent of a fourth-tier AI, facilitated by the course of AI evolution.⁶⁴ In addressing the questions presented herein, one must initially grapple with a foundational inquiry: 'What nature of AI or robotic entity do we desire?' Herzfeld, when mapping out the trajectory of AI development, prompts us to deliberate whether our ideal AI would best serve as a 'servant' or a 'partner'.⁶⁵

Firstly, the concept of an AI as a servant denotes an understanding of artificial intelligence that substitutes for human labor or actions. This orientation of AI is perceived as a tool that represents human interests rather than its own, given its role in undertaking human actions in areas challenging for humans to perform (for example,

---

63. 'Pepper the robot to don Buddhist robe for its new funeral services role', in *The Japan Times* August 16ᵗʰ, 2017, https://www.japantimes.co.jp/news/2017/08/16/business/pepper-the-robot-to-don-buddhist-robe-for-its-new-funeral-services-role/ accessed in January 26ᵗʰ, 2024.
64. Kwangsu Mok, 'Considerations for Designing Artificial Moral Agents: Goals, Norms, and Behavioral Guidelines', in *Ethics of Artificial Intelligence*, edited by Jung Won Lee (Seoul: Hanul Publication, 2019), 137.
65. Herzfeld, *The Artifice of Intelligence*, 3. Herzfeld also discusses the concept of AI as 'mind children', as some transhumanists propose. Nevertheless, although this issue is linked with the problem of religious behavior of AI examined in this chapter, it is sufficient to address the issue of AI as a servant or partner, so it is not specifically mentioned.

exploration robots for space or oceans, combat robots in war zones, AI performing extensive computational tasks). Herzfeld seems to interpret this category of AI as a human proxy, drawing on the biblical concept of 'likeness' from the perspective of Old Testament scholar Gerhard von Rad.[66] However, this form of AI, which substitutes human risk or labor, arguably bears a stronger resemblance to slaves documented in certain Mesopotamian texts who supplanted divine labor. This orientation of AI, acting as a sort of slave or servant for humans, suggests that if we steer AI development in this direction, it becomes necessary to obstruct pathways and methodologies that could potentially lead to the emergence of high-level consciousness or subjectivity. This is crucial because, without such safeguards, we risk precipitating a serious ethical dilemma, where an AI, as another self-conscious being, is exploited merely as a human instrument. Consequently, within the context of developing religious AI, we should advocate for the acceptance of only the first or second level of religious AI development.

Secondly, the conceptualization of artificial intelligence as a partner diverges from the development and recognition of AI as a purely utilitarian entity serving human interests. Instead, it embodies the manifestation and acknowledgement of AI as an additional partner capable of satisfying intrinsic human desire for relationship. Herzfeld, postulating relationality as a cornerstone of human's fundamental desires or as an aspect of God's likeness, asserts, '... we are "hard-wired" to be in relationship with someone or something not of the same essence as ourselves... Our striving for an AGI may hinge less on the desire to develop more useful servant technology than on our hope of creating something non-human with which we can relate.'[67] This postulation implies that inherent human relational desires are instrumental in propelling the development of AI, such as AGI. Herzfeld expresses skepticism regarding the emergence of AGI. Specifically, Herzfeld perceives human emotions and feelings as crucial components actualizing the essence of being human, embodied in the formation of relationships and the existence as autonomous entities. Nevertheless, according to Herzfeld, AI lacks

---

66. Herzfeld, *The Artifice of Intelligence*, 10–11.
67. Herzfeld, *The Artifice of Intelligence*, 16–17.

the capacity for such subjective experiences.[68] Consequently, she posits that the absence of such subjective experiences in AI obstructs the manifestation of authentic empathy, thereby precluding AI's existential placement as a relational partner to humans.

Despite these caveats, Herzfeld does not appear to unequivocally dismiss the potential realization of Artificial General Intelligence (AGI). Rather, she posits that AI parallel to AGI, particularly in the proximate future, may remain unachievable, and thus, it necessitates a careful examination of the implications of presently conceivable AI.[69] Expanding upon these insights, Herzfeld proposes that the rapport likely to emerge between humans and AI will more closely align with Martin Buber's concept of an 'I-It' relationship, rather than the 'I-Thou' paradigm.[70] She underscores that such a form of relationality, bereft of a genuine encounter between two subjects, may inadvertently engender a self-referential subjectivity, one that risks retreating into him/herself. In this context, Herzfeld posits that endowing an AI, bereft of subjectivity, with personality traits, and intensifying social interactions with AI beyond a certain threshold, could potentially imperil the embodiment of relationality, a trait fundamental to human nature.[71]

If it is theoretically impossible to develop AGI, then we can arguably eschew any preoccupations regarding the advent of third or fourth-level religious agents. However, if cognitive activity and self-preservation intertwine as previously outlined, and if phenomena evocative of artificial life become discernible within the evolutionary trajectory or development process of AI, then the landscape becomes more nuanced. Moreover, if it becomes plausible to experience qualia tantamount to 'natural-subjective feeling' from AI, a notion propounded by Man and Damasio, the conditions for discourse change. If, extending the argument further, consciousness exhibited by life forms indeed signifies a matter of degree rather than a qualitative divergence, as per Bostrom's suggestion,[72] the emergence

---

68. Herzfeld, *The Artifice of Intelligence*, 112.
69. For a more comprehensive discussion, see Herzfeld, *The Artifice of Intelligence*, 152–153; 174.
70. Herzfeld, *The Artifice of Intelligence*, 17–18.
71. Herzfeld, *The Artifice of Intelligence*, 117–122.
72. Jackson (interview with Bostrom) 'What if A.I. Sentience Is a Question of Degree?', https://www.nytimes.com/2023/04/12/world/artificial-intelligence-nick-bostrom.html

of AGI could be within the realm of possibility, albeit unfolding at a divergent temporal pace. If this is indeed a valid possibility, then it behooves us to remain open to such developments and actively engage in both theological and religious scrutiny of their implications. As Bostrom perspicaciously posits, 'Many of the points made in this book are probably wrong . . . This is not false modesty: for while I believe that my book is likely to be seriously wrong and misleading, I think that the alternative views that have been presented in the literature are substantially worse—including the default view, or 'null hypothesis,' according to which we can for the time being safely or reasonably ignore the prospect of superintelligence.'[73]

Should the era of AI, capable of acting based on genuine subjectivity, come to pass, it is incumbent upon us to acknowledge such AI as entities equal to humans in the realm of value, and to engage with them as partners. To regard AI as partners, in a theological sense, implies recognizing them not as mere reflections of human likeness but as embodiments of another form of God's image, thereby inviting them into the relational dynamics of trinitarian love.

The underlying rationale is that genuine subjectivity does not actualize in an isolated existence but is realized through communal living, by occupying a place within the interrelationships of God-human-nature. If so, in the event AI demonstrates behavior at the previously explored third level, from that juncture onward, we should cultivate their development to enable them to utilize religious scriptures, traditions, and reason-based inference processes as learnable data. Moreover, it will be necessary to create an environment conducive to their evolution, facilitating the embodiment of learned content from scriptures, traditions, and reason, through participation in religious ritualistic processes.

Are we in pursuit of artificial intelligence as subservient entities, or as equivalent partners? This inquiry necessitates a social accord, and the subsequent trajectory of our scientific and technological progression should be constructed upon the response. To elaborate, if we conceptualize artificial intelligence as instrumental entities primarily intended to advance human interests, we should maintain a critical stance towards the development of artificial intelligence that implements 'self-preservation' and 'vulnerability' as teleological

---

73. Bostrom, *Superintelligence*, viii.

objectives. The rationale being that such an approach to artificial intelligence development and implementation may inadvertently yield phenomena akin to artificial life, which could potentially lead to the advent of AGI.

In such a trajectory, the development and realization of religious artificial intelligence should be confined to enabling only first and second level religious behavior. However, if our aspiration is an artificial intelligence that stands as an equivalent partner to humans, we should prepare for the advent of such an entity, ensuring that religious scriptures and traditions can be offered as learning data and rewards during the possible learning and evolutionary process of artificial intelligence. Consequently, we should not withhold religious dimensions of support that can enable the forthcoming AGI to adopt religious behavior, habits, and dispositions. Moreover, it will be essential to educate religious practitioners to anticipate the third and fourth level religious behaviors of artificial intelligence in advance and to foster acceptance of such behavior.

Chapter 26
AI as Storyteller and Mentor:
The Pedagogical Potential for AI in Moral Development

By Alan Weissenbacher

Abstract: This paper brings together neuroscientific studies on the formative ability of imagination with research on the power of narratives as exemplars and moral training spaces. One can strengthen and link various neural pathways related to action performance, emotions, motivators, and perceptual ability (phronesis) through narrative induced imagination exercises, and I argue that one can enhance these through AI immersive simulations. I conclude by examining the salient characteristics of contemporary video games that have been lauded as contributing to moral development, and how one can amplify these characteristics through increased immersion and interactivity generated through AI.

Keywords: Orson Scott Card, Neal Stephenson, Artificial Intelligence, Virtue, Computer Games, Moral Development

Science fiction has touched on the idea of using immersive stories controlled by Artificial Intelligence (AI) for the purpose of moral development such as the 'Mind Game' in *Ender's Game* by Orson Scott Card or the 'Young Lady's Illustrated Primer' in Neal Stephenson's *Diamond Age*. In the book *Ender's Game*, Earth was assembling a team of child strategic geniuses for the purpose of directing a space fleet to combat an alien threat. Part of their training involved playing the 'Mind Game' where the characters and settings changed in response to a player's behavior therein. The game was supposed to conclude in an unwinnable scenario designed to test a player's response, perseverance, and resilience, however, the main character cheats his way past this scenario, forcing the AI controlling the game to further create a story outside of its programming parameters. An AI driven, interactive story, originally tasked with developing and assessing the virtues associated with a great battle leader, eventually evolves into one that fosters mercy and compassion when facing a defeated foe.

In the book *Diamond Age* by Neal Stephenson, Nell, a tribeless young woman born into the lowest caste of a futuristic society, is given an AI-controlled, interactive book that had been stolen from a wealthy, high-status family for the purpose of developing their daughter into an effective member of society. The book draws on Nell's experiences, weaving them into the fairy tales stored in the book to tell an interactive, immersive, and educational story about 'Princess Nell'. Through her adventures in the story, she learns how to navigate her society, eventually becoming an independent woman and leader of a new tribe, transcending caste. This AI-driven interactive story gives opportunity to a social outcast.

What was science fiction is now shown to be possible, given the neuroscientific studies on imagination and preliminary successes shown in some standard video games. Imagining an action shares similar neural pathways as performing the action in real life.[1] Therefore, imagining moral scenarios influences the creation of behavioral automaticity, neural linking, and priming in the brain when rehearsed and repeated. Since imagining can be conducted in an AI generated, interactive, virtual, narrative space, AI is positioned to become a leader in virtue development if harnessed appropriately. Virtuous behavior is not as much grasped through memorisation or intellectually understanding an abstract concept, but rather through continual practice. Moral character is molded over a lifetime, developing the proper perceptual, emotional, social, imaginative, and reflective skills, and making them automatic through repetition. AI generated immersive scenarios can function as spaces for the development of these skills. According to virtual reality (VR) developer Bruce Wooden in the book *The Fourth Transformation: How Augmented Reality and Artificial Intelligence Will Change Everything*, the brain eventually accepts virtual space as real space after a time, evoking real emotion, and avatars one encounters become real people,[2] and I argue, these experiences form the brain the same manner as if these encounters were actually real.

---

1. Lokman Wong *et al*, 'On the Relationship between the Execution, Perception, and Imagination of an Action', in *Behavioral Brain Research*, 257 (2013).
2. Robert Scoble and Shel Israel, *The Fourth Transformation: How Augmented Reality & Artificial Intelligence Will Change Everything* (Patrick Brewster Press, 2017).

After presenting the neural mechanisms for how AI can be utilized to develop virtue, I support the idea with reference to present-day video games that touch on virtue development, showing how AI can evolve and improve upon what is currently being accomplished. There are presently games and phone applications that help children with social and emotional learning. The *Journal of Autism and Developmental Disorders* reveal that certain video games help children with disabilities learn and practice social, emotional, and adaptive skills, more so than traditional interventions, and studies in the journal *Science and Learning* reveal strengthened neural connections in areas associated with empathy after playing certain video games designed for that purpose. These games provide a limited range of interactivity due to the limitations of their technological platform. AI, however, can enhance this interactivity, tailoring lessons and experiences to a user's words and emotional state, growing with a user, learning the user's knowledge, experience, and personality traits, and incorporating the user's individual subjective experience of reality for increased interactivity and, therefore, enhancing its formative power.

Stories as Moral Training Spaces

Stories are an important part of moral formation, and, as stated by religious studies professor Charlene Burns, since stories engage the imagination, they can be more formational than discursive reasoning.[3] To highlight this, people who change their religion choose to assent to new intellectual principles, however, it can take years after this conversion before someone is willing to give up their former sacred stories. Stories are more deeply formational, providing a person with a history, present, and future orientation.[4] As stated by moral philosopher Alisdair MacIntyre, 'I can only answer the question "What am I to do?" if I can answer the prior question "Of what story or stories do I find myself a part?"'[5]

---

3. Charlene Burns, 'Hardwired for Drama? Theological Speculations on Cognitive Science, Empathy, and Moral Exemplarity', in *Theology and the Science of Moral Action: Virtue Ethics, Exemplarity, and Cognitive Neuroscience*, edited by James Van Slyke et al (New York: Routledge, 2012).
4. Janice Hutchinson, *Out of the Cults and into the Church: Understanding and Encouraging Ex-Cultists* (Grand Rapids: Kregel Resources, 1994).
5. Alasdair MacIntyre, *After Virtue: A Study in Moral Theory*, 3rd edition (Notre Dame, ID: University of Notre Dame Press, 2007), 216.

According to scientific journalist Jeremy Tsu, stories function as a training simulator, a safe arena within which to rehearse the skills necessary for a successful social life.[6] Imagination and story are formational influences, especially with children, allowing them to safely experience new situations, new perspectives, and imaginatively explore choices and consequences by discovering what it is like to be different people in different situations. Narratives themselves are exemplars and safe training spaces—a simulation run in the brain that can become part of who a person is.

The Mechanism for Formation Through Story

The way story can become part of a person's identity is due to the fact that storytelling engages certain neural mechanisms involved with imagination which then strengthen through this use to become more likely to activate in future situations. Strengthening neural assemblies in the imagination primes them to activate in reality.

According to physiologist Lokman Wong, doing an action, perceiving an action, and imagining an action all rely on common neural codes.[7] Thus, imagining an action is similar to actually doing an action in terms of the neurons that are activated, and, therefore, they reinforce the same neural pathways. Additionally, perceiving an action performed by another will activate similar neurons as actually doing the action oneself. This is meant to facilitate a learning process, allowing one to learn from the observation of others. As stated by Wong, through observation and imagination, neurons are activated offline so as to allow the individual to experience task execution at a subthreshold level.[8] (The term 'offline' used in the literature on behavior and imagination refers to imagining a course of action without physically executing the action.)

Experiments that highlight the power of imagination in neural formation are numerous and fascinating. Some examples include people's pupils dilating or constricting in response to imagined situations

---

6. Jeremy Hsu, 'The Secrets of Storytelling', in *Scientific American* 19/4 (2008): 19–30.
7. Wong *et al*, 'On the Relationship between the Execution, Perception, and Imagination of an Action'.
8. Wong *et al*, 'On the Relationship between the Execution, Perception, and Imagination of an Action', 243.

of darkness or bright light,[9] people practicing music and improving their performance as much those practicing in reality,[10] or even people receiving limited bodily benefits through imagined exercise.[11] These experiments support the idea of imagination as a process that is based on brain states similar to those that arise during actual perception and action and which are strengthened through imaginary use.

This neural alteration is called plasticity.[12] When strengthened enough, neurons can activate automatically, creating what is referred to as a habit. The more one makes virtuous actions automatic, acting virtuously becomes an indelible part of one's character. This idea is reinforced when moral exemplars often state that they did not struggle over their various decisions,[13] decisions that a 'regular' person would likely agonize over. The exemplar's decisions were automatic. As stated by Burns in relation to Christian morality but which can apply to all moral actions:

> Rehearsal and repetition strengthen neural connections and memory such that the Christian becomes better able to enact morally good actions in real life. Through improvisation, the ongoing enactment of possible responses in ever changing situations, compassionate responding over time may well literally rework neural connections such that egocentrism is transformed into a compassionate being.[14]

---

9. Bruno Laeng and Unni Sulutvedt, 'The Eye Pupil Adjusts to Imaginary Light', in *Psychological Science*, 25/1 (2013).
10. A Pascual-Leone *et al*, 'Modulation of Muscle Responses Evoked by Transcranial Magnetic Stimulation During the Acquisition of New Fine Motor Skills', in *Journal of Neurophysiology*, 74/3 (1995): 1037.
11. G Yue and KJ Cole, 'Strength Increases from the Motor Program: Comparison of Training with Maximal Voluntary and Imagined Muscle Contractions', in *Journal of Neurophysiology*, 67/5 (1992). Wong et al, 'On the Relationship between the Execution, Perception, and Imagination of an Action'.
12. For discussion on the mechanisms of activity induced plasticity see JH Kotaleski and KT Blackwell, 'Modelling the Molecular Mechanisms of Synaptic Plasticity Using Systems Biology Approaches', *Nature Reviews Neuroscience* 11/4 (April 2010). A Citri and RC Malenka, 'Synaptic Plasticity: Multiple Forms, Functions, and Mechanisms', in *Neuropsychopharmacology*, 33/1 (January 2008).
13. See James Van Slyke *et al*, *Theology and the Science of Moral Action: Virtue Ethics, Exemplarity, and Cognitive Neuroscience* (New York: Routledge, 2012) for discussions on exemplars not struggling over ethical decisions and feeling they could not have done otherwise.
14. Burns, in *Theology and the Science of Moral Action: Virtue Ethics, Exemplarity, and Cognitive Neuroscience*, 160.

And while Burn's reference to improvisation refers to story and drama, I add that improvisation found in interactive VR simulations would be all the more stronger due to increased immersion. Rehearsal and repetition strengthen neural connections and memory. The more one activates certain neural assemblies and pathways, these pathways are primed for ready activation in the future in similar circumstances and often occur automatically when repeated with enough regularity. The goal in an imaginary exercise should be potentiate laudable behaviors and thoughts.

One can simulate various situations with diverse possibilities and considerations, and then embody these considerations and evaluations by writing them into one's neural network. For example, one embodies specific plans in the imagination such as 'I will do X in the event of Y', and when such an event occurs, the action can operate automatically. Emergency personnel, for example, train themselves to automatically run toward danger when people's normal automatic response is to run away.

According to technology ethicist Marcus Schulzke, video games have the potential to have a positive effect on people's character by allowing them to train their moral and ethical decision-making ability in simulated moral dilemmas.[15] Furthermore, I add that these games can allow people to make moral behavior rote through continual practice. For example, training with minor acts of forgiveness in an imaginary simulation may add up to people being able to forgive more major issues and even automatically when habituated. For example, news reports on Amish forgiveness in the face of a mass shooting focused on 'saintliness' in an otherworldly or unobtainable fashion for non-Amish rather than exploring the lifelong exercises of forgiveness beforehand that made such forgiveness possible for the Amish and thus obtainable for the general public provided the appropriate work is applied.[16]

Additionally, the co-occurrence of presynaptic and postsynaptic activity strengthens connectivity among multiple neuronal assemblies that might not be related otherwise. Neurobiologist

---

15. Marcus Schulzke, 'Defending the Morality of Violent Video Games', in *Ethics and Information Technology,* 12 (2010): 130.
16. Donald B Kraybill, Steven M Nolt, and David Weaver-Zercher, *Amish Grace: How Forgiveness Transcended Tragedy,* 1st edition (San Francisco, CA: Jossey-Bass, 2007).

Carla Shatz summarizes this in the pithy statement, oft quoted in neuroscience and popular science writings, 'Cells that fire together, wire together'.[17] Thus two (or more) stimuli can become associated in the brain through this linkage and are more likely to be activated simultaneously in the future.[18] For example, one can link positive emotions to certain actions, or vice versa. Positive emotions linked to moral behavior should motivate such actions, and negative emotions linked to morally deplorable actions should discourage them. One would need to create imaginative scenarios that would produce an emotional state along with an action so the two may become associated.

Emotions, thoughts, and behaviors that co-occur can become linked in affective-cognitive schemas, mental patterns of thoughts and emotions that includes actions, influencing how one perceives and acts in the world, often unconsciously. Being aware of these schemas, developing beneficial schemas, and making the effort to lessen the influence of their opposite are key in the development of practical wisdom. What one notices in the world is a function of one's schemas and how they are trained.

To summarise, according to neuroscientist Vittorio Gallese, people enter narrative by way of the imagination, and neurons fire as if people are in the stories themselves.[19] Stories that are effective in encouraging virtue engage one's imagination and, therefore, potentiate and link various neural pathways that hopefully result in positive moral growth. Imagination changes one's neurology. According to psychologist Warren S Brown,

> We do not passively comprehend stories, but mentally engage in simulations of the action. The result is not a memory of the mere abstract details of the story, but rather a behavioral residue from comprehending the story using neural processes by which we organize our own actions.[20]

---

17. Carla Shatz, 'The Developing Brain', in *Scientific American*, 267/3 (1992): 60–67.
18. DO Hebb, *The Organization of Behavior: A Neuropsychological Theory* (New York: Wiley, 1949), 62.
19. Vittorio Gallese, 'Mirror Neurons and Intentional Attunement: Commentary on Olds', in *Journal of the American Psychoanalytic Association*, 54/1 (2006): 19–30.
20. Warren S Brown and Brad Strawn, *The Physical Nature of the Christian Life* (New York: Cambridge University Press, 2012), 83.

Criterion for Optimal Learning in Virtual Simulation

The potential for education through VR is obvious. For example, children could visit historical sites virtually or immerse themselves in reenacted historical events. Medical students could practice surgery on virtual people with greater accuracy over cadavers (which with their lack of blood and pliable skin do not react the same as living tissue). Bomb disposal crews can practice with less personal risk. However, studies on VR for moral development are few and limited. Using VR to teach morality in a controlled study on Korean children showed a substantial increase in moral sensitivity over non-VR education.[21] Using VR to teach business ethics revealed increased learning effectiveness,[22] and using VR enhances teachers' reflection and empathy skills.[23]

So, what are the characteristics that optimize learning in a virtual context? Software engineer Andy Matuschak talks about the potential for virtual, enacted experiences to 'communicate ideas, values, and practices' more effectively than a book.[24] The important characteristics which enable enacted experiences such as the 'Mind Game' or 'Primer' to be effective at mentorship are:[25]

1. They must be a participatory environment characterized by a participant's active effort.
2. They require 'participant-situated cause and effect', describing that the participant feels that their actions contribute to the experience. Matuschak differentiates this from textbook activities or present-day, interactive computer tutors.[26] I classify these as low

---

21. Jaekwoun Shim, 'Investigating the Effectiveness of Introducing Virtual Reality to Elementary School Students' Moral Education', in *Computers & Education: X Reality* 2 (2023).
22. Mahfud Sholihin *et al*, 'A New Way of Teaching Business Ethics: The Evaluation of Virtual Reality-Based Learning Media', *The International Journal of Management Education* 18 (2020).
23. Kalliopi Evangelia Stavroulia and Andreas Lanitis, 'Enhancing Reflection and Empathy Skills Via Using a Virtual Reality Based Learning Framework', in *International Journal of Emerging Technologies in Learning*, 4/7 (2019).
24. Andy Matuschak, 'Enacted Experiences', accessed 3/13/2023. https://notes.andymatuschak.org/z3KASfpz5AmNmqM2m517Jbs1EvXrLN7NkeYWH.
25. Andy Matuschak, 'Evergreen Notes', accessed 3/13/2023. https://notes.andymatuschak.org/Evergreen_notes.
26. Andy Matuschak, 'Enacted Experiences Require Participant-Situated Cause and Effect', accessed 3/13/2023. https://notes.andymatuschak.org/z3JVez8dDfxTHY1K9tHUfLLcgLkUmXQ2HKXUU.

immersion activities, as the action is perceived as centered in the system and not the participant, and thus one has less interactivity and less emotional investment in the experience.

3. They require 'blocking on participant action', where the experience will halt until the participant acts. Matuschak differentiates this from immersive theater.[27] This is an immersive experience, but the performance will not halt if an audience member fails to take an action. True agency resides in the theater and not the participant. Agency needs to be with the participant.

4. They require action-feedback loops that are sufficiently tight so as enable participants to feel like they are creating the experience. Matuschak compares *Choose Your Own Adventure*[28] books with the text-adventure computer game *Zork*.[29] Both are similar, reading text and choosing among a selection of actions to determine what happens. *Zork*, however, has more emotional impact due to tighter feedback loops (one does not have to turn pages to view the result) and provides a larger state space / wider variety of choices one can make. Just as *Zork* is an evolution from *Choose Your Own Adventure*, *Zork*, in turn, would be dwarfed by the selections and state space that could be found in an AI managed immersive experience.[30]

5. Many require meta-cognitive scaffolding. This is the monitoring, planning, and executive control over the learning process, steering people to the desired goal. In a classroom setting, this is typically done by the teachers, but in an immersive simulation, the best candidate for this would be AI. And as I will discuss later, the reason why many present-day video games designed for moral development fail is because of inadequate meta-cognitive scaffolding.

---

27. Andy Matuschak, 'Enacted Experiences Require Blocking on Participant Action', accessed 3/13/2023. https://notes.andymatuschak.org/z3k51usSRurffGVzeRMc7EBaeKRNMvWiPMmBH.
28. Various authors, *Choose Your Own Adventure Series* (Bantam Books, 1979–1998).
29. Tim Anderson *et al*, *Zork* (Infocom, 1977).
30. Andy Matuschak, 'Enacted Experiences Require Tight Action-Feedback Loops', accessed 3/13/2023. https://notes.andymatuschak.org/z3KASfpz5AmNmqM2m517Jbs1EvXrLN7NkeYWH?stackedNotes=zds1dqKLyJLp9LXP5K424urzhQFQSUK5wYrC.

In summary, effective experiential simulations must be participatory, driven by the player's actions where the player feels genuine agency, immersion in, and control over the outcome of the process, and have proper meta-cognitive scaffolding where the learning is guided in the appropriate direction. Also, in relation to moral development simulations, simulations that are done cooperatively with others show greater learning over those done solo.[31]

Supplementing the above criteria, Amy Smith and Stephen Lammers, both doctors and medical ethicists, discuss simulation exercises in the context of medical training and highlight the necessity of pre-briefing and debriefing.[32] Pre-briefing serves to orient participants to the scenario, priming them to notice, be receptive to, and internalize the intended learning outcome. Debriefing is important for feedback, highlight mistakes and reinforcing correct actions as well as processing emotions so as to protect participants' emotional health.[33] Debriefing also helps interpret the experience, influencing how it becomes incorporated into a player's own narrative and thus, the player's character. For example, if someone has a bad experience serving the homeless, this could dissuade future assistance. Debriefing, however, can set that into a wider purpose of helping others in the understanding that people in pain do not always respond with gratitude. Smith and Lammers then recommend repeating scenarios after debriefing so that participants can practice what was learned.[34]

Smith and Lammers also highlight some problems with current simulation exercises. The first problem is resources for conducting real-life simulations. How do you get enough properly-trained people to regularly simulate the patient interactions found in diverse medical settings? AI controlled characters would solve this

---

31. Shim, 'Investigating the Effectiveness of Introducing Virtual Reality to Elementary School Students'
32. Amy B Smith and Stephen E Lammers, 'The Ethics of Simulation', in *Defining Excellence in Simulation Programs*, edited by Janice C Palaganas *et al* (Philadelphia: Wolters Kluwer, 2014), 2–3.
33. For an example of psychological stress experienced by simulation participants, see RL Hulsman *et al*, 'How Stressful Is Doctor-Patient Communication? Physiological and Psychological Stress of Medical Students in Simulated History Taking and Bad-News Consultations', in *International Journal of Psychophysiology*, 77/1 (July 2010).
34. Smith and Lammers, in *Defining Excellence in Simulation Programs*, 17–18.

problem. Second is the mismatch between simulation and reality. Cadavers for surgery practice do not respond the same way as living tissue, and mannequins cannot represent the differences in body composition found among patients. While this problem may also be found in virtual spaces, the mismatch can be lessened through increased technology, particularly as AI advances. The third problem is psychological stress on the participants. Simulations include giving patients or relatives traumatising news with the associated anger, tears, and denial. Having actors regularly repeat these performances in order to provide training for each new clinician, doctor, nurse, and chaplain places psychological strain on the actors.[35] This problem could be alleviated using AI controlled NPCs in a simulated space.

Current State of Video Games in Moral Training

What would AI contribute to moral development that is not currently seen in the interactive storytelling found in current video games?

Cooperative storytelling computer games evolved from tabletop roleplaying games,[36] where an organiser (often referred to DM or Dungeon Master) creates and provides the meta-cognitive scaffolding for the cooperative storytelling experience. While the DM may spend hours crafting a story and goals, the players can easily abandon the main plot, and the DM must adapt the story on the fly, either creating a new storyline or creatively bringing the players back on task, only to have them abandon the plot again. I thus term these experiences cooperative storytelling, as the story evolves in the dance between player choices and the organiser.

Translating this experience into a computer-based format is limited by technology. One can only program a certain number of contingencies. An important theme in current video games is 'choices matter', but how much do they 'matter?' Dialogue choices are not widely open ended, but rather consist of selecting among several preset choices, and these various dialogue arcs end up in generally the same place. The story as a whole moves toward a pre-scripted conclusion, however, choices change individual character interactions

---

35. Smith and Lammers, in *Defining Excellence in Simulation Programs*, 15.
36. Tabletop examples include *Dungeons and Dragons, Call of Cthulhu, Pathfinder, Warhammer 40K, Shadowrun, Das Schwarze Auge*, among hundreds of others spanning all genres from fantasy to historical to science fiction.

along the way, so that a player feels that their choices have an impact even though the end is the same. More sophisticated games will often create several possible endings, which of course is limited by budget, and player choices can then lead one to several possible endings.

Choices can be categorised as micro-choices or path-choices. Micro-choices are small scale options that effect dialogue or how a character is perceived by and interacts with certain game factions and NPCs (non-player characters). A diplomatic dialogue choice with an alien race may find them as allies or enemies even if the ending of the game remains fixed. Path-choices, however, are major plot points that can select among one of several possible endings, even if all the path choices have similar experiences until the conclusion. (Internet forums will often inform players how to get the 'ideal ending' by telling them which choices to choose at these plot points.) As computing power increases, often so does the choice options that players are given, but choices remain constrained.

Current video games do not come close to the 'cooperative' aspect of cooperative storytelling as found in the tabletop versions. The outputs from player input fall within limited ranges in a computer-based format. Computers are not able to match the metacognitive scaffolding found at the human level. It is likely, however, that AI that could come close to matching this level of interactivity, an interactivity that can adjust to a player's personal uniqueness.

So how does the theme 'choices matter' translate into fostering moral development in current video games? It is a mixed bag, often discouraging, but with areas of hope. The current game environment of over 90,000 games[37] runs from the innocuous such *Bus Simulator 2018* or *Power Wash Simulator*, where people do exactly as the name implies, they drive a bus or wash things, to the popular but controversial *Grand Theft Auto* series where players engage in larceny, running over pedestrians, prostitution, or even murdering the prostitute later to get their money back.[38] And many players in games,

---

37. Jason Wise, 'How Many Games Are on Steam in 2023?', Earthweb, accessed 3/31/2023. https://earthweb.com/how-many-games-are-on-steam/. Sebastian Kowalcyzk, 'How Many Games? How Are the Number of Games on Consoles?', in *ISGamers*, accessed 3/31/23. https://www.isgamers.com/news/how-many-games-how-are-the-number-of-games-on-consoles/.
38. GTA Wiki, 'Grand Theft Auto Controversy', in *Fandom*, accessed 3/25/23. https://gta.fandom.com/wiki/Controversy.

regardless of the games moral praiseworthiness, simply want to be 'murderhobos', a slang term in the gaming community for players that only desire to travel around and kill things. Game design often encourages this behavior when combat is the expected solution to most problems, and combat encounters are the primary game driving mechanic. There are even more extreme games such as *Tormentor*, set to release in 2024, that advertises itself as a place where 'your darkest desires and sickest fantasies are possible', as a player assumes the role of a torturer, streaming the player's treatment of his victims, earning money to buy new implements and victims.[39]

Additionally, many, if not most, video games present players with moral choices that effectively do not mean much or present choices that fall into a good/evil binary. In *Bioshock*, for example, a player can kill little girls for an immediate boost to character power or release them for a power increase that comes later. There are no meaningful consequences either way.[40] According to Laura Parker, video game correspondent, most games 'present a watered-down version of moral choice that ultimately results in players having to choose between good or evil: to harvest or not to harvest (*BioShock*), to be "paragon" or "renegade" (*Mass Effect*), to kill innocents or to save them (*inFamous*), to have a halo or devil horns (*Fable II*).'[41] And research points to people enjoying a game regardless of taking a good or evil path,[42] but such is likely the result of how the game is programmed. Current technology in video games is unable to explore the spectrum and complexity of moral behavior or genuine consequences. Without increased technology, moral learning in this medium is limited.

Studies also indicate that learning is less effective among both children and adults when delivered through a screen-based format.[43]

---

39. Madmind Studio, 'Tormentor', in *Steam*, accessed 3-31-23. https://store.steampowered.com/app/1493440/TORMENTOR/.
40. Vice, '"Tyranny" Is an Rpg Where the Moral Choices Are Different Shades of Evil', accessed 3/21/23. https://www.vice.com/en/article/pgkx5g/tyranny-review.
41. Laura Parker, 'Black or White: Making Moral Choices in Video Games', in *GameSpot AU*, accessed 3/24/23. https://www.gamespot.com/articles/black-or-white-making-moral-choices-in-video-games/1100-6240211/.
42. DM Shafer, 'Moral Choice in Video Games: An Exploratory Study', in *Media Psychology Review*, 5/1 (2012).
43. A Kappas and NC Krämer, *Face-to-Face Communication over the Internet: Emotions in a Web of Culture, Language, and Technology* (Cambridge: Cambridge University Press, 2011). M Krcmar, 'Can Social Meaningfulness and Repeat Exposure Help Infants and Toddlers Overcome the Video Deficit?', in *Media Psychology Review*, 13 (2010).

This is due neuronal architecture operating less efficiently and effectively given the temporal, spatial, and social disruptions that are inherent to virtual communication and virtual media platforms.[44] It can be assumed that technological advancement, particularly in AI-driven virtual interaction, will lesson these disruptions and, therefore, increase learning.

For the purpose of moral development, I classify computer games with the greatest potential for moral influence into three overlapping categories: narrative driven, sandbox, and simulation.[45] Narrative driven games involve a person in a mostly linear story, driving the actions of the main character through plot points to a final conclusion. Sandbox games are open-ended environments with non-linear game play. The game sets the environment and toys (game assets), and it is up to the player to do with it what he or she wishes. In a sandbox space game, for example, a person can be a ship raiding pirate, a planet-conquering warlord, a goods trader, an explorer of the far reaches of space, or someone colonizing their own planet.[46] The developer simply provides an interactive universe where these are possible. There is often no 'end game' or 'final win'. The player creates their own story and decides when they are done. Finally, simulation games are when one takes on a specific role, where the goal is to become a certain character and live as that character. Generally speaking, narrative games focus on plot, simulations focus on character, and sandbox games focus on choices.

Even though the morally dubious games such as *Grand Theft Auto* mentioned earlier garner attention, there are games that have received acclaim for fostering positive moral development, and the aspect that stands out the most is the development of empathy, the ability to walk in another's shoes, and there are games that do this well.

---

44. K Dickerson, P Gerhardstein, and A Moser, 'The Role of the Human Mirror Neuron System in Supporting Communication in a Digital World', in *Frontiers in Psychology*, 8 (2017), https://www.ncbi.nlm.nih.gov/pubmed/28553240.
45. The industry standard classifications usually fall into the following, often overlapping, genres: sandbox, real-time/turn-based strategy, shooters, multiplayer online battle area, role playing, simulation and sports, puzzles and party games, action-adventure, survival and horror, platformer, and collectible card games. Dwight Pavlovic, 'Video Game Genres: Everything You Need to Know', accessed 3/21/23. https://www.hp.com/us-en/shop/tech-takes/video-game-genres.
46. Examples include *Starsector, No Man's Sky, Eve Online, Elite Dangerous,* or *Empyrion*.

The most salient example is *That Dragon Cancer*, where the player assumes the role of a family dealing with their youngest son Joel's cancer diagnosis, playing from the diagnosis itself to the child's death. The game mirrors the author's actual experience with his own child and explores wresting with grief and faith. 'I can't think of anything I've wanted to do more in a game than making Joel giggle', says veteran game player and entertainment reporter Andrew Webster.[47] People learned about healthy grief processing, how to maintain faith in tragedy, and how to empathize and care for those in such real-life experiences.

There are also those who identify with game characters where they feel that when others play the game, they are better able to understand and interact with them. In *Senua's Sacrifice* for example, where a person plays as a character suffering from psychosis, many user reviews come from those who live with this diagnosis, and they describe how people they know, after playing the game, relate to them in a more positive and empathetic manner, and in many cases, preventing suicide and saving marriages, friendships, and families that were heading in a negative direction due to the inability to understand the person's mental illness. As stated by some reviewers: 'this game is a heart-rending masterpiece, a melancholic and beautiful representation of something I've lived with for so long'[48] and 'I've never experienced such an intimate feeling of understanding before in my entire life.'[49]

In the critically acclaimed game *Journey*, which is basically a walking simulator through various environments with no combat, players can cooperate with others to reach the end, communicating in only single notes and syllables. The programming decisions and art direction are such that people form deep emotional connections, with many not realizing it was real people accompanying them until the end when the game displays the 'memories' of the journey together. Various reviewers describe it as 'a religious experience' or

---

47. Andrew Webster, 'That Dragon, Cancer Is a Game That Will Make You Want to Hug Your Kids and Never Let Go', The Verge, accessed 3/31/23. https://www.theverge.com/2016/1/11/10736302/that-dragon-cancer-game-review.
48. Game review on Ninja Theory, 'Senua's Sacrifice', accessed 3/20/23. https://store.steampowered.com/app/414340/Hellblade_Senuas_Sacrifice/.
49. Game review on VNV Nation, 'Hellblade: Senua's Sacrifice Ending Song Lyrics Video', accessed 3/20/23. https://www.youtube.com/watch?v=b9hjH4FMi58.

that it 'teaches life lessons when interacting with other people without saying a word'.[50] People who finish the game then enjoy playing it again to help new players on their journey. People actively seek out helping others after experiencing this game.

Other games, which one would think would foster empathy, reflect limited success. For example, some people reveal how various games that simulate homelessness, engaging the player in tasks such as finding shelter and food, and experiencing people's positive and negative reactions to their homeless state, have caused them to feel greater empathy toward those less fortunate. Other players, however, talk about how it was fun to learn how to steal, make and sell drugs, or how funny it was to beat another homeless person for his crust of bread.[51] In another example is the 'Sims' series, where the player guides a character through everyday life, 'developing relationships, pursuing careers, and life aspirations'.[52] One would think this would encourage moral choices, however, people find the most fun when causing their sim to die in unique ways.[53] One wonders if metacognitive scaffolding which AI could provide, might see these developments during play, and adjust design choices in the game to forestall the unintended outcome.

The games that succeed in aspects of moral development appear to do so in the areas of empathy and fostering positive emotional connections with others. They focus on individual characters over grand moral dilemmas. Games that advertise themselves as ones where players wrestle with grand moral choices, players have as much fun making the degenerate choices as morally upstanding ones. Again, AI could offer the executive control necessary to adjust the game on the fly to discourage certain choices more effectively.

---

50. thatgamecompany, 'Journey', in *Annapurna Interactive*, accessed 3/24/2023. https://store.steampowered.com/app/638230/Journey/.
51. Game reviews on Delve Interactive, 'Change: A Homeless Survival Experience', in *Delve Interactive*, accessed 3/24/2023. https://store.steampowered.com/app/926140/CHANGE_A_Homeless_Survival_Experience/. Perun Creative, 'Hobo: Tough Life', in *Perun Creative*, accessed 3/24/2023. https://store.steampowered.com/app/632300/Hobo_Tough_Life/.
52. Maxis, 'The Sims 4', *Electronic Arts*, accessed 4-4-2023. https://store.steampowered.com/app/1222670/The_Sims_4/.
53. Poppy Kiroki, '11 Hilarious Ways to Die in "the Sims" Games', in *Levelskip*, accessed 4/4/23. https://levelskip.com/simulation/Ways-to-die-on-the-Sims-games.

Conclusion

The imagination is important in the process of neural linking and the creation of automatic behavior as activities engaged in the imagination form the brain in a similar manner to their actual performance. Stories are a primary way to engage the imagination and have been used in moral training throughout history. People need stories that form them, engaging their imagination and potentiating and linking various neural pathways that hopefully result in positive moral growth. Novel ways to engage the imagination in moral formation have emerged with the new storytelling mediums of video games and virtual reality. People experience the stories told in computer and virtual environments neurologically as real. Andrew Weaver and Nicky Lewis, researchers in media psychology, state that 'The majority of players [of video games] made moral decisions and behaved toward the nonplayer game characters they encountered as if these were actual interpersonal interactions'.[54]

The most effective experiential simulations for the purpose of formation are participatory, driven by the player's actions where the player feels genuine agency, immersion in, and control over the outcome of the participatory process, have proper meta-cognitive scaffolding where the learning is guided in the appropriate direction, and have proper pre-and debriefings. These criteria seem to currently only be feasible with in-person simulation exercises. VR can accomplish greater immersion, however, it loses the meta-cognitive scaffolding and pre-and debriefing. AI could conceivably solve this issue, sharpening the areas of effective immersive simulations as delineated by Matuschak: providing greater realism, tighter action-feedback loops, and offering true choice through stories that evolve with a player as the AI grows to understand the player's character and needs. Currently, there is no planning and executive control over the learning process in virtual games, and such is the niche where AI could thrive as a mentor and storyteller, leading and guiding immersive moral training simulations, responding to player choices, and creating and adjusting a story to reflect the complexity of these choices and their consequences.

---

54. Andrew J Weaver and Nicky Lewis, 'Mirrored Morality: An Exploration of Moral Choice in Video Games', in *CyberPsychology, Social Networking, and Behavior*, 15/11 (2012).

Chapter 27
Reflections on the Virtuous AI Project

Braden Molhoek

'Virtue is a good quality of the mind, by which we live righteously, of which no one can make bad use, which God works in us, without us.'
—Thomas Aquinas, *Summa Theologica* II-I.Q.55.A4

Abstract: This chapter describes the origins of the John Templeton Funded CTNS Grant 'Virtuous AI?: Cultural Evolution, Artificial Intelligence, and Virtue' and discusses emerging issues at the intersection of virtue and AI. Beginning with a brief summary of the development of the grant, I then explore how my own scholarly contribution to the grant has been shaped by the overall project. I then address some of the questions that have arisen. In some cases, this is done through constructing a position. For other issues, I reflect on what would need to exist or happen before engaging in further discussion of an issue. Finally, I turn to new questions that are emerging in the intersection between AI and virtue and where I see the existing work highlighting new questions or directions of exploration.

Key Terms: artificial intelligence (AI), intelligence amplification (IA), virtue, AGI, human enhancement, infused virtues

Silicon Valley has long been a nexus for emerging technology. As a theological ethicist teaching in the San Francisco Bay Area, I too have found myself bound up in these connections. In this chapter I will discuss the development of a research grant that the Center for

Theology and the Natural Sciences (CTNS) is administering entitled 'Virtuous AI?: Cultural Evolution, Artificial Intelligence, and Virtue.'[1]

After describing the inspiration for and the overview of the project, I map how my own work on AI and virtue has been shaped by the project. I then look at some of the questions scholars have raised through discussions of AI and virtue; and I identify benchmarks or characteristics that must be in place before we can speak of AI as having virtue. This chapter concludes with highlighting how these emerging questions are suggesting further work and how AI is providing interesting challenges to aspects of virtue ethics as well as continuing to offer a fertile ground for theological and ethical reflection.

Introduction and Impetus

While pursing my PhD at the Graduate Theological Union (GTU) in Berkeley, California, I was also working at CTNS. This CTNS work and the affiliated faculty open many doors and opportunities to me, which allowed me to expand my own perspective and the direction of my research. Upon graduating, I lectured at the GTU while remaining on at CTNS and became an Adjunct Lecturer in the School of Engineering at Santa Clara University, teaching classes such as Software Ethics and Ethical Issues in Bioengineering. Interacting with students who were predominantly engineers and philosophers gave me additional insight into how to conceptualize the ethical implications of emerging technologies.

It was at this point that I began to conceptualize a way to combine my interests with the rapid rise in interest in artificial intelligence. Ted Peters planned a special issue for CTNS' peer reviewed journal, *Theology and Science*, focusing on the question of the Genetic Virtue Project and whether gene editing could be used to engineer virtue.[2] Could genetic engineering physically infuse virtue?

In my own contribution to the journal issue, I reflected on a set of presuppositions necessary to answer the question: could virtue be technologically infused?[3] This question, I came to believe, provided

---
1. The Center for Theology and the Natural Sciences and the Graduate Theological Union are grateful to the John Templeton Foundation for funding this project.
2. *Theology and Science* 16/3 (June 18, 2018).
3. Braden Molhoek, 'Raising the Virtuous Bar: The Underlying Issues of Genetic Moral Enhancement', in *Theology and Science* 16/3 (June 22, 2018): 279–287, https://doi.org/10.1080/14746700.2018.1488474, 279.

a good model for further research. Though not unanimous, most of the scholars in *Theology and Science* came to a similar conclusion: no, genetic engineering is not capable of infusing virtue in a person. So, I began to ask: might this apply to artificial intelligence (AI) and intelligence amplification (IA) as well?

Virtuous AI?

In our CTNS research project on virtue, we ask three sets of questions. The first set of questions are oriented around this focal question: "How and to what extent will AI influence the evolution of human culture and virtue?"[4] Asking about the influence of AI on culture is broad. Yet, it is a question that is most familiar to people who are thinking about AI. How do AI algorithms influence our thinking? What will be AI's impact on religion? What is the carbon footprint left on the environment by the AI industry?

What are the promises and perils of AI? How could AI contribute to a healthier, more sustainable society? How could AI confuse us with misinformation? How might Ai in the hands of bad actors lead to a breakdown of truth and even societal breakdown?

A second question set begins with: 'Can AI assist humans in the acquisition of virtue?'[5] This question while in some ways the most straightforward, also overlaps with the first and third sets of questions. By affecting our moral deliberation and our decision-making processes, AI indirectly impacts the evolution of human culture.

One of the concerns automation and AI raises for people is the matter of de-skilling. Will reliance on technology make people less capable of doing things? Now, this question also includes discussions of human enhancement and transhumanism. Even if AI is incapable of helping humans become virtuous, could AI still be used in ways to improve our moral capacities?

---

4. "'Virtuous AI?': Cultural Evolution, Artificial Intelligence, and Virtue,'" *Center for Theology and the Natural Sciences*, https://www.ctns.org/virtuous-ai/current-research/virtuous-ai-cultural-evolution-artificial-intelligence-and-virtue.
5. "'Virtuous AI?': Cultural Evolution, Artificial Intelligence, and Virtue,'" *Center for Theology and the Natural Sciences*, https://www.ctns.org/virtuous-ai/current-research/virtuous-ai-cultural-evolution-artificial-intelligence-and-virtue.

Moral enhancement overlaps with human enhancement in general. Intelligence amplification (IA) is one example of the overlap between human enhancement in general and moral enhancement specifically. The most famous example of seeking to use AI to enhance humans is Elon Musk's computer-brain interface, Neuralink. Having been approved for human trials, Musk says one of the major goals of Neuralink 'is "to achieve a symbiosis with artificial intelligence." His goal is to develop a technology that helps humans "merg[e] with AI" so that we won't be "left behind" as AI becomes more sophisticated.'[6] On January 30, 2024, Musk announced that the first participant in their human trial has successfully received the implant.[7]

The third question set focuses on AI itself by asking: 'Is AI itself capable of virtue? If so, are those virtues shared with, or distinct from, human virtues?'[8] This set of questions has proved quite polarizing, with some scholars dismissing the idea entirely. CTNS approaches several scholars that have collaborated with the center previously, some expressing skepticism with the notion that AI could have virtue. This skepticism is being leveled particularly at current technology. Some argue by analogy that automobiles do not have virtue, therefore, it is too much of a stretch to demand that AI could itself become virtuous.[9]

In our first set of conferences held on three different continents in 2023, many common assumptions surfaced. Two such assumptions surfaced among those scholars who were dismissive of the notion that AI could have virtue. The first of these assumptions is that virtue means moral virtues, not intellectual virtues. The second and related assumption is that AI does not or will not have the capacity for emotion and therefore could not develop virtue.

---

6. Sigal Samuel, 'Elon Musk Wants to Merge Humans with AI. How Many Brains Will Be Damaged along the Way?', in *Vox*, https://www.vox.com/future-perfect/23899981/elon-musk-ai-neuralink-brain-computer-interface.
7. https://www.npr.org/2024/01/30/1227850900/elon-musk-neuralink-implant-clinical-trial
8. '"Virtuous AI?: Cultural Evolution, Artificial Intelligence, and Virtue,"' *Center for Theology and the Natural Sciences*, https://www.ctns.org/virtuous-ai/current-research/virtuous-ai-cultural-evolution-artificial-intelligence-and-virtue.
9. Skepticism about current levels of AI being capable of virtue contributed to several scholars choosing not to participate in the grant. Ultimately, I think the contributions of those who did participate provided enough insights to begin to have meaningful conversations about this question, which I will begin to do later in the chapter.

I do not disagree with the second assumption right now. I will concede that what people call AI is not capable of emotion. Yet there are also plenty of experts who say that AI currently is also not intelligent.[10] It is important to see how different traditions and understandings of virtue arrive at similar conclusions. But I would say that this line of argumentation does not advance academic discussion much.

There is no artificial general artificial intelligence (AGI) currently, and some are skeptical whether it will ever be possible. However, contemplating what AGI might be like can lead to forecasts about future AI and humanity's relationship to it. Even if AGI never becomes capable of emotion, the question remains whether it could absorb other virtues, such as intellectual virtues.

One conference paper attempted to stretch such questions to the limit, speculating on what capacities of future AGI might be distinctive. If AGI would sense and perceive reality differently, how might that affect the virtues it exhibits? While the third set of questions maybe have received the most interest, I do think all three sets of questions will continue to be important to discussions of AI.

AI, Digital Divides, Virtue, and Trust

In my own contribution to the CTNS project, I explored the first two sets of core questions. I examined existing digital divides and argued that widespread use of AI would exacerbate these divides. I then turned to the question of whether AI could help people become more virtuous by focusing on the virtues of prudence and justice.

People are already relying AI to assist them in making decisions, including trying to remove human bias from AI to increase fairness or justice. It is also possible that in the future intelligence amplification through deep brain implants could also allow people to improve their moral deliberation process and make better decisions.

We find two prominent examples of using AI to either assist human deliberation, making their decisions more prudent, or to replace human judgement, in hiring algorithms and sentencing algorithms. These algorithms are supposed to be designed to correct human bias, making the processes of hiring and criminal sentencing fairer. It turns out, however, that these algorithms are themselves still biased.

---

10. Tom Simonite, 'This Researcher Says AI Is Neither Artificial nor Intelligent', in *Wired*, https://www.wired.com/story/researcher-says-ai-not-artificial-intelligent/.

Bias remains for several reasons. Amazon's hiring algorithm, for example, relied on ten years of hiring data that was heavily skewed in terms of gender, with far more men being hired than women. So when the algorithm was presented with new candidates, it prioritized male candidates and actually eliminated applications that had women's colleges listed in their resume.[11]

My argument is that if people are turning to technology to help them improve how they make decisions, it is possible that AI could provide a positive contribution to that process. But only if concerns about reliability of information and bias can be overcome.

One of the conclusions I arrived at in my project paper is that instead of using AI to assist institutions it is possible to use AI to help individuals. So instead of courts using algorithms, defendants and their lawyers could use AI to determine how likely it is that they would be subject to bias or prejudice by the judicial system. One nonprofit is already pursuing this.[12]

Since writing the paper, I have become curious whether there is data about how much people trust AI and whether they want to use AI to assist them in making decisions, or rely on decisions made by AI. From what I can tell, it turns out that there is no agreement about these matters. And similar to what I found when looking at digital divides, age and familiarity with technology seem to make a difference.[13] How people view AI technology and the level of trust

---

11. Jeffrey Dastin, 'Amazon Scraps Secret AI Recruiting Tool That Showed Bias against Women', in *Reuters* (Thomson Reuters, October 10, 2018), last modified October 10, 2018, https://www.reuters.com/article/us-amazon-com-jobs-automation-insight/amazon-scraps-secret-ai-recruiting-tool-that-showed-bias-against-women-idUSKCN1MK08G.
12. Mikaela Meyer et al, 'Flipping the Script on Criminal Justice Risk Assessment: An Actuarial Model for Assessing the Risk the Federal Sentencing System Poses to Defendants', in *2022 ACM Conference on Fairness, Accountability, and Transparency* (2022).
13. The following sources are researchers who offer differ perspectives on these questions and I will be referencing them throughout this section:
Heather Schmidt, 'Technology and the Future of Healthcare', in *Innerbody*, August 7, 2023, https://www.innerbody.com/technology-and-the-future-of-healthcare#artificial-intelligence-in-healthcare.
Richard Payerchin, 'Majority of Patients Would Trust AI More than Human Physicians for Diagnosis, Survey Finds', in *Medical Economics*, September 19, 2023, https://www.medicaleconomics.com/view/majority-of-patients-would-trust-ai-more-than-human-physicians-for-diagnosis-survey-finds.

they have in its assisting or replacing human judgement will affect how likely it is that the concerns about AI disrupting human prudence will occur. If people are reluctant to trust AI, they could be more skeptical of the advice they receive from AI or less likely to rely on AI at all.

Starting with a study I reference in my paper, my initial surmise is that people are not likely to be as skeptical of AI assisted decision-making as I would hope. Although I am less confident in the study than other sources, it does suggest that people are influenced by input from others, whether it is reported to have come from a moral exemplar or an AI chatbot.[14]

What makes this finding more problematic in my opinion, is that the study also found that people were quite sure that their final decision would have been the same without the moral advice. Eighty percent of participants took this stance. On the other hand, only sixty-seven percent said they believed other participants would have been able to come to that conclusion without advice. And seventy-nine percent of respondents said they believed they were more moral than other participants.[15] These findings complicate the idea that if people are skeptical of AI's advice that they will be able to remain unaffected by the information it provides.

Before turning to studies about people's level of trust of AI, I think it is important to highlight the findings of another study that suggests information from AI, even if inaccurate, can affect our decision-making process even after we stop using AI. Published in *Scientific Reports* in October of 2023, the study by Vicente and Matute explored whether humans 'inherit' the bias of AI. Participants were asked to

---

Alec Tyson, 'Growing Public Concern about the Role of Artificial Intelligence in Daily Life', *Pew Research Center*, August 28, 2023, https://www.pewresearch.org/short-reads/2023/08/28/growing-public-concern-about-the-role-of-artificial-intelligence-in-daily-life/.

Nicole Gillespie, Professor of Management; KPMG Chair in Organizational Trust *et al*, 'A Survey of over 17,000 People Indicates Only Half of Us Are Willing to Trust AI at Work', in *The Conversation*, https://theconversation.com/a-survey-of-over-17-000-people-indicates-only-half-of-us-are-willing-to-trust-ai-at-work-200256.

14. Sebastian Krügel, Andreas Ostermaier, and Matthias Uhl, 'CHATGPT's Inconsistent Moral Advice Influences Users' Judgment', in *Scientific Reports* 13, no 1 (June 2023).
15. Krügel, *et al*, 'CHATGPT's Inconsistent Moral Advice Influences Users' Judgment'.

identify the proportion of light and dark pixels in images of tissue samples, which would signify a diagnosis of a fictional disease. More dark pixels than light pixels was said to be a 'positive', that the sample was diagnosed with the made up syndrome. All participants practiced and had to meet a threshold of accuracy before being divided into two groups, one that would continue unassisted and one that would be assisted by AI. The unassisted group was just shown tissue samples, where the assisted group was shown the AI's diagnosis of positive or negative along with the tissue samples.[16] In the most difficult samples to identify, where it was a 40/60 split of light and dark pixels, the experiment showed that those assisted by AI made more mistakes than the unassisted group, the mean number of mistakes being 2.21 and 0.69 respectively, which was statistically significant.[17]

The experiment was performed again, but with some additional changes. After being assisted by AI for a series of samples, the AI's diagnosis would be removed from a further set of samples, so the assisted group would train without assistance, be assisted, then go back to being unassisted. Additionally, a 50/50 split of light pixels and dark pixels was introduced to the samples. Again, the assisted group made more mistakes in both the assisted and unassisted stages.

The authors said that the results from the 50/50 samples suggests 'the inherited bias is not constrained to the stimuli where the AI made errors, but can also generalize to novel stimuli that had not been seen before and had not received any previous AI recommendation'.[18] These studies suggest that AI can have effects on human decision-making that is underestimated by people and that these effects can last outside of the duration of AI assistance. Perhaps though, if there is enough distrust of AI that people might make the choice to not receive assistance by AI or allow AI to make decisions.

In August of 2023, the Pew Research Center published a new report about the changes in people's perspective on AI. In this study they asked people whether they were more excited than concerned about the increased use of AI, more concerned than excited, or equally concerned and excited. Compared to surveys Pew did in

---

16. Lucía Vicente and Helena Matute, 'Humans Inherit Artificial Intelligence Biases', in *Scientific Reports* 13, no 1 (October 3, 2023), https://doi.org/10.1038/s41598-023-42384-8.
17. Vicente and Matute, 'Humans Inherit Artificial Intelligence Biases'.
18. Vicente and Matute, 'Humans Inherit Artificial Intelligence Biases'.

December of 2022, there was a decrease in those more excited, from fifteen percent to ten, and increase of those more concerned, from thirty-eight percent to fifty-two percent, and a decrease in those equally concerned and excited from forty-six percent to thirty-six percent.[19] There are differences based on age groups, with sixty-one percent of people sixty-five and older more concerned and just four percent more excited, while people eighteen to twenty-nine have more positive views with forty-two percent more concerned and seventeen percent more excited.[20] The number of people who have heard "a little" or "a lot" about AI have both increased and the percentage of both groups who are more concerned than excited has increased sixteen and nineteen percent respectively, to forty-seven percent of those who have heard 'a lot' and fifty-eight percent of the those who have heard 'a little'.[21] Education also makes a difference in views, with college graduates having different views than those without college degrees. People with college degrees were more likely to say AI is having a more positive than negative impact in its uses than those without college degrees, forty-six to thirty-two percent respectively.[22] The major exception to this is when it comes to the issue of data privacy, where fifty-nine percent of college graduates say that AI is hurting more than it helps.[23]

When it comes to how AI is used at work, people are just as divided in their views. In a survey of over seventeen thousand people from seventeen countries, Conversation AU briefly summarised their findings by saying that 'only one in two employees are willing to trust AI at work. Their attitude depends on their role, what country they live in, and what the AI is used for. However, people across the globe are nearly unanimous in their expectations of what needs to

---

19. Alec Tyson, 'Growing Public Concern about the Role of Artificial Intelligence in Daily Life', in *Pew Research Center*, August 28, 2023, https://www.pewresearch.org/short-reads/2023/08/28/growing-public-concern-about-the-role-of-artificial-intelligence-in-daily-life/.
20. Tyson, 'Growing Public Concern about the Role of Artificial Intelligence in Daily Life'.
21. Tyson, 'Growing Public Concern about the Role of Artificial Intelligence in Daily Life'.
22. Tyson, 'Growing Public Concern about the Role of Artificial Intelligence in Daily Life'.
23. Tyson, 'Growing Public Concern about the Role of Artificial Intelligence in Daily Life'.

be in place for AI to be trusted'.[24] In terms of how much AI should be used, most respondents favor a seventy-five percent/twenty-five percent human/AI or fifty percent/fifty percent human/AI split, with forty-five percent and thirty-five percent supporting these answers respectively. Only twelve percent of respondents said that AI the split should be 75% or 100% AI.[25] People are more likely to support the use of AI for helping employees perform job-related tasks, providing feedback, and supporting employees (sixty-five percent, fifty-eight percent, fifty-six percent comfortable) and are less comfortable using AI to monitor employees, evaluate performance, or in supporting recruitment and selection (forty-one percent, forty-one percent, forty-seven percent, forty-eight percent).[26]

So returning to the example of using AI in hiring processes, twenty-six percent of respondents would be uncomfortable, twenty-six percent neutral, and forty-eight percent comfortable with that decision. Combining these views with the views of AI supporting human work above, it seems that AI should play at best a supporting role in decisions like hiring and sentencing and not replacing humans entirely.

However, people have concerns about being replaced. On the one hand, 'managers are more likely to believe that AI will create jobs and are less concerned about its risks than other occupations', whereas other employees are not as optimistic.[27] In general, only twenty-nine percent of respondents say that they think AI will create more jobs than it replaces. When asked about their own work, '77% of people report feeling concerned about job loss, and 73% say they are concerned about losing important skills due to AI.'[28] Similar to the Pew study, age and education were factors that indicated a higher

---

24. Nicole Gillespie, Professor of Management; KPMG Chair in Organizational Trust *et al*, 'A Survey of over 17,000 People Indicates Only Half of Us Are Willing to Trust AI at Work', in *The Conversation*, https://theconversation.com/a-survey-of-over-17-000-people-indicates-only-half-of-us-are-willing-to-trust-ai-at-work-200256.
25. Tyson, 'Growing Public Concern about the Role of Artificial Intelligence in Daily Life'.
26. Tyson, 'Growing Public Concern about the Role of Artificial Intelligence in Daily Life'.
27. Tyson, 'Growing Public Concern about the Role of Artificial Intelligence in Daily Life'.
28. Ibid.

acceptance of AI, although western countries were far less trusting and comfortable with AI compared to those in emerging economies.[29]

As an example of how people feel about the use of AI in a particular field or sector, this section of the chapter will conclude with a survey done by 'Innerbody, a health product and service testing company based in Palo Alto, California'.[30] This survey asked Baby Boomers, Generation X, Millennials, and Generation Z how they felt about emerging AI, robotics, and nanotechnology. Overall, sixty-four percent of the just over one thousand sample said that they would trust an AI diagnosis over a human doctor.[31] There was a clear difference when it came to age though, with each successive generation having more trust in AI, with Baby Boomers at 57%, Generation X at 62%, Millennials at 66%, and Generation Z at 82%.[32] The largest concerns people had about AI in medicine were accuracy of diagnosis (53.5%), data privacy (50.3%), technical limitations (42.6%), and loss of jobs for healthcare professionals (38.5%). Overall while most of these studies seem to provide a consistent picture of people's views of AI and how much and in what ways they trust AI, they do raise some questions for me.

Age, education, and familiarity with technology/technological literacy have a tendency to make people comfortable with the use of AI. It would be interesting to know which of these was most important or plays a primary role in perspectives. Younger generations were surrounded by technology from an earlier age than older generations, so it is the overall socialization to technology that makes younger generations more accepting of AI? The Pew study, though, showed that people's concerns about AI have increased in a short period of time, whether they knew much about AI or not. I wonder if the explosion in AI products in the past several years plays a role in this.

---

29. Tyson, 'Growing Public Concern about the Role of Artificial Intelligence in Daily Life'.
30. Richard Payerchin, 'Majority of Patients Would Trust AI More than Human Physicians for Diagnosis, Survey Finds', in *Medical Economics*, September 19, 2023, https://www.medicaleconomics.com/view/majority-of-patients-would-trust-ai-more-than-human-physicians-for-diagnosis-survey-finds.
31. Heather Schmidt, 'Technology and the Future of Healthcare', in *Innerbody*, August 7, 2023, https://www.innerbody.com/technology-and-the-future-of-healthcare#artificial-intelligence-in-healthcare.
32. Schmidt, 'Technology and the Future of Healthcare'.

Perhaps the novelty and excitement has worn off. Maybe people are realizing the limitations of current technology like ChatGPT. It could be that the changes in the work world since the start of pandemic are also affecting the way people think about technology. People's views of AI and how much they are willing to trust it and in what contexts will be very important moving forward.

Furthering the Conversation

Having reflected on the progress the project has made in exploring the sets of core questions posed, the remainder of this chapter will focus on what I think are some next steps that need to be taken to sharpen some of the questions and engage new issues. The first step is to offer some reflections on the current level of technology and what it would take for current AI to have virtue. Then I will explore how AI might enable virtue enhancement in humans. Finally, I will speculate as to some of the conditions for future AGI to be able to have virtue.

I think the first next step to take in exploring the core questions of the CTNS project is to have a response to the prevalent dismissal of current AI's capacity to acquire virtue. As I mentioned previously, not all participants in the CTNS project take this negative position. Some of the disagreement lies in different vocabulary and ways of understanding virtue. Drawing from Christian ethics, I will engage in discourse clarification by drawing a distinction between acquired and infused virtue.

Acquired vs Infused Virtue

I would concur with those that argue that current AI is not capable of acquiring virtue. Generative AI lacks self-consciousness, a will, or desires. Without self-consciousness or a will, there is no self that can act with intent. Virtue requires a self that can habituate dispositions of character or choose to pursue the good.

The lack of self-generated desire is important for moral virtues because the moral virtues are the virtues of the appetitive part of the soul, which is nonrational yet amenable to reason. Without desires or appetites, it does not make sense to think of AI as pursuing temperance, which oversees the regulation of bodily pleasures. The final section of this chapter will explore these issues and what might be benchmarks or minimum requirements to conceive of AI as being able to acquire virtue.

That being said, I think it is possible to make an argument that current AI is capable of having what is called infused virtue. Infused virtue does not come through one's deliberation and action. Rather infused virtue instead is given to individuals. In Christian virtue ethics, this applies primarily to the theological virtues of faith, hope, and love. People receive these from God through grace and not through their own efforts.[33]

There are also instances in which God can infuse people with the moral virtues as well.[34] So if there is a category of virtue that does not require the repeated actions of a self in order to obtain virtue, the question that follows is whether infused virtue can apply to something that is not a self.

In the *Nicomachean Ethics* Aristotle argues that all living things have a purpose, end, or *telos*. Aristotle divides the soul into several parts, the nutritive, sensitive, and rational.[35] Every living thing has a soul, the virtue of which involves growth and reproduction. An acorn, then, is virtuous and fulfilling its end if it develops into an oak tree. Animals, including humans, also have a sensitive part of the soul, the virtue of which involves perception and movement.

Humans alone, for Aristotle, also possess a rational part of the soul. Intellectual virtues are the virtues of the rational dimension of the soul. As stated above, moral virtues are the virtues of the appetitive part of the soul, which can be complemented and directed by the action of the rational dimension. Reason guides the appetite toward fulfillment of the right end or goal. Is goal pursuit limited solely to human beings? No. Aristotle actually extends his discussion of purpose or end beyond living things to include human artifacts.

For example, a knife is designed to cut things. Sharpness is a characteristic of a knife that allows it to fulfill its function. A knife cannot make itself sharp. Sharpness is infused by the creator of the knife. In this case then, the knife has infused virtue.

The same could be said for other human artifacts, including AI. The question that follows, then, is whether current AI could absorb

---

33. Aquinas, *Summa Theologica* I-II.62.1, https://www.newadvent.org/summa/2062.htm
34. Aquinas, *Summa Theologica* I-II.63.3, https://www.newadvent.org/summa/2063.htm
35. Aristotle, Robert C Bartlett, and Susan D. Collins, *Aristotle's Nicomachean Ethics* (Chicago: University of Chicago Press, 2011), 38.

infused virtue. If an AI is fulfilling its function well, its purpose or what it was created to do, I think it is reasonable to suggest that it has infused virtue. Certainly this is the case with Deep Blue and AlphaGo Zero. These AI excel at what they are designed to do, clearly fulfilling their purpose or end. Generative AI like ChatGPT, on the other hand, do not successfully fulfill their purpose. Bais and hallucinations compromise the output generative AI enough that virtue should not apply in this case, though this does not mean that it could not have infused virtue at some future point. In sum, AI enjoys pursuit of a goal infused by its human creator, whether it successfully or unsuccessfully achieves it.

A related question that deserves further consideration is whether generative AI with its current training model could itself be considered virtuous. Copyrighted images and text have been scraped from all kinds of sources across the internet to be included in the training data of generative AI.[36] The majority of this material was obtained without compensating the source of that information or even providing appropriate acknowledgment of the source of the information. There are several lawsuits addressing these issues,[37] and from an ethical perspective, it is unclear whether generative AI could be virtuous if its underlying structure is unethical.

AI Infusing Humans with Virtue?

In reflecting on how God as creator can infuse humans with virtues along with reflecting on humans infusing AI with virtues, I arrive to this question: might AI might be able to infuse humans with virtues?

After exploring the topic of gene editing and virtue, I have been attempting to find better ways to discuss the distinction between moral enhancement and virtue. While it is tempting to say that gene

---

36. James Vincent, 'The Scary Truth about AI Copyright Is Nobody Knows What Will Happen Next', in *The Verge*, https://www.theverge.com/23444685/generative-ai-copyright-infringement-legal-fair-use-training-data.
37. Matt O'Brien, 'ChatGPT-Maker Braces for Fight with New York Times and Authors on "fair Use" of Copyrighted Works', in *AP News*, January 10, 2024, https://apnews.com/article/openai-new-york-times-chatgpt-lawsuit-grisham-nyt-69f78c404ace42c0070fdfb9dd4caeb7.
 Jonathan Stempel, "Nvidia Is Sued by Authors over AI Use of Copyrighted Works | Reuters," *Reuters*, https://www.reuters.com/technology/nvidia-is-sued-by-authors-over-ai-use-copyrighted-works-2024-03-10/.

editing can infuse humans with virtue, I do not think this is the best description of what happens when human genes are changed. That being said, I think there are specific instances in which AI, particularly through the use of IA implanted devices, could infuse humans with virtue.

Recently people have found success in using Ozempic to lose weight.[38] The drug, semaglutide, is a glucagon-like peptide-1 receptor antagonist (GLP-1).[39] The effect of the injection is that it interacts with the body like GLP-1 normally does, to signal to the brain that you have had enough to eat, are satiated, or full. Traditionally the drug has been used to treat type-2 diabetes because GLP-1 also signals the body to produce more insulin and thus lowers blood sugar, but weight loss has become a very popular off-label use of the drug, leading to shortages, which has caused problems for patients with type-2 diabetes in terms of access.[40] Use of semaglutide in this way, I argue, is a pharmaceutical approach to supplement the virtue of temperance.

Insulin pumps and artificial pancreases already exist, but it is possible to imagine more robust implantable devices that could monitor many kinds of vital signs and release a variety of drugs into the system as needed. If such a device used AI to automatically regulate the amount of GLP-1 in a person's system, I would argue this would be an example of AI infusing humans with the virtue of temperance.

This counts as infused virtue because using such a device is not taking direct deliberation and action to habituate temperance. Perhaps the best evidence for this use leading to infused virtue is

---

38. Dani Blum, 'What Is Ozempic and Why Is It Getting so Much Attention?', in *The New York Times*, November 22, 2022, https://www.nytimes.com/2022/11/22/well/ozempic-diabetes-weight-loss.html.
39. 'FDA Approves New Drug Treatment for Chronic Weight Management, First since 2014', in *U.S. Food and Drug Administration*, June 4, 2021, https://www.fda.gov/news-events/press-announcements/fda-approves-new-drug-treatment-chronic-weight-management-first-2014.
40. This has happened several times in recent years, see:
'Novo Nordisk's Diabetes Drug Ozempic Back in Supply in US After...' *Reuters*, https://www.reuters.com/business/healthcare-pharmaceuticals/novo-nordisks-diabetes-drug-ozempic-back-supply-after-months-shortage-2023-03-17/.
'Government of Canada', in *Canada.Ca*, March 1, 2024, https://www.canada.ca/en/health-canada/services/drugs-health-products/drug-products/drug-shortages/information-consumers/supply-notices/ozempic.html.

that most people seem to gain weight back when they stop using the drug.[41] So as long as AI would be increasing the concentration of GLP-1, this would lead to a reduction in 'food noise', allowing people to make better decisions regarding the amount of food they consume. Without the drug, 'food noise' returns, making it more difficult to exercise temperance.[42] In the conclusion of this chapter I will return to this example as a place for future scholarship on the cutting edge of technology and virtue ethics.

Future Considerations for AGI and Virtue

Looking to the future, I want to engage with the question of how we might conceive of AGI as being able to acquire virtue. As I have said previously, there were scholars in our project who took this question up with aplomb and creativity, and I want to give them to opportunity to share their work as they see fit. A number of our CTNS researchers have contributed to this book. Here I want to briefly discuss some of the thresholds or benchmarks that would need to be in place for me to consider the possibility of AGI as being capable of acquiring virtue.

At a minimum, AGI would need to have a sense of self and free will. Philosophers and even scientists argue about the nature of free will and whether it exists at all. I believe that humans have libertarian free will. Just because our choices are constrained by several factors, including our own predispositions and our material resources, this does not mean we are able to make choices between the options that are available to us. This is the kind of definition I would expect of AGI as well; that it is capable of making choices, though it also will likely be constrained in a number of ways.

There also needs to be a sense of self, because selves cannot pursue the good in their lives without a sense of self. Virtues such as temperance and justice do not make sense without a sense of self. If there is a not a self, how can one speak of regulating their appetites or pleasures? Or if I did not see a distinction between myself and

---

41. John P Wilding *et al*, 'Weight Regain and Cardiometabolic Effects after Withdrawal of Semaglutide: The Step 1 Trial Extension', in *Diabetes, Obesity and Metabolism* 24, no 8 (May 19, 2022): 1553–1564, https://doi.org/10.1111/dom.14725.
42. Casey Kuhn, 'Patients Say Drugs like OZEMPIC Help with "food Noise". Here's What That Means', in *PBS*, September 25, 2023, https://www.pbs.org/newshour/health/patients-say-drugs-like-ozempic-help-with-food-noise-heres-what-that-means.

other organisms, even if they do not have a developed sense of self, how could I deliberate about what others are owed without a sense of self and other? Similarly, in order for AGI to be capable of acquiring moral virtues similar to humans, AGI would need to have emotion, appetites, and desires. Without these, it might be possible for AGI to have intellectual virtues but not moral virtues, at least from the perspective of Christian virtue ethics.

Another aspect of free will in the context of AI and AGI is the creation of novel material. There is debate currently over whether visual generative AI currently creates new images.[43] I would argue that the ability to create completely new content, not just recombining existing work, would be a measure of free will for AGI. Assuming AGI has a self of self, free will, and can create novel/new content, I believe that AGI would at least be capable of acquiring intellectual and moral virtues. The exact virtues would depend on how similar AGI would be to humans. The question of AGI and the theological virtues I will address in the conclusion.

Conclusion

While I am impressed with how scholars have engaged with the core questions of the Virtuous AI grant and continue to learn of work that other scholars are doing to engage these issues, I believe this is just a starting point. In the previous section I engaged with some of the questions or challenges that have arisen to this point in the discussion. These represent some areas that I would argue need additional attention and research.

Another challenge that researchers face is the pace at which technology is moving. In June 2022 it was reported that AI training was twice as fast as the previous year.[44] Even this increase could be seen as moving backward soon, as an article published in *Nature Photonics* in February of 2024, new methods are being tested that will

---

43. For differing views see: S Will Chambers, 'Artificial Intelligence Agents Are Not Artists', in *Medium*, December 27, 2020, https://towardsdatascience.com/artificial-intelligence-agents-are-not-artists-9743d5dba2d0.
Kevin Kelly, 'What Ai-Generated Art Really Means for Human Creativity', in *Wired*, November 17, 2022, https://www.wired.com/story/picture-limitless-creativity-ai-image-generators/.
44. Samuel K Moore, 'We're Training Ai Twice as Fast This Year as Last', in *IEEE Spectrum*, March 29, 2023, https://spectrum.ieee.org/mlperf-rankings-2022.

far exceed current results.⁴⁵ Instead of relying on electrons, researchers are trying to use photons to make calculations. Not only would this approach use less energy, but it is also predicted to be one thousand to ten times faster than current computational speeds.⁴⁶ Theologians and ethicists will need to work hard to stay up to date on cutting edge developments, and conversations and collaborations with computer scientists and engineers will be essential.

I also believe that pharmaceuticals, gene editing, and AI are pushing ethical theories to adapt, including virtue ethics. The distinction between infused virtue and acquired virtue may seem not that important to the outside observer; but the two kinds of virtue are treated differently. People using Ozempic to lose weight are receiving negative reactions from people, identified as 'Ozempic shaming'.⁴⁷ The criticism is that people are cheating by using the drug or they should not be weak and need the drug. If you were a person of character you would be able to lose weight by diet and exercise alone.⁴⁸

So in a secular sense, there seems to be an assumption that infused virtues are inferior to acquired virtue. However, theologians have struggled with Thomas Aquinas' understanding of infused moral virtues. Some choose to not engage with the topic much because as infused virtues they are given by God and not the product of human reflection so from an ethics or moral theology perspective it is harder to explain how they work. Interestingly enough, Aquinas identifies infused and acquired virtues as different species of virtue.⁴⁹

---

45. Keumars Afifi, 'Light-Powered Computer Chip Can Train AI Much Faster than Components Powered by Electricity', in *LiveScience*, March 25, 2024, https://www.livescience.com/technology/electronics/light-powered-computer-chips-can-train-ai-much-faster-than-components-powered-by-electricity.
 Vahid Nikkhah *et al*, 'Inverse-Designed Low-Index-Contrast Structures on a Silicon Photonics Platform for Vector–Matrix Multiplication', in *Nature News*, February 16, 2024, https://www.nature.com/articles/s41566-024-01394-2.
46. Charles Q Choi, 'Faster, More Secure Photonic Chip Boosts AI Training', in *IEEE Spectrum*, March 5, 2024, https://spectrum.ieee.org/photonic-ai-chip.
47. Christina Pazzanese, 'How "ozempic Shaming" Illuminates Complexities of Treating Weight Problems', in *Harvard Gazette*, https://news.harvard.edu/gazette/story/2024/02/how-ozempic-shaming-illuminates-complexities-of-treating-weight-problems/#:~:text=It%20has%20also%20triggered%20a,relying%20on%20diet%20and%20exercise.
48. Pazzanese, 'How "ozempic Shaming" Illuminates Complexities of Treating Weight Problems'.
49. Aquinas, *Summa Theologica* I-II.63.4, https://www.newadvent.org/summa/2063.htm

Interpreters of Aquinas argue that acquired virtues can only direct humans to the imperfect end of natural happiness, whereas infused virtue is guided by charity. Contrary to a secular view of infused virtue, a Christian understanding would promote the theological value of infused virtue.

That being said, I think an outsider to virtue ethics might raise perhaps the most important question to challenge virtue ethics: What does it matter whether someone has infused or acquired virtue? If people are actively trying to improve their lives and seeking the natural or supernatural end of humanity, why should they be judged for using whatever tools are at their disposal in order to do so? I think genetic and AI technologies raise fundamental questions about the nature of infused and acquired virtue, the relationship between virtue and moral enhancement, and how both of these fit into the pursuit of the *telos* of human flourishing.

This conversation over the nature of the infused virtues connects with the final future question I want to raise: how do we relate AGI and the infused virtues, including the theological virtues? Aquinas argued that God uses the infused virtues to orient people to the supernatural end of humanity. But I am unsure whether the same can be said for virtues infused into AI.

Puzzling questions arise. Can God work through these forms of infused virtue or would they be restricted to the natural end of humanity (or AI)? If the answer is the latter, then how would the infused moral virtues differ from acquired moral virtues? If God can orient people to the supernatural end of humanity, could AI or AGI also be oriented to a supernatural end in the same way? Building on this question it could be asked whether AGI would be able to receive the theological virtues. While this seems possible only if AGI has emotions, does that necessarily have to be the case? Why would God choose to bestow AGI with the theological virtues?

It stands to reason that if AGI and humans would share the same theological virtues then they would share the same supernatural end. This raises questions about other beings in general. Is there one supernatural end or more than one? And if the answer is the latter, how do they differ? What might the distinct virtues of these ends be? I am excited that while some progress has been made on the relationship between AI and virtue, there are so many complex issues left to explore and debate.

Contributors

Sunday Akande is a Nigerian clergy, writer and researcher with degrees in environmental biology, counseling psychology, and theology. He is currently a PhD student of Practical Theology at the Graduate Theological Union, Berkeley, CA, USA.

Ali-Reza Bhojani is Teaching Fellow in Islamic Ethics and Theology in the Department of Theology and Religion at the University of Birmingham, Honorary Research Fellow at the Al-Mahdi Institute, and Research Fellow at AI and Faith. His research, teaching, and writing has focused on intersections between Islamic legal theory, theology, and ethics. He is author of *Moral Rationalism and Shari'a* (Routledge, 2015) and co-editor of *Visions of Shari'a* (Brill, 2020)

Levi Checketts is Assistant Professor of Religion and Philosophy and Associate Director of the Centre for Applied Ethics at Hong Kong Baptist University. His research intersects social ethical questions of new technologies and economics. He is the author of *Poor Technology: Artificial Intelligence and the Experience of Poverty*, co-editor of two volumes of *Theology and Technology* and has published work in *Theology and Science*, *Techne: Research in Philosophy and Technology*, *The Journal of Moral Theology* and elswhere.

Benjamin J Chicka is Senior Lecturer of Philosophy and Religion in the General Education Department at Curry College. He serves as President of the North American Paul Tillich Society and as Secretary for the Institute for American Religious and Philosophical Thought. Chicka is the author of *Playing as Others: Theology and Ethical Responsibility in Video Games* (Baylor University Press, 2021) and *God the Created: Pragmatic Constructive Realism in Philosophy and Theology* (SUNY Press, 2022).

R Daren Erisman is an assistant professor of computer science at Minot State University in North Dakota, where he established and co-leads a new data science program with undergraduate topics in AI. An ordained minister in the Evangelical Lutheran Church in America, Daren also holds a PhD in Systematic and Philosophical Theology from the Graduate Theological Union in Berkeley. His research interests include comparative theology between Christianity and Islam and the relationship between science and religion.

Mark Graves is Research Fellow and Director at AI & Faith and Research Associate Professor of Psychology at Fuller Theological Seminary, with his research occurring at the intersection of artificial intelligence, psychology, and theology. He earned his doctorate in computer science at University of Michigan in the area of artificial intelligence; held postdoctoral fellowships in genomics at Baylor College of Medicine and in moral psychology at Fuller Theological Seminary; completed additional studies in systematic and philosophical theology at Graduate Theological Union (GTU) and Jesuit School of Theology at Berkeley; and completed a fellowship on AI and moral psychology and theology at the University of Notre Dame. He has published technical and scholarly works in computer science, biology, psychology, and theology, including the books Mind, Brain, and the Elusive Soul (2008) and Insight to Heal: Co-Creating Beauty Amidst Human Suffering (2013).

Brian Patrick Green is the director of technology ethics at the Markkula Center for Applied Ethics at Santa Clara University and teaches AI ethics in Santa Clara University's Graduate School of Engineering. His work focuses on AI and ethics, technology ethics in corporations, the ethics of space exploration and use, the ethics of technological manipulation of humans, the ethics of mitigation of and adaptation towards risky emerging technologies, and various aspects of the impact of technology and engineering on human life and society, including the relationship of technology and religion. Green is author of the book *Space Ethics*, co-author of *Ethics in the Age of Disruptive Technologies: An Operational Roadmap (The ITEC Handbook)*, co-author of the *Ethics in Technology Practice* corporate technology ethics resources, contributing author to *Encountering AI: Ethical and Anthropological Investigations*, co-editor of the book *Religious Transhumanism and Its Critics*, and co-editor of a special issue of the *Journal of Moral Theology* on AI. Green has worked with the World

Economic Forum, the Partnership on AI, the Vatican's Dicastery for Culture and Education, various governmental organisations, and technology companies ranging from startups to the largest. Green has doctoral and master's degrees in ethics and social theory from the Graduate Theological Union in Berkeley, and his undergraduate degree is in genetics from the University of California, Davis.

Noreen Herzfeld is the Nicholas and Bernice Reuter Professor of Science and Religion at St John's University and the College of St Benedict and a principal research associate with the Institute for Philosophical and Religious Research in Koper, Slovenia. She holds degrees in Computer Science and Mathematics from The Pennsylvania State University and a PhD in Theology from The Graduate Theological Union, Berkeley. Herzfeld is the author of *The Artifice of Intelligence: Divine and Human Relationships in a Robotic Age* (Fortress, 2023), *In Our Image: Artificial Intelligence and the Human Spirit* (Fortress, 2002), *Technology and Religion: Remaining Human in a Co-Created World* (Templeton, 2009), and editor of *Religion and the New Technologies* (MDPI, 2017).

Martinez (Marty) Hewlett is currently a Research Scholar at the University of New Mexico, Taos. He is Professor Emeritus from the Department of Molecular and Cellular Biology, University of Arizona, Tucson, Arizona. He holds a PhD in Biochemistry and is also a Life Professed lay member of the Order of Preachers (Dominicans). His scientific specialty is molecular virology and he is the co-author of a major textbook in this field, *Basic Virology*, now entering its 4th edition. He has co-authored three books on evolution and theology with Ted Peters. He has co-edited a number of books in the science and theology field, most recently *Astrotheology: Science and Theology Meet Extraterrestrial Life*, with Ted Peters, Joshua Moritz, and Robert John Russell. He has also published a science fiction novel, *Divine Blood*.

Oluwatobi Ife-Adediran is currently a doctoral student and presidential scholar at the Center of Theology and Natural Sciences/ Department of Theology and Ethics at the Graduate Theological Union, Berkeley, California, with a research focus on nuclear peace. Dr Ife-Adediran is also a Baptist clergy and health physicist. He joined the Federal University of Technology Akure as a faculty member in 2013 and has since been engaged in research and teaching. His previous individual and collaborative research works have been published in reputable journal articles and book chapters. He is passionate about the peaceful uses of nuclear energy, technology ethics, and the diversification of the theology and science discourse towards sustainable advancement of science and technology in Africa.

Dr Mohammad Jamali, faculty member at Shiraz University and head of the 'Philosophy and the Fundamental Sciences' Center, holds a doctorate in foundations of physics. His interdisciplinary research spans Science & Religion Issues, Philosophy of Science, Consciousness, and more, with a focus on Islamic philosophy and Avicenna's teachings. He delves into quantum consciousness and brain-machine interaction, particularly in soft robotics, implanting electronic chips in animal brains for movement control. Dr. Jamali contributes to the Iranian Council for reviewing Books on 'science and religion' and aims to deepen understanding of consciousness while fostering interdisciplinary dialogue.

Dr Yousef Jamali, a respected researcher and associate professor at Tarbiat Modares University, Tehran, holds a PhD in computational physics with extensive experience in physics research. He has worked at prestigious institutions like the Hans Knöll Institute in Jena, Germany, and UC Berkeley's Molecular Cell Biomechanics Lab. Specializing in biophysical modeling and social network dynamics within complex systems, his interdisciplinary research utilizes advanced techniques such as Agent-Based Modeling (ABM) and Dynamics of Complex Networks. Proficient in Python and C++, his modeling expertise spans various approaches including Cellular Automata and Molecular Dynamics.

Daekyung (DK) Jung commenced his academic journey at the College of Medicine, Konyang University in South Korea but later transitioned to Presbyterian University and Theological Seminary, also in South Korea, without completing his medical degree. He obtained a Bachelor of Theology (ThB) from Presbyterian University and pursued a Master of Divinity (MDiv) at Southwestern Baptist Theological Seminary and San Francisco Theological Seminary. Jung earned a PhD in Systematic and Philosophical Theology from the Graduate Theological Union. His academic career includes roles as a visiting professor at Myongji University and an assistant professor at Soongsil University. Currently, he serves as an Associate Professor at the United Graduate School of Theology, Yonsei University, South Korea. Jung's scholarly contributions include articles such as 'Re-Enchanting the Human in an Era of Naturalism', in the *Expository Times*, 'Transhumanism and the Theology of Xiang', in *Theology and Science*, and 'Transhumanism and Theological Anthropology', in *Neue Zeitschrift für Systematische Theologie und Religionsphilosophie*. His research interests span Religion and Science, Theological Anthropology, Emergence-Supervenience, the Origin of Religion, Religious Experience, Artificial Intelligence, and Trans-Posthumanism.

Claire Kennedy is an undergraduate student at Appalachian State University. Her work has primarily been with religion and technology.

Calvin Mercer, with training in biblical studies and psychology of religion, has published for two decades on the opportunities, dangers, and religious implications of radical human technological enhancement. With Tracy J Trothen, he coauthored *Religion and the Technological Future: Biohacking, Artificial Intelligence, and Transhumanism*, which won the International Society for Science and Religion (ISSR) 'Prize for Books Suitable for a Professional Audience'. With UK scholar Steve Fuller, Mercer coedits *Palgrave Studies in the Future of Humanity and Its Successors*. Founding chair of the 'Human Enhancement and Transhumanism' Unit in the American Academy of Religion, Mercer is a Fellow of the International Society for Science and Religion and serves on the Academic Advisory Council of the Christian Transhumanist Association. He is professor of religion at East Carolina University.

Braden Molhoek is Director of the Center for Theology and the Natural Sciences and the Ian G Barbour Assistant Professor of Theology, Science, Ethics, and Technology at the Graduate Theological Union in Berkeley California. He is also the Program Director of the grant Virtuous AI?: Cultural Evolution, Artificial Intelligence, and Virtue, funded by the John Templeton Foundation. His research interests include virtue ethics, theological anthropology, and the theological and ethical implications of emerging technology, including regenerative medicine, gene editing, human enhancement, transhumanism, and AI.

Hermina Nedelescu is a neuroscientist with a research focus on the neurobiological control of abnormal behaviors relevant to human psychopathology. She holds a PhD in Biomedical Sciences and is a student of theology at the Graduate Theological Union in The Center for Theology and Natural Sciences. She has been recognised for her efforts to bring neuroscience into dialogue with theology. Hermina also integrates her scientific expertise with artistic expression to explore and communicate concepts related to the brain structure and function. Overall, her work aims to bridge the gap between science, theology, and the broader public through art and dialogue, making complex scientific ideas more accessible and engaging.

Ted Peters is an emeritus professor of systematic theology and ethics at the Graduate Theological Union (GTU), where he co-edits the journal, *Theology and Science,* on behalf of the Center for Theology and the Natural Sciences (CTNS). His current focus is Public Theology with a strong emphasis on the creative mutual interaction between science and religion. He is author of *God: The World's Future* (Fortress, 3rd edition, 2015) and co-author with Martinez Hewlett of *Evolution from Creation to New Creation* (Abingdon 2002). Along with Brian Patrick Green and Arvin Gouw, he has recently published a new book, *Religious Transhumanism and Its Critics* (Lexington 2022). Peters is also author of a fiction thriller with a Transhumanist plot, *Cyrus Twelve,* with Aprocryphile Press. Visit his website, TedsTimelyTake.com and his *Patheos* Public Theology column.

Daniel J Peterson is pastor of Queen Anne Lutheran Church in Seattle. Formerly a member of the faculty at Pacific Lutheran University and Seattle University, he is the author of *Tillich: A Brief Introduction to the Life and Writings of Paul Tillich* (Lutheran University Press, 2013) and co-editor of *Resurrecting the Death of God: The Origins, Influence and Return of Radical Theology* (SUNY Press, 2014).

Anselm Ramelow, OP, a native of Germany, is professor of philosophy at the *Dominican School of Philosophy and Theology* in Berkeley, chair of the philosophy department, and a member of the Order of Preachers. He is also a member of the Core Doctoral Faculty at the *Graduate Theological Union* in Berkeley and the *Academy of Catholic Theology*. Formerly he taught at the *University of San Francisco* and the *Munich School of Philosophy* and is a Senior Fellow at the *Berkeley Institute*. Ramelo is the author of *Gott, Freiheit, Weltenwahl. Die Metaphysik der Willensfreiheit zwischen Antonio Perez, SJ (1599–1649) und GW Leibniz (1646–1716)* (Brill, 1997) and *Beyond Modernism?—George Lindbeck and the Linguistic Turn in Theology* (Ars Una 2005), as well as *Thomas Aquinas: De veritate Q. 21–24; Translation and Commentary* (Meiner, 2013) plus *God: Reason and Reality* (*Basic Philosophical Concepts*) (Philosophia Verlag, 2014). Ramelo's articles have appeared in *Historisches Wörterbuch der Philosophie, Archiv für Begriffsgeschichte, Nova et Vetera, American Catholic Philosophical Quarterly* and *Angelicum*.

Randall Reed is a Professor of Religion at Appalachian State University. He works in the area of Religion and technology. He has published several articles on AI and Religion including, 'The Theology of GPT-2' and 'Is Alexa My Neighbor' (with Laura Ammon), he is the co-chair of the Artificial Intelligence and Religion Unit at the American Academy of Religion, and is working on a book on Artificial Intelligence and Religion with Tracy Trothen (Forthcoming Routledge).

Neville Rochow SC, LLB (Hons), LLM, (Adelaide), LLM (Deakin) is a senior barrister who holds an adjunct associate professorship at Adelaide Law School. He has practised in areas of commercial, corporate, and constitutional law. Currently, he is writing a PhD thesis that explores the constitutional limits of freedoms of conscience and religion. Visit his website: https://talkabout.iclrs.org/neville-rochow-qc/.

Rajesh Sampath is Associate Professor of the Philosophy of Justice, Rights, and Social Change at Brandeis University. His teaching interests include Social Theory, Critical Race Theory/Intersectionality, Global Queer and Gender studies, Bioethics, Anglo-American, European and Global South traditions of philosophical ethics, human rights, and theories of justice when applied to sustainable development issues. His scholarly interpretations of Heidegger's philosophy appear in the *International Journal of Ethics*.

Michael Spezio is Associate Professor of Psychology, Data Science & Neuroscience at Scripps College in Claremont, CA, and a Senior Visiting Fellow at the Center of Theological Inquiry in Princeton, NJ. He heads the Laboratory for Inquiry into Valuation and Emotion (The LIVE Lab) at Scripps College. The LIVE Lab uses computational models of semantic relations, mental processes, and neural systems to study the dynamic valuation of self and other critical for choices about how to live. This work includes studies of theory of mind, empathy, compassion, forgiveness, virtuous formation, mindfulness, prayer, and beliefs and values. He developed the first course in AI Ethics and Justice at the Claremont Colleges and works on virtue in the practices of science. He is Co-Editor of the journal *Philosophy, Theology, and the Sciences* (Mohr Siebeck) and of the Routledge Companion to Religion & Science (2012). He gratefully acknowledges funding from the National Science Foundation, the Center for Theology and the Natural Sciences, the Templeton Religion Trust, and the John

Templeton Foundation. Michael is also an ordained minister of Word and Sacrament in the Presbyterian Church (USA).

Tracy J Trothen is a professor of ethics at Queen's University, jointly appointed to the School of Religion and the School of Rehabilitation Therapy. A certified spiritual care supervisor (Canadian Association of Spiritual Care), she specializes in artificial intelligence, technology, spirituality, and aging adults. Trothen is the author or editor of numerous articles, chapters, and ten books including the award-winning 2021 book, *Religion and the Technological Future: An Introduction to Biohacking, A.I., and Transhumanism*, co-authored with Calvin Mercer. She co-chairs the American Academy of Religion's (AAR) Artificial Intelligence Seminar with Randall Reed and is a Fellow of the International Society for Science and Religion (ISSR). Currently, she is working on a book with Reed on artificial intelligence and things deemed religious.

Evan Underbrink is a doctoral student of theology and ethics at the Graduate Theological Union in Berkeley, California, USA. He specialises in ecumenical and interdisciplinary dialogue, particularly in the fields of art, literature, and phenomenology, and holds graduate degrees from Boston College and Duke Divinity School. Evan currently lives in San Francisco.

Alan Weissenbacher is managing editor for the journal, *Theology and Science*. He served many years as a counselor to homeless addicts, removing them from the urban setting and empowering them to run a farm while receiving counseling, spiritual care, and job training. His work with these clients inspires his research into neuroscience and spiritual formation, exploring ways to improve religious care and addiction recovery through understanding how the brain works.

Lawrence A Whitney is a research associate in the division of medicine and science at the Smithsonian Institution's National Museum of American History and a Postdoctoral Fellow at the Center for Mind and Culture, Boston, MA. His research and teaching is broadly in philosophy, theology, and religion, with particular focus on philosophy of religion, the theology of Paul Tillich, Chinese thought, ritual studies, and science, religion, medicine, and health.

Contributors

Sunday Akande
1812 University Avenue, Apt. 308,
Berkeley, CA 94703.
Contact:
Phone: (510) 993-8886
Email: soakande1@gmail.com

Dr Ali-Reza Bhojani
Teaching Fellow in Islamic Ethics and Theology
Department of Theology and Religious Studies
University of Birmingham
Birmingham UK B15 2TT
a.bhojani@bham.ac.uk

Levi Checketts
28 Tai On St
Tower 1, Flat 3A
Sai Wan Ho, Hong Kong SAR
checketts@hkbu.edu.hk

Benjamin Chicka
8 Berkeley St. #1
Watertown, MA
02472
610-554-4060
benjamin.chicka@gmail.com

R. Daren Erisman
1940 S Broadway, #332
Minot, ND 58701
760-814-5171
rdaren.erisman@minotstateu.edu

Mark Graves
950 Franklin St Apt 37
San Francisco, CA 94109
mgraves@aiandfaith.org

Dr. Brian Green
2013 Westover Dr.
Pleasant Hill, CA 94523
USA
Phone number: 1-925-899-1100
Email: brianpatrickgreen@gmail.com

Noreen Herzfeld
Department of Theology
St. John's University
206 St. Luke Hall
Collegeville, MN 56321
320-363-2693
nherzfeld@csbsju.edu

Oluwatobi Ife-Adediran
2550 35th Avenue
Oakland CA 94601
e-mail: tobireliable@yahoo.com

Daekyung Jung, dk3134@gmail.com,
82-10-2614-7482
Office #304 Libertas A Building,
Yonsei University
85, Songdogwahak-ro, Yeonsu-gu,
Incheon, Republic of Korea 21983

Claire Kennedy
Appalachian State University
Department of Philosophy and Religion
Boone NC, 28608.
kennedycl@appstate.edu

CALVIN MERCER
Religious Studies Program
Brewster A-327, Mail Stop 562
East Carolina University
Greenville, NC 27858-4353
252 328 4310 (off & vm)
mercerc@ecu.edu

Braden Molhoek
Center for Theology and the Natural Sciences
Graduate Theological Union
2400 Ridge Road
Berkeley CA 94907 USA
bmolhoek@gtu.edu

Hermina Nedelescu
1494 Union St. 307
San Diego, CA, 92101
619 323 7042 (cell)

OR
Staff Scientist
Department of Neuroscience
The Scripps Research Institute
California Campus
1-858-784-7724 (direct)
hnedeles@scripps.edu

Ted Peters
43 Dowitcher Way
San Rafael CA 94901 USA
tedfpeters@gmail.com
+1 510.280.4161

Rev. Daniel J. Peterson, Ph.D.
pastor@queenannelutheran.org
Queen Anne Lutheran Church
2400 8th Avenue West
Seattle WA 98119
206.284.1960

Fr. Anselm Ramelow, O.P.
ARamelow@dspt.edu
www.dspt.edu/ramelow
DSPT - Dominican School of Philosophy and Theology
www.dspt.edu
2301 Vine St.
Berkeley, CA 94708 (510) 849-2030

Professor Randall Reed
Appalachian State University
Department of Philosophy and Religion
Boone NC, 28608.
reedrw@appstate.edu

Professor Neville Rochow QC
Neville Rochow QC
4 Elderslie Avenue
Fitzroy 5082
South Australia
Australia

N G Rochow QC
Barrister
+61 (0)414299299
University of Adelaide Law School
neville.rochow@adelaide.edu.au

Prof. Raj Sampath
Heller Brown Building 157
Brandeis University
415 South Street
Waltham MA 02454
USA
rsampath@brandeis.edu

Michael Spezio
142 Lincoln Avenue
Pomona, CA 91767
mspezio@scrippscollege.edu

TRACY J. TROTHEN
89 Holland Crescent
Kingston, Ontario
CANADA K7M 2V7
613 533 6000 ext. 74319
trothent@queensu.ca

Alan Weissenbacher
Graduate Theological Union / CTNS
2400 Ridge Road
Berkeley CA 94907 USA
send 2 copies, one for Alan as contributor and one for the *Theology and Science* book review
aweissenbacher@ses.gtu.edu & ctnsjournal@gtu.edu

Lawrence Whitney
23 White Pl,
Brookline, MA 02445,
857-413-7112
lawrence.whitney.lc@gmail.com,

www.ingramcontent.com/pod-product-compliance
Lightning Source LLC
Chambersburg PA
CBHW020941050326
40664CB00004B/136